Essentials of Management

11th Edition

Andrew J. DuBrin

Professor Emeritus of Management
Saunders College of Business
Rochester Institute of Technology

www.wessexlearning.com

Essentials of Management 11e
by Andrew J. DuBrin

Copy Editor : Mark Misercola

Book / Cover Design / Production : Anna Botelho

Indexer : Judi Gibbs—Write Guru®

ISBN: 978-0-9897013-0-3 (hardcover)
        978-0-9897013-1-0 (softcover)

Wessex Press, Inc.
www.wessexlearning.com

Noel Capon, R.C. Kopf Professor of International Marketing, Columbia Business School, founded Wessex Press, Inc. in 2007. Wessex Press is a publishing company, located in New York, that makes textbooks, simulations, and other learning materials more accessible to college students and life-long learners globally. We operate at the cutting edge of technology, and provide traditional and e-learning tools to students and professors at affordable prices. We focus primarily on Marketing, Sales, and other higher-education textbooks, and continue to expand into other business areas, covering subjects as diverse as Management, Finance, Human Resources, and Sociology.

Preface

Essentials of Management is written for newcomers to the field of management and for experienced managers seeking updated information and a review of the fundamentals. It is also written for the many professionals and technical people who work closely with managers and who take their turn at performing some management work. An example would be the member of a cross-functional team who is expected to have the perspective of a general manager.

Based on extensive research about curriculum needs, the design of *Essentials of Management* addresses itself to the needs of introductory management courses and supervision courses offered in educational settings. Previous editions of the text were used in the study of management in colleges and universities, as well as in career schools in such diverse programs as hospitality and tourism management, and nursing. The book can also be used as a basic resource for management courses that rely heavily on lecture notes, PowerPoint presentations, and videos rather than an encyclopedia-like text.

Comments made by Jack and Suzy Welch over fifteen years ago support the intent and relevance of this text in both the present and previous editions. (The late Jack Welch was the long-time chairman and CEO of GE and Suzy Welch is a former *Harvard Business Review* editor.) They both wrote:

> *In the past two years, we've visited 35 B-schools around the world and have been repeatedly surprised by how little classroom attention is paid to hiring, motivating, team-building, and firing. Instead B-schools seem far more invested in teaching brainiac-concepts—disruptive technologies, complexity modeling, and the like. Those may be useful, particularly if you join a consulting firm, but real managers need to know how to get the most out of people.*

(*BusinessWeek*, December 11, 2006, p. 112)

ASSUMPTIONS UNDERLYING THE BOOK

The approach to synthesizing knowledge for this book is based on the following four assumptions:

1. A strong demand exists for practical and valid information about solutions to managerial problems. The information in this text reflects the author's orientation toward translating research findings, theory, and experience into a form useful to both the student and the practitioner.

2. Managers and professionals need both interpersonal and analytical skills to meet their day-to-day responsibilities. Although this book concentrates on managing people, it also provides ample information about such topics as decision making, job design, organization structure, communication technology, budgeting, and inventory management.

3. The study of management should emphasize a variety of large, medium, and small work settings, as well as profit and not-for-profit organizations. Many

management students, for example, intend to become small business owners. Examples and cases in this book therefore reflect diverse work settings, including retail and service firms.

4 Introductory management textbooks tend to become unrealistically comprehensive. Many introductory texts today are more than 800 pages long. Such texts overwhelm students who attempt to assimilate this knowledge in a single quarter or semester. The goal with *Essentials of Management* was to develop a text that realistically—in terms of time and amount of information—introduces the study of management. Also, this text is not merely a condensation of a larger text, but a concise and comprehensive treatment of management since the first edition.

FRAMEWORK OF THE BOOK

The first three chapters present an introduction to management. Chapter 1, "The Manager's Job," explains the nature of managerial work with a particular emphasis on managerial roles and tasks. Chapter 2, "Ethics and Corporate Social Responsibility," examines the moral aspects of management. Chapter 3, "International Management and Cultural Diversity," describes how managers and professionals work in a multicultural environment.

The next three chapters address the subject of planning. Chapter 4, "Essentials of Planning and Strategy," presents a general framework for planning—the activity underlying almost any purposeful action taken by a manager. Chapter 5, "Decision Making, Creativity, and Innovation," explores the basics of decision making, with an emphasis on creativity, innovation, and other behavioral aspects. Chapter 6, "Quantitative Techniques for Problem Solving and Decision Making," describes several adjuncts to planning and decision making, such as break-even analysis, PERT, and production-scheduling methods used for both manufacturing and services.

Chapters 7–9 focus on organizing, culture, and staffing. Chapter 7, "Job Design and Arranging Work," explains how jobs are laid out and work schedules arranged to enhance productivity and customer satisfaction. Chapter 8, "Organization Structure, Culture, and Change," explains how work is organized from the standpoint of the enterprise, how culture profoundly influences an organization, and how to cope with and capitalize on change. Chapter 9, "Human Resource and Talent Management," explains the methods by which people are brought into the organization, trained, and evaluated.

The following four chapters, on leading, deal directly with the manager's role in influencing group members. Chapter 10, "Leadership in Organizations," focuses on different approaches to leadership available to a manager and on the personal characteristics associated with leadership effectiveness. Chapter 11, "Motivation," describes what managers can do to increase or sustain employee effort toward achieving work goals. Chapter 12, "Individual and Organizational Communication," deals with the complex problems of accurately sending and receiving messages. Chapter 13, "Teams, Groups, and Teamwork," explains the nature of teams and how managers can foster group members' working together cooperatively.

The next two chapters, on controlling, each deal with an important part of keeping performance in line with expectations. Chapter 14, "Essentials of Control" presents an overview of measuring and controlling performance, and also describes how managers work with a variety of financial measures to monitor performance. Chapter 15, "Managing Substandard Performers," describes current approaches to dealing with substandard performers, with an emphasis on elevating performance.

The final chapter in the text, Chapter 16, "Enhancing Personal Productivity and Managing Stress," describes how personal effectiveness can be increased by developing better work habits and time management skills and keeping stress under control. A major theme of the chapter is that good work habits help prevent and manage stress.

PEDAGOGICAL FEATURES

Essentials of Management is designed to aid both students and instructors in expanding their interest in and knowledge of management. The book contains the following features:

- Learning objectives coordinate the contents of each chapter. They preview the major topics and are integrated into the text by indicating which major topics relate to the objectives. The end-of-chapter *Summary of Key Points*, based on the chapter learning objectives, pulls together the central ideas in each chapter.

- An opening case example illustrates a major topic to be covered in the chapter.

- The *Management in Action* feature presents a portrait of how specific individuals or organizations practice an aspect of management covered in the chapter.

- Concrete, real-world examples with which the reader can readily identify are found throughout the text. Some examples are original, while others reference research information from magazines, newspapers, journals, and Internet sources.

- Figures, which include figures, tables, and self-assessment quizzes, aid in the comprehension of information in the text.

- Key terms and phrases highlight the management vocabulary introduced in each chapter with definitions that appear in the margin.

- Questions at the end of each chapter assist learning by encouraging the reader to think about some of the major and minor topics presented in the chapter.

- Skill-building exercises, including Internet activities appear at the end of each chapter.

- Self-assessment quizzes appear throughout the text, designed to help students think through their standing on important dimensions of behavior that influence managerial and professional work.

- Case problems, also located at the end of each chapter, can be used to synthesize the chapter concepts and simulate the practice of management.

NEW TO THE ELEVENTH EDITION

The eleventh edition is an updating of the tenth edition which incorporated more major changes. A brief listing of the changes in this new edition is as follows:

- All 16 chapters contain new information where appropriate, and many older research findings and several topics of lesser interest today have been deleted.

- New examples are added throughout the 16 chapters.

- Thirteen of the 32 end-of-chapter cases are new, and three cases from the previous edition are updated with new developments.

- Twelve of the chapter-opening cases are new, with the four other chapter-opening cases updated with new developments.

- Thirteen *Management in Action* boxes are new, with two updated with new developments.

- There is one new end-of-chapter exercise called *Management Now: Online Skill-Building Exercise*. These exercises will encourage students to use the Internet to obtain up-to-the-minute information, ideas, and applications directly related to each chapter's topic.

- Five of the skill-building exercises are new.

- One new self-quiz has been added.

New Topics Added to the Text

- Chief transformation officer as new management position (Chapter 1)

- Entrepreneurial mode of thinking (Chapter 1)

- The fourth industrial revolution (Chapter 1)

- Additional information about the meaning of virtue as it relates to ethics (Chapter 2)

- Wells Fargo account fraud as example of corporate unethical behavior (Chapter 2)

- Triple bottom line as measure of corporate social responsibility (Chapter 2)

- Creating a desirable workplace as corporate social responsibility initiative (Chapter 2)

- United States, Mexico, and Canada agreement (USMCA) (Chapter 3)

- Tariffs as a key factor in international trade (Chapter 3)

- Whether or not to put deal in writing as a cross-cultural difference in negotiating style (Chapter 3)

- Self-reinvention as a business strategy (Chapter 4)

- The application of artificial intelligence (AI) to decision making (Chapter 5)

- How candid feedback contributes to creativity (Chapter 5)

- The role of artificial intelligence (AI) in business forecasting (Chapter 6)

- The role of robots in the automation of work (Chapter 7)

- The potential negative consequences of job crafting (Chapter 7)

- The nine day/two weeks form of compressed workweek (Chapter 7)

- Organization structure of Procter & Gamble as an example of product structure (Chapter 8)

- Joy and happiness as a dimension of organization culture (Chapter 8)

- Gaining acceptance for change by presenting and inspiring vision of the future (Chapter 8)
- Use of texting to replace preliminary screening interview by some employers (Chapter 9)
- Replacements for traditional job interviews such as hiring on the basis of a phone interview (Chapter 9)
- The importance of leaders being humble (Chapter 10)
- Optimum level of intelligence for leadership effectiveness (Chapter 10)
- Work addiction and entrepreneurial leadership (Chapter 10)
- Personal toll of being a transformational leader (Chapter 10)
- Optimistic view of percentage of employees who are engaged in their work (Chapter 11)
- Influence of worker personality on engagement (Chapter 11)
- Use of discretionary rewards for employee motivation (Chapter 11)
- Mirroring or imitating a conversation partner as a form of nonverbal communication (Chapter 12)
- Employee "voice" as a form of upward communication (Chapter 12)
- Excessive use of jargon as a communication barrier (Chapter 12)
- Use of emojis to overcome cross-cultural communication barriers (Chapter 12)
- Leader setting the tone for an effective meeting (Chapter 12)
- Stealing credit for ideas as an unethical political tactic (Chapter 12)
- High-performance work team as newer version of self-managed work team (Chapter 13)
- How to collaborate effectively with other members of a virtual or remote team (Chapter 13)
- Appropriate degree of collaboration as characteristic of effective work group or team (Chapter 13)
- Opportunity for learning and growth as a positive consequence of conflict (Chapter 13)
- The use of EBITDA to evaluate a company up for sale, as well as for taking bold management actions (Chapter 14)
- How substandard performance often goes unobserved by supervisors (Chapter 15)
- On-the-spot positive feedback as part of coaching to improve performance (Chapter 15)
- The workplace bully as a type of difficult person (Chapter 15)
- Not feeling shamed or intimidated as a way of dealing with a workplace bully (Chapter 15)
- The manager not shifting blame when firing an employee (Chapter 15)
- Choosing the most important performance metrics as personal goals (Chapter 16)

- The importance of self-discipline for improving personal productivity (Chapter 16)
- The time-box as a variation of the to-do list (Chapter 16)
- Getting perfectionism under control as a way of combatting procrastination (Chapter 16)
- Nomophobia as an individual factor contributing to work stress (Chapter 16)

New Skill-Building Exercises

Every chapter contains two skill-building exercises, with five new exercises added to the eleventh edition, as follows:

- *Dealing with the Homeless* (Chapter 2)
- *Developing Business Strategy for Canned Goods* (Chapter 4)
- *Helping a Company that Arranges Booking a Hotel by the Minute* (Chapter 5)
- *Reactions to Organizational Change* (Chapter 8)
- *How Does a Person Qualify as a Workplace Jerk?* (Chapter 15)

New Management Now – Online Skill-Building Exercise

Every chapter contains an Internet-based skill-building exercise designed to connect students to websites that will boost their knowledge of management topics and issues. The one new skill builder is:

- *Checking Out the Profit of Your Favorite Companies* (Chapter 14)

Self-Quizzes

Not only will students enjoy taking the self-quizzes, they will also learn about their strengths and areas for improvement in the process. Chapter 10 has a new self-quiz about humility for leadership. Your students will benefit from taking the following:

- *My Managerial Role Analysis* (Chapter 1)
- *Cross-Cultural Skills and Attitudes* (Chapter 2)
- *The Ethical Reasoning Inventory* (Chapter 3)
- *How Strategic Is My Thinking?* (Chapter 4)
- *How Involved Are You?* (Chapter 7)
- *Attitudes Toward Bureaucracy Self-Quiz* (Chapter 8)
- *Self-Evaluation of my Humility* (Chapter 10)
- *My Self-Leadership Tendencies* (Chapter 10)
- *How Much Do I Crave Recognition?* (Chapter 11)
- *The Positive Organizational Politics Questionnaire* (Chapter 12)
- *My Effectiveness as a Team Member* (Chapter 13)
- *The Self-Sabotage Questionnaire* (Chapter 15)
- *Procrastination Tendencies* (Chapter 16)
- *The Stress Questionnaire* (Chapter 16)

New Action Inserts

Students will find one *Management in Action* insert in every chapter. Thirteen inserts are completely new and two are an update of an insert from the tenth edition. A complete list follows:

- *Rite Aid CEO Heyward Donigan Hopes to Revitalize the Company* (Chapter 1)
- *Walmart Managers Take the High Road and the Low Road* (updated) (Chapter 2)
- *Ultimate Software Has a Culture of Real Inclusion* (Chapter 3)
- *Mars Petcare is a Purpose-Driven Organization* (Chapter 4)
- *Inventory Management at McDonald's Restaurants* (Chapter 6)
- *Flexible Work Arrangements at Upwork* (Chapter 7)
- *Former Home Depot CFO, Carol Tomé Helped Renovate the Corporate Culture* (Chapter 8)
- *KitchenAid and Whirlpool Invest in their Promising Workers* (Chapter 9)
- *Merck CEO Kenneth Frazier Pushes Hard to Grow the Company and Help Humanity* (updated) (Chapter 10)
- *Employee Recognition at Yogurt Maker Chobani* (Chapter 11)
- *The San Diego Humane Society & SPCA Relies on FeTCH, Its Intranet* (Chapter 12)
- *Dell Inc. Implements Virtual Teams* (Chapter 13)
- *Netflix Tackles Cash Flow Issue* (Chapter 14)
- *Amazon.com Systematically Approaches Substandard Performance* (Chapter 15)
- *German Tech Consulting Firm Decreases Wasted Time to Enable Five-Hour Workday* (Chapter 16)

New End-of-Chapter Cases

Thirteen of the cases in the eleventh edition are new and three are updated as follows:

- *The Uber Drivers and Their Algorithm Bosses* (Chapter 1)
- *Just Inc Wants to Revolutionize the Egg Industry* (Chapter 2)
- *Candor at Anti-Bias Training* (Chapter 3)
- *What Exactly Is Our Purpose?* (Chapter 4)
- *Lenovo Implements Its Strategy of Protect and Attack* (updated) (Chapter 4)
- *The Blade Knife Company Seeks a Cutting-Edge Innovation* (Chapter 5)
- *7-Eleven Wants a Chunk of e-Commerce* (updated) (Chapter 5)
- *The Alarming Walk-In Bathtub Forecast* (Chapter 6)
- *Dental Hygienist Kelsey Crafts her Job* (Chapter 7)
- *Some Uber Drivers Want to Be Employees* (updated) (Chapter 7)
- *Aspiring Hotel Executive Annabelle Wants to Know if She Would Fit the Culture* (Chapter 8)
- *Abigail Believes in As-Needed Evaluations* (Chapter 9)

- *Servant Leader Nicole* (Chapter 10)
- *The 10-for-10 Program at Mason Appliances* (Chapter 11)
- *Lone Wolf Pamela Gets Passed Over* (Chapter 12)
- *Kevin Cultivates His Coworkers* (Chapter 13)
- *Business Owner Jeremy Needs More Cash* (Chapter 14)
- *Blunt Manager Elijah* (Chapter 15)
- *Harper, The Busy Office Manager* (Chapter 16)

INSTRUCTIONAL RESOURCES

Essentials of Management is accompanied by comprehensive instructional support materials, and all the resources are prepared by the textbook's author.

- *Instructor's Manual with Test Bank.* The instructor's manual provides resources to increase the teaching and learning value of *Essentials of Management.* For each chapter, the manual provides a statement of purpose and scope, outline and lecture notes, lecture topics, comments on the end-of-chapter questions and activities, responses to case questions, and an experiential exercise. The test bank contains 25 multiple choice questions, 25 true/false questions, and five essay questions. The test bank is also available in a computerized format at *www.wessexlearning.com.*

- *PowerPoint Slides.* A set of 350 PowerPoint slides accompanies the text. This slide package is designed for easy classroom use and includes reproductions of many of the figures found in the text.

A NOTE TO THE STUDENT

The information in the general preface is important for students as well as instructors. Here I offer additional comments that will enable you to increase the personal payoffs from studying management. My message can be organized around several key points.

- *Management is not simply common sense.* The number one trap for students in studying management is to assume the material is easy to master because many of the terms and ideas are familiar. For example, just because you have heard the word *teamwork* many times, it does not automatically follow that you are familiar with specific field-tested ideas for enhancing teamwork.

- *Managerial skills are vital.* The information in the course you are studying and in the textbook itself are vital in today's world. People with formal managerial job titles, such as *supervisor, team leader, department head,* or *vice president* are obviously expected to possess managerial skills. But many other people in jobs without managerial titles also benefit from managerial skills. Among them are people with titles, such as *administrative assistant, customer-service representative,* and *inventory-control specialist.*

- *The combination of managerial, interpersonal, and technical skills leads to outstanding career success.* A recurring myth is that it is better to study "technical" or "hard" subjects than management because the pay is better. In reality, the people in business making the higher salaries and other compensation are those who combine technical skills with managerial and interpersonal skills. Executives and business owners, for example, can earn incomes rivaled only by leading professional athletes and entertainment personalities. Furthermore, business graduates are among the highest paid in terms of starting salaries.

- *Studying management, however, has its biggest payoff in the long run.* Entry-level management positions are in short supply. Management is a basic life process. To run a major corporation, manage a restaurant or a hair salon, organize a company picnic, plan a wedding, or run a good household, management skills are an asset. We all have some knowledge of management, but formally studying management can multiply one's effectiveness.

Take advantage of the many study aids in this text. You will enhance your learning of management by concentrating on such learning aids as the chapter objectives, summaries, discussion questions, self-quizzes, skill-development exercises, and the glossary. Carefully studying a glossary is an effective way of building a vocabulary in a new field. Studying the glossary will also serve as a reminder of important topics. Activities, such as the cases, discussion questions, and skill-building exercises facilitate learning by creating the opportunity to think through the information. Thinking through information, in turn, leads to better comprehension and long-term retention of information.

ACKNOWLEDGMENTS

Any project as complex as this text requires a team of dedicated and talented people to see that it gets completed effectively. Many reviewers made valuable comments during the development of this new edition as well as the previous editions of the text. I appreciate the helpful suggestions of the following colleagues:

Thelma Anderson
Montana State University–Northern

Zay Lynn Bailey
SUNY—Brockport

Tom Birkenhead
Lane Community College

Genie Black
Arkansas Tech University

Thomas M. Bock
Baruch College

Brenda Britt
Fayetteville Technical Community College

Murray Brunton
Central Ohio Technical College

Michel Cardinale
Palomar College

Gary Clark
North Harris College

Jose L. Curzet
Florida National College

Rex Cutshall
Vincennes University

Robert DeDominic
Montana Tech University

Robert Desman
Kennesaw State College

Kenneth Dreifus
Pace University

Ben Dunn
York Technical College

Debra Farley
Ozark College

Thomas Fiock
Southern Illinois University at Carbondale

Dan Geeding
Xavier University

Shirley Gilmore
Iowa State University

Philip C. Grant
Hussen College

Randall Greenwell
John Wood Community College

David R. Grimmett
Austin Peay State University

Robert Halliman
Austin Peay State University

Paul Hegele
Elgin Community College

Thomas Heslin
Indiana University

Peter Hess
Western New England College

Nathan Himelstein
Essex County College

Kim T. Hinrichs
Minnesota State University—Mankato

Judith A. Horrath
Lehigh Corbon Community College

Lawrence H. Jaffe
Rutgers University

Steven Jennings
Highland Community College

B. R. Kirkland
Tarleton State University

Margaret S. Maguire
SUNY—Oneonta

Patricia Manninen
North Shore Community College

Noel Matthews
Front Range Community College

Christopher J. Morris
Adirondack Community College

Ilona Motsiff
Trinity College of Vermont

David W. Murphy
University of Kentucky

Robert D. Nale
Coastal Carolina University

Christopher P. Neck
Virginia Tech

Ronald W. Olive
New Hampshire Technical College

George M. Padilla
New Mexico State University—Almogordo

J. E. Pearson
Dabney S. Lancaster Community College

Joseph Platts
Miami-Dade Community College

Larry S. Potter
University of Maine—Presque Isle

Thomas Quirk
Webster University

Jane Rada
Western Wisconsin Technical College

James Riley
Oklahoma Junior College

Robert Scully
Barry University

William Searle
Asnuntuck Community Technical College

William Shepard
New Hampshire Technical College

Howard R. Stanger
Canisius College

Lynn Suksdorf
Salt Lake Community College

John J. Sullivan
Montreat College

Gary Tilley
Surry Community College

Bernard Weinrich
St. Louis Community College

Blaine Weller
Baker College

Mara Winick
University of Redlands

Alex Wittig
North Metro Technical College

Marybeth Kardatzke Zipperer
Montgomery College

The production of this edition of *Essentials of Management* was a team effort, and I thank my team members as follows: Mark Misercola, copy editor and proofreader, Anna Botelho, designer, Judi Gibbs, indexer.

Writing without loved ones would be a lonely task. My thanks therefore go to my family: Drew, Heidi, Rosie, Clare, Douglas, Gizella, Camila, Sofia, Eliana, Julian, Melanie, Carson, and Owen. In addition, I thank another part of my family, Stefanie, the woman in my life, and her daughter Sofia for their contribution to my well-being.

Andrew J. DuBrin

ABOUT THE AUTHOR

 Andrew J. DuBrin is Professor Emeritus of Management in the Saunders College of Business at the Rochester Institute of Technology, where he has taught courses and conducted research in management, organizational behavior, leadership, and career management. He has also served as department chairman and team leader in previous years. He received his Ph.D. in Industrial Psychology from Michigan State University. DuBrin has business experience in human resource management and consults with organizations and individuals. His specialties include career management leadership and management development. DuBrin is an established author of textbooks, scholarly books, and trade books, and he also contributes to professional journals, and online media. He has written textbooks on management, leadership, organizational behavior, and human relations. His scholarly books include the subjects of impression management, narcissism in the workplace, the proactive personality, and crisis leadership. His trade books cover many management issues, including charisma, team play, office politics, overcoming career self-sabotage, and coaching and mentoring.

Brief Table of Contents

Table of Contents

Part Four : Leading

Part One

Introduction to Management

CHAPTER 1

The Manager's Job

OBJECTIVES

After studying this chapter and doing the exercises, you should be able to:

1 Explain the term *manager* and identify different types of managers.

2 Describe the process of management, including the functions of management.

3 Describe the various managerial roles.

4 Identify the basic managerial skills and understand how they can be developed.

5 Identify the major developments in the evolution of management.

Ryan Carson is an entrepreneur and co-founder of Treehouse Island, a successful online coding school based in Portland, Oregon. He is open to experimentation in terms of the services he offers the public, and his approach is to keep employees job-satisfied, work-engaged, and productive. At Treehouse, staff members worked four days per week, only worked on projects they found interesting, were infrequently required to send e-mails, and had no direct managers.

As the business grew to more than 100,000 online students and 100 employees, Carson recognized that not having managers was counterproductive. In the absence of project managers, supervisors and work deadlines, productivity was declining in comparison to the competition. Staff members were also unsure of their responsibilities. Carson told a reporter from *The Wall Street Journal* that the experiment with no bosses failed.

After assigning middle managers to the company, revenues increased, and the time it took customer support agents to respond to online student questions dropped from seven to three-and-one-half hours.

Craig Dennis, a teacher at Treehouse says he appreciates having a manager provide him direction and praise him for a job well done. He misses having the opportunity to pitch a new project to colleagues, but life with a boss is "light years better."

Four years later Carson decided a modification of Treehouse's mission was necessary. The company had been offering a $25 per month product that can be signed up for online. The company learned, however, that the low-price product was not "the most effective way to empower people to get jobs in the tech future." A shift would be made to place people into jobs through apprenticeship. As a result, the product team focusing on the $25 per month training in coding was downsized with 12 people losing their jobs. Carson said that it was a tough decision that affected some great folks who worked super-hard to serve the company's students.[1]

The story about the CEO of an online coding school illustrates that a manager makes things happen, such as enabling the growth of the firm and keeping employees pointed in the right direction. Unfortunately, pointing the company in the right direction could mean a change in mission that results in layoffs. Also illustrated is that managers play an important role in providing employee recognition. As will be described in this chapter, and throughout the book, the manager carries out a large number of demanding activities.

Explain the term **manager** and identify different types of managers.

manager
A person responsible for the work performance of group members.

management
The process of using organizational resources to achieve organizational objectives through planning, organizing and staffing, leading and controlling.

WHO IS A MANAGER?

A **manager** is a person responsible for the work performance of group members. Approximately 10 percent of the U.S. workforce holds a managerial position of one type or another. A manager holds the formal authority to commit organizational resources, even if the approval of others is required. For example, the manager of a Jackson-Hewitt income tax and financial service outlet has the authority to order the repainting of the reception area. The income tax and financial services specialists reporting to that manager, however, do not have that authority.

The concepts of manager and managing are intertwined. The term **management** in this book refers to the process of using organizational resources to achieve organizational objectives through the functions of planning, organizing and staffing, leading and controlling. These functions represent the broad framework for this book and will be described later. In addition to being a process, the term *management* is also used as a label for a specific discipline, for the people who manage and for a career choice.

You probably would not be reading this book or taking its related course if you did not think that managers make a contribution to an organization. Nevertheless, it is reassuring to know that scientific evidence demonstrates that managers make a contribution to the good of an organization. At Google it was found that knowledge workers (those who work with ideas) often doubted that managers had much to contribute, particularly for technical jobs. Management was even regarded as a distraction from their regular job responsibilities such as designing and debugging.

To investigate the value of managers and management, Google's people analytics team made a convincing data-based argument. The team scrutinized employee surveys, performance evaluations and interview responses to verify that management really did make a contribution. Three of these useful behaviors of managers are as follows: "Is a good coach," "Expresses interest in and concern for team members' success and personal well-being," and "Has key technical skills that help him or her advice the team." Most Google engineers ("Googlers") now value management.[2]

Levels of Management

Another way of understanding the nature of a manager's job is to examine the three levels of management shown in Figure 1-1. The pyramid in this figure illustrates progressively fewer employees at each higher managerial level. The largest number of people is at the bottom organizational level. (Note that the term *organizational level* is sometimes more precise than the term *managerial level*, particularly at the bottom organizational level, which has no managers.) It is important to recognize that levels of management do not correspond exactly with the levels of influence and compensation. Individual contributors, such as coders and corporate attorneys, might have more influence and earn higher compensation than many middle managers and first-level managers.

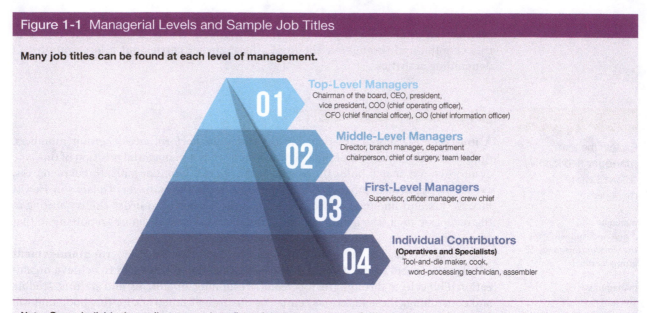

Figure 1-1 Managerial Levels and Sample Job Titles

Many job titles can be found at each level of management.

Top-Level Managers
Chairman of the board, CEO, president, vice president, COO (chief operating officer), CFO (chief financial officer), CIO (chief information officer)

Middle-Level Managers
Director, branch manager, department chairperson, chief of surgery, team leader

First-Level Managers
Supervisor, officer manager, crew chief

Individual Contributors
(Operatives and Specialists)
Tool-and-die maker, cook, word-processing technician, assembler

Note: Some individual contributors, such as financial analysts and administrative assistants, report directly to top-level managers or middle managers.

Top-Level Managers

Most people who enter the field of management aspire to become **top-level managers**—managers at the top one or two levels in an organization. **C-level manager** is a current term to describe a top-level manager because these managers usually have *chief* in their title, such as *chief operating officer*. Top-level managers are empowered to make major decisions affecting the present and future of the firm. Only a top-level manager, for example, would have the authority to purchase another company, initiate a new product line, or hire hundreds of employees. Top-level managers are the people who give the organization its general direction; they decide where it is going and how it will get there. The terms *executive, top-level manager, senior-level manager*, and *c-level manager* can be used interchangeably.

Because management is an evolving field, new job titles for c-level managers continue to surface. Often these titles reflect a new emphasis on what needs to be accomplished for an organization to run successfully. Here are a few of the recent c-level positions often found in large organizations:

- *Chief Culture Officer.* A major responsibility of the chief culture office is to ensure that all departments align with the mission and vision of the company. He or she also works to enhance communication in the company, as well as plans and carries out events, such as annual meetings, for employees.[3]

- *Chief Transformation Officer.* A chief transformation officer oversees the organization to bring about major changes. This job role first appeared at McDonald's Corp. when a single point of contact, the chief transformation officer, helped each franchise build business plans and obtain the corporate resources they need to solve problems. The chief transformation officer is aided by a team of field consultants who spend at least half their time helping franchisees improve their business.[4]

top-level managers
Managers at the top one or two levels in an organization.

c-level manager
A current term to describe top-level managers because they usually have *chief* in their title.

- *Chief Innovation Officer.* A chief innovation officer (CINO) or chief technology innovation officer (CTIO) is a person in a company who is primarily responsible for managing the formal process of innovation in an organization and ensuring ideas at every level of the organization are encouraged and evaluated.
- *Chief Privacy Officer.* The chief privacy officer works on such problems as safeguarding customer information in the digital world. He or she also deals with consumer concerns about the use of personal information, including financial and medical information. With concerns about cyber security, the position of chief privacy officer has gained in importance.

Middle-Level Managers

middle-level managers
Managers who are neither executives nor first-level supervisors, but who serve as a link between the two groups.

Middle-level managers are managers who are neither executives nor first-level supervisors, but who serve as a link between the two groups. Middle-level managers conduct most of the coordination activities within the firm, and they are responsible for implementing programs and policies formulated by top-level management. The jobs of middle-level managers vary substantially in terms of responsibility and income. A branch manager in a large firm might be responsible for more than 100 workers. In contrast, a general supervisor in a small manufacturing firm might have 20 people reporting to him or her. Other important tasks for many middle-level managers include helping the company undertake profitable new ventures and finding creative ways to reach goals. A major part of a middle manager's job is working with teams to accomplish work and execute on goals articulated by senior management. Middle-level managers play a major role in operating an organization, and therefore continue to be in demand, as suggested in the chapter opener.

Although advances in information technology have reduced the communication requirements of the middle manager position, the need for middle managers is still strong. Ethan Mollick, Wharton management professor, explains that the influence of middle managers stems from their key role in project management. This includes tasks and responsibilities, such as resource allocation and monitoring of deadlines. Middle managers also play a key role in fostering environments that facilitate creativity and innovation.[5]

First-Level Managers

first-level managers
Managers who supervise operatives (also known as first-line managers or supervisors).

Managers who supervise operatives are referred to as **first-level managers**, first-line managers, or supervisors. Historically, first-level managers were promoted from production or clerical (now called staff support) positions into supervisory positions. Rarely did they have formal education beyond high school. A dramatic shift has taken place in recent years. Many of today's first-level managers are career school graduates and four-year college graduates who are familiar with modern management techniques. The current emphasis on productivity and cost control has elevated the status of many supervisors.

To understand the work performed by first-level managers, reflect back on your first job. Like most employees in entry-level positions, you probably reported to a first-level manager. Such a manager might be a supervisor of newspaper carriers, dining room manager, service station manager, maintenance supervisor, or department manager in a retail store. Supervisors help shape the attitudes of new employees toward the firm. Newcomers who like and respect their first-level manager tend to stay with the firm longer. Conversely, new workers who dislike and disrespect their first supervisor tend to leave the firm early.

TYPES OF MANAGERS

The functions performed by managers can also be understood by describing different types of management jobs. The management jobs discussed here are functional and general managers, administrators, entrepreneurs and small business owners and team leaders. (The distinction between line and staff managers will be described in Chapter 8 when we discuss organization structure.)

Functional and General Managers

Another way of classifying managers is to distinguish between those who manage people who do one type of specialized work and those who manage people who engage in different specialties. *Functional managers* supervise the work of employees engaged in specialized activities, such as accounting, engineering, information systems, food preparation, marketing and sales. A functional manager is a manager of specialists and of their support team, such as office assistants.

General managers are responsible for the work of several different groups that perform a variety of functions. The job title, "plant general manager" offers insight into the meaning of general management. Reporting to the plant general manager are various departments engaged in both specialized and generalized work, such as manufacturing, engineering, labor relations, quality control, safety and information systems. Company presidents are general managers. Branch managers are also general managers if employees from different disciplines report to them. The responsibilities and tasks of a general manager highlight many of the topics contained in the study of management. These tasks will therefore be introduced at various places in this book.

Administrators

An *administrator* is typically a manager who works in a public (government) or nonprofit organization, including educational institutions, rather than in a business firm. Among these managerial positions are hospital administrator and housing administrator. Managers in all types of educational institutions are referred to as administrators. The fact that individual contributors in nonprofit organizations are sometimes referred to as administrators often causes confusion. An employee is not an administrator in the managerial sense unless he or she supervises others.

Entrepreneurs and Small Business Owners

Millions of students and employees dream of turning an exciting idea into a successful business. Many people think, "If Jeff Bezos started Amazon.com from a tiny office using a desk made out of an old door, and he might be the wealthiest person in the world today, why can't I do something similar?" Success stories such as Bezos' kindle the entrepreneurial spirit. By a strict definition, an **entrepreneur** is a person who founds and operates an innovative business. After the entrepreneur develops the business into something bigger than he or she can handle alone or without the help of a few people, that person becomes a general manager.

entrepreneur
A person who founds and operates an innovative business.

Similar to an entrepreneur, the owner and operator of a small business becomes a manager when the firm grows to include several employees. **Small business owners** typically invest considerable emotional and physical energy into their firms. Note that entrepreneurs are (or start as) small business owners, but that the reverse is not necessarily true. You need an innovative idea to fit the strict definition of an entrepreneur. Simply

small business owner
An individual who owns and operates a small business.

running a franchise that sells sub sandwiches does not make a person an entrepreneur, according to the definition presented here. Also, an entrepreneur may found a business that becomes so big it is no longer a small business. (In everyday language, anyone who founds a small business, including a food truck, is referred to as an *entrepreneur.*)

A major characteristic of both entrepreneurs and small business owners is their passion for the work. These types of managers will usually have a single-minded drive to solve a problem. Many corporate managers are passionate about their work also, but the passion of an entrepreneur appears to be highly pronounced, as success or failure rests solely on their shoulders.

Team Leaders

team leader
A manager who coordinates the work of a small group of people, while acting as a facilitator and catalyst.

A major development in types of managerial positions during the last 35 years is the emergence of the **team leader.** A manager in such a position coordinates the work of a small group of people, while acting as a facilitator or catalyst. Team leaders are found at several organizational levels, and are sometimes referred to as project managers, program managers and task force leaders. Note that the term *team* could also refer to an executive team, yet a top executive almost never carries the title *team leader*. You will be reading about team leaders throughout this text.

All of the managerial jobs described above vary considerably on the demands placed on the job holder. All workers carrying the job title *chief executive officer* may perform similar work, yet the position may be much more demanding and stressful in a particular organization.[6] Imagine being the CEO of an American auto parts manufacturer that is facing extinction because of overseas competition. His or her job is more demanding than that of the CEO of a company like Binney & Smith, the subsidiary of Hallmark Cards, which produces Crayola crayons among other popular products for children. With over three billion crayons produced each year, and a fan base in the millions, Binney & Smith is not threatened with extinction. A lot of children have switched to tablet computers instead of crayons but not enough to make a huge difference in crayon, chalk and marker sales. So at least the CEO can enjoy his or her golf outings while the auto parts CEO worries about losing customers and laying off employees.

LEARNING OBJECTIVE **2**

Describe the process of management including the functions of management.

THE PROCESS OF MANAGEMENT

A helpful approach to understanding what managers do is to regard their work as a process. A process is a series of actions that achieves something—making a profit or providing a service, for example. To achieve an objective, the manager uses resources and carries out four major managerial functions. These functions are planning, organizing and staffing, leading and controlling. Figure 1-2 illustrates the process of management.

Resources Used by Managers

Managers use resources to accomplish their purposes, just as a carpenter uses resources to build a terrace. A manager's resources can be divided into four types: human, financial, physical and informational.

Human resources are the people needed to get the job done. Managers' goals influence which employees they choose. A manager might set the goal of delivering automotive

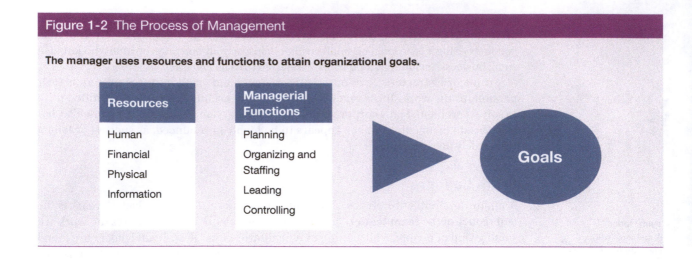

Figure 1-2 The Process of Management

The manager uses resources and functions to attain organizational goals.

Resources	Managerial Functions
Human	Planning
Financial	Organizing and Staffing
Physical	Leading
Information	Controlling

Goals

supplies and tools to auto and truck manufacturers. Among the human resources he or she chooses are manufacturing technicians, sales representatives, information technology specialists and a network of dealers.

Financial resources are the money the manager and the organization use to reach organizational goals. The financial resources of a business organization are profits and investments from stockholders. A business must occasionally borrow cash to meet payroll or to pay for supplies. The financial resources of community agencies come from tax revenues, charitable contributions and government grants.

Physical resources are a firm's tangible goods and real estate, including raw materials, office space, production facilities, office equipment and vehicles. Vendors supply many of the physical resources needed to achieve organizational goals.

Information resources are the data that the manager and the organization use to get the job done. For example, to supply leads to the firm's sales representatives, the sales manager of an office supply company reads local business newspapers and Internet postings to learn about new firms in town. These newspapers and websites are information resources. Merchandising managers at physical and online stores regularly scan published articles and blogs searching for new trends in products and potential products.

As originally formulated by the famous management thinker, Peter Drucker, managers are knowledge workers. As a result of being knowledge workers, managers rely heavily on information resources. Drucker also observed that managers are quite skilled at obtaining data, but they are less skilled at converting these data into useful information. According to Drucker, few executives will ask, "What new tasks can I tackle, now that I have all these data? Which old tasks should I abandon?"[7] Imagine that a middle manager is wondering about how to best motivate workers. She inserts into Bing.com the question, "How do you motivate workers?" She receives close to 31 million entries. She must then understand how to sort out the most useful of these entries. (Or, she could study the chapter about motivation of a management textbook.)

THE FOUR MANAGERIAL FUNCTIONS

Figure 1-2 shows the four major resources in the context of the management process. To accomplish goals, the manager performs four managerial functions. These functions are planning, organizing and staffing, leading, and controlling.

Planning

Planning involves setting goals and figuring out ways of reaching them. Planning, considered the central function of management, pervades everything a manager does. In planning, a manager looks to the future, saying, "Here is what we want to achieve, and here is how we are going to do it." Decision making is usually a component of planning, because choices have to be made in the process of finalizing plans. The importance of planning expands, as it contributes heavily to performing the other management functions. For example, managers must make plans to do an effective job of staffing the organization. Planning is also part of marketing. For example, cereal maker Kellogg Corp. established plans to diversify further into the snack food business to reach its goal of expanding market share.

Organizing and Staffing

Organizing is the process of making sure the necessary human and physical resources are available to carry out a plan and achieve organizational goals. Organizing also involves assigning activities, dividing work into specific jobs and tasks and specifying who has the authority to accomplish certain tasks. Another major aspect of organizing is grouping activities into departments or some other logical subdivision. The staffing function ensures the availability of necessary human resources to achieve organizational goals. Hiring people for jobs is a typical staffing activity. Staffing is such a major activity that it is sometimes classified as a function separate from organizing.

Leading

Leading means influencing others to achieve organizational objectives. As a consequence, it involves engaging, directing, persuading others, and creating a vision. Leadership involves dozens of interpersonal processes: motivating, communicating, coaching and showing group members how they can reach their goals. Leadership is such a key component of managerial work that management is sometimes seen as accomplishing results through people. The leadership aspect of management focuses on inspiring people and bringing about change, whereas the other three functions focus more on maintaining a stable system. According to prominent management thinker, Henry Mintzberg, effective leaders develop the sense of community or shared purpose that is essential for cooperative effort in all organizations.[8]

Although leadership deals heavily with persuasion and inspiration, the leader also executes the visions and other ideas for change he or she formulates. Visionaries often fail because they do not translate their strategies (master plans) into results. Also, it has been said that *execution* has become an important new buzzword in business because leaders in the past placed too much emphasis on spinning grand visions without really taking care of business. A survey of CEOs indicated that chief executives are so concerned about executing strategy that they rated it as their most challenging issue.[9]

Controlling

Controlling generally involves comparing actual performance to a predetermined standard. Any significant difference between actual and desired performance would prompt a manager to take corrective action. He or she might, for example, increase advertising to boost lower-than-anticipated sales.

A secondary aspect of controlling is determining whether the original plan needs revision, given the realities of the day. The controlling function sometimes causes a manager to return to the planning function temporarily to fine-tune the original plan. For example, many retailers in the current era have found that sales volume in stores was not enough to earn the company a profit. So they closed the stores and shifted all sales to online, as well as selling their product to other retailers.

One important way in which the jobs of managers differ is in the relative amounts of time spent on planning, organizing and staffing, leading and controlling. Executives ordinarily spend much more time on strategic (high-level and long-range) planning than do middle- or first-level managers. Lower-level managers are more involved with day-by-day and other short-range planning. Also, lower-level managers spend the most time in face-to-face leadership such as coaching and disciplining workers. This is true because entry-level workers are likely to need more assistance than those workers who have advanced higher in the organization.

THE SEVENTEEN MANAGERIAL ROLES

To further understand the manager's job, it is worthwhile to examine the various roles managers play. A **role**, in the business context, is an expected set of activities or behaviors stemming from a job. Mintzberg conducted several landmark studies of managerial roles.[10] Other researchers extended his findings.[11] In the sections that follow, the roles delineated by these researchers are associated with the major managerial functions to which they most closely pertain. Roles and functions are closely related. They are both activities carried out by people. (In current business jargon, a *role* often refers to the position held by a person, such as the role of the customer care manager,) The description of the 17 roles should help you appreciate the richness and complexity of managerial work, and also serve as a generic job description for a manager's position. These roles are described next and listed in Figure 1-3.

LEARNING OBJECTIVE 3

Describe the various managerial roles.

role
An expected set of activities or behaviors stemming from a job.

Figure 1-3 The Seventeen Managerial Roles

Planning
1 Strategic planner
2 Operational planner

Organizing and Staffing
3 Organizer
4 Liaison
5 Staffing coordinator
6 Resource allocator
7 Task delegator

Leading
8 Motivator and coach
9 Figurehead
10 Spokesperson
11 Negotiator
12 Team builder
13 Team player
14 Technical problem solver
15 Entrepreneur

Controlling
16 Monitor
17 Disturbance handler

Planning

Two managerial roles—strategic planner and operational planner—relate to the planning function.

1 *Strategic Planner.* Top-level managers engage in strategic planning, usually assisted by input from others throughout the organization. Specific activities in this role include: (a) setting a direction for the organization, (b) helping the firm deal with the external environment, and (c) developing corporate policies.

2 *Operational Planner.* Operational plans relate to the day-to-day operation of a company or unit. Two such activities are: (a) formulating operating budgets and (b) developing work schedules for the unit supervised. Middle-level managers are heavily involved in operational planning; first-level managers are involved to a lesser extent.

Organizing and Staffing

Five roles that relate to the organizing and staffing function are organizer, liaison, staffing coordinator, resource allocator, and task delegator.

3 *Organizer.* As a pure organizer, the manager engages in activities such as: (a) designing the jobs of group members, (b) clarifying group members' assignments, (c) explaining organizational policies, rules, and procedures, and (d) establishing policies, rules, and procedures to coordinate the flow of work and information within the unit.

4 *Liaison.* The purpose of the liaison role is to develop and maintain a network of work-related contacts with people. To achieve this end, the manager: (a) cultivates relationships with clients or customers, (b) maintains relationships with suppliers, customers, and other persons or groups important to the unit or organization, (c) joins boards, organizations, or public service clubs that might provide useful, work-related contacts, and (d) cultivates and maintains a personal network of in-house contacts through visits, telephone calls, e-mail, text messages, social media and participation in company-sponsored events.

5 *Staffing Coordinator.* In the staffing role, the manager tries to make sure competent people fill positions. Specific activities include: (a) recruiting and hiring staff, (b) explaining to group members how their work performance will be evaluated, (c) formally evaluating group members' overall job performance, (d) compensating group members within the limits of organizational policy, (e) ensuring group members are properly trained, (f) promoting group members or recommending them for promotion, and (g) terminating or demoting group members.

6 *Resource Allocator.* An important part of a manager's job is to divide resources in the manner that best helps the organization. Specific activities to this end include: (a) authorizing the use of physical resources (facilities, furnishings, and equipment), (b) authorizing the expenditure of financial resources, and (c) discontinuing the use of unnecessary, inappropriate, or ineffective equipment or services.

7 *Task Delegator.* A standard part of any manager's job is assigning tasks to group members. Among these task-delegation activities are: (a) assigning projects or tasks to group members, (b) clarifying priorities and performance standards for task completion, and (c) ensuring group members are properly committed to effective task performance.

Leading

Eight managerial roles relate to the leadership function: motivator and coach, figure-head, spokesperson, negotiator, team builder, team player, technical problem solver, and entrepreneur.

8 *Motivator and Coach.* An effective manager takes time to motivate and coach group members. Specific behaviors in this role include: (a) informally recognizing employee achievements, (b) offering encouragement and reassurance, thereby showing active concern about the professional growth of group members, (c) providing feedback about both effective and ineffective performance, and (d) giving group members advice on steps to improve their performance.

9 *Figurehead.* Figurehead managers, particularly high-ranking ones, spend some of their time engaging in ceremonial activities or acting as a figurehead. Such activities include: (a) entertaining clients or customers as an official represen-tative of the organization, (b) serving as an official representative of the organi-zation at gatherings outside the organization, and (c) escorting official visitors.

10 *Spokesperson.* When a manager acts as a spokesperson, the emphasis is on answering inquiries and formally reporting to individuals and groups outside the manager's organizational unit. As a spokesperson, the manager keeps five key stakeholder groups informed about the unit's activities, plans and capabilities. These groups are: (a) upper-level management, (b) clients and customers, (c) other important outsiders (such as labor unions), (d) professional colleagues, and (e) the general public. Usually, top-level managers take responsibility for keeping outside groups informed.

11 *Negotiator.* Part of almost any manager's job is trying to make deals with others for needed resources. Three specific negotiating activities are: (a) bargaining with supervisors for funds, facilities, equipment, or other forms of support, (b) bargaining with other units in the organization for the use of staff, facilities and other forms of support, and (c) bargaining with suppliers and vendors about prices, services, schedules and delivery times.

12 *Team Builder.* A key aspect of a manager's role is to build an effective team. Activities contributing to this role include: (a) ensuring group members are recognized for their accomplishments (by issuing letters of appreciation, for example), (b) initiating activities that contribute to group morale, such as giving parties and sponsoring sports teams, and (c) holding periodic staff meetings to encourage group members to talk about their accomplishments, problems, and concerns.

13 *Team Player.* Three behaviors of the team player are: (a) displaying appropriate personal conduct, (b) cooperating with other units in the organization, and (c) displaying loyalty to superiors by fully supporting their plans and decisions.

14 *Technical Problem Solver.* It is particularly important for first- and middle-level managers to help group members solve technical problems. Two such specific activities related to problem solving are: (a) serving as a technical expert or advisor and (b) performing individual contributor tasks, such as making sales calls or fixing software problems on a regular basis. The managers most in demand today are those who combine leadership skill with a technical or business specialty. Note that the term *technical* refers to complex details in any specialty, not just information technology. For example, a construction supervisor might know the technology of using a five-story high crane.

15 *Entrepreneur.* Managers who work in large organizations have some responsibility for suggesting innovative ideas or furthering the business aspects of the firm. Three entrepreneurial role activities are: (a) reading trade publications and professional journals and searching the Internet to keep up-to-date, (b) talking with customers or others in the organization to keep abreast of changing needs and requirements, and (c) getting involved in activities outside the unit that could result in performance improvements within the manager's unit. These activities might include visiting other firms, attending professional meetings or trade shows, and participating in educational programs.

Controlling

The monitor role mentioned next fits the controlling function precisely, because the term *monitoring* is often used as a synonym for *controlling*. The role of disturbance handler is categorized under controlling because it involves changing an unacceptable condition to an acceptable stable condition.

16 *Monitor.* The activities of a monitor are: (a) developing systems that measure or monitor the unit's overall performance, (b) using information systems to measure productivity and cost, (c) talking with group members about progress on assigned tasks, and (d) overseeing the use of equipment and facilities (for example, vehicles and office space) to ensure that they are properly used and maintained.

17 *Disturbance Handler.* Four typical activities of a disturbance handler are: (a) participating in grievance resolution within the unit (working out a problem with a labor union, for example), (b) resolving complaints from customers, other units, and superiors, (c) resolving conflicts among group members, and (d) resolving problems about work flow and information exchange with other units. Disturbance handling might also be considered a leadership role.

Managerial Roles Currently Emphasized

Managerial work has shifted substantially away from the controller and director role to that of motivator and coach, facilitator and supporter. As reflected in the position of team leader, many managers today deemphasize formal authority and rank. Instead, they work as partners with team members to jointly achieve results. Managers today emphasize horizontal relationships and deemphasize vertical (top-down) relationships. We encourage you not to think that traditional (old) managers are evil, while new managers are good.

Professors of entrepreneurial management, Joseph Pistrul and Dimo Dimov, think that a required shift in managerial roles is for managers to develop an entrepreneurial mode of thinking. An entrepreneurial mode of thinking helps managers see things that are normally overlooked, and do things that are usually avoided. The two professors explain that, "Thinking like an entrepreneur simply means to expand your perception and increase your action—both of which are important for finding new gateways for development."[12]

Figure 1-4 gives you the opportunity to relate managerial roles to yourself, even if you are not presently working as a manager.

Figure 1-4 My Managerial Role Analysis

Here is an opportunity for you to think through your current level of skill or potential ability to carry out successfully the 17 managerial roles already described. Each role will be listed with a brief reminder of one of its key aspects. Check next to each role whether it is an activity you could carry out now, or something for which you will need more experience and preparation. For those activities you check as "capable of doing it now," jot down an example of your success in this area. For example, a person who checked "capable of doing it now" for Role 5, staffing coordinator, might have written, "I recruited three part-time servers to work in the restaurant where I worked as an assistant manager."

Few readers of this book will have had experience in carrying out most of these roles. So relate the specific roles to any management experience you may have had, including full-time work, part-time work, volunteer work, clubs, committees, and sports.

Managerial Role	Capable of Doing It Now	Need Preparation and Experience
1 *Strategic planner:* Set direction for others based on external environment.	_____	_____
2 *Operational planner:* Plan for running the organization or the unit.	_____	_____
3 *Organizer:* Design jobs for group members and clarify assignments.	_____	_____
4 *Liaison:* Develop and maintain network of work-related contacts.	_____	_____
5 *Staffing coordinator:* Recruit, hire, train, evaluate, and fire group members.	_____	_____
6 *Resource allocator:* Divide resources to help get job done.	_____	_____
7 *Task delegator:* Assign tasks to group members.	_____	_____
8 *Figurehead:* Engage in ceremonial activities, and represent the group to outsiders.	_____	_____
9 *Spokesperson:* Answer inquiries and report information about the group to outsiders.	_____	_____
10 *Negotiator:* Make deals with others for needed resources.	_____	_____
11 *Motivator and coach:* Recognize achievements, encourage, give feedback and advice.	_____	_____
12 *Team builder:* Contribute to group morale, hold meetings to encourage members to talk about accomplishments and concerns.	_____	_____
13 *Team player:* Correct conduct, cooperate with others, and be loyal.	_____	_____
14 *Technical problem solver:* Help group members solve technical problems; perform individual contributor tasks.	_____	_____
15 *Entrepreneur:* Suggest innovative ideas and further business activity of the group; search for new undertakings for the group.	_____	_____
16 *Monitor:* Measure performance and productivity, and review progress on tasks.	_____	_____
17 *Disturbance handler:* Resolve problems and complaints.	_____	_____

Interpretation: The more of the 17 roles you are ready to perform, the more ready you are to function as a manager or to perform managerial work. Your study of management will facilitate carrying out more of these roles effectively.

The Influence of Management Level on Managerial Roles

A manager's level of responsibility influences which roles he or she is likely to engage in most frequently. Information about the influence of level on roles comes from research conducted with 228 managers in a variety of private-sector service firms (such as banks and insurance companies) and manufacturing firms. The roles studied were basically those described in this chapter. One clear-cut finding was that, at the higher levels of management, four roles were the most important: liaison, spokesperson, figurehead, and strategic planner. Another finding was that the role of leader is critical at the first level of management.[13] Even though the study in question is 37 years old, it is consistent with current management practice. For example, today's organizations, first-level managers are expected to be effective leaders who motivate and coach subordinates.

Management as a Practice

A useful perspective on the nature of management is that it is a practice, rather than a science or a profession. Managers learn through both experience and study. As Mintzberg explains, science is about the development of systematic knowledge through research. In contrast, the major purpose of management is to help get things done in organizations.[14] Managers sometimes make use of systematic knowledge, yet they also rely on the intuition that stems from experience.

Management is not a profession in the sense of being a licensed occupation such as law, medicine, psychology, veterinary medicine, or electrician. If management were a profession in this strict sense, you would be forbidden to work as a middle manager or start a software firm without being licensed by your state or province. The fact that managerial work is not defined as a profession does not downgrade its importance. You don't need a license to be the president of the United States.

Another point of view is advanced by Harvard Business School professors, Rakesh Khurana and Nitin Nohria, who claim it is time to make management a true profession. In their opinion, to regain public trust, management needs to become a profession that follows an ethical code. Managers should have appropriate education, as with other professions.[15] (These authors appears to be referring to top-level executives.)

evidence-based management
The systematic use of the best available evidence to improve management practice.

One way in which the occupation of management can become more professionalized is for managers to base more of their decisions on systematically gathered evidence, such as surveys and experiments. **Evidence-based management** is the systematic use of the best available evidence to improve management practice.[16] The application of evidence-based management includes a critical evaluation of the best available research evidence.[17] You might regard evidence-based management as a professional form of managerial practice that relies on multiple sources of evidence. The evidence-based approach is growing in management education, as schools of business and management continue to enhance the knowledge and skills of present and future managers.

To use this approach, managers would rely on both scientific evidence as well as local business evidence. To illustrate, there are hundreds of articles published in professional journals about the usefulness of goals for improving performance and how best to use goals. (Chapter 11 contains information about goals and motivation.) The manager might also check out how well goals worked in local business firms. A manager who used some of this information would be working more professionally than a manager who relied only on common sense to boost motivation and performance.

Another perspective on the practice of management is that unless managers actively practice management, job, group, and organizational performance may suffer. Management writer Victor Lipman observes that the problem of managing people too closely, or micromanagement, gets most of the attention but under-management is an equally big problem. When not enough management is practiced, attaining results often suffers. According to Lipman, managers sometimes back off from playing an active role because they prefer to avoid conflict. Instead, managers should place high priority on delivering results, such as holding people accountable for strong performance.[18]

FIVE KEY MANAGERIAL SKILLS

To be effective, managers need to possess technical, interpersonal, conceptual, diagnostic, and political skills. The sections that follow will first define these skills and then comment on how they are developed. Whatever the level of management, a manager needs a combination of all five skills.

LEARNING OBJECTIVE **4**

Identify the basic managerial skills and understand how they can be developed.

Technical Skill

Technical skill involves an understanding of and proficiency in a specific activity that involves methods, processes, procedures, or techniques. Technical skills include the ability to prepare a budget, lay out a production schedule, prepare a spreadsheet analysis, upload information onto a social networking site, and demonstrate a piece of electronic equipment. Intricate knowledge of the business, such as developing a marketing campaign for a product can also be regarded as a technical skill. Technical skills are frequently referred to as *hard skills*. A well-developed technical skill can facilitate the rise into management. For example, Bill Gates of Microsoft Corp. launched his career by being a competent programmer (coder today).

Technical skill continues to grow in importance because it can also be considered a key part of the intellectual capital that drives an economy based on knowledge. The term *knowledge economy* has gained in popularity as companies have begun to harvest data and information rather than relying so heavily on the natural resources that once drove economic growth.[19] You have probably heard of people who have created a business from their tablet computer and smartphone, using a microscopic amount of natural resources.

Interpersonal Skill

Interpersonal (or human relations) skill is a manager's ability to work effectively as a team member and to build cooperative effort in the unit. Communication skills are an important component of interpersonal skills. They form the basis for sending and receiving messages on the job. Although interpersonal skills are often referred to as *soft skills*, it does not mean these skills are easy to learn or insignificant. Interpersonal skills are more important than technical skills in getting to the top and providing leadership to people. Many managers at all levels ultimately fail because their interpersonal skills do not match the demands of the job. For example, some managers intimidate, bully, and swear at group members. In the process, they develop such a poor reputation that it may lead to their being replaced. Have you ever worked for a manager who was so rude and insensitive that he or she damaged morale and productivity?

An interpersonal skill for managers that has recently captured attention is **empathy,** the ability to understand another person's point of view. Empathy is particularly important for positions involving human interaction, such as a manager, customer support agent, and nurse. The McKinsey Global Institute found that human interaction jobs are the most rapidly growing category of employment in advanced economies.[20] One reason is that so many other positions have been automated.

empathy
The ability to understand another person's point of view.

Conceptual Skill

Conceptual skill is the ability to see the organization as a total entity. It includes recognizing how the various units of the organization depend on one another and how changes in any one part affect all the others. It also includes visualizing the relationship of the individual business to the industry; the community; and the political, social, and economic forces of the nation as a whole. For top-level management, conceptual skill is a priority because executive managers have the most contact with the outside world.

Conceptual skill can also be framed as seeing the big picture, or purpose, of what the organization is intending to accomplish. For example, the big picture for a manager in a vehicle tire manufacturing plant is to help provide safe transportation.

Political Skill

An important part of being effective is the ability to obtain power and prevent others from taking it away. Managers use political skill to acquire the power necessary to reach objectives. Other political skills include establishing the right connections and impressing the right people. Furthermore, managers with strong political skills possess an astute understanding of people, along with a fundamental belief that they can control the outcomes of their interactions with people.

Political skill should be regarded as a supplement to job competence and the other basic skills. Managers who overemphasize political skill at the expense of doing work of substance focus too much on pleasing company insiders and advancing their own careers. Too much time invested in office politics takes time away from dealing with customer problems and improving productivity; and often leads to mistrust from peers and subordinates.

Diagnostic Skill

Managers are frequently called on to investigate a problem and then to decide on and implement a remedy. Diagnostic skill often requires other skills because managers need to use technical, human, conceptual, or political skills to solve the problems they diagnose. Much of the potential excitement in a manager's job centers on getting to the root of problems and recommending solutions. An office supervisor, for example, might attempt to understand why productivity has not increased in his office despite the installation of the latest office technology.

The accompanying *Management in Action* insert feature illustrates some of the management roles and skills described in this chapter.

DEVELOPMENT OF MANAGERIAL SKILLS

This text is based on the assumption that managerial skills can be learned. Education for management begins in school and continues in the form of training and development programs throughout a career. Examples of such programs might include a seminar about how to be an effective leader or a workshop about social media marketing.

Developing most managerial skills is more complex than developing structured skills such as computing a return on investment ratio or transferring images from a phone to a slide show. Nevertheless, you can develop managerial skills by studying this text and doing the exercises, which follow a general learning model:

1 *Conceptual knowledge and behavioral guidelines.* Each chapter in this text presents useful information about the practice of management, including step-by-step procedures for a method of group decision making called the nominal group technique.

MANAGEMENT IN ACTION

Rite Aid CEO Heyward Donigan Hopes to Revitalize the Company

In 2019, Rite Aid Corp. appointed longtime healthcare executive Heyward Donigan as Chief Executive Officer. At the time of her appointment Rite Aid Chairman Bruce Bodakenh said that Donigan's strong senior executive experience, proven leadership capabilities, and consistent track record of driving profitable growth, as well as her broad healthcare knowledge and digital shopping expertise make her unique. He also said that "Her skill set will be invaluable as we work to deliver on the full potential of our business and create additional long-term value for our shareholders, associates, customers and patients."

Previous to joining Rite Aid, Donigan was president and chief executive officer at Sapphire Digital, a business firm that develops omnichannel platforms to help consumers choose healthcare providers. Her other executive roles included president and CEO of ValueOptions, a behavior health improvement company. In addition, Donigan had held executive positions at Premera Blue Cross, Cigna Healthcare, General Electric, and U. S. Healthcare. Donigan was widely regarded as having an in-depth knowledge of the healthcare business.

Rite Aid is the third largest pharmacy chain, operating closed to 2,500 stores in 18 states, and also oversees pharmacy benefits manager EnvisionRxOptions. (A pharmacy benefit manager acts as a broker between health insurance providers and pharmaceutical companies.) CVS has ten times the sales volume of Rite Aid, and Walgreens has seven times the volume. To help cope with its financial struggles, in 2017 Rite Aid sold 1,932 of its stores to Walgreens.

When Donigan took over as CEO, Rite Aid and its two key rivals were battling to expand traditional pharmacy services and broaden their reach into provider services. These initiatives included online sales, walk-in clinics, and urgent-care centers. A financial analyst noted that Donigan faced a monumental turnaround effort, with the odds not being in her favor. He noted, however, that there is little doubt that the 58-year-old Heyward Donigan has "got the chops."

Donigan began her position with an optimistic outlook, saying, "I see tremendous opportunity to revitalize the company's position as a leader in meeting the health and wellness needs of customers and patients through our store and pharmacy benefit management platforms."

Industry observers noted that Donigan's primary task was to grow the company. One of her first initiatives was to strike a deal with Amazon.com to enable customers to pick up online orders at Rite Aid stores. She said she hoped to find additional incentives to persuade customers to visit the stores in person.

Donigan received an MPA finance degree from New York University, and an B.A. degree for the University of Virginia.

Questions

1 **Which management roles can you identify that Donigan has occupied?**

2 **Which management skills does Donigan appear to possess?**

3 **How does the statement about Donigan "having the right chops" relate to management skills?**

4 **Based on current industry reports, how well is Donigan doing in terms of her hopes to revitalize Rite Aid?**

Source: Original story based on facts and observations in the following sources: James Brumley, "New CEO Heyward Donigan Needs a Miracles to Revive Rite Aid Stock," *Investor Place* (www.investorplace.com), September 23, 2019, pp. 1–4; Heather Haddon, "Rite Aid Taps Tech Executive As CEO," *The Wall Street Journal*, August 13, 2019, p. B3; Anne Stych, "Rite Aid Names Health-Care Exec Heyward Donigan CEO," *bizwoman* (bizjournal.com), August 13, 2019, p. 1; Russell Redman, "Rite Aid Names Heyward Donigan as New CEO," *Super Market News* (www.supermarket.com), August 12, 2019, pp. 1–3; Katie Kushner-Hebert, "Rite Aid's Newest CEO Heyward Donigan Comes With a Proven Track Record," *Chief Executive* (www.chiefexecutive.net), pp. 1–3.

2 *Conceptual knowledge demonstrated by examples.* Brief descriptions of managers and professionals in action, including small business owners, are presented throughout the text.

3 *Skill-development exercises.* The text provides an opportunity for practice and personalization through cases and self-assessment exercises. Self-quizzes are included because they are an effective method of helping you personalize the information.

4 *Feedback on skill utilization, or performance from others.* Feedback exercises appear at several places in the text. Implementing some of these managerial skills outside of the classroom will provide additional opportunities for feedback.

5 *Frequent practice of what you have learned, including making adjustments from the feedback.* Soft skills as well as technical skills must be practiced frequently to develop expertise. If you also make the adjustments that feedback has suggested, the level of expertise is likely to be higher. Suppose you wanted to develop the managerial skill of giving praise and recognition to others. Not everybody is naturally good at giving praise and recognition so you would have to practice frequently. If several people told you your praise was too heavy, you might diminish the amount of praise you were heaping upon others.

Experience is obviously important in developing management skills. Yet experience is likely to be more valuable if it is enhanced with education. Consider this analogy to soccer. A person learning soccer might read and watch a video on the proper way to kick a soccer ball. With this education behind her she now kicks the ball with the side of her foot instead of toe first. She becomes a competent kicker by combining education and experience. People often make such statements as, "You can't learn to be a manager (or leader) from a book." However, you can learn managerial concepts from a book, or lecture, and then apply them. People who move vertically in their careers usually have both education and experience in management techniques.

A key reason for continuing to develop managerial skills is that the manager's job is more demanding than ever and the workplace keeps changing. A manager is likely to work in an intense, pressure-filled environment requiring many skills. Companies forced to keep up with competition are driving the demand for managers with updated skills. Rapid changes, such as developing an effective social networking presence, or responding to a major increase in the minimum wage, require managers to continually develop new skills.

Identify the major developments in the evolution of management.

THE EVOLUTION OF MANAGEMENT

Management as a practice has an almost unlimited history. Visualize a group of prehistoric people attempting to develop a device that would help transport heavy objects. Given a modern label, the cave person suggesting this development is the head of product research and development. The project of building the curious new circular device was turned over to a group of people who had hands-on access to raw material. Because the developers of the wheel did not constitute a business enterprise, they handed over the technology of the wheel to all interested parties. Also, in prehistoric times, patents were not available.

Management as a formal study, in comparison to a practice, began in the 1700s as part of the Industrial Revolution. Here we take a brief historical look at management, covering both historical developments and various approaches to understanding it. The anchor points to our discussion are as follows:

1 Classical approach (scientific management and administrative management)
2 The behavioral approach
3 Quantitative approaches to management and Big Data
4 The systems perspective
5 The contingency approach
6 The information technology approach and social media era
7 The Fourth Industrial Revolution

All of these approaches are mentioned here, but also appear in later sections of the book. For example, the study of leadership and motivation stems from both the classical and behavioral approaches. The historical approaches laid the foundation for understanding and practicing management.

Classical Approach to Management

The study of management became more systematized and formal as a by-product of the Industrial Revolution that took place from the 1700s through the 1900s. Approaches to managing work and people needed to be developed to manage all the new factories that were a central part of the Industrial Revolution. The classical approach to management encompasses scientific management and administrative management.

The focus of **scientific management** was on the application of scientific methods to increase individual workers' productivity. An example would be assembling a washing machine with the least number of wasted motions and steps. Frederick W. Taylor, considered the father of scientific management, was an engineer by background. He used scientific analysis and experiments to increase worker output. Other key contributors to scientific management were Henry Gantt and Frank and Lillian Gilbreth. (Gantt charts for scheduling activities are still used today.)

scientific management
The application of scientific methods to increase individual workers' productivity.

Scientific management is often regarded as a relic of the past, yet in reality many of the principles of this rigorous approach to accomplishing tasks are with us today. For example, principles of scientific management have been applied to reducing the time it takes for online stores to get packages shipped to customers.

Administrative management was concerned primarily with how organizations should be managed and structured. French businessman Henri Fayol and German scholar Max Weber were the main contributors to administrative management. Based on his practical experience, Fayol developed 14 management principles through which management engaged in planning, organizing, commanding, coordinating, and controlling. Two examples of his principles are: (1) *unity of command*—for any tasks, each worker should receive orders from only one supervisor, and (2) *esprit de corps*—promoting team spirit builds harmony and creates organizational unity. Weber proposed an ideal form of bureaucracy to improve upon inefficient forms of organization that included using favoritism to promote workers.[21] Among Weber's recommendations were to break each job down into simple, routine, and well-defined tasks.

administrative management
The use of management principles in the structuring and managing of an organization.

Alfred D. Chandler, Jr., Harvard University business historian, was a key figure in promoting the importance of the classical approach to management. He championed the study of modern bureaucratic administration, and influenced the thinking of executives about organizing large business firms. Many of the insights Chandler developed were based on the individual histories he gathered from Du Pont, General Motors, Standard Oil (now Exxon), and Sears, Roebuck & Co. The time period he chose for studying these organizations was between 1850 and 1920, and the most comprehensive version of his conclusions about major business firms was published in *Strategy and Structure* in 1962.

Chandler's book demonstrates the essential link between a company's strategy (master plan) and its structure (layout or division of work). His famous thesis is that a firm's structure is determined or chosen by its strategy—and unless structure follows strategy, inefficiency results. In other words, what a firm wants to accomplish determines how the company is organized. Chandler's insights contributed to the decentralization of many modern organizations.[22]

Consider today's Colgate-Palmolive Company, whose strategy might be stated as responding to the personal-care needs of people and animals throughout the world. To achieve this lofty goal, the company is divided into four mammoth divisions: Oral Care, Personal Care, Home Care, and Pet Nutrition. Each division is subdivided into product groups of its own, such as Personal Care including men's antiperspirant and deodorant, women's antiperspirant and deodorant, body wash, and liquid hand soap. If Colgate-Palmolive were not organized by divisions, the company would consist of major groups such as manufacturing, engineering, research and development, finance, and information systems.

The core of management knowledge lies within the classical school. As its key contribution, it studies management from the framework of planning, organizing, leading, and controlling—the framework chosen in this text. Many major historical developments in organizations, such as the decentralization of General Electric (GE) in the 1950s, were based on classical principles.

An article about the history of management, by Leon Prieto and Simone Phipps, observes that the contribution of African Americans to the evolution of management thought has been neglected by scholars. A key example is a 1927 newspaper article written by Charles Clinton Spaulding, the manager of the North Carolina Mutual Life Insurance Company. (At the time, all the customers and employees of the company were black.) Spaulding's ideas fit mostly the classical school, but his insights overlapped with the behavioral school of management. In brief, the eight fundamental necessities of management formulated by Spaulding were as follows[23]:

1 *Cooperation and teamwork.* (A team-based culture focused on the success of the organization is fundamental to success.)

2 *Authority and responsibility.* (Somebody has to make the final decision.)

3 *Division of labor.* (Departmentalization and specialization are essential.)

4 *Adequate manpower.* (A company can succeed only with sufficient quality and quantity of human resources.)

5 *Adequate capital.* (Money must be re-invested back into the business.)

6 *Feasibility analysis.* (Companies must assess if a new venture has a reasonable chance of succeeding.)

7 *Advertising budget.* (Products and services must be promoted.)

8 *Conflict resolution.* (Cooperation and goodwill can reduce conflict.)

The classical school provides a systematic way of managing people and work that has proven useful over time and represents its major strength. Its major limitation is that it sometimes ignores differences among people and situations. For example, some of the classical principles for developing an organization are not well-suited to fast-changing situations.

The Behavioral Approach

behavioral approach to management
An approach to management that emphasizes improving management through an understanding of the psychological makeup of people.

The **behavioral approach to management** emphasizes improving management through the psychological makeup of people. In contrast to the largely technical emphasis of scientific management, a common theme of the behavioral approach focuses on the need to understand people. The behavioral approach is sometimes referred to as the human resources approach because of the focus on making optimum use of workers in a positive way, such as making jobs motivational. One hope of the behavioral approach was to reduce some of the labor–management conflict so prevalent under the classical approach to management. The behavioral approach has profoundly influenced management, and a portion of this book is based on behavioral theory. Typical behavior and human resource topics include leadership, motivation, communication, teamwork, and conflict.

The most direct origins of the behavioral approach are set in the 1930s through the 1950s. Yet earlier scholars, such as Robert Owen and Mary Parker Follett, also wrote about the importance of the human element. Working in the textile industry in Scotland in the early 1800s, Owen criticized fellow managers for failing to understand the human element in the mills. He contended that showing concern for workers resulted in greater profitability while at the same time reducing hardship for workers. Owen reported that efforts to pay careful attention to the human element often resulted in a 50 percent return on his investment.[24]

Follett focused her attention on the importance of groups in managing people. Although she published her works during the period of scientific management, Follett did not share Taylor's view that organizations should be framed around the work of individuals. In contrast, she argued that groups were the basis on which organizations should be formed. Follett explained that to enhance productivity and morale, managers should coordinate and aid the efforts of work groups.[25]

Three cornerstones of the behavioral approach are the Hawthorne studies, Theory X and Theory Y, and Maslow's need hierarchy. These developments contributed directly to managers' understanding of the importance of human relations on the job. Yet again, practicing managers have probably always known about the importance of human relations. The prehistoric person who developed the wheel probably received a congratulatory pat on the back from another member of the tribe!

The Hawthorne Studies

The purpose of the first study conducted at the Hawthorne plant of Western Electric (an AT&T subsidiary located in Cicero, Illinois) was to determine the effects of changes in lighting on productivity.[26] In this study, workers were divided into an experimental group and a control group. Lighting conditions for the experimental group varied in intensity from 24- to 46- to 70-foot candles. The lighting for the control group remained constant.

As expected, the experimental group's output grew with each increase in light intensity. But unexpectedly, the performance of the control group also changed. The production of the control group increased at about the same rate as that of the experimental group. Later, the lighting in the experimental group's area was reduced. The group's output continued to increase, as did that of the control group. A decline in the productivity of the control group finally did occur, but only when the intensity of the light was roughly the same as moonlight. Clearly, the researchers reasoned something other than illumination caused the changes in productivity.

An experiment was then conducted in the relay-assembly test room over a period of six years, with similar results. In this case, relationships among rest, fatigue and productivity were examined. First, normal productivity was established with no formal rest periods and a 48-hour week. Rest periods of varying length and frequency were then introduced. Productivity increased as the frequency and length of rest periods increased. Finally, the original conditions were reinstated. The return to the original conditions, however, did not result in the expected productivity drop. Instead, productivity remained at the same high level.

Hawthorne effect
The phenomenon in which people behave differently in response to perceived attention from evaluators.

One interpretation of these results was that the workers involved in the experiment enjoyed being the center of attention. Workers reacted positively because management cared about them. The phenomenon is referred to as the **Hawthorne effect**. It is the tendency of people to behave differently when they receive attention because they respond to the demands of the situation. In a work setting, employees perform better when they are part of any program, whether or not that program is valuable. Another useful lesson learned from the Hawthorne studies is that effective communication with workers is critical to managerial success.

Theory X and Theory Y of Douglas McGregor

A widely quoted development of the behavioral approach is Douglas McGregor's analysis of the assumptions managers make about human nature.[27] Theory X is a set of traditional assumptions about people. Managers who hold these assumptions are pessimistic about workers' capabilities. They believe workers dislike work, seek to avoid responsibility, are not ambitious, and must be supervised closely. McGregor urged managers to challenge these assumptions about human nature because they are untrue in most circumstances.

Theory Y, the alternative, poses an optimistic set of assumptions. These assumptions include the idea that people do accept responsibility, can exercise self-control, possess the capacity to innovate, and consider work to be as natural as rest or play. McGregor argued these assumptions accurately describe human nature in far more situations than most managers believe. He therefore proposed that these assumptions should guide managerial practice.

Maslow's Need Hierarchy

Most readers are already familiar with the need hierarchy developed by psychologist Abraham Maslow. This topic will be presented in Chapter 11 in discussions about motivation. Maslow suggested that humans are motivated by efforts to satisfy a hierarchy of needs, ranging from basic needs to those for self-actualization, or reaching one's potential. The need hierarchy prompted managers to think about ways of satisfying a wide range of worker needs to keep them motivated.

The primary strength of the behavioral (or human resources) approach is that it encourages managers to take into account the human element. Many valuable methods of motivating employees are based on behavioral research. The primary weakness of the behavioral approach is that it sometimes leads to an oversimplified view of managing people. Managers sometimes adopt one behavioral theory and ignore other relevant information. For example, several theories of motivation pay too little attention to the importance of money in people's thinking.

Quantitative Approaches to Management and Big Data

quantitative approach to management
A perspective on management that emphasizes use of a group of methods in managerial decision making, based on the scientific method.

The **quantitative approach to management** is a perspective on management that emphasizes the use of a group of methods in managerial decision making, based on the scientific method. Today, the quantitative approach is often referred to as management science, operations research (OR), or analytics. Frequently used quantitative tools and techniques include statistics, linear programming, network analysis, decision trees and computer simulations. These tools and techniques can be used when making decisions regarding inventory control, plant-site locations, quality control and a range of other decisions where objective information is important. Several quantitative approaches to decision making including the use of Big Data are found in Chapter 6 (quantitative techniques for planning and decision making).

Frederick Taylor's work provided the foundation for the quantitative approach to management. However, the impetus for the modern-day quantitative approach was the formation of OR teams to solve a range of problems faced by the Allied forces during World War II. Examples of the problems considered by the OR team included the bombing of enemy targets, the effective conduct of submarine warfare and the efficient movement of troops from one location to another. Following World War II, many industrial applications were found for quantitative approaches to management. The approach was facilitated by the increasing use of computers. A representative problem tackled by a quantitative approach to management would be to estimate the effect of a change in the price of a product on the product's market share.

The current emphasis on Big Data and analytics is a manifestation of the quantitative approach to management. **Big Data** refers to the collection of enormous amounts of data in order to find patterns and insights that are useful in marketing products and dealing with customers and employees. Restaurant chains illustrate how Big Data is being used to enhance customer experience and improve sales volume. A case in point is when guests of Sweetgreen Inc. place an order on the chain's mobile app, they are prompted to choose from a list of dietary restrictions, such as soy and nuts. The choices cause menu items containing these ingredients to be marked with a red asterisk so the guests know to avoid them. The selections are saved for future orders. This use of Big Data is a first step in a long-term plan to collect a mass of specific data about what customers prefer and why.[28]

Analytics is about making use of data and statistics to gain insight into an organization's practices, and thereby improve planning. Analytics often makes use of Big Data, but can also be accomplished using smaller amounts of data. Analytics have also been applied to managing human resources, such as gathering substantial feedback data about employee performance rather than rely on a single performance review rating. Results of brief online surveys might be analyzed to help understand how well managers are performing.[29]

The primary strength of the quantitative approach to management is that it enables managers to solve complex problems that cannot be solved by common sense alone. For example, management science techniques are used to make forecasts that take into account hundreds of factors simultaneously. A weakness of management science is that the answers it produces are often less precise than they appear. Although quantitative approaches use precise methods, much of the data is based on human estimates, which can be unreliable.

The Systems Perspective

The **systems perspective** is a way of viewing problems more than it is a specific approach to management. It is based on the concept that an organization is a system, or an entity of interrelated parts. If you adjust one part of the system, other parts will be affected automatically. For example, suppose you offer low compensation to job candidates. According to the systems approach, your action will influence your product quality. The "low-quality" employees who are willing to accept low wages will produce low-quality goods. Figure 1-2, which showed the process of management, reflected a systems viewpoint.

Another aspect of systems theory is to regard the organization as an open system, one that interacts with the environment. As illustrated in Figure 1-5, the organization

Big Data
The collection of enormous amounts of data in order to find patterns and insights that are useful in marketing products and dealing customers and employees.

systems perspective
A way of viewing aspects of an organization as an interrelated system. It is based on the concept that an organization is a system, or an entity of interrelated parts.

transforms inputs into outputs and supplies them to the outside world. If these outputs are perceived as valuable, the organization will survive and prosper. The feedback loop indicates that the acceptance of outputs by society gives the organization new inputs for revitalization and expansion. Managers can benefit from this diagram by recognizing that whatever work they undertake it should contribute something of value to external customers and clients.

Two other influential concepts from the systems perspective are entropy and synergy. **Entropy** is the tendency of a system to run down and die if it does not receive fresh inputs from its environment. As indicated in Figure 1-5, the organization must continually receive inputs from the outside world to make sure it stays in tune with, or ahead of, the environment. **Synergy** means that the whole is greater than the sum of the parts. When the various parts of an organization work together, they can produce much more than they could by working independently. For example, over ten years ago product developers at Apple Inc. thought about building a stylish new smartphone called the iPhone. The developers consulted immediately with manufacturing, engineering, purchasing and dealers to discuss the feasibility of their idea. Working together, the units of the organization produced a highly successful product launch in a tightly competitive market.

The Contingency Approach

The **contingency approach to management** emphasizes that there is no single best way to manage people or work in every situation. A method that leads to high productivity or morale under one set of circumstances may not achieve the same results in another. The contingency approach is derived from the study of leadership and organization structures. With respect to leadership, psychologists have developed detailed explanations of which style of leadership would work best in which situation. An example would be for the manager to give more leeway to competent group members. Also, the study of organization structure suggests that some structures work better in different environments, such as a team structure being best for a rapidly changing environment. Common sense also contributes heavily to the contingency approach. Experienced managers know that not all people and situations respond identically to identical situations. The contingency approach is emphasized throughout this book.

entropy
A concept of the systems approach to management that states an organization will die without continuous input from the outside environment.

synergy
A concept of the systems approach to management that states the whole organization working together will produce more than the parts working independently.

contingency approach to management
A perspective on management that emphasizes no single way to manage people or work is best in every situation. It encourages managers to study individual and situational differences before deciding on a course of action.

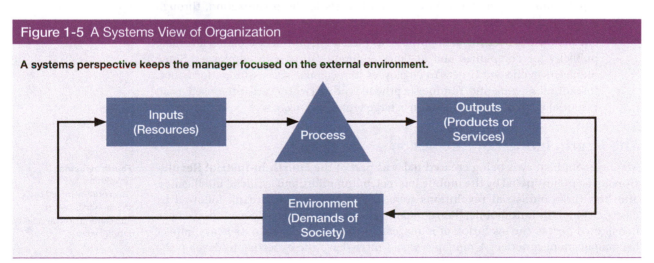

Figure 1-5 A Systems View of Organization

A systems perspective keeps the manager focused on the external environment.

The strength of the contingency approach is that it encourages managers to examine individual and situational differences before deciding on a course of action. Its major problem is that it is often used as an excuse for not acquiring formal knowledge about management. If management depends on the situation, why study management theory? The answer is because a formal study of management helps a manager decide which factors are relevant in a given situation.

The Information Technology and Social Media Era

The information technology era had relatively modest beginnings in the 1950s when electronic data processing first took over the manual processing of large batches of data and numbers. By the late 1980s, the impact of information technology and the Internet began to influence how managers manage work and people. A report by two economists concluded that the impact of the Internet on business is similar to the impact of electricity at the beginning of the 20th century.[30] Can you visualize what it must have been like to work in an office or factory without electricity?

The impact of information technology and the Internet on the work of managers is so vast that it is incorporated into most managerial activities, including customer satisfaction surveys and anonymous evaluations of managers. Information technology has modified managerial work in the following ways:

- Managers often communicate with people, even sending layoff notices, by e-mail rather than by telephone or in person. Managers send and receive messages more frequently than in the past because they are in frequent contact with the office through their smartphones and tablet computers.

- Many managers organize their sales and marketing efforts differently by using the Internet to conduct most transactions. Similarly, much purchasing of supplies and materials is conducted through the Internet. The current buzzword, *The Internet of Goods*, refers to the digitization of the production, sorting, and movement of physical products[31] (like ordering a mattress online and having it delivered to your door!) Almost every consumer-oriented business today has been drawn into using social networking sites such as Twitter and Facebook to market their products.

- Managers run their organizations more democratically because they receive input from so many workers at different levels in the organization, through e-mail and intranets.

- Social media is used for such purposes as marketing products, creating favorable publicity for companies and at times communicating with employees. Some managers even send tweets to employees to recognize successful performance. Instant messaging and Yammer (a private type of Twitter) are often used as an essential form of communication in large organizations.

The Fourth Industrial Revolution

Management history is being created today as part of the **Fourth Industrial Revolution**, an economy fueled by the mobile Internet, automation, and artificial intelligence. The first three industrial revolutions were driven by coal and steam, followed by electricity and the automobile, then computing.[32] The new Industrial Revolution can be considered part of the evolution of management thought because of its heavy impact on management practice. A manager would rarely have the expertise to develop the

Fourth Industrial Revolution
An economy fueled by the mobile Internet, automation, and artificial intelligence.

mobile Internet, automation, just as managers were never expected to design the industrial machinery in their department. Managers, however, had to incorporate these new technologies into their work.

artificial intelligence
The ability of a computer program or machine to think and learn in a manner that emulates human intelligence.

A key component of the Fourth Industrial Revolution is **artificial intelligence** (AI), the ability of a computer program or machine to think and learn in a manner that emulates human intelligence. An application of AI that impacts millions of people is targeted advertising on the Internet, that attempts to predict which products or services would interest a person based on his or her many clicks. We will describe how AI impacts managerial decision making in Chapter 5.

Thomas W. Malone, a professor of business management at the MIT Sloan School of Management, explains a key way in which AI impacts the manager's job. Given that AI can carry out large numbers of routine tasks, much of the remaining non-routine work is likely to be carried out by shifting groups of people with the combination of skills needed for whatever task needs to be carried out. The composition of groups will change depending on the type of task that needs to be accomplished. As AI becomes more dominant in organizations, the manager will be a facilitator of different groups of people performing non-routine work.[33] The impact of AI on the manager's job has already taken place to a slight extent, and Malone predicts a bigger impact in the future.

Be careful not to dismiss the evolution of management thought with historical information that is no longer relevant. Practicing managers can use all seven major developments in management thought. An astute manager selects information from the various schools of thought to achieve good results in a given situation. Visualize an executive making a large financial services firm more efficient and effective. The manager might rely on the classical school of management in restructuring company divisions. At the same time, the executive uses site visits and town hall meetings to communicate with employees, reflecting the behavioral approach to management.

The history of management is being written each year in the sense that the practice of management continues to evolve. As you study this book and listen to associated lectures you will learn about the new era in management, which emphasizes employee engagement, empowerment, outsourcing, and helping employees manage stress.

SUMMARY OF KEY POINTS

To facilitate your study and review of this and the remaining chapters, text summaries are organized around each chapter's learning objectives.

1 Explain what the term manager means and identify different types of managers.

A manager is a person responsible for work performance of other people. Management is the process of using organizational resources to achieve specific objectives through the functions of planning, organizing and staffing, leading and controlling. Organizational levels consist of top-level managers, middle-level managers, first-level managers, and individual contributors. New types of c-level managers continue to emerge, such as chief culture officer and chief transformation officer. Categories of managers include functional managers (who deal with specialties within the firm) and general managers, administrators (typically managers in nonprofit firms), entrepreneurs (those who start innovative businesses), small business owners, and team leaders. Entrepreneurs and small business owners are particularly passionate about their work.

2 Describe the process of management, including the functions of management.

To accomplish organizational goals, managers use resources and carry out the basic management functions. Resources are divided into four categories: human, financial, physical, and informational. The four managerial functions are planning, organizing, organization and staffing, leading and controlling.

3 Describe the various managerial roles.

The work of a manager can be divided into 17 roles that relate to the four major functions. Planning roles include strategic planner and operational planner. Organizing and staffing calls for the organizer, liaison, staffing coordinator, resource allocator, and task delegator roles. Leading roles include figurehead, spokesperson, negotiator, motivator and coach, team builder, team player, technical problem solver, and entrepreneur. Controlling involves the monitor

and disturbance handling roles. Managerial work has shifted substantially away from the controller and director role to that of coach, facilitator, and supporter. Top-level managers occupy more external roles than do lower-ranking managers. A useful perspective on the nature of management is that it is a practice rather than a science or profession. The use of evidence-based management helps professionalize the work of managers.

4 Identify the basic managerial skills and understand how they can be developed.

Managers need interpersonal, conceptual, diagnostic and political skills to accomplish their jobs. An effective way of developing managerial skills is to follow a general learning model. The model involves conceptual knowledge, behavioral guidelines, following examples, skill-development exercises, feedback and frequent practice. Management skills are also acquired through a combination of education and experience.

5 Identify the major developments in the evolution of management.

Management practice has an almost unlimited history, whereas the formal study of management began as part of the Industrial Revolution. The major developments in management thought and the history of management are: (1) the classical approach (scientific management and administrative management), (2) the behavioral or human resources approach, (3) quantitative approaches to management and Big Data, (4) the systems approach, (5) the contingency approach, (6) the information technology and social media era, and (7) the Fourth Industrial Revolution.

The best practices of managers today include elements of the seven major developments in management thought. Management thought continues to evolve, such as the current emphasis on employee engagement.

Key Terms and Phrases

manager 3

management 3

top-level managers 4

c-level manager 4

middle-level managers 5

first-level managers 5

entrepreneur 6

small-business owner 6

team leader 7

role 10

evidence-based management 15

empathy 16

scientific management 20

administrative management 20

behavioral approach to
management 21

Hawthorne effect 23

quantitative approach to
management 23

Big Data 24

systems perspective 24

entropy 25

synergy 25

contingency approach to
management 25

Fourth Industrial Revolution 26

artificial intelligence 27

Questions

Here, as in other chapters, groups or individuals can analyze the questions and cases. We strongly recommend using some small-group discussion to enhance learning.

1. In addition to a paid job, where else might a person develop managerial experience?

2. In recent years, many employers seek out technically trained job candidates who also have studied management. What advantages do you think employers see in a technical person studying management?

3. Why do large companies encourage many of their employees to, "think like an entrepreneur?"

4. During weather emergencies, such as a severe ice storm, some companies send out an alert that only "essential" employees should report to work. Explain why managers should or should not stay home on such emergency days.

5. Why might evidence-based management make an organization more competitive?

6. Why haven't loads of managers been replaced by apps and other software?

7. Describe any way in which your life has been changed by AI so far.

Skill-Building Exercise 1-A: Identifying Managerial Roles

Interview a manager at any level in any organization, including a retail store or restaurant. Determine which of the 17 managerial roles the manager you interview thinks apply to his or her job. Find out which one or two roles the manager thinks are the most important. Be ready to discuss your findings in class. You can often gain insight into which roles the manager emphasizes by asking about challenges the manager faces. For example, when asked about the biggest challenges in her job, a restaurant manager might say, "Turnover is a monster problem. It's so hard to find good servers who stick around for at least a year." The manager's comments indicate the organizing function.

Skill-Building Exercise 1-B: Managerial Skills of Athletic Coaches

The key managerial skills described in this chapter apply to managers in all fields. To help visualize these skills in action, individually or as a group, identify these skills as used by a coach during the next week. Perhaps you can watch a coach in person, on television, or read a newspaper report. Find a good example for each of the five skills and jot down the basis for your answer. To help point you in the right direction, consider the following example a student might furnish: "Last night I was watching a college basketball game on television. The score was tied with ten seconds to go, and a timeout was called. With the five players in the game in a huddle, the coach got out his clipboard and diagrammed a play using Xs, Os, and a marker. The play worked, and the team won in the final second. I would say the coach was using technical skill because he dug into the details of how to win."

For which skills was it easiest to find an example? For which skill was it the most difficult? What conclusions can you draw about the managerial skills of athletic coaches?

Technical Skill _____

Interpersonal Skill _____

Conceptual Skill _____

Diagnostic Skill _____

Political Skill _____

Management Now—Online Skill-Building Exercise: What Kind of Technology Skills Do Managers Need?

As explained in the chapter section *Five Key Managerial Skills*, managers need technical skills along with other skills. To dig further into this conclusion, conduct an informal investigation. Go to the career section of several of your favorite companies, but do not choose only high technology firms. Look under openings for managerial positions, and check out the qualifications needed. What demand do you see for technology skills? How encouraging do you find this information with respect to your own skill set and career?

Kevin Needs to Justify His Position

Twenty-nine-year-old Kevin holds what he considers an ideal position at this point in his career. He is the manager of the contingent workforce for a national waste disposal company, Clean Planet Forever, Inc. His employer basically picks up refuse from residences and small businesses, and then recycles whatever refuse is possible.

Clean Planet has both a full-time workforce and a contingent workforce. The latter includes part-time and temporary workers who load and unload refuse from residences and small businesses. A big part of Kevin's job is ensuring local operators have an ample supply of reliable workers. He also gives local managers suggestions for motivating and retaining workers. Kevin says he is proud of his management job for two reasons: "First of all we offer decent pay to a wide bunch of guys and gals who might otherwise go unemployed. I'm talking about decent people who may not have much formal education, but they have a great work ethic, and get the job done. Second, Clean Planet is literally helping save the planet. Garbage is a way of life in a civilized society, but these millions of tons of debris have to be disposed of or recycled safely."

Top-level management at Clean Planet has recently encountered some discouraging news. Competition has increased and many customers have cancelled their service. These are the "garbage-removal thieves" who haul their refuse away at night and dump it into the dumpsters of neighboring business firms, including restaurants and retail stores. As a result of these developments, company leadership has initiated a review of operations. The review includes an evaluation of which positions in the company can be cut. Just today Kevin received a long e-mail message from his boss, asking him to be prepared to justify to Clean Planet management why his position is necessary.

Kevin's initial reaction was that the request to justify his position was about as sensible as justifying why Clean Planet Forever needed to maintain trucks and hire drivers. That night however, Kevin said to his wife, "As wacko as it sounds, I'm going to get started tonight preparing a document to prove that I'm necessary."

Case Questions

1 If you were Kevin, how seriously would you take the demand to justify the necessity of your position to the company?

2 What suggestions can you offer Kevin to help him justify his position as "manager, contingent workforce"?

3 What do you think of the idea of Kevin making a PowerPoint presentation to upper management to help defend his position?

The Uber Drivers and their Algorithm Bosses

Amanda, a management professor at a college in Brooklyn, New York, decided to conduct research about how Uber drivers liked being managed by algorithms. She thought her research highly relevant because Uber has over one million drivers in the United States and Canada, and about 3 million globally. As part of her research, Amanda conducted a focus group of five Uber drivers who worked in Brooklyn. Her research grant enabled Amanda to pay the drivers $20 per hour for participating in the focus group, as well as providing refreshments.

The key question asked of the Uber drivers was, "How do you feel about being managed mostly by an algorithm rather than a human supervisor?" A partial transcript of the responses by the five drivers follows:

Sean: I kind of like being managed by an algorithm because it is more objective and impartial than a human supervisor. Yet, I have some issues. Above all, it's kind of creepy being under constant surveillance. As soon as I log in, my every move is being watched. Big Brother algorithm knows my GPS location, how fast I am driving, and my acceptance rate of customer requests. I thought that being a ride-hailing driver would make me feel independent. Instead, my every move is being watched.

Kaitlin: Being an Uber driver is a nice side hustle for me that brings me some needed extra bucks. Yet it is annoying to have to submit a complaint by e-mail or text message. The answer I get can seem like a canned response from customer service. A few weeks ago, one of my passengers was an overbearing middle-age man. He kept touching my hair even after I told him to please not do that after he did it once. He twirled my hair with his fingers three times after that. I would have liked to talk with a real supervisor about being harassed, but instead I had to write an e-mail to a call center in the Philippines about my problem. The answer I received from driver support was reasonable, but this was a frustrating experience that should have been talked over with a supervisor.

Boris: Uber is my only job so driving is a bigger part of my life than for part-time drivers. This focus group is fun for me because I get to interact face-to-face with other drivers. I guess the traditional taxi driver faces the same problem of being a lone wolf. You have no other drivers to talk with, and you are not part of a team. I don't even have a supervisor to give me a little encouragement, or to criticize me in person when I mess up.

Caleb: I find being an Uber driver dehumanizing in other ways, even though I generally like the freedom I have of not being chained to a regular job. I like to feel that I am an employee, even if part time. In one lawsuit against Uber, lawyers representing the company said that drivers are actually just consumers of Uber's technology, the same as passengers. This is crazy. Is a pilot for United Airlines just a consumer of airplane technology?

Jared: I like working about 20 hours a week for the world's leading ride-hailing service. My complaint is that Uber drivers are under so much political attack. In one city after another, some politicians are trying to ban Uber from operating in their city. If Uber management didn't have to spend so much money on legal fees to defend its existence, the drivers could be paid much more. Of course, we also have the problem that taxi cab drivers consider us to be their enemy. Uber and Lyft as well are being blamed for destroying the taxi-cab industry. I feel that I'm contributing to creating poverty for dozens of Brooklyn cab drivers and their families.

Amanda: Thank you so much guys. You are giving me tremendous qualitative data for my research.

Case Questions

1 **To what extent should Uber management take seriously a study like this about drivers being controlled by algorithms?**

2 **What, if anything, should Uber management do to build human contact into the job of the Uber driver?**

3 **What recommendations do you have for Uber management to deal with the perception of Uber drivers that they are under too much surveillance by algorithms?**

Source: Many of the facts in this case on based on the following sources: Mareike Möhlmann and Ola Henfridsson, "What People Hate About Being Managed by Algorithms, According to a Study of Uber Drivers," *Harvard Business Review* (https://hbr.org), August 30, 2019, pp. 1–5; Alex Rosenblat, "When Your Boss is an Algorithm" *www.nytimes.com*, October 12, 2018, pp. 1–2;Tim Simonite, "When Your Boss is an Uber Algorithm," *MIT Technology Review* (www.technologyreview.com), December 1, 2015, pp. 1–3; Isaac Chotiner, "When Your Boss Is an Algorithm," *Slate* (www.slate.com), October 26, 2018, pp. 1–4; John Koestler, "Uber Might Be The First AI-First Company, Which is Why They 'Don't Even Think About It Anymore'," Forbes (www.forbes.com) , pp. 1–2.

ENDNOTES

1. Original story based on facts and observations in the following sources: Rachel Feintzeig, "Radical New Idea: Middle Managers: When Experiments in Self-management Fall Flat, Companies Give Bosses another Try," *The Wall Street Journal*, August 10, 2015, p. B5; Olan Mochari, "When Even Flat Companies Need Managers," *Inc.com* (www.inc.com) August 19, 2015, pp. 1–3; "Middle Management Saves the Day," *The Healthy Leader* (http://healthycompanies.com), August 21, 2015. pp. 1–3; Malia Spencer, "Portland Online Code School Cuts Staff," *Portland Business Journal* (bizjournals.com), June 5, 2019, pp. 1–2.

2. David A. Garvin, "How Google Sold Its Engineers on Management," *Harvard Business Review*, December 2013, pp. 74–82.

3. "Chief Culture Officer: Job Description, Salary & ROI," *elm* (http://elearningmind.com, pp. 1–9. Accessed December 8, 2015.

4. Julie Jargon, "McDonald's Details Restructuring," *The Wall Street Journal*, June 12, 2018, p. B2.

5. "Why Middle Managers May Be the Most Important People In Your Company," *Knowledge@Wharton* (http://knowledge.wharton.upenn.edu), May 25, 2011, p. 1.

6. Donald C. Hambrick, Sydney Finkelstein, and Ann C. Mooney, "Executive Job Demands: New Insights for Explaining Strategic Decisions and Leader Behavior," *Academy of Management Review*, July 2005, pp. 472–491.

7. "An American Sage," *The Wall Street Journal*, November 14, 2005, p. A22.

8. Henry Mintzberg, *Managing* (San Francisco: Berrett-Koehler, 2009), p. 9.

9. Ed Barrows, "What is Strategy Execution?" *www.amanet.org*, August 6, 2014, p. 1.

10. This research is reported in Henry Mintzberg, *The Nature of Managerial Work* (New York: Harper & Row, 1973); Mintzberg, *Managing*, pp. 44–45.

11. Kenneth Graham Jr. and William L. Mihal, *The CMI Managerial Job Analysis Inventory* (Rochester, NY: Rochester Institute of Technology, 1987); Jeffrey S. Shippman, Erich Prien, and Gary L. Hughes, "The Content of Management Work: Formation of Task and Job Skill Composite Classifications," *Journal of Business and Psychology*, Spring 1991, pp. 325–354.

12. Joseph Pistrul and Dimo Dimov, "The Role of a Manager Has to Change in 5 Key Ways," *Harvard Business Review* (https://hbr.org), October 26, 2018, pp. 1–6.

13. Cynthia M. Pavett and Alan W. Lau, "Managerial Work: The Influence of Hierarchical Level and Functional Specialty," *Academy of Management Journal*, March 1983, pp. 170–177.

14. Mintzberg, *Managing*, p. 10.

15. Rakesh Khurana and Nitin Nohria, "It's Time to Make Management a True Profession," *Harvard Business Review*, October 2008, pp. 70–77.

16. Sara L. Rynes, Denise M. Rousseau, and Eric Barends, "Change the World: Teach Evidence-Based Practice!" *Academy of Management Learning & Education*, September 2014, pp. 305–321.

17. April L. Wright, Gemma Irving, Paul Hibbert, and Geoff Greenfield, "Student Understanding of Evidence-Based Management: Ways of Doing and Being," *Academy of Management Learning & Education*, December 2018, p. 453.

18. Victor Lipman, "Under-Management Is the Flip Side of Micromanagement—and It's a Problem Too," *Harvard Business Review* (https://hbr.org), November 8, 2018, pp. 1–5.

19. "A Driving Force in the Knowledge Economy." Article prepared and distributed by John Wiley & Sons, 2015.

20. Geoff Colvin, "Humans Are Underrated," *Fortune*, August 1, 2015, p. 108.

21. "Theory of Social and Economic Organization: Max Weber," in *Business: The Ultimate Resource* (Cambridge, MA: Perseus Publishing, 2002), p. 950.

22. Alfred Chandler, *Strategy and Structure* (New York: Doubleday, 1962); Albert Chandler, "Strategy and Structure: Albert Chandler," in *Business: The Ultimate Resource* (Cambridge, MA: Perseus Publishing, 2002), p. 950.

23. Leon Prieto and Simone Phipps, "Re-discovering Charles Spaulding's 'The Administration of Big Business': Insight into Early 20th Century African-American Management Thought," *Journal of Management History*, Volume 22, Issue 1, 2016, pp. 73–90.

24. Robert Owen, *A New View of Society* (New York: E. Bliss and F. White, 1825), p. 57.

25. Mary Parker Follett, *The New State: Group Organization of the Solution of Popular Government* (New York: Longmans Green, 1918), p. 28.

26. E. J. Roethlisberger and W. J. Dickson, *Management and the Worker* (Cambridge, MA: Harvard University Press, 1939).

27. Douglas McGregor, *The Human Side of Enterprise* (New York: McGraw-Hill, 1960), pp. 33–57.

28. Julie Jargon, "Restaurants See Value In Big Data," *The Wall Street Journal*, October 3, 2018, p. R5.

29. Mae Anderson, "Amazon's Data-Driven Approach Becoming More Common," *Associated Press*, August 30, 2015.

30. Martin Brooks and Zakhi Wahhaj, *Is the Internet Better Than Electricity?* Goldman Sachs report cited in Gary Hamel, "Inside the Revolution—Edison's Curse," *Fortune*, March 5, 2001, p. 176.

31. Michael Mandel, "Get Ready for the Internet of Goods," *The Wall Street Journal*, October 16, 2017, p. A17.

32. Christopher Mims, "Inside the New Industrial Revolution," *The Wall Street Journal*, November 13, 2018, pp. R1-R2; Klaus Schwabel, "The Fourth Industrial Revolution," *www.weforum.org.*, January 14, 2016, pp. 1–5.

33. Thomas W. Malone, "What AI Will Do To Corporate Hierarchies," *The Wall Street Journal*, April 2, 2019, p. R6.

CHAPTER 2

Ethics and Corporate Social Responsibility

OBJECTIVES

After studying this chapter and doing the exercises, you should be able to:

1 Identify the philosophical principles behind business ethics.

2 Explain how values relate to ethics.

3 Identify factors contributing to lax ethics and common violations.

4 Apply a guide to ethical decision making.

5 Describe the stakeholder viewpoint of social responsibility and the triple bottom line.

6 Present an overview of corporate social responsibility initiatives.

7 Summarize how managers can create an environment that fosters ethically and socially responsible behavior, promote such behavior, and the benefits of such activity.

Zillow Group, Inc. has been named by *Fortune* as one of the 100 Best Companies to work for based on employee surveys of how the workplace culture including trust in managers, compensation, and fairness. You may be familiar with Zillow as an online tool to obtain an estimate of what a particular house is worth. Zillow Group houses a portfolio of the largest real estate and home-related brands on mobile and the web. The company helps consumers with buying, renting, selling, and financing homes. In addition, Zillow provides a suite of marketing software and technology solutions to help real estate workers maximize business opportunities, and connect with millions of consumers. Zillow will also purchase homes from sellers, and quickly refurbish houses for resale.

Top-level management at Zillow places considerable emphasis on building a workplace that facilitates its employees having an enriched workplace experience. This is accomplished both through how managers treat their employees, and specific programs developed by the HR group.

The Zillow benefits package reflects what employees and their families think are important. The primary focus of the benefits package is to encourage work-and-personal life balance by addressing all facets of an employee's life. Among the highlights are payment of total premiums of medical, dental, and eye care, 16 weeks paid maternity leave, eight weeks parental leave for non-delivering parents, infertility treatment covered by insurance. Add to the list, a 401K plan that matches employee contributions, generous time off, and six weeks of sabbatical after six years of employment.

The Learning & Development team at Zillow empowers employees to increase their knowledge, build job-related skills, and take ownership for their careers. The internal mobility team helps employees navigate new job opportunities at Zillow.

Diversity is a core value of Zillow Group. Management recognizes that the unique perspective and experiences of employees are as valuable as their skills. The company strives to maintain a culture that is both open and inclusive, with an emphasis on building a work environment that is representative of the diversity with the communities in the various company locations.

Dan Spaulding, Chief People Officer of the People Group, says that there are four qualities most associated with being a great manager. As a result, managers are encouraged to do the following:

- *Show They Care.* Managers should show interest in their team member's lives outside of work, and have sympathy for employees who are having a bad day.

- *Empower Their Teams.* Managers should give employees the tools and information they need to feel confident in the work they are performing, so they can be successful contributors.

- *Know How to Get It Done.* Effective managers know how to make things happen, who to talk to, and how to navigate the organization.

- *Communicate.* Effective managers make sure the team is informed, know what is going on, and what is expected of each member.

Zillow CEO Spencer Rascoff perceives employee recruitment and retention as the company's top priority. If a star employee leaves the firm, Rascoff or another high-level manager will attempt to convince the employee to return.[1]

Based on how employees at the company are treated, Zillow Group, Inc. can be considered a socially responsible employer. The purpose of this chapter is to explain the importance of and provide insights into ethics and social responsibility. To accomplish this purpose, we present various aspects of ethics and social responsibility, including organizational activities to help create a sustainable (green) environment. We also present guidelines to help managerial workers make ethical decisions and to conduct socially responsible acts.

BUSINESS ETHICS

Understanding and practicing good business ethics is an important part of a manager's job. **Ethics** is the study of moral obligation, or separating right from wrong. Although many unethical acts are illegal, others are legal and issues of legality vary by nation. An example of an illegal, unethical act in the United States is giving a government official a kickback for placing a contract with a specific firm. An example of a legal, yet unethical practice is making companies more profitable by eliminating their pension plans.

One of the many reasons that ethics are important is that customers, suppliers and employees prefer to deal with ethical companies. Prudential, the insurance and financial services giant, is a representative example. The company has been in business for 140 years. Part of Prudential's longevity is because it is perceived to be an ethical institution that gives high priority to the welfare of people who are insured by or place their investments with the company.

A useful perspective in understanding business ethics emphasizes **moral intensity**, or the magnitude of an unethical act.[2] When an unethical act is not of large consequence, a person might behave unethically without much thought. However, if the act is of large consequence, the person might refrain from unethical or illegal behavior. For example, a manager might plagiarize someone else's speech or make an unauthorized copy of software (both unethical and illegal acts). The same manager, however, might hesitate to dump toxins into a river or sexually harass a business intern.

Business ethics will be mentioned at various places in this text. Here we approach the subject from several perspectives: philosophical principles, values, contributing factors to ethical problems, common ethical problems and a guide to ethical decision making. To better relate the study of ethics to you, take the self-quiz presented in Figure 2-1.

moral intensity
The magnitude of an unethical act.

Philosophical Principles Underlying Business Ethics

A standard way of understanding ethical decision making is to know the philosophical basis for making these decisions. When attempting to decide what is right and wrong, managerial workers can focus on: (1) consequences, (2) duties, obligations, and principles, or (3) integrity.[3]

Focus on Consequences and Pragmatism

When attempting to decide what is right or wrong, people can sometimes focus on the consequences of their decisions or actions. According to this criterion, if no one gets hurt, the decision is ethical. The decision maker is concerned with the utility of the decision. What really counts is the net balance of good consequences over bad. An automotive body shop manager, for example, might decide that using low quality replacement fenders is ethically wrong because the fender will rust quickly or damage under light impact. To focus on consequences, the decision maker would have to be aware of all the good and bad consequences of a given decision. The body-shop manager would have to estimate such factors as how angry customers would be whose cars were repaired with inferior parts and how much negative publicity would result.

Closely related to focusing on consequences is *pragmatism*, the belief that there are no absolute principles or standards, no objective truth and no objective reality. "Truth" is whatever works, or helps you attain the goals you want. Edwin A. Locke, professor emeritus of leadership and management at the University of Maryland, believes that pragmatism is the most prevalent ethical theory in use.[4] Unfortunately, being a pragmatist can land an executive in prison. A classic example is Bernard L. Madoff, the former Nasdaq chairman, and later head of his own investment company, who pretended to customers that he was making true investments with their money. Madoff apparently thought that lying to customers was pragmatic.

Focus on the Rights of Individuals (Deontology)

Another approach to making an ethical decision is to examine one's duties in making the decision. The theories underlying this approach are referred to as *deontology*, from the Greek word *deon*, or duty. Deontology also refers to moral philosophies that center on the rights of individuals and the intentions associated with a particular behavior. A fundamental idea of deontology is that equal respect must be given to all persons.

Figure 2-1 The Ethical Reasoning Inventory

Describe how much you agree with each of the following statements, using the following scale: disagree strongly (DS); disagree (D); neutral (N); agree (A); agree strongly (AS). Circle the answer that best fits your level of agreement.

Managerial Role	DS	D	N	A	AS
1 When applying for a job, I would cover up the fact that I had been fired from my most recent job.	5	4	3	2	1
2 Cheating just a few dollars in one's favor on an expense account is okay if the person needed the money.	5	4	3	2	1
3 Employees should inform on each other for wrongdoing.	1	2	3	4	5
4 It is acceptable to give approximate figures for expense account items when one does not have all the receipts.	5	4	3	2	1
5 I see no problem with conducting a little personal business, such as shopping online, on company time.	5	4	3	2	1
6 A business owner has the right to take family members on a business trip and claim the cost as a business expense.	5	4	3	2	1
7 To make a sale, I would stretch the truth about a delivery date.	5	4	3	2	1
8 I would flirt with my boss just to get a bigger salary increase.	5	4	3	2	1
9 If I received $200 for doing some odd jobs, I would report it on my income tax returns.	1	2	3	4	5
10 I see no harm in taking home a few office supplies.	5	4	3	2	1
11 It is acceptable to read the e-mail and instant messages of co-workers even when not invited to do so.	5	4	3	2	1
12 It is unacceptable to call in sick to take a day off, even if only done once or twice a year.	1	2	3	4	5
13 I would accept a permanent, full-time job even if I knew I wanted the job for only six months.	5	4	3	2	1
14 I would check company policy before accepting an expensive gift from a supplier.	1	2	3	4	5
15 To be successful in business, a person usually has to ignore ethics.	5	4	3	2	1
16 If I were physically attracted to a job candidate, I would hire him or her over another better qualified candidate.	5	4	3	2	1
17 I tell the truth all the time on the job.	1	2	3	4	5
18 Software should never be copied, except as authorized by the publisher.	1	2	3	4	5
19 I would authorize accepting an office machine on a 30-day trial period, even if I knew I had no intention of making a purchase.	5	4	3	2	1
20 I would never accept credit for a co-worker's ideas.	1	2	3	4	5
21 I would park my car in the parking lot of another company just to make use of that company's wi-fi for my laptop computer.	5	4	3	2	1
22 I would see no problem in taking debris from our company and placing it in another company's dumpster just to save us hauling fees.	5	4	3	2	1

Scoring and interpretation: Add the numbers you have circled to obtain your score.

90–100 You are a strongly ethical person who may take a little ribbing from co-workers for being too straightlaced.

60–89 You show an average degree of ethical awareness, and therefore should become more sensitive to ethical issues.

41–59 Your ethics are underdeveloped, but you have at least some awareness of ethical issues. You need to raise your level of awareness about ethical issues.

20–40 Your ethical values are far below contemporary standards in business. Begin a serious study of business ethics.

Rights, such as the rights for privacy and safety are the key aspect of deontology. From a deontological perspective, the principles are more important than the consequences. If a given decision violates one of these universal principles, it is automatically unethical even if nobody gets hurt. An ethical body shop manager might think, "It just isn't right to use replacement fenders that are not authorized by the automobile manufacturer. Whether or not these parts rust quickly or fare poorly in a crash is a secondary consideration."

Focus on Integrity (Virtue Ethics)

The third criterion for determining the ethics of behavior focuses on the character of the person involved in the decision or action. If the person in question has good character, and genuine motivation and intentions, he or she is behaving ethically. The ingredients making up character will often include the two other ethical criteria. One might judge a person to have good character if she or he follows the right principles and respects the rights of others.

The decision maker's environment or community helps define what integrity means. You might have more lenient ethical standards for a person selling you a speculative investment than you would for a bank vice president who accepted your cash deposit.

Virtue is more complicated than its everyday meaning. According to a scholarly analysis of the concept, **virtue** is the "human inclination to feel, think, and [behave in] ways that express moral excellence and contribute to the common good."[5] A virtuous manager or professional would therefore have to believe strongly in carrying acts that most people think are good. At the same time, he or she would be a role model for others and provide output that helps many people.

virtue
The human inclination to feel, think, and [behave in] ways that express moral excellence and contribute to the common good.

The virtue ethics of managers and professionals who belong to professional societies can be judged readily. Business-related professions having codes of ethics include accountants, purchasing managers and certified financial planners. To the extent the person abides by the tenets of the stated code, he or she is behaving ethically. An example of such a tenet would be for a financial planner to be explicit about any commissions gained from a client accepting the advice.

When faced with a complex ethical decision, you are best advised to incorporate all three philosophical approaches. You might think through the consequences of a decision, along with an analysis of duties, rights, principles and intentions. It would also be helpful to display virtue.

Values and Ethics

Values are closely related to ethics. Values can be considered clear statements of what is critically important. Ethics become the vehicle for converting values into actions, or doing the right thing. For example, a clean environment is a value, whereas not littering is practicing ethics. Many firms contend that they "put people before profits" (a value). If this assertion was true, a manager would avoid actions such as delaying payments to a vendor just to hold on to money longer, or firing a group member for having negotiated a deal that lost money. Values are also closely tied to the character of a person, or being moral. A person of good character would do the right things despite outside pressures to do the opposite.[6] A pharmaceutical executive of good character would reduce pressures to create false early expiration dates on some over-the-counter medicines just to enhance sales as demanded by outside investors.

LEARNING OBJECTIVE 2

Explain how values relate to ethics.

An example of company values that facilitate ethical behavior are those espoused by Gunderson Health System, a Wisconsin-based nonprofit healthcare network. Company leaders specified their values as respect for individuals, excellence, compassion, innovation, and integrity. The CEO at the time the values were articulated, Jeff Thompson, said it is important that everyone from billing department associates to senior executives be clear about the values that unite company employees.[7] It would be equally important for employees to implement these values.

A person's values also influence which kind of behaviors he or she believes are ethical. An executive who strongly values profits might not find it unethical to raise prices more than needed to cover additional costs. Another executive who strongly values family life might suggest the company invest money in an on-premises child-care center.

Values are important because the right values can lead to a competitive advantage. An example of a winning value is building relationships with customers. A major contributor to the success of Mary Kay is that associates are taught to build relationships with their direct customers and try extra hard to please them.

ethically-centered management
Management that emphasizes that the high quality of an end product takes precedence over its scheduled completion.

The concept of **ethically-centered management** helps put some teeth into an abstract discussion of how values relate to ethics. Ethically-centered management emphasizes that the high quality of an end product takes precedence over its scheduled completion. At the same time, it sets high quality standards for dealing with employees and managing production. The concept of ethically-centered management is helpful in understanding what went wrong in the many product recalls. A product such as a baby crib is shipped to distributors before all the possible hazards are removed. The product developers and the manufacturers might have been given such a tight deadline for product delivery that a thorough, field-tested inspection was not possible.

LEARNING OBJECTIVE **3**

Identify factors contributing to lax ethics and common violations.

Sources of Unethical Decisions and Behavior

Ethical problems remain a major concern in the workplace. Many factors contribute to these types of unethical behavior. A team of researchers pulled together 30 years of research to conclude that drivers of unethical behavior fall into characteristics of the: (a) individual, (b) moral issue facing the person, and (c) organizational environment.[8] Here we will present several of the possibilities under each source of unethical decisions and behavior.

Individual Characteristics

Self-interest continues to be a factor that influences ethics, often taking the form of greed and gluttony, or the desire to maximize self-gain at the expense of others. For example, when a company is losing money is it justified for a CEO to maneuver his or her way into a $20 million compensation package for that year? Greed and gluttony are sometimes attributed to having a Machiavellian personality, which relates to a desire to manipulate others for personal gain. For example, a person with strong Machiavellian tendencies would be willing to claim that somebody else was responsible for his or her spreadsheet analysis containing serious errors.

Another individual driver of unethical behavior is *unconscious biases that lead us to behave in unjust ways toward others*. More than two decades of psychological research indicates that most of us harbor unconscious biases that differ from our consciously held beliefs. The flawed judgments from these biases create ethical problems and can interfere with a manager's intention to recruit and retain high-level talent, among other problems. Suppose a real estate manager holds the common stereotype that women are more suited to real estate sales because they are more home oriented and more responsive to the needs of customers. When the manager is recruiting new agents, he or she might unjustly exclude a qualified male for the position. If the male candidate is equally or better qualified than a given women candidate, the real estate manager is behaving unethically.

It is difficult to overcome an unconscious bias because it is below the level of awareness. However, if you carefully analyze the decisions you have made recently, you might find a pattern of slightly unethical behavior.[9] For example, a worker might say, "Of the last six people I recommended to work for our company, all are the same nationality and race as mine. Have I been excluding other good candidates without meaning to do so?"

The most pervasive reason for unethical behavior is *rationalization*, or making up a good excuse for poor ethics. In this context, a rationalization can be regarded as a mental strategy that enables employees, and others around them, to view their corrupt acts as justified.[10] Many of the reasons already presented for unethical behavior involve an element of rationalization, such as blaming the organizational culture for a personal misdeed.

The person who commits an unethical act might dismiss its significance by observing that other people in comparable positions are doing the same thing, such as cheating on an expense account. At the top of the organization, a CEO and CFO might team together to lie to outside analysts about accumulating debt and plunging sales with the rationalization they are trying to save the company.

Job dissatisfaction can also contribute to unethical behavior. A worker who is strongly dissatisfied might behave unethically as a way of getting revenge on the employer. For example, a manager who is strongly dissatisfied with his pay might use his company-paid smartphone to make a series of personal calls.

Another reason that some people in a work environment behave unethically is that they have a tendency to *morally disengage*, or think in such a way as to avoid being moral without feeling distress. The person who morally disengages cognitively reconstructs his or her harmful behavior by ignoring, minimizing, or challenging the harmful effects. As a result, the person does not feel guilty.[11] A product development specialist might morally disengage from selling a trade secret to a competitor by rationalizing that he or she is underpaid and therefore merits supplementary income from working so hard.

The Nature of the Moral Issue

The moral intensity of the issue is a driver of unethical behavior, with many people willing to behave unethically when the issue does not appear serious. Visualize Gus, preparing a vat of soup at a food company. If one mosquito flies into the vat, Gus might go ahead and send the soup off for placement into cans. However, if a nest of hornets flew into the soup, Gus might blow the whistle even if his supervisor might not be happy about the hornets.

Another issue-related driver of unethical behavior is **moral laxity**, *a slippage in moral behavior because other issues seem more important at the time*. The implication is that the businessperson who behaves unethically has not carefully planned the immoral behavior but lets it occur by not exercising good judgment. For example, many deaths from fires in nightclubs result from management not paying careful enough attention to fire regulations, such as having adequate escape exits or fireproofing.

moral laxity
A slippage in moral behavior because other issues seem more important at the time.

The Ethical Climate in the Organization

Another major contributor to unethical behavior is an *organizational atmosphere that condones such behavior*. A group of case histories of unethical behavior in business detected the underlying theme of a management culture that fostered ethical misdoing—or at least permitted it to happen—even when the organization espoused a code of ethics. One such ethical lapse was hiring undocumented immigrant workers.[12]

Unethical behavior is often triggered by *pressure from higher management to achieve goals*. Too much emphasis on meeting financial targets can push workers toward meeting financial targets in questionable ways. Visualize a chain of hearing centers for which management places difficult-to-attain sales goals on each unit. Some associates might be inclined to exaggerate the necessity for hearing aids for some potential customers who visit the center to find out if their hearing needs improvement.

An unethical decision or behavior can sometimes stem from a combination of individual, issue-related, and organizational factors. In 2010, Toyota recalled millions of vehicles worldwide to repair accelerators that stuck while eight models of Toyota vehicles were being driven. A related problem was that accelerators were sometimes catching on floor mats. The company had received more than 2,000 complaints of unintended acceleration during an eight-year period. Toyota management discounted early reports of the problem. Also, management was not entirely truthful about supporting evidence from the National Highway Traffic Safety Administration for its dismissal of the gravity of the problem. An ethical issue here might be that Toyota management did not pay serious enough attention to seriousness of the sticking accelerator problem.[13]

In 2015, Toyota recalled another 6.5 million cars, this time for a faulty window switch that was not properly lubricated during manufacturing. When the switch wears down over time it could cause a short circuit that could overheat the car part, leading to a potential fire, although none were reported.[14]

An individual factor contributing to this unethical behavior might have been that Toyota executives wanted to escape blame. An issue factor is that at first it appeared the number of problem accelerators was quite small considering the total number of Toyota vehicles on the road. An organizational climate factor is that Toyota had developed such a great reputation for its meticulous approach to building cars and servicing customers. It might therefore have seemed unbelievable to Toyota top-level managers that the company was facing a true safety and quality issue. An organization can develop a climate or culture of smugness.

Frequent Ethical Violations

Certain ethical violations, including illegal actions, recur in the workplace. Familiarizing yourself with these behaviors can be helpful in managing the ethical behavior of others as well as monitoring individual behavior. A list of commonly found ethical temptations and violations, including criminal acts follows[15]:

1　*Stealing from employers and customers.* Employee theft costs U.S. companies about $50 billion annually. Retail employees steal goods from their employers and financial service employees steal money. Examples of theft from customers include airport baggage handlers who steal from passenger suitcases, as well as bank employees, stockbrokers and attorneys who siphon money from customer accounts. Many corporate security specialists estimate that 25 to 40 percent of all employees steal from their employers.

Customers also steal from companies in many forms, including purchasing an expensive item intended for a single use, and then returning the product. One example is a customer who purchases a dress for a special purpose and then returns the dress because "it does not fit." Another example is purchasing an expensive digital camera to record an event, and then returning it after the event has been uploaded.

2 *Illegally copying software.* A rampant problem in the workplace is making unauthorized copies of software for either company or personal use. The penalties for violating software licensing agreements can be stiff, reaching over $500,000. Similarly, many employees make illegal copies of videos, books and magazine articles instead of purchasing these products.

3 *Treating people unfairly.* Being fair to people includes equity, reciprocity and impartiality. Fairness revolves around the issue of giving people equal rewards for accomplishing the same amount of work. The goal of human resource legislation is to make decisions about people based on their qualifications and performance—not on the basis of demographic factors such as gender, race, or age. A fair working environment is where performance is the only factor that counts (equity). Employer-employee expectations must be understood and met (reciprocity). Prejudice and bias must be eliminated (impartiality).

4 *Sexual harassment.* Sexual harassment involves making compliance with sexual favors a condition of employment, or creating a hostile, intimidating environment related to sexual topics. Harassment violates the law and is also an ethical issue because it is morally wrong and unfair. Sexual harassment is widespread in the U.S. workplace and in other countries as well. The U.S. Equal Employment Opportunity Commission (EEOC) reported about 7,500 charges are filed annually, with about 16 percent of these charges from men.[16] Recognize that very few incidents of sexual harassment result in formal charges to the EEOC.

5 *Conflict of interest.* Part of being ethical is making business judgments only on the basis of the merits in a situation. Imagine you are a supervisor who is romantically involved with a worker within the group. When it came time to assigning raises, it would be difficult for you to be objective. A **conflict of interest** occurs when your judgment or objectivity is compromised. Most of the major financial scandals in brokerage firms in recent years have stemmed from blatant conflicts of interest. An example would be a research analyst from an investment firm giving a recommendation to purchase a stock from a company who is an investment banking client of the analyst's firm. If the analyst makes "buy" recommendations about the company's stock, that company will more likely continue to be a lucrative client of the analyst's firm.

conflict of interest
A situation that occurs when your judgment or objectivity is compromised.

The Sarbanes–Oxley Act of 2002 attempted to reduce many conflicts of interest in business, such as requiring a company auditing a firm must not receive money for other services from that firm. Also, companies are required to assign certain consulting and auditing work to different firms.

6 *Accepting kickbacks and bribes for doing business with another company.* Also referred to as "payola," accepting cash payments, special deals on stocks and lavish gifts from industrial customers is a perennial temptation in business. Sending a manager and his or her family on a week's vacation after the manager closes a deal to make a huge purchase from the vendor is an example of a kickback. Giving gifts to curry favor in business has long been standard

practice in business, yet is unethical because it creates a conflict of interest described above.

7 *Divulging confidential information.* Other people can trust an ethical person not to divulge confidential information unless the welfare of others is at stake. The challenge of dealing with confidential information arises in many areas of business, including information about performance evaluation results, compensation, personal problems of employees, disease status of employees and co-worker bankruptcies. A serious betrayal of confidence took place when Anil Kumar, a former senior partner at the consulting firm McKinsey & Co. was paid more than $1 million to provide tips on McKinsey's clients to the hedge fund firm, Galleon Group. The tips were useful to the hedge fund firm (one that deals in complex investments) because they could make profitable trades based on that information.[17]

8 *Misuse of corporate resources.* A corporate resource is anything the company owns, including its name and reputation. Assume a woman named Jennifer Yang worked as a financial consultant at Bank of America, Merrill Lynch. It would be unethical for her to establish a financial advisory service and put on her website, "Jennifer Yang, financial consultant, Bank of America, Merrill Lynch." Using corporate resources can fall into the gray area, such as whether to borrow a notebook computer to prepare income taxes for a fee.

An ethical violation, particularly among top-level executives is to misuse corporate resources in an extravagant, greedy manner. The temptation is greater for top executives because they have more control over resources. Examples of the greedy use of corporate resources include using the corporate jet for personal vacations, or for friends and family members; paying for personal items with an expense account; and paying exorbitant consulting fees to friends and family members.

9 *Extracting extraordinary compensation from the organization.* Related to the misuse of corporate resources is extraction of a disproportionate share of compensation from a company. A person usually has to be a CEO to engage in this type of ethical violation. Two examples: In 2019, Safra Catz, co-CEO of Oracle Corporation, was paid $108.3 million, and Robert Iger, CEO of Disney was paid $65.6 million.[18] Some management writers, however, do not regard such payouts as unethical. One argument for the high compensation is that unless a talented executive is highly paid, he or she will join the competition. Another argument is that some of these high executive payouts are in stock, and the stock can lose value rapidly.

10 *Corporate espionage.* An entrenched unethical practice is to collect competitive information to the extent that it constitutes spying on competitors. Among the common forms of spying are computer hacking, bribing present employees to turn over trade secrets and prying information from relatives of workers with useful information. Outright stealing of information about rivals is obviously unethical. A less obvious form of espionage would be to leave your company, join a competitor, and then reveal key insider information about the first company to your new employer.

11 *Poor cyberethics.* The Internet creates considerable potential for unethical behavior, thereby making it important for all employees to resist the temptation of practicing poor cyberethics. One example of questionable ethics would

be to send a giant e-mail file with a video containing your opinion about a non-work-related issue to everyone in your company. If many people send such attachments, the servers would be blocked from conducting legitimate company business. An ethical breach of greater consequences would be to steal personal identities from job résumés online. A scam in this area is to contact the author of a résumé claiming to be an employer. The scam artist then asks for additional personal information such as the person's social security number and bank account number.

Business Scandals as Ethical Violations

Major ethical and legal violations in business have taken place forever. The best-known scandals are associated with infamous executives. Yet scandals are also perpetuated by hundreds of players, including the Internet frauds of identity theft and work-at-home scams (such as making you an agent for transferring funds received from customers). Identity theft and virus-spreading is rampant on Facebook and Twitter.

These major financial scandals have caused mammoth job losses, wiped out pension funds, triggered huge investment losses by individuals and the bankruptcy of vendors who supplied the companies that went bankrupt. Furthermore, the families of some of the unethical executives were badly hurt when the primary breadwinner consumed family resources on legal fees and then went to prison. People who worked for scandalized companies sometimes find it difficult to find work elsewhere. Another problem is that distrust of managers could lead to fewer talented people wanting to enter the field of business. At times scandals are embarrassing but do not have huge negative financial consequences. A brief description of two well-publicized scandals follows.

Emission Cheating Scandal of Volkswagen. In 2015 Volkswagen admitted to installing software in more than 11 million diesel vehicles so their engines temporarily ran cleaner when being tested for pollution. The specific purpose of the software was to conceal emissions of harmful nitrous oxide and give the public an inflated view of the environmental friendliness of their vehicles as a way of stimulating sales. The scheme was exposed by the United States Environmental Protection Agency and triggered investigations and lawsuits around the globe. Nine Volkswagen managers were suspended and sales of VWs plunged in the United States and the United Kingdom.

Hans Dieter Pötsch, the VW chairman, attributed the scandal to a combination of individual misconduct and mistakes. He said company engineers had installed the "defeat" devices in engines—or software that could detect when they were being tested—after concluding they could not meet the emissions targets for diesel cars in the United States by "permissible means."[19] The diesel-emissions problems continued into the future for the company. In December of 2019, German prosecutors raided Volkswagen's Wolfsburg, Germany headquarters as part of a fresh investigation into diesel VWs, particularly a four-cylinder engine.[20]

The scandal was particularly bizarre because VW is one of Germany's most important companies with approximately 230,000 employees, and had a reputation as an honorable and reputable manufacturer. Furthermore, VW and its several brands ranks as one of the world's largest automobile manufacturers. The VW brand is so well respected and admired, that the company has been able to rebuild its reputation.

Wells Fargo and Bogus Customer Accounts. In 2016, federal investigators revealed that Wells Fargo had opened more than two million bank and credit card accounts for customers without obtaining their consent from 2011 t0 2015. As a result of these bogus accounts, customers paid $2.6 million in unwarranted fees (such as draft overcharges) for tens of thousands of unaware customers. Then CEO John Stumpf and the executive team agreed to pay $185 million in penalties. Several years later the settlement reached $575 million. The bank fired 5,300 employees for creating unauthorized bank and credit-card accounts. Stumpf gave back $41 million of his compensation, and said, "We never directed nor wanted our team members to provide products and services to customers that they did not want." Stumpf resigned in 2016, receiving a $134.1 million retirement package. In 2018, the successor CEO, Tim Sloan, told Congress that he was sorry for how the bank abused customers.[21] In 2020, the U.S. government announced that Stumpf had been barred from ever working at a bank and will pay $17.5 million in connection to scandals at Wells Fargo.[22]

A person reading these two examples of unethical behavior of managers might wonder how wealthy, intelligent people could exercise such poor judgment. The answer lies partially in the explanations for unethical behavior presented earlier, with particular attention to greed, gluttony and avarice. For a deeper level explanation, recognize that emotion can cloud anybody's judgment. Think of all the young professional football players who ruin their careers by driving under the influence or illegally using handguns.

A Guide to Ethical Decision Making

A practical way of improving ethical decision making is to run contemplated decisions through an ethics test when any doubt exists. The ethics test presented next was used at the Center for Business Ethics at Bentley College as part of corporate training programs. Other guides to ethical decision making ask similar questions. Decision makers are taught to ask themselves[23]:

1 *Is it right?* This question is based on the deontological theory of ethics that there are certain universally accepted guiding principles of rightness and wrongness, such as "thou shall not steal."

2 *Is it fair?* This question is based on the deontological theory of justice, implying that certain actions are inherently just or unjust. For example, it is unjust to fire a high-performing employee to make room for a less competent person who is a personal friend.

3 *Who gets hurt?* This question is based on the notion of attempting to do the greatest good for the greatest number of people.

4 *Would you be comfortable if the details of your decision were reported on the front page of your local newspaper, on a popular website or blog, or through your company's e-mail system?* This question is based on the universalist principle of disclosure.

5 *Would you tell your child (or young relative) to do it?* This question is based on the deontological principle of reversibility, referring to reversing who carries out the decision.

6 *How does it smell?* This question is based on a person's intuition and common sense. For example, underpaying many accounts payable by a few dollars to save money would "smell" bad to a sensible person.

A decision that was obviously ethical, such as donating some managerial time for charitable organizations, would not need to be run through the six-question test. Neither would a blatantly illegal act, such as not paying employees for work performed. But the test is useful for decisions that are neither obviously ethical nor obviously unethical. Among such gray areas would be charging clients based on their ability to pay and developing a clone of a successful competitive product.

Another type of decision that often requires an ethical test is choosing between two rights (rather than right versus wrong).[24] Suppose a blind worker in the group has personal problems so great that her job performance suffers. She is offered counseling but does not follow through seriously. Other members of the team complain about the blind worker's performance because she is interfering with the group achieving its goals. If the manager dismisses the blind worker, she might suffer severe financial consequences. (She is the only wage earner in her family.) However, if she is retained the group will suffer consequences of its own. The manager must now choose between two rights, or the lesser of two evils.

CORPORATE SOCIAL RESPONSIBILITY

LEARNING OBJECTIVE 5

Describe the stakeholder viewpoint of social responsibility and the triple bottom line.

Many people believe that firms have an obligation to be concerned about outside groups affected by an organization. **Corporate social responsibility** is the idea that firms have obligations to society beyond their economic obligations to owners or stockholders and also beyond those prescribed by law or contract. Both ethics and social responsibility relate to the goodness or morality of organizations. However, business ethics is a narrower concept that applies to the morality of an individual's decisions and behaviors. Corporate social responsibility is a broader concept that relates to an organization's impact on society, beyond doing what is ethical.[25] To behave in a socially responsible way, managers must be aware of how their actions influence the environment.

corporate social responsibility
The idea that firms have obligations to society beyond their economic obligations to owners or stockholders and also beyond those prescribed by law or contract.

A continuing debate concerns what obligations companies have toward being socially responsible. One position is that business firms should take action on issues ranging from pollution and global warming to AIDS, illiteracy and poverty. The other position is that many investors want companies in which they invest to focus on the bottom line so they can maximize their returns. In reality, these positions can be mutually supportive. Many socially responsible actions are the by-products of sensible business decisions. For instance, it is both socially responsible and profitable for a company to improve the language and math skills of entry-level workers and invest in local schooling. Literate and numerate entry-level workers for some jobs may be in short supply, and employees who cannot follow written instructions and do basic math may be unproductive. Also, a business firm that is environmentally friendly might attract the type of workers who are talented enough to help the firm become more profitable.

A practical problem in practicing corporate social responsibility is that not all interested parties agree on what constitutes responsible behavior. Target stores might have many customers who believe that citizens have a constitutional right to defend themselves with handguns against home intruders. To this group of customers, a retailer selling handguns to the public would reflect corporate social responsibility. Another customer group might believe strongly in tight gun controls. A group like this would view Target as socially responsible for not selling handguns to the public.

This section will examine three aspects of corporate social responsibility: (1) the stockholder versus stakeholder viewpoints of social responsibility, (2) corporate social performance, and (3) a sampling of social responsibility initiatives.

Stockholder versus Stakeholder Viewpoints

stockholder viewpoint
The viewpoint of social responsibility that business firms are responsible only to their owners and stockholders.

stakeholder viewpoint
The viewpoint of social responsibility contending that firms must hold themselves responsible for the quality of life of the many groups affected by the firm's actions.

The **stockholder viewpoint** of social responsibility is the traditional perspective. It holds that business firms are responsible only to their owners and stockholders. The job of managers is therefore to satisfy the financial interests of the stockholders. By so doing, says the stockholder view, the interests of society will be served in the long run. Socially irresponsible acts ultimately result in poor sales. According to the stockholder viewpoint, corporate social responsibility is therefore a by-product of profit seeking.

The **stakeholder viewpoint** of social responsibility contends that firms must hold themselves responsible for the quality of life of the many groups affected by the firm's actions. These interested parties, or stakeholders, include those groups composing the firm's general environment. Two categories of stakeholders exist. Internal stakeholders include owners, employees and stockholders; external stakeholders include customers, labor unions, consumer groups and financial institutions. The stakeholder viewpoint reflects the modern viewpoint of the corporation. Today, a company's assets are likely to be found in the employees who contribute their time and talents rather than in the stockholders who invest their money. The modern company should be a wealth-creating community whose members have certain rights. In this way the various stakeholders will be more willing to cooperate with each other.[26] Figure 2-2 depicts the stakeholder viewpoint of social responsibility.

Many organizations regard their various stakeholders as partners in achieving success, rather than as adversaries. The organizations and the stakeholders work together for their mutual success. An example of a company partnership with a labor union is the establishment of joint committees on safety and other issues of concern to employees.

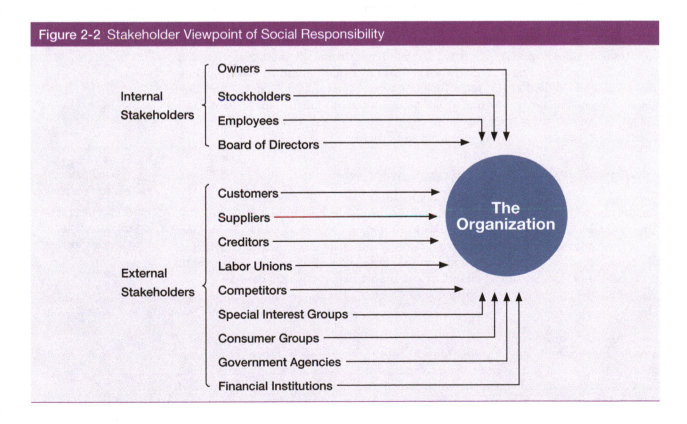

Figure 2-2 Stakeholder Viewpoint of Social Responsibility

Part of understanding the stakeholder viewpoint is to recognize that not all stakeholders are the same. Instead, they can be differentiated along three dimensions. Some stakeholders are more powerful than others, such as the United Auto Workers (UAW) union being more powerful than a small group of protesters. Some stakeholders are more legitimate than others, such as the Food and Drug Administration (FDA), which is a well-established and legal entity. Some stakeholders are more urgent than others because they require immediate attention. A group of protesters chaining themselves to a company fence because they believe the company is polluting the soil would require immediate attention.[27]

Kenneth Frazier, the long-time CEO of Merck, places the stockholder versus stakeholder view in practical perspective, in these words: "While a fundamental responsibility of a business leader is to create value for shareholders, I think businesses also exist to deliver value to society." He points out that the salient purpose of Merck in the world is to deliver medically important vaccines and medicines that make a huge difference for humanity.[28]

Triple Bottom Line: Profit, People, and Planet

A comprehensive perspective about corporate social responsibility is for an organization to focus on the **triple bottom line**. The idea is that organizations should prepare three different and separate bottom lines: the corporate bottom line; people in terms of their well-being; and the planet, referring to environmental responsibility.[29] Many businesses of all sizes make a conscious effort to focus on the triple bottom line. Keeping costs below revenue pays attention to the corporate bottom line. Many programs described in this book, such as employee engagement and stress management, attempt to enhance worker well-being. A focus on the planet takes many forms, such as recycling waste or a package-delivery service such as UPS using algorithms to find efficient truck routes, thereby reducing the amount of pollutants sent into the air.

Amazon pays attention to profits and the planet simultaneously by attempting to ship each order in one correctly sized package instead of multiple boxes. Shipping costs are reduced, and at the same time, Amazon responds to consumers' concerns about the negative environmental impact and general nuisance of all the cardboard. Suppliers are involved in the process because Amazon requests that they make smaller packaging specifically for online sales, not store shelves.[30]

triple bottom line
The idea that companies should prepare three different and separate bottom lines: the corporate bottom line; people in terms of their well-being; and the planet, referring to environmental responsibility.

Corporate Social Responsibility Initiatives

Creating opportunities for a diverse workforce, described in Chapter 3, is an important social responsibility initiative. Here we look at positive corporate responses to other important social issues. A firm that takes initiatives in these areas can be considered socially responsible. The five social responsibility initiatives described here are: creating a desirable workplace, work and personal life balance programs, environmental protection and sustainability, philanthropy, and acceptance of whistleblowers.

LEARNING OBJECTIVE **6**

Present an overview of corporate social responsibility initiatives.

Creating a Desirable Workplace

Creating a comfortable, pleasant, and intellectually stimulating work environment is a social responsibility initiative that directly affects employees' well-being. The introductory story about Zillow describes a company considered to be a top place to work. Because many people invest about one-third of their time at work, a pleasant work environment increases the chances that their lives will be enriched. Robert Levering and Milton Moskowitz of the Great Place to Work® Institute, in cooperation with *Fortune*, have institutionalized the idea of being a "best company to work for." Employers nominate themselves, and two-thirds of the score is based on how randomly selected employees respond to the Great Place to Work Trust Index®, a survey measuring organizational culture. An evaluation of the Culture Audit by staff members at the Great Place to Work Institute determines the rest of the score.

The focus is on employee satisfaction, yet the firms that fall into "the 100 best companies to work for" are also typically profitable. Among the benefits these companies offer are flexible working hours; on-site day care; concierge services, such as dry-cleaning pickup; domestic-partner benefits to same-sex couples; and fully paid sabbaticals. Following are two of the most highly-rated companies[31]:

Hilton. Ranked number one, Hilton listens to employee suggestions about changes, such as making uniforms more comfortable and practical. Employee spaces have comfortable furnishings, are well lit, and contain massage chairs. Line-level workers, such as cleaning and kitchen staff, are treated well and recognized as major contributors to the reputation of this giant hotel-and-resort chain. The company offers outstanding management development programs that facilitate workers to be promoted into management. Hilton has over 62,000 employees worldwide.

Nationwide. Ranked number 57, this major insurance company spends over $90 million annually on employee staff development, that encompasses more than 1,700 courses for employees. Employees enjoy enormously the mentoring they receive. The history and culture of this 97-year-old company is a source of employee pride. Nationwide has over 30,000 employees across the United States.

Work and Personal Life Balance Programs

Organizations take a major social responsibility initiative when they establish programs that help employees balance personal and work demands. The intent of these programs is to help employees lead more balanced lives and be more satisfied and productive on the job. (These programs are often referred to as "work/life" but this term implies that work and life are separate entities. In reality, work is a key part of life for all members of the workforce.) Figure 2-3 lists a variety of work and personal life balance programs. The most popular of these programs remains flexible work schedules, which often include the opportunity to work remotely about one day per week. Flexible work schedules have grown in popularity because evidence suggests it reduces turnover, improves morale and helps recruit talent.

Creating Job Opportunities for Unemployed People in Poor Neighborhoods

A corporate responsibility initiative that directly affects the lives of people is to create job opportunities for qualified people in poor neighborhoods, such as many inner cities in North America. Creating job opportunities includes providing the necessary training in job skills and attitudes toward work that help people become qualified job candidates. Many companies have independently created job opportunities for people in need. Some of the more significant initiatives include establishing a large retail store, building a brewery, construction company, or bus depot in economically disadvantaged areas. The federal government program called Opportunity Zones initiated in 2017 encourages business firms to locate in low-income, urban areas.

Figure 2-3 A Variety of Work and Personal Life Balance Programs

- Flexible work schedules
- Opportunity to work from home or other remote location, full-time or part-time
- Onsite childcare
- Seasonal childcare (such as spring break, holiday break, or winter break)
- Eldercare initiatives (may include assessment of problem, referral programs, or seminars and support groups)
- Job sharing between two employees
- "Family sick days" that permit employees to stay home and care for sick children, parents, or relatives

- Parental leave for adoptive parent
- Family leave policies
- Employee assistance programs (aid with personal problem that affect job performance)
- Onsite physical fitness facilities, or financial aid for membership in physical fitness club
- Family leave policies
- Concierge service where the company runs errands for employees
- Electronic breast pumps for mothers of infants who want to return to work and continue breast feeding

---

The Chicago-based technology and design firm, Rightpoint, is considered a leader in creating inner city employment. With annual revenues of approximately $28 million, Rightpoint creates jobs at all skill levels, with many workers being recruited directly from the inner city. Business firms that locate in the inner city are considered to be essential drivers of economic development and job creation, thereby exhibiting corporate social responsibility.[32]

Environmental Protection and Sustainability

A major corporate thrust toward ethical and socially responsible behavior is for business firms, as well as not-for-profit organizations to be *green*, or make a deliberate attempt to create a sustainable environment. In more technical detail, green is an approach to defining and creating processes that are: (1) environmentally friendly, (2) economically viable, and (3) pragmatic in the long term. *Environmentally friendly* refers to reducing the generation of pollution at its source, and minimizing life risks to humans, animals and plants. *Economically viable* refers to such financial benefits as attaining reduced costs from energy savings, gaining governmental subsidies and avoiding penalties. *Pragmatic* refers to sustainability by means of a positive impact on the global or local environment, community, society or economy.[33] Sustainability refers to the idea that the physical environment can be sustained, or kept safe such as a new tree growing in place of a tree that has been harvested for wood.

Several management scholars believe that human-induced climate change is one of the most daunting challenges today.[34] Nevertheless, people sometimes disagree about whether global warming exists, or that humans are creating the problem, but almost nobody disagrees that a clean, safe environment is desirable. Here we highlight five illustrative approaches to environmental protection. You will notice that many of the approaches to being green overlap and support each other. For example, a lawn mower manufacturer might produce a lawn mower that increases fuel efficiency, while at the same time reducing carbon dioxide emissions in its plant by using solar energy.

1   *Commit to low carbon dioxide emissions, as well as other hazardous emissions.*
    A major thrust in going green is to emit fewer toxins into the atmosphere. In one initiative, 67 companies including General Electric and Siemens agreed

to create a, "low emitting society." In response to criticism of the amount of petroleum consumed in plastic bottles, Coca-Cola unveiled a new plastic bottle made partially from plants. Pepsi, also, now has bottles containing less plastic. Another aspect of committing to low carbon dioxide emissions is for a company to develop biofuels, such as ethanol from agribusiness waste and plants. Making existing fuels burn cleaner is a related green initiative.[35]

Renewable energy sources, particularly solar and nuclear, are very low in carbon emissions. Yet a complete switch to these sources can have undesirable consequences from the standpoint of social responsibility. The shift away from carbon emissions has created deep economic problems in coal regions such as Central Appalachia. Twenty-seven coal-mining companies in the region filed for bankruptcy in a three-year period, and 332 mines were closed.[36]

2   *Develop a green supply chain.* In addition to management reducing emissions from their own company, pressure can be placed on supply-chain members to reduce their emissions. The Supply Chain Leadership Collaboration is composed of a group of companies to pressure suppliers to disclose greenhouse gas emissions and reduce them. About 60 percent of the 500 largest companies participate in this voluntary emissions-disclosure program, with more companies joining regularly. For example, Nestlé places strict quality controls on its suppliers that includes limiting potential contaminants.[37]

3   *Make sustainability and eco-friendly policies part of your business plan.* A strategic approach to being a green company is to build sustainability into the organization's business plan or strategy. Xerox Corp. has followed this approach for many years. The company was an early adopter of eco-friendly policies long before it was about economics or regulation or remanufacturing. Xerox invented two-sided copying, and focused on forestry standards. The EPA (Environmental Protection Agency) lists Xerox as the top purchaser of clean energy. Eco-friendly policies are perceived by company management as a way of taking care of employees, customers and the community.[38]

4   *Implement a four-day workweek.* The less time employees spend driving to work in their own vehicles, the more energy is saved, and the less the air is polluted with carbon dioxide emissions. Also, when offices are closed, less energy is required to heat or cool the office building. The city of Bacoor in the Philippines operates on a four-day workweek to save energy. The city information officer said, "Just imagine how much electricity we can save when air conditioners and electric fans are turned off."[39] Many business firms have offered four-day workweeks to employees.

5   *Invest heavily in recycling.* A high-impact way of sustaining the environment also involves recycling but on a grander scale. Waste Management, the trash hauler, combined with its wholly-owned subsidiary, Recycle America, is North America's largest recycler. Management estimates that the company recycles enough paper to save more than 41 million trees annually. The landfills of Waste Management provide more than 17,000 acres of protected habitat for wildlife. This activity fits into the green movement because many people believe that protecting wildlife is an important component of building a sustainable environment.

Another way in which a company can invest heavily in recycling is to manufacture and sell products made from recycled materials. Among these products are jeans made from recycled plastic bottles, furniture made from recycled plastics and walkways made from recycled tires. Pratt Industries is a major player in the cardboard box industry, and makes these boxes using 100 percent recycled paper, from newspapers and pizza boxes.[40]

A strategic view of sustainability programs is they are more likely to work when they take into account the interests of all stakeholders: investors, employees, customers, governments NGOs (non-governmental organizations) and society at large.[41] This is a major challenge but take this example: A major restaurant chain such as Kentucky Fried Chicken (KFC) decides to improve the environment by adjusting the temperature in all its franchise and company-owned stores. During cold-weather months all stores must keep the thermostat at 67 degrees F; and during warm-weather months, the stores must keep the thermostat at 75 degrees F. The energy savings will be enormous, but would there be so many complaints from customers that sales drop? So many complaints from employees that turnover increases? If these complaints materialize, investors might be unhappy and government will have less revenue. And maybe an NGO will like the environmental protection but will complain about KFC workers and employees not having a comfortable place to eat or work.

In addition to top-level management taking the initiative to protect the environment, companies often trigger many employees into thinking about environmental protection in ways such as carpooling, being a good recycler and not littering.

Philanthropy

A standard approach to social responsibility is to donate money to charity and various other causes. Most charities are heavily dependent on corporate support. Colleges, universities and career schools also benefit from corporate donations. Many corporate donors want their charitable investments to benefit the end consumer, not get lost in red tape and overhead and show measurable results. The new breed of philanthropist studies each charitable cause as he or she would a potential business investment, seeking maximum return in terms of social impact. This philanthropist might also seek follow-up data, for example, on how many children were taught to read or by what percentage new cases of AIDS declined. The type of corporate response to natural disasters shown by many other large firms, might also be classified as philanthropy.

An extraordinary example of philanthropy is Warren Buffet, the legendary investor and CEO of Berkshire Hathaway, who is one the world's richest people. He has pledged to give 99 percent of his wealth to philanthropic causes. He has designated approximately 83 percent of the donation to the Bill & Melinda Gates Foundation, with much of the rest going to his children. The mission of the Foundation is to help all people lead healthy, productive lives in developing countries. It concentrates on improving the physical health of people and giving them the chance to lift themselves out of hunger and extreme poverty.[42]

Acceptance of Whistleblowers

A **whistleblower** is an employee who discloses organizational wrongdoing to parties who can take action. A whistleblower has to be patient because it usually takes years to resolve a claim, including an agonizing court procedure. Another problem is that whistleblowers are often ostracized and humiliated by the companies they hope to improve by such means as no further promotions or poor performance evaluations. More than half the time the pleas of whistleblowers are ignored. It is therefore important

whistleblower
An employee who discloses organizational wrongdoing to parties who can take action.

for leaders at all levels to create a comfortable climate for legitimate whistleblowing. Also, it is preferable to deal with a problem internally rather than ignore the whistleblower thereby prompting him or her to report the misdeeds to an outside agency.

The manager needs the insight to sort out the difference between a troublemaker and a true whistleblower. Careful investigation is required. Only an organization with a strong social conscience would embrace employees who inform the public about its misdeeds. Yet some companies are becoming more tolerant of employees who help keep the firm socially responsible by exposing actions that could harm society.

The accompanying *Management in Action* insert describes a well-known company and how it is perceived to be socially responsible by many, and socially irresponsible by many others.

MANAGEMENT IN ACTION

Walmart Managers Take the High Road and the Low Road

Walmart Inc. is the world's largest retailer and one of the best-known companies, with annual sales of over $514 billion and a payroll of 2.2 million associates worldwide, with 1.5 million U.S. employees. Every week, 270 million customers and members visit Walmart in 11, 766 stores in 27 countries. The company has thousands of suppliers, who, in turn, employ millions of workers.

About 10 percent of all consumer money spent on goods other than vehicles goes to a Walmart or Sam's Club store. Many people perceive Walmart to be a wonderful corporate citizen because of the jobs it creates, the suppliers it helps keep in business, its endless amount of site construction and real-estate purchases, its corporate philanthropy and its responsiveness to natural disasters. The many critics of Walmart, however, regard the super-giant as an unethical and evil force that suppresses wages and health benefits and combats labor unions, and should be dismantled. Here we present a sampling of some of the evidence and opinion on the positive and negative aspects of Walmart's ethics and social responsibility.

The Ethical and Socially Responsible Side of Walmart

Walmart is a great boon for low-income and middle-income people in every location they serve. The purpose of Walmart is to save people money so they can live better. Customers can stretch their dollars, and afford things they could not previously buy easily without the mega-retailer. Walmart has wrung tens of billions of dollars in cost efficiencies out of the retail supply chain, passing many of these savings on to shoppers. The company's low prices on generic drugs have forced other chain stores to follow suit. The low prices at Walmart have gradually attracted more middle-income and higher-income shoppers who have become more interested in saving money than the status of where the items were purchased.

Walmart is an excellent corporate citizen as evidenced by its quest to help build a green (environmentally friendly) environment. The company strives to be supplied 100 percent by renewable energy; to minimize waste; and to sell products that sustain resources and the environment. The chain encourages customers to purchase energy-saving light bulbs, thereby helping to fight global warming. Walmart has taken many steps to reduce excess packaging.

Walmart has established an emergency relief team that responds quickly and more effectively than the U.S. government to natural disasters. In response to Hurricane Katrina, Walmart contributed $20 million in cash donations, 1,500 truckloads of free merchandise, food for 100,000 meals and the promise of a job for each one of its displaced workers.

Walmart has taken the initiative to help small businesses in the communities it serves. The Jobs and Opportunity Zones assist nearby small business enterprises, sponsor local training programs and support the local chamber of commerce. Most of the company's charitable donations are made at the local level.

Walmart provides one-stop shopping, including groceries, furniture, pharmaceuticals and even health clinics for individuals whose busy lives make it difficult to visit several stores during a shopping trip. Walmart thereby saves consumers time, a precious resource for many.

Walmart encourages free trade because it forces suppliers to go offshore for its products, and Walmart buys directly from many overseas suppliers. The company forces those it does business with to become more efficient and focused, leaner and faster. The suppliers learn the art of continuous improvement.

continues on next page

MANAGEMENT IN ACTION (continued)

Walmart provides stable employment for many members of the workforce who might not qualify for jobs in higher-end retail stores or offices. Walmart creates jobs for people who need them the most, and offers them mobility. Walmart is a leading source of employment for minority group members in terms of the percent of minorities on the payroll. About 75 percent of store management teams started as hourly associates. Store managers can earn between $70,000 and $150,000 per year. During a recent year, Walmart promoted more than 215,000 people to positions with greater responsibility and higher pay.

The wages, benefits and job security offered by Walmart surpass those typically offered by smaller enterprises such as mom-and-pop stores, as well as many large retailers. Walmart provides health insurance to more than 1 million associates and family members. Walmart raised its minimum wage to $11 for 2018, thereby spending about $1.5 billion to increase pay for approximately 500,000 workers. The average hourly compensation including benefits for workers is $17.50.

Walmart welcomes diversity, as evidenced by it joining the corporate council of the National Gay and Lesbian Chamber of Commerce. The company conducts workshops for gay and lesbian business owners on how to become Walmart suppliers.

The Unethical and Socially Irresponsible Side of Walmart

Walmart encourages its suppliers to rely on low-paid offshore workers so it can make large profits on its general merchandise, allowing it to give away toys at below cost. As a result, several toy stores have gone bankrupt. To remain a Walmart supplier, many companies are forced to lay off employees and close U.S. plants in favor of sending production offshore. Many Walmart suppliers face such a price squeeze that they are forced to produce goods of lower quality.

A few years ago, Walmart management initiated a program called "On-Time, In Full" that increases pressure on suppliers through tighter delivery scheduling. Fines of about 3 percent are imposed on suppliers who are late or early, who deliver goods on time but packaged improperly. The goal of the program is to add $1 billion in annual revenue by improving product availability at stores. Walmart felt a sense of urgency as the company increased salaries, cut prices, and had more competition from Amazon.com. A retail analyst noted, "Walmart has to find efficiencies wherever it can. They're trying to squeeze, and squeeze and squeeze."

Walmart is a poor corporate citizen because its presence leads to the deterioration of many small downtown areas. The company often abandons stores to pursue lower taxes in another county, leaving behind an ugly, limited-use big box building. Also, the presence of a Walmart store cheapens the image of a city or village.

Walmart keeps hundreds of thousands of employees in low-wage jobs and meager health benefits, making it difficult for them to move up the economic ladder. The anti-union stance of the company has contributed to low wages in retailing throughout North America.

The company forces many supermarkets as well as other merchants out of business. The failures of so many stores forces thousands of storeowners and employees out of work. As Walmart takes away business from traditional grocery chains, more and more union workers will lose their jobs paying decent wages.

Walmart faces a continuing stream of lawsuits for mistreating employees, including sex discrimination and forcing employees to work unpaid overtime. Many people protest in the streets demanding that Walmart pay workers a minimum of $15 per hour.

Another concern about Walmart is that it seeks to reduce U.S. taxes by overseas tax dodges. Walmart holds about $76 billion of its assets through a web of affiliates in tax havens around the world. The overseas operations have helped Walmart reduce its U.S. income taxes by about $3.5 billion during a recent six-year period.

Questions

1 **If many of these charges about Walmart being unethical and socially irresponsible are true, why does the company keep growing in size and profits?**

2 **Recommend several additional actions Walmart might take to develop a better reputation for ethics and social responsibility.**

3 **Many families and individuals who suddenly face financial difficulty shift much of their shopping to Walmart and away from traditional retailers. What message does this shift send to you about Walmart's social responsibility?**

4 **Has the information just presented had any impact on your propensity to shop or *not* shop at Walmart? Explain.**

Source: Original story based on facts and observations in the following sources: Company Facts, *http://corporate.walmart.com*, updated June 2019, pp. 1–4; *Walmart Global Responsibility Report*, (http://corporate.wqalmart.com), 2015; Phil Wahba, "If Walmart and 7-Eleven Had a Baby," *Fortune*, June 1, 2019, pp. 142–148; Matthew Boyle, "Wal-Mart Cracks the Whip on Suppliers," *Bloomberg Businessweek*, July 24, 2017, pp. 14–15; "Waste Not: Walmart's H. Lee Scott Jr., on What the Company is Doing to Reduce Its Carbon Footprint—and Those of Its Customers," *The Wall Street Journal*, March 24, 2008, p. R3; Ann Zimmerman, "Walmart's Emergency-Relief Team Girds for Hurricane Gustav," *The Wall Street Journal*, April 30-31, 2008, p. A3; "Haiti Earthquake Relief," *http://walmartstores. com/CommunityGiving/9596.aspx*, January 30, 2010; Jesse Drucer and Renee Dudley, "Walmart Has Found a New Discount: Its Taxes," *Bloomberg Businessweek*, June 29–July 5, 2015, pp. 25–26.

LEARNING OBJECTIVE **7**

Summarize how managers can create an environment that fosters ethically and socially responsible behavior, promote such behavior, and the benefits of such activity.

CREATING AN ETHICAL AND SOCIALLY RESPONSIBLE WORKPLACE

Establishing an ethical and socially responsible workplace is not simply a matter of luck and common sense. Top-level managers, assisted by other managers and professionals, can develop strategies and programs to enhance ethical and socially responsible attitudes and behavior. We turn now to a description of several of these initiatives.

Formal Mechanisms for Monitoring Ethics

The majority of companies with 500 or more employees have ethics programs of various types. Large organizations frequently set up ethics committees to help ensure ethical and socially responsible behavior. Committee members include a top management representative plus other managers throughout the organization. An ethics and social responsibility specialist from the human resources department might also join the group. The committee establishes policies about ethics and social responsibility, and may conduct an ethical audit of the firm's activities. In addition, committee members might review complaints about ethical violations.

The Lockheed Martin Corporation's ethics and compliance program has received much favorable publicity. Elements of the Lockheed Martin program include the following:

- *Make ethics training mandatory.* Mandatory means for every employee, including the CEO.
- *Develop multiple channels for raising questions and voicing concerns.* These mechanisms include a toll-free hotline, a formal ethics office at the corporate level and a culture that welcomes discussing ethical issues.
- *Act decisively on legitimate ethical problems reported by employees.* Demonstrate to employees that the company's commitment to good ethics is serious.[43]

The point of these suggestions is that they should be incorporated into a manager's way of thinking and behaving. To encourage using these ideas, Lockheed Martin managers have ethics discussions with their direct reports annually.

Written Organizational Codes of Conduct

Written codes of ethical conduct require people to behave with integrity and candor. A helpful example is the Kraft Heinz code of ethics that contains 12 short rules of ethical behavior that all employees must follow, with each rule accompanied by detailed instructions and examples of its implementation:

1 We prioritize safety in our workplace.

2 We handle non-public information privately and confidentially.

3 We do not tolerate discrimination or harassment.

4 We make delicious, safe and high-quality food.

5 We market and communicate responsibly.

6 We maintain the integrity, accuracy and reliability of our books, records, and controls.

7 We protect and ensure proper use of company assets.

8 We do not use or disclose information for personal gain.

9 We do not take action that conflicts or appears to conflict with the company's best interest.

10 We do not accept gifts as company employees.

11 We do not tolerate bribery and corruption.

12 We comply with competitive and antitrust laws.[44]

In many organizations, known code violators are disciplined. If the violation is serious enough, such as insider trading, the employee might be fired.

Widespread Communication about Ethics and Social Responsibility

Extensive communication about the topic reinforces ethical and socially responsible behavior. Top management can speak widely about the competitive advantage of being ethical and socially responsible. Another effective method is to discuss ethical and social responsibility issues in small groups. In this way the issues stay fresh in the minds of workers. A few minutes of a team meeting might be invested in a topic such as, "What can we do to help employees in our company whose families experience food insecurity?

Leadership by Example and Ethical Role Models

A high-powered approach to enhancing ethics and social responsibility is for top management to behave in such a manner themselves. If people throughout the firm believe that behaving ethically is "in" and behaving unethically is "out," ethical behavior will prevail. Visualize a scenario in which key people in an investment-banking firm vote themselves a $3 million year-end bonus. Yet to save money, entry-level clerical workers earning $15 an hour are denied raises. Many employees might feel that top management has a low sense of ethics and therefore, being ethical and socially responsible is not important.

A new perspective on creating an ethical organization culture is to encourage good behavior. A strong initiative in this direction is to remind employees of the importance of *prosocial values* as they make decisions.[45] Prosocial values are aimed at helping other people, such as explaining to co-workers how their work contributes to the good of the organization.

Leading by example is particularly useful in encouraging ethical behavior because it provides useful role models. Employees are often influenced by the people they work with every day, such as a supervisor or team leader. In contrast, top executives are distant figures who the worker rarely observes directly. Role modeling an immediate manager might proceed in this manner: A worker observes a manager consistently treating others fairly (and not playing favorites). In future dealings, the worker treats people fairly, modeling the behavior of his or her manager.

Encouragement of Confrontation about Ethical Deviations

Unethical behavior may be minimized if every employee confronts anyone seen behaving unethically. For example, if you spotted someone making an unauthorized copy of software, you would ask the software pirate, "How would you like it if you owned a business and people stole from your company?" The same approach encourages workers to ask about the ethical implications of decisions made by others in the firm.

Training Programs in Ethics and Social Responsibility

Training about ethics and responsibility can include messages about ethics from executives, classes on ethics at colleges and exercises in ethics. In some companies, ethics training is mandatory. Understanding the company's code of ethics is usually incorporated into the training. Knowledge or relevant legislation, such as anti-discrimination laws, is another key subject. A current approach is to conduct ethics training through e-training, and videos about ethics followed by small-group discussions with a manager often leading the discussion group.

Ethics training programs reinforce the idea that ethical and socially responsible behavior is both morally right and good for business. Discussing ethical issues combined with factual knowledge helps raise workers' level of awareness. Much of the content of this chapter reflects the type of information communicated in such programs. In addition, Skill-Building Exercise 3-A represents the type of activity included in ethical training programs in many companies.

Social Entrepreneurship

A direct approach to corporate social responsibility is to reach into the environment to find new ways of doing social good as an entrepreneur or as a unit within a larger organization. Social entrepreneurship is an entrepreneurial approach to social problems such as homelessness, contaminated drinking water and extreme poverty. Businesspeople who take an entrepreneurial approach to solving social problems are classified as *social entrepreneurs*.

A key aspect of social entrepreneurship in contrast to entrepreneurship in general is that social entrepreneurship addresses important social needs in a way that is not dominated by direct financial payoffs to the entrepreneur.[46] Social entrepreneurs are reformers and revolutionaries with a social mission, such as Muhar Kent, the former chairman and CEO of the Coca-Cola Company, who founded the Coca-Cola African Foundation to improve drinking water and sanitation in underdeveloped countries within Africa. One of the goals of the foundation is to reduce the number of children who die from preventable diseases.[47]

An analysis of social enterprises concluded that to be effective they must be financially sustainable to avoid being dependent on a constant flow of subsidies from taxpayers or charitable givers.[48] A social enterprise sponsored by a business corporation would avoid these problems.

Benefits Derived from Ethics and Social Responsibility

Highly ethical behavior and socially responsible acts are not always free. Initiatives such as programs for balancing work and family life and creating job opportunities for disconnected youths may not have an immediate return on investment. Here we look at evidence and opinions about the advantages of ethics and social responsibility.

Research demonstrates that companies that focus on the social and environmental bottom line in addition to the financial bottom line, on average, generate greater shareholder value over the mid-to-long term, according to one review of studies. "Adopting a broad triple bottom line approach is more than just good corporate citizenship—it is simply good business management."[49]

An analysis was made of the results obtained by companies that practice sustainability, have a positive reputation for dealing well with company insiders and outsiders, and that are well-managed and with regulations. These activities were found to link to cash flow (money available to spend) in five important ways: (1) facilitating top-line growth, (2) reducing costs, (3) minimizing regulatory and legal interventions, (4) increasing employee productivity, and (5) optimizing investment and capital expenditures.[50] Recognize, however, that such outstanding results can be attributed in part to a company that has enough revenue to invest in being socially responsible.

Being ethical also helps avoid the costs of paying huge fines for being unethical, including charges of discrimination and class-action lawsuits because of improper financial reporting. Charges of age and sex discrimination are two leading sources of lawsuits against companies.

Finally, organizations with strong reputations for being socially responsible will attract a large number of people who want to work for them. For example, business firms high on the *Fortune* list of best companies to work for are flooded with résumés of job applicants.

SUMMARY OF KEY POINTS

1 **Identify the philosophical principles behind business ethics.**

When deciding on what is right and wrong, people can focus on consequences and pragmatism; duties, rights of individuals; or integrity. Focusing on consequences judges the impact of a decision. Examining the rights of individuals in making a decision is the deontological approach and is based on universal principles such as honesty and fairness. According to the integrity (or virtue) approach, if the decision maker has good character and genuine motivation and intentions, he or she is behaving ethically. Pragmatism (whatever works) is closely related to focusing on the consequences.

2 **Explain how values relate to ethics.**

Ethics becomes the vehicle for converting values into action, or doing the right thing. A firm's moral standards and values also influence which kind of behaviors managers believe are ethical. According to ethically centered management, the high quality of an end product takes precedence over meeting a delivery schedule. Catastrophes can result when management is not ethically centered.

3 **Identify factors contributing to lax ethics, and common ethical temptations and violations.**

Drivers, or sources of unethical behavior fall into the characteristics of the individual, moral issue facing the person and the organizational environment. Individual factors include contributing to unethical behavior include greed and gluttony, a Machiavellian personality, unconscious biases and rationalization. Moral issue factors include the gravity of the issue and moral laxity (other issues seem more important at the time), and moral disengagement. An organizational factor includes an organizational atmosphere that condones unethical behavior, and pressure from higher management to achieve goals.

Recurring ethical violations, including criminal acts, include the following: stealing from employers and customers, illegally copying software, treating people unfairly, sexual harassment, conflict of interest, accepting kickbacks and bribes, divulging confidential information, misusing corporate resources. Three other problems are extracting extraordinary compensation, corporate espionage and poor cyberethics. Business scandals are ethical and legal violations that have created mammoth job losses, the wiping out of pension funds, high investment losses and bankruptcy of some vendors of the bankrupt companies.

4 **Apply a guide to ethical decision making.**

When faced with an ethical dilemma, ask yourself: Is it right? Is it fair? Who gets hurt? Would you be comfortable with the deed exposed? Would you tell your child to do it? How does it smell?

5 **Describe the stakeholder viewpoint of social responsibility and the triple bottom line.**

Social responsibility refers to a firm's obligations to society. Corporate consciousness expands this view by referring to values that guide and motivate individuals to act responsibly. The stakeholder viewpoint of social responsibility contends that firms must hold themselves accountable for the quality of life of the many groups affected by the firm's actions. The triple bottom line means that organizations should prepare three different and separate bottom lines: the corporate; people in terms of their well-being; and the planet, or environmental responsibility. Walmart makes an excellent case study of corporate social responsibility.

6 **Present an overview of social responsibility initiatives.**

Creating opportunities for a diverse workforce is a major social responsibility initiative. Also important are creating a desirable workplace, work and personal life balance programs, creating job opportunities for unemployed people in poor neighborhoods, environmental protection and sustainability, philanthropy, and acceptance of whistleblowers. Initiatives for environmental protection and sustainability include (a) commit to low hazardous emissions, (b) develop a green supply chain, (c) make sustainability and eco-friendly policies part of the business plan, (d) implement a four-day workweek, (e) invest heavily in recycling. Climate change can have an impact on a manager's job, such as setting a goal for reducing carbon emissions.

7 | **Summarize how managers can create an environment that fosters ethically and socially responsible behavior, and the benefits of such activity.**

Initiatives for creating an ethical and socially responsible workplace include: (a) formal mechanisms for monitoring ethics, (b) written organizational codes of conduct, (c) communicating about the topic, (d) leadership by example and ethical role models, (e) confrontation about ethical deviations, (f) training programs in ethics and social responsibility, and (g) social entrepreneurship.

More profitable firms can invest in good corporate social performance. Ethical leadership behavior is associated with many outcomes that contribute to organizational effectiveness. Being ethical helps avoid big fines for being unethical, and ethical organizations frequently attract more employees.

Key Terms and Phrases

ethics 35

moral intensity 36

virtue 38

ethically centered management 39

moral laxity 40

conflict of interest 42

corporate social responsibility 46

stockholder viewpoint 47

stakeholder viewpoint 47

triple bottom line 48

whistleblower 52

Questions

1. A frequent use of Zillow is to find the value of a neighbor's or friend's house. To what extent do you think Zillow facilitates "spying on" neighbors and friends?

2. What is your reaction to the following statement made by many business students? "It may be nice to study ethics, but in the real world the only thing that counts is money."

3. Some people believe that a parent should be able to take a young child to work on a given day when childcare is not available. What is your opinion on this issue?

4. The Vitium Global Fund is a mutual fund that favors products or services often considered socially irresponsible, including investments in tobacco, alcoholic beverages, gambling companies, as well as defense contractors. Discuss whether you would be willing to invest in this fund (its returns vary considerably).

5. What do you think of the ethics of a CEO making public announcements about his/her political preferences, such as why he/she favors one candidate for president of the United States?

6. Get together with a group of people and rank the occupations listed next in terms of your perception of their ethical reputations. The most ethical occupation receives a rank of one. (The list that follows is presented in random order.) Use the average rank of the group members if consensus is not reached.

____ Cosmetic (plastic) surgeon

____ Computer coder

____ Business executive, major firm

____ Criminal lawyer

____ Veterinarian for domestic animals

____ Business school professor

____ Family court judge

____ Small business owner

____ New car sales representative

____ Stockbroker/financial consultant

7. To avoid getting trapped in the politically-charged argument of whether global warming really exists and to defend its initiatives for reducing carbon dioxide emission, a company will say, "Cleaning up the environment is a good idea in its own right, whether or not we truly have global warming." What do you think of the preceding argument?

Skill-Building Exercise 2-A: Ethical Decision Making

Working in small groups, take the following two ethical dilemmas through the six steps for screening contemplated decisions. You might also want to use various ethical principles in helping you reach a decision.

Scenario 1: The Budget Furniture

You are the office manager at a company that does considerable business with the federal government. You put together a proposal for purchasing $25,000 of new furniture for the office, including desks, chairs, sofas and filing cabinets. You have asked for several bids on the furniture, including investigating several business-to-business portals. You have identified a supplier whom you think offers the best combination of price and quality. You submit your proposal to your manager for final approval. He says, "I have studied your proposal and I think we can do much better. Through our contacts with the government, we can purchase the same furniture for about $6,500 through Unicorn. All their goods are manufactured with prison labor. The inmates are paid between $.35 (35 cents) and about $1.50 per hour, so a lot of the cost savings would go directly to us. Besides, these jobs keep the inmates out of trouble and teach them valuable skills they can use in the future."

You begin to reflect, "Yes, Unicorn furniture may be a bargain, but what about the honest furniture company employees who are losing their jobs? Their employers cannot compete well with Unicorn."

What do you do now? Do you fight for your proposal for spending $25,000 for furniture manufactured by workers not in the prison system? Or do you go along with the idea of purchasing from Unicorn? Explain your position.

Scenario 2: The Bistro Shrimp Pasta

You and three other students are placed on an ethics task force at the popular upscale restaurant chain, The Cheesecake Factory. The Bistro Shrimp Pasta served by the restaurant has 3,120 calories and 89 grams of saturated fat. Although the meal may be delicious it exceeds the recommended daily calories and fat for an average-size adult. The U.S. Food and Drug Administration recommends about 2,000 calories per day for a woman of moderate physical activity and 2,700 calories for a male of moderate physical activity. About 70 grams of fat per day would be recommended for the adult of average size. You and your teammates are asked to present top management with an evaluation of the ethics of continuing the Bistro Shrimp Pasta.

Skill-Building Exercise 2-B: Dealing with the Homeless

You work for a company that is the major tenant of a large office building in downtown New York. Many homeless people congregate outside the building, and some employees complain that the homeless people badger them for money, and also create sanitary problems. Yet many other employees are concerned about the well-being and even survival of home-less people outside the building. Several employees have suggested that during extremes in heat or cold, the homeless should be invited to spend time in the lobby to avoid suffering the consequences of extreme cold or heat.

Your company CEO wants to do something about the homeless problem, but has no good answers. The CEO says that up to now the city government has provided very little help, so the company has to take action. She appoints you as the task force leader to come up with a solution to the problem. You and four other classmates who are part of the homeless solution task force spend about 30 minutes finding a solution to the problem. Answer the following questions about your proposed solution to the homeless problem:

1. How well does your proposed solution meet the needs of the various stakeholders involved?

2. What impact on your company's profitability might your solution have?

3. How well will your proposed solution help the homeless people in the long run?

Management Now—Online Skill-Building Exercise: Creating Employment in Poor Neighborhoods

Many economists, management specialists and politicians (both liberal and conservative) believe a corporate activity of high social responsibility is to create employment in poor areas. The area or region can be within cities or rural areas. Small enterprises, such as convenience stores and hair salons, routinely create such opportunities, yet large businesses and government agencies are less likely to establish a presence in economically distressed areas. Search the Internet to find at least one example of a large company or government agency that has established a presence in a poor area. See if you can find any information regarding the success of the project, such as the number of people employed and the profitability of the enterprise.

JUST, Inc. Wants to Revolutionize the Egg Industry

Joshua Tetrick, the founder and CEO of JUST, Inc. launched his company in 2011 when it was named Hampton Creek. The purpose of the San Francisco-based company was to create healthier, affordable food, with less of a negative impact on the environment than foods such as natural eggs, chicken, and beef. Early products included plant-based Just Mayo and Just Cookie Dough, with ingredients such as Canadian yellow pea and sorghum which were designed to be sustainable, less expensive alternatives to eggs.

Just Mayo is an egg-free mayonnaise substitute. JUST, Inc. has varied its product mix several times, and today concentrates on spreads, dressings, cookie dough, and its key product Just Egg (described below). Billionaire investors jumped in on this trendy food idea shortly after Hampton Creek was founded.

During its early years, Hampton Creek was mired in scandal and legal battles. The company was accused of having employees purchase Just Mayo from retail stores in order to inflate sales. Employees were instructed to pose as doubtful or noncommittal consumers, and to buy large quantities of their own mayonnaise. At the same time, Hampton Creek contractors were instructed to telephone store managers and inquire about Just Mayo while pretending to be interested customers. Tetrick told news reporters that the purchases were simply an unorthodox method of testing the quality of the product. The CEO later informed employees about a subsequent investigation by the Justice Department and the Securities and Exchange Commission.

The U. S. Food and Drug Administration issued an official warning in 2015 demanding that Hampton Creek modify its label over inaccurate health and nutrition claims. Many anonymous Hampton Creek employees accused the company of overlooking the science related to its products, and misrepresenting the research it cited. The FDA complaint was resolved later in 2015 when the company agreed to change its labeling while keeping the "Just Mayo" branding intact.

In 2017, Target removed the brand from its shelves, pointing to food safety concerns about the Just products. One of the allegations was that Hampton Creek products were being mislabeled as non-genetically modified organisms (GMO).

In June 2017 the company faced another challenge. Actor Jaden Smith, the son of actor and former rapper Will Smith, filed suit against Just and Joshua Tetrick. Jaden Smith is the co-founder of the sustainable water bottle company, Just Water. Smith's lawsuit alleged that Tetrick copied his company name and violated a 2014 trademark agreement between his company and the mayonnaise brand that specified the conditions under which the word "Just' could be used.

In 2019, JUST, Inc. was seeking more than $200 million in new funding, while simultaneously trying to downplay any past mistakes, notably not exercising careful quality control over ingredients or giving the impression of inflating sales figures at the retail level. While the company was seeking new funding, demand was strong for the key product, Just Egg. The product is an egg substitute, or vegan egg, that contains the same amount of protein as a chicken egg, with zero cholesterol. JUST Egg is claimed to look, cook, and taste just like scrambled eggs. Although JUST Egg performs best as an egg substitute, it can also be used for French toast, fried rice, quiches, and omelets.

The egg substitute is a successful product, for sale in over 5,000 stores in the United States. The grocery chain Kroger sells JUST Egg in the egg department, rather than being shelved in the alternative protein section. In 2019, Tetrick said, "Right now the company is JUST Egg and JUST Egg is the company."

About 77 percent of the consumers who buy JUST Egg are not vegans or vegetarians. About 35 percent of people who purchase JUST Egg arc purchasing it instead of plant-based proteins such as veggie burgers, or beef, chicken, and pork. Tetrick pointed that that many college-educated women like JUST Egg, saying that they are trying to eat good, clean protein products that are free of antibiotics, and sustainable.

Case Questions

1. What, if any, ethical violations do you think JUST, Inc. committed?

2. In what ways is JUST, Inc. showing good corporate social responsibility?

3. In what ways is JUST, Inc. showing poor corporate social responsibility?

4   **What would you recommend to JUST, Inc. management so that the company stays out of future legal trouble and embarrassments?**

Source: Original case based on information in the following sources: Ian Agar, "Just Inc. Raising $200M Amid Controversial Past," *Pitch Book* (www.pitch.com), February 20, 2019, pp. 1–3; Elaine Watson, "Just, Inc. CEO: 'The Company is JUST Egg, and JUST Egg is the Company,'" *Foodnavigator-USA.com*, August 21, 2019, pp. 1–3; Monica Watrous, "What Happened to Hampton Creek?" *Food Business News* (www.foodbusinessnews.net), October 4, 2018, pp. 1–2; "The Startup Scandal Scale," *Fortune*, January 1, 2017, p. 75; Nick Wingfield and Katie Benner, "Hampton Creek, Maker of Just Mayo, Is Sold Under Inquiry," *www.nytimes.com*, August 19, 2016, pp. 5–6.

Case Problem 2-B

Urban Financial Feels the Squeeze

Troy is the CEO of Urban Financial, a payday lender with 25 locations. The core business at Urban is to lend consumers advances of between $100 and $500 against their paycheck for short periods of time, usually about one week to 10 days. Urban also offers other financial services, such as check-cashing and wiring money. Similar to other payday lenders, Urban charges approximately $15 for a two-week loan to their borrowers who tend to be high risk. If the loan interest were calculated on an annual basis, the rate would be 390 percent. Some states, including New York, cap interest rates at 16 percent for loans, even though store credit cards often charge over 20 percent for their loans. (Both 16 and 20 refer to annual rates.)

Troy informs his management team during a meeting that he, along with them, is worried about the future of the business. He notes that 15 states have already banned payday loans and more and more politicians are condemning the business. He reminds the team that some of the accusations against the industry are preposterous.

"My favorite example is that a modest-priced hotel room is about $150 per night before taxes," said Troy. "If somebody stayed the entire year in the hotel, or 365 nights, the annual fee would be $54,750 plus taxes. Yet no politician complains about the exorbitant rates charged by these hotels. My biggest concern right now is that the state is going to shut us down."

Troy then had a problem-solving session with the group, exploring alternatives that could be pursued to stay in business. One alternative that emerged was to set up online operations overseas in a country that welcomed such businesses (e.g., Malta or the West Indies). The suggestion was to still keep a few offices open to catch street traffic and offer services for wiring money. In this way, state regulations could be avoided.

Another alternative the group formulated was to base the business on a Native American reservation, again to avoid state regulations. A handful of payday lenders have successfully made this transition.

Troy concluded the meeting by saying, "We cannot forget that our mission is to help financially troubled people in need. Without our loans, many of our potential customers would have their cars repossessed or their homes foreclosed. Equally bad, they would have to use loan sharks to get money. Our interest rates may seem high to the outside world, but we have to charge enough to cover our risks and earn a small profit."

The team nodded in agreement with Troy.

Case Questions

1   **What is your evaluation of the ethics of Urban Financial making payday loans?**

2   **What do you think of the ethics of the two alternatives mentioned to avoid state regulations: locating offshore or on a Native American reservation?**

3   **What do you recommend to Troy to make the business model of Urban Financial ethical enough to avoid being attacked by politicians?**

ENDNOTES

1. Original story based on facts and observations in the following sources: Michael C. Bush and Christopher Tkaczyk, "The 100 Best Companies to Work For 2019, *Fortune*, March 1, p, p. 74; "Zillow Group Named One of Fortune's 2019 Best Companies to Work For," *prnewswire.com*, February 14, 2019, pp. 1–2; "Want to Know What It's Really Like to Work At Zillow?" *www.indeed.com*, 2019, pp. 1–4; Phil La Duke, "Zillow group," *Thrive Global* (www.thriveglobal.com), April 18, 2019, pp. 1–5; Maggie McGrath, "Competition is the New Union," *Forbes*, December 26, 2017, pp. 56–57.

2. Thomas M. Jones, "Ethical Decision Making by Individuals in Organizations," *Academy of Management Review*, April 1991, p. 391.

3. Linda K. Treviño and Katherine A. Nelson, *Managing Business Ethics: Straight Talk About How to Do It Right* (New York: Wiley, 1995), pp. 66–70; O. C. Ferrell, John Fraedrich, and Linda Ferrell, *Business Ethics: Ethical Decision Making and Cases* (Boston: Houghton Mifflin Company, 2000), pp. 54–60.

4. Edwin A. Locke, "Business Ethics: A Way Out of the Morass," *Academy of Management Learning & Education*, September 2006, pp. 324–332.

5. Toby Newstead, Rob Macklin, Sarah Dawkins, and Angela Martin, "What Is Virtue? Advancing the Conceptualization of Virtue to Inform Positive Organizational Inquiry," *Academy of Management Perspectives*, November 2018, pp. 443–457.

6. Cassie B. Barlow, Mark Jordan, and William H. Hendrix, "Character Assessment: An Examination of Leadership Levels," *Journal of Business and Psychology*, Summer 2003, p. 563.

7. Jeff Thompson, "Like Our Values? Then Sign Them," *Executive Leadership*, April 2017, p. 3.

8. Jennifer J. Kish-Gephart, David A. Harrison, and Linda Klebe Treviño, "Bad Apples, Bad Cases, and Bad Barrels: Meta-Analytic Evidence About Sources of Unethical Decisions at Work," *Journal of Applied Psychology*, January 2010, pp. 418.

9. Vikas Anand, Blake E. Ashforth, and Mahendra Joshi, "Business as Usual: The Acceptance and Perpetuation of Corruption in Organizations," *Academy of Management Executive*, November 2005, p. 9. Reprinted from 2004, Vol. 18, No. 3.

10. Literature reviewed in Sejin Keem, et al., "Are Creative Individuals Bad Apples? A Dual Pathway Model of Unethical Behavior," *Journal of Applied Psychology*, April 2018, p. 416.

11. Mahzarin R. Banaji, Max H. Bazerman, and Dolly Chugh, "How (Un) ethical Are You?" *Harvard Business Review*, December 2003, pp. 56–64.

12. Ann Pomeroy, "The Ethics Squeeze," *HR Magazine*, March 2006, p. 48.

13. Bill Vlasic, "Toyota's Slow Awakening to a Deadly Problem," *The New York Times* (nytimes.com) February 1, 2010.

14. Jess McHugh, "Toyota Recall 2015: Is Your Car Affected? How to Check Model, Year To See if You're One Of 6.5 M Affected," *www.ibtimes.com*, December 14, 2015, p. 2.

15. The first seven items on the list are from Treviño and Nelson, pp. 47–57; *Reference for Business*, 2nd ed. "Employee Theft" (*www.referenceforbusiness.com*), 2010; Matt Villano, "Sticky Fingers in the Supply Closet," *The New York Times* (http://www.nytimes.com), April 30, 2006.

16. "Charges Alleging Sex-Based Harassment (Charges Filed with EEOC) FY 2010–FY 2018, *U.S. Equal Employment Opportunity Commission* (www.eeoc.gov), 2018, p. 1.

17. Chad Bray, "Kumar Said He Was Paid for Tips," *The Wall Street Journal*, January 8, 2010, p. C3.

18. Michael B. Sauter, "These Are the Highest-Paid CEOs at America's Largest Companies," *USA Today* (www.usatoday.com), April 30, 2019, p. 21.

19. Jack Ewing, Graham Bowley, and Melissa Eddy, "Sarcasm and Doubt Precede VW's Update on Cheating Inquiry," *The New York Times* (www.nytimes.com). December 6, 2015, pp. 1–5; Graham Ruddick, "VW Admits Emissions Scandal Was Caused by a 'Whole Chain' of Failures, *The Guardian* (www.theguardian.com), December 10, 2015. pp. 1–3.

20. Clifford Atiyeh, "Everything You Need to Know about the VW Diesel-Emissions Scandal," *Car and Driver* (www.caranddriver.com), December 4, 2019, p. 1.

21. "In Brief," *Bloomberg Businessweek*, January 7, 2019, p. 7; Laura J. Keller and Shahien Nasiripour, "Wells Fargo's Uphill Battle," *Bloomberg Businessweek*, March 5, 2018, pp. 31–32; Matt Krantz, "Under Cloud of Scandal, Wells Fargo CEO Retires, Gets $134M," *USA Today*, October 13, 2016, p. 1B.

22. Source: CNBC, https://www.cnbc.com/2020/01/23/former-wells-fargo-ceo-stumpf-barred-from-industry-to-pay-17point5-million-over-sales-scandal.html.

23. James L. Bowditch and Anthony F. Buono, *A Primer on Organizational Behavior*, 5th ed. (New York: Wiley, 2001), p. 4.

24. Joseph L. Badaracco Jr., *Defining Moments: When Managers Must Choose Between Right and Wrong* (Boston: Harvard Business School Press, 1997).

25. "Corporate Social Responsibility: Good Citizenship or Investor Rip-off?" *The Wall Street Journal*, January 9, 2006, p. R6.

26. Charles Handy, "What's Business For?" *Harvard Business Review*, December 2002, pp. 49–55. For an expansion on this point of view, see Stuart Cooper, *Corporate Social Performance: A Stakeholder Approach* (Burlington, VT: Ashgate, 2004).

27. Ronald K. Mitchell, Bradly R. Agle, and Dona J. Wood, "Toward a Theory of Stakeholder Identification and Salience: Defining the Principle of Who and What Really Counts," *Academy of Management Review*, October 1997, p. 869.

28. Adi Ignatius, "A Conversation with Merck CEO Kenneth Frazier," *Harvard Business Review*, March–April 2018, p. 84.

29. J. Alberto Aragon-Correa, et al., "Sustainability Management Teaching Resources and the Challenge of Balancing Planet, People, and Profits," *Academy of Management Learning & Education*, September 2017, pp. 469–483; "Triple Bottom Line," *The Economist*, November 17, 2009, pp. 1–2.

30. Laura Stevens and Erica E. Phillips, "More Amazon Orders, Fewer Boxes," *The Wall Street Journal*, December 21, 2017, p. B2.

31. Michael C. Bush and Christopher Tkaczyk, "The 100 Best Companies to Work For 2019," *Fortune*, March 1, 2019, pp. 57–80.

32. "Rightpoint Ranks among ICIC And FORTUNE's Inner City 100 Winners for Second Consecutive Year," *Inner City 100 2015* (www.rightpoint.com), October 13, 2015, pp. 1–3.

33. Probal DasGupta, "A Practical Inquiry Into the New Green Revolution," *Newark Business Strategies Examiner* (www.examiner.com) January 30, 2010.

34. Jeffrey G. York, Siddharth Vedula, and Michael J. Lenox, "It's Not Easy Building Green: The Impact of Public Policy, Private Actors, and Regional Logics on Voluntary Standards Adoption," *Academy of Management Journal*, August 2018, p. 1492.

35. Jeremiah McWilliams, "Companies Producing Lighter, Greener Water Bottles," *The Atlanta-Journal Constitution* (www.ajc.com), January 20, 2010; Peter A. Heslin and Jenna D. Ochoa, "Understanding and Developing Strategic Corporate Responsibility," *Organizational Dynamics*, April–June 2008, p. 135.

36. Paul H. Tice, "Obama's Appalachian Tragedy," *The Wall Street Journal*, December 1, 2015, p. A19.

37. David Roberts, "Carbon Copy," *Fast Company*, December 2007/January 2008, p. 78; Doug Collins, "Sustainability: Realizing Supply Chain Leadership through Collaborative Innovation" (*www.innovationmanagement.se*), June 25, 2013, pp. 1–5.

38. "Paper Trail," *The Wall Street Journal*, March 9, 2009, p. R7; *2014 Report on Global Citizenship*, www.xerox.com, 2014.

39. Maricar Cinco, "Bacoor Goes On 4-Day Workweek to Save Energy," *Inquirer Southern Luzon*, newsinfo.inquirer.net, March 21, 2015, pp. 1–3.

40. Chase Peterson-Wothorn, "Thanks Jeff Bezos!" *Forbes*, August 17, 2015, p. 36.

41. Robert G. Eccles and George Serafeim, "Innovating for a Sustainable Strategy," *Harvard Business Review*, May 2013, p. 52.

42. "Warren Buffet – Inside Philanthropy," *www.insidephilanthropy.com*, 2019; PMNCH, Bill & Melinda Gates Foundation, *www.who.int/pmnch.com*, 2019.

43. "Ethics," *www.lockheedmartin*.com, © Copyright Lockheed Martin, 2015. Erin White, "What Would You Do? Ethics Courses Get Context," *The Wall Street Journal*, June 12, 2006, p. B2.

44. "The Kraft Heinz Company Employee Code of Conduct 2019," *www.kraftheinzcompany.com*, 2019.

45. Nicholas Epley and Amit Kumar, "How to Design an Ethical Organization," *Harvard Business Review*, May–June 2019, p. 146.

46. Johann Mair and Ignasi Marti, "Social Entrepreneurship Research: A Source of Explanation, Prediction, and Delight," *Journal of World Business*, Issue 1, February 2006, pp. 36–44.

47. "WaterAid Joins Forces with the Coca-Cola Africa Foundation to Bring Safe Drinking Water," *Financial News Making Money* (*www.finchannel.com*), May 11, 2013, pp. 1–3.

48. Roger L. Martin and Sally R. Osberg, "Two Keys to Sustainable Social Enterprise," *Harvard Business Review*, May 2015, p. 94.

49. Research reported in June Rogers, "The Growing Field of Corporate Social Responsibility," *The Star* (www.thestar.com), September 8, 2014, p. 2.

50. Thomas W. H. Ng and Daniel C. Feldman, "Ethical Leadership: Meta-Analytic Evidence of Criterion-Related and Incremental Validity," *Journal of Applied Psychology*, May 2015, pp. 948–965.

CHAPTER 3

International Management and Cultural Diversity

OBJECTIVES

After studying this chapter and doing the exercises, you should be able to:

1 Explain the extent of involvement in international trade.

2 Identify and summarize several trade agreements among countries.

3 Recognize the importance of sensitivity to cultural differences in international enterprise.

4 Identify major challenges facing the global managerial worker.

5 Pinpoint success factors in the global marketplace, and several positive and negative aspects of globalization.

6 Describe the scope of diversity, the competitive advantage, and potential problems of a culturally diverse workforce.

7 Summarize organizational practices to encourage diversity.

Doretha Leftwood, a 71-year-old customer at a Dollar Tree store in Louisville, Kentucky, said, "Oh please don't let them raise prices. I don't get but one Social Security check a month, and when it's gone, it's gone. Who can afford to go to CVS anymore? When I shop here, I can really stretch my money." Leftwood's concern, as that of millions of other consumers, stemmed from tariffs that were being imposed on Chinese imports by President Donald Trump in order to pressure the Chinese government into fairer trade practices.

Dollar Tree operates about 15,000 stores. A key part of the company business model is to purchase bottom-level price products from China, ship them to the United States in bulk, and then sell them in their stores at a fixed price point of $1. The 10 percent tariffs that began in 2018 slashed profit margins, forcing the company to find savings elsewhere.

CEO Gary Philbin said in March 2019 that a proposed 25 percent tariff on Chinese products could eventually cost the company $140 million. To mitigate the cost, Dollar Tree management negotiated with vendors, and sourced from other countries that produce inexpensive merchandise. Yet it is difficult to find other countries that offer goods that can be sold for less than one dollar. Even before the imposition of tariffs, the company had been considering selling items priced at $2 to $5, a move made more urgent by the new tariffs. Phiblin was concerned about company profitability, as well as the impact of the tariffs on its customers. He also noted that Dollar Tree customers are so accustomed to paying $1 for products that passing along cost increases to them would be difficult.

Dollar Tree was pondering the offset of the effect of tariffs on its costs by boosting prices in its own stores as well as in its Family Dollar subsidiary. Dollar Tree was also making changes in its product line to keep prices at $1 even if competitor dollar stores had priced many of their goods above $1. A retail analyst pointed out that the Dollar Tree model is "Everything is a Dollar," so the company would have to make changes in its merchandise assortment and in the supply chain. For example, a 24-count box of crayons could be reduced to 20 crayons so shoppers would still be paying $1 for a box of crayons.

Top-level managers at Dollar Tree and many other discount retailers were relieved when, in December 2019, trade representatives of the U.S. and China had agreed to a truce on the tariff conflict. The truce included the U.S. not imposing a new round of tariffs.[1] As a Dollar Tree manager said, "I am so happy that we won't have to raise the price of shampoo to $1.25 from $1. That 25-cent price boost would turn away a lot of our faithful customers."

The Dollar Tree example illustrates how sensitive certain industries are to developments in international business and how managers in these firms might have to make quick adjustments to trade conflicts. In this chapter we describe major aspects of the international and culturally diverse environment facing managers. Among the topics covered are methods of entry into the global marketplace, tariffs, and success factors in globalization and the advantages and disadvantages of going global. We also highlight cultural diversity, including its competitive advantage and the skills required to become a multicultural manager. Globalization and cultural diversity are such major forces in the workplace that they must receive some attention throughout our study of management.

INTERNATIONAL MANAGEMENT

LEARNING OBJECTIVE **1**

Explain the extent of involvement in international trade.

The internationalization (or globalization) of business and management exerts an important influence on the manager's job. Approximately 10 to 15 percent of all jobs in the United States are dependent upon trade with other countries. Another way of understanding the impact of globalization is to recognize that many complex manufactured products are built with components from several countries. The mix of components can sometimes confuse the national identity of a product, with automobiles being a prime example. The Jeep Wrangler is often perceived as the most American of vehicles, yet 30 percent of its content is made outside the United States and Canada. The manual transmission is sourced from Germany.[2]

The internationalization, or globalization, of management is part of the entire world becoming more global, representing challenges for workers at every level. For example, a financial analyst in Bangalore, India, can perform the work of a financial analyst in Columbus, Ohio, at a lower wage rate. A counterforce to the global economy is that jobs involving personal contacts and relationships are less subject to competition from another country.

The aspects of international business covered here are: (a) extent of involvement in international trade, (b) trade agreements among countries, (c) global outsourcing, (d) trade tariffs, and (e) sensitivity to global business.

Extent of Involvement in International Trade

Firms involve themselves in international trade in several different ways, and new approaches continue to evolve. The extent of involvement can also be regarded as a method of entry. At one time a small firm relied on importer-exporters or distributors to enter the world market. Now many home-based businesses sell worldwide through a website. Two broad purposes of foreign commerce are to enhance sales and to produce goods and services. A physical presence in another country might enhance sales, and goods and services might be produced less expensively in another country such as a technical support center located overseas.

The initial entry mode used to penetrate a foreign market must be chosen carefully because of its potential effects on the success of the venture. Another factor is the difficulty in changing the mode without considerable loss of time and money. Six methods of entry into world markets are described next.

1 *Trading Companies.* Goods produced in one country are then sold for direct use or resale to one or more companies in foreign countries. Many small firms specialize in helping companies gain entry into foreign markets through exporting. An overseas distributor can be quite helpful, but one must be chosen carefully to determine compatibility and perhaps the integrity of the proposed partner.

2 *Contract manufacturing.* Companies of all sizes from startups to major companies rely on companies in other countries to manufacture part or all of their products. A producer of a designer line of tee-shirts in Boston for example, might design the shirts at home but contract the production to a clothing manufacturer in New Delhi, India. Most smartphones with the Apple logo are manufactured in China.

3 *Strategic alliances and joint ventures.* Instead of merging formally with a firm of mutual interest, a company in one country pools resources with one or more foreign companies. A major reason for the willingness of so many firms to form alliances is the enormous expense and effort necessary for a single organization to accomplish a full range of business activities. In a joint venture, the companies in an alliance produce, warehouse, transport and market products. A joint venture is thus a special type of strategic alliance. Profits or losses from these operations are shared in some predetermined proportion.

   Strategic alliances also take the form of brand partnerships, in which two companies from different countries jointly market their brands to the advantage of both. BMW partnered with Louis Vuitton to have luggage designed to fit perfectly in the rear parcel shelf of the BMW i8. The luggage includes a business case and two other pieces.

4 *Direct foreign investment.* The most advanced stage of multinational business activity takes place when a company in one country produces and markets products through wholly owned facilities in foreign countries. Toyota Motor Co. and Ford Motor Co., two well-known multinational corporations, conduct business in this manner. A positive perspective on direct foreign investment is that the multinational corporation exports jobs to other countries, such as the substantial manufacturing facilities of Honda, Toyota, Hyundai and Mercedes-Benz in the United States. These overseas companies have helped turn the United States into the center of a global industry. Foreign players are said to have reinvigorated the U.S. auto industry.

5 *The multinational corporation.* The highest level of involvement in international trade is the **multinational corporation** (MNC), a firm with units in two or more countries in addition to its own. An MNC has headquarters in one country and subsidiaries in others. However, it is more than a collection of subsidiaries that carry out decisions made at headquarters. A multinational corporation

multinational corporation
A firm with operating units in two or more countries in addition to its own.

sometimes hires people from its country of origin (expatriates) for key positions in facilities in other countries. At other times, the MNC will hire citizens of the country in which the division is located (host-country nationals) for key positions. Most of the best-known companies are MNCs, including PepsiCo, IBM and Microsoft among hundreds of others.

6   *Global startup.* A **global startup** is a small firm that comes into existence by serving an international market. By so doing, the firm circumvents the previous methods. Selling over the Internet facilitates creating a global startup because customers can be reached directly without a distributor. Almost every week some small business owner attempts a global startup such as attempting to sell waterproof socks or decorative smartphone covers. However, trade restrictions such as paying tariffs and obtaining approval from the foreign governments usually apply.

global startup
A small firm that comes into existence by serving an international market.

Trade Agreements Among Countries

Trade agreements are important for understanding international management because these agreements facilitate business in exporting, importing and building goods in other countries. Also, the agreements have triggered considerable controversy often leading to anti–trade-agreement demonstrations. Four of these agreements are described next.

LEARNING OBJECTIVE **2**

Identify and summarize several trade agreements among countries.

The USMCA and NAFTA

The United States, Mexico, and Canada Agreement (USMCA) was ratified by the three countries in 2020 to improve and strengthen its preceding agreement, the North American Free Trade Agreement (NAFTA). Among the modifications in the new agreement were more protection for U.S. labor and stronger enforcement provisions. Seventy-five percent of the value of automobiles and trucks must originate in North America to qualify as duty-free. A major new provision is that 40 percent of a car's value, and 45 percent of a light truck's value must be manufactured in North American facilities. The salaried workers in these facilities must be paid an average of a minimum of $16 per hour. (Critics felt these higher wages could put Mexico at a disadvantage with Asian competitors.)

The USMCA gives biologic drugs in North America a minimum of 10 years of intellectual property protection from generic competitors. To modernize NAFTA, tariffs on digital products are prohibited, and companies can protect proprietary software. A new feature of the agreement is the establishment of labor panels to monitor if Mexico is following the new regulations. Also new is a provision allowing for independent labor unions in Mexico.

Industry analysts believe that the USMCA will bring about tangible benefits for agriculture, technology, manufacturing, as well as other business sectors. Among the groups who anticipated major benefits from USMCA were dairy farmers who would be allowed to sell three times as much milk to Canada as they did previously. Mining companies also saw major benefits from the USMCA because tariffs were to be removed from steel and aluminum.[3]

NAFTA established liberal trading relationships among the United States, Canada, and Mexico. The pact also called for the gradual removal of tariffs and other trade barriers on most goods produced and sold in the United States. NAFTA went into effect in Canada, Mexico, and the United States on January 1, 1994. The agreement created a giant trading zone extending from the Arctic Ocean to the Gulf of

Mexico. NAFTA forms the world's second largest free trade zone, bringing together a total population of 485 million in the three countries, with an unknown number being potential consumers. The largest free trade zone is the European Union.

Many companies benefited from NAFTA because of better access to the two other countries in the pact. Consequently, U.S. trade with Mexico and Canada has increased dramatically. Many U.S. companies have expanded sales of industrial and consumer products to Canada and Mexico. These products include computers, consumer electronics and machine tools. As a result of NAFTA, Canadian and Mexican firms have sold more products to the United States. More Canadian and Mexican beer now flows in the United States, as well as the sale of electronic products and furniture. Much of the surge in the Mexican auto industry can be attributed to the substantial drop in tariffs between the United States and Mexico. (Mexico assembles autos for the U.S. market.)

Large American manufacturers benefited from NAFTA as they slashed production costs and boosted profits by opening factories in Mexico, where workers are paid about $4 an hour. In addition to auto manufacturers, computer and electronic companies have used Mexico as a platform for fast, inexpensive, and flexible production facilities.[4]

Opponents of NAFTA, including both presidents Obama and Trump, believed that the agreement led to the shuttering of factories in Rust Belt states because companies fled to inexpensive labor Mexico. As a result, millions of U.S. workers lost their jobs or were forced to accept lower wages.[5]

The European Union

The European Union is a 27-nation alliance that virtually turns member countries into a single marketplace for ideas, goods, services, and investment strategies. Brussels, Belgium is the headquarters of the EU. The EU was a 15-nation alliance for many years, but continues to incorporate new nations, and has become the world's largest economic entity. The EU trades with member nations, the United States and Canada, and other countries throughout the world. In addition, Japanese firms are now investing extensively in Europe. An example of the unity created among nations is the Schengen Agreement. It ended passport control and customs checks at many borders, creating a single space where EU citizens can travel, work, and invest.

The EU faced a major challenge in 2020 when the United Kingdom exited, a departure referred to as Brexit (British exit!). A concern was that British exports to the Continent will face customs checks and tariffs that will result in delays and added costs.[6] Furthermore, with the U.K. departing, other members of the EU might follow suit, seeking independence from the alliance and its central control by a parliament. On the positive side, the U.K. was expected to forge its own trade alliance with the United States.

A major step for the European Union is its monetary union in which 11 countries traded their national money for currency called the Euro. The Euro fluctuates in value, but in 2020 was worth about $1.15.

The World Trade Organization (WTO)

The World Trade Organization is the only international agency overseeing the rules of international trade, and it liberalizes trade among many nations throughout the world. The idea is to lower trade barriers, thereby facilitating international trade, with the ultimate goal of moving the world toward free trade and open markets. The WTO facilitates trade throughout the world and ensures that goods flow smoothly through trade agreements. According to the *most favored nation* clause, each member country is supposed to grant all other member countries the most favorable treatment it grants any country with respect to imports and exports. As a result, all countries are supposed to make trade with other member countries quite easy.

An important function of the World Trade Organization is to settle trade disputes between two countries. The decisions of the WTO are absolute, and all members must abide by its rulings. For example, when the U.S. and the European Union are in conflict over imports and exports of beef and lumber, the WTO acts as judge and jury. Countries that violate trade rules are subject to sanctions such as substantial fines.[7]

The WTO now has about 164 member countries, which accounts for about 95 percent of world trade. Lower trade barriers eliminate the artificially high prices consumers previously paid for imported goods. A continuing problem for the WTO is the distrust of developing countries that claim they are bullied by rich countries. Instead, developing countries want trade agreements that will also help poor nations.

One issue in facilitating trade is that global trade liberalization leads to continuous job cuts and downward pressures on wages in industrialized nations. The concern about global trade contributing to worker exploitation is so strong that riots frequently take place outside WTO meetings. Rioters regularly pelt security workers with rocks and smash the windows of American-owned stores, or U.S. franchises abroad. McDonald's restaurants are a frequent target because McDonald's symbolizes American trade overseas.

The counterargument to objections to overseas trade is that free trade, in the long run, creates more job opportunities by making it possible to export more freely, such as the U.S. exporting pork to China. A related argument is that when companies shift manufacturing to low-wage countries, the companies can remain more cost competitive. As a consequence of globalizing production, the companies stay in business and keep more domestic workers employed.

Among the criticisms of the WTO is that it does not resolve disputes efficiently, such as taking 15 years to resolve the dispute about Airbus receiving unfair subsidies. Another problem is that WTO rules do not cover digital trade, cross-border data flows, and many services, such as commercial aviation. Many American politicians and business executives believe that the WTO has an anti-American bias, but their counterparts in other countries disagree. The WTO is in the early stages of making reforms so it can play a stronger role in world trade. By 2020, the Trump administration was seriously considering a U.S. withdrawal from the WTO.

Global Outsourcing as Part of International Trade

The trade agreements described above have made it much easier for companies to have manufacturing and many services performed in other countries. In general, **outsourcing** refers to the practice of hiring an individual or another company outside the organization to perform work. Here we are concerned with global outsourcing, sometimes referred to as **offshoring**. We will visit outsourcing again in Chapter 8, as part of the discussion of organization structure.

Outsourcing continues to grow in scope, thereby increasing trade among countries. Some knowledge work, including financial analysis and legal work is also globally outsourced. For example, in Gurgaon, India, Copal partners conduct equity, fixed income and trading research for big name banks, such as Goldman Sachs and JP Morgan.[8] Transactional work, such as accounting, billing and processing of HR and insurance claims are common. Legal outsourcing to law firms in India has also grown considerably in recent years to help hold down legal fees in the United States. Small

outsourcing
The practice of hiring an individual or another company outside the organization to perform work.

offshoring
Global outsourcing.

domestic law firms as well as middle-class individuals are using the Internet to hire foreign lawyers at low prices for such activities as legal research, intellectual property advice and helping with child custody disputes.[9]

A major force behind global outsourcing is the pressure that discount retailers such as Walmart, Target and Dollar General exert on manufacturers to keep their prices low. Visualize a mermaid doll being sold for $1.00 at a discount store in the United States. The distributor of these dolls has to rely on an extremely low-priced manufacturer to be able to sell the doll to the retailer for about 50 cents. So, the doll is made in China where the cost of production is extremely low. Sending so much manufacturing and service work (such as coding and call centers) continues to create heated controversy. Here we look briefly at the major arguments for and against outsourcing. Some of these arguments are also included in the discussion later of the pros and cons of globalization.

The Case for Global Outsourcing

Sending jobs overseas can create new demand for the lower-priced goods, ultimately leading to new jobs in the United States. Consumer electronics is a germane example. In the United States and Canada, people consume an enormous quantity of electronic products, such as smartphones, video games, and laptop computers made overseas. As a result, many retail stores and jobs are created as well as technicians to service all the equipment. If these products were manufactured domestically, high prices might limit demand.

The proponents who favor global outsourcing are also part of the argument for free trade. Slashing costs of production through global outsourcing can help a company become more competitive and win new orders. Many consumer products companies would have to charge much higher prices if they did not globally outsource their customer service and tech support centers.

Outsourcing to other countries sometimes creates a favorable climate for reciprocity on the part of countries that are the major beneficiaries of global outsourcing, such as India. A case in point is the Tata Group conglomerate from India. The Tata Consultancy Services unit hired 1,300 employees who are American, among its 14, 000 employees in the U.S. The vast majority of these U.S. employees are Indian Americans.[10]

The Case Against Global Outsourcing

Many Americans believe offshoring is responsible for the permanent loss of jobs in the United States, as well as slow job creation. Yet, increased productivity through information technology has created the vast majority of lost jobs. Furthermore, scores of jobs disappear because of information technology, such as those of travel agents, newspaper journalists and door-to-door sales representative. Another problem tied with global outsourcing is that American employers can offer low wages to domestic employees because their work could be sent offshore.

A notable problem some American companies have with outsourcing customer-service centers to foreign countries is that language barriers may make it difficult to resolve customer problems. Although the call center workers in the other country might be fluent in English, some Americans have difficulty understanding English as spoken in other countries. Art O'Donnell, the executive vice president of customer service at Monster, offers this explanation: "We're really dealing with people putting together a résumé or posting a job and you need to be able to do trouble-shooting, problem analysis and provide directions. And you can't do that if there is a language barrier."[11]

Tariffs as a Key Factor in International Trade

As implied for the trade agreements already described, tariffs play a key role in the globalization of business. Tariffs are essentially fees charged against importers by the government to which a product or service is exported. The imposition of tariffs helps some firms but hurts others, and are often furiously debated by businesspeople and politicians. A key purpose of tariffs is to protect an industry in one's own country. For example, a U.S. aluminum company would be a competitive disadvantage if a Canadian aluminum company were able to import aluminum into the country at two-thirds the price of the American company. If the U.S. imposes a 40 percent tariff on Canadian companies, American firms that use aluminum would be more likely to purchase domestically-produced aluminum.

Tariffs have been in use since the 1840s, so they have offered useful protection for some companies in some industries. Yet tariffs can backfire in several ways. An immediate impact is that consumers pay more for the same product, such as the price of a hairdryer increasing if tariffs are increased against Chinese domestic electronic products. Another problem is that trading partners tend to retaliate. If the United States imposes heavy tariffs on electronic components made in China, the Chinese government will impose heavy tariffs on Cadillacs (a vehicle in much demand by wealthy Chinese). Tariffs can also force a company to be less profitable. When the United States imposed tariffs on the European Union a few years ago, Europe imposed a new 25 percent tariff on U.S. motorcycles. Harley-Davidson management said it would have to eat the approximately $2,200 price per vehicle to avoid losing European customers.[12]

A major example of the impact of tariffs on world trade took place in 2020, when the United States and China reached agreement on some aspects of their trade dispute that had been running for 21 months. China's government agreed to postpone planned punitive tariffs on U.S. manufactured automobiles and other goods. Washington had agreed to postpone a planned tariff hike on $160 billion of Chinese imports, and to reduce other tariffs to 7.5 percent from 15 percent. China also committed to purchase $40 billion of American farm products during a two-year period.[13] As a result of the end of this tariff conflict, consumer confidence in the United States rose, business executives increased their investments, and overall economic growth began to climb. Positive results of this nature could be interpreted as an indicator of how high tariffs hold back the economy.

Sensitivity to Cultural Differences

The guiding principle for people involved in international enterprise is sensitivity to cultural differences. **Cultural sensitivity** is awareness of local and national customs and their importance in effective interpersonal relationships. Ignoring the customs of other people creates a communications block that can impede business and create ill will. For example, Americans tend to be impatient to close a deal while businesspeople in many other cultures prefer to build a relationship slowly before consummating an agreement.

Cultural sensitivity can also take the form of adapting your behavior to meet the requirements of people from another culture. A frequent challenge in international business is speaking slowly enough in your own language, so workers for whom your language is not their native tongue can understand you readily. To not adapt your rate of speech can be a sign of cultural insensitivity.

LEARNING OBJECTIVE **3**

Recognize the importance of sensitivity to cultural differences in international enterprise.

cultural sensitivty
Awareness of local and national customs and their importance in effective interpersonal relationships.

multicultural worker
An individual who is aware of and values other cultures.

Cultural sensitivity is also important because it helps a person become a **multicultural worker**. Such an individual is convinced all cultures are equally good, and enjoys learning about other cultures. Global migration suggests that multicultural employees already make up a sizeable chunk of the workforce.[14]

Multicultural workers are usually people who have been exposed to more than one culture in childhood. A person from another culture is likely to accept a multicultural person. A theoretical analysis concludes that multiculturalism is the virtue of being open to others.[15] The multicultural worker is open to people who harbor different beliefs and customs.

Being culturally sensitive and multicultural is important because it is challenging to manage employees with dissimilar backgrounds and cultures, yet attaining business goals while adapting to these differences. According to the research of Development Dimensions International, *how* a manager manages people in different cultures can influence results. One potential area for culture conflict occurs between East and West. In Japan, communication about change tends to be more subtle and indirect than in the United States. Japanese managers often use consensus-building techniques to bring about acceptance of change before executing the change. An American manager in Japan might fall back on his or her natural pattern of being much more authoritarian and direct as a way of bringing about change.[16]

Candidates for foreign assignments generally receive training in the language and customs of the country they will work in, as a way of enhancing cultural sensitivity. International workers are also sensitized to positive cultural behaviors as well as cultural mistakes to avoid, as shown in Figure 3-1.

LEARNING OBJECTIVE 4

Identify major challenges facing the global managerial worker.

CHALLENGES FACING THE GLOBAL MANAGERIAL WORKER

Managerial workers on assignment in other countries, as well as domestic managers working on international dealings, face a variety of challenges. Rising to these challenges can be the difference between success and failure. Among the heaviest challenges are developing global leadership skills, currency fluctuations, human rights violations, culture shock, differences in negotiating style, and national culture influences on a management technique. (See Figure 3-2).

Developing Global Leadership Skills

global leadership skills
The ability to effectively lead people of other cultures.

Managerial workers occupying leadership positions need to develop **global leadership skills**, the ability to effectively lead people from other cultures. Having such skills is a combination of cultural sensitivity and leadership abilities in general. An attitude of welcoming other cultures is perhaps more important than overseas experience itself in becoming an effective global leader. The global leader manages across distance, countries, and cultures. To be effective as a global leader, the manager must inspire others, such as getting workers in another country excited about the future of the multinational corporation. Good interpersonal relationships are required, as they are of all leaders.

Another aspect of global leadership skill is to understand how well management principles from one's own culture transfer to another. The point about understanding cultural differences as part of cultural sensitivity made above is a variation on the same

Figure 3-1 Protocol Dos and Don'ts in Several Countries

Several specialists in cross-culture etiquette suggest adhering to the following dos and don'ts in the countries indicated. Remember, however, these suggestions are not absolute rules.

Great Britain

- DO say "please" and "thank you" often.
- DO arrive promptly for dinner.
- DON'T ask personal questions because the British protect their privacy.
- DON'T gossip about British royalty. Allow the British to take the initiative with respect to gossiping about royalty, such as mentioning juicy stories in the tabloids.

France

- DO shake hands when greeting. Only close friends give light, brushing kisses on cheeks.
- DO dress more formally than in the United States. Elegant dress is highly valued.
- DON'T expect to complete any work during the French two-hour lunch.
- DON'T chew gum in a work setting.

Italy

- DO write business correspondence in Italian for priority attention.
- DO make appointments between 10:00 a.m. and 11:00 a.m. or after 3:00 p.m.
- DON'T eat too much pasta, as it is not the main course.
- DON'T hand out business cards freely. Italians use them infrequently.

Greece

- DO distribute business cards freely so people will know how to spell your name.
- DO be prompt even if your hosts are not.
- DON'T expect to meet deadlines. A project takes as long as the Greeks think is necessary.
- DON'T address people by formal or professional titles. The Greeks want more informality.

Japan

- DO present your business cards with both hands and a slight bow as a gesture of respect.
- DO present gifts, American-made and wrapped.
- DON'T knock competitors.
- DON'T present the same gift to everyone, unless all members are the same organizational rank.
- DON'T attempt to kiss or hug work asscoiates.

China

- DO reach for your Chinese boss's hand first. A high-ranking person in the company should never initiate a handshake. A limp grip connotes humility and respect.
- DO be impressed by a business card from a Chinese businessperson. Place the card on a table in front of you so you can continue to admire it.
- DON'T point with one finger because it is considered very rude.
- DON'T give clocks as gifts because the pronunciation of the Chinese phrase, "to give clocks" could also mean, "to attend to a dying relative."
- DO wrap gifts in gold or red paper and present them with both hands.
- DON'T wrap gifts in black or white.

Most Asian Countries

- DO be polite and respect authority. Most Asian cultures emphasize polite gestures such as gentle bowing and smiling to indicate acceptance or agreement.
- DON'T emphasize the number "4," such as giving a pack of four bottles of cologne or cigars as a gift, and do not rent a conference room on the fourth floor of a hotel. The number "4" connotes death in many Asian cultures.

Source: *Inc. Magazine's Going Global: Japan Inc.*, January 1994; Alan Morrell, "Helping to Navigate 'Cultural Icebergs'," *Democrat and Chronicle*, December 14, 2015, p. 9A; "Etiquette Abroad," *Executive Leadership*, July 15, 2015, p. 1; Christina Larson, "The Chinese Take Their Etiquette Seriously," *Bloomberg BusinessWeek*, June 3–9, 2013, pp. 15–16; Eric Spitznagel, "Impress Your Chinese Boss," *Bloomberg Businessweek*, January 9–15, 2012, pp. 80–81; "How to Research Culture Before Moving Abroad," *Personal Business* (online.westernunion.com) © 2016 Western Union Holdings Inc.

Note: A cultural mistake for Americans to avoid when conducting business in most countries outside the United States and Canada is to insist on getting down to business quickly. North Americans in small towns also like to build a relationship before getting down to business.

Figure 3-2 Challenges Facing the International Managerial Worker

theme. A specific example is supply-chain management. According to Kim Tae Woo, a management advisor from South Korea, most Western companies are quite willing to switch parts suppliers to cut costs. Switching suppliers is a tougher sell in Japan, where executives frequently have long-term or personal relationships with key people at their suppliers.[17]

The nature of what constitutes global leadership skills is a vast topic, yet consider this example: You are the manager of a unit of a company that expects employees to give utmost attention to meeting customer deadlines, even if it means working 70 hours per week. In your group are several workers from overseas who are from a culture that gives family life much higher priority than work life, so workers are not disposed to work more than 37 and one-half hours per week. During crunch time, it is your job to cultivate the overseas worker to become more work oriented.

Currency Fluctuations

A frequent challenge to the international manager is adjusting business practices in response to changes in the value of currencies in the home country and elsewhere. If the currency of a country suddenly *gains* in value, it may be difficult to export products made in that country. However, when a country's currency *weakens* versus the currency of other countries, it is easier to export goods because they are significantly less expensive and competitive in other countries. The strengthening of the U.S. dollar in recent years made it easier for U.S. citizens to purchase foreign goods. For example, the U.S. dollar rose to 1.35 cents against the Canadian dollar in 2020. (A leather jacket made in Canada for 200$ would cost $133 U.S. In contrast, a handbag priced at $200 U.S. would cost 270$, excluding differences in sales taxes. So, Americans would find the Canadian leather jacket to be a relative bargain, and Canadians would find the American handbag quite expensive.

A related example with a strong U.S. dollar is that profits from overseas operations reported in U.S. dollars shrink. The idea is that it takes more foreign currency to create the same amount of profits in U.S. dollars. For several years the Canadian dollar and the U.S. dollar were close to equivalent, so a $100,000 profit from a Canadian subsidiary would be about $100,000 in profit expressed in U.S. dollars. In contrast, in 2020, the same profit would only be $74,000 in U.S. profits.

Currency fluctuations are always a concern for workers in marketing. Yet, managers in manufacturing and in services must also pay close attention to currency fluctuations. For example, when a currency drops in value, the manufacturing manager might be forced to find ways to lower the manufacturing cost of a product to compete better against imports. As a country's currency rises in value, exporting companies must become more and more efficient at lowering costs.

Human Rights Violations, Corruption, and Violence

International managers face potential ethical problems when their customers and suppliers reside in countries where human rights are violated. Should a U.S. manufacturer of batteries for high-tech devices purchase cobalt from a supplier that employs 10-year-old children who work as miners for the equivalent of $4 U.S. per day? Should a U.S. shoe manufacturer buy components from a country that uses political prisoners as free labor? Ethical issues require careful thought, especially when they are not always clear-cut. To a child in an underdeveloped country, receiving $4 per day can mean the difference between malnutrition and adequate food.

The subject of human rights violations is complicated and touchy. Multinational corporations based in the United States are often accused of profiting from the labor of employees exploited in less-developed countries. Also, many U.S. companies hire undocumented aliens at below minimum wage, and maintain substandard and dangerous working conditions. The United States sets high standards when it comes to human rights in other countries. Yet, according to Amnesty International, these standards are sometimes violated, such as unfair treatment of indigenous people including Inuits (the preferred term for "Eskimo") and Native Americans, as well as capital punishment.[18]

Another ethical and legal problem the international manager faces is dealing with corruption by foreign officials. To conduct business in some countries, a string of officials demand payments to facilitate allowing foreigners to conduct business or speed approval of an operating license. Corruption is considered to be a significant risk for foreign companies doing business in Mexico. The Business Anti-Corruption Portal contends that collusion among the police, judges, and criminal groups is extensive, leading to widespread crime. Bribery is often necessary to obtain construction permits and licenses.[19] However, the United States is not immune to corruption as evidenced by how frequently public office holders are convicted of accepting bribes from construction firms. The bribes are based on the construction firm receiving a contract to build part of the infrastructure such as a highway or the bridge.

A life-threatening risk for U.S. multinational companies is for its employees to be trapped in violent acts in the overseas country. A chilling example is the large number of people killed in the drug-fueled wars gripping cities that are home to U.S. factories in Mexico. During a recent year, over 33,000 homicide victims of the Mexican drug cartel violence were reported.[20] Civil unrest, such as in Iran and Iraq can also create loss of life and severe disruption of the business.

Culture Shock

Many managers and professionals on overseas assignments face **culture shock**. The condition refers to a group of physical and psychological symptoms that may develop when a person is abruptly placed in a foreign culture. Among them are excessive hand-washing and concern for sanitation, fear of physical contact with others, fear of being mugged and strong feelings of homesickness.[21] Another potential contributor to culture shock is that the expatriate may work in one time zone while contacts in company headquarters work in a time zone with a difference of six or more hours. As a result, the expatriate is often expected to answer e-mails, text messages and respond to phone calls during his or her typical evening or sleeping hours. For example, a person from headquarters in Los Angeles might place an urgent phone call at 5 p.m. his time to a worker in London whose time is 3 a.m. Frequent disruptions to personal life of this nature contribute to making the international assignment uncomfortable for the expatriate.

Differences in Negotiating Style

A recurring challenge in other countries is that the international managerial worker may have to use a different negotiation style. A do-or-die attitude is often self-defeating. American negotiators, for example, often find they must be more patient, use a team approach and avoid being too informal. Patience is a major factor in negotiating outside the United States. Asian negotiators are willing to spend many days negotiating a deal. Much of their negotiating activity seems to be ceremonial (including elaborate dining) and unrelated to the task. This protracted process can frustrate many Americans. Although members of another culture spend a long time working a deal, they may still take a tough stance, such as insisting on a reasonable profit.

Another relevant aspect of cultural differences in negotiating style is knowing whether to put the final deal in writing. According to cross-cultural specialist Erin Meyer, in the United States and Northern Europe, summarizing the agreement is standard practice. Yet this seemingly efficient practice can backfire in Africa or in Asia. A spoken agreement is preferable in African and Asian countries, where relationships are more important than written contracts. A Nigerian manager explained, "If the moment we come to an agreement, you pull out a contract, I start to worry. Do you think I won't follow through? Are you trying to trap me?"[22]

Recognizing National Culture May or May Not Influence the Effectiveness of a Management Technique

A general challenge confronting the international manager is that techniques that work well in one culture may not necessarily work well elsewhere. For example, in a culture that highly respects the authority of the boss, granting decision making authority to the group may not be so effective. In cultures like India and Japan, the manager is supposed to make most decisions. Most workers in India and Japan would therefore consider it a sign of weakness if the manager called on them to make most decisions.

The international manager should also be aware of management practices that are likely to work well in many cultures. A group of researchers conducted a large-scale investigation on how the effectiveness of a well-established management technique and high-performance work practices are influenced by national culture.[23] *High-performance work practices* enhance employee ability, motivation, and opportunity to contribute. High-performance work systems (HPWS) include such practices as rigorous methods of employee selection, pay for performance and employee participation in decisions. The investigation aggregated 156 studies of the relationship between HPWS and business performance on 35,767 companies in 29 countries.

A major finding of this massive study was that high-performance work systems are associated with good business performance in all the countries. A high-performance work system therefore does not have to be adapted to a national culture. One reason this finding is not so surprising is that a HPWS is typically based on well-researched and fair human resource procedures that people from any culture would appreciate.

SUCCESS FACTORS IN THE GLOBAL MARKETPLACE

LEARNING OBJECTIVE 5

Pinpoint success factors in the global marketplace, and several positive and negative aspects of globalization.

Success in international business stems from the same factors that lead to success at home. The ultimate reason for the success of any product or service is its ability to satisfy customer needs. Additional strategies and tactics, however, are required for success in the global marketplace. It is important to recognize that internationalization of business is not always successful. Most of these strategies and tactics extend logically from the topics discussed previously in this chapter.

Think Globally, Act Locally

A competitive enterprise combines global scale and world-class technology with deep roots in local markets. Local representatives of the firm behave as though their primary mission is to serve the local customer. Multinational corporations implementing a local market focus face the challenge of adapting a product to local trends and preferences. Often the differences are subtle and require a careful study of the local market. For example, Mary Kay, a direct seller of cosmetics, has adapted its products to Chinese culture, which perceives smooth white skin as the essence of beauty, said Paul Mak, president of Mary Kay China. As a result, sunless tanners or bronzers are not distributed in China. Instead Mary Kay markets skin whiteners and is developing a line of botanical lotions that include traditional Chinese herbs.[24]

A major aspect of thinking globally, yet acting locally, is for the multinational corporation to compete successfully against well-established, well-managed domestic (local) companies. Two members of the Boston Consulting Group studied this challenge. One of the key principles is for the multinational company to create customized products and services for the local market—as does Mary Kay.[25]

Recruit and Select Talented Nationals

A major success factor in building a business in another country is to hire talented citizens of that country to fill important positions. After the host-company nationals are hired, they must be taught the culture of the parent company. By teaching the overseas managers the values and traditions of the firm, those managers can better achieve corporate objectives. Networking with contacts in the other country is important. One way to network would be to make a list of other companies from your country already established in your destination country. These people might include bankers, lawyers, suppliers and distributors.

Staffing in other countries may require a modification of U.S. ideas about good candidates. An international human resources manager observes that, "One of the most common mistakes companies make when hiring and recruiting employees in China is to judge candidates based on U.S. perceptions and criteria. Chinese employees often have different ways of communicating their interests and skills during an interview, and they consider it unbecoming to place too much emphasis on their skills and experience." An interviewer not familiar with this mindset could miss hiring an excellent candidate.[26]

Hire or Develop Multicultural Workers

A contributing factor to success in global markets is to hire multicultural workers. Multiculturalism enhances acceptance of a firm by overseas personnel and customers. Included in multiculturalism is the ability to speak the language of the target (or host) country. Even though English is the official language of business and technology, overseas employees should develop the right foreign language skill. Being able to listen to and understand foreign customers speaking in their native language about their requirements may reveal nuances that would be missed by having them speak in English. Showing that one has made an effort to learn the native language can earn big dividends with employees, customers, prospective customers, bankers and government officials. To be impressive, however, it is important to go beyond the most basic skill level.

The presence of multicultural workers can also help with the pesky problem of having website information translated correctly into the predominant language in another country. Computerized translations often create embarrassing gaffes. For example, the American word "clutch" for handbag might be translated by computer into the automotive mechanism for shifting gears.[27] The point here is not that machine translations are typically incorrect, but that a multicultural worker might catch a translation that does not convey the proper meaning. How about translating a "fall sale" into a word in another language that means a "tumbling down sale?"

To help workers and their family members become multicultural, many companies offer cultural training. Joerg Schmitz, a global management training expert, shares an illuminating example of the impact of culture on an employee's job performance: "The U.S. culture is extraordinarily task oriented. Northern Europe is perhaps the closest to the type of task orientation you'll find in the United States. But about every other country in the world is relationship oriented."[28] Expatriates must understand this observation as they work hard to build rapport and gain credibility with business colleagues in other cultures.

Research and Assess Potential Markets

Another basic success strategy in international markets is to acquire valid information about the firm's target market. Trade statistics usually provide a good starting point. If the company manufactures sweaters, raincoats and boots for dogs, it must research where such items sell best. Basic trade data are often available at foreign embassies, banks with international operations and departments of commerce. Much of this information can be ferreted out with a skilled Internet researcher. Walmart invests enormous energy and money into researching which overseas markets—and consumer reaction—would fit its retailing model. In general, the planning has worked well. For example, Walmart has been highly successful in Mexico and Canada, and has stayed out of Paris (as well as New York City!). The company, however, stumbled in Germany and eventually sold its stores in that country over ten years ago.

The Advantages and Disadvantages of Globalization

Many managers and scholars believe that globalization of business is both inevitable and highly desirable. Yet for other managers, business owners and individual workers, the internationalization of the workplace has created more problems than opportunities. Many of the advantages and disadvantages of globalization depend upon an individual's vantage point. An executive in an MNC might receive a generous bonus because shifting a call center to India saves the company $5 million per year in labor costs. As a consequence, she welcomes globalization. The middle-aged customer-service center supervisor who lost his enjoyable, well-paying job, and is now a greeter at a discount department store would view globalization more negatively. Figure 3-3 outlines the major pros and cons of globalization.

Figure 3-3 The Pros and Cons of Globalization

Advantages

- By sending jobs overseas, a country such as the United States is better able to compete globally, thus saving jobs in the long run. A company frequently cannot get the contracts it needs to survive, if it cannot reduce prices, so global outsourcing becomes a necessity. Construction outsourcing can cut costs by 10–20 percent on a major project.

- Productivity grows more quickly when countries produce goods and services in which they have a comparative advantage. Living standards go up faster. Productivity in high-wage companies also increases because they are forced to reduce the cost of production to survive world-wide competition.

- Global integration helps reduce world-wide poverty, as poorer countries become wealthier because of new employment and exports. At the same time, economic growth around the world contributes to economic stability and peace because impoverished people are more likely to revolt and attack wealthier people and institutions.

- Global competition and inexpensive imports set a ceiling on prices, so inflation is less likely to be too high.

- When one country buys goods from and sends jobs to another country, the second country is better able to purchase goods from the first country. For example, India furnishes its customer service centers for U. S firms with U.S. computers and software.

Disadvantages

- Millions of Americans have lost jobs due to imports or production shifts abroad. Most find lower-paying jobs. Most of the jobs sent overseas from the United States are permanent losses. Many service and professional jobs, such as financial analysis and design engineering, are now sent to other countries.

- Millions of others fear losing their jobs, especially at those companies operating under competitive pressure. Workers are forced to compete against foreign workers in countries like Pakistan and Malaysia where workers are paid, on average, one-tenth as much as their American counterparts.

- To stay competitive in a global economy, many companies reduce wages, close plants rather than have a unionized workforce, reduce health and retirement benefits, and eliminate some pension plans.

- Profits and executive salaries increase while workers toil in overseas sweatshops. Many of these workers are vulnerable to human rights violations.

- National pride is hurt as many Americans lament, "Nothing is 'made in the USA' any longer. We used to be such a great country." At the same time, many American consumers resent call center workers from 6,000 miles away responding to their requests for information and service. Many Americans have a difficult time understanding workers who speak English with a foreign accent.

continues on next page

Figure 3-3 The Pros and Cons of Globalization (continued)

Advantages

- An open economy spurs innovation with fresh ideas from abroad. Innovation at home receives a boost because the domestic company has to become more specialized and creative to compete against international rivals.

- When research and development jobs are moved overseas, products reach the market faster because work can be done 24/7, as scientists and engineers in one part of the world pass off their project at the end of the day to research workers just starting the workday overseas.

- Workers become broader in their outlook and profit from the opportunity to become multicultural, including foreign travel.

- With many jobs shipped overseas, talent is freed up within the United States, which can be re-skilled and used elsewhere during a tight labor market. At the same time, many people whose jobs are outsourced, or fear being outsourced, start small enterprises of their own, helping to revitalize the economy.

- It is possible for an American company to promote fair trade around the world by choosing foreign vendors who pay beyond the minimum wage, and also offer workers bonuses and medical benefits.

- To stave off foreign competition, domestic companies are forced to increase the quality of their goods and services.

- Taxes are lower and financial incentives for establishing manufacturing are often higher in countries such as Malaysia and Singapore than they are in the U.S., making it easier for American firms to operate profitably. Also, it is often easier for U.S. companies to find inexpensive funding overseas.

Disadvantages

- American high-tech companies are occasionally levied heavy fines by the European Union for employing unfair trade practices, not paying their fair share of taxes, or being monopolistic. For example, in 2019 the European Commission fined Google approximately $1.7 billion U.S. for "abusive practices" in online advertising, such as preventing or limiting its rival from working with companies that had deals with Google.

Source: Bruce Einhorn and Matthew Phillips, "Need a New Building?: Call the Philippines," *Bloomberg Businessweek*, September 9–September 16, 2013, p. 14; Brian Blackstone, "Fed Chairman Expects Globalization to Enhance Living Standards," *The Wall Street Journal*, August 26–27, 2006, p. A3; "Don't Discount the Positive Side of Globalization," *Toronto Star* (www.thestar.com); Douglas A. Irwin, "Outsourcing Is Good for America," January 28, 2004, *The Wall Street Journal*, p. A16; Pete Engardio, "Can the Future Be Built in America?" *Business Week*, September 21, 2009, pp. 046–051; Bill Chappell, "EU Fines Google $1.7 Billion Over 'Abusive' Online Ad Strategies," *NPR* (www.npr.org), March 20, 2019, p. 1.

LEARNING OBJECTIVE 6

Describe the scope of diversity, the competitive advantage, and potential problems of a culturally diverse workforce.

diversity
A mixture of people with different group identities within the same work environment.

THE SCOPE, COMPETITIVE ADVANTAGE, AND POTENTIAL PROBLEMS OF MANAGING DIVERSITY

The globalization of business means that managerial workers must be able to deal effectively with people from other countries. At the same time, it is important to deal effectively with different cultural groups within one's own country and company. Both the international and domestic workforces are diverse. In the present context, **diversity** refers to a mixture of people with different group identities within the same work environment. The term *diversity* includes two subtypes, demographic and cultural.

Demographic diversity refers to the mix of group characteristics of the organization's workforce. Demographic characteristics include such factors as age, sex, religion, physical status and sexual orientation. *Cultural diversity* refers to the mix of cultures and subcultures to which the organization's workforce belongs. Among these cultures are the Hispanic culture, the deaf culture, the Muslim culture, the Jewish culture, the Native American culture and the Inuit culture. It is possible for people with the same demographic characteristics not to share the same cultural characteristics. A deaf person who went to school with hearing people, whose parents are hearing, and most of whose friends can hear, may be deaf from a demographic standpoint, yet the person does not identify with the deaf culture. Following common practice in this text, the term *diversity* is used to reflect both demographic and cultural diversity.

Here and in the next section, we study diversity in the workplace from five perspectives: (1) the scope of diversity, (2) its competitive advantage, (3) potential disadvantages, (4) organizational practices for capitalizing on diversity, and (5) an analysis of how the English language is used to unify people in business. Before reading further, take the self-quiz about cross-cultural skills and attitudes presented in Figure 3-4.

Figure 3-4 Cross-Cultural Skills and Attitudes

Various employers and cross-cultural experts believe the following skills and attitudes are important for relating effectively to co-workers in a culturally diverse environment.

	Applies to Me Now	Not There Yet
1 I have spent some time in another country.	_____	_____
2 At least one of my friends is deaf, blind, or uses a wheelchair.	_____	_____
3 I know how much at least two foreign currencies are worth in comparison to the money of my country.	_____	_____
4 I can read in a language other than my native tongue.	_____	_____
5 I can speak in a language other than my native tongue.	_____	_____
6 I can write in a language other than my own.	_____	_____
7 I can understand people speaking in a language other than my own.	_____	_____
8 I use my second language regularly.	_____	_____
9 My friends include people of races different from my own.	_____	_____
10 My friends include people of different ages.	_____	_____
11 I feel (or would feel) comfortable having friends with a sexual orientation different from mine.	_____	_____
12 My attitude is that although another culture may be different from mine, that culture is equally good.	_____	_____
13 I would be willing to (or already do) hang art from various countries in my home.	_____	_____
14 I would accept (or have already accepted) a work assignment of more than several months in another country.	_____	_____
15 I have a passport.	_____	_____
16 I sometimes eat in restaurants that serve the food of a country quite different from mine, and/or I prepare such food at home.	_____	_____

Interpretation: If you answered "Applies to Me Now" to ten or more of the questions, you most likely function well in a multicultural work environment. If you answered "Not There Yet" to ten or more of the questions, you need to develop more cross-cultural awareness and skills to work effectively in a multicultural work environment. You will notice that being bilingual gives you at least five points on this quiz.

Source: Several of the statements are based on Ruthann Dirks and Janet Buzzard, "What CEOs Expect of Employees Hired for International Work," *Business Education Forum*, April 1997, pp. 3–7; Gunnar Beeth, "Multicultural Managers Wanted," *Management Review*, May 1997, pp. 17–21.

The Scope of Diversity

Improving cross-cultural relations includes appreciating the true meaning of diversity. To appreciate diversity, a person must go beyond tolerating and treating people from different racial and ethnic groups fairly. Valuing diversity means respecting and enjoying a wide range of cultural, demographic, and individual differences. A current trend in the workplace is for people of color not just to be stirred into the melting pot, but to be recognized and appreciated for their cultural differences.[29] To be diverse is to be different in some measurable way. Although the diversity factor is measurable in a scientific sense, it may not be visible on the surface. Upon meeting a team member, it may not be apparent that the person is diverse from the standpoint of being dyslexic, color-blind, gay, lesbian, or vegetarian. However, all these factors are measurable.

As just implied, some people are more visibly diverse than others because of physical features or disabilities. Yet the diversity umbrella is supposed to include everybody in an organization. People who are neuro-diverse, such as those with autism or dyslexia, are recognized as another component of diversity to be recognized. The goal of a diverse organization then, is for persons of all cultural backgrounds to achieve their full potential, not restrained by group identification, such as sex, nationality, age, race, physical status (abled and disabled), or sexual orientation.

A diverse organization is also thought to be inclusive, where the contributions of every employee is valued, appreciated, and leveraged in the sense of being capitalized upon.[30] *Inclusion*, therefore, refers to being accepted and welcomed, and for people to feel that they belong to the organization. An organization might be diverse, without making an effort to reach out to all of its diverse members. Another aspect of inclusiveness is to make accommodations for people with physical disabilities, such as making desks high enough for the wheelchair user to slide the wheelchair under.

Working well with different generations has become an important part of both cultural and demographic diversity in organizations, with the goal of people of all ages working well together. The two extremes are the traditionalists (or veterans) born between 1922–1945 and the millennials born from 1981–2000. One cultural difference between the groups is that traditionalists are likely to prefer to communicate by telephone and e-mail, whereas millennials prefer sending text messages.

Another cultural and demographic group being emphasized for full inclusion in the workforce is people who are lesbian, gay, bisexual, and transgender (LGBT). For example, more people in key managerial positions now openly announce they are gay or lesbian. Furthermore, some transgender people who hold a position as a member of one sex, then one day return to work announcing they have changed their sexual identification. For example, Sam in customer service returns from his summer vacation as Sally, and now wears women's clothing to work.

Cultural diversity also includes having a diverse group of suppliers.

The Competitive Advantage of Diversity

Encouraging diversity within an organization helps an organization achieve social responsibility goals. Also, diversity brings a competitive advantage to a firm. Before diversity can offer a competitive advantage to a firm, it must be woven into the fabric of the organization. This stands in contrast to simply having a "diversity" or "anti-bias" program offered on rare occasions by the human resources department. Instead, the human resource efforts toward accomplishing diversity become part of organizational strategy. The potential competitive (or bottom-line) benefits of cultural diversity, as revealed by research and observations, are described next:

1 *Managing diversity well offers a marketing advantage, including increased sales and profits.* A representational workforce facilitates reaching a multicultural market. A study or more than 1,000 companies covering 12 countries found that gender diversity in top-level management was associated with higher profits. Business firms in the top quartile in gender diversity were 21 percent more likely to have above-average profits than those companies in the fourth quartile. The same study found that companies with the most ethically diverse teams are more likely to outperform comparable companies on profitability.[31]

2 *Effective management of diversity can reduce costs.* More effective management of diversity may increase job satisfaction of diverse groups, thus decreasing turnover and absenteeism and their associated costs. A diverse organization that welcomes and fosters the growth of a wide variety of employees will retain more of its minority and multicultural employees.

3 *Companies with a favorable record in managing diversity are at a distinct advantage in recruiting talented people.* Those companies with a favorable reputation for welcoming diversity attract the strongest job candidates among women and racial and ethnic minorities. A shortage of workers gives extra impetus to diversity. During a tight labor market, companies cannot afford to be seen as not welcoming any particular group.

4 *Workforce heterogeneity may also offer a company a creativity advantage.* Creative solutions to problems are more likely when a diverse group attacks a problem due to the variety of perspectives that contribute to creative alternatives. For example, if a company is going to launch products that fit the needs of young people, it is best to include young people in generating ideas for these products. Peter Fasolo, the chief human resources officer at Johnson & Johnson, explains how diversity enhances creativity: "Because we are an innovation company, we need a global workforce that not only represents our customers and patients but also constantly brings in new insights."[32]

The accompanying *Management in Action* insert offers several insights into how a business firm strives to be diverse and inclusive.

Potential Problems Associated with Diversity

In addition to understanding the competitive advantages of diversity within an organization, a brief look at some of the potential problems is also helpful. Rich Karlgaard, the publisher of *Forbes*, has identified what he considers the paradox and challenge of diversity. An organization's best chance to create a successful, productive team involves diverse membership. Yet the more diverse the membership, the lower the chance the team will survive long enough to produce those positive results.[33]

Cultural diversity initiatives are usually successful in assembling heterogeneous groups, but the group members do not necessarily work harmoniously. The potential for conflict is high. In general, if the demographically different work group members are supportive toward each other, the benefits of group diversity, such as more creative problem solving will be forthcoming. Group members must also share knowledge with each other for the heterogeneous groups to be successful. Another problem is that diverse groups may be less cohesive than those with less diverse composition.

MANAGEMENT IN ACTION

Ultimate Software Has a Culture of Real Inclusion

Ultimate Software Group, Inc., based in Weston, Florida, is a leading provider of human capital management (HCM) software in the cloud, and maintains more than 51 million people records. The company employs more than 5,400 professionals, and has more than 4,500 customers, with employees in 160 countries including Red Roof Inn, Subway, and Texas Roadhouse.

In 2018, Ultimate Software ranked number 5 in the *Best Workplaces for Diversity* list developed by *Fortune* and Great Place to Work. The ranking is based on responses from employees surveyed across the United States. The survey analyzes the daily work experiences of women, people of color, members of the LGBTQ community, Baby Boomers, older generations, and people with disabilities. In 2019, Ultimate Software was named a top-scoring company in the *Disability Equality Index* by Disability:IN, the leading nonprofit resource for business disability inclusion worldwide.

The *Disability Equality Index*, working with the American Association of People with Disabilities, grades organizations on the merits of their policies, programs, and practices aimed at hiring, including, and better serving people with disabilities across the business.

Vivian Maza, chief culture officer at Ultimate Software, said "Diversity, inclusion, and equality are at the heart of who we are at Ultimate, and it's our unique people who keep our culture strong every day." Maza also noted that Ultimate is one family, working together to help improve the lives of people everywhere through innovative HR technology, personalized customer support, and dedicated community service.

For many years, Ultimate has included diversity and inclusion training as part of its leadership development program called LeadUS for current and potential managers. The curricula includes workshops on creating environments of safety and trust, recognizing and minimizing unconscious biases in dealing with employees, and embracing differences in creative thinking to drive innovation. As part of the company's orientation program, new hires receive training in Whole Brain Thinking and learn how to conduct conversations that respects diverse ways of thinking and processing information.

Another diversity initiative is to encourage employee participation in companywide Communities of Interest, consisting of four diverse groups: PRIDEUS for LGBTQIA individuals;

Women in Leadership for women at all organizational levels; ULtiVETS for veterans and active service members, and UltiHOPE that provides a support network for cancer patients, survivors of cancer and caregivers of people with cancer. As part of inclusion, "Allies" are welcome to join any Community of Interest they choose to support and advocate.

The Ultimate benefit package is also geared toward diversity and inclusion. The company pays the entire healthcare premium for employees and their families (including same-sex married couples), with coverage for in-vitro sterilization (IVF) treatments and transgender reassignments.

The "U Belong" program is dedicated to ensuring that all Ultimate employees are comfortable bringing their whole, authentic self to work. U Belong hosts a variety of events and workshops to raise awareness and further educate employees about employees with disabilities, both visible and invisible. One such recent panel discussion focused on "Life on the Autism Spectrum."

Questions

1 **How might the diversity and inclusion initiatives at Ultimate contribute to the success of the company?**

2 **How should an Ultimate manager deal with an employee who says that he or she objects to several of the diversity and inclusion programs (such as payment for sex reassignment treatment) based on his or her religious beliefs?**

3 **If Ultimate Software is really so diverse and inclusive, should the company purposely hire a few people who strongly dislike information technology?**

Source: Original story based on facts and observations in the following sources: Christina Austin, "The Ten Best Workplaces for Diversity," *Fortune*, January 1, 2018, p. 16; Ultimate Software Ranks #5 on *Fortune*'s Best Workplaces for Diversity List for 2018, pp. 1–4; "Ultimate Software Named Top-Scoring Company on 2019 Disability Equality Index," *Business Wire* (www.business wire.com), October 11, 2019, pp. 1–2; Cecil Alper-Leroux, "A Culture of Real Inclusion," blog.ultimastesoftware.com, June 21, 2018, pp. 1–3.

A problem with diversity from a business standpoint is that having a diverse workforce does not always translate into profits. Many large retailers with diverse employees have gone out of business in recent years. The problems of too many retail stores, and the shift to online shopping could not be overcome by diversity alone.

ORGANIZATIONAL PRACTICES TO ENCOURAGE DIVERSITY

Summarize organizational practices to encourage diversity.

The combined forces of the spirit of the times and the advantages of valuing diversity spark management initiatives to manage diversity well. Four representative practices that enhance diversity management are: (1) corporate policies favoring diversity, (2) employee network groups, (3) diversity training, and (4) anti-bias training.

Corporate Policies Favoring Diversity

Many companies formulate policies that encourage and foster diversity. A typical policy is, "We are committed to recruiting, selecting, training and promoting individuals based solely on their capabilities and performance. To accomplish this goal, we value all differences among our workforce." To create a culturally and demographically diverse organization, some companies monitor recruitment and promotions to assure diverse people are promoted into key jobs. After they are promoted, minority group members are eligible to be coached by an external consultant in terms of becoming a successful leader—as is frequently done with majority group members.

A leading example of a company whose policies favor diversity is MGM Resorts. The company consistently wins national diversity honors. "For nearly two decades, we have worked to weave inclusion into the core of our very identity and our operations," said Phyllis A. James, the company's Executive Vice President and Chief Corporate Responsibility Officer.

Since 2001, MGM Resorts has invested $1.8 billion with Minority-and-Women-Owned Business Development Enterprisers suppliers representing eleven percent of MGM's total spending on biddable projects for goods and services. An example of a specific resort diversity initiative is the MGM Mirage Bellagio in Las Vegas. The Bellagio resort unit runs a nine-month executive mentoring program designed to prepare high-potential minority employees in management positions for advancement into the executive level. The hotel also offers a six-month management associate program—six months of training to prepare recent minority graduates for careers in management through mentoring, classroom instruction, job-shadowing and hands-on experience.[34]

Employee Network Groups

A company approach to recognizing cultural differences is to permit and encourage employees to form **employee network groups**, as mentioned in the *Management in Action* insert. The network group is composed of employees throughout the company who affiliate on the basis of group characteristics such as race, ethnicity, gender, sexual orientation, or physical ability status. Group members typically have similar interests and look to groups as a way of sharing information about succeeding in the organization. Although some human resource specialists are concerned that network groups can lead to divisiveness, others believe they play a positive role. They often increase morale and retention, and can also provide ideas for products and services based on their demographic or cultural background. Visualize an affinity group of Vietnamese women in the corporate headquarters of a retailer. The employee network group members group might make suggestions to the design group about effective styles for petite women.

Employee network groups, as with any other diversity initiative, are likely to be more successful with top-level management support. Interviews were conducted

employee network group
A group composed of employees throughout the company who affiliate on the basis of group characteristics such as race, ethnicity, gender, sexual orientation, or physical ability status.

with 24 CEOs in companies known for their success with cultural diversity, such as MasterCard, Merck, and Nissan. Managers supported diversity initiatives by meeting regularly with employee network groups and diversity councils.[35]

Diversity Training

Cultural training, as described in the section about international business, aims to help workers understand people from another culture. **Diversity training** has a slightly different purpose. It attempts to bring about workplace harmony by teaching people how to get along better with diverse work associates. Quite often the program is aimed at minimizing open expressions of racism and sexism. A more strategic goal of diversity training is to gain acceptance on all types of diversity with the belief that enhanced business performance will result.[36] All forms of diversity training center on increasing people's awareness of and empathy for people who are different from themselves.

Diversity training sessions focus on ways that men and women, or people of different races, reflect different values, attitudes, and cultural backgrounds. These sessions can vary from several hours to several days. Sometimes the program is confrontational, sometimes not.

An essential part of relating more effectively to diverse groups is to empathize with their point of view. To help training participants develop empathy, representatives of various groups explain their feelings related to workplace issues. During one of these training sessions, a Chinese woman said she wished people would not act so shocked when she is assertive about her demands. She claimed that many people she meets at work expect her to fit the stereotype of the polite, compliant Chinese woman.

A related approach to diversity training is to emphasize tolerance of the values and viewpoints of other people. Participants are encouraged to understand different values even if they are not incomplete accord with the values.[37] For example, a Native American might express the view that white people have stolen their land, and that business firms and the government should pay reparations to Native Americans. Another participant listening to this point of view may not agree but should try to understand the values built into the opinion.

Many other exercises are used in diversity training. In one exercise, a nationality is mentioned, such as Italian. All group members then describe what comes to mind when the nationality "Italian" is mentioned. Later, the group discusses how their stereotypes help and hinder diversity. Another type of diversity training focuses on cross-generational diversity, or relating effectively to workers much older or younger than you.

A study found that diversity training is likely to have a strong impact on retaining people of color when the program is tied to business strategy and the CEO is committed to the program.[38] Nevertheless, diversity training can still make a contribution in terms of better understanding among diverse workers.

Anti-Bias Training

Closely related to diversity training are programs to help employees discover their unconscious biases that may adversely affect certain demographic and cultural groups. Examples include being more likely to call back a white applicant than a black applicant for a second interview, and automatically not inviting a worker in his or her sixties to join a team on a high-tech venture. An unconscious bias is a hidden, reflex-like preference that can shape a person's view of the world. Such biases also can shape diversity by rejecting people for certain assignments and not valuing their ideas. For example, a project manager at a mine in northern Alaska might not give a key assignment to an Inuit because the manager has an unconscious bias suggesting that an Inuit has a weak work ethic. Facebook and Google make extensive use of unconscious bias training.

Unconscious bias training usually includes administration of the Implicit Association Test that follows the logic of the example about "Italian" presented above. Research conducted at Google indicates almost everyone is a little bit sexist or racist. Training can help us become aware of our unconscious biases and make appropriate adjustments.[39] For example, a manager might have the bias that Chinese workers want to occupy strictly technical roles, and are therefore not well suited for supervisory roles. After training, the manager would recognize that many Chinese American workers are interested in and skilled at supervisory positions. (The CEO of BlackBerry, turnaround specialist John Chen, is Chinese in origin.)

Anti-bias training received extensive publicity in 2018 when it was administered at 8,000 Starbucks stores (cafés) during one afternoon. The trigger event for the anti–racial bias training was the arrest of two African American men at a Starbucks in Philadelphia. The two men were asked to leave after one was denied access to the restroom. Neither had yet ordered a beverage or food, but they were waiting for a business meeting. A Starbucks employee called the police, who arrested the men but released them almost immediately with no charges. The anti-bias training was combined with diversity training in such forms as presenting a video about the civil rights movement.[40]

A major concern about anti-bias training is that just because a person has an unconscious or hidden bias, it does not always follow that the bias will lead to discrimination. Take Jason, for example, a construction site manager whose family has been in the construction business for generations. Jason's hidden bias is that he believes that only Native Americans are highly skilled steeplejacks (good at dangerous climbing). Yet this bias does not stop Jason from hiring other ethnic group members for these high-paying construction jobs.

The English Language as a Force for Unity

Although differences among people are important to business firms around the world, international workers have to communicate effectively with each other. To compete globally, more and more European businesses are making English their official language. In this way, workers of different European nationalities can communicate with each other. In many Asian countries also, English is widely used in business. The majority of managerial, professional, technical and support positions in Europe require a good command of English.

One reason English maintains the edge as the official language of business in so many countries is that English grammar is less complex than that of many other languages. The Internet, and information technology in general, with its heavy emphasis on English, is another force for making English the language of business.

An effective approach to the complexities of language in a multicultural world is for leaders to develop a language strategy that fits the needs of the organization. The idea is to build language skills and cultural awareness throughout the organization to acquire and develop the kind of talent needed to compete globally and locally. The language strategy should fit the company's goals.[41] A company might use English throughout a world-wide organization to facilitate communication across geographically dispersed units. Yet part of the language strategy would be for workers throughout the world to still communicate with customers and the majority of workers in the local language. (The goal here would be to simultaneously have a smooth-functioning global organization as well as one that worked smoothly with local personnel.)

Although English may have emerged as the official language of business, the successful international manager needs to be multicultural. Furthermore, if business associates throughout the world are fluent in their native tongue as well as English, command of a second language remains an asset for North Americans. Also, for certain purposes it can be helpful for American companies to communicate with workers in their native language. One such situation is advising workers of dangerous situations on construction sites and on oil rigs. Also, some employers are providing banking, healthcare, and retirement information in Spanish to help Latino workers become more knowledgeable about money matters.[42] The perceptive manager knows when being bicultural and bilingual is helpful.

Explain the extent of involvement in international trade.

Firms involve themselves in international trade in several different ways that also reflect a method of entry into international markets. The extent of involvement includes trading companies, contract manufacturing, strategic alliances and joint ventures, direct foreign investment, the multinational corporation and the global startup.

 Identify and summarize several trade agreements among countries.

Trade agreements are an important part of international management because they facilitate trade. Key trade agreements include the Unites States, Mexico, and Canada Agreement (formerly NAFTA), the European Union, and the World Trade Organization. Concern has been expressed that free trade agreements have shrunk the number of middle-class jobs in the United States, and leads to downward pressures on wages in industrialized nations. Sending work offshore, or global outsourcing has become a key part of international trade. However, global outsourcing has both advantages and disadvantages.

 Recognize the importance of sensitivity to cultural differences in international enterprise.

The guiding principle for people involved in international enterprise is sensitivity to cultural differences. Cultural sensitivity can take the form of adapting your behavior (such as speaking more slowly) to meet the requirements of people from another culture. Candidates for foreign assignments generally receive training in the language and customs of the country in which they will work. Another approach to developing cross-cultural sensitivity is to learn cultural mistakes to avoid in the region in which you will be working.

 Identify major challenges facing the global managerial worker.

Challenges facing global managerial workers include the following: developing global leadership skills, currency fluctuations, human rights violations corruption and violence, culture shock, differences in negotiating style, and recognizing that national culture may or may not influence the effectiveness of a management technique.

 Pinpoint success factors in the global marketplace, and several positive and negative aspects of globalization.

Success factors for the global marketplace include (a) think globally, act locally, (b) recruit and select talented nationals, (c) hire or develop multicultural workers, and (d) research and assess local markets. Many of the advantages and disadvantages of globalization depend upon an individual's point of view. For example, profits may increase at the cost of many workers' jobs.

6 Describe the scope of diversity and the competitive advantage and potential problems of a culturally diverse workforce.

To be diverse is to be different in some measurable way, but not necessarily in a visible way. Valuing diversity means to respect and enjoy a wide range of cultural, demographic, and individual differences. A diverse organization is thought to be inclusive in which the contribution of every employee is valued, appreciated, and leveraged in the sense of being capitalized upon. Diversity often brings a competitive advantage to a firm, including the following: marketing advantage, lowered costs due to turnover and absenteeism, improved recruitment and a creativity advantage. A potential problem is that diverse group members may not get along well with each other, and sometimes diversity does not translate into profits.

7 Summarize organizational practices to encourage diversity.

Four representative practices that enhance diversity management are corporate policies about diversity, employee network groups, diversity training, and anti-bias training. Although cultural diversity is welcomed, the English language has become a force for unity throughout the world of business. To deal with the complexities of a multicultural world, it is helpful for a company to develop a language strategy.

Key Terms and Phrases

multinational corporation (MNC) 69

global startup 70

outsourcing 72

offshoring 72

cultural sensitivity 74

multicultural worker 75

global leadership skills 75

culture shock 79

diversity 83

employee network group 88

diversity training 89

Questions

1. Assume a person living in the United States thinks international trade is important for the economy, yet still believes that U.S. manufacturers of consumer goods must survive. What percent of that person's purchases should therefore be of goods made in the U.S.?

2. Identify a profit-making enterprise that does not have to be bothered with international trade, and for whom international competition is not a threat.

3. What can you do in your career to help reduce the threat that your job will be outsourced to another country?

4. Due to a law on the books for over 50 years, the United States imposes a tariff of 25 percent on pickup trucks manufactured in other countries. How justified is this practice?

5. What steps can you take, starting this week, to ready yourself to become a multicultural worker?

6. Suppose an African American couple opens a restaurant that serves African cuisine, hoping to appeal mostly to people of African descent. The restaurant is a big success, yet the couple finds that about 50 percent of its clientele is Caucasian or Asian. Should the restaurant owners then hire several Caucasians and Asians so the employee mix will match the customer mix? (The wait staff dresses in African attire.)

7. If English has become the universal language of business and science, why should an American international business specialist bother learning another language?

Skill-Building Exercise 3-A: Coping with Cultural Values and Traditions

The purpose of this exercise is to develop sensitivity to how cultural values and traditions create problems for people from other countries. Find three fellow students, co-workers, friends, or acquaintances from another country who are willing to be interviewed digitally or in-person for about ten minutes on the subject of adapting to a new culture. An alternative is to interview people from a far-away region in the same country, such as interviewing somebody from New York City if you are taking this course in Salt Lake City. Dig for answers to the following questions:

1. Which cultural values and traditions in this (the country or region in which you are taking this course) country (or regions) do you find the most unusual?

2. In what way are these values unusual?

3. What adaptations have you had to make to cope with these values?

4. In what ways are these values unusual?

5. What adaptations have you had to cope with these traditions?

Be prepared to have a class discussion of your findings and conclusions. Identify any lessons you have learned that will help you be more effective as a multicultural worker.

Skill-Building Exercise 3-B: How Pervasive is Global Outsourcing?

Although reading about the extent of global outsourcing is authoritative and convincing, collecting some data on your own is a good supplement to such information. Look at the label or identifying information on the next ten products you see and count how many are manufactured outside the country in which you are now living. You might collect the data by examining products, such as clothing or electronic devices in your own home or while visiting a store. Or take a stroll through a vehicle parking lot. To enlarge your sample, you might share results with several classmates. Based on your micro-study, what conclusion do you reach about the extent of global outsourcing in the country in which you are living now?

Management Now—Online Skill-Building Exercise: Becoming Multicultural

A useful way of developing skills in a second language and learning more about another culture is to use a foreign language website as your homepage. In this way, each time you go the Internet on your own computer, your homepage will contain fresh information in the language you want to develop. Or, simply make the foreign language site a favorite or bookmark so you can easily and routinely access the site.

Enter a key word like, "Mandarin newspaper" or "Mexican current events" in your search engine. Once you find a suitable choice, enter the edit function for, "Favorites" or "Bookmarks" and insert that newspaper as your home page or cover page. For example, imagine that French were your choice; your search might have brought you to *http://www.france2.fr*, or *http://www.lapresse.ca*. These websites keep you abreast of French (or Canadian) international news, sports and cultural events—written in French. Another example is to find a Spanish language version of a U.S. newspaper such as found on *http://www.elpasotimes.com*.

Typically, these foreign language websites have accompanying videos in your target language. Now every time you access the Internet, you can spend five minutes becoming multicultural. You can save a lot of travel costs and time using the Internet to help you become multicultural. Also, you will have a daily, up-to-date source of information about your target language and culture.

Triumph Services Wants to Go Global

Triumph Services Inc. is a company based in the United States that helps other companies with their sales and marketing, sometimes taking almost full responsibility for both functions. Clients usually approach Triumph with the hope of growing their businesses, perhaps 10 percent in one year. Triumph will provide the client, usually a small firm, with the sales and marketing personnel, along with a marketing and execution plan to accomplish the goal. Triumph relies heavily on information technology, including analytics and a telepresence system to help attain the growth goal of the client.

CEO Jason has been satisfied with Triumph's growth since he founded the firm six years ago. During the 10 years, Jason has grown from two employees, including Jason, to 75 employees today. During a recent Saturday morning meeting, Jason said to his management team, "Triumph is a great company in helping other companies with their growth. We can be proud of our outstanding reputation. But we lack a global presence. We have clients in 15 states but none in Canada, Mexico, or overseas.

"What I want us to get started doing this morning, is coming up with a plan for international expansion. Just placing ads on social media and search-engine websites is not good enough. Let's develop a plan for becoming an international marketing and sales solutions firm."

Case Questions

1 Why should Jason be concerned about international expansion when Triumph Services is already a prosperous firm?

2 Explain which method of entry you would recommend for Triumph.

3 Identify a couple of major challenges Triumph would face in attempting to assist clients in other countries.

Candor at Anti-Bias Training

Niki, an HR consultant, is conducting an onsite workshop in anti-bias training for Ventura Inc., a telecommunications equipment manufacturer. Although Ventura was not deluged with complaints about discrimination against or limited growth opportunities for any particular group, company management wanted to foster a climate of cultural diversity and inclusion. The CEO commented, "We are hiring Niki as much for prevention of problems as for resolving problems that have taken place."

After delivering a 20-minute PowerPoint presentation on the meaning of implicit bias and how it might impact workplace relationships, Niki gives the ten workshop participants this assignment: "I want each of you, one by one to tell the group any bias you might possibly have. Nothing you say will be recorded on a hidden video and reported to management. You can therefore be as candid as you want. I want us to all learn what biases might exist at Ventura." Although they showed visible signs of being nervous, the workshop participants complied with Niki's request.

Calvin: I'll go first at the risk of being hated by the other people at this training session. As a sales manager, when I am interviewing a candidate for a sales position and she is a total beauty, I think she might not be so sharp intellectually. I apologize folks, but that's my bias.

Tamara: When I'm at a physical retail store purchasing something complicated like a smart refrigerator or smart TV receiver, I'll approach an Asian sales associate first if possible, especially an Indian American or a Chinese American—because my bias is that they are smart and efficient.

Clayton: If I see a young African American in our company wearing a lot of expensive "bling," my hunch is that he or she might be involved in crime on the outside. I know that's a horrible insult, but Niki asked us to be totally honest.

Marvin: A few months ago, I was given the assignment of putting together a men's basketball team to play in an industrial league. My first initiative was to talk to or send texts to African American or African guys in the company. I figure they have more interest and ability in basketball. I hope that I didn't upset anybody with my comments.

Lindsay: When I needed technical advice, I never ask anybody in the company over age 50. I assume that if you are not a digital native, you won't be helpful with a difficult technology problem.

Bianca: I never thought of myself as biased, bit I do have one bias. If I need something done in a hurry, I don't ask an obese person. I think that obese people are lazy.

Fred: When Venture recently announced that the new CEO had an MBA from Harvard, I was delighted. I figure that the best financial minds have attended elite schools.

Vanessa: Six months I had an opportunity to transfer to one of two departments. I avoided the department headed by a recently-divorced middle-aged male because I thought there was a possibility he would sexually harass me.

Omar: Three weeks ago, I had to visit our affiliated urgent-care clinic because I had cut a capillary in my thumb. I asked to be treated by a female nurse because I believe that nursing is a job for a woman.

Georgia: I needed to add another member to my project. I purposely avoided inviting a millennial to join because I think they have poor attendance records or are too self-centered.

Lance: We had to order some new, complex AI equipment. I suggest that we order then equipment from a German firm because I believe that Germans are the best manufacturing engineers.

Nicki said, "Thanks for being so open and honest. Let's reflect together on what we have just learned about bias at Ventura."

Case Questions

1 To what extent do you think that the staff members' expression of their conscious biases in a workshop accomplishes anything worthwhile?

2 Which one or two of biases revealed do you think might be harmful to a culture of diversity at Ventura?

3 If you were at this workshop, explain whether or not you would express any conscious bias you might have.

0

ENDNOTES

1. Original story based on facts and observations in the following sources: Patrick Thomas, "Dollar Tree Feels Sting From Tariffs," *The Wall Street Journal*, November 27, 2019, p. B2; Natasha Frost, "Trump's Tariffs are Hurting the Stores Where the Poorest Americans Shop," *Quartz* (www.qz.com), March 6, 2019, p. 1–2; "Dollar Store Customers to Feel the Impact of Trump's Tariffs," *USA Today*, October 8, 2018; Abha Bhattarai, "Trump's Tariffs are Hitting the Country's Most Vulnerable Shoppers," *Washington Post* (www.washingtonpost.com), May 31, 2019, pp. 1–2; Sarah Min, "Dollar Tree CEO Warns that More China Tariffs Will Hurt Shoppers," *cbsnewsw.com*, May 30, 2019, pp. 1–3.

2. "Jeep Wrangler is 'Most American-Made' Vehicle," *Body-Shop Business* (www.bodyshopbusiness.com), June 26, 2017, p. 1.

3. Ted Budd, "Got Trade? Dairy Farmers Stand to Gain From the USMCA," *The Wall Street Journal*, December 14-15, 2019, p. A15; Timothy Puko, "Businesses Prepare to Reap Trade Gains," *The Wall Street Journal*, December 11, 2019, p. A6; Michelle Collins and David Jackson, "Both Sides Hail Deal to Replace NAFTA," *USA Today*, December 11, 2019, p. 8A.

4. "Obama Continues NAFTA Criticism," *MSNBC* (http://firstread.msnbc.com), February 23, 2015.

5. Roger Yu, "NAFTA Scorecard: Who Gained, who was Pained," *USA Today*, May 4, 2017, p. 4B.

6. Joe Mayes, "A Costly Farewell," *Bloomberg Businessweek*, May 20, 2019, pp. 34–36.

7. Thomas J. Duesterberg, "Now Is a Good Time to Modernize the WTO," *The Wall Street Journal*, December 2, 2019, p. A12.

8. Heather Timmons, "Cost-Cutting in New York, but a Boom in India," *The New York Times* (nytimes.com), August 12, 2008, p. 1.

9. Legal Skills Prof, "Small Firms and Private Individuals are Now Outsourcing Legal Work to India," *lawprofessors.typepad.com*, October 5, 2013, p. 1.

10. Mehul Srivastava and Moira Herbst, "The Return of the Outsourced Job," *Bloomberg Businessweek*, January 11, 2010, p. 16; Patrick Thibodeau, "IT Worker's Lawsuit Accuses Tata of Discrimination," *Computerworld* (www.computerworld.com). April 15, 2015, p. 1.

11. Jeremy Smerd, "India on the Outs?" *Workforce Management*, May 18, 2009, p. 32.

12. Peter Coy, "Who Really Pays for Tariffs," *Bloomberg Businessweek*, pp. 32–34.

13. "China Delays Tariffs After Trade Accord," *Associated Press*, December 16, 2019.

14. Stacey R. Fitzsimmons, "Multicultural Employees: A Framework for Understanding How They Contribute to Organizations," *Academy of Management Review*, October 2013, p. 545.

15. Blaine J. Fowers and Barbara J. Davidov, "The Virtue of Multiculturalism," *American Psychologist*, September 2006, pp. 581–594.

16. Dianne Nilsen, Brenda Kowske, and Kshanika Anthony, "Managing Globally," *HR Magazine*, August 2005, pp. 111–115.

17. Phred Dvorak, "Making U.S. Management Ideas Work Elsewhere," *The Wall Street Journal*, May 22, 2006, p. B3.

18. "Rights Trampled for Indigenous Peoples Across the Americas," *http://www.amnesty.org*, August 8, 2014.

19. "Business Corruption in Mexico," *Business Anti-Corruption Portal* (www.business-anti-corruption.com), May 2015, p. 1.

20. Eli Meixler, "Cartel-Ravaged Mexico Sets a New Records for Murders," *Time* (www.timje.com), January 22, 2019, p. 1.

21. Harry C. Triandis, *Culture Shock and Social Behavior* (New York: McGraw-Hill, 1994), p. 263.

22. Erin Meyer, "Getting to Si, Ja, Oui, Hai, and Da," *Harvard Business Review*, December 2015, p. 79.

23. Tanja Rabl, Mevan Jayasinghe, Barry Gerhart, and Torsten M. Kühlmann, "A Meta-Analysis of Country Differences in the High-Performance Work System-Business Performance Relationship: The Roles of National Culture and Managerial Discretion," *Journal of Applied Psychology*, November 2014, pp. 1011–1041.

24. Julia Glick, "China Market Helps Mary Kay Stay in the Pink," *Associated Press*, August 6, 2006; Daniel Gross, "How Do You Say 'Pink Cadillac' in Mandarin?" *www.slate.com*, November 17, 2009, pp. 1–5.

25. Arindam K. Bhattacharya and David C. Michael, "How Local Companies Keep Multinationals at Bay," *Harvard Business Review*, March 2008, p. 90.

26. Mary E. Medland, "Setting Up Overseas," *HR Magazine*, January 2004, p. 72.

27. Steven Norton, "Websites Lost in Translation: Machines Can Translate—but Only Up to a Point," *The Wall Street Journal*, October 14, 2015, p. R6.

28. Andrea C. Poe, "Selection Savvy," *HR Magazine*, April 2002, p. 78.

29. Susan G. Hauser, "The Clone Danger," *Workforce Management*, April 2013, p. 39.

30. Susan Meisinger, "Diversity: More Than Just Representation," *HR Magazine*, January 2008, p. 8.

31. Vivian Hunt, Larsina Yee, Sara Prince, and Sundiatu Dixon-File, "Delivering through Diversity," *McKinsey & Company* (www.mckinsey.com), January 2018, p. 8.

32. Quoted in Novid Parsi, "Diversity and Innovation," *HR Magazine*, February 2017, p. 45.

33. Rich Karlgaard, "Diversity's Central Paradox," *Forbes,* May 5, 2015, p. 34.

34. "MGM Resorts International Named Among Nation's 2018 Top Regional Companies for Diversity by DiversityInc." *http:newsroom.mgmresorts.com*, May 18, 2018, pp. 1–2; "MGM International Named a 'Best Company for Diversity' by Leading Hispanic Business Publication," *MGM Resorts International Investor Room* (http://mgmresorts.investorroom.com), October 24, 2014, pp. 1–2.

35. Boris Groysberg and Katherine Connolly, "Great Leaders Who Make the Mix Work," *Harvard Business Review*, September 2013, p. 76.

36. Rohini Ahand and Mary-Frances Winters, "A Retrospective View of Corporate Diversity Training From 1964 to Present," *Academy of Management Learning & Education,* September 2008, p. 356.

37. Diether Gebert, Claudia Buengeler, and Kathrin Heinitz, "Tolerance: A Neglected Dimension in Diversity Training?" *Academy of Management Learning & Education*, Septermber 2017, pp. 415–438.

38. Research cited in Ahand and Winters, "A Retrospective View of Corporate Diversity," p. 367.

39. Farhad Manjoo, "Exposing Hidden Bias at Google," *New York Times* (www.nytimes.com), September 24, 2014, pp. 1–4; Jessica Guynn, "Facebook Develops Unconscious Bias Training," *USA Today*, July 30, 2015, p. 3B.

40. Terry Tang, "Starbucks Training a First Step, Experts Say," *Associated Press*, May 29, 2018.

41. Tsedal Neely and Robert Steven Kaplan, "What's Your Language Strategy?" *Harvard Business Review*, September 2014, pp. 70–76.

42. Kathryn Tyler, "Financial Fluency," *HR Magazine*, July 2006, pp. 76–81.

Part Two

Planning

CHAPTER 4

Essentials of Planning and Strategy

OBJECTIVES

After studying this chapter and doing the exercises, you should be able to:

1 Summarize a general framework for planning and apply it to enhance your planning skills.

2 Explain how business strategy is developed, including a SWOT analysis.

3 Identify levels of business strategy and types of business strategies.

4 Explain the strategy execution through the use of operating plans, policies, procedures, and rules.

5 Present an overview of management by objectives.

Elon Musk has been referred to as the modern-day Thomas Edison. Musk was one of the founders of PayPal, and then went on to become the founder and CEO of Tesla, and SpaceX, and the chairman of SolarCity. He has also been involved at an executive level with Neuralink and the Boring Company (for digging tunnels). Several years ago, at age 44, he held a public gathering at the Tesla design studio in Hawthorne, California. Musk walked onto the stage as hard rock music blared in the background. He began his presentation by showing an image of thick, yellowish smoke pouring out of a number of industrial chimneys. At the same time, Musk displayed a chart indicating how an accumulation of carbon dioxide in the air is moving the earth toward an almost inevitable calamity. He informed the crowd, "What I am going to talk about tonight is a fundamental transformation of how the world works."

The purpose of the meeting was to launch a new product line of large batteries that store energy in homes, plus even larger batteries that that store energy for utilities and businesses. For a medium-picture thinker, the meeting would have focused on this new line of batteries. Yet for the big-picture-thinking Elon Musk, the evening presentation was about changing the world. An additional grand purpose of the new line of batteries was to eliminate the world's dependence on power plants.

Musk is devoted to the preservation of both planet Earth and the human species, and has therefore been an inspiring figure for many people inside and outside the world of business and technology. Each one of Musk's endeavors is accompanied by a vision and mission more ambitions and far sighted than the previous one. For example, his Hyperloop vision imagines customers traveling around the world through high-speed tubes with speeds of up to 600 miles per hour.[1]

The story about the inventor and business executive Elon Musk illustrates one of the themes of this chapter. Thinking big and developing a vision and strategy contribute to organizational success. These three activities can be considered part of planning. The purpose of this chapter is to describe the planning function in such a way that you can use what you learn to plan more effectively as a manager or individual contributor. First the chapter looks at a framework for the application of planning. You will also learn about high-level, or strategic planning, including how strategy is developed and the types of strategy that result from strategic planning. We then describe operating plans, policies, procedures and rules, and a widely used method for getting large numbers of people involved in implementing plans: management by objectives.

A GENERAL FRAMEWORK FOR PLANNING

LEARNING OBJECTIVE 1

Summarize a general framework for planning and apply it to enhance your planning skills.

strategic planning
A firm's overall master plan that shapes its destiny.

tactical planning
Planning that translates a firm's strategic plans into specific goals by organizational unit.

operational planning
Planning that requires specific procedures and actions at lower levels in an organization.

Planning is a complex and comprehensive process involving a series of overlapping and interrelated elements or stages, including strategic, tactical and operational planning. **Strategic planning** establishes master plans that shape the destiny of the firm. An example of strategic planning is when the executive team at Harley-Davidson Inc. planned how to deal with the demographic shift of their customer base becoming much older. The strategic issue it faced was whether to change its iconic product line to win over young buyers.

A second type of planning is needed to support strategic planning, such as how to build motorcycles that fit the preferences of younger motorcyclists. **Tactical planning** translates strategic plans into specific goals and plans that are most relevant to a particular organizational unit. Tactical plans also provide details on how the company or business unit will compete within its chosen business area. Middle managers have the primary responsibility for formulating and executing tactical plans. These plans are based on marketplace realities when developed for a business. Conditions can change rapidly in competitive fields, such as a South Korean company suddenly developing a substantially lower-priced sports bike. The scope of tactical plans is broader than operational plans (described next), but not as broad as that of strategic plans.

A third type of planning is aimed more at day-to-day operations or the nuts and bolts of doing business. **Operational planning** identifies the specific procedures and actions required at lower levels in the organization. If Harley-Davidson wants to revamp an assembly line to produce more sports bikes, operational plans would have to be drawn. In practice, the distinction between tactical planning and operational planning is not clear-cut. However, both tactical plans and operational plans must support the strategic plan, such as revamping manufacturing and marketing to capture a larger group of young cyclists.

The framework presented in Figure 4-1 summarizes the elements of planning. With slight modification the model could be applied to strategic, tactical and operational planning. A planner must define the present situation, establish goals and objectives and analyze the environment in terms of aids and barriers to goals and objectives. The planner must also develop action plans to reach goals and objectives, develop budgets, implement the plans and control the plans.

This chapter examines each element separately. In practice, however, several of these stages often overlap. For example, a manager might be implementing and controlling the same plan simultaneously. Also, the planning steps are not always followed in the order presented in Figure 4-1. Planners frequently start in the middle of the process, proceed forward, and then return to an earlier step. This change of sequence frequently

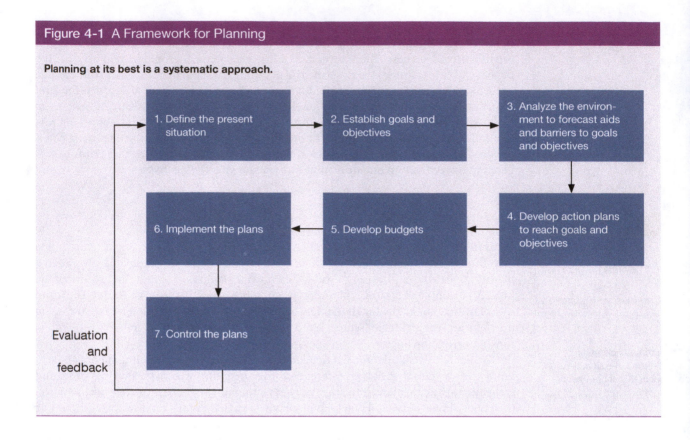

Figure 4-1 A Framework for Planning

Planning at its best is a systematic approach.

1. Define the present situation

2. Establish goals and objectives

3. Analyze the environment to forecast aids and barriers to goals and objectives

4. Develop action plans to reach goals and objectives

5. Develop budgets

6. Implement the plans

7. Control the plans

Evaluation and feedback

happens because the planner discovers new information or because objectives change. Also, many managers set goals before first examining their current position.

To illustrate the general framework for planning we turn again to Harley-Davidson, that is dealing with the planning challenge presented by its aging customer base, and an effort to attract a greater number of younger buyers. The challenge was expressed about a decade ago by Joe Mammolito, a tow truck company owner from Dix Hills, N.Y., and a Harley devotee for 30 years: "I have about 14 guys driving trucks for me. The younger guys ride sports bikes, the older fellows like a big bike. I think they should get guys in their 20s and 30s accustomed to riding Harleys. They need to get the younger guys accustomed to the name, the products, and the dealership network."[2]

In 2015, Harley CEO Matt Levatich framed the challenge a little differently. He said that electronic devices, such as smartphones and video games were distracting potential young bikers from the call of the open road, and using lower-cost bikes now, and electric bikes in the future. Four years later the American icon was still struggling to reach a young audience with its heavy motorcycles, so a shift was made to offer a line of smaller, lighter motorcycles.[3]

Define the Present Situation

Knowing where you are is critical to establishing goals for change. Defining the present situation includes measuring success and examining internal capabilities and external threats. Harley-Davidson has had a long tradition of success. At one time the motorcycle had a youth-oriented counterculture mystique. By the mid-2000s, Harley had become a middle-aged nostalgia brand. Because of so many loyal customers, Harley had been able to turn small product improvements into sustained growth. Many Harley-Davidson customers own multiple—sometimes even 12—Harley motorcycles. The moment the new, bigger Twin Cam engine and six-speed transmission was announced in July 2006, orders began pouring into dealers. Another capability of Harley is a fast-growing overseas fan base that perceives the Harley-Davidson brand in the best possible sense, associating it with being powerful and free. Today, over one-fifth of Harleys are sold outside the United States.

A major external threat facing Harley-Davidson was the long-time prediction that a demographic time bomb would blow up the company. In the U.S., Harley as well as other manufacturers were balancing two customer demographic trends: Millennials who had a limited interest in being part of the motorcycle lifestyle and Boomers who are concerned that they are too old to keep motorcycling. As a result, sales were declining for about six years with weak sales still being a problem in 2019 when about 220,000 motorcycles were sold.

Establish Goals and Objectives

The second step in planning is to establish goals and identify objectives that contribute to the attainment of goals. (Goals are broader than objectives, whereas objectives function as smaller goals that support the bigger goals.) A major goal Harley management might establish is to continue to cultivate people over 30 who prefer the big loud bikes that allow for smooth rides on long trips. Another goal would be to promote the Harley as a retirement treat, especially for young Baby Boomer retirees. An additional goal would be to promote its all-electric LiveWire cycle introduced in 2019 that eliminates the familiar engine roar without sacrificing power or speed. The LiveWire weighs only 549 pounds and should appeal to riders who are concerned about motorcycle emissions polluting the air.

A Harley 10-year goal is to train two million new U.S. riders. The company was also planning five additional electric motorcycles, all to be introduced by 2022. More broadly, the company plans to introduce 100 new models through 2027, and to grow international business to 50 percent of its sales. Harley also began manufacturing some motorcycles overseas for sales in the international market. One example was a small bike built in China.

Genevieve Schmitt, founding editor of *WomenRidersNow.com*, believes Harley should establish the goal of continuing to focus on what they do best. She says, "They've responded to the needs of smaller, less muscular riders by offering motorcycles with lower motors. They realize women are an up-and-coming segment and that they need to accommodate them. They don't market to a specific gender, but are gender-neutral. They market a lifestyle, with daughters and moms, dads and sons." Following this thought, Harley might establish the goal of making their marketing more gender-neutral.

Analyze the Environment to Forecast Aids and Barriers to Goals and Objectives

As an extension of defining the present situation, the manager or other planner attempts to predict which internal and external factors will foster or hinder attainment of the desired ends. A key strength of Harley being able to retain its prominence in the motorcycle business is that its brand is so well established. The loyal and talented Harley-Davidson workforce will be able to adapt to any shift toward smaller, sportier bikes, including the LiveWire.

A barrier to Harley-Davidson's prosperity became evident around 2018. Too many used Harleys were on the market, with three used motorcycles being sold for every new one.[4] Another external threat is that many individuals are concerned about motorcycle safety and the disturbance to the environment from the loud exhaust blast. The Hell's Angels image of motorcyclists is a potential barrier. Yet the barrier is offset somewhat by the fact that many would-be drivers are attracted to the rebellious image.

Develop Action Plans to Reach Goals and Objectives

Goals and objectives are only wishful thinking until action plans are drawn. An **action plan** consists of the specific steps necessary to achieve a goal or objective. The planners must figure out specifically how they will accomplish such ends as encouraging Harley users to keep motorcycling until later in life. The major action plan was mentioned above, in the form of the company releasing almost a dozen small, lightweight bikes including the electric vehicles. The intent of his action plan was to appeal to young, urban, and not necessarily American-born riders. Harley wants international riders to constitute one-half its customer in the next ten years.

action plan
The specific steps necessary to achieve a goal or an objective.

Other action plans might include more advertising aimed at women, including the objective of featuring women celebrities in advertisements for Harley-Davidson. Additional action plans could offer free seminars for seniors about the joy of motorcycle driving and more extensive promotion of the new, smaller motorcycle. By 2008, Harley-Davidson began purposely reaching out to younger drivers in its marketing campaigns.

Develop Budgets

Planning usually results in action plans that require money to implement. Among the expenses would be larger advertising and promotion budgets geared to younger people and women. Another budget item would include safe driving campaigns to help soften the image of motorcycling being so dangerous. Development of all the new motorcycle represented a major capital expenditure for Harley-Davidson.

Implement the Plans

If the plans developed in the previous five steps are to benefit the firm, they must be put to use. A frequent criticism of planners is they develop elaborate plans and then abandon them in favor of conducting business as usual. Furthermore, execution is considered to be a specific set of behaviors and techniques that companies need to master in order to maintain a competitive advantage.[5] Research with over 12,000 firms in 24 countries has shown that there are vast differences in how well companies execute basic tasks like setting targets that stem from planning. Firms that follow through with their plans perform significantly better on high-level metrics such as productivity, profitability, growth, and longevity.[6]

Harley managers and specialists seem poised to execute because their planning sessions heavily emphasize turning plans into action. Harley-Davidson management desperately wants the success of the Harley line of motorcycles to continue.

Control the Plans

Planning does not end with implementation because plans may not always proceed as conceived. The control process measures progress toward goal attainment and indicates corrective action if too much deviation is detected. The deviation from expected performance can be negative or positive. Progress against all of the goals and objectives mentioned above must be measured. One goal was to hold on to much of the existing customer base. Mark Barnett, an El Paso, Texas, Harley dealer believes Harley is attaining this goal. He observes: "When they get into their 30s and 40s, people slow down and get tired of sports bikes. If you look at the sport bike demographics, the number of them over 40 is pretty low. As long as people don't quit riding motorcycles altogether, they're going to be our customer when they turn 40." Company management needs more time to know if the goal for getting more young riders to purchase sports cycles in the Buell line has been attained.

In Figure 4-1, note the phrase, "Evaluation and Feedback" on the left. The phrase indicates that the control process allows for the fine-tuning of plans after their implementation. One common example of the need for fine-tuning is a budget that has been set too high or too low in the first attempt at implementing a plan. A manager controls by making the right adjustment.

Make Contingency Plans

contingency plan
An alternative plan to be used if the original plan cannot be implemented or a crisis develops.

Many planners develop a set of backup plans to be used in case things do not proceed as hoped. A **contingency plan** is an alternative plan to be used if the original plan cannot be implemented or a crisis develops. (The familiar expression "Let's try plan B" gets at the essence of contingency planning.) One potential crisis for Harley management would be substantial climate changes in the form of much more rain, snow and ice that would make motorcycle riding less feasible in many parts of the world. Another crisis would be the escalation of motorcycle insurance premiums to the point that the demand for on-the-road motorcycles would decline sharply. Heavy tariffs imposed on American motorcycles would force Harley to manufacture more motorcycles overseas to sell in those markets.

Contingency plans are often developed from objectives in earlier steps in the planning process. The plans are triggered into action when the planner detects, however early in the planning process, deviations from objectives. Construction projects, such as building an airport hangar, are particularly prone to deviations from completion dates because so many different contractors and subcontractors are involved. In practice, planning also involves spotting problems that need to be fixed, and then taking appropriate action.

An *exit strategy* might be part of the contingency plan. If the demand for both the Harley big bikes and sports bikes declined to the point of major losses, the Harley facilities and dealerships might be sold to Suzuki. Harley management, of course, does not envision this crisis.

LEARNING OBJECTIVE 2

Explain how business strategy is developed, including a SWOT analysis.

strategy
The organization's plan for achieving its vision, mission, and goals.

THE DEVELOPMENT OF BUSINESS STRATEGY

Elaborate methods of planning are often used to help develop business strategy. (**Strategy** is the organization's plan for achieving its vision, mission, and goals.) The planning model presented earlier in the chapter contains the foundation of these tools, and SWOT analysis presented later is another planning tool. In the opinion of some management specialists, the best strategy emerges from an organization having a grand purpose.[7] A company's purpose can be interpreted as a bold affirmation of its reason for existing. The effective leader, and often the founder, sets the purpose of the firm. Coca-Cola began this way, as did Apple Inc., and the Sloan Kettering Cancer

Institute. After the firm's purpose is established, the leader also becomes the steward of the strategy. Mintzberg argues that if you want good strategy, skip all the elaborate planning and just focus on having a great vision.[8]

According to researchers at the Gallup Organization, managers and leaders face the ongoing challenge of making that purpose real. Southwest Airlines provides a relevant example. The airline's stated purpose is "to connect people to what's important in their lives through friendly, reliable and low-cost air travel." In the spirit of carrying out that purpose, Southwest does not charge people for their first two pieces of luggage.[9]

The accompanying *Management in Action* insert illustrates how purpose can facilitate the success of a major business enterprise.

Strategic planning encompasses those activities that lead to the statement of goals and objectives and the choice of strategies to achieve them. The final outcomes of strategic planning are statements of vision, mission, strategy, and policy. A **vision** is an idealized picture of the future of the organization. The more concrete the vision, the more it is likely to inspire employees. In contrast, vision statements laden with abstract terms are frequently ignored. A concrete vision might be, "We aim to bring smiles to customers." A blurry vision might be, "We aim to impact the world."[10] The visions shown in Figure 4-2 would be perceived as concrete by most employees.

vision
An idealized picture of the future of an organization.

MANAGEMENT IN ACTION

Mars Petcare is a Purpose-Driven Organization

Mars Inc. is one of the world's largest family owned business enterprises with more annual sales exceeding $34 billion. The 109-year-old company is best known for its iconic candy brands including Milky Way, Snickers, and M&Ms and Twix, Mars also makes common household brands such as Uncle Ben's Rice. In recent years, however, the company's biggest business has been pet care. Mars bought Veterinary Care of America (VCA), which manages 800 veterinary hospitals, for $9 billion in 2017. Other pet care acquisitions include Blue Pearl Veterinary Partners and Pet Partners. Pet foods made by Mars include Iams, Nutro, Pedigree, and Whiskas.

Mars chairman Stephen Badger, the great-grandson of founder Franklin Mars, said: "We used to be very much a pet food company. Now we're a pet care company with businesses like VCA and Banfield, where we are actually doing day-to-day treatment of animals all the way through to quite serious diagnostics and treatment of animals." Managing the portfolio of brands has become a key part of operating Mars.

The growth of Mars Petcare has been driven in part by the growing concern among pet owners regarding their pet's health, resulting in more money being spent on nutritious pet food. Millennials are another driving force for the business. As a demographic group, they are more focused on pets than previously, and therefore demand nutritious pet food, as well as accurate information about the food. Humanization of animal care is another trend driving Mars' strategy. Food trends for humans, such as organic food and fewer chemical additives, have drifted over into preference for pet food.

A group of researchers concluded that Mars Petcare succeeded where other companies have failed because every move it has made has been aligned with the same core purpose: "A better world for pets." The same purpose is expanding into pet activity monitoring with "smart" collars.

Questions

1 **Mars was one of the oldest companies in the world, had enormous brand recognition, and was also highly successful. So why the need for diversifying into pet care?**

2 **In terms of brand strategy, what do you think of the idea of Mars creating the products, "Milky Way for dogs," and "M&Ms" for cats?**

3 **Visualize a dog and cat nail-clipping technician working in a VCA clinic. How easy would it be for the technician to identify with the purpose of Mars PetCare?**

Source: Original story created from facts and observations in the following sources: Thomas W. Malnight, Ivy Buche, and Charles Dhanaraj, "Put Purpose at the Core of Your Strategy," *Harvard Business Review*, September–October 2019, pp. 70–79; Ger Hofstee, "Mars' Forward Vertical Integration Strategy!" *Business Matters* (www.veterinarybusienssmztters.com), November 23, 2018, pp. 1–3; Cadie Thompson, "The Company Behind Some of the Most Popular Candies in the World is Quietly Taking Over the Pet-Care Industry," *Business Insider* (www.businessinsider.com), June 13, 2018, pp. 1–3; Jennifer Semple, "Mars Petcare Shares Strategy to Keep Pace with Trends," *Food Business News* (www.foodbusinessnews.net), April 15, 2018, pp. 1–4.

mission

The firm's purpose and where it fits into the world.

The **mission** identifies the firm's purpose and where it fits into the world. Specifying a mission answers the question, "What business are we really in?" A mission is more grounded in present-day realities than a vision, but some companies use the terms interchangeably. One of the most practical aspects of a mission is that it provides direction, and sometimes inspiration to employees. For example, an inter-city bus company might have this mission: "To provide safe, reliable transportation to our passengers."

A firm's mission may not be apparent to the casual observer. For example, Godiva Chocolates (the company that produces high-priced chocolate sold in separate displays in retail outlets) would appear to be in the candy business. In reality, their real mission places them in the luxury and pampering business. Figure 4-2 presents a few examples of company vision and mission statements. You will observe that companies vary considerably in what should be included in a mission or vision statement.

As mentioned above, planning alone does not create strategy because strategy can also stem from inspired thinking. Inspired thinking includes creativity. As explained by Adam Brandenburger, a professor at the NYU Stern School, the field of strategy over focuses on analytic rigor and places too little emphasis on creative thinking. Analytic tools help strategists develop business ideas that are close to implementation, but less effective at discovering strategies that transform an organization or industry. Elon Musk provides an example of how creativity is the basis for strategy: With SpaceX he has overthrown major assumptions about space travel: "That it must occur on a fixed schedule, be paid for by the public, and use onetime rockets."[11] Analytic tools play a major role in refining the creative idea behind the strategy, such as developing a marketing strategy for selling seats on a space rocket.

Corporate values also influence strategy because well-managed organizations tend to develop strategy to fit what the people in power think is important. If the company highly values innovation, it will not adopt a strategy of being successful by imitating other successful products. Piaget, for example, has remained successful for more than 200 years by staying with its own high-quality watches, and not imitating other trends in the watch industry.

While strategy often stems from planning, many firms choose a strategy prior to strategic planning. Once the firm has the strategy, a plan is developed to implement it. A chief executive might say, "Let's compete by becoming the most recognizable company in our field." The executive team would then develop specific plans to implement that strategy, rather than strategic planning leading to the conclusion that brand recognition would be an effective strategy. For many medium-sized and small organizations it is strategy first, followed by planning.

Figure 4-2 Sample Vision and Mission Statements

Google Inc. (a division of Alphabet)	*Mission:* "Organize the world's information and make it universally accessible and useful."
Warby Parker	*Mission:* "To offer designer eyewear at a revolutionary price, while leading the way for social conscious businesses."
Teach for America	*Vision:* "One day, all children in this nation will have the opportunity to attain an excellent education."
Starfire Systems	*Vision:* "Starfire Systems will pioneer the creation of new advanced materials through enabling technology based on a wide range of ceramic forming polymers that meet the needs of customers."

The Importance of Strategic Thinking

Strategic planning as well as setting the vision without the planning share an important purpose. It is to get managerial workers throughout the organization thinking strategically and wondering about how the firm adapts to its environment and how it will cope with its future. One of the central challenges of modern organizations is for leaders at all levels of the firm to think strategically—including seeing the overall picture as they go about their work.[12]

A strategically-minded worker at any level would think, "How does what I am doing right now support corporate strategy?" The customer-care-center worker at Hewlett-Packard Inc. might say to himself, "Each time I help a customer solve a problem I am contributing to the strategy of having the highest quality products in all the markets we serve."

An example of high-level strategic thinking is the company leadership at Google saying it will continue "pursuing moonshots." The phrases refer to the idea that as part of its strategy, the company will continue to pursue improbable projects that will require enormous amounts of cash and great leaps of faith. Among these moonshots are self-driving cars, anti-aging drugs and computerized glucose-sensing contact lenses for diabetics.[13]

A study of 231 upper level leaders in a large global company found that global work experience was associated with a stronger tendency to think strategically. The effect was more pronounced when the experience was in a culture distant from one's own, such as an American being on assignment in Japan.[14]

Because effective strategy begins with strategic thinking, you are invited to think through your tendencies toward being a strategic thinker by taking the self-quiz in Figure 4-3. A recommendation for becoming a strategic thinker is to take some time to think strategically every working day. For example, you might take the time to understand the unique information and perspective that your role contributes to the larger organization.[15]

Next, we describe three major approaches to developing strategy: gathering multiple inputs, analyzing the realities of the business situation and doing a SWOT analysis. All three of these approaches are consistent with, and extensions of, the basic planning model presented in Figure 4-1.

Gathering Multiple Inputs to Formulate Strategy

Strategic managers and leaders are often thought of as mystics who work independently and conjure up great schemes for the future. In reality, many strategic leaders arrive at their ideas for the organization's future by consulting with a wide range of parties at interest. Strategy theorist Gary Hamel advises executives to make the strategy-creation process more democratic. He reasons that imagination is scarcer than resources. As a consequence, "We have to involve hundreds, if not thousands, of new voices in the strategy process if we want to increase the odds of seeing the future."[16]

Conversations about strategy with people from different organizational units facilitate companies to look at the big picture. The result of gathering strategic input can be useful in understanding what is happening in the market place.[17] For example, a store manager might contribute the input to a retail executive that too many customers are grumbling, "Why bother visiting stores any longer? I would rather shop from home with my smartphone."

Figure 4-3 How Strategic Is My Thinking?

Indicate your strength of agreement with each of the following statements:
SD – strongly disagree; D – disagree; N – neutral, A – agree; SA –strongly agree.

		SD	D	N	A	SA
1	I get upset if my checkbook does not balance even to the dollar.	5	4	3	2	1
2	I often think about the meaning and implications of news stories.	1	2	3	4	5
3	A top-level manager is usually better off finding ways to cut costs than thinking about the future of the business.	5	4	3	2	1
4	I like to argue (or used to) with an instructor about what should be the correct answer to a multiple-choice question.	5	4	3	2	1
5	So long as a company provides good customer service with its present product line, its future is very secure.	5	4	3	2	1
6	I prefer acquiring knowledge and skills that can help me with my job during the next month rather than those that might help me in the future.	5	4	3	2	1
7	It makes me laugh when a CEO says a big part of his or her job is creating visions.	5	4	3	2	1
8	The most successful people in most fields are visionaries.	1	2	3	4	5
9	I am a "big picture" thinker.	1	2	3	4	5
10	If workers take care of today's problems, the company does not have to worry about the future.	5	4	3	2	1
11	Once a company hits a certain size, such as $50 million in annual sales, it does not have to worry much about competition.	5	4	3	2	1
12	An organization cannot become great without an exciting vision.	1	2	3	4	5

Scoring and interpretation: Find your total score by summing the point values for each question.

52–60	You probably already think strategically, which should help you as a top-level manager.
30–51	You probably have a neutral, detached attitude toward thinking strategically.
12–29	Your thinking probably emphasizes the here and now and the short term. People in this category are usually not ready to provide strategic leadership to group members.

crowdsourcing
The use of collective intelligence gathered from the public, often by the use of social media.

An extreme form of gathering multiple inputs for strategy is **crowdsourcing**, the use of collective intelligence gathered from the public, often by the use of social media. The company might gather thousands of suggestions to sort out a few nuggets of wisdom. Crowdsourcing can involve a range of stakeholders including employees, customers, suppliers and investors. An example of crowdsourcing would be if PepsiCo sent out an inquiry to thousands of people, "We've been a highly successful beverage and snack company for many years. What do you think we should do next as a company?"

Inputs to strategy are helpful, particularly in encouraging debate. Strategy consultant, Melissa Raffoni advises however, that if staff members are asked what direction the organization should take, the executive weakens his or her leadership.[18]

Analyzing the Realities of the Business Situation

To develop an effective business strategy, the strategist must make valid assumptions about the environment. When the assumptions are incorrect, the strategy might backfire. Let's get preposterous for a moment. Assume Krispy Kreme believes online sales will soon become the dominant approach to selling retail. The company therefore halts its plans to vend its donuts through stores of its own, in grocery stores and service stations. Instead, Krispy Kreme develops websites so people can purchase donuts and coffee online, and pay for quick delivery service. The wrong assumption is that potential Krispy Kreme customers throughout the world own computers, are online, have credit cards, and will pay a premium to have donuts and coffee delivered to their home or office. The new e-commerce strategy fails because assumptions about the potential customer base were flawed.

The general point here is that firms must constantly change in order to be aligned with their key environments.[19] Sometimes management can shape the nature of the business to match the external environment, such as Harley-Davidson crafting motorcycles that its aging customer base can continue to drive. (What about motorcycle tricycles such as the police vehicles with a side car?) The assumption Harley would be making here is that motorcyclists want to continue driving motorcycles as late in life as possible.

Accurately analyzing the environment in terms of understanding customers, potential customers, production capability and the relevant technology is a time-consuming and comprehensive activity. Yet for a strategy to work well, the manager has to understand both the external environment and the capabilities of the firm, as already implied from the basic planning model.

Performing a SWOT Analysis

Quite often strategic planning takes the form of a **SWOT analysis**, a method of considering the strengths, weaknesses, opportunities, and threats in a given situation. The strengths and weaknesses take into account internal resources and capabilities, whereas opportunities and threats refer to factors external to the organization. SWOT is considered most applicable to the early stages of strategic and marketing planning. Elements of a SWOT analysis are included in the general planning model. Given SWOT's straightforward appeal, it has become a popular framework for strategic planning. The framework, or technique can identify a niche the company has not already exploited. The framework is outlined in Figure 4-4.

SWOT analysis
A method of considering the strengths, weaknesses, opportunities, and threats in a given situation.

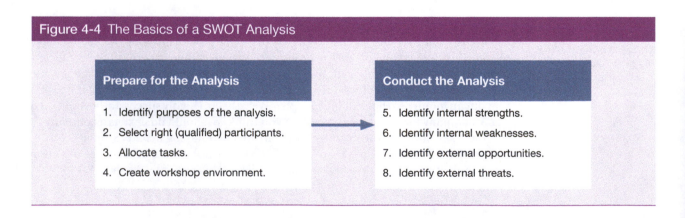

Figure 4-4 The Basics of a SWOT Analysis

Prepare for the Analysis

1. Identify purposes of the analysis.
2. Select right (qualified) participants.
3. Allocate tasks.
4. Create workshop environment.

Conduct the Analysis

5. Identify internal strengths.
6. Identify internal weaknesses.
7. Identify external opportunities.
8. Identify external threats.

Typical SWOT Analysis Matrix

Preparing for the Analysis

Four steps are recommended to bring about a successful SWOT analysis.[20] First, it is important to be clear about what you are doing and why. The purpose might be to fine-tune a present strategy or to point the business in a new direction. Second, it is important to select appropriate contributors. Select people with appropriate experience, talent and enthusiasm. Imaginative people are particularly useful for a SWOT analysis. Usually six to ten people are enough, but involving more people can be helpful to get more people involved in the changes that SWOT might trigger. Third, allocate research and information-gathering tasks. Several members of the team might concentrate on analyzing the firm, whereas others might concentrate on analyzing the outside environment. Step four is to create a workshop environment by encouraging open communication among participants. All present should feel free to criticize the status quo, even questioning what most people think is a company strength. A SWOT team member of a group at Starbucks might say, "Is having so many stores such a great strength? Could we be losing out to the coffee lovers who want a more unique, intimate experience?"

Conducting the Analysis

To illustrate the use of the model, we turn to Ulysse Nardin, a Swiss manufacturer of fine watches founded in 1846. The price range of Ulysse Nardin watches is between approximately $6,000 and $66,000. Assume top executives at Ulysse Nardin are thinking about finding another niche by manufacturing luxury pens in the $200 to $500 range. Some of their thinking in regard to a SWOT analysis might proceed as follows:

- **Internal Strengths.** *What are the good points about a particular alternative? Use your judgment and intuition; ask knowledgeable people.* Selling luxury pens appears to be a reasonable fit with the watch line because a luxury pen is often worn as jewelry. We are great at making small-size luxury items. People who just want a writing instrument could settle for a Bic or competitive brand.

The profit margins on luxury pens are quite good, and they are not likely to be deeply discounted in department stores or discount stores. We can also maintain low inventories until we assess the true demand. As our sales representatives and distributors receive orders, we can manufacture the pens quickly. Our beautiful website, *http://www.ulysse-nardin.com*, could easily incorporate a line of luxury pens.

- **Internal Weaknesses.** *Consider the risks of pursuing a particular course of action, such as getting into a business you do not understand.* We are watch makers, pure and simple. We would need to train our skilled craftspeople to make pens, or hire new workers. If only a handful of companies manufacture luxury pens, it could be because it is a tough market to crack. We are so well known for watches, that our clientele might not perceive us to be a crafter of fountain pens. (We will need to do some market research here.) Another risk is that we will cheapen the Ulysse Nardin name. The average price of a Ulysse Nardin product is now about $7, 000. With a brand of luxury pens, a person could take home a Ulysse Nardin brand product for about $400, which could result in a scaling down of our image. Another problem is that we are not presently linked to all the distribution channels that sell luxury pens, such as office supply stores. We might have to rely on new distributors to get us into that channel. We do not sell over the Internet from our factories to customers, and selling pens might move us in this direction. (Many of our dealers sell our watches over the Internet.)

- **External Opportunities.** *Think of the opportunities that welcome you if you choose a promising strategic alternative.* Use your imagination and visualize the opportunities. The opportunities could be quite good in terms of snob appeal. Maybe large numbers of consumers would welcome the opportunity to carry a Ulysse Nardin anything in their shirt pocket, handbag, or attaché case. Many of the people who become Ulysse Nardin luxury pen customers might want to take a step up to become a Ulysse Nardin watch owner.

- **External Threats.** *Every alternative has its downside, so think ahead to allow for contingency planning.* Ask people who have tried in the past what you are attempting now. But don't be dissuaded by the naysayers, heel draggers and pessimists. Just take action. Several manufacturers of high-end products in jewelry, clothing, and automobiles have cheapened their image and lost market share when they spread their brand names too thin. Following this approach, we could wind up having Ulysse Nardin pens, wallets and handbags. At that point the high prestige of the Ulysse Nardin brand would be at risk.

As a result of this SWOT analysis, Ulysse Nardin sticks to its knitting (or watch making) and continues to make world class watches. Do you think they are making the right decision? Or do you think the brand equity (value of the brand name) warrants putting the Ulysse Nardin label on another product?

A caution about the SWOT analysis is that it is sometimes viewed as too superficial, and may rely on descriptions instead of analyses and ignores prioritizing the alternatives it generates. Another potential problem with the SWOT analysis is it might give the false impression that just running through the complicated steps will result in an effective strategy. In reality, strategy requires a high level of imagination and creativity.

Ask Five Strategic Questions and Take Risks

Strategy formulation is a vast topic with many different recommended approaches. Yet a recent attempt to synthesize and simplify the formulation of strategy appear to have particular merit. Strategy expert, Ken Favaro, advises that strategy formulations in companies need to address the "strategic five" fundamental and difficult questions: For illustrative purposes take the example of management at a chain of budget motels answering these questions.[21]

1 What business or businesses should you be in? (We are in the business of providing short-term lodging for people with limited travel budgets.)

2 How do you add value to your businesses? (Our rooms are cleaner and better maintained than the competition. We also do not have rooms with doors facing the outside, thereby enhancing security.)

3 Who are the target customers for your business? (Among our target customers are construction workers on assignment, college students, seniors with modest incomes, moderate-income families on vacation and groups of high-school students on field trips.)

4 What are your value propositions to those target customers? (We offer an acceptable level of the service for the price, including Wi-Fi, relative safety, satellite TV service with a reasonable section of channels and room furnishings in good shape.)

5 What capabilities are essential to adding value to your businesses and differentiating their value propositions? (We need to control costs yet still provide a comfortable low-cost motel experience.)

Even though the strategy has been effective, and the chain of budget motels is prospering, the unique competitive position may not last a long time. New strategic initiatives may have to be launched again to meet a changing environment and new competitive threats.[22] An example is Macy's, at one time the most successful and best-known department stores chains in the United States. Macy's has done well from time to time in recent years, but has had to reformulate its strategy to compete. with discount and online retailers. Part of Macy's strategy has to become both a traditional retailer and a discounter at the same time, while building its e-commerce.

Asking the five questions just presented, going through a SWOT analysis or formulating strategy by any other method, usually results in taking risks and facing the unknown.[23] For example, GM committing to the development and distribution of self-driving cars is a large risk. Suppose large numbers of serious accidents occur with the driverless cars. The consequence could be many local ordinances outlawing such vehicles for public use.

Levels of Strategy and Types of Strategies

LEARNING OBJECTIVE 3

Identify levels of business strategy and types of business strategies.

The nature of strategy and how it is developed may appear complex. Yet strategy statements themselves, as expressed by managers and planners are usually straight-forward and expressed in a few words, such as, "We will be cost leaders," or, "We will be competitive by offering superior service." Keep in mind that businesspeople are likely to have a less precise and less scientific meaning of strategy than do strategy researchers. A variety of business strategies have already been mentioned in this chapter. Here we look at levels and types of business strategies.

Levels of Business Strategies

A strategy chosen to reach an important goal depends considerably on the level of the organization. At the highest level of the overall firm, Amazon.com might decide that its strategy is to allow people throughout the world to purchase as many products online as they wish. The Amazon vision states, "Our vision is to be the earth's most customer-centric company, to build a place where people can come to find and discover anything they might want to buy online." Yet at the level of the distribution centers, theses managers must develop a strategy for enabling world-wide distribution of products at a reasonable cost. Figure 4-5 provides a few details about strategy levels.

Two major concerns of *corporate-level strategy* are articulating the overall direction of the enterprise, and the selection of specific businesses that serve that purpose. Usually the total direction of the enterprise begins with the founding of the company, such as Boeing Co. being founded as an airplane company. Later, a variety of businesses may emerge, such as Boeing forming a commercial division, a military division and a service division. Executives in large, diversified firms invest considerable time in deciding which businesses to enter; such as Yahoo! moving into various types of entertainment.

Business-level strategy focuses on the question of how to compete in each of the businesses that make up an organization. Several of these strategies will be mentioned in the next section.

Functional-level strategies are formulated to specify actions required to success-fully implement strategies at the corporate and business level. An example is that a corporate-level strategy of Google is to be a leading innovator in any business it enters. The human resources function must then assist in attracting, selecting and retain-ing imaginative workers. Fit among the various functions is another major consider-ation. For example, if the human resources department at Google recruits imaginative workers, these workers must be placed in functions such as marketing and finance that provide stimulating work for these people.

Under ideal circumstances, the activities of managers and other workers at the functional level support the business-level and corporate-level strategies. For example, if top-level management wants the firm to be world-recognized for its quality products

---

Figure 4-5 Strategy Levels for Diversified and Single-Business Firms

Diversified Business Firms	Single-Business Firms
Corporate-Level Strategy	*Corporate-Level Strategy*
• What direction do we pursue for the total enterprise?	• Which business should we be in?
• Which businesses should we enter?	• How do we compete within the market we have chosen?
Business-Level Strategy	*Functional-Level Strategy*
• How do we compete within each of the businesses we have chosen?	• How can each function best support each of our businesses?
	• How do we get the various functions working together smoothly?
Functional-Level Strategy	
• How can each function best support each of our businesses?	
• How do we get the various functions working together smoothly?	

and services (such as Dell), business units would not engage in such businesses as selling refurbished office furniture). At the functional level, all Dell departments would hire talented people who can help deliver quality goods and services.

Types of Business Strategies

Companies use a variety of strategies to survive and prosper. We present here eight widely-used business strategies.

1 *Strategic alliances.* A widely used business strategy is to form alliances, or share resources with other companies to exploit a market opportunity. A major factor contributing to the growth of alliances is the enormous costs and time involved in developing and distributing products if a company starts from zero.

  Macy's & Google formed an alliance for local inventory search. Shoppers who use Macy's website can see if the items they might want to search are in stock at a specific Macy's store, and they can order it for immediate in-store pick up. The feature increases the probability a consumer will visit the store, and perhaps make a few additional purchases. Google benefits from higher ad rates for this type of search because it is more targeted and valuable to Macy's than traditional search.[24]

2 *Diversification of goods and services.* "Don't put all your eggs in one basket" is a standard business strategy. One of the many reasons that diversification is an effective strategy is that it serves as a hedge in case the market for one group of products or services softens. Another advantage of diversification is that it can lead to immediate growth at the same time. Samsung is one of the world's most prominent companies with an active diversification strategy. The company is well known for its smartphones, table computers and television receivers. Samsung also manufactures military hardware, apartment buildings, ships, and also operates an amusement park in South Korea. Coca-Cola Co. engages in a slight diversification strategy with its coffee-infused variant and an energy-drink version of Coke, and also sells water, juice, and other drinks.

3 *Sticking to core competencies.* It may be valuable not only to not put all your eggs in one basket, but also to guard against spreading yourself too thin. Many firms of all sizes believe they will prosper if they confine their efforts to business activities where they perform best—their core competencies. At one time Walmart attempted to lure higher-income shoppers with trendier fashions, and the experiment flopped, eroding profit. The company then returned to its low-price roots which helped it prosper during the Great Recession. As Walmart re-strengthened its reputation for very low prices, many higher-than-average income shoppers traded down.[25] Eleven years later the core competency strategy was still working in terms of higher-than-average income shoppers thinking it is cool or chic to wear clothing purchased at Walmart.

4 *Product Differentiation.* A differentiation strategy attempts to find a niche or offer a product or service perceived by the customer as different from available alternatives. Most companies believe they have a differentiated product unless their strategy is to imitate another product or service, or produce *knock off* merchandise. Luxury brands often stem from a differentiation strategy. An example of a low-price luxury brand that has honed a differentiation strategy is Etón Corporation of Palo Alto, California. Their Grundig AM/FM/Shortwave radio retails for about $100 and offers the remarkable feature of receiving AM and FM stations from several hundred miles away.

An extension of the product differentiation strategy is to create a new market in which competition does not exist, referred to as a blue ocean strategy. A prime example is Cirque du Soleil. They increased revenue 22 fold in a ten-year period by reinventing the circus with extravagant shows that combine several forms of entertainment at once.[26] Many people would perceive the iPhone to be a modern example of the blue ocean strategy.

5 *Focus.* In a focus strategy, the organization concentrates on a specific regional or buyer market. To gain market share, the company uses either a differentiation or a low-cost approach in a targeted market. Some companies have several products or services catering to a buyer market, such as vitamins for seniors, but it does not constitute a full focus strategy. Specialized medical products, such as leg and arm prostheses are based on a focus or niche strategy. Payday loan stores are based on a focus strategy. Typically these stores, such as Advance America, focus on the working poor who live paycheck to paycheck. Yet in recent years, these payday loan stores have developed a presence in some affluent neighborhoods. The real focus of payday loan stores is people in financial need, and perhaps have already used up their credit or have poor credit.

6 *Self-reinvention.* To survive many business enterprises have to radically alter their business model. A leading example is how Intuit, the tax-software maker stays on top of the competition by rethinking its business model. The company's original product, Quicken personal finance had to be recreated when Microsoft Windows replaced its DOS operating system. QuickBooks for small business and Turbo tax for tax preparation remained product leaders when Intuit management moved them from PCs to online in the early days of the Internet. About six years ago, Intuit re-invented itself again by becoming an open platform so developers could add apps that would be useful to its customers.[27]

7 *Cost leadership.* The cost leader provides a product or service at a low price in order to gain market share. Discount stores that sell both general merchandise and food are obvious examples of the cost-leadership strategy. The retail operations of Amazon are driven by a cost-leadership strategy. Many of the millions of products sold through Amazon.com are offered at lower prices than what could be attained by purchasing directly from the manufacturer of the product or its distributors. To attain the cost leadership strategy, Amazon executives, headed by CEO and founder Jeff Bezos, have spent billions of dollars building a distribution-center infrastructure as a world-class system for online shopping. Because of the heavy investments in building the Amazon infrastructure, it took time for the company to generate profits consistently.

8 *Find and retain the best people.* A foundation strategy for becoming and remaining a successful organization is to find and retain highly competent people. Such people will help the organization develop products and services that are in demand, and will find ways to reduce costs and behave ethically. Top management at Microsoft and Amazon.com attribute most of their success to hiring only intelligent, motivated job candidates. *Fast Company* magazine offered this advice to modern business executives' years ago, and the advice is equally relevant today.

"Yes, you need an Internet strategy. Sure, you've got to stay on the good side of Wall Street. But when it comes to building great companies, the most urgent business charge is finding and keeping great people. In an economy driven by ideas and charged by the web, brainpower is the real source of competitive advantage."[28]

So now that you are a top executive, or an advisor to a top executive, which combination of strategies should you choose to triumph? Strategies must be selected carefully and given a chance to work. When a strategy is agreed upon, it must be executed carefully. Jumping from strategy to strategy in the hopes of revitalizing a company has been cited as a major reason why companies fail.

Strategic plans and strategy must also remain flexible to adapt to changing circumstances. Most strategies are only effective for about five years, and adverse circumstances and shorten their useful cycle. A few companies have gone to the extreme of establishing "situation rooms" in which staffers are glued to computer screens to monitor developments affecting sales and finance. In this way, the implementation of the strategy can change rapidly, even if the basic strategy remains stable. For example, a drop in the price of gasoline might increase the likelihood that many consumers will make purchases in physical stores rather than online. As a result, merchandising executives would have less need to sell merchandises at high discounts.

STRATEGY EXECUTION THROUGH OPERATING PLANS, POLICIES, PROCEDURES, AND RULES

The strategy execution, or converting it into action, is necessary for any strategy formulation to be successful. As we discussed, tactical plans are used to execute strategies as are operating plans, policies, procedures and rules, which are described in this next section. An executive once commented, "I could leave a copy of our strategy on a seat in the airport and our company wouldn't have to worry. The competition wouldn't know how to execute it."

A study of strategy execution based on 8,000 managers in more than 250 companies concluded that execution works best when it is framed in these terms: "The ability to seize opportunities aligned with strategy while coordinating with other parts of the organization on an ongoing basis."[29] Assume a company wants to execute a cost-leadership strategy. This requires all organizational units to search for opportunities where a company product or service could be offered at a low price. Managers and other workers throughout the organization need to coordinate to tightly control costs so it is possible to offer goods and services at a low cost, and still be profitable.

Another essential part of strategy execution is for C-suite executives to frequently and effectively communicate the strategy. Communication might feature frequent digital messages, but must also include face-to-face communication, such as town hall meetings. For example, if top-level management agrees that product diversification is their strategy for the future, this topic must be explored in depth throughout the organization. Louis D'Ambrosio has been the CEO of several firms including the clean-tech company, Sensus. He says that you have to repeat a sales strategy at least ten times for an organization to fully internalize it. He held monthly, "all-hands calls" to keep everyone informed about strategy."[30]

Widespread communication of the strategy also connects employees to the purpose and identity of the organization. Articulating the strategy in terms of what capabilities the company will need to build and the skills required to do so, enables employees to understand how their roles role fits into the overall strategy.[31] Assume that a chain of golf courses develops the strategy of appealing to younger as well as older people to survive. Golf course employees will need to develop the skills and sensitivity to work well with members of the youngest adult demographic group. This means appealing to their need to stay connected to their mobile devices while golfing, and for some employees to wear body art and body piercings.

Operating Plans

Operating plans are the means through which strategic plans alter a firm's destiny. Operating plans involve organizational efficiency (doing things right), whereas strategic plans involve effectiveness (doing the right things). Both strategic and operational plans involve exploring alternatives and evaluating the effectiveness of the plan. In a well-planned organization, all managers take responsibility for developing operating plans that mesh with the strategic business plans. Operating plans provide the details of how strategic plans will be accomplished. In many firms, operating plans incorporate suggestions that stem from employees at lower levels.

operating plans
The means through which strategic plans alter a firm's destiny.

Operating plans tend to look internally; focusing more on the firm than on the external environment. To illustrate, the strategic plan of a local government might be to encourage the outsourcing of certain functions to the private sector. One unit within the local government might then formulate an operating plan to subcontract, refuse removal to private contractors, and phase out positions for civil service sanitation workers.

Operating plans tend to span shorter time periods than strategic plans. The local government plan for increasing the private sector's involvement in activities might be a 10-year plan. In contrast, the phasing out of government sanitation workers might take two years.

Policies

Policies are general guidelines to follow in making decisions and taking action; as such, they are plans. Many policies are written; some are unwritten or implied. Policies, designed to be consistent with strategic plans, must allow room for interpretation by the individual manager. An important managerial role is interpreting policies for employees. Here is an example of a policy and an analysis of how it might require interpretations.

policies
General guidelines to follow in making decisions and taking action.

Policy: When hiring employees from the outside, consider only those candidates who are technically competent or show promise of becoming technically competent and who show good personal character and motivation.

A manager attempting to implement this policy with respect to a given job candidate would have to ask the following questions:

- What do we mean by "technical competence?"
- How do I measure technical competence?
- What do we mean by "show promise of becoming technically competent?"
- How do I rate the promise of technical competence?
- What do we mean by "good personal character and motivation?"
- How do I assess good personal character and motivation?

Policies are developed to support strategic plans in every functional area of the firm. Many firms have strict policies against employees accepting gifts and favors from vendors or potential vendors. For example, many schools endorse the Code of Ethics and Principles advocated by the National Association of Educational Buyers. One of the specific policies states that buyers should, "decline personal gifts or gratuities which might in any way influence the purchase of materials."

When policies do not align with strategy (or do not keep the strategy in mind), the system tends to break down. For example, if a restaurant chain serves extra-healthy food, it would hurt the business if franchise owners did not have strong policies about serving only healthy, non-contaminated food.

Procedures

procedure
A customary method for handling an activity. It guides action rather than thinking.

Procedures are considered plans because they establish a customary method of handling future activities. They guide action rather than thinking, in that they state the specific manner in which a certain activity must be accomplished. Procedures exist at every level in the organization, but tend to be more complex and specific at lower levels. For instance, strict procedures may apply to the handling of checks by store associates; whereas the procedures for check handling by managers may be much less explicit. Procedures are very important, such as in a surgical ward carefully marking which knee is to be replaced. Although difficult to believe, before this procedure was established a few patients left the hospital with the wrong knee replaced—or wrong leg amputated!

Rules

rule
A specific course of action or conduct that must be followed. It is the simplest type of plan.

A **rule** is a specific course of action or conduct that must be followed; it is the simplest type of plan. Ideally, each rule fits a strategic plan. In practice, however, many rules are not related to organizational strategy. When rules are violated, corrective action should be taken. Two examples of rules follow:

- Any employee engaged in an accident while in a company vehicle must report that accident immediately to his or her supervisor.
- No employee is authorized to use company photocopying machines for personal use, even if he or she reimburses the company for the cost of the copies.

Some workers think policies, procedures and rules are rigid, bothersome and old-fashioned. The other point of view is that policies and procedures protect company assets and provide a guide for employee actions. Business consultant, Susan Kastan provides this example:

Several laptops were stolen from an office by a group of people pretending to be part of the cleaning company. Every laptop stolen contained sensitive client data. After the theft, all clients had to be notified that their personal information may have been compromised. The breach of security prompted 25 percent of the company's clients to close their accounts. One laptop had the company's identifications and passwords taped to the bottom, which the thieves used to gain access to the plans for an upcoming product. The information was then sold to a competitor.

If the company had policies on how computer ID and passwords should be stored, and how laptops should be secured, these problems would most likely have been avoided.[32]

MANAGEMENT BY OBJECTIVES: A SYSTEM OF PLANNING AND REVIEW

LEARNING OBJECTIVE **5**

Present an overview of management by objectives.

management by objectives (MBO)
A systematic application of goal-setting and planning to help individuals and firms be more productive.

Management by objectives (MBO) is a systematic application of goal-setting and planning to help individuals and firms be more productive. MBO is also interpreted to be a strategic management model. The system began in the 1950s, and continues to contribute to organizational effectiveness. An MBO program typically involves people setting many objectives for themselves as well as management imposing key organizational objectives upon people. An MBO program usually involves sequential steps, which are cited in the following list. (Note that these steps are related to those in the basic planning model shown in Figure 4-1.)

1 *Establishing organizational goals.* Top-level managers set organizational goals to begin the entire MBO process. Quite often these goals are strategic. A group of hospital administrators, for example, might decide upon the strategic goal of improving healthcare for poor people in the community. After these broad goals are established, managers determine what the organizational units must accomplish to meet these goals. When only one to three objectives are established at a time, employees are more focused on what their essential priorities should be.[33]

2 *Establishing unit objectives.* Unit heads then establish objectives for their units. A cascade of objectives takes place as the process moves down the line. Objectives set at lower levels of the firm must be designed to meet the general goals established by top management. Lower-level managers and operatives provide input because a general goal usually leaves considerable latitude for setting individual objectives to meet that goal. The head of inpatient admissions might decide that working more closely with the county welfare department must be accomplished if the healthcare goal cited earlier in this list is to be met. Figure 4-6 suggests ways to set effective goals.

Figure 4-6 Guide to Establishing Goals and Objectives

Effectives goals and objectives have certain characteristics in common. Effective goals and objectives:

- Are clear, concise, and unambiguous. An example of such an objective is: "Reduce damaged boxes of printer paper from April 27 to April 30."

- Are accurate in terms of the true end state or desired condition. An accurate objective might state, "The factory will be as neat and organized as the front office after the cleanup is completed."

- Are achievable by competent workers. Goals and objectives should not be so high or rigid that the majority of competent team members will become frustrated and stressed by attempting to achieve them.

- Include three difficulty levels: routine, challenging, and innovative. Most objectives deal with routine aspects of a job, but they should also challenge workers to loftier goals.

- Are achieved through team-member participation. Subordinates should participate actively in setting objectives.

- Relate to small chunks of accomplishment. Many objectives should concern small, achievable activities, such as uncluttering a work area. Accomplishing small objectives is the building block for achieving larger goals.

- Specify what is going to be accomplished, who is going to accomplish it, when it is going to be accomplished, and how it is going to be accomplished. Answering the what, who, when, and how questions reduces the chance for misinterpretation.

3 *Reviewing group members' proposals.* At this point, group members make proposals about how they will contribute to unit objectives. For example, the assistant to the manager of inpatient admissions might agree to set up a task force to work with the welfare department. Each team member is also given the opportunity to set objectives in addition to those that meet the strategic goals.

4 *Negotiating or agreeing.* Managers and team members confer together at this stage to either agree on the objectives set by the team members or negotiate further. In the hospital example, one department head might state that he or she wants to reserve ten beds on the ward for the exclusive use of indigent people. The supervisor might welcome the suggestion but point out that only five beds could be spared for such a purpose. They might settle for setting aside seven beds for the needy poor.

5 *Creating action plans to achieve objectives.* After the manager and team members agree upon objectives, action plans must be defined. Sometimes the action plan is self-evident. For example, if your objective as a call-center manager is to hire three new customer service representatives this year, you would begin by consulting with Human Resources.

6 *Reviewing performance.* Performance reviews are conducted at agreed-upon intervals. (A semiannual or annual review is typical.) People receive good performance reviews based on how well they attain most of the major objectives. When objectives are not attained, the manager and group member mutually analyze what went wrong. Equally important, they discuss the corrective actions. New objectives are then set for the next review period. Because establishing new objectives is part of an MBO program, the process of management by objectives can continue for the life of an organization.

SUMMARY OF KEY POINTS

 Summarize a general framework for planning and apply it to enhance your planning skills.

A generalized planning model can be used for strategic planning, tactical planning and operational planning. The model consists of seven related and sometimes overlapping elements: defining the present situation, establishing goals and objectives, analyzing the environment in terms of forecasting aids and barriers to goals and objectives, developing action plans, developing budgets, implementing the plan and controlling the plan. Contingency plans should also be developed.

 Explain how business strategy is developed, including a SWOT analysis.

Business strategy usually develops from planning but can also stem from a vision. Strategy is influenced by values. The best strategy emerges from an organization having a grand purpose. An important part of business strategy is to get managerial workers throughout the organization thinking strategically and wondering about how the firm adapts to the environment and will cope with its future.

Gathering multiple inputs, including the technique of crowdsourcing is important in developing strategy. Strategists must also analyze the realities of the business situation to guard against false assumptions about customers, production capability and the relevant technology. Strategy development often begins with a SWOT analysis, but first the group must prepare for the analysis. The SWOT analysis considers the strengths, weaknesses, opportunities and threats in a given situation.

Strategy formulations need to address five fundamental and difficult questions, including "What business or business should you be in?" and "Who are the target customers for your business?" After strategy is formulated, it is still necessary for the organization to take risks and face the unknown.

 Identify levels of business strategy and types of business strategies.

In a diversified business firm, strategy is formulated at the corporate level, the business level and the functional level. The activities of managers and other workers at the functional level should support the business-level and corporate-level strategies.

Types of business strategies include strategic alliances, diversification of goods and services, sticking to core competencies, product differentiation, focus, self-reinvention, cost leadership and finding and retaining the best people.

The right strategy or combination of strategies must be chosen with care. Current thinking suggests strategic plans and strategy must remain flexible enough to adapt to changing circumstances.

 Explain the strategy execution through the use of operating plans, policies, procedures, and rules.

The execution of strategy is necessary for strategy formulation to be successful, usually requiring coordination throughout the organization and frequent communication of the strategy. Operating plans provide the details of how strategic plans will be accomplished or implemented. They deal with a shorter time span than strategic plans. Policies are plans set in the form of general statements that guide thinking and action in decision making. Procedures establish a customary method of handling future activities. A rule sets a specific course of action or conduct and is the simplest type of plan.

5 **Present an overview of management by objectives.**

Management by objectives (MBO) is a well-established formal system of goal-setting, planning and review. In general, it has six elements: establishing organizational goals, establishing unit objectives, obtaining proposals from group members about their objectives, negotiating or agreeing to proposals, developing action plans and reviewing performance. After objectives are set, the manager must give feedback to team members on their progress toward reaching the objectives.

Key Terms and Phrases

strategic planning 101

tactical planning 101

operational planning 101

action plan 104

contingency plan 105

strategy 105

vision 106

mission 107

crowdsourcing 109

SWOT analysis 110

operating plans 118

policies 118

procedure 119

rule 119

management by objectives (MBO) 120

Questions

1. In what way does planning control the future?

2. What is your evaluation of the opinion expressed by Harley-Davidson's CEO that the fascination of young people with electronic gadgets is limiting their interest in owning motorcycles?

3. Imagine yourself as the founder of a company in a field that interests you, and you want to develop a strategy for your firm. How effective would it be for you to search the Internet for a suitable strategy?

4. What is the purpose of your present employer or your most recent employer? Was this purpose communicated to employees throughout the organization?

5. Some business owners believe and have been known to say, "We're too busy to bother with strategy. We have to take care of the present." What might be wrong with their reasoning?

6. Some companies place their vision statement on a small plastic card that employees can attach to their key chain, or on coffee mugs given to employees. How effective do you think these gimmicks are in guiding the work activities of employees?

7. Give an example of how a rule could fit the corporate strategy of cost leadership.

Skill-Building Exercise 4-A: Conducting a SWOT Analysis

In this chapter you have read the basics of conducting a SWOT analysis. Now gather in small groups to conduct one. Develop a scenario for a SWOT analysis, such as the group starting a chain of coffee shops, pet care service centers, or treatment centers for online addictions. Or, conduct a SWOT analysis for reorganizing a company from being mostly hierarchical to one that is mostly team-based. Keep in mind one of the biggest challenges in doing a SWOT analysis—differentiate between internal strengths and weaknesses, and external opportunities and threats. Because most of your data are hypothetical, you will have to rely heavily on your imagination. Group leaders might share the results of the SWOT analysis with the rest of the class.

Skill-Building Exercise 4-B: Developing Business Strategy for Canned Soup

Imagine yourself as part of a strategy development team for Campbell Soup Co. The industry data show a steady decline in sales of canned soup. Consumers are shifting more toward products they perceive to be fresher and healthier. Fresh food often costs less than a can of soup. Furthermore, many nutritionists think they are healthier than soup because of their lower sodium content. Work as part of small team to recommend a business strategy that will help invigorate the company. Your final strategy statement should be about 25 words long, yet powerful enough to generate millions of dollars in annual profits for Campbell Soup.

Management Now—Online Skill-Building Exercise: Business Strategy Research

The purpose of this assignment is to find three examples of business strategy by searching the Internet. Choose several companies that interest you, and search for online news articles about their strategies posted within the last 90 days. Examples would include strategies for increasing sales, introducing a new product, or combating the negative impact of a scandal or controversy. Compare the strategic plans described in the articles to the section of this chapter called "Types of Business Strategies." Attempt to match the company strategy to a type of strategy listed in the chapter.

What Exactly Is Our Purpose?

Todd is the CEO of Protecto, a manufacturer and seller of vinyl floormats, trunk organizers, and smartphone holders for cars and trucks. The products are sold to consumers in automobile parts stores, department stores, and through telephone orders, and online. As people tend to keep their cars and trucks longer today than in the past, Proteco's business has thrived. Todd recently read in an article on the Internet that enduring and successful companies have a purpose, or a reason for being. He reflected that the purpose of Protecto seems obvious, but maybe a Friday afternoon meeting with the management team could articulate the company's true purpose. Todd also noted that a company with a purpose has more committed employees and customers, and sometime suppliers.

Todd sent an e-mail message to the management team indicating that the purpose of the meeting was to discuss the purpose of Protecto. To start the meeting, Todd said, "Okay folks, let's take turns describing what you think is the purpose of Protecto. Why are we here? What are we trying to do? What is our *raison d'etre* (reason for being)? A partial transcript of the meeting follows:

Brandy (chief marketing officer): I've been thinking a little about this topic for a while, so I thank Todd for calling this meeting. As I've tried to communicate in some of my marketing efforts, the purpose of Protecto is to make driving cars and trucks a more esthetic and enjoyable experience.

Tony (chief financial officer): From my standpoint, we have the same purpose as any sensible business. We are trying to make a profit and survive.

Derek (head of manufacturing): Our purpose is clear to me. We are in the business of protecting car and truck interiors. That's common sense.

Lori (chief engineering officer): Derek is on the right track. Protecto's purpose is to design and distribute high-quality protective devices for vehicle interiors that will help sustain the appearance and functionality of those vehicles.

Maria (customer support manager): Let's not get too fancy or unrealistic. Our purpose is to help our customers enjoy a more comfortable experience with their vehicles.

Quincy (head of logistics and shipping): You folks might be overlooking our ultimate purpose. We are helping sustain the planet by making car and truck interiors more durable thereby reducing the need for replacing the vehicles.

Todd: I'll be sending you an e-mail after I integrate these thoughts. Maybe we will vote on which one or two final contenders should be our purpose.

Case Questions

1 Which of the suggested purposes of Protecto do you think would be the most effective in enhancing the commitment of the company's customers, employees, and suppliers?

2 Which of the suggested purposes of Protecto do you think would be the least effective in enhancing the commitment of the company's customers, employees, and suppliers?

3 To what extent do you think that Todd is just wasting time? Does Protecto really need a written purpose?

Lenovo Implements its Strategy of Protect and Attack

Lenovo, the Chinese technology company, designs, manufactures, and sells personal computers, tablets, smartphones, smart televisions, workstations, and servers. Since its founding in 1984, Lenovo has become one of the world's largest technology companies. Although not yet as well-known as Apple or Samsung, you will find loads of business and government offices equipped with banks of Lenovo PCs.

A major part of Lenovo's path to growth has been to purchase money-losing divisions of major companies, and then make them profitable. Key examples include the purchase of the PC division of IBM on 2005, and IBM's low-end server division in China in 2014. The next major acquisition was the purchase of the handset division of Google (formerly part of Motorola). Lenovo also purchased NEC's PC operations in Japan, enabling the company to become the PC market leader in Japan. The acquisition strategy of Lenovo has been described as "cannily scavenging other companies' castoffs."

Lenovo has created a brand name recognizable around the world, an achievement no other Chinese technology company has been able to achieve. The company is vertically integrated in the sense that it does almost all its own manufacturing. Another distinguishing characteristic of Lenovo is that it is not strictly a low-cost producer. For example, its ThinkPad laptop and Yoga four-position ultrabook are premium priced.

The core of Lenovo's growth has come from its strategy, which is known as "protect and attack." CEO Yang Yuanging (known as "YY" to company personnel), initiated this strategy in 2009. The "protect" or defensive part of the strategy seeks to build on Lenovo's success in China, where it is the leading vendor of PCs. At the same time Lenovo has become the world's largest manufacturer of PCs, claiming almost a 25 percent market share, well ahead of HP Inc., Dell, and Apple. The "attack" or offensive aspect of the business strategy is to grow internationally by levering the assets derived from acquiring other companies, or parts of companies, and expanding sales to emerging markets, such as in underdeveloped countries where the markets have strong growth potential. The attack part of the strategy also refers to taking riskier bets outside of its PC business.

The phrase "protect and attack" is found everywhere in the company, with employees at all levels frequently repeating the phrase. To implement a protect and attack strategy, Lenovo relies on two interrelated business models, referred to by company executives as "transactional" and "relationship." The transactional model emphasizes sales to retail customers, as well as small and medium-sized businesses. The sales come directly from online and Lenovo stores, and indirectly through distributors and retailers.

The relationship model is geared toward sales on a larger scale, including large businesses and educational and governmental institutions. Sales of large number of products are accompanied by a high degree of personalized service by Lenovo staff. A combination of internal sales representatives and business partners are engaged in the personalized service.

A major component of the protect part of the strategy in China is Lenovo's enormous network of distribution channels. A few years ago, a Lenovo executive bragged that the company had access to 13,000 sales points in its Chinese distribution network, with 80 percent selling only Lenovo products. Protecting these competitive advantages is a top strategic priority.

The attack part of the strategy includes expanding Lenovo's presence in emerging markets such as India, Russia and Brazil. The company is willing to lose money initially in order to gain a stronghold in another country. Lenovo executives recognize that being successful in the international markets is not easy. The Americas, Europe, Africa and the Middle East have unique consumer preferences, as well as differences in government regulations. Acquiring companies in different markets is part of the attack strategy. For example, Lenovo doubled its share of the PC market in Germany and Brazil by acquiring computer makers in those two countries.

Although much of Lenovo's rise to prominence as a technology firm has been attributed to it success in personal computers, the company has developed new revenue streams. CEO Yang says PCs are moving toward the "PC + Era." In this stage of the evolution of

PCs, they will exist as central hubs linking interconnected devices including tablet computers, smartphones and smart TVs. The strategy of expanding into new markets has moved Lenovo into a distant third position in the global smartphone and tablet markets behind Samsung and Apple. By implementing its protect and attack strategy, Lenovo plans to overtake Apple and Samsung.

Case Questions

1 How does the protect-and-attack strategy fit any of the other business strategies mentioned in this chapter?

2 How do you imagine Lenovo can be successful with its scavenger strategy? For example, if a major company like IBM was losing money on selling PCs, how could Lenovo make a profit with this product?

3 What strategy could Lenovo management possibly develop so the company would surpass Apple and Samsung in the mobile device industry?

4 By the way, have you or anybody you know used a Lenovo product? What do you think of the quality?

Source: Original story based on facts and observations in the following sources: Jason Fernando, "A Look at Lenovo's Strategy & Business Model," *www.investopedia.com*, November 30, 2019, pp. 1–11; Drake Bennett, "Are You Done with That?" *Bloomberg Businessweek*, May 12–May 18 2014, pp. 46–51; William J. Holstein, "Lenovo Goes Global," *Strategy + Business* (www.strategy-business.com), Issue 76, Autumn 2014, pp. 1–2; "Executing a Global Growth Strategy at Lenovo," *www.bts.com*, Copyright © 2015, BTS, pp. 1–2.

ENDNOTES

1. Original story based on facts and observations in the following sources: Jason Heckl, "Strategic Planning Lessons from Elon Musk," *Strategic Planning and Management Insights* (www.smestrategy.net), July 16, 2019, pp. 1–2; Max Chafkin, "Elon Musk Thinks Bigger," *Fast Company*, December 2015/January 2016, pp. 112–113; Christopher Mims, "Tesla's Problem: Pushing Boundaries Too Far," *The Wall Street Journal*, July 5, 2016, p. B4.

2. The facts about Harley-Davidson and the quotes are from Claire Buddath, "The Hog of Tomorrow," *Bloomberg Businessweek*, August 27, 2018, pp.44–49; "Harley-Davidson Reports 2008 Results, Plans Lower 2009 Shipments and Unveils Strategy for Current Environment," *www.harley-davidson.com*, 2009; Dan Neil, "Harley's LiveWire Whispers 'Hello' to Next-Gen Riders," *The Wall Street Journal*, July 20–21, 2019, p. D10; Micah Toll, "The LiveWire Electric Motorcycle Won't Save Harley-Davidson, but THIS Might," *electrek* (https:/electrek.com), October 11, 2019, pp. 1–10; Austen Hufford, "Harley Revs Up Overseas Plan With Small Bike Built in China," *The Wall Street Journal*, June 20, 2019, p. B1; "In Brief," *Bloomberg Businessweek*, February 4, 2019, p. 8.

3. Rick Barrett, "Harley, Other Motorcycle Makers Face Big Challenges as Sales Sputter," *USA Today — Democrat and Chronicle*, January 18, 2018, p. 3B; Alexander C. Kaufman, "Harley-Davidson CEO Wants Young People to 'Live for Real' on a Motorcycle," *The Huffington Post* (www.huffingtonpost.com). June 19, 2015, p. 1; James R. Hagerty, "Harley-Davidson's Hurdle Attracting Young Motorcycle Riders," *The Wall Street Journal* (edn.expublic.com), June 19, 2015, p. 1.

4. Bob Tita, "Glut of Used Hogs Drags on Harley," *The Wall Street Journal*, October 2, 2018, p. B5.

5. Larry Bossidy and Ram Charan with Charles Burck, *Execution: The Discipline of Getting Things Done* (New York: Crown Business, 2002).

6. Raffaella Sadun, Nicholas Bloom, and John Van Reenan, "Why Do We Undervalue Competent Management?" *Harvard Business Review*, September–October 2017, p, 122.

7. Cynthia A. Montgomery, "Putting Leadership Back Into Strategy," *Harvard Business Review*, January 2008, pp. 54–60.

8. Henry Mintzberg, *Managing* (Berrett-Koehler, 2009), pp. 162–163.

9. Nate Dvorak and Bryant Ott, "A Company Purpose Has to Be a Lot More than Words," *www.gallup.com*, July 28, 2015, pp. 1–2.

10. "So Your Company Has a Vision: Why Can't Everyone See It?" *Knowledge@Wharton*, (https://knowledge.wharton.upenn.edu) July 15, 2019, p. 1.

11. Adam Brandenburger, "Strategy Needs Creativity: An Analytic Framework Alone Won't Reinvent Your business," *Harvard Business Review*, March–April 2019, pp. 61–62.

12. James R. Bailey, "The Mind of the Strategist," *Academy of Management Learning and Education*, December 2003, p. 385.

13. Jessica Guynn, "Google to Keep Shooting for the Moon" *USA Today Money*, June 4, 2015, p. 4B.

14. Lisa Dragnoni, et al., "Developing Leaders' Strategic Thinking through Global Work Experience: The Moderating Role of Cultural Distance," *Journal of Applied Psychology*, September 2014, pp. 867–882.

15. Nina Bowman, "4 Ways to Improve Your Strategic Thinking," *Harvard Business Review* (hbr.org), December 27, 2016, pp. 1–5.

16. Cited in John A. Byrne, "Three of the Busiest New Strategists," *Business Week*, August 26, 1996, p. 50.

17. Chris Ertel and Lisa Kay Solomon, "Go Ahead, Strategize," *The Wall Street Journal*, March 27, 2014, p. A 15.

18. Cited in "4 Subtle Leadership Traps to Avoid," *Executive Leadership*, October 2015, p. 8.

19. Bob De Wit and Ron Meyer, *Strategy Synthesis: Resolving Strategy Paradoxes to Create Competitive Advantage* (London, UK: Thomson Learning, 2005).

20. "Performing a SWOT Analysis," in *Business: The Ultimate Resource* (Cambridge, MA: Perseus Publishing, 2002), pp. 468–469.

21. Ken Favaro, "How Leaders Mistake Execution for Strategy (and Why that Damages Both)", *Strategy + Business* (www.strategy-business.com) February 11, 2013, pp. 2–3.

22. Rita Gunther McGrath, "Transient Advantage," *Harvard Business Review*, June 2013, pp. 62–70.

23. Roger L. Martin, "The Big Lie of Strategic Planning," *Harvard Business Review*, January–February 2014, p, 81.

24. Michelle Greenwald, "11 of the Best Strategic Brand Partnerships in 2014," *www. forbes.com*, December 11, 2014, p. 2.

25. Ann Zimmerman and Miguel Bustillo, "Walmart Angles to Keep Those Who Traded Down," *The Wall Street Journal*, October 2, 2009, p. B1.

26. W. Chan Kim and Renée Mauborgne, "Blue Ocean Strategy," *Harvard Business Review*, October 2004, pp. 76–84.

27. Geoff Colvin, "How Intuit Reinvents Itself," *Fortune*, November 1, 2017, pp. 76–81.

28. Bill Breen and Anna Mudio, "Peoplepalooza," *Fast Company*, January 2001, pp. 80–81.

29. Donald Sull, Rebecca Homkes, and Charles Sull, "Why Strategy Execution Unravels—and What to Do About It," *Harvard Business Review*, March 2015, p. 66.

30. Cited in Frank Cespedes, "Putting Sales at the Center of Strategy," *Harvard Business Review*, October 2014, p. 25.

31. Paul Leinwand and Joachim Retering, "How to Excel at Both Strategy and Execution," *Harvard Business Review* (https://hbr.org), November 17, p. 4.

32. Susan Kastan, "Policies, Procedures Serve Real Purpose," *Democrat and Chronicle*, December 27, 2009, p. 2E.

33. "What is MBO (Management by Objectives)?" *Workfront* (www.workfront.com), February 12, 2019, pp. 1–4.

CHAPTER 5

Decision Making, Creativity, and Innovation

OBJECTIVES

After studying this chapter and doing the exercises, you should be able to:

1 Explain the steps involved in making a complex decision.

2 Understand the key influences on decision making in organizations.

3 Appreciate the value and potential limitations of group decision making.

4 Understand the nature of creativity and how it contributes to managerial work.

5 Describe organizational programs for improving creativity and innovation.

6 Implement several suggestions for becoming a more creative problem solver.

About five years ago, a concept in condominium complexes arose in Detroit, Michigan—constructing them from abandoned shipping containers used for shipping goods by sea. Since that time, other urban communities in the United States have converted shipping containers into single-family and multiple-family homes. Deviating from traditional construction material, a team in Newark, New Jersey, built a three-family home out of 18 shipping containers on a vacant lot.

Europe has had offbeat dwellings, such as tiny homes that pre-dated the shipping container concept. Frederick Cooke of C + C Architecture in Newark, said: "It's a little different here. As Americans, our living standards are different. One of the challenges we've faced in doing this has been creating a very typical floor plan for a traditional three-bedroom apartment and figure out how to make the containers work with that."

The floor plan of the container module apartment includes an open living room, dining room and kitchen space, three bedrooms and two bathrooms, with a laundry suite in each unit. The floors are constructed with poured concrete, and the walls are insulated with cell foam that exceed current standards. Other sustainability features include a base structure built on pile footings to permit better rainwater absorption, and an option for installing solar panels in the future. In Portland, Oregon, a developer called Relevant Buildings, has built a two-story, eight-unit condominium complex made entirely out of shipping containers.

Cooke also mentions that he is trying to reinvigorate the urban neighborhood and create affordable homes for middle-class families. The container-build home sells for around $200,000, about 10 percent less than, typical two-family condos in Newark. The containers for the home are sourced from the Port of Newark, with tens of thousands of these containers tacked wherever possible, and sitting idle. The cost of a container that has made only one ocean voyage is about $2,000. Multiple-voyage containers have already begun to rust In Portland, Oregon, container-home developers pay between $2,500 and $4,500 for the containers.

Much of what is made inside the container-homes in various communities across the United States is either recycled, upcycled, or super-energy efficient. The homes are designed to be earth-friendly and affordable. Cooke said he is hoping to attract artists and people who think about living in a urban environment "as a cool and creative thing to do."[1]

The story about the developers of container-based homes illustrates how creativity and innovative thought can launch an enterprise and help society. Also illustrated is that business creativity does not necessarily focus on esoteric technology. This chapter explores how managerial workers solve problems and make decisions individually and in groups. We emphasize the role of creativity and innovation in problem solving because useful new ideas are the lifeblood of most organizations.

A **problem** is a discrepancy between ideal and actual conditions. For example, a hospital might have too many beds unoccupied. The ideal would be to have an occupancy rate of 90 percent or greater. A **decision** is choosing among alternatives, such as affiliating with more doctors so as to receive more patient referrals.

Problem solving and decision making are required to carry out all management functions. For example, when managers control, they must make a series of decisions about how to solve the problem of getting performance back to standard. Decision making may also be seen as the heart of management. A distinguishing characteristic of a manager's job is the authority to make decisions.

problem
A discrepancy between ideal and actual conditions.

decision
A choice among alternatives.

STEPS IN PROBLEM SOLVING AND DECISION MAKING

Learning how to solve problems and make decisions properly is vitally important. A McKinsey & Company survey of 1,259 managers found that few companies excel at decision making. The companies that did excel made high-quality decisions at high velocity (making and executing the decision quickly), leading to better financial results.[2] The basic purpose of making a decision is to solve a problem, but one must analyze the problem prior to making the decision. As shown in Figure 5-1, and described next, problem solving and decision making may be divided into steps.

LEARNING OBJECTIVE **1**

Explain the steps involved in making a complex decision.

Identify and Diagnose the Problem

Problem solving and decision making begins with the awareness that a problem exists. In other words, the first step in problem solving and decision making is identifying a gap between desired and actual conditions. Being attentive to the environment helps the manager identify problems, such as noticing that the department is receiving frequent criticism from outsiders and insiders. At times, a problem is imposed on a manager, such as when customer complaints increase. At other times, he or she has to search actively for a worthwhile problem or opportunity. For example, a sales manager actively pursues a problem by conducting an audit to find out why former customers stopped buying from the company.

A thorough diagnosis of the problem is important because the real problem may be different from the one that a first look suggests. The ability to think critically helps a person get at the real problem. The critical thinking manager might listen to

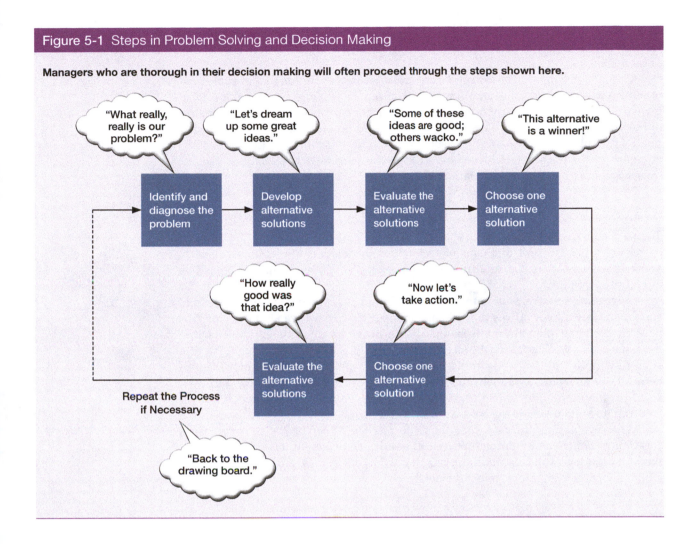

Figure 5-1 Steps in Problem Solving and Decision Making

Managers who are thorough in their decision making will often proceed through the steps shown here.

the evidence of the problem, and then ask what is missing from the description.[3] For example, "Let's dig further into why our shipments are late so frequently."

As Albert Einstein said, "If I were given one hour to save the planet, I would spend 59 minutes defining the problem and one minute resolving it."[4] To diagnose a problem properly, you must clarify its true nature. A frequent example is that a manager might attempt to reduce turnover by increasing wages. The manager assumes that the workers would stay with the company longer if their wages were higher. Yet the real problem is inflexible working hours that are triggering turnover.

Develop Alternative Solutions

The second step in decision making is to generate alternative solutions. In this intellectually freewheeling aspect of decision making, all kinds of possibilities are explored, even if they seem unrealistic. Often the difference between good and mediocre decision makers is that the former do not accept the first alternative that occurs to them. Instead, they keep digging until they find the best solution. A classic example is when Jeff Bezos, the founder of Amazon.com, was searching for a way to commercialize the Internet: he made a list of the top 20 mail-order products; he then looked for where he could create the most value for customers; and finally, he decided on the alternative of selling books.[5]

Often the problem solver will find a creative alternative solution to the problem. At other times, a standard solution will work adequately. For example, one small-business owner needing money to expand the business might choose the standard alternative of borrowing money from a bank or finance company. Another small-business owner might attempt the creative alternative of raising money by selling private shares of the company to friends and family members. (If the company fails, however, the business owner will have put important relationships at risk.)

Evaluate Alternative Solutions

The next step involves comparing the relative value of the alternatives. The problem solver examines the pros and cons of each one and considers the feasibility of each. Some alternatives may appear attractive but implementing them would be impossible or counterproductive.

Comparing relative value often means performing a cost and savings analysis of each alternative. Alternatives that cost much more than they save are infeasible. The possible outcome of an alternative should be part of the analysis. If an unsatisfactory outcome is almost a certainty, the alternative should be rejected. For example, if a firm is faced with low profits, one alternative would be to cut pay by 20 percent. The outcome of this alternative would be to lower morale drastically and create high turnover, so a firm should not implement that alternative. High employee turnover is so expensive that it would override the cost savings.

When evaluating alternative decisions, it is often helpful to look at all your options together rather than evaluating them one at a time.[6] For example, a facilities manager might lay out five proposals for improving traffic flow out of the factory parking lot and study them together, rather than individually.

Choose One Alternative Solution

The process of weighing each alternative must stop at some point. You cannot solve a problem unless you choose one of the alternatives—that is, make a decision. Several factors influence the choice. A major factor is the goal the decision should achieve. The goals sought for in making the decision are also referred to as the *decision criteria*. The alternative chosen should be the one that appears to come closest to achieving it. If two alternatives appear almost equally good after considerable deliberation, it may be helpful to seek the opinion of one more person to decide which alternative is slightly better.

Despite a careful evaluation of alternatives, ambiguity remains in most decisions. The decisions faced by managers are often complex, and the factors involved in them are often unclear. Even when quantitative evidence strongly supports a particular alternative, the decision maker may be uncertain. Human resource decisions are often the most ambiguous because making precise predictions about human behavior is so difficult. Deciding which person to hire from a list of several strong candidates is always a challenge no matter how much data have been collected about the candidates.

Implement the Decision

Converting a decision into action is the next major step. Until a decision is implemented, it is not really a decision. A fruitful way of evaluating the merit of a decision is to observe its implementation. A decision is seldom a good one if people resist its implementation or if it is too cumbersome to implement. Suppose a firm tries to boost productivity by decreasing the time allotted for lunch or coffee breaks. If employees resist the decision by eating while working and then take the allotted lunch break, productivity will decrease. Implementation problems indicate that the decision to boost productivity by decreasing break-time would be a poor one.

Another perspective on implementation is that it represents execution, or putting plans into action, as described in Chapter 4. For example, a smartphone company might decide to distribute many of its phones through general retailers such as supermarkets, general stores, and pharmacies. The marketing and sales group would then have to systematically sell their plans to merchandising managers at the outlets mentioned.

Evaluate and Control

The final step in the decision-making framework is to investigate how effectively the chosen alternative solved the problem. Controlling means ensuring that the results the decision obtained are the ones set forth during the problem-identification step. Evaluating and controlling your decisions will help you improve your decision-making skills. You can learn important lessons by comparing what actually happened with what you thought would happen. You can learn what you could have improved or done differently and use this information the next time you face a similar decision.

LIMITS TO RATIONALITY IN DECISION MAKING

Decision making is usually not entirely rational, because so many factors influence the decision maker. Awareness of this fact stems from the research of psychologist and economist Herbert A. Simon. He proposed that bounds (or limits) to rationality are present in decision making. These bounds are the limitations of the human mind, particularly related to the processing and recall of information.[7]

The field of behavioral economics for many years has challenged the popular view in economics that individual decision making is rational and predictable, and easily modeled.[8] The field emphasizes that people are not entirely rational decision makers, such as when they try hard to avoid losing money in the stock market rather than focus on increasing profits. An individual might hang on to a losing stock or mutual fund too long, and a manager might hang on to a losing product for too long.

An example of irrationality in decision making is that people are superstitious about numbers. For example, an affluent condominium apartment building in Hong Kong omits the 13th floor to cater to Western tastes.[9] Have you noticed that most hotels do not have a floor labeled 13? The developer who avoids assigning number 13 to a floor is being rational about catering to the irrationality of guests and potential guests.

Research and opinion on bounded rationality emphasizes that humans use problem solving strategies that are reasonably rapid, reasonably accurate, and fit the quantity and type of information available. In short, people do the best with what they have while making decisions. For example, an important decision facing a marketing manager in a large consumer products company is whether to sell products in discount stores because of concerns about cheapening its image. Samsung marketers moved quickly on this decision instead of agonizing over years of studies. As a result, many of their smartphones are sold in discount stores.

Partly because of limits to rational decision making, decision makers often use simplified strategies, also known as **heuristics**. A heuristic becomes a rule of thumb in decision making, such as the policy to reject a job applicant who does not smile during the first three minutes of the job interview. A widely used investing heuristic is as follows: The percent of equity in your investment portfolio should equal 100 minus your age, with the remainder being invested in fixed-income investments including cash. (Because people live longer today, 110 is sometimes used instead of 100.) A 25-year-old would therefore have a portfolio consisting of 25 percent interest-bearing securities, such as bonds, and 75 percent in stocks. Heuristics help the decision maker cope with masses of information, but their oversimplification can lead to inaccurate or irrational decision making. For example, the hiring manager cited might miss out on a highly capable candidate just because he or she is introverted and rarely smiles.

heuristics
A rule of thumb used in decision making.

KEY INFLUENCES ON THE QUALITY OF DECISION MAKING

The quality of decision making is influenced by many factors. These same influences on the decision-making process contribute to bounded rationality, such as not being able to take a sensible risk because of being too cautious. We describe nine such influences, as outlined in Figure 5-2.

LEARNING OBJECTIVE **2**

Understand the key influences on decision making in organizations.

Figure 5-2 Factors Influencing Decision Making

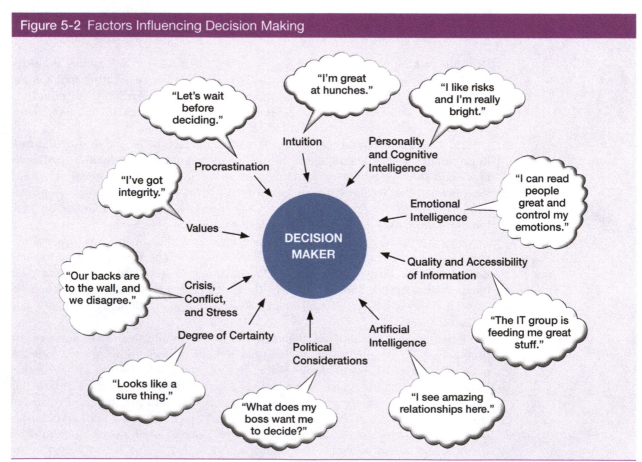

Intuition

Effective decision makers do not rely on analytical and methodological techniques alone. They also use their hunches and intuition. Intuition is an experience-based way of knowing or reasoning in which weighing and balancing evidence are done unconsciously and automatically. **Intuition** is also a way of arriving at a conclusion without using the step-by-step logical process. Intuition can be based mostly on experience or feeling. The fact that experience contributes to intuition means that decision makers can become more intuitive by solving many difficult problems because accumulated facts are an asset to intuition. It also means that decision makers will have better intuition if they perform the same work for a relatively long period of time.[10] Intuition would help point the executive in the right direction, such as sizing up the overall merits of the company to be acquired.

The surge in in use of big data, analytics, and artificial intelligence has not diminished the role of intuition in making major decisions. A survey of CEOs conducted by the consultancy KPMG LLP showed that 35 percent of executives highly trust data provided by the organization. Yet 65 percent of CEOs ignored insights provided by data analysis or computer models because it contradicted their intuition. Brad Fisher, the U.S. leader of data and analytics at KMPG, said that companies enlarging their analytics units must also find ways to sharpen executives' instincts (intuition).[11]

Major decisions, including strategic ones, usually begin with intuition. Tim Cook, CEO of Apple Inc. believes that intuition is a key part of his job. In his words, "The most important things in life, whether they're personal or professional, are decided on intuition.... You can do a lot of things that are quantitative in nature. But... the things that are most important are always gut calls."[12]

Personality and Cognitive Intelligence

The personality and cognitive intelligence of the decision maker influence his or her ability to find effective solutions. A particularly relevant personality dimension is a person's propensity for taking risks. A cautious, conservative person typically opts for a low-risk solution. An extremely cautious person may avoid making major decisions for fear of being wrong. Organizational pressures can also influence a person's propensity for risk taking. In addition to being related to risk taking, cautiousness and conservatism influence **decisiveness**—the extent to which a person makes up his or her mind promptly and prudently. Good decision makers, by definition, are decisive.

Perfectionism exerts a notable impact on decision making. People who seek the perfect solution to a problem are usually indecisive because they hesitate to accept the fact that a particular alternative is good enough. Optimism versus pessimism is another relevant personality dimension. Optimists are more likely than pessimists to find solutions. Pessimists are more likely to give up searching, because they perceive situations as being hopeless.

Cognitive (or traditional) intelligence carries a profound influence in decision making effectiveness. Today psychologists recognize other types of intelligence also, such as being imaginative and adapting well to the environment, or having practical intelligence. In general, intelligent and well-educated people are more likely to identify problems and make sound decisions than those who have less intelligence and education. A notable exception applies, however. Some intelligent, well-educated people have such a fondness for collecting facts and analyzing them that they suffer from "analysis paralysis." One plant manager put it this way: "I'll never hire a genius

intuition
An experience-based way of knowing or reasoning in which weighing and balancing evidence are done unconsciously and automatically.

decisiveness
The extent to which a person makes up his or her mind promptly and prudently.

again. They dazzle you with facts, figures, and computer graphics. But when they get through with their analysis, they still haven't solved the problem."

As mentioned in relation to evaluating alternatives, critical thinking plays a major role in decision making. As part of cognitive intelligence, the effective decision maker takes time to evaluate a potential decision from all sides. For example, in developing a new business strategy, it is helpful to ask, "Why is this the best way forward? What does market research say about the future of the market?"[13]

It is helpful for you to size up the environment in terms of how much analysis is required before making a decision. It is good to avoid being both impulsive (jumping too quickly to a decision) and indecisive because of over-analysis.

A person will typically make best use of cognitive intelligence when he or she is well rested, or at least not highly fatigued. That is one reason why airlines have strict regulations about the hours of sleep pilots need before flying. An analysis of many studies and theories concluded that executive teams making decisions under chronically shortened sleep or working late at night are likely to solve problems poorly and make inaccurate decisions.[14] During crisis conditions many decisions are unfortunately made with limited sleep.

Emotional Intelligence

How effective you are in managing your feelings and reading other people can affect the quality of your decision making. For example, if you cannot control your anger you are likely to make decisions motivated by retaliation, hostility, and revenge. An example would be shouting and swearing at your team leader because of a work assignment you received. **Emotional intelligence** refers to qualities such as understanding one's own feelings, empathy for others, and the regulation of emotion to enhance living. This type of intelligence generally affects the ability to connect with people and understand their emotions. If you cannot read the emotions of others you are likely to make some bad decisions involving people, such as pushing your boss too hard to grant a request.

emotional intelligence
The ability to connect with people and understand their emotions.

One component of emotional intelligence particularly linked to decision making is self-management, the ability to control one's emotions and act with honesty and integrity in a consistent and adaptable manner.[15] The right degree of self-management helps prevent a person from throwing temper tantrums when activities do not go as planned. Effective workers do not let their occasional bad moods ruin their day. A manager with high self-management would not suddenly decide to fire a group member because of one difference of opinion.

Quality and Accessibility of Information

Reaching an effective decision usually requires high-quality, valid information. The ability to supply managers with high-quality information forms the major justification for information systems. Part of having quality information is being able to base decisions upon solid data. The discussion in Chapter 1 about evidence-based management emphasizes collecting information before making a decision, and the mention of Big Data is also relevant.

A major potential contribution of Big Data to the quality of information is how smart or insightful the data might be.[16] Big Data might be one of the hottest topics in management, but it does not improve the quality of decision making unless it adds valid insights. The decision maker therefore has to sort out kernels of information from data so vast that it will not fit a spreadsheet.

UPS (United Parcel Service) illustrates a company that makes effective use of Big Data. A major Big Data tool is ORION (On-Road Integrated Optimization and Navigation) for optimizing delivery routes. The advanced algorithms of this tool create optimal routes for UPS drivers from the data furnished by customers and drivers. The trucks can alter the routes on the fly based on changing weather conditions or road accidents. Time savings, costs, and emission reductions from the application of ORION are extraordinary. UPS anticipates reducing delivery miles by 100 million annually.[17]

A potential downside of Big Data is that it can lead to information overload and analysis paralysis (mentioned in relation to cognitive intelligence). McKinsey consultants Aaron De Smet and Greg Jost point out that Big Data and analytics might create a belief that decision-making can be entirely rational. In reality, emotion can be helpful in determining what is good and desirable and what is the opposite.[18]

Accessibility may be even more important than quality in determining what information is used or not used. Sometimes it takes so much time and effort to search for quality information that the manager relies on lower-quality information that is close at hand. A frequent accessibility problem is relying on information from the Internet because it is easy to access, without stopping to investigate the date or the source of the information. Quite often the information comes from blogs with content from uninformed writers.

Closely related to quality and accessibility of information is the tendency to be influenced by the first information we receive when attempting to solve a problem or make a decision. **Anchoring** occurs during decision making when the mind gives too much weight to the first information it receives. Initial impressions, estimates, or data hold back, or anchor, later thoughts and judgments.[19] The manager who uses old or inaccurate information found on the Internet may be overly influenced by this information. As the first received, the anchored information becomes the standard against which to judge other information. Anchoring can therefore lead to wasting useful information received after the first information.

anchoring
In the decision making process, placing too much value on the first information received and ignoring later information.

The Application of Artificial Intelligence (AI)

Managerial decision makers often rely on Big Data and its use of artificial intelligence. In the words of technology writer Ted Greenwald, "AI is anything a computer can do that formerly was considered a job for a human."[20] The machine learning aspect of AI means that the program learns from the pattern and associations it detects. Managers are consumers of AI rather than producers in the sense that few managers are expected to have the skills to be coders or develop software that provides artificial intelligence. Computer science is the field most directly responsible for the development of AI.

Artificial intelligence can have a major impact on decision making because it provides additional data for making many types of decisions. Examples include deciding on advertising appeal or selecting among hundreds of job candidates. A variety of companies have reported that the algorithms produced by AI make them more efficient and give employees increased opportunities to perform new types of work. The same software has taken on managing tasks such as scheduling and guiding strategic projects. Here are three specific examples of the managerial application of artificial intelligence in making business decisions[21]:

- The national real-estate firm Keller Williams enables individual realtors to work more efficiently and effectively on their own by giving home buyers the opportunity to automatically search listing photos for specific features such as "bay windows."

- The financial services major player HSBC uses AI to detect fraud rapidly by screening vast amounts of customer data against publicly available data in the search for suspicious activity.

- Amazon.com uses algorithms to help decide which size box to use and how many items can be packed together to decrease both shipping costs and the amount of cardboard entering into recycling.

Artificial intelligence is spreading so rapidly that it might already be considered an everyday technology, but it has not replaced the role of judgment in management decision making. The manager or corporate professional still has to decide which data are useful. For example, an HR specialist might use AI to identify the ideal candidate for the company's chief diversity officer vacant position. Yet members of the management team should decide for themselves on such vital factors as how well they would enjoy working with the candidate and whether he or she would be a good fit for the company culture.

Political Considerations

Under ideal circumstances, managers make organizational decisions on the basis of the objective merits of competing alternatives. In reality, many decisions are based on political considerations, such as favoritism, alliances, or the desire of the decision maker to stay in favor with people who wield power.

Political factors sometimes influence which data are given serious consideration in evaluating alternatives. The decision maker may select data that support the position of an influential person whom he or she is trying to please. For instance, one financial analyst, asked to investigate the cost-effectiveness of owning versus leasing the corporate headquarters. She knew that the CEO thought the firm would be better off selling the building and leasing it from the new owner, thereby giving the firm more cash on hand. The analyst then gathered facts that supported a company leasing rather than owning a building, thereby pleasing the CEO.

The *status quo* trap ties decisions to political factors. Failure to challenge the status quo often stems from worry that being critical will invite criticism from key people. Breaking away from the status quo requires action, and when we take action, we take responsibility, thus opening ourselves up to criticism.[22] A barrier many sales representatives face in selling against a dominant product in the industry results from managers' fear of being criticized if the new product fails. As one system administrator said, "You can never get fired for buying Cisco." (The implication is that if the manager bought Internet equipment from a smaller competitor, he would risk being reprimanded.)

A person with professional integrity arrives at what he or she thinks is the best decision and then makes a diligent attempt to convince management of the objective merits of that solution. The person with integrity is aware of not alienating people in power yet supports what he or she thinks is the best decision.

Degree of Certainty

The more certain a decision maker is of the outcome of a decision, the more calmly and confidently the person will make the decision. Degree of certainty is divided into three categories: certainty, risk, and uncertainty. A condition of certainty exists when the facts are well known, and the outcome can be predicted accurately. A retail store manager may predict with certainty that more hours of operation will lead to more sales.

A condition of risk exists when a decision must be made based on incomplete, but accurate, factual information. Effective managers often accept a condition of risk. A calculated risk is where the potential return is well worth the cost that will be incurred if the effort fails. Tesla's expansion into manufacturing batteries that are sold to other automobile manufacturers, homeowners, commercial properties, and utilities represents a prudent risk. Uncertainty occurs when the decision outcomes are unknown.

Crisis, Conflict, and Stress

In a crisis, many decision makers panic. They become less rational and more emotional than they would in a calm environment. Decision makers who are adversely affected by crisis perceive it to be a stressful event. As a consequence, they concentrate poorly, use poor judgment, and think impulsively. Under crisis, some managers do not bother dealing with differences of opinion because they are under so much pressure. A smaller number of managers perceive a crisis as an exciting challenge that energizes them toward their best level of problem solving and decision making.

A recommendation for becoming more adept at making decisions under crisis conditions is to anticipate crises. Visualize ahead of time how you will react to the situation. Visualization serves somewhat as a rehearsal for the real event. A hospital administrator might think to herself, "Here is what I would do if a patient dies during routine surgery, and the media grab hold of the story."

Conflict relates to crisis because both can be emotional experiences. When conflict is not overwhelming, and is directed at real issues, not personalities, it can be an asset to decision making. By virtue of opposing sides expressing different points of view, problems can be resolved more thoroughly, which leads to better decisions. Conflict is also a major source of stress, so the decision maker facing conflict may also have to deal with his or her stress. The problem is that heavy stress can impair decision making. (Dealing with stress is covered in Chapter 16.)

Values of the Decision Maker

Ultimately, all decisions are based on values. A manager who places a high value on the personal welfare of employees tries to avoid alternatives that create hardship for workers and implements decisions in ways that lessen turmoil. Another value that significantly influences decision making is the pursuit of excellence. A manager who embraces the pursuit of excellence will search for the high-quality alternative solution.

Attempting to preserve the status quo mentioned above as a political factor is also a value. If you value the status quo too highly, you may fail to make a decision that could bring about major improvements. For example, a supermarket executive might not want to bother shifting most of the company's marketing efforts to social media. As a result, other supermarkets who have a strong presence on Facebook and comparable websites gain a few percentage points in market share.

Procrastination

procrastinate
To delay taking action without a valid reason.

Many people are poor decision makers because they **procrastinate**, or delay taking action without a valid reason. Procrastination results in indecisiveness and inaction and is a major cause of self-defeating behavior. Procrastination is a deeply ingrained behavior pattern and may be based on such factors as being concerned about being judged as poorly. For example, if the oil company manager delays making a decision about drilling, he or she cannot be accused of having wasted resources on an oil source of limited value.

Although too much procrastination may interfere with effective decision making, rapid decision making is not always the most effective. When too much emphasis is placed on speed, financial data become less reliable, customer service might be compromised, and productivity suffers. Furthermore, critical information may not be shared, alternative solutions are dismissed too readily, and risks are ignored. Good decision makers recognize the balance between procrastination and impulsiveness. We will return to the problem of procrastination in Chapter 16.

Decision-Making Styles

The various factors that influence the quality of decision making also contribute to a manager's typical pattern of making decisions, or **decision-making style**. For example, a manager who relies heavily on intuition will tend to make decisions quickly without agonizing over data. And a manager with procrastination tendencies will ponder over as much information as possible and consult many people before reaching a decision. You may refer to these opposite tendencies as being impulsive versus reflective. Most analyses of decision-making styles incorporate these two dimensions. Kenneth R. Brousseau, the CEO of Decision Dynamics, and his colleagues have studied executive decision-making styles, using a database of 120,000 people.

According to the Decision Dynamic research, decision styles differ in two fundamental ways: how information is used, and how options are created. In terms of information, some managers want to pore over reams of information before making a decision. The opposite approach is to come to a decision as soon as enough information is available. In terms of creating options, single-focus decision makers are committed to taking one course of action. In contrast, their multi-focused counterparts generate lists of possible options and may pursue multiple courses.[23]

John Flint, the former CEO of HSBC Holdings PLC, illustrates the problem of being too reflective in making decisions. He was dismissed in part because of his pondering over alternatives to decisions without taking decisive action. According to observers, when Flint was faced with a problem, he spent time considering it and would jot down potential actions on a piece of paper.[24] Although this approach may be sound, Flint did not act quickly enough on a potential solution to a problem to suit the HSBC board.

A key suggestion in relation to decision-making styles is to be aware that they exist. Next, reflect on your style, including receiving feedback from others. You may recognize, for example, that you tend to collect too much data before making a decision. You are much like the potential homebuyer who collects so much information before making a purchase offer that the property is sold to someone else.

decision-making style
A manager's typical pattern of making decisions.

GROUP PROBLEM SOLVING AND DECISION MAKING

We have described how individuals go about solving problems and making decisions. Yet because so much emphasis has been placed on teams in organizations and participative decision making, an increasing number of decisions are made by groups rather than individuals. **Group decisions** result when several people contribute to a final decision. Group decision making is often used in complex and important situations, such as developing a new product or producing a list of the employees with the best potential for promotion. We will examine the advantages and disadvantages of

LEARNING OBJECTIVE 3

Appreciate the value and potential limitations of group decision making.

group decision
The process of several people contributing to a final decision.

group decision making, describe when it is useful, and present a specific group decision making technique.

Advantages and Disadvantages of Group Decision Making

Group decision making offers several advantages over the same activity carried out individually. First, the quality of the decision may be higher because of the combined wisdom of group members. Integrating the perspectives of the group members increases the chances that one of the group's ideas will be a radical, breakthrough creative product.[25] The idea is that by combining and synthesizing the best thinking of each group member, an exceptional idea can emerge. The mixture of good ideas leads to a result that is bigger than the sum of the parts. A product developer at the LEGO Group, for example, might consider asking ten people to dream up another version of the basic product. The combined best thinking of group members could result in yet another version of Lego that is a winner with children and adults.

A second benefit is a by-product of the first. Group members evaluate each other's thinking, so that major errors are likely to be avoided. The marketing vice president of a company that sells small appliances such as microwave ovens, toasters and coffee pots decided the company should sell online directly to consumers. Before asking others to begin implementing the decision, the executive brought up the matter for group discussion. A sales manager in the group pointed out that direct selling would enrage their dealers and damage the vast majority of their sales. The marketing vice president then decided she would back off on direct marketing until a new product was developed that would not be sold through dealers. The dealers, however, would be free to sell the products online.

Third, group decision making is helpful in gaining acceptance and commitment. People who participate in making a decision will often be more committed to the implementation than if they were not consulted. Fourth, groups can help people overcome blocks in their thinking, leading to more creative solutions to problems.

Group decision making also has some notable disadvantages. The group approach consumes considerable time and may result in compromises that do not really solve the problem. An intelligent individual may have the best solution to the problem and relying on his or her judgment could save time.

groupthink
A psychological drive for consensus at any cost.

Flawed decisions have generally been attributed to **groupthink**, a psychological drive for consensus at any cost. Groupthink makes group members lose their ability to evaluate bad ideas critically. Glen Whyte believes that many instances of groupthink are caused by decision makers who see themselves as choosing between inevitable losses. The group believes that a sure loss will occur unless action is taken. Caught up in the turmoil of trying to make the best of a bad situation, the group takes a bigger risk than any individual member would.[26] Some of the groups of financial executives who sell securities based on subprime mortgages and credit card loans may think that without a hot new financial product on the market, their investment banks would lose out on profits. Furthermore, the executives would lose out on generous bonuses. As a consequence, high risk investments are sometimes sold to the public.

The negative aspects of groupthink can often be avoided if the team leader encourages group members to express doubts and criticisms of proposed solutions. It is helpful to show by example that you are willing to accept criticism. It is also important for someone to play the role of the devil's advocate. This person challenges the thinking of others by asking such questions as, "Why do you think so many employees, investors, and regulators are so stupid they will not find out that we virtually stole billions from the corporation with our wacky schemes?"

Because group decision making takes more time and people than individual decision making, it should not be used indiscriminately. Group decision making should be reserved for complex decisions of reasonable importance. Too many managers use the group method for solving such minor questions as "What should be on the menu at the company picnic?"

A Specific Method of Group Problem Solving: The Nominal Group Technique

A manager who must make a decision about an important issue sometimes needs to know what alternatives are available and how people would react to them. Another important consideration is for the group to reach consensus. An approach called the **nominal group technique (NGT)** has been developed to fit this situation. The term *nominal* means that, for much of the activity, the participants are a group in name only; they do not interact. A version of the steps in the nominal group technique used by the Centers for Disease Control of the U.S. Department of Health and Human Services, proceeds as follows:

nominal group technique (NGT)
A group decision making technique that follows a highly structured format.

1   *Generating Ideas:* The moderator presents the question or problem to the group in written form and reads the question to the group. The moderator directs everyone to write ideas in brief phrases or statements and to work silently and independently. Each person silently generates ideas and writes them down.

2   *Recording Ideas:* Group members engage in a round-robin feedback session to concisely record each idea, without discussion or debate at this point. The moderator writes an idea from a group member on a flip chart, or a digitized equivalent, that is visible to the entire group. He or she proceeds to ask for another idea from the next group member, and so on. There is no need to repeat ideas; however, if group members believe that an idea provides a different emphasis or variation, it can be included. The moderator proceeds until all members' ideas have been documented.

3   *Discussing Ideas:* Each recorded idea is then discussed to determine clarity and importance. For each idea the moderator asks, "Are there any questions or comments group members would like to make about the item?" This step provides an opportunity for members to express their understanding of the logic and the relative importance of the item. The creator of the idea need not feel obliged to clarify or explain the item. Any member of the group can play that role.

4   *Voting on Ideas:* Group members vote privately to prioritize the idea. The votes are tallied to identify the ideas that are rated highest by the group as a whole. The moderator establishes what criteria are used to prioritize the ideas. To start, each group member selects the five most important or valuable ideas from the group list and writes one idea on each index card. Next, each member ranks the five ideas selected, with the most important or valuable receiving a rank of 5, and the least important or valuable receiving a rank of 1.

5   *Selecting the Highest-Ranking Alternative:* After members rank their responses in order of priority, the moderator creates a tally sheet on a flip chart, or computerized equivalent, with numbers down the left-hand side of the chart,

which correspond to the ideas from the round robin. The moderator collects all the cards from the participants and asks one group member to read the idea number and total points allocated to each one while the moderator records and then adds the scores on the tally sheet. The ideas that are the most highly rated by the group are the most favored actions or ideas in response to the question posed or problem presented by the moderator.[27]

The NGT has met with acceptance because it results in a disciplined decision. An advantage of this technique is that it combines the merits of individual reflection with the scrutiny of collective thought. Also, the NGT helps introverted people become actively involved in group activity.

The accompanying *Management in Action* insert illustrates the voting and tallying aspects of the nominal group technique.

Up to this point, we have explored how decisions are made and characteristics that influence the decision-making situation; we have also studied group decision making. Next, we study in depth the aspect of decision making that moves organizations forward and helps them stay competitive.

MANAGEMENT IN ACTION

Pleasant Valley Heating, Ventilation, and Air Conditioning (HVAC) Uses the Nominal Group Technique

Based on an outstanding year, Pleasant Valley HVAC has $75,000 available to invest in a constructive purpose. Founder and CEO Larry brings the group together to decide what to do with the funds. Larry had used the NGT previously when he was a project manager at a large commercial HVAC company. He was impressed with the fact that the method tends to reduce bickering about reaching a decision. Each member of the group presented a preferred alternative, followed by some explanation and discussion.

Larry presented the five alternatives chosen by the group as follows: (1) Build a rooftop garden for the warehouse and garage; (2) paint and refurbish the office and reception area; (3) donate the funds to a shelter for homeless families in the city; (4) purchase two new pickup trucks; and (5) build a new locker room for the HVAC workers. The alternatives were presented in an e-mail attachment, and voting was as shown in the worksheet below. Table 1 lists the alternatives, the rankings of 1 to 5 made by the top-management team, and the tallying of the ranks.

Alternative C was ranked highest: donate the funds to a shelter for homeless families in the city. After the decision was reached, Marcy and Laurie clapped, and each of the other four managers said that they were pleased with the decision. Larry concluded, "We had five good alternatives. As a company that improves living conditions, we will be proud of our effort to help build new lives."

Table 1: Alternatives Chosen by Group Members

A. Build a rooftop garden for the warehouse and garage.
B. Paint and refurbish the office and reception area.
C. Donate the funds to a shelter for homeless families in the city.
D. Purchase two new pickup trucks.
E. Build a new locker room for the HVAC workers.

Nominal Group Worksheet: Ranks (5 is highest) by Members and Tallying

Choice	Luke	Maria	Ron	Janine	Tom	Lauren	Sum of Ranks
A	2	4	3	5	2	2	18
B	1	2	5	2	5	4	19
C	3	5	4	4	3	5	24
D	5	1	2	3	1	1	13
E	4	3	1	1	4	3	16
Row and Column Sums	15	15	15	15	15	15	90

Questions

1 **To what extent do you think Pleasant Valley made effective use of the nominal group technique?**

2 **Would a better decision have been for Larry to divide the $75,000 equally among the five alternatives just to please all group members?**

3 **Was Larry abdicating his management and leadership responsibilities by using the NGT instead of making the decision by himself?**

CREATIVITY AND INNOVATION IN MANAGERIAL WORK

Creativity is an essential part of problem solving and decision making. To be creative is to see new relationships and produce imaginative solutions. **Creativity** is the process of developing novel ideas that can be put into action. By emphasizing the application of ideas, creativity is closely linked to innovation. To be innovative, a person must produce a new product, service, process or procedure. Innovation can also be regarded as the commercialization or implementation of creative ideas. Another key characteristic of an innovation is that it must depart significantly from a prior product, service, or production process.[28] By this strict criterion of innovation, the product "LEGOs for Girls" might be successful and useful but not innovative because it does not depart significantly from traditional LEGOs. Also, many people regard food trucks as innovative, but people have been selling hot dogs from pushcarts for probably 130 years.

An aspect of innovation that has permeated through society is **disruptive innovation**. The term refers to the way a new product or service transforms an existing market by bringing new simplicity, convenience, and affordability. The late Harvard Business School professor Clayton M. Christensen coined the term *disruptive innovation* in his book *The Innovator's Dilemma*. In its original meaning, *disruption* refers to a process whereby a smaller company with fewer resources can successfully challenge established business enterprises.[29] Famous disruptions include PCs decreasing the demand for mainframe computers, mobile phones decreasing the demand for landline phones and small computers, and home-sharing services decreasing the demand for traditional hotels. A less publicized disruption is sports clothing manufacturers selling directly to consumers, decreasing the demand for retail stores selling their clothing lines. A disruptive technology sometimes results in a free product or service. As a result, a company that charges for the service that is now available for free may lose considerable revenue. One example of such a disruption is a mobile app that functions as a GPS for a vehicle, making it difficult to now sell the GPS device.

Disruptive technology is supposed to develop a new market that replaces the old one; but that rarely happens. We therefore use the term *decreased demand*, because disruptive technologies usually do not totally eliminate the demand for a product; for example, vinyl records still have a market niche, and PCs still are essential for most organizations including small businesses.

Managers play a key role in today's innovation-driven economy because finding ways to generate powerful ideas is an urgent managerial priority.[30] Leaders both generate these ideas themselves and encourage idea-generation among subordinates. (Some of these methods will be described in the following pages.)

Our discussion of managerial creativity focuses on the creative personality, the necessary conditions for creativity, the creative and innovative organization, creativity programs, and suggestions for becoming more creative.

The Creative Personality

Creative people tend to be more emotionally open and flexible than their less-creative counterparts. People who rarely exhibit creative behavior suffer from "hardening of the categories" and cannot overcome the traditional way of looking at things. The cliché is that creative people can "think outside the box," meaning that they get beyond the usual constraints when solving problems. Individuals with a strong need to grow psychologically want to learn new things, stretch themselves, and strive to do better in their jobs.[31] It follows that such workers look around for useful new ideas that can be applied to their jobs. Yet another way of characterizing creative thinkers is that they break the rules—or otherwise disrupt the status quo.

A key part of being creative is to think laterally. **Lateral thinking** spreads out to find many alternative solutions to a problem. **Vertical thinking**, in contrast, is an analytical, logical process that results in few answers. A problem requiring lateral thinking would be to specify a variety of ways in which a small-business owner could increase income. A vertical thinking problem would be to calculate how much more money the small-business owner needs each month to earn a 10 percent profit. Lateral thinking can also be framed as divergent thinking, in which the creative problem solver reaches out to different points of view and ideas from people not directly in his or her field.

Conditions Necessary for Creativity

Certain individual and organizational conditions are necessary for, or at least enhance the production of, creative ideas. The most consistent of these conditions are described here and in the next section about the creative and innovative organization.

Expertise, Creative-Thinking Skills, Internal Motivation, and Curiosity

Creativity researcher Teresa M. Amabile summarized 22 years of research about the conditions necessary for creativity in organizations. Creativity takes place when three components join together: expertise, creative-thinking skills and motivation.[32] Expertise refers to the necessary knowledge to put facts together. The more facts floating around in your head, the more likely you are to combine them in some useful way.

A relevant example is entrepreneur Neil Dipaola, the founder and CEO of Auto-camp. He observed that "Not much has changed in the camping industry since the beginning of time." His pioneering hotel company hosts travelers in stylish aluminum Airstream travel trailers in attractive camping areas such as Santa Barbara, California. AutoCamp locations include a luxurious clubhouse and a communal fire pit. Dipaola says it costs 30-40 percent less to construct an AutoCamp than a traditional hotel, and that rooms are easy to set up and move.[33] To launch and maintain his creative business Dipaola had to have a lot of facts in is head a lot about camping, trailer construction, and the hotel business.

If you know how to keep digging for alternatives, and to avoid getting stuck in the status quo, your chances of being creative multiply. Persevering, or sticking with a problem to a conclusion, is essential for finding creative solutions. A few rest breaks to gain a fresh perspective may be helpful, but the creative person keeps coming back until a solution emerges.

The right type of motivation is the third essential ingredient for creative thought. A fascination with, or passion for, the task is more important than searching for external rewards. People will be the most creative when they are motivated primarily by the satisfaction and challenge of the work itself. The ultimate involvement in work is referred to as the **flow experience**, a condition of heightened focus, productivity, and happiness. You are experiencing flow when you are "in the zone."

A fourth notable internal factor associated with creativity is curiosity. The entrepreneur just described must have been curious about the camping industry. A group of artisans selling goods through an e-commerce website were asked several

lateral thinking
A thinking process that spreads out to find many alternative solutions to a problem.

vertical thinking
An analytical, logical process that results in few answers.

flow experience
The ultimate involvement in work or a condition of heightened focus, productivity, and happiness.

questions aimed at measuring their curiosity. The study participant's creativity was then measured by the number of items they created and listed over a two-week period. A one-point increase on the curiosity measure was associated with 34 percent greater creativity.[34]

Environmental Need Plus Conflict and Tension

In addition to the internal conditions that foster creativity, two factors outside the person have a significant effect. An environmental need must stimulate the setting of a goal, which is another way of saying, "Necessity is the mother of invention." A man named David Werner had an "aha moment" when he almost crashed into a motorcyclist who was stopped in front of him behind a van. The cyclist's helmet blended into the van, but a third light on the van alerted Werner to the cyclist. Werner wondered, "Why doesn't a motorcycle have a third light, like a van does?" As a result, Werner formed a company, Third-Eye Design, that makes a wireless brake-and turn signal light mounted on the back of motorcycle helmets. The need here is that the most frequent reason for car-motorcycle crashes is that that car drivers do not see the motorcycle.[35]

An environmental need also stimulates creativity and innovation because with a problem lurking in the back of your mind, you are more likely to have an "aha moment." This means that a problem-solving alternative may pop into your mind while doing an unrelated activity such as cleaning your car or bicycle.

Enough conflict and tension to put people on edge might also foster creativity. A practical way to create this conflict is for people to challenge each other's thinking, such as saying, "Offering construction workers tents as temporary housing won't attract enough of them to come down to this hurricane-ravaged city. Let's try harder for a housing solution."

Encouragement from Others

Another external factor in creativity is encouragement, including a permissive atmosphere that welcomes new ideas. A manager who encourages imaginative and original thinking, and does not punish people for making honest mistakes, is likely to receive creative ideas from employees.

Another aspect of encouragement that enhances creativity is to encourage risk taking. Employees are sometimes hesitant to make creative suggestions for fear of being zapped if their new idea fails when implemented. In contrast, if risk taking is encouraged by informing employees that it is okay to fail, more people will take chances. For people to sustain creative effort, they need to feel that their work matters to the employer. The manager might say, "I love your idea for reducing shipping costs. Keep up the good work." In this way, the employee might be encouraged to take a risk.

The Creative and Innovative Organization

Another perspective on the conditions necessary for creativity is to recognize that certain managerial and organizational practices foster creativity. When thinking about organizational creativity and innovation, recognize that the two concepts apply to services and processes, as well as products. An example of a service innovation is small clinics in discount department stores and pharmacies that treat medical problems. Continuous innovation of processes are also a key part of profitability, such as the extraordinary computer network used by Google, and the inventory management system deployed by Amazon.

Seven categories of activities summarize much of what is known about what managers can do to establish a creative atmosphere, as described below. The combination of all or several of these activities contribute to a culture of innovation, and therefore a community that is willing and able to innovate. Convincing evidence for the importance of the organizational culture comes from a study of 750 publicly held companies across 17 nations. The major finding was that a corporate culture that fosters innovation is the single most important factor in determining if a company will produce radical innovations.[36]

1 *Challenge.* Giving employees the right type and amount of challenge helps provide a creative atmosphere. Employees should be neither bored with the simplicity of the task nor overwhelmed by its difficulty. A good creativity-inducer for a new sales representative might be for the manager to say, "How would you like to go through our ex-customer file, and attempt to bring back 5 percent of them? It would have a great impact on profits."

   A refreshing approach to challenging employees to be creative is to encourage workers that anything is possible, or to dream big. Jenni Hogan, chief media officer at Tagboard, explains, "Creativity is not doing things the way they have been done before. A key to this is simply asking the questions: What is your dream solution?"[37]

2 *Freedom.* To be creative, employees should have the freedom to choose how to accomplish a goal, but not which goal to accomplish. For example, creativity would be encouraged if a manager said to a group member, "I would like to improve our Facebook presence, and I want you to figure out how." A creative result would be less likely if the manager said, "I would like you to improve our service, and this is what I want you to do."

   Although freedom about choosing a goal is important, companies still need to place some constraints on how much time an innovative project can take before it produces tangible results. Google, for example, now terminates some projects if they do not produce useful (and therefore innovative) results within two years.[38]

3 *Resources.* Managers need to allot time and money carefully to enhance creativity. Tight deadlines can get the creative juices flowing, but people still need enough time to let creative ideas swirl around in their heads. Employees also need large enough budgets to purchase the equipment and information necessary to get the job done. It is also important that the budget approval process for funding worthwhile ideas not be overly restrictive.

4 *Rewards and recognition for innovative ideas.* Even if internal motivation is important for innovation, external rewards and recognition are helpful. Borrego Solar Systems in San Diego holds quarterly employee contests promoting original thinking, each with a $500 prize. One contest seeks the best business innovation, which must be carefully documented in terms of the problem the idea solves, as well as its costs, risks, and benefits. The other competition rewards the best "knowledge brief" which encourages employees to share information that can benefit the entire company.[39]

5 *Allocating time for innovative thinking.* Workers need time to think to be creative. Several large information technology companies offer employees time to pursue pet-project programs as a way of enhancing creativity and innovation. At Google, for example, coders and other knowledge workers have "20 percent time" in which they are free to pursue projects they are passionate about.

This policy has led to products such as Google News, Gmail, and AdSense, an advertising engine. Over the years more restrictions have been placed on who gets 20 percent of time to pursue passionate projects, with managers having the authority to approve or disapprove which employees are selected for the thinking time.[40]

6 *Candid feedback.* Encouragement may facilitate creativity, but candid feedback also plays a key role in developing and sustaining a culture of innovation. Harvard Business School professor Gary P. Pisano says that unvarnished candor is essential for innovation because it facilitates the evolvement and improvement of ideas. Providing and accepting frank criticism shows respect, rather than disrespect.[41] An example of candid, yet respectful, feedback would be, "Your idea for using chartreuse labels on our spaghetti sauce certainly would attract attention. Yet my understanding is that most people have a negative physiological reaction when chartreuse is associated with food."

7 *Greater diversity in groups.* Managers can also cultivate creativity by establishing a group of people with diverse backgrounds. Intellectual diversity, in particular, fans the fire of creativity. A variety of perspectives leads to thinking outside the box and challenging existing frames of reference. The best boosts to creativity in groups come from deep-level diversity—personality, values, and abilities.[42] Cultural diversity often results in deep-level diversity. As was mentioned in Chapter 3, forming diverse groups to enhance creative thinking has become standard practice.

Here are two companies that have been successful in fostering creativity and innovation, as designated by Fast Company. The two make use of many of the practices mentioned in the last several pages.[43]

- Warby Parker was the first company to sell fashionable eyeglasses over the Internet and has since added 64 physical boutiques. By designing and manufacturing their own frames and selling directly to consumers (you send in your optical prescription), they are able to charge as little as $95 for a pair of eyeglasses.

- Domino's has been an innovator in pizza delivery for 45 years. Recently, the company has added delivery to park benches, the New Year's Eve celebration in New York, and ball fields.

Organizational Programs for Improving Creativity and Innovation

Another aspect of the creative organization is formal programs or mechanisms for creativity improvement. Four such mechanisms include creativity training, brainstorming, systematically gathering ideas, and appropriate physical surroundings.

Creativity Training

A standard approach to enhancing individual and organizational creativity is to offer creativity training to many workers throughout the organization. Much of creativity training encompasses the ideas already covered in this chapter, such as learning to overcome traditional thinking and engaging in some type of group problem solving activity. A variety of techniques are used to encourage more flexible thinking, such as engaging in child play, and scavenger hunts. An extreme technique is to deprive

LEARNING OBJECTIVE 5

Describe organizational programs for improving creativity and innovation.

participants of food and rest for 24 hours, so their defenses are weakened, and they are then mentally equipped to "think differently." Other creativity-training techniques are more cerebral, such as having participants solve puzzles and ask "what if" questions.

Brainstorming

brainstorming

A group method of solving problems, gathering information, and stimulating creative thinking. The basic technique is to generate numerous ideas through unrestrained and spontaneous participation by group members.

The best-known method of improving creativity, as well as working on real problems, is **brainstorming**. This technique is a method of problem solving carried out by a group. Brainstorming is standard practice for solving real problems facing a company and is also a creativity-training technique. Group members spontaneously generate numerous solutions to a problem, without being discouraged or controlled. Alex Osborn, the founder of modern brainstorming, believed that one of the main blocks to organizational creativity was the premature evaluation of ideas. The presence of a trained facilitator greatly enhances the productivity of brainstorming meetings.[44]

Brainstorming produces many ideas, but it is not a technique for working out details during the first meeting. Some types of business problems are well suited to brainstorming, such as coming up with a name for a new sports car, identifying ways to attract new customers, and making cost-cutting suggestions. People typically use brainstorming when looking for tentative solutions to non-technical problems; yet the technique is also used to improve software and systems.

By brainstorming, people improve their ability to think creatively. To achieve the potential advantages of brainstorming, the session must be conducted properly. Figure 5-3 presents rules for conducting a brainstorming session, yet the technique continues to evolve. Another suggestion is to allow natural light into the brainstorming workspace. A sterile, windowless room may not be conducive to idea generation.

Figure 5-3 for Conducting a Brainstorming Session

Rule 1   Enroll five to eight participants. If you have too few people, you lose the flood of ideas; if you have too many, members feel that their ideas are not important, or too much chatter may result. Set a meeting limit of about 60 minutes because creativity tends to come in intense bursts, and these bursts are mentally draining.

Rule 2   Give everybody the opportunity to generate alternative solutions to the problem. Have them call out these alternatives spontaneously. Encouraging members to prepare for the meeting will often help participation. One useful modification of this procedure is for people to express their ideas one after another, to decrease possible confusion.

Rule 3   Do not criticize ideas when they are first introduced or show value judgments during the brainstorming session. Make all suggestions welcome Above all, members should not laugh derisively or make sarcastic comments about other people ideas. Constructive criticism may work well when ideas are being edited and refined.

Rule 4   Encourage freewheeling. Welcome bizarre ideas. It is easier to tone down an idea than it is to think one up.

Rule 5   Strive for quantity rather than quality. The probability of discovering really good ideas increases in proportion to the number of ideas generated.

Rule 6   Encourage members to piggyback, or build, on the ideas of others.

Rule 7   The facilitator should record each idea or audio-record the session. Disallow participants from taking notes on a computer or smartphone rather than actively participating. Written notes should not identify the author of an idea because participants may worry about saying something foolish.

Rule 8   After the brainstorming session, edit and refine the list of ideas and choose one or two for implementation.

Source: Parts of rules 1 and 8 are from "Finding Inspiration in a Group," *Business 2.0*, April 2005, p. 110.

Criticizing the ideas of others has also become more acceptable as a brainstorming refinement.

An advantage of brainstorming is that it encourages collaboration and building on the ideas of each other. Liz Matthews, the chief food and beverage innovation officer at Taco Bell, puts it his way, "Creativity is about exploring, collaborating and pushing your boundaries of comfort. That doesn't happen at your desk alone."[45]

Brainstorming can also be conducted through e-mail and other online collaboration tools, generally referred to as electronic brainstorming. The online collaboration tool might include video, audio, file sharing, and sketch pads. In brainstorming by e-mail, group members simultaneously enter their suggestions into a computer. The ideas are distributed to the screens of other group members. Or ideas can be sent back at different times to a facilitator who passes the contributions along to other members. In either approach, although group members do not talk to each other, they are still able to build on each other's ideas and combine ideas.

Systematically Gathering Ideas

A powerful approach to developing an innovative organization is to systematically gather ideas from people inside and outside the firm. Gathering ideas is essential because it takes a lot of ideas to find a good one. As Thomas Alva Edison said, "I have not failed; I've just found 10,000 ways that won't work." An intra-company technique is to set quotas for employee suggestions, including the demand that employees bring a useful idea to a meeting. Being creative therefore becomes a concrete work goal. The oldest approach to systematically gathering ideas is the humble suggestion box in which employees insert ideas on paper into a box and are often given cash awards for useful ideas. The modern era's equivalent to wooden boxes are online systems for offering suggestions. Quite often the suggestions gathered have to do with human resources management, but many product and process ideas emerge also. Energy-saving suggestions often show up in suggestion systems.

Appropriate Physical Surroundings

Creativity is facilitated when the physical environment allows for the flow of ideas, including a room with natural light as previously mentioned. Physical spaces for innovation should be designed that encourage informal conversations. Break rooms are useful, and so are atriums. The presence of whiteboards throughout the corridors encourages the sudden exchange of complicated ideas that benefit from a diagram. Open work areas that allow for desks turning toward each other also facilitate the exchange of idea though conversation.

Despite the merits of physical spaces for idea sharing, many workers need private space to do their best creative thinking. After developing a creative idea, the person might want to refine the idea by interacting with others. Yet the time for independent thinking, away from the buzz and interruptions of the office, is important. Many companies make sure that employees required to do creative work have access to private space, as well as the opportunity for group interaction. Recent research suggests that with open-office plans, workers don't necessarily interact more, or they interact in unproductive ways. Among the unproductive ways of interacting is to avoid eye contact, or become so engrossed in their tasks that they are selectively deaf.[46]

As has been described, creativity and innovation are highly valued in most organizations. Yet, a caution is in order. A company has to focus on the most important creative ideas and not attempt every good idea. Too many products and services at the same time can lead to more complexity than the company can manage. The company needs to optimize revenues and profits by focusing on the most promising new offerings.[47] Yet if creativity and innovation are ignored, a company will not have promising new offerings like the typewriter (a huge innovation in its time), personal computer, GPS, and smartphone upon which to concentrate.

Self-Help Techniques for Improving Creativity

In addition to participating in organizational programs for creativity improvement, you can help yourself become more creative. Becoming a more creative problem solver and decision maker requires that you increase the flexibility of your thinking. Reading about creativity improvement or attending one or two brainstorming sessions is insufficient. You must also practice the methods described in the following sections. As with any serious effort at self-improvement, you must exercise the self-discipline to implement these suggestions regularly. Creative people must also be self-disciplined to carefully concentrate on going beyond the obvious in solving problems.

Six Specific Creativity-Building Suggestions

To develop habits of creative thinking, you must regularly practice the time-proven suggestions described in the list that follows.[48]

1 Keep track of your original ideas by maintaining an idea notebook, computer file, or phone app. Few people have such uncluttered minds that they can recall all their past flashes of insight when they need them.

2 Stay current in your field and be curious about your environment. Having current facts at hand gives you the raw material to link information creatively. (In practice, creativity usually takes the form of associating ideas that are not associated, such as associating the idea of selling movie tickets with the idea of selling through vending machines.) The person who routinely questions how things work (or why they do not work) is most likely to have an idea for improvement.

3 Improve your sense of humor, including your ability to laugh at your own mistakes. Humor helps reduce stress and tension, and you will be more creative when you are relaxed.

4 Adopt a risk-taking attitude when you try to find creative solutions. You will inevitably fail a few times. A key aphorism about creativity is that it is a "numbers game."

5 Identify which times of day or the week when you are most creative and attempt to accomplish most of your creative work during that period. Most people are at their peak of creative productivity after ample rest, and so try to work on your most vexing problems at the start of the workday. Schedule routine decision making and paperwork for times when your energy level is lower than average.

6 When faced with a creativity block, step back from the problem and engage in a less mentally demanding task for a brief pause, or even a day. Sometimes by doing something quite different, your perspective will become clearer and a creative alternative will flash into your head when you return to your problem. Although creative problem solvers are persistent, they will sometimes put a problem away for a while so they can come back stronger. The solution will eventually emerge, as an "aha" experience.

Play the Roles of Explorer, Artist, Judge, and Lawyer

One method for improving creativity incorporates many of the suggestions discussed so far. It requires you to adopt four roles in your thinking. First, you must be an *explorer*. Speak to people in different fields to get ideas you can use. Second, be an *artist* by stretching your imagination. Strive to spend about 5 percent of your day asking "what if?" questions. For example, an executive in a swimsuit company might ask, "What if the surgeon general decides that since sunbathing causes skin cancer, we have to put warning labels on bathing suits?" Third, know when to be a *judge*. After developing some wild ideas, evaluate them. Fourth, achieve results with your creative thinking by playing the role of a *lawyer*. Negotiate and find ways to implement your ideas within your field or place of work. You may spend months or years getting your best ideas implemented.[49] One the biggest hurdles in bringing about innovation in an organization is to obtain funding for your brainchild.

Engage in Appropriate Physical Exercise

A well-accepted method of stimulating creativity is to engage in physical exercise. Stephen Ramocki, a marketing professor at Rhode Island College, found that a single aerobic workout is sufficient to trigger the brains of students into high gear—and that the benefit lasted for a minimum of two hours. One explanation of why exercise facilitates creativity is that exercising pumps more blood and oxygen into the brain. Exercise also enhances activity in the frontal lobe, the region of the brain involved in abstract reasoning and attention.[50]

The fact that physical exercise can boost creative thinking should not be interpreted in isolation. Without other factors going for the manager, such as a storehouse of knowledge and passion for the task, physical exercise will not lead to creative breakthroughs.

Solicit Feedback on Your Performance

Another effective way of enhancing creativity on the job is to seek feedback on your performance from both your manager and your co-workers. Even if you are not asking for feedback on creative suggestions exclusively, the feedback process is likely to sharpen your imagination. An example of a feedback-seeking question would be "What did you think of my suggestion for reducing energy costs by encouraging employees to bring sweaters to the office?" The feedback refines your thinking, helping you develop ideas that others perceive to be imaginative.

A study demonstrating the link between feedback seeking and job creativity was conducted with 456 supervisor–employee pairs in four management consulting firms. Employees who asked for feedback directly and looked around for indirect feedback tended to be rated more highly on displaying creativity.[51] Examples of indirect feedback would be seeing positive mention of your performance in an e-mail or hearing a spontaneous comment about your work during a meeting.

1 Explain the steps involved in making a complex decision.

The recommended steps for solving problems and making complex decisions call for a problem solver to identify and diagnose the problem, develop alternative solutions, evaluate the alternatives, choose an alternative, implement the decision, evaluate and control and repeat the process if necessary.

2 Understand the key influences on decision making in organizations.

Bounds (or limits) to rationality are present in decision making. Partly because of these limits, people often make use of heuristics. People vary in their decision-making ability, and the situation may influence the quality of decisions. Factors that influence the quality of decisions are intuition; personality and cognitive intelligence; emotional intelligence; quality and accessibility of information; artificial intelligence; political considerations; degree of certainty; crisis, conflict, and stress; values of the decision maker; and procrastination. Decision-making style focuses on a combination of how information is used and how options are created. The two options are single-focused, and multi-focused.

3 Appreciate the value and potential limitations of group decision making.

Group decision making often results in high-quality solutions, because many people contribute. It also helps people feel more committed to the decision. However, the group approach consumes considerable time, may result in compromise solutions that do not really solve the problem, and may encourage groupthink. This occurs when consensus becomes so important that group members lose their ability to evaluate ideas. It is likely to occur when decision makers have to choose between inevitable losses. Group decision making should be reserved for complex decisions of reasonable importance.

The nominal group technique (NGT) is recommended for a situation in which a manager who wants consensus needs to know what alternatives are available and how people will react to them. Using the technique, a small group of people contribute written thoughts about the problem. Other members respond to their ideas later. Members rate each other's ideas numerically, and the final group decision is the value of the pooled individual votes.

4 Understand the nature of creativity and how it contributes to managerial work.

Creativity is the process of developing novel ideas that can be put into action. Creative people are generally more open and flexible than their less-creative counterparts, and they are willing to break the rules. They are also better able to think laterally.

Creativity takes place when three components join together: expertise, creative-thinking skills, internal motivation, and curiosity. Perseverance in digging for a solution is also important, and so is an environmental need that stimulates the setting of a goal. Conflict and tension can also prompt people toward creativity. Encouragement contributes to creativity.

Certain managerial and organizational practices foster creativity and innovation. To establish a creative atmosphere, managers can: (a) provide the right amount of job challenge; (b) give freedom on how to reach goals; (c) provide the right resources; (e) give rewards and recognition for creative ideas; (e) allocate time for innovative thinking; (f) provide candid feedback, and (g) promote greater diversity in groups, especially deep-level diversity.

5 Describe organizational programs for improving creativity and innovation.

One organizational program for improving creativity is to conduct creativity training. Brainstorming is the best-known method of improving creativity. The method can also be conducted by e-mail and online collaboration tools. Systematically gathering ideas inside and outside the company often enhances creativity, as does appropriate physical surroundings.

6 Implement several suggestions for becoming a more creative problem solver.

Self-discipline improves creative thinking ability. Techniques for creativity-building include staying current in your field and being curious about your environment, improving your sense of humor, and having a risk-taking attitude. A broad approach for improving creativity is to assume the roles of an explorer, artist, judge, and lawyer. Each role relates to a different aspect of creative thinking. Engaging in appropriate physical exercise can stimulate the brain to think creatively. Soliciting feedback on your performance can enhance your job creativity.

Key Terms and Phrases

problem 130	anchoring 137	creativity 144
decision 130	procrastinate 139	disruptive innovation 144
heuristics 134	decision-making style 140	lateral thinking 145
intuition 135	group decision 140	vertical thinking 145
decisiveness 135	groupthink 141	flow experience 145
emotional intelligence 136	nominal group technique (NGT) 142	brainstorming 149

Questions

1. Describe a problem the manager of a new restaurant might face, and point to the actual and ideal conditions in relation to this problem.

2. How might the use of Internet search engines help you make better decisions on the job?

3. Assume that the director of a social agency was exploring different alternatives for decreasing the number of homeless people in the area. Describe how a political factor might influence his or her decision making.

4. Describe the general approach a firm of five real-estate developers might take to use the nominal group technique for deciding which property to purchase next.

5. Why should a manager worry about being a creative business thinker, when he or she can hire creative people?

6. To what extent do you think that homes built out of used shipping containers is a creative and innovative idea?

7. It is widely accepted that the generation of creative and innovative ideas is important for the survival of an organization. But what should management do with the bunch of apparently useless ideas it receives?

Skill-Building Exercise 5-A: Helping a Company that Arranges Booking a Hotel by the Minute

A few years ago, a company named Recharge (now called Globe) launched a mobile app that allows fatigued travelers and anyone else in need of a quick shower or nap the opportunity to book a high-end hotel in San Francisco by the minute. The service is now also offered in New York City. The average stay is approximately two hours, and the room costs for less than one dollar to $3 per minute. Some hotels impose a minimum fee, such as $25.

You have been assigned to a team to help Globe think of a way of expanding their market. You might conceptualize your session as brainstorming for the purpose of product development. Top-level management instructs you not to be concerned about coming up with foolish ideas because silly ideas can become the germ of an idea for a breakthrough use of their service. By the end of your brainstorming session, present management with at least five suggestions for new uses (or users) of the Globe app.

Skill-Building Exercise 5-B: Choosing an Effective Domain Name

Using brainstorming, huddle in small groups. Your task is to develop original domain names for several products or services. An effective domain name is typically one that is easy to remember and will capture potential customers in an uncomplicated web search. One reason this exercise is difficult is because "cybersquatters" grab unclaimed names they think business owners might want and then sell these names later. For example, a cybersquatter (a domain name exploiter) might develop or buy the domain name *www.dogfood.com*, hoping that a dog-food company will want this name in the future. The owner of dogfood.com would charge a company like Pet Smart every time a surfer looking to purchase dog food over the Internet entered dogfood.com and was linked to Pet Smart.

After your team has brainstormed a few possible domain names, search the Internet to see if your domain name is already in use. Simply enter "www" plus the name you have chosen into your browser. You may also visit the site of a company like Domain.com or Godaddy.com. After you have developed your list of domain names not already in use, present your findings to the rest of the class.

- Hair salons specializing in bald men
- Replacement parts for antique or classic autos
- A used-car chain
- Yoga salons
- Personal loans for people with poor credit ratings
- Recycled steel for manufacturers
- Choose one of your own

Management Now—Online Skill-Building Exercise: Finding an Innovative Idea for a Product or Service

Imagine yourself as a company CEO, a middle manager, or somebody who wants to launch a business. Your problem is that you do not have an idea for a product or service that appears to be worth pursuing. See what help for identifying innovative ideas for products or services you might find on the Internet. Also, identify a consulting firm that provides ideas for products and services. Another way of looking at this assignment is that you are attempting to discover the feasibility of outsourcing innovation. If you are able to identify a website that can help you identify an innovative idea for a product or service, make a judgment about the credibility of the website.

The Blade Knife Company Seeks a Cutting-Edge Innovation

The Blade Knife company is a medium-size manufacturer of kitchen knives, chef knives, and pocket knives. The carefully-designed knives are made one at a time in a rural community in Portland, Oregon. Each knife is made of stainless steel, and ground to a perfect edge. The higher-end knives have beautifully crafted handles. Sales have been stable for about five years, but Mia, the CEO and founder of the Blade Knife Company is worried. During a Friday afternoon meeting with the management team, Mia said to the group:

"I am so proud of the high quality and beauty of our knives. I am also proud of our management team and our hard-working, highly-skilled employees. But I am worried about the future of Blade Knife. Our product mix is about the same as it was when I founded this company 25 years ago. What do you think is blocking our sales growth? What can we do to innovate our product line?"

Fred (manufacturing vice-president): A major reason our sales are flat is that our products are too high quality and too durable. Some of our customers keep our knives in their kitchen permanently unless they are thrown out accidentally. Even if someone sells a restaurant, our knives are likely to be included in the deal. Maybe we could innovate by making scissors, tweezers, and manicure kits. Or, how about stainless steel beer kegs?

Lola (chief marketing officer): A big problem I face in marketing our knives is that there are lower-priced alternatives available. At the extreme, you can purchase a decent set of three kitchen knives at Dollar General for four dollars. Maybe a gourmet cook, or a chef in an upscale restaurant wouldn't like those knives, but for the average person the inexpensive knives get the job done. We also are underpriced by decent quality knives

made in China, Malaysia, and Vietnam. For now, the only innovation I can think of is diversifying into pots and pans, but I am working on the problem.

Sean (chief financial officer): Our sales are flat because we are in a stable market. A big driver to our revenue is people setting up new households. With population growth being flat, I don't see much growth there. Our financials are good, so I am not too worried about Blade Knife. I would worry about investing a ton of money in innovation that might not pay off.

Melissa (head of administration and HR): I love our products, but I realize that we are not in an expanding industry or a hot market. A great strength I see of our company is our people, at all job levels. Let's unleash the talent of all our employees by asking them to submit creative ideas that could lead to a breakthrough innovation for us. I think we might all be pleasantly surprised by the innovative capacity of our employees.

Mia: We are now in the preliminary stage of developing an innovation that will spur revenue and growth for our company. We have to think big and disrupt what we are doing. We will make innovation a top company priority.

Case Questions

1   What is your evaluation of the suggestions offered for product diversification instead of innovation?

2   Which one of the suggestions offered do you think has the best chance of bringing an innovation to Blade Knife?

3   In what way could Blade Knife possibly come up with a *disruption* for kitchen cutlery?

7-Eleven Wants a Chunk of e-Commerce

A few years ago, management of 7-Eleven, a Tokyo-based company with 68,250 convenience stores in the United States, Canada, and the rest of the world, was worried about online shopping. Although purchasing beer, milk, and candy bars over the Internet might not be practical, 7-Eleven was losing out a little to e-commerce. Many consumers choose to purchase items such as beauty products, razors, and even batteries online. With more purchases online, 7-Eleven would expect fewer sales and less foot traffic in their stores. About two-thirds of the 8,500 7-Eleven stores in the United States and Canada are franchise-owned.

7-Eleven leadership decided to get a slice of online revenue by installing lockers for e-commerce pickups at 200 stores in North America, and the program continues to expand. The company announced that it would hold packages from Amazon, FedEx, UPS, Walmart, and several other retailers in these lockers. The placements are part of its Amazon Hub Lockers program. Amazon also places its lockers in locations such as Whole Foods, Stein Mart, and Sprint Stores, college campuses and apartment buildings. Amazon defines its hub locker as a "secure, self-service kiosk that allows you to pick up your package at a place and time that's convenient for you. No more worrying about packages left at your door while you're out."

Customers who find it inconvenient or not possible to have packages delivered to their doorsteps, can open the lockers by scanning bar codes sent over e-mail to their smartphones.

The lockers are placed against a wall, and each unit consumes about the same amount of space as a large shelf. Both 7-Eleven and the franchise operator receive a small commission from the package delivery service for each unit placed in a locker.

In facing the tradeoff between shelf space and higher foot traffic, 7-Eleven management chose the latter with the installation of more lockers. Company management believes that a larger number of potential customers will increase sales, particularly through impulse purchases. Each square foot in a typical convenience store generates about $600 in annual sales.

Other retailers have experimented with package pickup services in their stores with mixed results. Walgreens and Rite Aid Corp. host lockers, and many parking garages in New York City have lockers placed against the wall near the entrance to the garage.

The head of a household in a medium-size city was asked her opinion about the 7-Eleven locker program. She responded, "A good idea. Package drop-offs at private houses have become a joke. Thieves follow the delivery trucks into our neighborhood and then pick up the packages lying next to the front door. Unless you are home at the time the UPS, FedEx, or USPS truck drops by, you can forget about receiving your package."

Case Questions

1 What problem or problems is the locker program supposed to solve?

2 How would you rate the 7-Eleven program in terms of creativity and innovation?

3 What do you think about the tradeoff between 7-Eleven renting locker space versus having the space available to sell more goods?

4 How big a problem is theft of delivered packages for online retailers? If this is a valid problem, what creative solution can you offer?

Source: Original story created from facts and observations in the following sources: Loretta Chao, "7-Eleven Wants to Be Your Post Office," *The Wall Street Journal*, November 13, 2015, pp. B1, B2; Karl Utermohlen, "7-Eleven Adds More Lockers for E-Commerce Pickups," *www.investorplace.com*, November 12, 2015; "7-Eleven Endorses e-Commerce by Explaining the Number of Online Lockers at its North American Stores," *Island Pump & Tank* (www.islandpumpandtank.com), 2019, p. 1; "Everything You Need to Know about Amazon Hub Locker," *www.amazon.com*, June 21, 2018, pp. 1–2; Dan Berthiaume, "Report: Amazon Seeks Aggressive Locker Expansion," *Chain Store Age* (www.chainstoreage.com), September 17, 2019, p. 12.

ENDNOTES

1. Original story created from facts and observations in the following sources: Keely Chalmers, "Portland Developer Builds Homes from Shipping Containers," *KGW8* (kgw.com), November 6, 2018, pp. 1–2; Erin O'Neil, "The Chic Condos Made from Shipping Containers are Coming to Newark," *NJ.com*, updated January 17, 2019, pp. 1–3; "Condos Made of Shipping Works In Detroit," *www.chicagotribune.com*, May 18, 2015, pp. 1–2.

2. "Decision Making in the Age of Urgency," *McKinsey & Company Quarterly* (www.mckinsey.com), May 2019, p. 2.

3. Thomas Wedell-Wedellsborg, "Are You Solving the Right Problems?" *Harvard Business Review*, January–February 2017, p. 82.

4. Quoted in Dwayne Spradlin, "Are You Solving the Right Problem?" *Harvard Business Review*, September 2012, p. 85.

5. Joshua Quittner, "An Eye on the Future: Jeff Bezos Merely Wants Amazon.com to Be Earth's Biggest Seller of Everything," *Time*, December 27, 1999, p. 57.

6. Shanka Basu and Krishna Savani, "To Make Better Choices, Look at All Your Options Together," *Harvard Business Review*, June 28, 2017, pp. 1–4.

7. Herbert A. Simon, "Rational Choice and the Structure of the Environment," *Psychological Review*, 63 (1956), pp. 129–138.

8. Ben Leubsdorf and David Gauthier-Villars, "Nobel Goes to Economist Richard Thaler," *The Wall Street Journal*, October 7, 2017, p. A2.

9. Carl Bialik, "Number Crushing: When Figures Get Personal," *The Wall Street Journal*, October 28, 2009, p. A19.

10. Erik Dan and Michael G. Pratt, "Exploring Intuition and its Role in Managerial Decision-Making," *Academy of Management Review*, January 2007, pp. 33–35.

11. John D. Stoll, "'Feel then Force': Gut Instinct, Not Data Is the Thing," *The Wall Street Journal*, October 19–20, 2019, p. B4.

12. Interview by Josh Tyrangiel, "Tim Cook's Freshman Year," *Bloomberg Businessweek*, December 10–December 16, 2012, p. 76.

13. Helen Lee Bouygues, "3 Simple Habits to Improve Your Critical Thinking," *Harvard Business Review* (www.harvardbusinessreview.org), May 6, 2019, pp. 1–5.

14. Christopher M. Barnes and John R. Hollenbeck, "Sleep Deprivation and Decision-Making Teams: Burning the Midnight Oil, or Playing with Fire?" *Academy of Management Review*, January 2009, pp. 56–66.

15. Daniel Goleman, Richard Boyatzis, and Annie McKee, "Primal Leadership: The Hidden Driver of Great Performance," *Harvard Business Review*, December 2001, pp. 42–51.

16. From the Editors, "Big Data and Management," *Academy of Management Journal*, April 2014, p. 321.

17. Bernard Marr, "The Brilliant Ways UPS Uses Artificial Intelligence, Machine Learning and Big Data," *Forbes* (www.forbes.com), June 16, 2018, pp. 1–6.

18. Aaron De Smet and Greg Jost, "Keys to Unlocking Great Decision-Making," *www.mckinsey.com*, April 19, 2018, pp. 3–4.

19. John S. Hammond, Ralph L. Keeney, and Howard Raffia, "The Hidden Traps in Decision Making," *Harvard Business Review*, September–October 1998, p. 48.

20. Ted Greenwald, "What Exactly Is Artificial Intelligence, Anyway?" *The Wall Street Journal*, April 30, 2018, p. R2.

21. Andrew Moore, "When AI Becomes an Everyday Technology," *Harvard Business Review*, June 7, 2019, p. Laura Stevens and Erica E. Phillips, "More Amazon Orders, Fewer Boxes," *The Wall Street Journal*, December 21, 2017, p. B3.

22. Hammond, Keeney, and Raffia, "The Hidden Traps," pp. 48–49.

23. Kenneth R. Brousseau, Michael J. Driver, Gary Hourihan, and Rikard Larsson, "The Seasoned Executive's Decision-Making Style," *Harvard Business Review*, February 2006, pp. 110–121.

24. Margot Patrick, "Lack of Action Led to CEO's Ousting," *The Wall Street Journal*, August 8, 2019, p, B2.

25. Sarah Harvey, "Creative Synthesis: Exploring the Process of Extraordinary Group Creativity, *Academy of Management Review*, July 2014, pp. 324–343.

26. Glen Whyte, "Decision Failures: Why They Occur and How to Prevent Them," *Academy of Management Executive*, August 1991, p. 25.

27. Adapted from "Gaining Consensus among Stakeholders through the Nominal Group Technique," *Evaluation Briefs*, No. 17, 2006, Department of Health and Human Services, Centers for Disease Control and Prevention.

28. William McKinley, Scott Latham, and Michael Braun, "Organizational Decline and Innovation: Turnarounds and Downward Spirals," *Academy of Management Review*, January 2014, p. 91.

29. Clayton M. Christensen, The Innovator's Dilemma (Boston: Harvard Business School Press, 1997); Clayton M. Christensen, Michael Raynor, and Rory McDonald, "Disruptive Innovation," *Harvard Business Review*, December 2015, p. 46.

30. Teresa M. Amabile and Mukti Khaire, "Creativity and the Role of the Leader," *Harvard Business Review*, October 2008, p. 100.

31. Christina E. Shalley, Lucy L. Gilson, and Terry C. Blum, "Interactive Effects of Growth – Need Strength, Work Contest, and Job Complexity on Self-Reported Creative Performance," *Academy of Management Journal*, June 2009, pp. 489–505.

32. Teresa M. Amabile, "How to Kill Creativity," *Harvard Business Review*, September–October 1998, pp. 78–79.

33. "For Putting the Boutique Hotel Outdoors," *Fast Company*, Summer 2019, p. 58.

34. "The Business Case for Curiosity," *Harvard Business Review*, September-October 2018, p. 50.

35. Alan Morrell, "Motorcycle Helmets with Signal Lights Designed to Save Lives," *Democrat and Chronicle*, June 30, 2019, p. 3E.

36. Gerard Tellis, Jaideep Prabhu, and Rajesh Chandy, "Radical Innovation Across Nations: The Preeminence of Corporate Culture," *Journal of Marketing*, January 2009, pp. 3–23.

37. Quoted in Matt Villano, "Creative Genius," *Entrepreneur*, April 2015, p. 59.

38. Megan Caponetto and Sam Kaplan. "Where Google Ventures is Pinning Its Hopes," *Fortune*, January 13, 2014, pp. 76–79.

39. Teri Evans, "Entrepreneurs Seek to Elicit Workers' Ideas," *The Wall Street Journal*, p. B7.

40. Ryan Tate, "Google Couldn't Kill 20 Percent Time Even if It Wanted To," *Wired* (www.wired.com), August 20, 2013, pp. 1–12.

41. Gary P. Pisano, "The Hard Truth about Innovative Cultures," *Harvard Business Review*, January–February 2019, p. 68.

42. Tomas Chamorro-Premuzic, "Does Diversity Actually Increase Creativity?" *Harvard Business Review*, June 28, 2017, pp. 3–4.

43. "The World's 50 Most Innovative Companies," *Fast Company*, March/April 2019, p. 41; and March 2015, pp. 66–80.

44. Leigh Thompson, "Improving the Creativity of Organizational Work Groups," *Academy of Management Executive*, February 2003, p. 97.

45. Quoted in Matt Villano, "Creative Genius," *Entrepreneur*, April 2015, p. 60.

46. Ethan Bernstein and Ben Waber, "The Truth about Open Offices," *Harvard Business Review*, November–December 2019, pp. 82–91.

47. Mark Gottfredson and Keith Aspinall, "Innovation Versus Complexity," *Harvard Business Review*, November 2005, pp. 62–71; Robin Hanson, "The Myth of Creativity," *Business Week*, July 3, 2006, p. 134.

48. Eugene Raudsepp, "Exercises for Creative Growth," *Success*, February 1981, pp. 46–47; Mike Vance and Diane Deacon, *Think Out of the Box* (Franklin Lakes, NJ: Career Press, 1995); "What's Your Best Creative Time?" *Executive Leadership*, July 2012, p. 2.

49. "Be a Creative Problem Solver," *Executive Strategies*, June 6, 1989, pp. 1–22

50. Richard A. Lovett, "Jog Your Brain: Looking for a Creative Spark? Hop to the Gym," *Psychology Today*, May/June 2006, p. 55

51. Katleen D. De Stobbeleir, Susan J. Ashford, and Dirk Buyens, "Self-Regulation of Creativity at Work: The Role of Feedback-Seeking in Creative Performance," *Academy of Management Journal*, August 2011, pp. 811–831.

CHAPTER 6

Quantitative Techniques for Problem Solving and Decision Making

OBJECTIVES

After studying this chapter and doing the exercises, you should be able to:

1 Explain how managers use data-based decision making.

2 Explain the use of forecasting techniques in planning.

3 Describe how to use Gantt charts, milestone charts, and PERT planning techniques.

4 Describe how to use break-even analysis and decision trees for problem solving and decision making.

5 Describe how to manage inventory by using the economic order quantity (EOQ) and the just-in-time (JIT) system.

6 Describe how to identify problems using a Pareto diagram.

Michael Ringelsten is the owner and operator of Shorewood Liquidators Inc., a 91-employee business that helps online retailers clean up some of the inventory mess that would otherwise be created by returns. The problem is especially urgent in the first two or three months following Christmas because between 10 to 40 percent of online purchases are returned. Sorting and restocking all the returned merchandise could be an enormous headache for retailers. For example, many purchases made through Amazon.com really come from a third-party vendor, such as a jeweler. A watch sent back to Amazon would then have to be mailed back to the jeweler.

Ringelsten describes Shorewood as a re-processor of store returns. The company helps many online retailers salvage some value on their returned and also closeout inventory. After returned merchandise is sent to Shorewood, it is sold on online auction platforms, and is eventually sold in deep discounters and even flea markets.

Shorewood buys truckloads of returned merchandise, sorts the items into categories, and then resells as much as the company can at bargain-bin prices. Merchandise is also available for auction on the company website, sliBuy.com. Some of the returned merchandise comes about because customers change their minds, receive an unwanted gift, or the merchandise is flawed. Ringelsten says his business is in the "reverse logistics industry" because of the focus on reversing the flow of products.

Some of the returned merchandise does not go back to the original retailer but is collected at centralized return centers run by Shorewood, as well as other logistics companies. A portion of the merchandise is sold at substantial discounts to liquidators and small businesses. Some of the unprocessed returns from retailers are sold in truckloads at a time, at about 10 cents and 20 cents on the dollar. There is strong demand for some categories of merchandise, such as children's toys, sporting goods, housewares, and consumer electronics.

Rebecca Smithers, an industry analyst, said a contributor to the problem of so many returns is that online shopping has built-in drawbacks for certain types of purchases. Not being able to see, touch, or check the item you are buying may lead to disappointment when it arrives at your door or mailbox. Another problem is the same size; "large" is not uniform across all clothing items. Approximately 88 percent of purchases are made in stores, a reality that is probably driven by the interest in trying on clothing, and looking first hand at the quality of merchandise.

Ringelsten says dealing with returned merchandise is a volume game. "If we can make 10 percent profit, we are jumping up and down." Because the profit margin is low, Shorewood employees have to be productive, and sometimes carry out two tasks simultaneously. A former Shorewood floor manager said that he had to help with loading and unloading a fork lift while monitoring employees at the same time.[1]

The story about the "reverse logistics" company illustrates that managing inventory, including getting rid of unwanted inventory, is part of being a successful business. To make planning and decision making about inventory and other matters more accurate, a variety of techniques based on the scientific method, mathematics and statistics have been developed. This chapter will provide sufficient information for you to acquire basic skills in several popular techniques for planning and decision making. You can find more details about these techniques in courses and books about production and operations management and accounting. All these quantitative tools are useful, but they do not supplant human judgment and intuition. For example, a decision-making technique might tell a manager that it will take four months to complete a project. She might say, "Could be, but if I put my very best people on the project, we can beat that estimate."

As you read and work through the various techniques, you will probably recognize that software is available to carry them out. However, before using a computer to run a technique, it is best to understand the technique and try it out manually or with a calculator. Such firsthand knowledge can help you have a more mature understanding of forces affecting the firm. A manager at a restaurant in Italy was asked the exchange rate between the American dollar and the Euro. She said, "I don't have to know. The cash register does the calculation." The problem here is that an up-to-date manager should understand how currency fluctuations might affect the tourism and restaurant industry.

DATA-DRIVEN DECISION MAKING

LEARNING OBJECTIVE 1

Explain how managers use data-based decision making.

data-driven decision making
An attitude and approach to management rather than a specific technique that stems from data-based decision making.

Numbers and facts often influence managerial decision making. **Data-driven decision making** refers to the idea that decisions are based on facts rather than impressions or guesses. In other words, data informs the decision maker. The idea is straightforward. Before making a decision of consequence, the managerial worker should gather facts that could influence the outcome of the decision. Analyzing the facts could lead to discovering a relevant pattern. A construction manager might note, for example, that the least turnover among construction supervisors takes place with supervisors who have two-year degrees in a related field, such as engineering technology. The manager would therefore emphasize recruiting graduates of two-year schools with a degree in a field closely related to construction.

A survey of more than 1,000 senior executives conducted by the consulting firm PwC provides some evidence for the contribution of data-driven decision making. The survey found that highly data-driven organizations are three times more likely to report improvements in decision-making compared to firms that rely less on data.[2] The quantitative techniques described in this chapter assist the process of data-driven management, yet simply gathering relevant facts can make data-driven management possible.

The discussion about using high quality information and Big Data in making decisions (Chapter 5) is part of data-driven management. Also, people who are scientifically oriented use data-driven management quite naturally. Many managers want to see the data before accepting a suggestion from a subordinate. For example, during a video conference, the chief operations officer might say, "We need to increase our entry-level wages for production technicians because our turnover is too high with this group." The data-driven CEO might respond, "Give me the facts on how our entry-level wages compare to the industry. Then we can have a serious discussion."

Data-driven management is more of an attitude and approach rather than a specific technique, and it is hardly new. You attempt to gather relevant facts before making a decision of consequence. Suppose a small business owner wants to repaint the walls inside the office. The office manager suggests buying a premium brand of paint because such paint stays fresher-looking longer and does not chip as readily. The data-driven manager would say, "Where is the evidence that if we have the painter use premium paint the walls will look better longer and resist chipping? Show me the evidence."

Although data-driven management is preferable in most situations, intuition and judgment still contribute to making major decisions. At times relevant data may not be available, so acting on hunches can be essential. A major new source of recruiting for truckers is early retiree couples who enjoy heavy travel. A growing number of American couples aged 50 and over are choosing trucking as a second career. According to the Bureau of Labor Statistics, 203,000 men and women truck drivers in the United States are 65 or older.[3] The American Trucking Association developed a billboard, print and television campaign urging older couples to drive together. A key reason is that putting two drivers in one cab doubles the number of miles driven, thereby making quicker deliveries.[4]

Before actively recruiting older people as potential truckers to help with the acute trucker shortage, several trucking association executives guessed this demographic group might be attracted to trucking. Now trucking managers have some data to work with in terms of recruiting retiree couples as truckers.

FORECASTING METHODS

LEARNING OBJECTIVE **2**

Explain the use of forecasting techniques in planning.

All planning involves making forecasts or predicting future events. Forecasting is important because if a manager fails to spot trends and react to them before the competition does, the competition can gain an invaluable edge. Recognizing the importance of understanding the future, almost every large business or government agency performs some type of formalized forecasting.[5] The forecasts used in strategic planning are especially difficult to make because they involve long range trends.

Unknown factors might crop up between the time the forecast is made and the time about which predictions are made. This section will describe approaches to and types of forecasting.

Qualitative and Quantitative Approaches

Forecasts can be based on both qualitative and quantitative information. Most of the forecasting done for strategic planning relies on a combination of both. *Qualitative* methods of forecasting consist mainly of subjective hunches. For example, an experienced executive might predict the high cost of housing will create a demand for small, less expensive homes, even though this trend cannot be quantified. One qualitative method is a **judgmental forecast**, a prediction based on a collection of subjective opinions. It relies on analysis of subjective inputs from a variety of sources, including consumer surveys, sales representatives, managers and panels of experts. For instance, a group of potential homebuyers might be asked how they would react to the possibility of purchasing a compact, less expensive home.

judgmental forecast
A qualitative forecasting method based on a collection of subjective opinions.

Quantitative forecasting methods involve either the extension of historical data or the development of models to identify the cause of a particular outcome. A widely used historical approach is **time-series analysis**. This technique is simply an analysis of a sequence of observations that have taken place at regular intervals over a period of time (hourly, weekly, monthly and so forth). The underlying assumption of this approach is the future will be much like the past. Figure 6-1 shows a basic example of a time-series analysis chart. This information might be used to make forecasts about when people would be willing to take vacations. Such forecasts would be important for the resort and travel industry. A time-series forecast works best in a relatively stable situation. For example, an unusually strong or weak hurricane season makes it difficult to predict the demand for home improvement materials. If you use a spreadsheet program to make forecasts, you will find the input data are part of a time-series analysis. The future trends projected are based on historical data.

time-series analysis
An analysis of a sequence of observations that have taken place at regular intervals over a period of time (hourly, weekly, monthly and so forth).

Many firms use both quantitative and qualitative approaches to forecasting. Forecasting begins with a quantitative prediction, which provides basic data about a future trend. An example of a quantitative prediction is forecasting a surge in demand for smart television receivers 50 inches or greater. Next, the qualitative

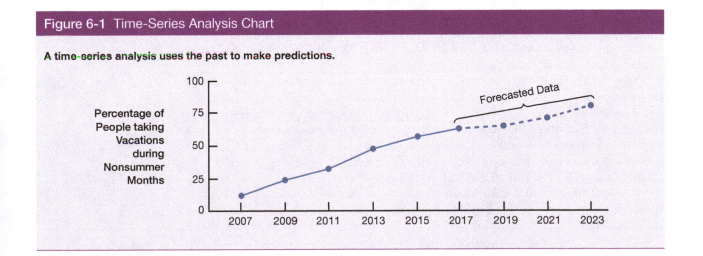

Figure 6-1 Time-Series Analysis Chart

A time-series analysis uses the past to make predictions.

Percentage of People taking Vacations during Nonsummer Months

Forecasted Data

forecast is added to the quantitative forecast, somewhat as a reality check. For example, a quantitative forecast might predict that if the current growth trend continues, 90 percent of households in North America will contain at least one 50-inch smart TV by 2025.

The quantitative forecast is then adjusted according to the subjective data supplied by the qualitative forecast. In this case, it could be reasoned that the growth trend was extrapolated too aggressively. In many instances, a quantitative forecast will serve as a reality check on the qualitative forecasts because numerical data is more accurate than intuition.

Three errors or traps are particularly prevalent when making forecasts or estimates.[6] One is the *overconfidence trap*, whereby people overestimate the accuracy of their forecasts. A CEO might be so confident of the growth of her business that she moves the company into expensive new headquarters. Based on her confidence, she does not prepare contingency plans in case the estimated growth does not take place. A second problem is the *prudence trap* in which people make cautious forecasts, "just to be on the safe side." Being safe can mean taking extra measures not to be caught short, such as a restaurant owner buying ten extra boxes of strawberries, "just to be safe." If the strawberry desserts go unsold, the owner is stuck unless he can make strawberry pudding for tomorrow's menu.

A third problem is the *recallability trap*, whereby our forecasts are influenced by extremely positive or negative incidents we recall. If a manager vividly recalls success stories from global expansion to Singapore, he might overestimate the chances of succeeding in that country.

Being aware these traps can help you take a more disciplined approach to forecasting. For example, to reduce the effect of the overconfidence trap, start by considering the extremes—the possible highs and lows. Try to imagine a scenario in which your forecast could be way too high or way too low and make appropriate adjustments if necessary. For a reality check, discuss your forecasts with other knowledgeable people. To become a good forecaster, you need to make a large number of predictions and then look for feedback on the accuracy of these predictions.

The Role of Artificial Intelligence in Forecasting

Artificial intelligence plays a major role in quantitative approaches to forecasting by providing data about associations among possibly thousands of facts and observations. Hernân Orsey, the chief data officer at Salesforce, says that the human and technological sides must work together to make effective use of Big Data and artificial intelligence. Orsey says that when Salesforce missed its sales goals one quarter, the company turned to AI, and more accurate forecasts ensued.

For forecasting to be considered scientific, data and facts should be the basis for conclusions, and AI amasses data and facts. With AI, the decision maker can use data-driven rationale to explain how the result was found.[7] For example, a sales manager for high-priced recreation vehicles (RVs) might prepare a chart based on AI indicating that even a slight uptick in the economy leads to a minimum 15 percent increase in the sales of RVs. Assuming that the economy was improving, manufacturing might ramp up, for the anticipated sales increase.

An advantage of AI for forecasting is that it is brutally honest, providing cold, hard truth. The facts provided by AI can be used to verify hunches, but the decision maker must decide if the facts are relevant. In the RV example, AI might reveal that 85 percent of RV owners have purchased all-weather boots. The fact might be true, but people who do not own outdoor boots might also be potential purchasers of RVs.

Types of Forecasts

Three types of forecasts are used most widely: economic, sales and technological. Each of these forecasts can be made by using both qualitative and quantitative methods. Forecasts that are updated regularly with fresh data are referred to as *rolling forecasts*. The presence or absence of hurricanes, as mentioned above, would be useful in updating a yearly sales forecast in the building-supply industry.

Economic Forecasting

No single factor is more important in managerial planning than predicting the level of future business activity. Strategic planners in large organizations rely often on economic forecasts made by specialists they hire. Planners in smaller firms are more likely to rely on government forecasts, industry analysts, or speaking to other business-people. However, forecasts about the general economy do not necessarily correspond to business activity related to a particular product or service. Assume you are a manager at an office supply company, such as Office Depot or Staples. Optimistic forecasts about the growth of remote working may prompt you to stock up on home office systems.

A major factor in the accuracy of forecasts is time span: Short-range predictions are more accurate than long-range predictions. Strategic planning is long-range planning, and many strategic plans have to be revised frequently to accommodate changes in business activity. For example, a sudden recession may abort plans for diversification into new products and services.

Sales Forecasting

The sales forecast is usually the primary planning document for a business. Even if the general economy is robust, an organization needs a promising sales forecast before it can be aggressive about capitalizing on new opportunities. Sales forecasts are also important because they contribute heavily to an earnings forecast. When sales improve, so do earnings if costs are kept under control. If sales decrease, earnings will decrease unless costs are reduced.

Strategic planners themselves may not be involved in making sales forecasts, but to develop master plans they rely on forecasts from the marketing unit. For instance, the major tobacco companies have embarked on strategic plans to diversify into a number of non-tobacco businesses, such as soft drinks and food products. An important factor in the decision to implement this strategic plan was a forecast of decreased demand for tobacco products in the domestic market. The cause for decreased demand was health concerns of the public, and numerous anti-smoking campaigns. The major shift to vaping products was another response to health concerns about tobacco use.

Feedback from the field sales force often provides useful input for forecasts. The people in the field know the realities of consumer demand, and might have an inkling of what customers will want in the future.[8] One of the reasons many television sets now have an Internet capability is because customers often said to store associates something to the effect, "I wish I didn't have to get up from watching television just to check my e-mail or stream my favorite movies or sporting events."

Technological Forecasting

A technological forecast predicts what types of technological changes will take place. Technological forecasts allow a firm to adapt to new technologies and thus stay competitive. For example, forecasts made in the late 1990s about the explosive growth of e-commerce have enabled many firms to ready themselves technologically for the future. At first a lot of the activity was unprofitable, yet the majority of industrial and consumer companies that prepared to buy and sell over the Internet soon found it to be profitable. By mid-2000 technological forecasts were made based on the abundant availability of Wi-Fi at places of work, airports, hotels and restaurants. This forecast encouraged the manufacturing and marketing of portable computers and smartphones suited for the wireless environment. (*Wi-Fi* refers to Wireless Fidelity, a high-speed, high-capacity network built on radio signals.)

Scenario Planning to Make Good Use of Forecasts

Forecasting is a way of predicting what will happen in the future. To make effective use of such knowledge it is helpful to plan how to respond to the forecasted events. **Scenario planning** is the process of preparing responses to predicted changes in conditions.[9] With scenario planning, you prepare for what the future might look like. The practice of scenario planning was pioneered in the U.S. military in the 1950s and gained popularity in a few major business corporations in the 1970s. With the turbulence in the modern era, including the airplane attacks on the World Trade Center on September 11, 2001, ISIS attacks around the world a decade later, and continuing threats of nuclear warfare, scenario planning has made a comeback.

scenario planning
The process of preparing responses to predicted changes in conditions.

A good use of scenario planning would be to figure out in advance how to deal with a serious disruption in business, such as damage caused by a hurricane. At the same time, it would be helpful to plan for a substantial increase in business that may be caused by the same hurricane. A building supply company might face the latter problem.

One business giant making serious use of scenario planning is Royal Dutch Shell. The company has used this technique for 50 years because predicting the future is vital for an energy company. A Shell scenario developed in 2013 for the future is "Oceans." The prediction was that strong economic growth would accelerate energy demands. Power would be more widely distributed, and governments would be slower to agree on major decisions. Market forces rather than policies will shape the future of energy systems. Oil and coal will remain part of the mix, and greenhouse gases will bring about dramatic change.[10] Although the price of petroleum dropped drastically a few years after the scenario was developed, and then recovered, the scenario is playing out to be quite accurate.

The Delphi Technique for Increasing the Accuracy of Forecasts

The approaches to forecasting can be made more systematic, and a little more quantitative, if those making forecasts on the same trend are pooled. Each forecaster commenting on the forecast made by the other forecasts can also increase accuracy. Using the **Delphi Technique**, a facilitator gathers all the forecasts, as well as the reasons for them, from the specialists in the panel. (The Delphi Technique is a form of group decision making designed to provide group members with one another's ideas and feedback while avoiding some of the problems associated with interacting groups.) All the panelists then receive each other's forecasts and reasons for the forecasts, and

Delphi Technique
A form of group decision making designed to provide group members with one another's ideas and feedback while avoiding some of the problems associated with interacting groups.

comment on this information. After several rounds of reviews, the forecasts are refined, and the facilitator submits the final forecast. Ideally, the forecasters attain consensus on the final forecast. An example of a final forecast might be, "By 2025, one half of car buyers in the United States and Canada will want to purchase a hybrid vehicle."

Forecasting has its merits but also can reach a point of diminishing returns. Scott Cook is the co-founder and chairman of Intuit, the company that helps executives make decisions using his financial management software. He believes employees should not invest too much time in forecasting. Cook would rather have employees engage in more productive activities, such as innovating and executing the company's strategic plan.[11]

LEARNING OBJECTIVE **3**

Describe how to use Gantt charts, milestone charts, and PERT planning techniques.

GANTT CHARTS AND MILESTONE CHARTS

Two basic tools for monitoring the progress of scheduled projects are Gantt charts and milestone charts. Closely related to each other, they both help a manager keep track of whether activities are completed on time. Both techniques include the use of numbers, so they can be classified as quantitative.

Gantt Charts

Gantt chart
A chart that graphically depicts the planned and actual progress of work during the life of the project.

During the era of scientific management, Henry Gantt developed a chart for displaying progress on a project. An early application was tracking the progress of building a ship.[12] A **Gantt chart** graphically depicts both the planned and actual progress of work over the period of time encompassed by a project. Gantt charts are especially useful for scheduling one-time projects, such as constructing buildings, making films, or building an airplane. Charts of this type are also called time-and-activity charts, because time and activity are the two key variables they consider. Time is plotted on the horizontal axis; activities listed on the vertical axis.

Despite its simplicity, the Gantt chart is a valuable and widely used control technique. It also provides the foundation for more sophisticated types of time-related charts, such as the PERT diagram described later.

Figure 6-2 shows a Gantt chart used to schedule the opening of a small office building. Gantt charts used for most other purposes have a similar format. During the planning phase of the project, the manager lays out the schedule by using rectangular boxes. As each activity is completed, the appropriate box is shaded. At any given time, the manager can see which activities have been completed on time. For example, if the building owner has not hired a contractor for the grounds by August 31, the activity would be declared behind schedule.

The Gantt chart also depicts dependent activities, such as in Figure 6-2, hiring contractors being dependent on first getting the building permit. The dependent activities must be completed in sequence. However, some of the activities are nondependent or "parallel." For example, some developers obtain leases before a building is completed.

The Gantt chart presented here is quite basic. On most Gantt charts, the bars are movable strips of plastic. Different colors indicate scheduled and actual progress. Mechanical boards with pegs to indicate scheduled dates and actual progress can also be used. Some managers and specialists now use computer graphics to prepare their own high-tech Gantt charts. You can also use a spreadsheet to readily construct a Gantt chart, and many different software packages are available for preparing these charts.

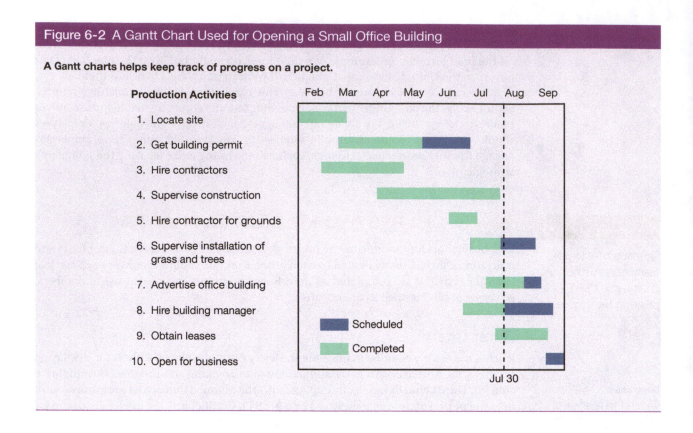

Figure 6-2 A Gantt Chart Used for Opening a Small Office Building

A **Gantt charts** helps keep track of progress on a project.

Production Activities								
1. Locate site								
2. Get building permit								
3. Hire contractors								
4. Supervise construction								
5. Hire contractor for grounds								
6. Supervise installation of grass and trees								
7. Advertise office building								
8. Hire building manager								
9. Obtain leases								
10. Open for business								

Because Gantt charts are used to monitor progress, they also act as control devices. When the chart shows that the building permit activity has fallen behind schedule, the manager can investigate the problem and solve it. The Gantt chart gives a convenient overall view of the progress made against the schedule. However, its disadvantage is that it does not furnish enough details about the sub-activities that need to be performed to accomplish each general item.

Milestone Charts

A **milestone chart** is an extension of the Gantt chart, and some more advanced Gantt charts make provisions for the milestones. The milestone chart provides a listing of the sub-activities that must be completed to accomplish the major activities listed on the vertical axis. The inclusion of milestones, which are the completion of individual phases of an activity, adds to the value of a Gantt chart as a scheduling and control technique. Each milestone serves as a checkpoint on progress. In Figure 6-3, the Gantt chart for constructing a small office building has been expanded into a milestone chart. The numbers in each rectangle represent milestones. A complete chart would list each of the 33 milestones. In Figure 6-3, only the milestones for obtaining leases (including screening tenants) and the opening date are listed.

milestone chart
An extension of the Gantt chart that provides a listing of the subactivities that must be completed to accomplish the major activities listed on the vertical axis.

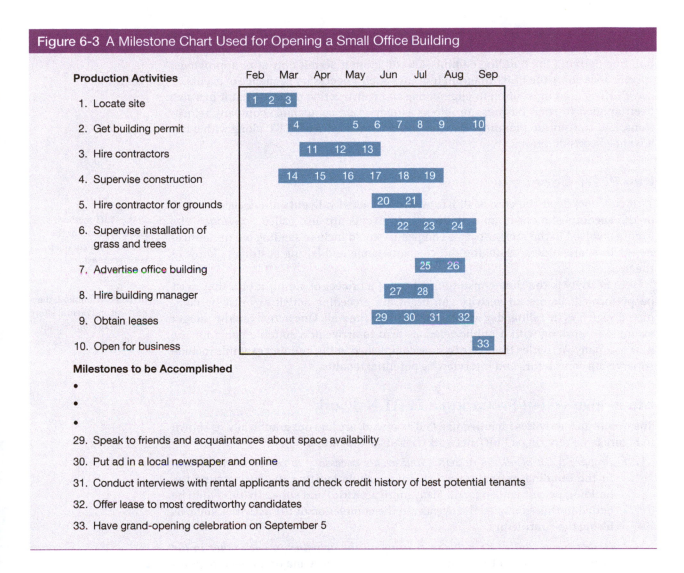

Figure 6-3 A Milestone Chart Used for Opening a Small Office Building

Production Activities

1. Locate site
2. Get building permit
3. Hire contractors
4. Supervise construction
5. Hire contractor for grounds
6. Supervise installation of grass and trees
7. Advertise office building
8. Hire building manager
9. Obtain leases
10. Open for business

Milestones to be Accomplished

- •
- •
- •

29. Speak to friends and acquaintances about space availability
30. Put ad in a local newspaper and online
31. Conduct interviews with rental applicants and check credit history of best potential tenants
32. Offer lease to most creditworthy candidates
33. Have grand-opening celebration on September 5

PROGRAM EVALUATION AND REVIEW TECHNIQUE

program evaluation and review technique (PERT)
A network model used to track the planning activities required to complete a large scale, nonrepetitive project. It depicts all of the interrelated events that must take place.

Gantt and milestone charts are basic scheduling tools, exceeded in their basic versions only in simplicity by a to-do list. A more complicated method for scheduling activities and events is the use of a network model. This model depicts all the inter-related events that must take place for a project to be completed. The most widely used network-modeling tool is the **program evaluation and review technique (PERT)**. It is used to track the planning activities required to complete a large scale, non-repetitive project.

Quite often Gantt charts and PERT are used together, with the Gantt chart being laid out first because it provides a useful list of all the activities that need to be performed in a project. PERT has the potential to reduce the time and costs required to complete a project because activities can be sequenced efficiently. A scheduling technique such as PERT is useful when certain tasks have to be completed before others if the total project is to be completed on time. In the small office building example, the site of the building must be specified before the owner can apply for a building permit. (The building commission will grant a permit only after approving a specific location.) The PERT diagram indicates such a necessary sequence of events.

PERT is used most often in engineering and construction projects. But it has also been applied to such business problems as marketing campaigns, company relocations, and convention planning. Here we examine the basics of PERT, along with a few advanced considerations.

Key PERT Concepts

Two concepts lie at the core of PERT: events and activity. **Events** are decision points or the accomplishment of an activity or task. Events are also called *milestones*. The events involved in the merger of two companies would include sending out announcements to shareholders, changing the company name and letting customers know of the merger.

An **activity** is the time-consuming aspect of a project or simply a task that must be performed. Before an activity can begin, its preceding activities must be completed—such as installing dry wall before painting the wall. One activity in the merger example is working with a public relations firm to arrive at a suitable name for the new company. Activities that have to be accomplished in the building example include supervising contractors and interviewing potential tenants.

events
In the PERT method, decision points or the accomplishment of an activity or task.

activity
In the PERT method, the physical and mental effort required to complete an event.

Steps Involved in Preparing a PERT Network

The events and activities included in a PERT network are laid out graphically, as shown in Figure 6-4. Preparing a PERT network consists of four steps:

1 *Prepare a list of all the activities and events necessary to complete the project.* In the building example, the activities include locating the site, getting the building permit and so forth. Many more activities and sub-activities could be added to this example. The events are the completion of the activities such, as hiring the contractors.

2 *Design the actual PERT network, relating all the activities to each other in the proper sequence.* Anticipating all the activities in a major project requires considerable skill and judgment. In addition, activities must be sequenced— the planner must decide which activity must precede another. In the building example, the owner would want to hire a grounds contractor before hiring a building manager.

3 *Estimate the time required to complete each activity.* This step must be done carefully because the major output of the PERT method is a statement of the total time required by the project. Because the time estimate is critical, several people should be asked to make three different estimates; optimistic time, pessimistic time and probable time.

Optimistic time (O) is the shortest time an activity will take if everything goes well. In the construction industry, the optimistic time is rarely achieved because so many different trades are involved in completing a project.

Pessimistic time (P) is the amount of time an activity will take if everything goes wrong (as it sometimes does with complicated projects, such as installing a new subway system).

Most probable time (M) is the most realistic estimate of how much time an activity will take. The probable time for an activity can be an estimate of the time taken for similar activities on other projects. For instance, the time needed to build a cockpit for one aircraft might be based on the average time it took to build cockpits for comparable aircraft in the past.

After the planner has collected all the estimates, he or she uses a formula to calculate the **expected time**. The expected time is the time that will be used on the PERT diagram as the needed period for the completion of an activity. As the following formula shows, expected time is an "average" in which most probable time is given more weight than optimistic time and pessimistic time.

expected time
The time that will be used on the PERT diagram as the needed period for the completion of an activity.

$$\text{Expected time} = \frac{O + 4M + P}{6}$$

(The denominator is six because O counts for one, M for four and P for one.)

Suppose the time estimates for choosing a site location for the building are as follows; optimistic time (O) is two weeks, most probable time (M) is five weeks, and pessimistic time (P) is eight weeks. Therefore,

$$\text{Expected time} = \frac{2 + (4 \times 5) + 8}{6} = \frac{30}{6} = 5 \text{ weeks}$$

As each event or milestone is completed, the project manager can insert the actual time required for its completion. The updates are helpful because if the completion time turns out to be the pessimistic one, more resources can be added to shorten the activity required to attain the next event.

critical path
The path through the PERT network that includes the most time-consuming sequence of events and activities.

4 *Calculate the* **critical path**, *the path through the PERT network that includes the most time-consuming sequence of events and activities.* The path with the longest elapsed time determines the length of the entire project. To calculate the critical path, you must first add the times needed to complete the activities in each sequence. The logic behind the critical path is this: A given project cannot be considered completed until its lengthiest component is completed. For example, if it takes six months to get the building construction permit, the office building project cannot be completed in less than one year, even if all other events are completed earlier than scheduled. Sudden changes in the time required for an activity can change the critical path, such as unanticipated delays in obtaining enough plywood for the building project.

Figure 6-4 shows a critical path that requires a total elapsed time of 93 weeks. This total is calculated by adding the numerals that appear beside each thick line segment. Each numeral represents the number of weeks scheduled to complete the activities between each lettered label. Notice that activity completion must occur in the sequence of steps indicated by the direction of the arrows. In this case, if 93 weeks appeared to be an excessive length of time, the building owner would have to search for ways to shorten the process. For example, the owner might be spending too much time supervising the construction.

When it comes to implementing the activities listed on the PERT diagram, control measures play a crucial role. The project manager must ensure all critical events are completed on time. If activities in the critical path take too long to complete, the overall project will not be completed on time. If necessary, the manager must take

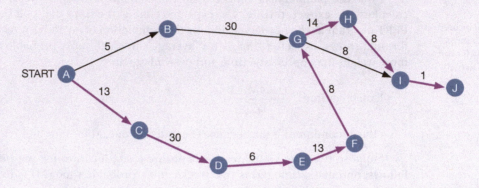

Figure 6-4 A PERT Network for Opening a Building

Each numeral in the diagram equals the expected time for an activity, such as 5 weeks to locate site (between circles A and B) and 13 weeks to supervise installation of grass and trees (between circles E and F). The critical path is the estimated time for all the activities shown above the thick arrows (13+30+6+13+8+14+8+1 = 93).

corrective action to move the activity along. Such action might include hiring additional workers, dismissing substandard workers, or purchasing more productive equipment.

Advanced Considerations in PERT

Considering that PERT is used for projects as complicated as building a new type of airliner, the process can become quite complex. In practice, PERT networks often specify hundreds of events and activities. Each small event can have its own PERT diagram. Commercial software is available to help perform the mechanics of computing paths. Here we look at two concepts that are used in complex applications of PERT.

Refined Calculation of Expected Times

The optimistic, pessimistic and most probable times should be based on a frequency distribution of estimates. Instead of using one intuitive guess as to these durations, a specialist collects all available data about how long comparable activities took. For example: wiring a cockpit took seven weeks in 10 different cases, six weeks in five cases, five weeks in three cases, and so forth. The optimistic and pessimistic times are then selected as the lower and upper ten percentiles of the distribution of times. In other words, it is optimistic to think an event will be completed as rapidly as suggested by the briefest 10 percent of estimates. Also, it is pessimistic to think the event will be completed in the longest 10 percent of estimated times. (Remember, the expected time is calculated based on a weighted average of the optimistic, most probable and pessimistic times.)

It is often difficult to obtain data for comparable activities, so quantified guesswork will be required. To illustrate, a project manager might guess, "If we attempted to drill a hole for oil through that ice cap 100 times, I think it would take us 60 days 15 times, 90 days 20 times, 110 days 25 times, and 140 days 40 times." The guesses provided by this project manager might be combined with the guesses of another specialist, before calculating the pessimistic, optimistic and most probable times.

Resource and Cost Estimates

In addition to estimating the time required for activities, advanced applications of PERT estimate the amount of resources required. Before a building contractor would establish a price for erecting a building, it would be prudent to estimate how much and what types of equipment would be needed. It would also be essential to estimate how many workers of different skills would be required. Considering payroll runs about two-thirds of the cost for manufacturing, miscalculating people costs can eliminate profits.

Resource and cost estimates can be calculated in the same manner as time estimates. Both can then be attached to events, thereby suggesting at which point in the project they will most likely be incurred. For example, the building contractor might estimate siding specialists will not be needed until 90 days into the project.

BREAK-EVEN ANALYSIS

break-even analysis
A method of determining the relationship between total costs and total revenues at various levels of production or sales activity.

"What do we have to do to break even?" is asked frequently in business. Managers often find the answer through **break-even analysis**, a method of determining the relationship between total costs and total revenues at various levels of production or sales activity. Managers use break-even analysis because—before adding new products, equipment, or human resources—they want to be sure the changes will pay off. Break-even analysis tells managers the point at which it is profitable to go ahead with a new venture.

Figure 6-5 illustrates a typical break-even chart. It deals with a proposal to add a new product to an existing line. The point at which the Total Costs line and the Revenue line intersect is the break-even point. Sales shown to the right of the break-even point represent profit. Sales to the left of this point represent a loss.

Break-Even Formula

The break-even point (BE) is the situation in which total revenues equal fixed costs plus variable costs. It can be calculated with the following standard formula:

$$BE = \frac{FC}{P - VC}$$

where

P = selling price per unit

VC = variable cost per unit, the cost that varies with the amount produced

FC = fixed cost, the cost that remains constant no matter how many units are produced

The chart in Figure 6-5 is based on the plans of a small company to sell furniture over the Internet. For simplicity, we provide data only for the dining room sets. The average selling price (P) is $1,000 per unit; the variable cost (VC) is $500 per unit, including Internet commission fees for sales made through major websites. The fixed costs are $300,000.

$$BE = \frac{\$300,000}{\$1,000 - \$500} = \frac{\$300,000}{\$500} = 600 \text{ units}$$

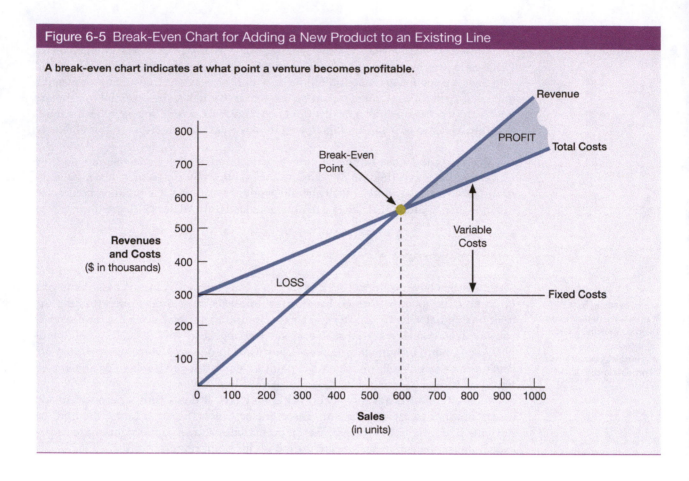

Figure 6-5 Break-Even Chart for Adding a New Product to an Existing Line

A break-even chart indicates at what point a venture becomes profitable.

Under the conditions assumed and for the period of time in which these costs and revenue figures are valid, a sales volume of 600 dining room sets would be required for the furniture company to break even. Any volume above that level would produce a profit and anything below it would result in a loss. (We are referring to online sales only. Sales through their customary channels would have to be figured separately.) If the sales forecast for dining room sets sold through e-commerce is above 600 units, it would be a good decision to sell online. If the sales forecast is less than 600 units, the furniture company should not attempt e-commerce for now. However, if the husband-and-wife team is willing to absorb losses now to build for the long range, they might start e-commerce anyway. Break-even analysis would tell the owners how much money they are likely to lose. An encouraging note is that small operations like the furniture company in question have typically profited from e-commerce.

Break-even analyses must be calculated frequently because fixed and variable costs may change quite suddenly. Imagine you were the manager of a package delivery service. One of your variable costs, gasoline, might fluctuate weekly. And a fixed cost like truck insurance might change every six months. Also, as an enterprise grows, new fixed costs may arise, such as needing to hire a human resources outsourcing firm to take care of payroll and benefits administration.

Advantages and Limitations of Break-Even Analysis

Break-even analysis helps managers keep their thinking focused on the volume of activity that will be necessary to justify a new expense. The technique is also useful because it applies to a number of operations problems. Break-even analysis can help a manager decide whether to drop an existing product from the line, to replace equipment, or to buy rather than make a part.

Break-even analysis has some drawbacks. First, it is only as valid as the estimates of costs and revenues managers use to create it. Second, the relationship between variable costs and sales may be complicated. Figure 6-5 indicates that variable costs and sales increase together in a direct relationship. In reality, unit costs may decrease with increased volume. It is also possible that costs may increase with volume: Suppose that increased production leads to higher turnover because employees prefer not to work overtime. A caution about break-even analysis, rather than a limitation, is that the break-even point is a calculation not a forecast. Just because the business owner above needs to sell 600 dining room sets to break even, it does not mean there is a demand for this many units.

Break-even analysis relates to decisions about whether to proceed or not to proceed. The next section will examine a more complicated decision-making technique that relates to the desirability of several alternative solutions.

DECISION TREES

decision tree
A graphic illustration of the alternative solutions available to solve a problem.

Another useful planning tool is called a **decision tree**, a graphic illustration of the alternative solutions available to solve a problem. Analyzing the outcomes of a few alternative actions before making a decision is useful because it helps predict if you have made a decision that produces the most favorable, or least painful, consequences.[13] Decision trees are designed to estimate the outcome of a series of decisions. As the sequences of the major decision are drawn, the resulting diagram resembles a tree with branches.

A decision tree extends from a starting point through a series of branches, until two or more final results are reached at the opposite end. The diagram may continue to branch, as more options are chosen. Using this information, the manager computes the expected values and adds them for the two alternatives. An **expected value** is the average value incurred if a particular decision is made a large number of times. Sometimes the alternative would earn more, and sometimes less, with the expected value being the alternative's average return.

expected value
The average return on a particular decision being made a large number of times.

To illustrate the essentials of using a decision tree for making financial decisions, consider a manager from a mining company in Alaska who is deciding on the feasibility of digging for gold. Discussions with staff accountants and mining engineers on the project suggest the following expected outcomes (conditional values) for a first gold dig; 10% chance of having a great very successful dig, 20% chance of having moderately successful dig, 10% chance of breaking even, and 60% chance of losing a moderate amount of money. These figures are conditional because they depend on such factors as the amount of gold in the ore under the ground and the reliability of the equipment. Liking the conditional values, the manager therefore decides to take a chance with mining for gold, and lays out the decision tree show in Figure 6-6.[14]

The expected financial outcome from the first dig is a profit of $40,000, calculated as follows: $.10 \times \$600,000 + .20 \times \$400,000 + .10 \times \$200,000 - .60 \times \$200,000 = \$40,000$. Or,

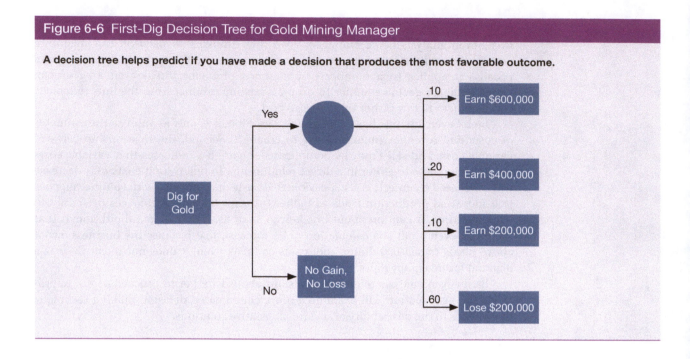

Figure 6-6 First-Dig Decision Tree for Gold Mining Manager

A decision tree helps predict if you have made a decision that produces the most favorable outcome.

Dig for Gold

Yes

No

No Gain, No Loss

.10 Earn $600,000

.20 Earn $400,000

.10 Earn $200,000

.60 Lose $200,000

$60,000 + $80,000 + $20,000 − $120,000 = $40,000. Our manager says, "Sounds good. I will go for the gold for the first dig."

The advantage of a decision tree is it can be used to help make sequences of decisions. After one dig for gold, the manager may think of expanding. One of the many ways in which the decision tree could continue would be for the manager to use more advanced equipment, or to conduct two digs at the same time. New conditional values would have to be calculated for these branches.

INVENTORY CONTROL TECHNIQUES

LEARNING OBJECTIVE **5**

Describe how to manage inventory by using the economic order quantity (EOQ) and the just-in-time (JIT) system.

Managers of manufacturing and sales organizations face the problem of how much inventory to keep on hand. If a firm maintains a large inventory, goods can be made quickly, customers can make immediate purchases, or orders can be shipped rapidly. However, stocking goods is expensive. The goods themselves are costly, and the money tied up in inventory cannot be invested elsewhere. Target is an example of a company that owes some of their competitive advantage to their efficient management of inventory. The company collaborates with its suppliers to keep shelves stocked with the right amount and quantity of merchandise to minimize inventory accumulation.

This section will describe two decision-making techniques used to manage inventory and control production, the economic order quantity (EOQ), and the just-in-time (JIT) system.

Economic Order Quantity

The **economic order quantity (EOQ)** is the inventory level that minimizes both administrative costs and carrying costs. The EOQ represents the reorder quantity of

economic order quantity (EOQ)
The inventory level that minimizes both administrative costs and carrying costs.

the least cost. Carrying costs include the cost of loans, the interest foregone because money is tied up in inventory and the cost of handling the inventory. EOQ is expressed mathematically as

$$EOQ = \sqrt{\frac{2DO}{C}}$$

where

D = annual demand in units for the product

O = fixed cost of placing and receiving an order

C = annual carrying cost per unit
    (taxes, insurance, storage, interest and other expenses)

The economic order quantity is found to be the most useful when a company has repetitive purchasing and demand for an item, such as truck tires or hospital supplies. Let us return to our furniture example. Assume the annual demand for coffee tables is 100 units and that it costs $1,000 to order each unit. Furthermore, suppose the carrying cost per unit is $200. The equation to calculate the most economic number of coffee tables to keep in inventory is

$$EOQ = \sqrt{\frac{2 \times 100 \times \$1,000}{\$200}}$$

$$EOQ = \sqrt{\frac{\$200,000}{\$200}}$$

$$EOQ = \sqrt{1,000}$$

$$= 32 \text{ coffee tables (rounded figure)}$$

Therefore, the owners of the online furniture store conclude the most economical number of coffee tables to keep in inventory during the selling season is 32. (The assumption is that the company has a large storage area.) If the figures entered into the EOQ formula are accurate, EOQ calculations can vastly improve inventory management.

Just-in-Time System

just-in-time (JIT) system
A system to minimize inventory and move it into the plant exactly when needed.

An important thrust in manufacturing is to keep just enough parts and components on hand to fill current orders. The **just-in-time (JIT) system** is an inventory control method designed to minimize inventory and move it into the plant exactly when needed. Note also that JIT is part of a manufacturing system that focuses on making manufacturing more efficient by eliminating waste wherever possible.

The key principle of the system is to eliminate excess inventory by producing or purchasing parts, subassemblies and final products only when—and in the exact amounts—needed. JIT helps a manufacturing division stay *lean* by minimizing waste. JIT is often referred to as lean manufacturing because waste of "fat" is minimized. A lean manufacturing organization adopts a culture of continuously looking for ways to be more efficient. A specific example would be redesigning a work area from a linear operation to a U-shaped station to improve efficiency.[15]

Just-in-time is not simply reducing inventory down to as small as possible, an activity that could be counterproductive. A case study of the automotive industry in China concluded that the whole logistics system and the relationship with suppliers are of vital importance. In this way the manufacturer and other members of the supply chain work in synchrony.[16] A negative use of JIT would be to make suppliers feel they are being exploited because they are expected to warehouse inventory for the manufacturer.

The JIT is quantitative in the sense that it relies heavily on numbers, such as specifying the number of parts and components accumulated as inventory. Also, under JIT the company would track data, such as the number of hours or days of accumulated inventory. Imagine the small furniture company having raw wood delivered to its door within an hour or so after an order is received over the Internet. JIT is generally used in a repetitive, single-product, manufacturing environment. However, the system is now also used to improve operations in sales and service organizations.

Reducing waste is the core of JIT philosophy. Three such wastes are overproduction, waiting and stock. *Overproduction waste* can be reduced by producing only what is needed when an order is received. *Waiting waste* can be reduced by synchronizing the workflow, such as technicians preparing a housing for a computer monitor when the internal mechanisms are coming down the line. *Stock waste* can be reduced by keeping inventory at a minimum.

Three noteworthy principles of just-in-time inventory management are presented next.

1 *Short production lead times.* A JIT system minimizes the time between the arrival of raw material or components in the plant and the shipment of a finished product to a customer.

2 *High inventory turnover (with the goal of zero inventory and stockless production).* The levels of finished goods, work in process and raw materials are purposely reduced. Raw material in a warehouse is regarded as waste, and so is idle work in process. (A person who applied JIT to the household would regard backup supplies of ketchup or motor oil as shameful!)

3 *Neatness.* A JIT plant that follows Japanese tradition is immaculate. All unnecessary materials, tools, rags and files are discarded. The factory floor is as neat and clean as the showroom.

Advantages and Disadvantages of the JIT Inventory System

Manufacturing companies have realized several benefits from adopting JIT. The expenses associated with maintaining a large inventory can be dramatically reduced, providing suppliers do not raise their prices for making deliveries as needed. JIT controls can lead to organizational commitment to quality in design, materials, parts, employee management and supplier–user relations and finished goods. With minimum levels of inventory on hand, finished products are more visible and defects are more readily detected. Quality problems can therefore be attacked before they escalate to an insurmountable degree. Low levels of inventory also shorten cycle times.

Despite the advantages, JIT management can offer large manufacturers some potential disadvantages. Above all, a JIT system must be placed in a supportive or compatible environment. JIT is applicable only to highly repetitive manufacturing operations, such as cars or residential furnace manufacturing. Also, product demand must be predictable with a minimum of surges in demand. Reliable suppliers are also needed.

Small companies with short runs of a variety of products may suffer financial losses from JIT practices. One problem they have is suppliers are often unwilling to promptly ship small batches to meet the weekly needs of a small customer.

The savings from JIT management can be deceptive. Suppliers may simply build up inventories in their own plants and add that cost to their prices. JIT inventory practices also leave a company vulnerable to work stoppages, such as a strike. With a large inventory of finished products or parts, the company can continue to meet customer demand while the work stoppage is being settled. Finally, just-in-time may lead to manufacturing efficiencies, but efficiency alone does not make for a great organization. You also need great products to move a company forward.

The accompanying *Management in Action* insert describes how inventory management is a key part of operating the world's best-known fast-food restaurant.

PARETO DIAGRAMS FOR PROBLEM IDENTIFICATION

LEARNING OBJECTIVE **6**

Describe how to identify problems using a Pareto diagram.

Pareto diagram
A bar graph that ranks types of output variations by frequency of occurrence.

Managers and professionals must frequently identify the major causes of their problem, such as: "What features of our product are receiving the most complaints from consumers?" or "Our agency is offering more services to the public than we can afford. Which services might we drop without hurting too many people?" One problem-identification technique uses a **Pareto diagram**, a bar graph (or histogram) that ranks types of output variations by frequency of occurrence. Managers and other workers often use Pareto diagrams to identify the most important problems or causes of problems that affect output quality. Identification of the "vital few" allows management or product improvement teams to focus on the major cause of a production or service problem. Based on quantitative data, effort is then directed where it will do the most good.

An example of Pareto analysis is an investigation of the delay associated with processing credit card applications. The data are grouped in the following categories[17]:

- No signature
- Residential address not valid
- Non-legible handwriting
- Already a customer
- Other

The cause of a problem is plotted on the x-axis (horizontal). The cumulative effects both in frequency and percent are plotted on the y-axis (vertical). In a Pareto diagram, the bars are arranged in descending order of height (or frequency of occurrence) from left to right across the x-axis. As a consequence, the most important causes are at the left of the chart. Priorities are then established for taking action on the few causes that account for most of the effect. According to the Pareto principle, generally 20 percent or fewer of the causes contribute to approximately 80 percent or more of the effects. It is widely recognized, for example, that about 20 percent of the customers of an industrial company account for 80 percent of sales. And also, about 20 percent of customers account for about 80 percent of complaints.

MANAGEMENT IN ACTION

Inventory Management at McDonald's Restaurants

McDonald's is one of the world's best-known brands. Relying on franchise operators, the company has approximately 38,000 restaurants (also referred to as "stores") in 120 countries and territories, 210,000 workers, and serves over 68 million customers daily. Managing inventory or stock is therefore a key element in the profitability of each restaurant. Corporate profitability is also affected because franchisees pay a royalty on their profits to McDonald's Corporation. Stock management focuses on creating a balance between meeting customer demands, while minimizing waste.

The general approach to inventory management at McDonald's restaurants is usually to have all the ingredients on hand to assemble, and do not assemble unless an order is taken. An exception are a few finished products such as milk, coffee, and pastries. One goal of this approach to inventory is to make the process so standardized that customers have the same experience each time they visit a McDonald's.

Inventory or stock, management is a challenge for all McDonald's franchise operators and restaurant managers. Stock management has two components: forecasting demand so that food will not be wasted, and control stock accurately for raw materials. The store manager receives guidance from regional stock-control specialists, all of whom have had restaurant experience.

Each regional planner works with 100 restaurants, and communicates with them regularly through e-mail messages and teleconferences. Regional planners work with a stock control system to ensure there are sufficient raw materials on hand, including beef, chicken, potatoes, bread, lettuce, and tomatoes. Calculations about stock have to adjust for special promotions, such as the increased demand for Big Macs during the campaign, "Buy One, Get One Free." All factors that could affect the foot traffic in the restaurants are communicated to the manager. For example, during spring break, a surge in customers might be anticipated.

A basic part of the inventory control is the Work-in-Progress that consists of stock that is in the process of being converted into finished product. The famous Big Mac is composed of a bun, two beef patties, lettuce, cheese, pickles, onions, sauce, and a sprinkling of seasoning. The restaurant associate combines the items immediately after the customer orders a Big Mac so the burger is served hot and fresh.

A stock control system called Manguistics uses a few years' worth of product sales history to generate time series forecasts for each restaurant. The regional planner apples a specific factor the time series analysis for the forecast. One such factor would be population growth or decline. After the calculation is completed, the time-series graph can generate a forecast for future inventory level.

Key benefits from the stock-management system include the following: (1) Restaurants avoid running out of stock, (2) less waste translates into reduced food costs, (3) the need for emergency food deliveries is reduced, saving money, (4) the amount of stock ordered for promotions is more accurate because it based on past experience.

McDonald's also makes extensive use of just-in-time inventory management. When a customer orders a hamburger, a MacDonald's associate does not start to cook. Instead, he or she heats and assembles the burger according to the specifics of the order. With the help of the inventory management system, McDonald's pre-cooks a batch of hamburgers and keeps them under heat lamps. The just-in-time system helps reduce the quantity of meat that must be discarded. Waiting time for customers is also reduced. This is essential to serving a large number of customers in a short period of time during high-demand periods, such as lunch.

Restaurant managers play a key role in providing relevant data to the inventory management systems. For example, each day the restaurant manager records opening and closing stocks of key food item, and other items are recorded weekly. Entering data is a minor activity in comparison to store managers having to do all of the stock management work themselves.

A researcher studying the McDonald's approach to inventory management notes that the society's resources are being used efficiently with less food winding up in landfills. The researcher concludes, "The reduction of waste products provides a win/win/win solution for McDonald's, its customers, and wider society."

Questions

1 If you, a friend, or family member eats at McDonald's, what is your evaluation of how the stock-control system contributes to being served rapidly with tasty food?

2 How does keeping some food, such as beef patties, in the freezer contribute to inventory management at McDonald's?

Source: Original story based on facts and observations in the following sources: Sandro Dzananovic, "How Does McDonald's Manager their Inventory?" *www.academia.edu*, accessed January 5, 2020, pp. 1–5; "Analyzing Top Examples of Just in Time Inventory and Production Management," *www.davidkigerinfo.wordpress.com*, January 22, 2016, p. 4: "Managing Stock to Meet Customer Needs: A McDonald's Restaurants Case Study," *http:businesscasestudies.co.uk*, pp. 1–4, accessed January 5, 2020, pp. 1–4.

In the credit card example, the manager might find that about 80 percent of the credit card applications are being rejected because the signature is missing. Customer service agents would therefore coach customers to do a better job of signing their applications.

The root of a Pareto analysis is to identify which activities are producing most of the results. As a result of the analysis, the manager or staff professional may also find opportunities in addition to problems. Figure 6-7 presents a Pareto analysis of customer sources for a security system designed for small businesses and homes. As a result of the analysis, the security system official might decide where to best allocate funds for marketing and advertising.

Figure 6-7 A Pareto Analysis of Customer Sources for a Security System

The table of results presented below is based on the source of the last 100 customers to purchase a security system, who actually paid for at least two years of service. The analysis assumes the customers accurately recalled how they heard of the security company.

Source of Customer	Number of Customers Using this Source
1 Word of mouth from satisfied customer	35
2 Search engine results about security system	32
3 Observed sign outside other installation	14
4 Customer purchased system when in previous location	5
5 Company employee who wanted system installed in his or her home	4
6 Television advertisement	3
7 Newspaper advertisement	2
8 Advertisement in Yellow Pages of a phone book	2
9 Direct mail advertising flyer to home or office	2
10 Had relative or family member working for the company	1

Total = 100 sales, with the first three sources producing 81 percent of the sales

SUMMARY OF KEY POINTS

 Explain how managers use data-based decision making.

Using data-driven management, decisions are based on facts rather than impressions or guesses. Many managers want to see the data before accepting a suggestion from a subordinate. Data-driven decision making is more of an attitude and approach rather than a specific technique. Although data-driven decision making is preferable in most situations, intuition and judgment still contribute to making major decisions.

2 **Explain the use of forecasting techniques in planning.**

All planning includes making forecasts, both qualitative and quantitative. A judgmental forecast makes predictions on subjective opinions. Time-series analysis is a widely used method of making quantitative forecasts. Artificial intelligence plays a major role in quantitative approaches to forecasting by providing data about extensive facts and observations.

Three widely used forecasts are economic, sales, and technological. Scenario planning helps managers prepare for the outcomes of forecasts, both negative and positive. The Delphi Techniques can improve the accuracy of forecasts because specialists working alone prepare forecasts, and also comment on the forecasts prepared by others in the group.

3 **Describe how to use Gantt charts, milestone charts, and PERT planning techniques.**

Gantt and milestone charts are simple methods of monitoring schedules that are particularly useful for one-time projects. Gantt charts graphically depict the planned and actual progress of work over the period of time encompassed by a project. A milestone chart lists the sub-activities that must be completed to accomplish the major activities.

Managers use PERT networks to track complicated projects when sequences of events must be planned carefully. In a PERT network, an event is a point of decision or accomplishment. An activity is the task that must be performed to complete an event. To complete a PERT diagram, a manager must sequence all the events and estimate the time required for each activity. The expected time for each activity takes into account optimistic,

pessimistic and probable estimates of time. The critical path is the most time-consuming sequence of activities and events that must be followed to implement the project. The duration of the project is determined by the critical path. Frequency distributions are sometimes used to calculate expected times, and PERT can also be used to estimate resources and costs that will be needed.

4 **Describe how to use break-even analysis and decision trees for problem solving and decision making.**

Managers use break-even analysis to estimate the point at which it is profitable to go ahead with a new venture. It is a method of determining the relationship between total costs and total revenues at various levels of sales activity or operation. Break-even analysis determines the ratio of total fixed costs to the difference between the selling price and the variable cost for each unit. The results of break-even analysis are often depicted on a graph. Break-even analysis has to be done frequently, as fixed and variable costs change.

A decision tree provides a quantitative estimate of the best alternative. It is a tool for estimating the outcome of a series of decisions. When the sequences of the major decisions are drawn, they resemble a tree with branches.

5 **Describe how to manage inventory by using the economic order quantity (EOQ) and the just-in-time (JIT) system.**

The economic order quantity (EOQ) is a decision-support technique widely used to manage inventory. The EOQ is the inventory level that minimizes both ordering and carrying costs. The EOQ technique helps managers in a manufacturing or sales organization decide how much inventory to keep on hand.

Just-in-time (JIT) inventory management minimizes stock on hand. Instead, stock is moved into the plant exactly when needed. Although not specifically a decision-making technique, JIT helps shape decisions about inventory. The key principle underlying JIT systems is the elimination of excess inventory by producing or purchasing items only when and in the exact amounts they are needed. JIT is part of lean manufacturing.

Just-in-time processes involve: (1) short production lead times, (2) high inventory turnover, and (3) neatness throughout the factory.

JIT inventory management is best suited for repetitive manufacturing processes. One drawback of JIT is that it places heavy pressures on suppliers to build up their inventories to satisfy the sudden demands of their customers who use the system.

 Describe how to identify problems using a Pareto diagram.

Problems or causes of problems can often be identified by a problem-identification technique called the Pareto diagram. The Pareto principle stems from the diagram and suggests that about 20 percent or fewer of the causes contribute to 80 percent or more of the effects.

Key Terms and Phrases

data-driven decision making 161

judgmental forecast 163

time-series analysis 164

scenario planning 166

Delphi Technique 166

Gantt chart 167

milestone chart 168

program evaluation and
   review technique (PERT) 169

events 170

activity 170

expected time 171

critical path 171

break-even analysis 173

decision tree 175

expected value 175

economic order quantity (EOQ) 176

just-in-time (JIT) system 177

Pareto diagram 179

Questions

1. When a middle manager was asked if he was good at arithmetic, he replied, "Why should I be? I make all my calculations by computer." What is your evaluation of his response to the question?

2. Visualize yourself as the manager of an athletic club. Give three examples of data you might be able to use in making decisions about how to improve the profitability of the club.

3. Gantt charts have been around for more than 100 years, even though they are now implemented with software. Why do Gantt charts have such staying power?

4. How might you apply break-even analysis to estimate the payoff from your post-secondary school education?

5. How might the Pareto principle apply to merchandise returned from online shoppers?

6. At least one half of new restaurants fail within the first couple of years, even when these restaurants appear to be busy much of the time. Describe how two of the techniques described in this chapter might help a person prevent opening a restaurant that is doomed to fail.

7. An important part of management is dealing with people. Where is the human touch in any of the techniques described in this chapter?

Skill-Building Exercise 6-A: Developing a PERT Network

Use the following information about a company fitness center project to construct a PERT diagram. Be sure to indicate the critical path with a dark arrow. Work individually or in small groups.

Event	Description	Time Required (units)	Preceding Event
A	Complete audit of employee interest	6	none
B	Compare to other companies	15	A
C	Collect internal information	6	A
D	Identify fitness needs	3	B, C
E	Identify features of the center	7	D
F	Elicit employee participation	20	A
G	Implement fitness program	6	E, F
H	Measure participation in center	8	G

Skill-Building Exercise 6-B: Break-Even Analysis

On recent vacation trips to Juarez, Mexico, you noticed retail stores and street vendors selling inexpensive blood pressure monitors (sphygmomanometer). The prices for the inexpensive monitors ranged from $25 to $40 U.S. A flash of inspiration hits you. Why not sell Mexican-assembled blood pressure monitors back home to Americans, using a van as your store? Every three months you would drive the 350 miles to Mexico and load up on these novelty blood pressure cuffs. You are thinking of negotiating to receive large quantity discounts.

You would park your van on busy streets and nearby parks, wherever you could obtain a permit. You would typically display the monitors outside the van, but on a rainy day people could step inside. Your intention is to operate your traveling monitor sale about 12 hours per week. If you could make enough money from your business, you could attend classes full-time during the day. You intend to sell the blood pressure monitors at an average of $65 per unit.

Based on preliminary analysis, you have discovered your primary fixed costs per month would be: $550 for payments on a van, $175 for gas and maintenance, $75 for insurance and $60 for a street vendor's permit. You will also be driving down to Mexico every three months at $600 per trip, resulting in a $200 per month travel cost. Your variable costs would be an average of $30 per monitor and 45¢ for placing each monitor in an attractive box.

1. How many monitors will you have to sell each month before you start to make a profit?

2. If the average cost of your monitors rises to $35, how many monitors will you have to sell each month if you hold your price to $65 per unit?

Management Now—Online Skill-Building Exercise: The Reality of the Pareto Principle

The Pareto principle, which states that 80 percent of effects are created by 20 percent of causes, has become entrenched in management thinking. We regularly hear such glib statements as, "20 percent of our customers account for 80 percent of our sales." Conduct research on the Internet to find at least one example of the 80/20 rule that has taken place in the last several years. Perhaps a recent product recall will prove fruitful, such as one model of a product creating the vast majority of the problems. At the same time, see if you can find any evidence that refutes the reliability of this principle or rule. In other words, can you find a current example of a situation in which 20 percent of the causes did not produce 80 percent of the effects?

CEO Baxter Strives for Data-Based Decision Making

CEO Baxter was conducting a quarterly review of operations with his top-management team. One of the subjects he introduced, as well as informing the participants in advance of the meeting, was what the company was doing with its powerful new analytics capability. Baxter explained he was already aware of how advanced analytics, or Big Data, were helping make good decisions in marketing and selling many of its consumer products.

"At the moment, I would like to review what we are doing with analytics to help us do a better job of managing operations and human resources. We are paying large sums of money to collect and analyze data, but what's the payoff? We want to make good use of data-based decision making."

Roger, the manufacturing vice-president said some new machine analytics were providing precise data about when to schedule maintenance on machines, including the optimal time to lubricate machines with hundreds of parts. Baxter replied, "Not very impressive. You and your staff were doing a good job maintaining complex machinery before we hired the analytics consultants."

Samantha, the vice president of information technology explained that recent advances in analyzing vast amounts of data have provided her and her staff with a ton of facts about how employees use computers, the Internet, and mobile devices provided by the company. Samantha said, "We can now tell you which websites our employees visit, when they visit the sites, how much time they spend sending and receiving e-mails, and which employees receive the most e-mails. We even know which employees use our IT equipment after hours and on vacation." Baxter responded, "And in what way are these data telling us anything useful for operating the company more efficiently?"

Charlotte, the HR vice president, explained that her department was receiving a lot of information for HR analytics. She said, "We have a precise picture of which employees are using which benefits, and which employees are most likely thinking about retiring or quitting. We have even developed a data set of which employees are the most likely to participate in company training, or participate in MOOC, and who is most likely to have to take care of an elderly parent."

Baxter responded, "Charlotte, you have put us in the realm of Big Brother. But why should our company care? Why do we really need information about which employees are most likely to participate in training? When they ask us for training, and we ask them to participate in training, then we will have the information we need."

After shaking his head for a few seconds, Baxter said, "Maybe I'm a little dense. But will somebody give me a clear explanation of how our investment in Big Data is doing anything but making our consultants happy? We want to make data-based decisions, but why waste time?"

Case Questions

1 What advice can you offer Roger, Samantha, and Charlotte to better impress Baxter about the usefulness of analytics and Big Data at the company?

2 What advice can you offer Baxter to help him be more realistic about the use of Big Data and data-based decision making at the company?

3 What, if any, ethical issues are involved in this case?

The Alarming Walk-In Bathtub Forecast

Marvin is the product manager for walk-in bathtubs at a major manufacturer of bathroom fixtures and interiors. The walk-in bathtubs his company manufactures are distributed by home-supply retailers, home renovation companies, and companies that advertise walk-in bathtubs over television, Sunday newspaper supplements, and online. Marvin is pleased with the steady growth in the sales of walk-in tubs over the last several years. Today he has a meeting with Chloe, the company market researcher, to discuss future demand for walk-in bathtubs.

Marvin says to Chloe that he is eager to meet with her to help forecast the growth in future demand for the walk-in tubs. Smiling, he says, "If the trend continues in five years, walk-in tubs will be in more demand than the standard sit-in type. People want safety, and even those hold-on bars in our tubs generate sales."

Chloe responded, "Please don't shoot the messenger, but I have some news that might cool your enthusiasm. With the help of an outside data scientist, we just ran an AI report on the future demand for walk-in tubs, and the results are now what you would suspect. The future demand for our tubs will be at best stable, but is most likely to decrease." With an expression of surprise, Marvin responded, "Chloe your AI report is counterintuitive. The population is aging. Thousands of baby boomers are retiring each day. Walk-in bathtubs are poised for a sales boom."

Chloe explained, "My report is based on science, not common sense. Our artificial intelligence analysis examined hundreds of variables simultaneously that could affect future demand for walk-in tubs. Yes, the population is aging, but there are other factors that could decrease the demand for your tubs. With all the emphasis on physical fitness, better nutrition, and better medical care, millions of people are remaining fully mobile longer. So standard tubs fit them just fine.

"Another factor that could limit demand is that many of the least mobile people are moving into residence for assisted living. As a result, existing individual houses are less likely to have walk-in bathtubs installed. Yet another counter-intuitive factor is that many older people want to main a self-image of youth and health. Purchasing a walk-in bathtub runs counter to that image.

"Putting all these AI findings to together, the best you can hope for in the next five years is a stable demand for our line of walk-in bathtubs."

Marvin concluded, "Your AI-based forecast casts a gray cloud over the future of our product. But before I present a forecast of future demand for walk-in tubs to upper management, I'm going to think this over. Maybe the artificial intelligence report could benefit from a little practical intelligence."

Case Questions

1 How seriously should Marvin take the AI forecast of declining or stable demand for walk-in bathtubs?

2 What do you think Chloe should do to better convince Marvin of her findings?

3 When Marvin submits his sales forecast for walk-in tubs to upper management, what ethical obligation does he have to incorporate the AI findings submitted by Chloe?

ENDNOTES

1. Original story created from facts and observations in the following sources: Serena No and Laura Stevens, "Unwanted Presents Pile Up: Goods Account for a Quarter of Web Sales are Due to Be Returned this Holiday Season," *The Wall Street Journal*, December 28, 2015, pp. B1, B7; Courtney Reagan, "That Sweater You Don't Like is a Trillion-Dollar Problem for Retailers. These Companies Want to Fix It," *CNBC* (www.cnbc.com), January 12, 2019, pp. 1–2; "About us," *www.shorewoodliquidators.com*, 2020; "Shorewood Liquidators, *www.indeed.com*, January 2020, p. 2; "e-Commerce Share of Retail Sales in United States from 2013-2021," *www.statista.com*, January 4, 2020, p. 1.

2. "The Advantages of Data-Driven Decision-Making," *HBS Online* (https://online.hbs.ed), August 26, 2019, p. 1

3. Reported in "Am I too Old to Become a Truck Driver?" *Roadmaster* (www.roadmaster.com), p. 1. Accessed January 6, 2020.

4. Dan Woog, "Couples Aged 50-Plus Turn to Trucking as a Second Career," *http://career-advice.monster.com* © 2016; Stephanie Chen, "How Baby Boomers Turn Wanderlust Into Trucking Careers," *The Wall Street Journal*, August 24, 2006, pp. A1, A8.

5. "Forecasting in Business," *Encyclopedia.com* (www.encyclopedia.com), updated December 30, 2019. P. 1.

6. John S. Hammond, Ralph L. Keeney, and Howard Raiffa, "The Hidden Traps in Decision Making," *Harvard Business Review*, September–October 1998, pp. 55–58.

7. Hernân Asorey, 'How AI Is Transforming Forecasting for the Better," *www.saleforce.com*, pp. 1–3. Accessed January 6, 2020.

8. Gopinathan Thachappilly, "Revenue Forecasts Initiate Business Plan November 15, 2009 *http://forecastinginfo.blogspot.com/2010/07/revenue-forecasts-initiate-business.html*, November 15, 2009.

9. Cari Tuna, "Pendulum Is Swinging Back on 'Scenario Planning'," *The Wall Street Journal*, July 6, 2009, p. B6.

10. Angela Wilkinson and Roland Kupers, "Living in the Future: How Scenario Planning Changed Corporate Strategy," *Harvard Business Review*, May 2013, pp. 118–127.

11. "Why Inuit CEO Says Forget Forecasting," *Executive Leadership*, November 2014, p. 1.

12. "Gantt Chart," *NetMBA* (http://www.netmba.com/operations/project/gantt). © 2002–2010.

13. Carole Matthews, "Decision Making with Decision Trees," *Inc.com*, April 2003, p. 1.

14. The idea for this particular layout of a basic decision tree is based on "Decision Tree," *www.referenceforbusiness.com*.

15. Neal Haldene, "Novi Center Teaches Lean Way of Working," *Detroit News* (http://www.detnews.com), September 21, 2006.

16. Bo Hou, Hing Kai Chan, and Xiaoju Wang, "An Account for Implementing Just-In-Time: A Case Study of the Automotive Industry in China," *International Journal of Engineering and Technology Innovation*, Vol. 3, No. 3, 2013, pp. 156–167.

17. Kerri Simon, "Pareto Chart," *Six Sigma* (http://www.isixsigma.com), accessed January 6, 2020.

Part Three

Organizing

CHAPTER 7

Job Design and Arranging Work

OBJECTIVES

After studying this chapter and doing the exercises, you should be able to:

1 Describe the importance of job specialization and job design including automation and robots.

2 Describe job enrichment, including the job characteristics model.

3 Describe job involvement, enlargement, and rotation.

4 Explain how workers use job crafting to modify their jobs.

5 Illustrate how ergonomic factors can be part of job design.

6 Summarize the various modified work schedules.

7 Explain how job design can contribute to a high-performance work system.

An Amazon worker named Amanda Taillon was working with a robot at a company warehouse in Connecticut during the busy pre-Christmas period. She commented that the robot sure weighs a lot. Close by, a fleet of 6-foot-tall roving robot shelves moved swiftly around behind a chain-link fence. Taillon's key responsibility was to enter a cage and slow down the wheeled warehouse robots long enough so they can pick up a fallen piece of merchandise or halt a traffic jam. She strapped a light-up utility belt around her waist that functions like a superheroine's force field commanding the robot closest by to stop suddenly. Taillon's belt also commands other robots to slow down or adjust their routes.

Taillon said when you are out there on the floor, and you can hear them moving but can't see them, she would often wonder, "Where are they going to come from? It's a little nerve wracking at first."

Beth Gutelius, a professor at the University of Illinois at Chicago, interviewed warehouse workers around the country. She found that warehouses powered by robotics and AI software can trigger burnout by adding more work and putting heavy pressure on workers to rev up their performance. Gutelius also notes that although workers are usually trained on how to work with robots safely, "The problem is it becomes very difficult to do so when the productivity standards are se so high."

Frank Hearl, a staff member at the Center for Occupation Robotics Research, (a division of the National Institution of Safety and Health) said that workers have to learn to trust robots in order to minimize their concerns. He said, "It's the same type of trust that one builds in any co-worker. At first, you're watching the new person perform, and then as you see that he or she is doing the job correctly and safely over and over again. That's how you build trust."

Tye Brady, the chief technologist at Amazon Robotics, thinks that human problems with warehouse robots are surmountable. He says, "The efficiencies we gain from our associates and robotics working together harmoniously—what I like to call a symphony of humans and machines working together—allows us to pass along a lower cost to our customers."[1]

The anecdote and report about the human problems that robots sometimes create illustrates how managers often have to deal with the impact of job design and technology on the workforce. This chapter will explain basic concepts relating to job design, such as making jobs more challenging and giving employees more control over their working hours and workplace. We also look at how workers often shape their own jobs, the importance of ergonomics, and job designs for high-performance work systems. The next chapter will describe how work is divided throughout an organization.

JOB SPECIALIZATION AND JOB DESIGN

LEARNING OBJECTIVE **1**

Describe the importance of job specialization and job design including automation and robots.

job specialization
The degree to which a job holder performs only a limited number of tasks.

A major consideration in job design is how specialized the job holder must be. **Job specialization** is the degree to which a jobholder performs only a limited number of tasks. Specialists handle a narrow range of tasks especially well. High occupational-level specialists include the investment consultant who specializes in municipal bonds and the surgeon who concentrates on liver transplants. Specialists at the first occupational level are often referred to as entry-level workers, production specialists, support workers, or operatives.

A generalized job requires the handling of many different tasks. An extreme example of a top-level generalist is the owner of a small business who performs such varied tasks as making the product, selling it, negotiating with banks for loans, and hiring new employees. An extreme example of a generalist at the first (or entry) occupational level is the maintenance worker who packs boxes, sweeps, shovels snow, mows the lawn, and cleans lavatories.

Advantages and Disadvantages of Job Specialization

Job specialization allows for the development of expertise at all occupational levels. When employees perform the same task repeatedly, they become highly knowledgeable. Many employees derive status and self-esteem from being experts at some task. Specialized jobs at lower occupational levels require less training time and less learning ability, which can prove to be a key advantage when the available labor force lacks special skills. For example, McDonald's could never have grown so large if each restaurant needed expert chefs. Instead, newcomers to the workforce can quickly learn such specialized skills as preparing hamburgers and French fries. These newcomers can be paid entry-level wages, enabling many workers to have their first opportunity to enter the workforce.

Job specialization also has disadvantages. Coordinating the workforce can be difficult when several employees do small parts of one job. Somebody must take responsibility for pulling together the small pieces of the total task. Some employees prefer narrowly specialized jobs, but the majority prefers broad tasks that give them a feeling of control over what they are doing. Although many technical and professional workers join the workforce as specialists, they often become bored by performing a narrow range of tasks.

Automation, Robots, and Job Specialization

Automation has been used to replace some aspects of human endeavor in the office and the factory ever since the Industrial Revolution. Automation typically involves a machine that performs a specialized task previously performed by people. Automation is widely used in factories, offices, and stores. A major purpose of automation is to increase productivity by reducing the labor required to deliver a product or service. A representative example is robotic equipment that can polish automobile parts.

Two automation devices used in the retail store are optical scanners and the automatic recording of remaining inventory when a customer checks out. The computerization of the workplace represents automation in hundreds of ways, such as personal computers decreasing the need for clerical support in organizations. Today, only high-level managers have personal office assistants. Others rely on their computers and mobile devices to perform many chores.

E-mail and text messaging have automated the delivery of many types of messages once sent by postal mail or messenger service, including sending photos and graphics around the world. As a result, government-run postal services have much less mail to deliver. Similarly, online shopping is an automated activity that has eliminated many retail sales positions.

Automation enhances job satisfaction when annoying or dangerous tasks are removed, and automation does not result in job cuts. When automation helps a business become more productive, the net result is often the creation of more jobs. For example, an insurance or financial company that automates an increasing number of routine transactions has more money to invest in new branches and new services, such as the wealth management division of Allstate.

Robots are a major part of automation, and now perform may tasks outside of the factory. An advanced example is that drones and algorithms are performing many home appraisals that were performed in the past by human appraisers. (A drone can be classified as a robot.) The justification of the use of these robots is that lenders and home buyers save money, and the appraisal can be completed more quickly.[2]

A major advance in the business use of robots is collaborative robots (cobots) that work alongside humans performing specialized tasks, such as the Amazon robot mentioned in the chapter opener. Cobot arms are programmed to brake when they touch humans, to minimize accidents. An example of a cobot in action is a robot programmed to do visual inspections of automotive parts made by Kay Manufacturing in Calumet City, Illinois. A machine operator at the company said he will not miss doing the task himself, just as he does not miss the manual work in his job taken over by robots. The manual work contributed to arthritis in his hands and feet.[3]

As robots and cobots perform an increasing number of specialized tasks, there is widespread concern that unemployment will rise dramatically, such as when a manufacturing floor is run almost entirely by robots. Many labor economists, however, think that while robots displace many workers, they, along with other forms of automation, wind up creating different types of jobs. Giant distribution centers staffed with many humans continue to be built, and so do factories that produce robots. In recent years, many counties have experienced a labor shortage suggesting that robots have not eliminated so many jobs. Another argument is that robots make remaining workers more productive and their companies more profitable. In turn, more money is available for consumer purchases and investment, leading to more jobs and more spending on luxury goods.[4]

Despite this optimistic thinking about macro-trends, many people do lose their jobs to robots and other forms of automation, and suffer negative consequences. The real estate appraisers mentioned above are one example, and so are bartenders who have been replaced by robots that prepare mixed drinks.

Job Description and Job Design

job description
A written statement of the key features of a job along with the activities required to perform it effectively.

Before choosing a job design, managers and human resource professionals develop a job description. The **job description** is a written statement of the key features of a job, along with the activities required to perform it effectively. Sometimes a description must be written to fit the critical features of a position. For example, the job description of a customer-service representative might call for an excessive amount of listening to complaints, thus creating possible stress. Figure 7-1 presents a job description of a middle-level manager.

With today's emphasis on empowerment and employee creativity, job descriptions have been losing their stature and importance. Nevertheless, a carefully written job description can give employees the structure and direction they might need.

LEARNING OBJECTIVE 2

Describe job enrichment, including the job characteristics model.

JOB ENRICHMENT AND THE JOB CHARACTERISTICS MODEL

job enrichment
An approach to including more challenge and responsibility in jobs to make them more appealing to employees.

Job enrichment is an approach to including more challenge and responsibility in jobs to make them more appealing to most employees. At its best, job enrichment gives workers a sense of ownership, responsibility, and accountability for their work. Because job enrichment leads to a more exciting job, it often increases employee job satisfaction and motivation. People usually work harder at tasks they find enjoyable and rewarding, just as they put effort into a favorite hobby. The general approach to enriching a job is to build into it more planning and decision making, controlling, and responsibility. Most managers have enriched jobs; most data entry specialists do not.

Characteristics of an Enriched Job

The design of an enriched job includes as many of the characteristics in the following list as possible, based on the pioneering work of Frederick Herzberg, as well as updated research.[5] (Figure 7-2 summarizes the characteristics and consequences of enriched jobs.) The person holding the job must perceive these characteristics as part of the job. Supervisors and group members frequently have different perceptions of job characteristics. For example, supervisors are more likely to think a job has a big impact on the organization.[6] A worker who is responsible for placing used soft-drink cans in a recycling bin might not think his job is significant. Yet the supervisor might

Figure 7-1 Job Description for Branch Manager, Insurance

Manages the branch office, including such functions as underwriting, claims processing, loss prevention, marketing, and auditing, and resolves related technical questions and issues. Hires new insurance agents, develops new business, and updates the regional manager regarding the profit-and-loss operating results of the branch office, insurance trends, matters impacting the branch-office function, and competitor methods. The manager makes extensive use of information technology to carry out all of these activities, including spreadsheet analyses and establishing customer databases.

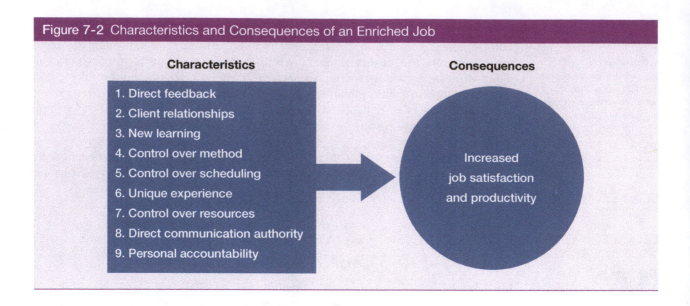

Figure 7-2 Characteristics and Consequences of an Enriched Job

Characteristics

1. Direct feedback
2. Client relationships
3. New learning
4. Control over method
5. Control over scheduling
6. Unique experience
7. Control over resources
8. Direct communication authority
9. Personal accountability

Consequences

Increased job satisfaction and productivity

perceive the individual to be contributing to the social-responsibility goal of creating a cleaner, less-congested environment—a green job.

1 *Direct feedback.* Employees should receive an immediate evaluation of their work. This feedback can be built into the job (such as the feedback that closing a sale gives a sales representative) or provided by the supervisor.

2 *Client relationships.* A job is automatically enriched when an employee has a client or customer to serve, whether that client is inside or outside the firm. Serving a client is more satisfying to most people than performing work solely for a manager.

3 *New learning.* An enriched job allows its holder to acquire new knowledge. The learning can stem from the actual job experiences or from training programs associated with the job. An aspect of new learning affecting many managerial and professional positions is to acquire knowledge abut how to use data analytics. One example would be a loan officer for automobiles using AI to estimate the credit-worthiness of a loan applicant who has no credit history.

4 *Control over method.* When workers have some control over which method to choose to accomplish a task, their task motivation generally increases. An office manager, for example, might be told to decrease energy costs by 10 percent in the building. She would have control over the method if empowered to decide how to decrease costs, such as adjusting the thermostat or finding a lower-cost energy supplier.

5 *Control over scheduling.* The ability to schedule one's own work contributes to job enrichment. Scheduling includes the authority to decide when to tackle which assignment and having some say in setting working hours.

6 *Unique experience.* An enriched job exhibits some unique qualities or features. A public-relations assistant, for example, has the opportunity to interact with visiting celebrities.

7 *Control over resources.* Another contribution to enrichment comes from some control over resources, such as money, material, or people.

8 *Direct communication authority.* An enriched job provides workers the opportunity to communicate directly with other people who use their output. A software engineer with an enriched job, for example, handles complaints about the software he or she developed. The advantages of this dimension of an enriched job are similar to those derived from maintaining client relationships.

9 *Personal accountability.* In an enriched job, workers take responsibility for their results. They accept credit for a job done well and blame for a job done poorly.

A highly enriched job with all nine of the preceding characteristics gives the jobholder an opportunity to satisfy high-level psychological needs, such as self-fulfillment. Sometimes the jobs of managers are too enriched, with too much responsibility and too many risks. A job with some of these characteristics would be moderately enriched. An impoverished job has none. Information technology workers are another occupational group that may suffer from over-enriched jobs. Working with computers and software at an advanced level may represent healthy job enrichment for many workers—working with information technology often gives a person direct feedback, new learning, and personal accountability. However, many other computer workers feel stressed by the complexity of information technology, the amount of continuous learning involved, and frequent hardware and software breakdowns beyond the control of the worker.

Many of the characteristics of an enriched job are now incorporated into managerial approaches such as empowerment and employee engagement. Formal programs of job enrichment are relatively rare today, at least in the sense of using the term job enrichment.

The Job Characteristics Model of Job Enrichment

job characteristics model
A method of job enrichment that focuses on the task and interpersonal dimensions of a job.

Expanding the concept of job enrichment creates the **job characteristics model**, a method of job enrichment that focuses on the tasks and interpersonal dimensions of a job.[7] As Figure 7-3 shows, five measurable characteristics of jobs improve employee motivation, satisfaction, and performance. All five characteristics have been incorporated into the four major dimensions of job design and were defined previously. The job characteristics model is considered to be the most influential model of work design, and still has considerable relevance in the modern organization.

As Figure 7-3 reports, these core job characteristics relate to critical psychological states or key mental attitudes. Skill variety, task identity, and task significance lead to a feeling that the work is meaningful. As will be described in Chapter 11 about motivation, meaningful work is a major driver of employee engagement or commitment. Quite often when employees feel overqualified for their jobs, such as a chemistry major working as a checkout associate in a supermarket, work will be perceived as less significant. An interesting twist to this observation was found in a study of professional workers in information technology companies located in China. It was found that when workers felt their peers were also overqualified, their own work was perceived to have more task significance.[8] If our chemistry major feels other physical science majors are checkout clerks in the supermarket, he might feel, "Not bad temporary work for a chemistry grad. At least I am helping feed people."

The task dimension of autonomy leads quite logically to a feeling of responsibility for work outcomes. And the feedback dimension leads to knowledge of results. According to the model, a redesigned job must lead to these three psychological states for

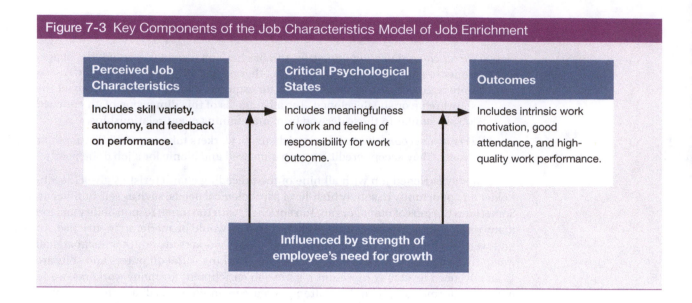

Figure 7-3 Key Components of the Job Characteristics Model of Job Enrichment

workers to achieve the outcomes of internal motivation, job satisfaction, low turnover and absenteeism, and high-quality performance.

JOB INVOLVEMENT, ENLARGEMENT, AND ROTATION

Job enrichment, including the job characteristics model, requires a comprehensive program. Managers can also improve the motivational aspects of job design through less complicated procedures: job involvement, job enlargement, and job rotation. All three processes are built into the more comprehensive job enrichment.

Job involvement is the degree to which individuals identify psychologically with their work. It also refers to the importance of work to a person's total self-image. If an insurance claims examiner regards his job as a major part of his identity, he experiences high job involvement. For example, at a social gathering the claims examiner would inform people shortly after meeting them, "I'm a claims examiner with Nationwide." The employee-involvement groups in quality management are based on job involvement. By making decisions about quality improvement, the team members ideally identify psychologically with their work. A person who experiences job involvement will usually be committed to his or her position and employer. Figure 7-4 gives you an opportunity to think about job involvement as it applies to you.

Job enlargement refers to increasing the number and variety of tasks within a job. The technique was developed to help workers combat boredom. Because the tasks are approximately at the same level of responsibility, job enlargement is also referred to as horizontal job loading. In contrast, *job enrichment* is referred to as vertical job loading, because the jobholder takes on higher-level job responsibility. The claims examiner would experience job enlargement if he were given additional responsibilities, such as examining claims for boats and motorcycles, as well as automobiles.

As responsibilities expand in job enlargement, jobholders usually find themselves juggling multiple priorities. Two, three, four, or even more demands might be facing the worker. In one approach to handling multiple priorities, a jobholder ranks them in order of importance and then tackles the most important one first. With this approach,

LEARNING OBJECTIVE **3**

Describe job involvement, enlargement, and rotation.

job involvement
The degree to which individuals identify psychologically with their work.

job enlargement
Increasing the number and variety of tasks within a job.

Figure 7-4 How Involved Are You?

Indicate how strongly you agree with the following statements by circling the number that appears below the appropriate heading: DS = disagree strongly; D = disagree; N = neutral; A = agree; AS = agree strongly. Respond in relation to a present job, the job you hope to have, or schoolwork.

		DS	D	N	A	AS
1	My work is the biggest contributor to my self-image.	1	2	3	4	5
2	Work is only a way of getting other things in life that I want.	5	4	3	2	1
3	The most meaningful things that happen to me involve my work.	1	2	3	4	5
4	I often concentrate so hard on my work that I'm unaware of what is going on around me.	1	2	3	4	5
5	If I inherited enough money, I would spend the rest of my life in leisure activities.	5	4	3	2	1
6	I attempt to minimize interruptions in my work, such as shifting my attention to a website unrelated to the task at hand.	1	2	3	4	5
7	I am very much emotionally involved personally in my work.	1	2	3	4	5
8	Most things in life are more important than work.	5	4	3	2	1
9	Working full time blocks me from doing a lot of things in life I would prefer to do.	5	4	3	2	1
10	My work is usually the most exciting part of my day.	1	2	3	4	5
	Score					

Scoring and interpretation: Total the numbers circled, and then use the following guide to interpret.

45–50	Your attitudes suggest intense job involvement. Such attitudes should contribute highly to productivity and satisfaction.
28–44	Your attitudes suggest a moderate degree of job involvement. To sustain a high level of productivity, you would need to work toward becoming more involved in your work.
10–27	Your attitudes suggest a low degree of job involvement. It would be difficult to sustain a successful, professional career with such low involvement.

Source: The idea for the job involvement scale stems from Myron Gable and Frank Dangello, "Job Involvement, Machiavellianism, and Job Performance," *Journal of Business and Psychology*, Winter 1994, p. 163.

the lowest-priority tasks may be neglected. With a more recommended approach, the jobholder finishes the top-priority task, and then moves immediately to all other tasks. Top-priority items can be tackled again after the lesser tasks are completed. Yet, if the manager or team leader insists that a specific task must be done immediately, it is good office politics to work on that task. Some catch-up time at night or on weekends may then be invested in work to avoid falling behind on other projects.

An approach to job enlargement has surfaced as a way for companies to reduce compensation costs when new positions are filled. In one variation of this approach, a mid-level position is combined with a more junior one. The position is then advertised and offered at a lower salary. In another variation of job enlargement, more senior people are hired and later find they are responsible for performing their own work as well as tasks that were formerly the responsibility of subordinates. A specific example of adding responsibilities to a position to save the company compensation costs surrounds hiring. For example, after being hired, a chief marketing officer might be expected to also handle ordinary media tasks, such as negotiating rates for advertising.[9]

Job rotation is a temporary switching of job assignments. Formal programs of job rotation usually last about one year.[10] In this way, employees develop new skills and learn about how other aspects of the unit or organization work. However, the potential advantages of job rotation are lost if a person is rotated from one dull job to another. A motivational form of job rotation would be for the claims examiner to investigate auto and small-truck claims one month, and large trucks the next. When a worker is rotated from one job to another, the position he or she left behind should be adequately staffed. When two competent workers switch jobs, the potential problem takes care of itself.

job rotation
A temporary switching of job assignments.

Job rotation helps prevent workers from feeling bored or in a rut. In addition to learning new skills, job rotation gives workers an opportunity to learn more about how the organization operates. A marketing specialist who was rotated into a finance position for six months commented, "Now I really understand firsthand how every penny counts when the company is attempting to obtain a good return on investment."

Job enlargement and job rotation offer similar advantages and disadvantages to the individual and the organization. Through job enlargement and job rotation, workers develop a broader set of skills, making them more valuable and flexible. Job rotation offers the career-boosting advantage of obtaining broad experience, such as a bank manager having the opportunity to work with both retail and commercial lending. Pushed to extremes, however, job enlargement and rotation lead to feelings of being overworked.

JOB CRAFTING AND JOB DESIGN

LEARNING OBJECTIVE **4**

Explain how workers use job crafting to modify their jobs.

In the traditional view of a job, a competent worker carefully follows a job description, and good performance means the person accomplishes what is specified in the job description. A contemporary view sees a job description as only a guideline: the competent worker exceeds the constraints of a job description. He or she takes on constructive activities not mentioned in the job description.

Workers sometimes deviate from their job descriptions by modifying their job to fit their personal preferences and capabilities. According to the research of Amy Wrzesniewski and Jane E. Dutton, employees craft their jobs by changing the tasks they perform and their contacts with others to make their jobs more meaningful.[11] A major point is that the changes made in the job are self-initiated.[12] To add variety to her job, for example, a team leader might make nutritional recommendations to team members. The team leader alters her task of coaching about strictly work-related issues to also coaching about personal health. In this way, she broadens her role in terms of her impact on the lives of work associates.

Job crafting refers to the physical and mental changes individuals make in the task or relationship aspects of their job. Three common types of job crafting include: (1) the number and types of job tasks, (2) the interactions with others on the job, and (3) one's view of the job. The most frequent purpose of crafting is to make the job more meaningful or enriched. A cook, for example, might add flair to a meal, which was not required, just to inject a little personal creativity. Job crafting is therefore modeled after the pride that craftsman and craftswomen take in their work, such as a person who makes boots or furniture by hand. At its best, job crafting can increase job performance, job satisfaction, and feelings of well-being.

job crafting
The physical and mental changes individuals make in the task or relationship aspects of their job.

Current research on job crafting identifies two broad dimensions, *role crafting* and *resource crafting*, with both having sub-dimensions. The *work-role expansion* component of role crafting focuses on self-initiated expansion of the incumbent's work role to include elements of work not included in the formal job description. (This is the same as type 1 mentioned above.) The difference is that under work-role expansion, people can add personally relevant content such as physical exercise to the job. The *social expansion* part of role expansion involves the proactive use of people to make the job more meaningful, such as enlarging one's social network in the organization. The *work-role reduction* part of role crafting involves deliberately reducing certain job requirements, like an office assistant no longer ordering food for office luncheons.

The *work-organization* component of resource crafting involves organizing the tangible elements of work. An example would be laying out all the tooling needed and making sure everything is organized. The *adoption* component refers to the use of technology and other sources of knowledge to alter and improve the job. An example would be finding software to help organize a project. The *metacognition* component of work organization includes making sense of things and manipulating one's psychological state. For example, if someone is angry at you, do not focus on the anger, instead focus on finding a solution to the problem. The *withdrawal crafting* component of resource crafting is changing the job in order to remove oneself mentally or physically form a person, situation, or event. An example would be taking a brief walk away from a nasty coworker.[13]

Job crafting can also take place at the group level, whereby the group collaboratively decides how to improve and enlarge the position. A study with teachers and aides in 62 childcare centers found that crafting by the group resulted in better job satisfaction and performance.[14] An example of job crafting by childcare teachers and aides would be offering guidance to parents on how they can involve their children in activities at home other than watching television and playing video games.

A concern about job crafting is that it can actually lower performance as well as cooperation with co-workers. The major problem is that crafting can take time away for job duties that are useful to the organization and for job performance. Small amounts of crafting do not create these problems. Yet research conducted with 295 individuals enrolled in an MBA course, suggested that moderate levels of crafting create the most problems. An example of how crafting could lower job performance is for the job holder to spend too much time searching the Internet for job-related information. When job crafting reaches a high level, the incumbent will often receive feedback from co-workers and the manager that will help reduce the crafting to useful levels.[15] The customer care supervisor might say to an extensive job crafter, "You are spending too much time in general conversation with customers. As a result, your productivity is falling behind."

The various approaches to job crafting provide useful information about how jobs can be made more satisfying and lead to higher productivity. However, another explanation of why workers are attracted to particular jobs and perform well is missing. **Job embeddedness** refers to the array of forces attaching people to their jobs. Three dimensions are included in job embeddedness.[16] First, are links—the formal or informal connections to people in the organization or community. (You might stick with a job because you love your city.) Second is sacrifice, or the perceived cost of material or psychological benefits you would forfeit if you left the job. (You might decide that relocation to another geographic area to find new employment would not be worth the many associated costs.) Third, is fit, the compatibility or comfort with the organizational environment and the external environment. (You might not find your job to be fascinating but you think highly of the company and enjoy your community.)

job embeddedness
The array of forces attaching people to their jobs.

ERGONOMICS AND JOB DESIGN

A key principle of job design is that the job should be laid out to decrease the chances that it will physically harm the incumbent. According to the U.S. Occupational and Health Agency (OSHA), **ergonomics** is the science of fitting the worker to the job. Ergonomics seeks to minimize the physical demands on workers and optimize system performance, and therefore has considerable relevance to job design. Three principles of ergonomics are recommended when designing physically-demanding jobs:

- Workers should be able to adopt several different postures that are safe and comfortable.

- When workers exert muscular force, they should be encouraged to use the largest muscle groups (such as using the legs and body to help lift a box rather than only the arms).

- Whenever possible, workers should be able to perform regular work activities with their joints, in the middle range of movement.[17]

It is important for managers to help prevent ergonomic problems for ethical and humanitarian reasons. In addition, injuries and illnesses stemming from ergonomic problems drive up health costs, including insurance premiums.

Musculoskeletal Disorders Including Carpal Tunnel Syndrome

A frequent problem in factories, mills, supermarkets and offices is work-related musculoskeletal disorders, or problems involving muscle and bones. Musculoskeletal disorders represent more than 100 injuries that take place when there is a mismatch between the physical requirements of the job and the physical capacity of the human body. Overuse is a common problem. A supermarket cashier might stay in good shape working a few hours a day but lifting several hundred bags of groceries in eight hours may create a severe back injury. OSHA recommends designing check-out counters to reduce ergonomic risk factors, such as twisting or extended reaching, can improve cashier effectiveness and productivity.

Solutions to some potential ergonomic problems can be quite simple. For example, working the back of a deep display case to face or stock merchandise can be awkward and uncomfortable, especially when heavy items are involved. One solution that OSHA recommends for this problem is display cases that are stocked from the back (as is common practice today). The product, such as cartons of milk, slides down an inclined shelf so that it is always in front of the customer. The employee stocking the shelf experiences less physical strain.[18]

Musculoskeletal disorders also include **cumulative trauma disorders**—injuries caused by repetitive motions over prolonged periods of time. These disorders now account for almost half of all occupational injuries and illnesses in the United States. Any occupation involving excessive repetitive motions, including bricklayer and meat cutter or fishery worker, can lead to cumulative trauma disorder. Vibrating tools, such as jackhammers, also cause such disorders. The use of computers and other high-tech equipment, such as price scanners, contributes to the surge in the number of cumulative trauma disorders.

Extensive keyboarding places severe strain on hand and wrist muscles, often leading to **carpal tunnel syndrome**. This syndrome occurs when frequent bending of the wrist causes swelling in a tunnel of bones and ligaments in the wrist. The nerve that gives feeling to the hand is pinched, resulting in tingling and numbness in the fingers.

LEARNING OBJECTIVE **5**

Illustrate how ergonomic factors can be part of job design.

ergonomics
The science of fitting the worker to the job.

cumulative trauma disorders
Injuries caused by repetitive motions over prolonged periods of time.

carpal tunnel syndrome
The most frequent cumulative trauma disorder that occurs when frequent wrist bending results in swelling, leading to a pinched nerve.

Overuse of the computer mouse is a major contributor to wrist and tendon injuries. The symptoms of carpal tunnel syndrome are severe. Many workers suffering from the syndrome are unable to differentiate hot and cold by touch and lose finger strength. They often appear clumsy because they have difficulty with everyday tasks, such as tying their shoes or picking up small objects. Treatment of carpal tunnel syndrome may involve surgery to release pressure on the median nerve. Another approach is anti-inflammatory drugs to reduce tendon swelling. You have probably seen many students and co-workers wearing braces on their wrists, or who have had operations to ease carpal tunnel syndrome.

To help prevent and decrease the incidence of cumulative trauma disorders, many companies select equipment designed for that purpose. Figure 7-5 depicts a workstation based on ergonomic principles developed to engineer a good fit between person and machine. In addition, the following steps should be taken to prevent cumulative trauma disorders[19]:

- Analyze each job with an eye toward possible hazards on that job, including equipment that is difficult to operate.

- Install equipment that minimizes awkward hand and body movements. Try ergonomically designed keyboards to see whether they make a difference.

- Encourage workers to take frequent breaks, and rotate jobs so repetitive hand and body movements are reduced.

- Encourage workers to maintain good posture when seated at the keyboard. Poor posture can lead to carpal tunnel syndrome from extending the wrists too far, as well as to neck ache and backache.

Figure 7-5 An Ergonomically Designed Workstation

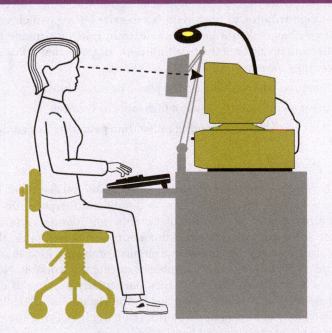

- Screen is below eye level.

- Elbows are on same level with the home key row, keeping wrists and lower arms parallel to the floor.

- Back and thighs are supported.

- Upper legs are parallel to the floor.

- Feet are placed flat on the floor.

- Task lamp supplements adequate room lighting.

- Keep wrists flat and straight in relation to the forearms and centered to the body when using a keyboard and mouse.

- Make less use of the mouse by using more key commands. Overuse of the mouse can cause repetitive motion injury. Find ways to use the left hand more, such as for tapping function keys. On-screen touch commands are helpful unless they create tendinitis of the index finger.

Workers must also recognize that if they spend many non-working hours using a keyboard, they increase the probability of developing carpal tunnel syndrome. Other factors that predispose workers to carpal tunnel syndrome are obesity, particularly when the obese person is diabetic, and shortages of vitamins B6 and C.[20]

Back Problems

Back pain remains one of the most common complaints in the workplace. According to the federal Bureau of Labor Statistics, the back injuries of more than one million workers account for nearly 20 percent of all injuries and illnesses in the workplace. Only the common cold accounts for more lost days of work.[21] Many cases of back pain stem from ergonomics problems, including long periods of hunching over to focus on a computer monitor. The first step in preventing back pain is to examine workplace practices and then take administrative action.

The good posture shown in Figure 7-5 will help prevent back problems, and so will knowing how to lift properly, such as bending from the knee, rather than bending down from the waist. The initiatives taken by FedEx to prevent back injuries represent a useful illustration of how such injuries can be reduced. Delivery workers must be able to lift 75 pounds, and new employees have the most back problems. As a consequence, FedEx takes steps to get employees in better physical condition. Employees are taught to stretch prior to their shifts; how to lift and put down packages properly; and how to find alternatives to lifting, such as sliding and pushing or pulling. Employees also use back-support belts that are useful in conjunction with other safety initiatives.[22]

A key contributor to back pain is excessive sitting, which you may have experienced if you have taken a long bus ride, train ride, or airplane flight. James Levine, researcher and inventor of the treadmill desk, suggests that office workers try standing whenever they have the opportunity, including:

- Standing while talking on the phone or eating lunch.

- Use a standing desk or use a high table or counter.

- Walk laps during a meeting rather than gathering in a conference room.[23]

Noise Problems

Repetitive motion disorders and other musculoskeletal disorders, including tendinitis, sciatica, and lower-back pain are well-publicized ergonomic problems. Another recurring problem relates to uncomfortable noise levels. Although industrial noise problems are usually associated with manufacturing and mills, the constant buzz in offices can also create discomfort and physical problems. Also, many workers complain about the ringing of personal cell phones during the workday. Noise disruptions can also cause a downturn in productivity, particularly because of difficulty in focusing and concentrating. A study conducted at the Occupational Health Nursing Program at the University of Michigan demonstrated chronic noise in the workplace causes an increase in blood pressure and heart rate.[24]

modified work schedule
Any formal departure from
the traditional hours of
work, excluding shift work
and staggered work hours.

MODIFIED WORK SCHEDULES AND JOB DESIGN

A key characteristic of job enrichment gives workers authority in scheduling their own work. Closely related is the widespread practice of giving workers some choice in deviating from the traditional five-day, 40-hour workweek. A **modified work schedule** is any formal departure from the traditional hours of work, excluding shift work. Yet shift work presents enough unique managerial challenges that it will be described here. Modified work schedules include flexible working hours, a compressed workweek, job sharing, remote work, and part-time and temporary work.

Modified work schedules serve several important organizational purposes in addition to being part of job design. They potentially increase job satisfaction and motivation and attract workers who prefer to avoid a traditional schedule. Modified work schedules are also popular with the physically disabled because the rigors of commuting may decrease. Many single parents need flexible hours to cope with childcare. Flexible working hours are popular with many employees. Working remotely, most frequently at home, is popular with a subset of the workforce.

Flexible Working Hours

Many employees exert some control over their work schedules through a formal or informal arrangement of flexible working hours. Employees with flexible working hours work certain core hours, such as 10:00 a.m. to 3:30 p.m. However, they are able to choose which hours they work from 7:00 a.m. to 10:00 a.m. and from 3:30 p.m. to 6:30 p.m. Figure 7-6 presents a basic model of flexible working hours. Time-recording devices, such as a badge scanner, frequently monitor employees' required hours for the week.

Flexible working hours are far more likely to be an option for employees on the exempt payroll. Such workers receive additional pay for work beyond 40 hours per week and premium pay for Saturdays and Sundays. Managers, professional-level workers and salespeople generally have some flexibility in choosing their work hours. In addition, managers and professionals in corporations work on average 55 hours per week, making concerns about fitting in a 40-hour-per-week flextime schedule irrelevant.

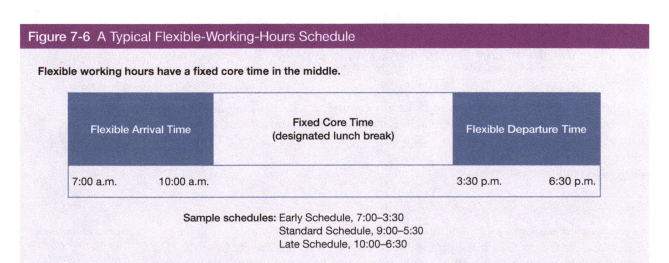

Figure 7-6 A Typical Flexible-Working-Hours Schedule

Flexible working hours have a fixed core time in the middle.

Flexible Arrival Time	Fixed Core Time (designated lunch break)	Flexible Departure Time
7:00 a.m. 10:00 a.m.		3:30 p.m. 6:30 p.m.

Sample schedules: Early Schedule, 7:00–3:30
Standard Schedule, 9:00–5:30
Late Schedule, 10:00–6:30

Many employers believe flexible working hours enhance productivity for reasons such as decreasing employee absenteeism and stress. Also, flexible working hours tend to increase efficiency during core times and decrease the need for overtime because more gets accomplished during the core.[25]

A major problem for the career-oriented employee who chooses flextime is that meetings may be held at times beyond the employee's scheduled quitting time. Suppose you have agreed to work from 7 a.m. until 4 p.m. on Thursday. The team leader schedules an important meeting at 4:30 for Thursday. You now face a conflict between taking care of personal obligations and appearing to be a dedicated worker.

Flexible schedules often come about after an employee requests the opportunity to participate in a program. Finding answers to the following questions can help the manager evaluate a flextime request[26]: (The same questions also apply generally to other types of modified work schedules.)

1   *Does the nature of the job allow for a flexible schedule?* Employees who must turn around work quickly or respond to crises might not be good candidates for flexible working hours. Negative indicators for flextime also include other employees being inconvenienced by the altered schedule, and a job that requires frequent interaction with others.

2   *Will this individual work well independently?* Some employees thrive on working solo, such as being in the office at 6 a.m. or 7 p.m. Others lose momentum when working alone. Does the employee have a high level of initiative and self-motivation?

3   *Are you comfortable managing a worker with flexible hours?* A manager who feels the need to frequently monitor the work of employees will become anxious when employees are working by themselves during non-core hours.

4   *Can you arrange tasks so the employee will have enough to do when you or other workers are not present?* Some employees can find ways to make a contribution on their own, while others must be fed work in small doses.

5   *Are you comfortable not seeing employees in the office, and empowering them?* For flexible work arrangements to be effective, the manager has to feel comfortable when workers with flexible hours are not present and are empowered to work without much supervision.

6   *Are you being fair when granting a flexible work schedule?* Giving just one or two people a flexible work schedule can lead to charges of favoritism. Unless unusual circumstances present themselves, such as a physical or family crisis, all workers who qualify should be given the opportunity to have flexible working hours.

Flexible working hours can also be attained outside a formal program by the manager granting flexibility as needed. For example, an accountant might ask her manager, "I have a house closing this Wednesday at 9 in the morning. Might I work two hours late on Thursday and Friday to make up for the lost time?" The manager would most likely respond positively.

Compressed Workweek

A **compressed workweek** is a full-time work schedule that allows 40 hours of work in less than five days. The usual arrangement is 4–40 (working four 10-hour days). Many employees enjoy the 4–40 schedule because it enables them to have three

compressed workweek
A full-time work schedule that allows 40 hours of work in less than five days.

consecutive days off from work. Employees often invest this time in leisure activities or part-time jobs. A 4–40 schedule usually allows most employees to take off Saturdays and Sundays. Important exceptions include police workers, hospital employees, and computer operators. As mentioned in Chapter 5 in relation to sustainability, the four-day workweek is gaining popularity in state and municipal government offices.

Another compressed workweek option is a nine-day/two-week arrangement. Two weeks of work are compressed into nine and a half days of work, instead of ten. A little extra time is built into the beginning or end of the workday in comparison to a 4–40 schedule.[27]

Treehouse, a firm that provides online education, implements a four-day work-week. The company has experienced major growth which CEO Ryan Carson attributes to the compressed workweek, "Thirty-two hours of higher quality work is better than 40 hours of lower-quality work" he said.[28]

Compressed workweeks are well liked by employees whose lifestyle fits such a schedule. (One logistics specialist humorously asked his manager if he could work a 2–20 schedule.) Morale sometimes increases because employees have more days off per month. However, the 4–40 week has many built-in problems. Some employees do not want so much time away from work each month. Many workers are fatigued during the last two hours and lose focus. From a personal standpoint, working for ten consecutive hours can be inconvenient. Also, the 4–40 workweek can create conflict with dependent care arrangements, and having an early dinner with the family.

The Remote Workforce and Telecommuting

**telecommuting
(or remote work)**
An arrangement with one's employer to use a computer to perform work at home, in a satellite office, or remote worksite.

An estimated 43 percent of people in the United States work at home, out of their cars, or another offsite location, at least part of the time.[29] **Telecommuting (or remote work)** is an arrangement in which employees use computers or mobile devices to perform their regular work responsibilities at home, in a satellite office, or remote worksite. In addition to using computers to communicate with their employer's office, telecommuters attend meetings on company premises and stay in contact by telephone and teleconferences. Such workers are often referred to as part of the remote workforce because they are located away from the traditional workplace. Self-employed people who work at home are not classified as remote workers. Remote working became mandatory for millions of workers during the coronavirus pandemic in 2020.

Telecommuting also takes place at cafés equipped with Wi-Fi, boats, and RVs (recreational vehicles). Microsoft is among the employers who provide remote touchdown spaces in suburban locations that allow workers to access secure networks and collaborate with other workers without having to drive long distances. Another possibility for working remotely is to work from a community center or co-working location alongside other telecommuters. A co-working location is an office site in which small amounts of space are rented, often for a day, to telecommuters or startup companies and freelancers.

Advantages of Telecommuting

Telecommuting can work well with self-reliant and self-starting employees who have relevant work experience. Work-at-home employees usually volunteer for such arrangements. As a result, they are likely to find telecommuting satisfying. Employees derive many benefits from working at home, including easier management of personal life; lowered costs for commuting, work clothing and lunch; much less time spent commuting and fewer distractions, such as office noise. Telecommuting offers the following advantages to the employer:

1 *Increased productivity.* Surveys consistently show telecommuting programs increase productivity, usually by at least 25 percent. A contributing factor to the productivity advantage of telecommuters is they tend to be well-educated and self-motivated.

2 *Low overhead.* Because employees provide some of their own office space, the company can operate with much less physical office space. A vice president of marketing research operations noted that, because of its work-at-home program, the company was able to greatly expand its client load without acquiring additional space.

3 *Access to a wider range of employee talent.* Companies with regular work-at-home programs are usually deluged with résumés from eager job applicants. The talent bank includes parents (mostly mothers) with young children, employees who find commuting unpleasant, and others who live far away from their firms. The Department of Labor regards telecommuting as an option for disabled workers who traditionally have few opportunities in the workplace. The disabled workers may have talents that otherwise might be overlooked.

4 *Direct contribution to sustainability initiatives.* Telecommuting makes a major contribution to sustaining the environment because people who work at home drive their vehicles less. As a result, air quality improves and atmospheric ozone levels decrease. Also, less congested highways and streets make for a better-looking environment.

Disadvantages of Remote Work

Work-at-home programs must be used selectively because they pose disadvantages for both employee and employer. The careers of telecommuters may suffer because they are not visible to management. Telecommuting may translate into less highway traffic and fewer meals eaten in restaurants. As a result, service-station owners and fast-service restaurant proprietors have less income.

Telecommuters can be exploited if they feel compelled to work on company problems late into the night and on weekends. The many potential distractions at home make it difficult for some telecommuters to concentrate on work. Telecommuters are sometimes part-time employees who receive limited benefits and are paid only for what they produce. As one telecommuter, a data entry specialist, said, "If I let up for an afternoon, I earn hardly anything."

Working at home can reinforce negative tendencies: It will facilitate a workaholic to work harder and longer, and it will give a procrastinator ample opportunity to delay work.[30] Telecommuting programs can be disadvantageous to the employer because building loyalty and teamwork is difficult when so many workers are away from the office. Telecommuters who are not performing measured work are difficult to supervise—working at home gives an employee much more latitude in attending to personal matters during work time. With so many teleworkers conducting business at coffee shops, many of them may drift away from being focused on company goals during the workday.

Another disadvantage of telecommuting is that home office-bound workers can feel lonely. Management professors Kevin W. Rockman and Michael G. Pratt conducted research at a Fortune 100 company in Silicon Valley that freely allowed off-site work. A key finding was that employees who continued to work in the home office wound up feeling lonely and disconnected. They found themselves deprived of energizing interactions, such as spontaneous hallway interactions and impromptu office conversations.[31]

A major concern is the organization may miss out on some of the creativity that stems from the exchange of ideas in the traditional office. Another problem is that telecommuting can impact a worker's identity toward being self-employed, and away from being part of the organization.[32] A worker who spends very little time on company premises is less likely to express a sentiment such as, "I am a Wells Fargo woman."

If you are in the process of building your career and want to develop valuable contacts on the job, minimize telecommuting. Establishing face-to-face relationships remains highly important for career advancement.

In recognition of the potential disadvantages or remote work, several major business organizations have reduced or eliminated their telework programs in recent years. Among these companies are The Bank of New York, Mellon Corp., IBM, Yahoo, Aetna, and Best Buy. The reasons offered for the cutback follow the disadvantages mentioned above. According to an interview study conducted by the Society for Human Resource Management, two major concerns about telework stand out. One reason is that collaborating remotely can be difficult. Proximity boosts productivity, particularly when collaboration is required. Creativity, as part of productivity, is often thought to be enhanced when people bat around ideas in person in the office. The second major concern is that remote workers feel less engaged in their work, and connected to the organization.[33]

Job Sharing

job sharing
A work arrangement in which two people who work part-time share one job.

Another way to accommodate workers is to give them half a job. **Job sharing** is a work arrangement in which two people who work part-time share one job. Salary and benefits are prorated for the half-time workers. The sharers divide up the job according to their needs. Each may work selected days of the workweek. Or, one person might work mornings and the other work afternoons. The job sharers may be two friends, a husband and wife, or two employees who did not know each other before sharing a job. For complex jobs, the sharers may spend work time discussing it.

Job sharing appeals mostly to workers whose family commitments do not allow them to work full time. Job sharing allows for a sense of balance in one's life yet being able to hold on to a career. A typical job-sharing situation involves two friends who want a responsible position but can only work part-time. Job sharing offers the employer an advantage in that two people working half-time usually produce more than one person working full time, which is particularly noticeable in creative work.

Part-Time and Temporary Work and the Gig Economy

Part-time work is a modified work schedule offered by about two-thirds of employers. The category of part-time workers includes employees who work reduced weekly, annual, or seasonal hours and those who have project-based occasional work. For example, a marketing brand manager might work full days on Mondays, Wednesdays and Fridays. Many people, such as students and semi-retired people, choose part-time work because it fits their lifestyles. Also, many people work part-time because they cannot find full-time employment.

Temporary employment is popular, with some employers even hiring part-time managers, engineers, lawyers, and other high-level workers. Part-time and temporary employees collectively constitute one-fourth to one-third of the workforce. Given they are hired according to, or contingent upon, an employer's need, they are referred to as **contingent workers**. Some contingent workers receive modest benefits.

Contingent employment now even takes place for executive positions, particularly for managers who can execute strategy and bring about operational efficiencies.[34] Another approach to contingent employment for executives is interim appointments. Interim executives are sometimes hired from outside a business organization to help a company through a restructuring or a scandal, such as top-level manager having been indicted for insider trading. Empty posts are also filled with interim company managers. If the manager performs well in the position, he or she might be awarded a permanent slot.[35]

Many employees enjoy part-time work, which allows them to willingly trade off the low pay for personal convenience. Employers, particularly in the retailing and restaurant industries, are eager to hire contingent workers to avoid the expense of hiring full-time workers. Paying limited or no benefits to part-time workers can save employers as much as 35 percent of the cost of full-time compensation. Also, contingent workers can be readily laid off if business conditions warrant. Some seasonally oriented businesses, such as gift catalog sales firms, hire mostly part-time workers.

A growing part of the workforce is referred to as the **gig economy**, or workers who are involved in some form of freelancing, contracting, temporary work, often based on outsourcing. The gig economy is also labeled as the Uber-economy because the ride-hailing company relies on freelance contractors for its workforce. Case B at the end of this chapter describes some of the controversy as to whether Uber drivers are contractors or traditional employees.

Because members of the gig economy are independent contractors, they receive benefits infrequently. A familiar example would be a plumber hired by a business owner to make a repair. The plumber sets the wage and receives no benefits. So many people working part-time without benefits is a concern to labor advocates and many politicians, as well as to the workers themselves. During a strong economy, however, gig employers, such as food-delivery companies are likely to offer benefits, a well a signing bonus.[36]

During a period of high employment, with ample full-time positions available, the gig economy tends to shrink. The reason is that many contract workers prefer full-time positions. Yet others enjoy the freedom of choosing how much they work each week, such as the many Uber drivers who work about 10 hours per week.

The size of the gig economy is difficult to specify accurately, but according to a recent estimate, 57 million workers in the United States are freelance workers. The average weekly earnings of these workers is $653 suggesting that they do not work full-time.[37]

The accompanying *Management in Action* insert describes a firm that offers flexible schedules.

Although modified work schedules can provide benefits to the individual and the organization, using these schedules can create problems for the worker. According to surveys, many employees who take advantage of flexible work schedules say they are made to feel like slackers. An Ernst & Young survey concluded that 10 percent of U. S. workers have experienced a negative consequence related to a flexible work schedule. The problem facing these workers is the perception that time spent in the office is associated with dependability and responsibility.[38]

contingent workers
Part-time or temporary employees who are not members of the employer's permanent workforce.

gig economy
Workers who are involved in some form of freelancing, contracting, temporary work, often based on outsourcing.

MANAGEMENT IN ACTION

Flexible Work Arrangements at Upwork

Upwork is a website that links organizations who want to hire freelance workers with freelancers who are looking for assignments. Upwork has 5 million registered client businesses, and 12 million registered freelancers. The company enables business firms and independent professionals to connect and collaborate remotely. With three million projects posted annually, Upwork is the world's largest freelance marketplace.

Upwork enables clients to interview, hire and work with freelancers through the company's platform. The platform features a chat function aimed at reducing the then time required to locate screen, and hire freelancers. A time-sheet application enables freelancers to track the specific amount of time spent working on projects with verified screenshots.

Upwork offers freelancers for short-term tasks, recurring projects, and full-time contract work. such as hiring someone to design a customer-satisfaction survey for a new product. Short-term tasks enable clients to build a pool of diverse talent for one-time tasks. For recurring projects clients have a go-to team with specialized skills. The full-time contract work offering provides clients an opportunity to supplement their full-time staffs with a dedicated team that works full-time as long as needed.

Given that Upwork is dedicated to enhancing the career of remote workers, the company also provides flexible work arrangements for its own employees. Company managers are aware that young workers in particular are attracted to firms that offer flexible work arrangements. One program is Work Online Wednesdays. Each "Hump Day," referring to the middle of the week. On Wednesdays every Upwork associate works wherever they want, as long as they want, provided Wi-Fi is present in their location. The majority of Upwork associates choose to work at least part of the day from their home. Yet many others work at cafés, restaurants, and possibly from a Wi-Fi enabled boat or campsite.

Flexible work arrangements are also offered on other workdays when needed. For example, a parent might need to stay home with a child who was too sick to attend school. Office hours are also super-flexible, providing the position does not require customer coverage during a specific time period. For example, a client-support technician might have to cover phone calls during a designated time period.

Questions

1 **What might Upwork management do to have evidence that flexible work arrangements are helping the company and employees?**

2 **Should Upwork management be concerned about some associates doing hardly any work on Wednesdays?**

Source: Original story based on facts and observations in the following sources: "10 Crazy Flexible Companies That Understand You Need Freedom," *The Muse* (www.themuse.com), pp. 3–4. Accessed January 9, 2020; "Get More Done with Top-Quality Freelancers," *www.upwork.com*. Accessed January 9, 2020; Isaac Kohen, "The 9-to-5 Myth: Why a 'Regular' Schedule Works Against Employees," *Upwork.com*, July 2, 2018, pp. 1–2.

Shift Work

To accommodate the needs of employers rather than employees, many workers are assigned to shift work. The U. S. Bureau of Labor Statistics reports that close to 15 percent of full-time workers work alternative shifts. The purpose of shift work is to provide coverage during nonstandard hours. The most common shift schedules are days (7 a.m. to 3 p.m.), evenings (3 p.m. to 11 p.m.), and nights (11 p.m. to 7 a.m.). Manufacturing uses shift work to meet high demand for products without having to expand facilities. It is more economical to run a factory 16 or 24 hours per day than to run two or three factories eight hours per day. Service industries make even more extensive use of shift work to meet the demands of customers around the clock, such as in a hotel and customer-care centers. Shift work is necessary in public service operations such as police work, firefighting and healthcare.

Catering to clients in faraway time zones may require some modification of a typical shift, such as a stockbroker in Seattle, Washington, being on call to converse with clients in Tokyo, Japan. Changes in the work shift affects circadian rhythm, which similar to jet lag, desynchronizes the body's sleep-wake schedule.[39]

Shift work involves more than a deviation from a traditional work schedule. It creates a lifestyle that affects productivity, health, family, and social life. Approximately 20 percent of shift workers report falling asleep during work, leading to more accidents and lower productivity. Many industrial catastrophes, such as shipwrecks, oil spills, and chemical leaks have taken place during the night ("graveyard") shift.[40] People who work nontraditional hours that interfere with their biological clock are also risking automobile crashes. A medical study found shift work can impair the functioning of the brain, including decreases in memory and overall brain functioning.[41]

Shift workers also have difficulty integrating their schedules with the social needs of friends and families. With proper training, employees can adjust better to shift work. A major consideration is to sleep well and comfortably, which often involves using draperies to create darkness in the room and sleeping at regular times.

JOB DESIGN AND HIGH-PERFORMANCE WORK SYSTEMS

LEARNING OBJECTIVE **7**

Explain how job design can contribute to a high-performance work system.

As implied throughout this chapter, a major purpose of job design is to enhance job performance and productivity. As such, job design contributes to work systems that perform exceptionally well. High-performing work systems were mentioned in Chapter 3 in terms of their fit with different national cultures. High-performing work systems based on the contribution of individual workers overlap with several of components of job enrichment and the job characteristics model. A **high-performance work system** is a way of organizing work so that front-line workers participate in decisions that have an impact on their jobs and the wider organization.

The United Auto Workers, as well as other labor unions, favor high-performance work systems as an option for saving jobs by boosting the productivity of U.S. manufacturing plants. However, for a plant to boost productivity, four workplace practices must be incorporated into the operation of the plant. First, workers must have a reasonable degree of autonomy in their jobs, such as making decisions about job tasks and work methods. A second practice is for workers to have access to co-workers, managers, and supporting professionals such as manufacturing engineers and product designers. Third, production floor teams must be self-managing to a large extent. Fourth is the presence of problem solving and quality-improvement teams that are exempt from assembly line responsibilities. Most of these ideas will be touched upon again when we study effective work groups in Chapter 13.

high-performance work system
A way of organizing work so that front-line workers participate in decisions that have an impact on their jobs and the wider organization.

Another consideration is that these four practices must be supported by the company's overall approach to human resource management. Among these supportive human resources practices are extensive screening of new employees to establish a high-quality workforce; increased training for production workers; a commitment to employment security; and financial incentives linked to group performance.[42]

An investigation of the impact of high-performing work systems looked at a subset of such a system, referred to as a high-commitment work system. These include employee participation, internal promotion, team rewards, extensive training and benefits, and job security. Together, these practices demonstrate commitment to the employee. The study took place in 55 high technology firms in China. A key finding was that a high-commitment work system was associated with higher employee creativity as measured by supervisory ratings. One such rating item was, "This subordinate seeks new ideas and ways to solve problem."[43]

The link between high-commitment work systems was supported in a more recent study. A survey conducted with over 2,600 employees in a variety of workplaces in Canada found that a high-commitment work system was associated with both product and process innovation.[44] The reason is probably that employees who are committed to their jobs and the organization are more willing to invest mental energy into their jobs.

SUMMARY OF KEY POINTS

1 Describe the importance of job specialization and job design including automation and robots.

A major consideration in job design is how specialized the job holder must be. Job specialization allows for the development of expertise at all occupational levels. Automation has been used to replace some aspects of human endeavor in the office and factory since the industrial revolution. Robots are a major part of automation, and now perform many tasks outside the factory. A major advance in the business use of robots is collaborative robots (cobots) that work alongside humans performing specialized tasks.

2 Describe job enrichment, including the job characteristics model.

Job enrichment is a method of making jobs that involve more challenges and responsibilities so they will be more appealing to most employees. The person holding the job must perceive these enriched characteristics of a job. An enriched job provides direct feedback, client relationships, new learning, control over methods, scheduling by the employee, unique experience, control over resources, direct communication authority, and personal accountability.

Expanding on the idea of job enrichment creates the job characteristics model that focuses on the task and interpersonal dimensions of a job. Five characteristics of jobs improve employee motivation, satisfaction and performance: skill variety, task identity, task significance, autonomy, and feedback. These characteristics relate to critical psychological states which, in turn, lead to outcomes, such as internal motivation, satisfaction, low absenteeism, and high quality.

3 Describe job involvement, enlargement, and rotation.

Job involvement reflects psychological involvement with one's work and how much work is part of the self-image. Job enlargement increases the number and variety of job tasks. Job rotation switches assignments and can contribute heavily to career development.

4 Explain how workers use job crafting to modify their jobs.

The rigidity of some job descriptions does not fit the flexible work roles carried out by many workers. A way of deviating from job descriptions is for workers to modify their jobs to fit their personal preferences and capabilities. Employees often craft their jobs by changing the tasks they perform and their contacts with others to make their jobs more meaningful. Crafting can take time away from job duties that are useful for the organization and job performance.

The idea of job embeddedness helps explain the many forces that attach people to their roles beyond job design.

5 Illustrate how ergonomic factors can be part of job design.

A key principle of job design is that the job should be laid out to decrease the chances it will physically harm the incumbent. Ergonomics seeks to minimize the physical demands on workers and optimize system performance. Musculoskeletal (muscle and bones) injuries include cumulative trauma disorders—injuries caused by repetitive motions over prolonged periods of time—that occur in many different types of work. Work stations can be designed to minimize these problems by such measures as supporting the back and thighs and placing the feet flat on the floor. Back problems are widespread in the workplace, and many of these problems can be prevented through ergonomics. Uncomfortable noise levels present another ergonomic problem to be addressed.

6 Summarize the various modified work schedules.

Work scheduling is another part of job design. A modified work schedule departs from the traditional hours of work. Modified work-scheduling options include flexible working hours, a compressed workweek, the alternative workplace and remote work, job sharing, and part-time and temporary work. Shift work involves more than a deviation from a traditional work schedule because it creates a lifestyle that affects productivity, health, family, and social life.

7 Explain how job design can contribute to a high-performance work system.

A high-performing work system organizes work so that front-line workers participate in decisions that have an impact on their jobs and the wider organization. Such a work system includes job autonomy, access to support from work associates, self-managing work teams, along with problem solving and quality-improvement teams. A subset of the high-performance work system, a high commitment work system, can enhance worker creativity.

Key Terms and Phrases

job specialization 191

job description 193

job enrichment 193

job characteristics model 195

job involvement 196

job enlargement 196

job rotation 198

job crafting 198

job embeddedness 199

ergonomics 200

cumulative trauma disorders 200

carpal tunnel syndrome 200

modified work schedule 203

compressed workweek 204

telecommuting (or remote work) 205

job sharing 207

contingent workers 208

gig economy 208

high-performance work system 210

Questions

1. Under what circumstances might a college graduate want to join the gig economy?

2. A while back, a few companies would hire talented people at a good salary, with the assignment of simply "doing something useful, and profitable." Were these hiring managers irresponsible? What kind of worker could perform well in such a position?

3. In about 35 words, write the job description for: (a) a restaurant manager, (b) the chief marketing officer at Tesla, and (c) the head coach of one of your favorite athletic teams.

4. What are the benefits of frequent job rotation for a person who would like to become a high-level manager?

5. What objections might labor unions have to the continuing growth of robot use?

6. Would you be satisfied as a remote worker? Why or why not?

7. How would a manager know if the jobs he or she supervises fit well into a high-performance work system?

Skill-Building Exercise 7-A: The Ideal Home-Based Office

Gather into teams of about five people to design an ideal office at home for a professional worker. Take about 20 minutes to develop suggestions for the following aspects of a home office: (1) hardware and software, (2) equipment other than computers and smartphones, (3) furniture, (4) ergonomics design, (5) office layout, and (6) location within the home. Consider both productivity and job satisfaction when designing your office. After the designs are completed, the team leaders may present the design to the rest of the class.

Skill-Building Exercise 7-B: The Ergonomic Audit of Heavy Users of Text Messages

Today you are a member of an ergonomics team working for the smartphone division of a large information technology company. Company leadership is worried that the obsessive amount of texting many consumers engage in could lead to serious ergonomics problems, such as tendinitis in the thumb or index finger. Your job is to collect fresh data on the extent of ergonomics problems associated with texting. Interview, or send an e-mail or text message to 10 people you know, including yourself, who text at least two hours a day. Inquire about what physical problems they have encountered because of their heavy texting. Be as specific as you can about any physical problems including headaches, visual problems, or tendinitis. Summarize your findings in about 25 words. Perhaps pool your results with classmates to help uncover whether there truly are ergonomics problems associated with texting.

Management Now—Online Skill-Building Exercise: Best Jobs

The assignment here is to gain insight into how intensely some people like their jobs, and to speculate what managers can do to create more of these jobs. Conduct an Internet search to find three jobs that could probably qualify for a "best job trophy." Focus your search on a written article or a blog posted within the last year. After finding these jobs (sometimes a work assignment that would inspire many people), identify what are the factors that make these jobs so rewarding and satisfying to people. Also, what interest might you have in holding one of these best jobs?

Dental Hygienist Kelsey Crafts Her Job

Twenty-nine-year-old Kelsey works full time as a dental hygienist at a thriving suburban dental practice, owned and operated by Dr. Malcolm. Many of the patients visit the clinic for a cleaning by Kelsey or the other dental hygienist rather than treatment by the dentist. Toward the end of a patient visit, Dr. Malcolm stops by for a quick checkup of the patient's teeth and gums. The work of dental hygienists is therefore an important source of revenue for the clinic. Jennifer is the office manager, assisted by Lila, a part-time associate.

Kelsey cleans teeth and removes plaque with enthusiasm, using the latest dental technology, such as displaying images on a large screen of potential problem areas with a patient's teeth. Kelsey says that taking care of teeth is obviously the key part of her job, but she also sees a broader role for herself as a healthcare provider. She remarked, "If I think a person is having dental problems because of bad eating habits such as too much sugar or carbohydrates, I'll let that patient know. I might even send the patient a follow-up text message with a diet recommendation."

A patient recently had an appointment with Kelsey, and she noticed that he was limping. The patient, Rob, said that he plays a lot of basketball and that an ankle ligament had a slight separation from a bone. Rob also said that his orthopedist thought the separation would heal naturally in a few months. Kelsey told Rob that he should get better care, and proceeded to write down the name and phone number of a foot specialist who was the best in the region.

Gia, a patient who came to the clinic for a routine teeth cleaning, was asked in a friendly manner by Kelsey how her family was doing. Gia said her son in the fifth grade was failing math, and the family and teacher were concerned. Kelsey responded that she had the perfect solution. She strongly recommended a franchise math tutoring service that would be of great benefit to her son.

As they were paying their bills, and scheduling an appointment into the future, a few patients questioned Jennifer, the office manager, about the nature of Kelsey's job responsibilities. Here are several examples: Rob commented, "Since when has my dental hygienist become a medical referral service?" Gia asked, "Is Kelsey connected to a math tutoring franchise?" Another patient, Samantha, said to Jennifer, "I know that I have lost too much weight recently. But I came here for a teeth cleaning, not a lecture by Kelsey about anorexia."

In thinking over these unusual comments, Jennifer thought that maybe she and Dr. Malcolm should have a candid discussion with Kelsey about her role at the dental clinic. Jennifer was also concerned that the dental practice might be facing legal problems if one of Kelsey's recommendations backfired.

Case Questions

1 In what way is Kelsey engaging in job crafting?

2 If Kelsey is crafting her job, how might it be contributing to her job satisfaction?

3 Advise Jennifer and Dr. Malcolm what they should do about Kelsey going beyond a traditional definition of the role of a dental hygienist.

Some Uber Drivers Want to Be Employees

Travis Kalanick, the former CEO of the app-driver, car-hailing service, Uber Technologies Inc., was used to engaging in legal battles and protests about his company. Many city governments have fought the right of Uber to exist in their city because they believe Uber does not conform to regulations for taxi services. Now many of the part-time drivers who use their own vehicles to transport customers are claiming they should have the same types of benefits as full-time employees. A handful of lawyers are encouraging some of these drivers to sue Uber to meet their demands, saying the company is violating labor laws. One driver who works about 20 hours per week said, "Life is tough enough as a cabbie without being treated like a second-class citizen."

Uber management pointed out that more than half of Uber's drivers work nine hours per week or less, therefore they should be classified as contractors, not employees. According to the CEO, driving for Uber is not a full-time job, but "a way to fill in the gaps." He also argued that the drivers want to be independent contractors because they enjoy being their own bosses.

One group of drivers filed a lawsuit against the company, with the contention that Uber is illegally classifying them as contractors to avoid paying them millions of dollars in expenses. In one specific suit, an Uber driver named Barbara Ann Berwick filed a wage complaint with the California Labor Commissioner. Among her demands was reimbursement for gas and bridge tolls. The Uber attorney argued that Berwick was not an employee and was therefore not entitled to reimbursement for business expenses. The California labor Commissioner disagreed and awarded Berwick over $4,000 in business expenses and back interest.

Among the many legal points raised was that drivers are not engaged in an occupation that is separate and distinct from Uber's core business. Also, the fact that the company provided drivers with iPhones and monitors their approval ratings by passengers moves the drivers closer to employee status.

Uber management's argument of classifying drivers as contractors was strengthened by a National Labor Relations Board advisory memo in May, 2019.

Peter Robb, the general counsel of the board, concluded that Uber drivers are independent contractors and not employees. He argued that the drivers set their hours, own their vehicles, and are free to work for Uber competitors, so they cannot be considered employees under federal law.

A pending California law later in 2019 threatened Uber's position that its drivers should be classified as contractors. The law states that a worker is only an independent contractor if (a) he or she is not under the control or direction of the company while working, (b) if the work is "outside the usual course" of the company's business, and (c) if he or she is "customarily engaged" in the same kind of work that he or she performs for the company. Yet Uber Chief Legal officer Tony West argued that the company should be able to continue to classify drivers as contractors. "Just because the test is hard doesn't mean we will not be able to pass it." One Uber argument is that the usual course of its business is to provide a technology platform to its drivers, in exchange for a service fee. Uber customers are therefore the drivers, not the riders.

To mollify the drivers a little, Uber management has given drivers some benefits, such as access to healthcare coverage and discounts on gasoline.

Case Questions

1 **What might Uber management do to keep Uber drivers happy, and not file lawsuits against the company?**

2 **How might the job of an Uber driver be enriched?**

3 **Why is this case significant for management throughout most of the modern world?**

Source: Original story created from facts and observations in the following sources: Sachi Barreiro, "Are Uber Drivers Employees Poor Independent Contractors in California?" *www.nolo.com*, 2016, pp. 1–4; Kia Kokalitcheva, "Uber CEO: Most Drivers Work Too Little to be Employees," *http://Fortune.com*. October 21, 2015, pp. 1–7; Douglas MacMillan, "Uber Drivers' Suit Given Status as a Class Action," *The Wall Street Journal*, September 2, 2015, pp. B1, B4; Daniel Wiessner, "Uber Drivers are Contractors, Not Employees, U. S. Labor Agency Says," *Reuters* (www.reuters.com), May 14, 2019, pp. 1–3; Aarian Marshall, "Why Uber Thinks It Can Still Call Its Drivers Contractors," *Wired* (www.wired.com), September 12, 2019, pp. 1–2.

ENDNOTES

1. Original story created from facts and observations in the following sources: Matt O'Brien, "Robots Creating Stress for Human Co-workers," *Associated Press*, January 5, 2020; O'Brien, "Robots Take Health Toll on Human Workers," *Daily Hampshire Gazette* (www.gazette.com), December 31, 2019; Susan Vargas, "Robots in the Workplace," *Safety + Health* (www.safetyandhealthmagazine.com), March 25, 2018, pp. 1–8; Erik Sherman, "New Study: Automation Makes Workers So Anxious that They Get Sick," *Inc.* (www.inc.com), March 20, 2018, pp. 1–3.

2. Ryan Dezember, "Robots Weigh In on Home Values," *The Wall Street Journal*, August 26, 2019, p. B4.

3. Alexia Elejalde-Ruz, "Collaborative Robots Helping Human Workers, Not Replacing Them," *Chicago Tribune Business*, October 21, 2018, p. 1.

4. Jerry Kaplan, "Don't Fear the Robots," *The Wall Street Journal*, July 22–23, 2017, p. C3.

5. Frederick Herzberg, "The Wise Old Turk," *Harvard Business Review*, September–October 1974, pp. 70–80; Nico W. Van Yperen and Mariët Hagedoorn, "Do High Job Demands Increase Intrinsic Motivation or Fatigue or Both? The Role of Job Control and Job Social Support," *Academy of Management Journal*, June 2003, pp. 339–348.

6. Marc C. Marchese and Robert P. Delprino, "Do Supervisors and Subordinates See Eye-to-Eye on Job Enrichment?" *Journal of Business and Psychology*, Winter 1998, pp. 179–192.

7. John Richard Hackman and Greg R. Oldham, *Work Redesign* (Reading, MA: Addison-Wesley, 1980), p. 77; Sharon K. Parker, Frederick P. Morgeson, and Gary Johns, "One Hundred Years of Work Design Research: Looking Back and Looking Forward," *Journal of Applied Psychology*, March 2017, pp. 407–408.

8. Jia Hu et al., "There Are Lots of Big Fish in This Pond: The Role of Peer Overqualification on Task Significance, Perceived Fit, and Performance for Overqualified Employees," *Journal of Applied Psychology*, July 2015, pp. 1228–1238.

9. Dana Mattioli, "Help Wanted: Senior-Level Job, Junior Title Pay," *The Wall Street Journal*, August 12, 2008, p. D1.

10. Margaret Fiester, "Job Rotation, Total Rewards, Measuring Value," *HR Magazine*, August 2008, p. 33.

11. Amy Wrzesniewski and Jane E. Dutton, "Crafting a Job: Revisioning Employees as Active Crafters of Their Work," *The Academy of Management Review*, April 2001, pp. 179–201.

12. Uta K. Bindl et al., "Job Crafting Revisited: Implications of an Extended Framework for Active Changes at Work," *Journal of Applied Psychology*, May 2019, p. 605.

13. Patrick F. Bruning and Michael A. Campion, "A Role-Resource Approach-Avoidance Model of Job Crafting: A Multimethod Integration and Extension of Job Crafting Theory," *Academy of Management Journal*, April 2008, pp. 499–522.

14. Carrie Leana, Eileen Appelbaum, and Iryna Shevchuk, "Work Process and Quality of Care in Early Childhood Education: The Role of Job Crafting," *Academy of Management Journal*, December 2009, pp. 1169–1192.

15. Erich C. Dierdorff and Jaclyn M. Jensen, "Crafting in Context: When Job Crafting Is Dysfunctional for Performance Effectiveness," *Journal of Applied Psychology*, May 2018, pp. 463–477.

16. Peter W. Hom et al., "Explaining Employment Relationships with Social Exchange and Job Embeddedness," *Journal of Applied Psychology*, March 2009, p. 281.

17. "Ergonomics," *http://www.referencesforbusiness.com/management/Em-Exp/Ergnomics.html*, Advameg Inc., 2016.

18. "Ergonomics for the Prevention of Musculoskeletal Disorders—Guidelines for Retail Grocers," *http://www.osha.gov/ergonomics/guidelines/retailgrocery/retailgrocery.html*, accessed November 26, 2006, p. 4.

19. Albert R. Karr, "An Ergo-Unfriendly Home Office Can Hurt You," *The Wall Street Journal*, September 30, 2003, p. D6; Amy Hamilton, "Cumulative Trauma Disorder," *Safety + Health* (www.safetyandhealthmagazine.com), June 1, 2013, pp. 1–2.

20. William Atkinson, "The Carpal Tunnel Conundrum," *Workforce*, September 2002, p. 17.

21. "Back Safety in the Workplace," *BLR* (www.blr.com), 2020, p. 1.

22. This section is mostly based on Nancy Hatch Woodward, "Easing Back Pain: Prevent Back Injuries from Crippling Your Business," *HR Magazine*, April 2008, pp. 56–60.

23. Mayo clinic post reported in Todd Clausen, "Workers Stand Up! Employees Enjoy Benefits of Standing Workstations," *Democrat and Chronicle*, July 12, 2015, p. 3E.

24. Research reported in Beth Rifkin, "The Effects of Noise in the Workplace," *smallbusinesschron.com*. (The Houston Chronicle) © Copyright 2016 Hearst Newspapers, LLC.

25. "Introducing Flexible Working Hours Into Your Organization," in *Business: The Ultimate Resource* (Cambridge, MA: Perseus Publishing, 2002), p. 358.

26. "A Time for Change? Maybe Not—Flextime Isn't for Everyone," *WorkingSMART*, September 1996, pp. 1–2; Jessica Marquez, "Citigroup to Train Managers on Flex-Work Arrangements," November 17, 2008, pp. 8, 10; Elise Marescaux and Sophie Ce Winne, "How to Allow Flexible Work Schedules Without Playing Favorites," *Harvard Business Review* (https://hbr.org), August 22, 2017, pp. 1–5.

27. "Compressed Work Schedules," *Duke Human Resources* (https://hr.duke.edu), p. 1. Accessed January 11, 2020.

28. "Amazon Has Joined These Companies in Offering Shorter Workweeks," *entrepreneur.co*, August 30, 2016, p. 2.

29. Dana Wilkie, "Why Are Companies Ending Remote Work?" *SHRM* (www.shrm.com), May 7, 2019, p. 2.

30. Jenny C. McCune, "Telecommuting Revisited," *Management Review*, February 1998, p. 13.

31. Research reported in Phyllis Korkki, "Telecommuting Can Make the Office a Lonely Place, a Study Says," *The New York Times* (www.nytimes.com), January 2, 2016, pp. 1–3.

32. Sherry M. B. Thatcher and Xiumei Zhu, "Changing Identities in a Changing Workplace: Identification, Identity, Enactment, Self-Verification, and Telecommuting," *Academy of Management Review*, October 2006, p. 1079.

33. Wilkie, "Why Are Companies Ending Remote Work?" pp. 1–6.

34. Sarah E. Needleman, "Employers Tap Executives for Temporary Jobs," *The Wall Street Journal*, May 13, 2008, p. D6.

35. Melissa Korn, "Making a Temporary Stint Stick," *The Wall Street Journal*, February 8, 2010, p. D6.; Michele Conlin, "Test-Drives in the C-Suite," *Business Week*, October 19, 2009, p. 054.

36. Kelsey Gee, "In a Hot Market, Gig Workers Vanish," *The Wall Street Journal*, August 9, 2017, p. B5.

37. "Gig Economy in the U.S.: Statistics and Facts," January 7, 2019, p. 1.

38. Rebecca Greenfield, "How to Make Flexible Work Schedules a Reality," *Bloomberg* (http://finance.yahoo.com), January 21, 2016, pp. 1–3.

39. "Shift Work Sleep Disorder," *http://www.sleepdisorderchannel.com/shiftwork*, accessed November 27, 2006.

40. "Shift Work," *www.sleepeducation.com*, updated July 10, 2007.

41. "The Impact of Shift Work on Health," *MNT* (www.medicalnewstoday.com), © 204-2020, pp. 1–2.

42. "High Performance Work Systems: What's the Payoff?" *http://www.uaw.org/publications/jobs_pay*, accessed November 22, 2006.

43. Song Chang et al., "Do High-Commitment Work Systems Affect Creativity? A Multilevel Combinational Approach to Employee Creativity," *Journal of Applied Psychology*, July 2014, pp. 665–680.

44. Yixuan Li et al., "From Employee-Experienced High-Involvement Work System to Innovation: An Emergence-Based Human Resource Management Framework," *Academy of management Journal*, October 2013, pp. 2000–2019.

CHAPTER 8

Organization Structure, Culture, and Change

....

OBJECTIVES

After studying this chapter and doing the exercises, you should be able to:

1 Describe the bureaucratic organization structure and discuss its advantages and disadvantages.

2 Explain the major ways in which organizations are divided into departments.

3 Describe four modifications of the bureaucratic structure.

4 Identify key factors that influence the selection of organization structure.

5 Specify how delegation, empowerment, and decentralization spread authority in an organization.

6 Identify major aspects of organizational culture.

7 Describe key aspects of managing change, including gaining support for change.

....

Satya Nadella became the third chief executive officer (CEO) in the history of Microsoft Corp. in 2014. His previous position in the company was executive vice president (EVP) of the cloud and enterprise group. He had also been with the company for 22 years, beginning as an electrical engineer. Nadella has steered the company away from a mobile strategy that was not going as well as planned. Instead he focused on other Microsoft products and services including cloud computing and AI.

Nadella's record of accomplishment as CEO of Microsoft has been widely lauded. Under his leadership, Microsoft had reversed its fortune and returned to being a growth stock after stagnating for nearly a decade. Nadella believes that much of Microsoft's surge in recent years can be attributed to cultural changes he has emphasized. One aspect of the cultural shift has focused on changing Microsoft from a "know-it-all" to a "learn-it-all" company. Nadella observed that when a company has enjoyed great success and invented many crucial concepts, it is tempted to believe it has mastered everything. That temptation needs to be resisted. "We aren't trying to be the cool kid or the cool company," said Nadella. "Our sole purpose is to build technology so that others can create more technology."

Nadella has received credit for transforming Microsoft's cautious, insular culture. Before Nadella, large teams would work for years on the next major version of a company-defining program like Windows or Word, leading to a risk-averse environment. Employees were hesitant to present new ideas for fear of breaking from what had already made Microsoft successful. In the modern era of "infrastructure on demand," dozens of new features and improvements need to be introduced each month. Endeavors like these require a culture of risk taking and exploration.

The culture Nadella has spearheaded engages and motivate employees to lead company-wide hackathons, and empowering them to work on projects they are passionate about. Enhanced employee engagement helped drive the expansion of Microsoft into cloud services and AI, which have become major sources of company revenue. Nadella also fosters engagement by his gentle approach to dealing with people. He believes that humans are naturally programmed to have empathy. Nadella also believes that empathy is essential not only for creating harmony in the workplace but for making products that will resonate with people.

Another Nadella approach to changing the culture through employee attitudes is to foster a growth mindset, as defined by psychologist Carol Dweck. A growth mindset refers to the idea that the true mark of success is the ability to learn. The walls of Microsoft's headquarter campus are filled with inspirational quotes about "inviting new ideas," and "fostering curiosity." The hackathon fosters a growth mindset because thousands of employees from different departments work together to experiment, learn, and build.

Another key issue Nadella tackled was Microsoft's culture of infighting and of treating competitors as if they were enemy warriors. The company's obsession with Windows, a cash-cow operating system, overlooked the boom in cloud service and software by subscription.

Nadella has also emphasized the important cultural shift of Microsoft now working with partners who were considered rivals in previous years. A key example was releasing a version of Microsoft Office for Apple's iPad. Before Nadella, partners and software developers talked about a hostile environment. It was difficult to get things done, and to obtain the resources they needed. Instead of cooperation, the attitude was hostility.

When Nadella was asked how he reinvented Microsoft in five years, he does not talk about cloud computing or the major acquisitions. Instead, he emphasizes that changing the direction of a ship carrying 130,000 employees could only be accomplished by changing the culture of the passengers and crew.

Nadella received a bachelor's degree in electrical engineering from the Manipal Institute of Technology (India), a master's degree in computer science from the University of Wisconsin-Milwaukee, and an MBA from the University of Chicago School of Business.[1]

The story about the new CEO of a major technology company illustrates how organizational change can be brought about by focusing on changing the organizational culture. The major topics we will cover in this chapter are organization structure, culture and change. All three are fundamental aspects of understanding how organizations function.

BUREAUCRACY AS AN ORGANIZATION STRUCTURE

LEARNING OBJECTIVE **1**

Describe the bureaucratic organization structure and discuss its advantages and disadvantages.

In Chapter 7, we described how the tasks of an organization are divided into jobs for individuals and groups. Companies also subdivide work through an **organization structure**—the arrangement of people and tasks to accomplish organizational goals. The structure specifies who reports to whom and who does what; and is also a method for implementing a strategy and accomplishing the purpose of the organization. For example, top management at Subway wants to sell millions and millions of sandwiches and beverages, so it places thousands of stores and counters in easily accessible locations, including convenience stores located in service stations.

A **bureaucracy** is a rational, systematic, and precise form of organization in which rules, regulations, and techniques of control are specifically defined. Think of bureaucracy as the traditional form of organization, with other structures as variations

organization structure
The arrangement of people and tasks to accomplish organizational goals.

bureaucracy
A rational, systematic, and precise form of organization in which rules, regulations, and techniques of control are specifically defined.

of, or supplements to bureaucracy. Do not confuse the word *bureaucracy* with bigness. Although most big organizations are bureaucratic, small firms can also follow the bureaucratic model. An example might be a small, carefully organized bank.

Principles of Organization in a Bureaucracy

The entire classical school of management contributes to our understanding of bureaucracy. Yet the essence of bureaucracy can be identified by these major characteristics and principles:

1   *Hierarchy of authority.* The dominant characteristic of a bureaucracy is that each lower organizational unit is controlled and supervised by a higher one. The person granted the most formal authority (the right to act) occupies the top place of the hierarchy. Figure 8-1 presents a bureaucracy as pyramid-shaped. The number of employees increases substantially as one moves down each successive level. Most of the formal authority concentrates at the top and decreases with each lower level.

unity of command
The classical management principle stating that each subordinate receives assigned duties from one superior only and is accountable to that superior.

2   *Unity of command.* A classic management principle, **unity of command**, states that each subordinate receives assigned duties from one superior only and is accountable to that superior. In the modern organization, many people serve on projects and teams in addition to reporting to their regular boss, thus violating the unity of command.

3   *Task specialization.* In a bureaucracy, division of labor is based on task-specialization. To achieve task specialization, organizations designate separate divisions or departments, such as new product development, customer service and information technology. Workers assigned to these organizational units employ specialized knowledge and skills that contribute to the overall effectiveness of the firm.

Figure 8-1 The Bureaucratic Form of the Organization

In a bureaucracy, power is concentrated at the top, yet many more employees occupy lower levels in the organization. Note that team leaders are typically found at the first level or middle level of management.

4   *Responsibilities and job descriptions.* Bureaucracies are characterized by rules that define the responsibilities of employees. In a highly bureaucratic organization, each employee follows a precise job description, and therefore knows his or her job expectations. Also, the responsibility and authority of each manager is defined clearly in writing. Responsibility, defined in writing, lets managers know what is expected of them and what limits are set to their authority.

5   *Line and staff functions.* A bureaucracy identifies the various organizational units as being line or staff. Line functions involve the primary purpose of an organization or its primary outputs. In a bank, line managers supervise work related to borrowing and lending money. Staff functions assist the line functions. Staff managers take responsibility for important functions, such as human resources and providing legal counsel. Although staff functions do not deal with the core business purposes of the firm, they play an essential role in achieving the organization's mission. For example, the legal department, a staff group at Apple Inc. plays a key role in defending the company against costly lawsuits related to patent infringements, thereby helping the company carry out its core mission.

Advantages and Disadvantages of Bureaucracy

Bureaucracy made modern civilization possible. Without large, complex organizations to coordinate the efforts of thousands of people, we would not have airplanes, automobiles, skyscrapers, universities, vaccines, smartphones, or space satellites. Many large bureaucratic organizations successfully continue to grow at an impressive pace, such as Microsoft and Bank of America. Here we look at a few key advantages and disadvantages of the bureaucratic form of organization structure.

Advantages

A major advantage of a bureaucracy is organizational members know who is responsible for what, and whether they have the authority to make a particular decision. For example, if a person develops a new idea for a product or service, it is reassuring to present that idea to a manager with the authority to implement the idea.

A major reason that hierarchies continue to thrive is that they fill the basic need for order and security. People want order, predictability, and structures they can understand, such as getting in touch with the tech center when a desktop computer breaks down. Hierarchies help us satisfy other psychological needs through such mechanisms as career ladders and giving us identity by belonging to a stable organization.[2] Also, organizations such as banks, pharmaceutical firms, and hospitals have to follow tight regulations for the good of the public.

Traditional bureaucracies facilitate vertical integration whereby a company controls materials, product development, manufacturing, and distribution. In an era of outsourcing and subcontracting, the 100-year-old strategy of vertical integration still has a place in building a strong, unified organization. For example, as a record store only, Virgin Records barely survived. After company management expanded into talent management and record production, Virgin Records became highly profitable.[3]

Two management professors, Daisy E. Chung and Beth Bechky, conducted a study demonstrating how a bureaucratic structure facilitates task accomplishment. The two production settings chosen for the study were a film set and a semiconductor manufacturing company, both of which had many bureaucratic elements. The study found that in both settings, workers were able to fulfil their bureaucratic expectations with a minimum of complaints or frustration. These expectations included adhering to a budget and tracking work across departments. The positive outcome took place because the specialists in both settings recognized that making bureaucracy work enabled them and their colleagues to maintain a sense of control over essential tasks.[4]

Disadvantages

Despite the contributions of bureaucracy, several key disadvantages exist. A bureaucracy can be rigid in handling people and problems. Its well-intended rules and regulations sometimes create inconvenience and inefficiency. For example, requiring several layers of approval to make a decision causes the process to take a long time. Another substantial problem in a pronounced bureaucracy is that many workers pass responsibility to another department for dealing with a problem. A typical comment is, "You will have to be in touch with (another department) to solve that problem."

Any structure in which strong divisions or departments exist lends itself to a silo mentality in which people of one group feel competitive with other groups to the extent that cooperation suffers. For example, the pharmaceutical group might compete for resources with the over-the-counter medicine group in a medical products company. The fatal ignition switch safety problem at GM that took place a few years ago was attributed in part to a silo mentality at the company. GM chief engineer Ray DeGiorgio flagged the ignition problem before the cars were ever released and called it "The Switch from Hell." He alerted management but GM leaders decided it was too expensive. Former U. S. Attorney General Anton Valukas concluded that GM did not fix its ignition switch rapidly or correctly because the company's many departments were not communicating with each other. A specific accusation was that the engineers who were investigating reports about vehicles stalling were not aware that engineers in other parts of GM had designed airbags that would not deploy when automobiles were technically off.[5]

Other frequent problems in a bureaucracy are frustration on the part of employees from sources such as red tape, slow decision making based on the layers of approval required and the occurrence of frequent meetings. During natural disasters, vitally needed medical supplies sent by other countries are sometimes blocked from getting through to people in need because of a lengthy customs procedure.

To examine your own orientation to the bureaucratic form of organization, take the self-quiz presented in Figure 8-2.

LEARNING OBJECTIVE **2**

Explain the major ways in which organizations are divided into departments.

....

departmentalization
The process of subdividing work into departments.

DEPARTMENTALIZATION

Bureaucratic and other forms of organization subdivide the work into departments, or other units to prevent total confusion. Can you imagine an organization of 300,000 people, or even 300 in which all employees worked in one large department? The process of subdividing work into departments is called **departmentalization**. This chapter uses charts to illustrate three frequently used forms of departmentalization: functional, geographic and product–service. In practice, most organization charts show a combination of these various forms, and therefore have hybrid organization structures.

Figure 8-2 Attitudes Toward Bureaucracy Self-Quiz

Indicate whether you mostly agree (MA) or mostly disagree (MD) with the following 10 statements.

Statement related to bureaucracy	MA	MD
1 I dislike having rules and regulations to guide me.	_____	_____
2 I enjoy working without the benefit of a carefully detailed job description.	_____	_____
3 I find it helpful to have a knowledgeable supervisor give me guidance and advice.	_____	_____
4 Regular working hours and regularly scheduled vacations are important to me.	_____	_____
5 I much prefer being expected to perform a variety of tasks than being assigned a job specialty.	_____	_____
6 I would much prefer working for a large, well-established organization than working for a startup company, even though the compensation was the same at both employers.	_____	_____
7 Having reasonably good job security is much more important to me than the opportunity to make much more money in an unknown company.	_____	_____
8 A person's rank in an organization should not bring him or her much respect.	_____	_____
9 I think that breaking company rules is fine, provided it is for a good purpose.	_____	_____
10 Major decisions should be made only after careful review by several layers of management.	_____	_____

Scoring and interpretation: Give yourself one point for each question you answered in the bureaucratic direction as follows: Mostly Agree, questions 2, 3, 4, 6, 7, and 10; Mostly Disagree, questions 1, 5, 8, and 9. The higher the number of statements that you answered in the bureaucratic direction, the more likely your attitudes and personality are suited to working in a bureaucracy. If your score is zero, look for employment in a startup, or start your own business. If you scored 10, get a position in a rule-oriented organization, such as a motor vehicle bureau.

Functional Departmentalization

functional departmentalization
An arrangement that defines departments by the function each one performs, such as accounting or purchasing.

Functional departmentalization defines departments by the function each one performs, such as accounting, purchasing, or final assembly. Dividing work according to activity is the traditional way of organizing the efforts of people. In a functional organization, each department carries out a specialized activity, such as information

Figure 8-3 Functional Departmentalization within the Davenport Machine Company

Observe that each box below the level of CEO indicates an executive in charge of a specific function or activity, such as sales and marketing.

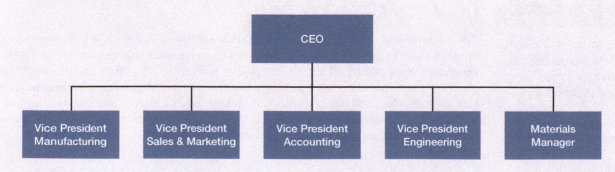

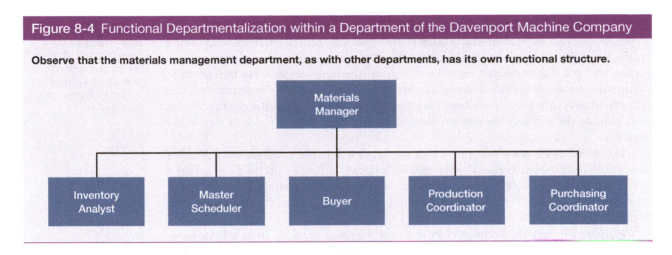

Figure 8-4 Functional Departmentalization within a Department of the Davenport Machine Company

Observe that the materials management department, as with other departments, has its own functional structure.

processing, purchasing, sales, accounting, or maintenance. Figure 8-3 illustrates an organization arranged on purely functional lines. The major subdivisions further divide along their own functional lines as shown in Figure 8-4. The figure shows the functional organization within the materials management department.

The list of advantages and disadvantages of the functional organization, the traditional form of organization reads the same as for bureaucracy. Functional departmentalization works particularly well when large batches of work have to be processed on a recurring basis and when the expertise of specialists is required. As with any form of departmentalization, a major problem is the people within a unit may not communicate sufficiently with workers in other units.

Geographic (or Territorial) Departmentalization

geographic (or territorial) departmentalization
An arrangement of departments according to the geographic area or territory served.

Geographic (or territorial) departmentalization is an arrangement of departments according to the geographic area or territory served. In this organization structure, people performing all the activities for a firm in a given geographic area report to one manager, often with a title like, "regional vice-president." Marketing divisions often use territorial departmentalization; the sales force may also be divided by region, such as the northeastern, southeastern, mid-western, northwestern and southwestern regions.

Geographic departmentalization that divides an organization into geographic regions generally works well for international business. For example, Burger King has the following four geographic divisions, each of which is headed by an executive vice president: North America; Europe, Middle East and Africa; Latin America and the Caribbean; and Asia Pacific.

A key advantage of geographic departmentalization is it allows for decision making at a local level, where staff members are most familiar with the problems and the local culture, including tastes in fashion, product styling and food. Geographic departmentalization also presents some potential disadvantages. The arrangement can be quite expensive because of duplication of costs and effort. For instance, each region may build service departments (such as for purchasing) that duplicate activities carried out at headquarters. A bigger problem arises if top-level management experiences difficulty controlling the performance of field units. To deal with this problem, many multinational corporations supplement the geographic structure by coordinating functional activities across regions. For example, a food processor might want to make sure the same health standards are followed in all parts of the world.

Product–Service Departmentalization

Product–service departmentalization is the arrangement of departments according to the products or services they provide. When specific products or services are so important that the units that create and support them almost become independent companies, product–service departmentalization makes sense. The departments of this size are usually labeled as divisions. With very successful products, the organizational unit making the product becomes a division, such as the wireless product division of Verizon.

Figure 8-5 presents a version of product–service departmentalization at Procter & Gamble (P&G). Notice that the ten global business units offer products or services with unique demands of their own. For example, the advertising campaign for personal healthcare is quite different than the campaign for fabric. Also, the manufacturing process would be quite different. (We hope!)

Notice also that the same customer might purchase services from one or more divisions, such as a supermarket chain making purchases from all ten divisions. As a consequence, the structure is not strictly oriented toward different customer groups.

Organizing by product line offers numerous benefits because employees focus on a product or service, which allows each division or department the maximum opportunity to grow and prosper. An important marketing and sales advantage is that sales representatives are assigned to one product or service group in which they become experts, rather than being sales generalists. For example, Dell has a specialist for different groups, such as servers, so generalist account reps are not sent into the field to compete with server specialists from Cisco Systems.

In a smooth-running organization with open communication, the various product or service units cooperate with each other for mutual benefit. A case in point is the healthcare giant Johnson & Johnson (J&J). A division that develops an improved method of delivering drugs (such as a skin patch) would typically share that development with another division. Human care could therefore improve pet care and vice versa! Similar to geographic departmentalization, grouping by product or service fosters

product–service departmentalization
The arrangement of departments according to the products or services they provide.

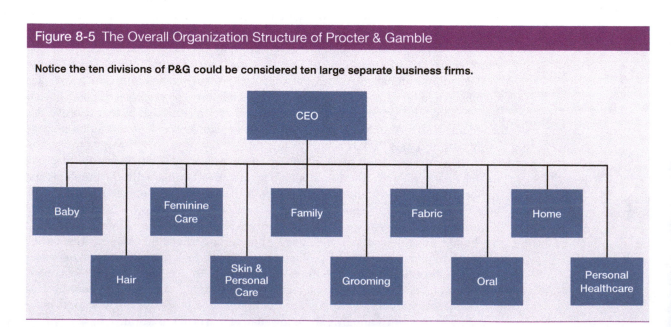

Figure 8-5 The Overall Organization Structure of Procter & Gamble

Notice the ten divisions of P&G could be considered ten large separate business firms.

CEO

Baby · Feminine Care · Family · Fabric · Home

Hair · Skin & Personal Care · Grooming · Oral · Personal Healthcare high morale, and allows decisions to be made at the local level. Departmentalization by product poses the same potential problems as geographic departmentalization. It can be expensive because of duplication of effort, and top-level management may find it difficult to control the separate units.

LEARNING OBJECTIVE **3**

Describe four modifications of the bureaucratic structure.

MODIFICATIONS OF THE BUREAUCRATIC ORGANIZATION

To overcome some of the problems of the bureaucratic (including the functional) structure, several other organization structures have been developed. Virtually all large organizations combine bureaucratic and less bureaucratic forms. This section describes three popular modifications of bureaucracy: the project and matrix organizations; flat structures, downsizing, and outsourcing; and the horizontal structure.

The Project and Matrix Organizations

project organization
A temporary group of specialists working under one manager to accomplish a fixed objective.

Departmentalization tends to be poorly suited to performing special tasks that differ substantially from the normal activities of a firm. **Project organization** is when a temporary group of specialists works under one manager to accomplish a fixed objective, and offers one widely used solution to this problem. A project can also be regarded as a special purpose team. Used most extensively in the military, aerospace, construction, motion picture and information technology industries, project management is so widespread that software has been developed to help managers plot out details and make all tasks visible.

The project manager is a central figure in getting major tasks accomplished, such as seeing a new product to completion. Another role emphasized for the project manager is being a linking pin between an organization providing service and the client.[6] An example would be a project manager at the General Electric division that services airplane engines spending time on the premises of United Airlines to help implement the service project.

matrix organization
A project structure superimposed on a functional structure.

The best-known application of project management form is the **matrix organization**, a project structure superimposed on a functional structure. Matrix organizations evolved to capitalize on the advantages of project and functional structures, while minimizing their disadvantages. Jay R. Galbraith, professor emeritus at the International Institute for Management Development, says that matrix organizations are a natural consequence of working in today's complex business environment.[7] The project groups act as mini-companies within the firm in which they operate. However, the group usually disbands after completing its mission. In some instances, the project proves so successful that it becomes a new and separate division of the company.

Figure 8-6 shows a popular version of the matrix structure. Notice that functional managers exert some functional authority over specialists assigned to the projects. For example, the quality manager occasionally meets with the quality specialists assigned to the projects to discuss their professional activities. The project managers hold line authority over the people assigned to their projects. For the matrix organization to work well, there should be an assumed balance of power between the two bosses.

The project managers borrow resources from the functional departments, a feature that distinguishes the matrix from other organizational structures. Also, each person working on the project reports to two superiors: the project manager and the functional manager. For example, observe the quality analyst in the lower right corner of Figure

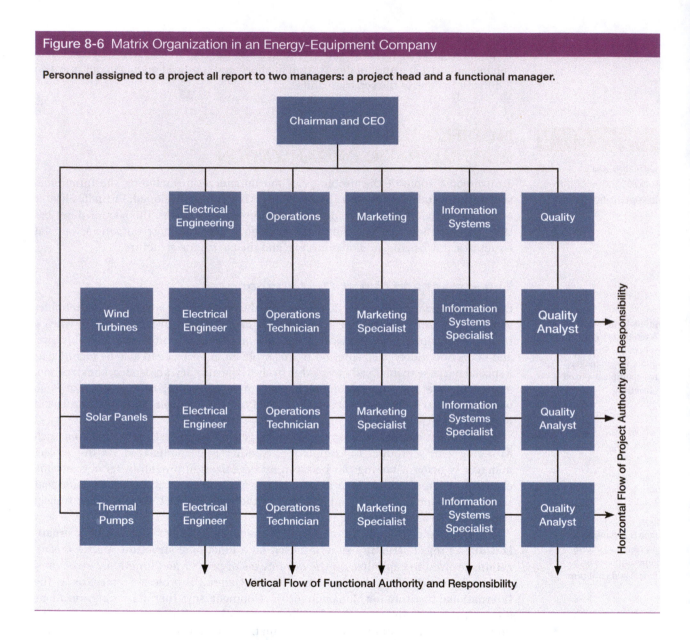

Figure 8-6 Matrix Organization in an Energy-Equipment Company

Personnel assigned to a project all report to two managers: a project head and a functional manager.

Horizontal Flow of Project Authority and Responsibility

Vertical Flow of Functional Authority and Responsibility

8-6. The analyst reports to the manager of quality three boxes above him or her and to the project manager for the thermal pumps project located five boxes to the left.

A survey of 4,000 employees conducted by consulting giant McKinsey & Company found a key strength of matrix organizations is collaboration—a positive finding because cross-company teamwork is a chief aim of many matrices. A problem reported with matrix structures, however, was that only a minority of workers in these structures agreed with the statement, "I know what is expected of me at work." This reflects the common complaint found in matrix organizations that the structure gives rise to unclear responsibilities, expectations and reporting relationships. Part of the problem is the complexity of the matrix structure.[8] The managers involved in a matrix should therefore invest more time in clarifying these issues for the team members.

Flat Structures, Downsizing, and Outsourcing

Three closely related approaches to simplifying an organization structure include creating flat structures, downsizing, and outsourcing. Reducing the number of layers typically makes an organization less bureaucratic.

Flat Structures

Organizations with a bureaucratic structure tend to accumulate many layers of managers, and often too many employees in general. For example, despite frequent reorganizations at General Motors, at last report the company had nine layers of management. To deal with the problems just mentioned, management may then decide to create a **flat organization structure**, a form of organization with relatively few layers. A flat organization structure acts less bureaucratically for two reasons. First, fewer available managers review the decisions of other workers. Second, a shorter chain of command means managers and workers at lower levels can make decisions more independently.

An important consequence of creating flat structures leaves the remaining managers with a larger **span of control**—the number of workers reporting directly to a manager. A large span of control works best with competent and efficient managers and group members. When group members do relatively similar work, the manager can supervise more people.

Sending digital information to workers has been a major force toward flattening organization structures. Workers have a lot of the information they need to accomplish their work without consulting a manager. Partly based on this ease of information sharing, a few firms have even attempted to operate without managers. Given the reality that the vast majority of workers including high achievers need some direction, guidance, and encouragement, many of these efforts at eliminating management have been abandoned.

Downsizing

Downsizing can be viewed as a way of simplifying an organization to make it less bureaucratic. Under ideal circumstances, downsizing also leads to better profits and higher stock prices. The motivation behind most downsizings of both assets (such as company divisions or buildings) and workers is generated by the company's need to reduce costs and increase profits. Yet, downsizing can be expensive. Among the costs associated with downsizing that need to be considered are severance pay, supplements to early retirement plans, disability claims, and lower productivity resulting from a possible decline in staff morale. Customer service can also suffer when an organization is thinned down; to the extent that most remaining employees are overloaded with responsibilities. A deep and widespread downsizing took place during the coronavirus pandemic in 2020.

A less obvious disadvantage of downsizing is that creativity may drop. In fear of becoming the next person downsized, employees tend to make less bold, creative moves in their jobs. Some employees may hold ideas in reserve in case they are downsized and need to find employment in another company. Less creativity often leads to less innovation, thereby preventing some productivity gains that might have stemmed from a useful new idea.[9] An employee might think, "Why risk suggesting an idea that might backfire? I could be downsized."

For downsizing to help the company in the long run, *it should be part of a business strategy to improve the company, not just a stopgap measure to save money.* Examples

flat organization structure
A form of organization with relatively few layers of management, making it less bureaucratic.

span of control
The number of workers reporting directly to a manager.

would be using downsizing to eliminate duplication of jobs after a merger, or to exit a business that does not fit a new strategy. *Eliminating low-volume and no-value activities* provides an early step in effective restructuring. This *activity-based reduction* systematically compares the costs of a firm's activities to their value to the customer. In searching for low-value activity, workers monitor the output of others. *Keeping future work requirements in mind* also contributes to effective restructuring. Letting go of people who will be an important part of the firm's future rarely provides an effective answer to overstaffing.

Sensible criteria should be used to decide which workers to let go. In general, the poorest performers should be released first. Offering early retirement and asking for voluntary resignations also leads to less disruption. At the same time, it is helpful to retain, or sometimes increase, the workers most needed for the company's success. During a 2019 downsizing, retail giant Macy's Inc. decided not to lay off sales associates. The CEO said, "We figured out how precious these sales associates are." In fact, the company added sales associates to some of the most profitable locations, which helped drive improvements in those stores.[10]

A comprehensive principle of downsizing or resizing a company is to *involve employees in the resizing process.* Top-level management may have to decide which employees will be terminated, yet workers can be involved in making suggestions about how the work should be reassigned. Laid-off workers should be *offered assistance in finding new employment or reorienting their careers.*

Outsourcing

Outsourcing is part of globalization but is also part of the organization structure by having other companies perform part of your work. Outsourcing to domestic companies is also a major part of hiring other firms to perform work. Outsourcing is part of a gradual and long-standing shift being undertaken by many business corporations in the United States and other countries. Starting in the 1960s, business firms began to focus more on their own core competencies, outsourcing many "non-core" functions and the jobs that go along with them to other firms. Payroll was one of the first functions to be outsourced. Today, many firms outsource accounting, customer support, web design, legal services and other functions.[11]

By outsourcing, a company can reduce its need for employees, physical assets and their associated costs. Outsourcing to low-wage regions also saves money, but only if the work is performed properly. Productivity can increase when work is performed more economically. The major justification for outsourcing is a company is likely to profit when it focuses its effort on activities it performs best, while noncore activities such as human resources, payroll processing and information systems are performed by outside experts.

Outsourcing also takes the form of subcontracting, in situations when another company functions like a complete manufacturing plant or operation—sometimes for high quality, expensive products. An example of this is Porsche, the German sports car manufacturer, who has contracted manufacturing to Valmet Automotive of Finland since 1997. Valmet produces about one-third of the total output of Porsche, including the Cayenne and the Boxster.[12]

United Parcel Service (UPS) exemplifies how far outsourcing has advanced. The world's largest delivery company provides a wide variety of services for other companies through its subsidiary, UPS Supply Chain Solutions. The services other companies outsource to UPS include emergency electronic repairs, fixing laptops, installing giant

X-ray machines, operating customer-service hotlines, packaging consumer electronics and issuing corporate credit cards. The type of work supply chain provides lends itself to domestic outsourcing because much of the work is needed urgently. UPS stores every conceivable part in its giant warehouse in Louisville, Kentucky, so it can perform repairs quickly. (For this type of operation, the just-in-time inventory system would be counterproductive because speed of repair is a success factor.) Outsourcing partners like UPS work so closely with their customers that they become virtually part of their client's business.[13]

Outsourcing is a form of organization structure that management must carefully evaluate. Outsourcing may save money and acquire expertise not available in-house, yet there is much to be said for building a company with a loyal workforce that has company pride. Great companies built in the past and the present, such as Colgate Palmolive and Google did not achieve their greatness through outsourcing every conceivable business process.

The Horizontal Structure (Organization by Team and Process)

In the traditional, or functional organization, people in various organization units are assigned specialized tasks, such as assembly, purchasing, marketing and shipping. In another approach to organization structure, a group of people concerns itself with a process, such as filling an order or developing a new product. Instead of focusing on a specialized task, all team members focus on achieving the purpose of all the activity, such as getting a product in the hands of a customer.

horizontal structure
The arrangement of work by teams that are responsible for accomplishing a process.

A **horizontal structure** is the arrangement of work by multidisciplinary teams that are responsible for accomplishing a process. Figure 8-7 illustrates a horizontal structure, as do the projects shown in Figure 8-6. The employees take collective responsibility for customers, and they work together to accomplish the task. Instead of one department handing off work to another department, the team members work together on the task of meeting customer requirements. A horizontal structure can therefore also be considered a team structure, which will be reintroduced in Chapter 13. It would be difficult today to find a business, governmental, not-for-profit, or educational organization that made no use of the team structure.

As with other modifications of the bureaucratic structure, the horizontal structure coexists with vertical structures. The process teams offer a balanced focus so employees can direct their effort and attention toward adding value for the customer.[14] The UPS groups that provide packaging services for clients use a horizontal structure because a project manager is responsible for making sure client needs are met. The team members focus on a single purpose, such as, "We have to get these Nikon cameras packed and ready for shipment."

Figure 8-7 A Horizontal Organization Structure

In a horizontal organization, even though specialists are assigned to the team, they are expected to understand one another's tasks and perform some of those tasks as needed.

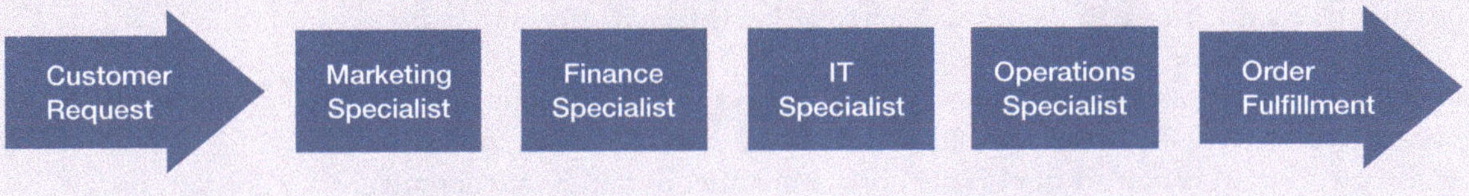

Customer Request → Marketing Specialist | Finance Specialist | IT Specialist | Operations Specialist | Order Fulfillment →

The push toward the horizontal structures and a process mentality should not be embraced without qualification. Having a task mentality remains important because expertise is still crucial in many endeavors. A building construction team, for example, still relies on highly proficient specialists, such as mechanical and electrical engineers. Wouldn't you prefer to ride in an elevator that was designed by a highly proficient mechanical engineer?

Informal Structures and Communication Networks

The formal structures described in this chapter are an essential part of planning how work is performed. Nevertheless, an organization chart does not tell the whole story of how work gets accomplished. The **informal organization structure** is a set of unofficial relationships that emerge to take care of events and transactions not covered by the formal structure. The informal structure supplements the formal structure by adding a degree of flexibility and speed. A widespread application of the informal structure is the presence of, "tech fixers" who supplement the technical support center. For example, marketing assistant Jason might be skilled at resolving software problems created by computer viruses. As a consequence, many people call on Jason for some quick assistance even though the formal organization indicates they should use the tech center for help with virus problems.

informal organization structure
A set of unofficial relationships that emerge to take care of events and transactions not covered by the formal structure.

Informal structures are also referred to as informal networks because of the focus on how people use personal contacts to obtain information in a hurry and get work done.[15] The informal networks reveal how well-connected people are, as well as how work really gets done. An application of mapping the informal network would be in spotting talent. Some of the most respected workers might not be found on the organization chart but could be indicated by a network map because of the number of times these individuals are consulted by other workers. The highly respected workers might be tapped for key projects.[16]

The informal organization can be revealed by **social network analysis**, the mapping and measuring of relationships and links between and among people groups, and organizations.[17] The nodes in the network are the people, and the links show relationships or flow between and among the nodes as shown in Figure 8-8. Notice that Rathin is an important node in the network because he is linked with Lisa, Anna and Brett. Social network analysis helps explain how work gets accomplished in a given unit, such as shown in the interactions among Susan, Tim and Tara on the right side of Figure 8-8. Perhaps the three of them mutually discuss credit risks. The interrelations can become quite complicated, because of the many number of people and interactions between and among them.

social network analysis
The mapping and measuring of relationships and links between and among people, groups, and organizations.

Social network analysis helps management survey the informal interactions among employees that can lead to innovative ideas. At the same time, the maps can point to areas where workers should be collaborating, but they are not. In this way, the maps help facilitate knowledge sharing. The maps can also be used to pinpoint the interactions one manager has so he or she can give the information to a successor.

Also, as part of informal networks, all organization structures described so far in this chapter are influenced by information technology. Workers from various units throughout an organization can solve problems together through information networks without being concerned with, "who reports to whom," as indicated by organization charts. Furthermore, entry-level workers can leapfrog layers of management and communicate directly with senior executives through e-mail. However, now, as in the past, entry-level workers almost never telephone a member of upper management.

Figure 8-8 A Basic Unit of a Social Network Analysis

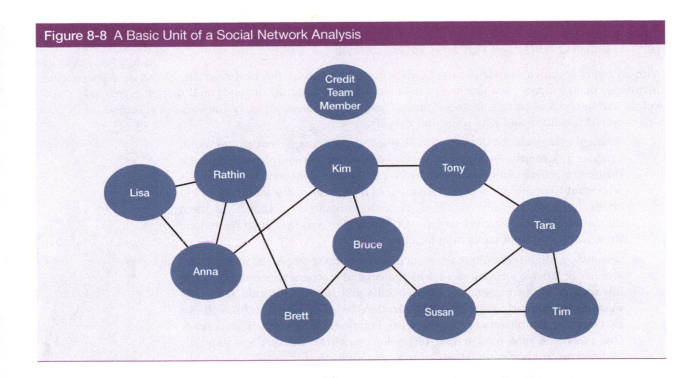

We have described many different organizational structures—enough to create some confusion and blurring. Figure 8-9 summarizes the unique aspect of each structure. We have added the conglomerate structure, referring to a collection of independent companies under one corporate roof. Although the term is fading from frequent use, conglomerates still exist, with General Electric being one of the best known.

Figure 8-9 Unique Feature of Various Organization Structures

Type of Structure or Modification	Unique Feature or Emphasis
Bureaucracy	Hierarchical, with clear rules and regulations.
Functional	Departments are defined by the function, or activity, they perform.
Geographic	Departments are defined by their geographic location.
Product-Service	Departments or divisions are defined by the major product or service they offer.
Matrix	A project, or program, structure is superimposed on a functional structure.
Flat and Downsized	One or more layers is removed from the structure, and the staff is reduced.
Outsourcing	Work activities are deployed outside the organization, including having it performed at peoples' homes.
Horizontal or Team	Work is performed by multidisciplinary teams, and communication among workers is enhanced.
Informal	People work cooperatively to fill in the gaps not taken care of by the formal organization.
Hybrid	A structure that combines several of the above structures, such as a traditional bureaucracy also having several product or service divisions.
Conglomerate	A large company that is really a collection of loosely related independent companies, with a minimum of direction and control from headquarters.

KEY FACTORS THAT INFLUENCE THE SELECTION OF AN ORGANIZATION STRUCTURE

LEARNING OBJECTIVE **4**

Identify key factors that influence the selection of organization structure.

With so many organization structures, how do managers choose the best one? The answer lies in contingency management—the most effective structure depends on the weight and analysis of certain factors. Among these factors are strategy, technology, size, financial condition and environmental stability.

1 *Strategy and goals.* As described in the history of management presented in Chapter 1, structure is supposed to follow strategy. Assume the strategy of a business machine company is to be the friend of small businesses and individuals who want to operate business equipment in their homes. The company would choose a geographically dispersed marketing organization that gives them maximum access to small customers, such as Staples and Best Buy. (We assume the customers do not make most purchases online.)

2 *Technology.* High-technology firms such as aerospace companies make extensive use of flexible structures, such as project and matrix structures. Relatively low-technology firms, such as lumber mills and refuse-collection firms rely more on bureaucratic structures. Organizations based on digital technology like Facebook and Amazon.com typically use horizontal and network structures. One reason is that information technology–oriented workers are naturally inclined toward horizontal, free-flowing communication.

3 *Size.* As an organization grows and matures, it inevitably needs centralized controls and some degree of bureaucracy, or formalization. Yet when the firm becomes very large, it is necessary to develop smaller, more flexible units, such as projects and task forces. These units help the firm remain adaptive and are found in every large organization.

4 *Financial condition of the firm.* Size influences structure, and the financial condition of the firm influences both size and structure. Many large business organizations have moved toward a flatter structure to trim costs. Trimming down the number of corporate positions influences structure because with fewer headquarter executives left to supervise divisions, decision-making authority becomes more decentralized.

5 *Environmental stability.* When a business firm faces an uncertain and unstable environment, such as the market for high-fashion clothing or consumer electronics, it needs a highly flexible structure. Task forces and projects are often called into action to deal with a rapidly changing marketplace. Conversely, a more bureaucratic structure is better suited to deal with more certain (stable) environments. An example is the market for Crayola Crayons and related products, which has proved to be both recession-proof and resistant to competitors.

DELEGATION, EMPOWERMENT, AND DECENTRALIZATION

LEARNING OBJECTIVE **5**

Specify how delegation, empowerment, and decentralization spread authority in an organization.

Collective effort would not be possible, and organizations could not grow and prosper if a handful of managers did all the work themselves. In recognition of this fact, managers divide up their work. Subdividing work through the process of departmentalization has already been described. The section that follows will discuss subdivision of work using the chain of command—specifically, delegation, empowerment, and decentralization.

Delegation of Responsibility and Empowerment

delegation
Assigning formal authority and responsibility for accomplishing a specific task to another person.

empowerment
The process by which managers share power with group members, thereby enhancing employees' feelings of personal effectiveness.

Delegation refers to assigning formal authority and responsibility for accomplishing a specific task to another person. If managers do not delegate any of their work, they are acting as individual contributors—not true managers. Some managers are hesitant to delegate because they dislike giving up control, which explains why *control* freaks are poor at delegation. Delegation relates closely to **empowerment**, the process by which managers share power with group members, thereby enhancing employees' feelings of personal effectiveness. Delegation is a specific way of empowering employees, thereby increasing motivation. In empowerment, however, the person performing the work has more control and authority.

A major goal of delegation is the transfer of responsibility as a means of increasing one's own productivity. At the same time, delegation allows team members to develop by learning how to handle more responsibility and to become more productive. Even though a manager may hold a group member responsible for a task, final accountability belongs to the manager. (To be accountable is to accept credit or blame for results.) If the group member fails miserably, the manager must accept the final blame; the manager chose the person who failed.

Delegation and empowerment lie at the heart of effective management. For example, a study was conducted with management teams in 102 hotel properties in the United States. A major finding was that empowering leadership increased the sharing of job knowledge among employees, and more effective teamwork. In turn, the improved knowledge-sharing and teamwork were related to good performance.[18]

Following the six suggestions presented next improves the manager's chance of increasing productivity by delegating and empowering individuals and teams.[19] (Note that teams as well as individuals can be the unit of delegation and power-sharing, such as asking a team to find a way of filling orders more rapidly.)

1 *Assign duties to the right people.* The chances for effective delegation and empowerment improve when capable, responsible, well-motivated group members receive the delegated tasks. The manager must be aware of the strengths and weaknesses of staff members to delegate effectively. However, if the purpose of delegation is to develop a group member, the present capabilities of the person receiving the delegated tasks are less important. The manager is willing to accept some mistakes as the cost of development.

2 *Delegate the whole task and step back from the details.* In the spirit of job enrichment, a manager should delegate an entire task to one subordinate rather than dividing it among several. This gives the group member complete responsibility and enhances motivation, and also gives the manager more control over results. After the whole task is delegated, step back from the details. If a manager cannot let go of details, he or she will never be effective at delegation or empowerment.

3 *Give as much instruction as needed.* Some group members will require highly detailed instructions, while others can operate effectively with general instructions. Many delegation and empowerment failures occur because instruction was insufficient. Dumping is the negative term given to the process of dropping a task on a group member without instructions. Under ideal circumstances, delegating should be an opportunity for coaching employees and sharing skills with them.

4   *Specify how much accountability the person has for the delegated assignment.* Delegation often fails because the person assigned the task does not know the amount of his or her responsibility.

5   *Retain some important tasks for yourself.* Managers need to retain some high-output or sensitive tasks for themselves. In general, the manager should handle any task that involves the survival of the unit or employee discipline. However, which tasks the manager should retain always depend on the circumstances. Strategy formulation is ordinarily not delegated except to obtain input from group members. Sales managers often keep one or two key accounts for themselves.

6   *Obtain feedback on the delegated task.* A responsible manager does not delegate a complex assignment to a subordinate, then wait until the assignment is complete before discussing it again. Managers must establish checkpoints and milestones to obtain feedback on progress.

Decentralization

Decentralization is the extent to which authority is passed down to lower levels in an organization. It comes about as a consequence of managers delegating work to lower levels. However, the term also refers to geographic decentralization, which often results in passing down authority because managers in the decentralized units are granted decision making authority. Unless so noted, this text uses the term decentralization in reference to authority. **Centralization** is the extent to which authority is retained at the top of the organization. Decentralization and centralization lie on two ends of a continuum. No firm operates as completely centralized or decentralized.

How much control top management wants to retain determines how much to decentralize an organization. Organizations favor decentralization when a large number of decisions must be made at lower organizational levels, often based on customer needs. J&J, the medical and personal care products giant, favors decentralization in part because the company consists of a collection of different businesses, many with vastly different customer requirements. Division management is much more aware of these needs than those at company headquarters. In general, a centralized firm exercises more control over organization units than a decentralized firm.

Many firms centralize and decentralize operations simultaneously. Certain aspects of their operations are centralized, whereas others are decentralized. Rapid-service franchise restaurants such as Subway, Long John Silver's and Wendy's illustrate this trend. Central headquarters exercises tight control over such matters as menu selection, food quality and advertising. Individual franchise operators, however, make human resource decisions, such as hiring.

An advanced technique of juggling the forces of centralization and decentralization simultaneously is for decentralized units to remain somewhat autonomous while cooperating with each other for the common good. For example, the basic structure of Johnson & Johnson is a decentralized firm with 250 nearly autonomous units organized into three business segments: consumer healthcare (such as Band-Aid and Johnson's Baby Powder), medical devices, and pharmaceuticals. J&J is considered by many to be the reference company for decentralization. The company emphasizes decentralized management because it believes workers closest to patients and

decentralization
The extent to which authority is passed down to lower levels in an organization.

centralization
The extent to which authority is retained at the top of the organization.

customers are best positioned to address their needs. The emphasis at J&J is for the autonomous divisions to cooperate with each other to achieve better products— such as sutures from one division being coated with drugs from another, to help prevent infections.[20]

LEARNING OBJECTIVE **6**

Identify major aspects of organizational culture.

ORGANIZATIONAL CULTURE

The structure of an organization is sometimes referred to as the "hard side" of how a firm operates; yet understanding the "soft side" of an organization is also essential. **Organizational culture (or corporate culture)** is the system of shared values and beliefs that actively influence the behavior of organization members. The term *shared* implies many people are guided by the same values and they interpret them in the same way. Values develop over time and reflect a firm's history and traditions. Organizational culture is important to understand because it is a major factor in the success of any company, as indicated in the chapter opener about Microsoft.

This section describes significant aspects of organizational culture: how it is learned, and its determinants, dimensions, consequences and management and maintenance.

organizational culture (or corporate culture)
The system of shared values and beliefs that actively influence the behavior of organization members.

Determinants of Organizational Culture

Many forces shape a firm's culture. Often its origin lies in the values, administrative practices and personality of the founder or founders. Also, the leader's vision can have a heavy impact on culture, such as John Chambers' dream of Cisco Systems becoming one of the world's greatest companies. Leaders play a key role in creating a positive culture, such as in displaying cooperative behavior among themselves, and being cordial and supportive toward workers throughout the company.[21]

The culture in which a society operates also helps determine the culture of the firm. Societal values are communicated through such means as the media, conversations and education. The emphasis on sexual and racial equality in U.S. society has become incorporated into the value culture of many employers. The introduction of values from another society into a retail business can be a competitive advantage. For example, the South Korean values of high quality, reliability, and spotless factories have helped fuel the success of the Hyundai and Kia car brands in the United States. The industry to which a firm belongs helps shape its culture. For example, a public utility's culture will be very different from a food manufacturer of comparable size. Heavy competition and low profit margins may force the food manufacturer to operate at a faster pace than the utility, which usually competes for customers with several other utilities.

Dimensions of Organizational Culture

The dimensions of organizational culture help explain the subtle forces that influence employee actions. In addition to the dominant culture of a firm, the sub-culture also influences behavior. A **subculture** is when the organizational culture differs from the dominant culture at the unit level, as well as other pockets of subculture within the company. A frequently observed difference in subcultures can be found between the marketing and production groups, even in such matters as dress and behavior. The marketing people are likely to be more style-conscious and people-oriented. Eight dimensions significantly influence organizational culture.[22]

subculture
A pocket in which the organizational culture differs from the dominant culture, as well as other pockets of the subculture.

1   *Values.* Values provide the foundation of any organizational culture. The organization's philosophy expressed through values guides behavior on a day-to-day basis. Representative values of a firm might include ethical behavior, concern for employee welfare, a belief that the customer is always right, a commitment to quality, and the importance of equality and independence. The emphasis placed on teamwork is another key value. A pervasive value is the importance of formality, with a heavily bureaucratic culture believing strongly in formality, including following procedures and protocol. Another value of significance is an emphasis on truthfulness and candor. In a culture characterized by candor, workers combat telling others what they want to hear.[23]

2   *Relative diversity of behavior.* The existence of an organizational culture assumes some degree of homogeneity. Nevertheless, organizations differ widely in terms of how much deviation can be tolerated. Many firms are highly homogeneous; executives talk in a similar manner and even look alike. Furthermore, these executives promote people from similar educational backgrounds and fields of specialty into key jobs.

3   *Resource allocations and rewards.* The allocation of money and other resources exerts a critical influence on culture. The investment of resources sends a message to people and units about what is valued in the firm. If a customer-service department is fully staffed and nicely furnished, employees and customers can assume the company values customer service.

4   *Degree of change.* The culture in a fast-paced, dynamic organization differs from that of a slow paced, stable one. A highly competitive environment might encourage a fast-paced climate. Top-level managers, by the energy or lethargy of their stance send signals about how much they welcome innovation. The degree of change also influences whether a culture can take root and how strong that culture can be.

5   *A sense of ownership.* An ownership culture increases loyalty, improves work effort and aligns worker interests with those of the company. A culture of this type can be reflected in such everyday actions as conserving electricity, making gradual improvements and not tolerating sloppiness by co-workers. An employee stock ownership plan or profit sharing contributes to an ownership culture.

6   *Organizational ambidexterity.* An aspect of organizational culture related to business strategy and innovation is the ability of an organization to simultaneously take advantage of existing market opportunities and innovating to meet the challenges of future markets.[24] Lenovo, as presented in Case Problem 4-B, shows its organizational ambidexterity through its strategy of protect and attack.

7   *Extent of fear.* In less prosperous organizations, workers face intense pressure to meet demanding goals with smaller teams and fewer resources, with negative consequences if they fall short of meeting the goals. Even during a prosperous economy, in some organizations fear and uncertainty remains, often fueled by advances in technology that are eliminating many jobs. Psychologist and business consultant Shelia M. Keegan said, "We have become much more brutal in organizations."[25]

8   *Joy and happiness.* An important dimension of organizational culture from the standpoint of the employee is the extent of joy and happiness that

pervades the organization. An outstanding example is Vail Resorts Inc., where management recognizes that cultivating joy among employees also facilitates customers having fun, which has a big impact in the hospitality business. (Vail, Colorado is a world-famous ski resort, but the company also has 13 other locations.) CEO Bob Katz proclaims "have fun" is a corporate value. Resort managers are a model of joy regularly and prescribe it for their teams. For example, ski-lift operators are often seen dancing, making jokes, and doing whatever is necessary to entertaining guests while maintaining ski safety.[26]

9 *Strength of the culture.* The strength of the culture, or how much influence it exerts, emerges partially as a by-product of the other dimensions. A strong culture guides employees in everyday actions. It determines, for example, whether an employee will inconvenience himself or herself to satisfy a customer or assist a team member. Without a strong culture, employees are more likely to follow their own whims—perhaps deciding to please customers only when convenient.

These dimensions represent a formal and systematic way of understanding organizational culture. In practice, people use more glib expressions in describing culture, as illustrated in Figure 8-10.

How Workers Learn the Culture

socialization

The process of coming to understand the values, norms, and customs essential for adapting to the organization.

Employees learn the organizational culture primarily through **socialization**, the process of understanding the values, norms, and customs essential for adapting to the organization. Socialization is therefore a method of indoctrinating employees into the organization in such a way that they perpetuate the culture. The socialization process takes place mostly by learning through imitation and observation.

Figure 8-10 Organizational Cultures of Three Well-Known Companies	
IKEA	Very informal culture with Swedish roots. Emphasis on informality, cost-consciousness, and a humble, down-to-earth approach. Workers are allowed considerable responsibility.
Apple Inc.	A strong cultural attitude of being winners who continue to change the world. Attitude of smugness and superiority, with a tendency to perceive other technology companies as mere imitators of the real thing (Apple), with these attitudes being strengthened with the extraordinary success of the iPhone. Pride dominates the organization. Intense fondness for innovation and free thinking, combined with a strong dislike for bureaucracy. The company thrives on secrecy and obsessive attention to detail.
Coca-Cola	Bureaucratic, slow-moving, with major changes taking a long time to implement. New CEO in 2017 wanted the company to shake off the culture of cautiousness that had gripped the company for more than a century. Continuing profits from beverages kept key employees in the past from seeing the need for change. For many years, Coca-Cola had a bloated staff. The company has gradually shifted to a faster-moving culture, willing to experiment on new products, acquisitions, and arrangements with suppliers. Employees tend to be loyal and are expected to drink Coke or other company beverages. Workers are geared toward professional behavior.

Sources: Katarina Kling and Ingela Goteman, "IKEA CEO Anders Dahlvig on International Growth and IKEA's Unique Corporate Culture and Brand Identity," *Academy of Management Executive*, February 2003, pp. 31–37; pp. 26–29; Angela Ahrendts, "First of All, Just Learn and Listen" *Fast Company*, February 2016, p. 63; Dylan Love, "Former Employee: 'At Apple, They Really Are After You'," *Business Insider* (www.businessinsider.com), January 9, 2013, p. 1; Jennifer Maloney, "Shaking the 'New Coke' Syndrome," *The Wall Street Journal*, May10, 2017, p. B1; Albrecht Rothacher, "Coke Nation Embodying Corporate Culture," *www.globalspec.com*, November 17, 2014, p. 3.

Organizational members learn the culture to some extent by observing what leaders pay attention to, measure and control. Suppose a co-worker is praised publicly for providing excellent customer service. You are likely to conclude that an important part of the culture is to go out of your way to help customers. Senior executives will sometimes publicly express expectations that help shape the culture of the firm, such as demanding data-driven decision making.

Workers also learn the culture by hearing repeated stories that illustrate company values. For example, at FedEx workers hear stories about how delivery workers went beyond the call of duty to deliver a package during a storm, or how a driver rescued a person caught in a flood. The value illustrated is outstanding service to customers and the community.

Consequences and Implications of Organizational Culture

The attention to organizational culture stems from its pervasive impact on organizational effectiveness. Figure 8-11 outlines several key consequences of organizational culture. The right organizational culture *contributes to gaining competitive advantage and therefore achieving financial success.* The consistently strong performance of Google can be partially attributed to its culture that values intelligence, imagination and hard work.

The right organizational culture can enhance *productivity*, *quality*, and *morale*. A culture that emphasizes productivity and quality encourages workers to be more productive and quality conscious. A synthesis of many studies found that organizational culture is related to quality practices related to attitudes (such as top management support for quality). In turn, these practices were related to manufacturing performance.[27] A culture that values the dignity of human beings fosters high morale and job satisfaction. A corporate culture that *encourages creative behavior contributes to innovation*, as described in Chapter 5 about problem solving and decision making. A key part of building a culture of innovation is for top-level managers to encourage an appetite for risk.[28]

Figure 8-11 Consequences and Implications of Organizational Culture

Although organizational culture is a soft concept, it has many hard consequences.

Organizational Culture

- Competitive Advantage and Financial Success
- Productivity, Quality, and Morale
- Innovation
- Compatibility of Mergers and Acquisitions
- Employee Recruitment
- Person–Organization Fit
- Influences Activity of Leaders

However, there can be a dark side to corporate culture. A culture that facilitates both high quality and business success can become too smug and complacent, believing it cannot fail. An example of how organizational culture can have negative consequences, is the problem Volkswagen AG experienced when it adjusted software in its diesel vehicles to make them appear more fuel efficient. Top-level management blamed the problem on a "culture of tolerance" for rule-breaking that enabled the deception to continue for a decade.[29]

A reliable predictor of success in merging two or more firms is *compatibility of their respective cultures*. When the cultures clash, such as a hierarchical firm merging with an egalitarian one, the result can be negative synergy. Similarly, a culture clash frequently happens when a bureaucratic organization acquires a startup with very few established rules, regulations and procedures. Mergers and acquisitions have a 50/50 chance of success, with some estimates of a failure rate of close to 80 percent, usually because the cultures of the two firms do not match.[30]

The reputation of an organizational culture, as perceived by outsiders has a *strong impact on employee recruitment* with job seekers gravitating toward organizations known for their positive culture. Being known as a company with integrity, as well as a fun place to work helps attract job candidates, assuming that pay and benefits are competitive.[31] The "Ohana" (the Hawaiian word for family) culture at Salesforce embraces, quality, service, and innovation which helps the company attract a steady stream of talented job applicants.

Individuals can contribute to their own success by *finding a good person–organization fit* to his or her personality. The person who finds a good fit is more likely to experience job satisfaction, commitment to the organization, and is less interested in quitting.[32] Similarly, an organization will be more successful when the personalities of most members fit its culture. Many companies today use cultural fit as a criterion in the hiring process. A major goal of finding people who fit the culture is to help build a cooperative, creative atmosphere that can make workdays more enjoyable and prevent interpersonal conflict.[33]

Organizational culture powerfully *influences the activity of leaders*. Top-level managers spend much of their time working with the forces that shape the attitudes and values of employees at all levels. Leaders in key roles establish what type of culture is needed for the firm and then shape the existing culture to match that ideal, which is why outsiders are sometimes brought in to head a company.

LEARNING OBJECTIVE **7**

Describe key aspects of managing change, including gaining support for change.

MANAGING CHANGE

To meet their objectives, managers must manage change effectively on a daily basis. Management consultant Robert H. Schaffer believes most management is really change management. The job of management often defines what changes need to be made and seeing that these changes are implemented.[34] An example would be identifying the need for increased sales, and developing a plan to attain the sales increase. Change in the workplace relates to any factor with an impact on people, including changes in technology, organization structure, organizational culture, competition, human resources and budgets.

We will explore aspects of managing change by looking at these six components: (1) change at the individual versus organizational level, (2) a model of the change process, (3) resistance to change, (4) gaining support for change, (5) bringing about planned change through Six Sigma. Knowledge of these components helps in managing change that affects oneself and others.

Creating Change at the Individual versus Organizational Level

Many useful changes in organizations take place every day at the individual and small group levels, in addition to the organizational level. Quite often, individual contributors, middle-level managers and team leaders identify a small need for change and make it happen. For example, a supermarket manager observed several meat department workers did not understand fractions. He therefore suggested that each supermarket should have a designated "fraction trainer" to assist meat workers who could not work with fractions.

Change at the organizational level receives much more attention than the small, incremental changes brought about by individuals that continuously improve processes and workplace productivity. Change at the organizational level usually is directed at modifying the culture, such as the company becoming more innovative and open to risk taking. Another key aspect of cultural change is to create values and attitudes that will support the organization's mission, such as developing a product or services of higher perceived value by customers.

A practical way of bringing about cultural change is to hold people accountable for the changes in behavior that support the shift. If top-level management decides customer service should receive top priority, employees at all levels should be measured on customer service in their performance reviews. If not, the cultural shift to placing a higher value on customer service will not take place.[35] Organizational culture consultant Bryan Kurey says, "As the leader, you need to set up the structures, processes, and incentives in your organization, and put your money where your mouth is."[36]

The chapter introduction described a far-reaching approach to bring about cultural change. The accompanying *Management in Action* insert describes a more modest approach to changing the organizational culture.

The Unfreezing-Changing-Refreezing Model of Change

Psychologist Kurt Lewin developed a three-step analysis of the change process widely used by managers to help bring about constructive change, as Illustrated in Figure 8-12.[37] *Unfreezing* involves reducing or eliminating resistance to change. As long as employees oppose a change, it will not be implemented effectively. To accept change, employees must first deal with and resolve their feelings about letting go of the old. Only after people have dealt effectively with endings can they readily make transitions. *Changing*, or moving on to a new level, usually involves considerable two-way communication, including group discussions. *Refreezing* includes pointing out the success of the change and looking for ways to reward people involved in implementing the change.

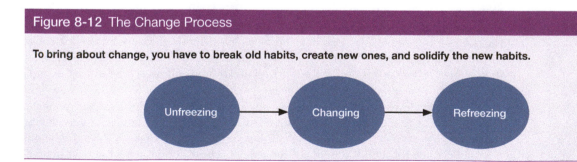

Figure 8-12 The Change Process

To bring about change, you have to break old habits, create new ones, and solidify the new habits.

MANAGEMENT IN ACTION

Former Home Depot CFO, Carol Tomé Helped Renovate the Corporate Culture

The Home Depot is the world's largest home-improvement retailer, and is known for its employee-centric, and store-centric culture. A major impact of the culture is that store associates are encouraged to be entrepreneurial and serve customers the best they can. Managers are trained and encouraged to occupy the role of coaches rather than traditional bosses.

Carol Tomé, was the company's chief financial officer for 18 years before she retired in 2019. During that time, she saw the company make a cultural shift, and then return to the culture established by the company's founders in 1979. According to Tomé, the most unique part of the culture is the inverted pyramid. The Home Depot executive team is placed at the bottom of the pyramid, and customers are at the top. The associates who service customers are placed at the second-to-top level.

At the end of 2000, the company tried to change the culture and it backfired. The Home Depot founders chose to bring in a former GE executive, Robert Nardelli, who they thought would help the company grow at an accelerated rate with more infrastructure and technology. He heavily emphasized efficiency measures. Nardelli decided to reverse the pyramid around so that leadership was at the top and associates were placed at the bottom. During Nardelli's reign, Home Depot's market share shrunk. Frank Blake was appointed CEO in 2007, and he flipped the pyramid back around to where it was.

The three major components of the Home Depot culture in addition to the inverted pyramid are excellence in service, people-centricity, and collaboration. "People-centricity" refers to encouraging employees to establish productive and enjoyable work relations and employee-customer relations. The collaboration dimension encourages store associates to perform as a team.

One of the changes Tomé favored was to sell HD Supply that emphasized selling in large quantities to contractors, and is now an industrial distributor. She felt that the company should get back to its core of dealing directly with end users and small contractors, such as home-repair specialists. During the housing crisis Home Depot had to close many stores, including the Expo business, a chain of high-end remodeling stores. Around 2007, the home-improvement market had become saturated with too few households per home-improvement store.

Tomé said that Blake and she had to convince employees that reverting back to Home Depot's original culture made sense. The company was undergoing a rough period. Between 2006 and 2009, company revenue decreased $13 billion, or 25 percent. Home Depot closed stores, exited a few lines of businesses, and laid off 1,000 people at the Store Support Center. Yet to support the company culture, hourly associates continued to receive merit increases, 401(k) contributions, and receive bonuses. Tomé believes that the investment in people paid off because seven years later Home Depot sales hit a record, and annual sales and profits have continued to grow. The vast majority of store managers and associates were pleased that we brought back our original culture.

Tomé emphasizes that a CFO must understand the business in addition to being a financial expert. She notes, "When I started working, I had to put on an apron and work in the store. You need to be able to speak the language of the business, not the language of finance."

Questions

1   If executives at Home Depot are paid more than store managers, and store managers are paid more than associates, how complete is the "reversed pyramid"?

2   If you, a family member, or friend have shopped at Home Depot a few times, what is your evaluation of the "excellence-in-service" dimension of Home Depot. (If you work for Home Depot, your input would be highly valuable.)

3   In what ways might Home Depot store associates all wearing an orange apron contribute to the corporate culture?

Source: Original story based on the following sources: Tatyana Shumsky, "Home Depot CFO to Retire After 18-Year Tenure," *The Wall Street Journal* (www.wsj.com), April 30, 2019; Sarah Nassauer, "Home Depot's CFO on How the Retail Giant Renovated Itself," *The Wall Street Journal*, August 10 11, 2019, p. B2; Andrew Thompson, "Home Depot's Organizational Culture: An Analysis," *Panmore Institute* (www.panmore.com), February 3, 2017, pp. 1–3; Kelly Spors, "How Home Depot Overcame a Difficult Cultural Shift," *Greenleaf Center for Servant Leadership* (www.greenleaf.org), July 10, 2015, pp. 1–3.

Resistance to Change

Before a company's managers can gain support for change, they must understand why people resist change. People resist changes for reasons they think are important, the most common being the fear of an unfavorable outcome, such as less money, personal inconvenience, or job insecurity. People also resist change for such varied reasons as not wanting to break well-established habits. Change may also be unwelcome because it upsets the balance of an activity, such as the old system of in-person meetings versus video conferencing. Underlying all forms of resistance to change are emotions and feelings, so the manager wanting to bring about change must make good use of his or her emotional intelligence.

Personality factors also contribute to resistance to change. For example, a rigid person might be more naturally disposed to maintaining the status quo. Workers who feel they lack the skills to deal effectively with the change, such as working in a team rather than individually, will sometimes resist change. Even when people do not view a change as potentially damaging, they may sometimes cling to a system they dislike rather than change. According to folk wisdom, "People would rather deal with the devil they know than the devil they do not know."

Workers may also resist change based on weaknesses in the proposed changes that may have been overlooked or disregarded by management. Jeffery D. Ford and Laurie W. Ford suggest that resistance is really a form of feedback, frequently provided by workers who know more about day-to-day operations than a high-level manager. For example, managers might not be aware of how upset many customers would be when a voice recognition system replaces live customer-service agents. Because workers have more contact with customers, they might predict the customer dissatisfaction.[38]

Gaining Support for Change

Gaining support for change, and therefore overcoming resistance is an important managerial responsibility. A case study at a consumer goods manufacturer showed that long-term benefits of change occur only when employees actively work to support the change and are aligned with the organization's goals and values.[39] Here we look at seven techniques for gaining support for change.

1 *Allow for discussion and negotiation.* Support for change can be increased by discussing and negotiating the more sensitive aspects of the change. It is important to acknowledge the potential hardships associated with the change, such as longer working hours or higher output to earn the same compensation. People should be given the opportunity to express their concerns about the changes. The two-way communication incorporated into the discussion helps reduce some employee concerns. Discussion often leads to negotiation, which further involves employees in the change process.

2 *Allow for participation.* To overcome resistance to change, allow people to participate in the changes that will affect them. In applying this concept, a manager can allow employees to set their own rules to increase compliance. A powerful participation technique is to encourage people who already favor the change to help in planning and implementation. These active supporters of the change will be even more strongly motivated to enlist the support of others. Participation is also useful because it gives the manager additional input into developing a careful plan for the change, including implementation.

3 *Point out the compelling reasons for change, including the financial benefits.* A good way to prepare employees for change is to point out the most compelling reasons why the status quo will no longer be effective, such as the competition gaining ground or new regulatory requirements. The compelling reason will often create a sense of urgency. Given that many employees express concern

about the financial effects of work changes, it is helpful to discuss these effects openly. If employees will earn more money as a result of the change, this fact can be used as a selling point.

4 *Establish a sense of urgency.* The presentation of compelling reasons for change will often create a sense of urgency, but the change agent may have to go even further. An appeal must be made to both emotions and reason. Telling a human-interest story about the need for change can help enlist emotions and the intellect.[40] For example, one division president explained how her uncle who owned a hotel was too slow to establish a Wi-Fi environment, and therefore experienced a decrease in occupancy rates.

5 *Avoid change overload.* Too much change too soon leads to negative stress. Too many sweeping changes in a brief period of time, or simultaneous changes also causes confusion, and it leads to foot dragging about workplace innovation. When change is perceived as excessive, employees often focus too much on the change and not enough on primary tasks, such as the product, service, or customers. Explaining how large-scale changes fit the company strategy can sometimes lessen the sting of change. An effective way of avoiding change overload is to focus on a few critical shifts in behavior at a time, particularly when attempting to bring about broad cultural change. The manager should ask about which new behaviors should be added, and which should be abandoned.[41] Assume company leadership wants to bring about a cultural shift toward welcoming ideas for improvement from a wider base of employees. Managers might be encouraged to send out e-mails once per month, asking all direct reports for one constructive idea to improve operations or increase sales. The behavior to be abandoned would be to pay limited attention to employee input about improvement.

6 *Get the best people behind the program.* A powerful tactic for bringing about change is to enlist the cooperation of people whom others in the organization respect, and who are flexible. For example, some workers enjoy change and are also influential among their peers. Such a person might be encouraged to communicate his or her attitudes about change, including posting them on a social networking site (without revealing company secrets). One person or a small group of trail blazers can provide the catalyst to bring about the desired changes.[42] The employees who welcome a particular change, and encourage others to join them have been labeled *champions of change.* These "champions" regard change as a positive challenge.[43]

7 *Inspire group members by presenting a compelling vision for the future.* During uncertain times, people want a clear view of the future. It is helpful for the manager to present the big picture of why the change is important, and the long-term benefits of the change.[44] Assuming that a small craft brewer is bought by a major beer company, the founder of the small brewery might explain how their brand will now go national. As a result, pride in the brand might grow, as well as the compensation of the craft division.

The above techniques for overcoming resistance to change are more likely to be successful when the manager has a good working relationship with staff members, including being trusted. For example, allowing for discussion and participation is less likely to be perceived as manipulation when the manager is trusted.

Six Sigma and Planned Change

The shift to a more quality-conscious firm can be classified as a total systems approach to organization change. Having high-quality goods and services is considered a necessary minimum to compete effectively. Most customers today require high-quality standards from vendors. One such standard is Six Sigma, or 3.4 errors in 1 million opportunities. (The figure is derived from the area under the normal curve from −6 to +6 standard deviations from the mean.) A number of organizations formalized this quality standard as part of company-wide programs for attaining high quality. **Six Sigma** refers to a philosophy of driving out waste and improving quality, and the cost and time performance of a company.

Six Sigma is regarded as a data-driven method for achieving near-perfect quality, with an emphasis on preventing problems. The focus is on identifying, quantifying, and eliminating errors in business processes. Six Sigma emphasizes statistical analysis and measurement in design, manufacturing and the entire area of customer-oriented activities. Decision making becomes heavily based on numbers, as in data-driven decision making. Six Sigma also contains a strong behavioral aspect, with a focus on motivating people to work together to achieve higher levels of productivity. Everybody in the company is supposed to be involved to some extent in the change effort.[45] As with all programs of organizational improvement, top management commitment is vital.

The Ford Motor Company Six Sigma initiative, called *Customer-Driven Six Sigma*, is a positive example of how the methodology can result in to major, positive organizational change. Ford began using Six Sigma strategy in the late nineties. The company wanted to enhance product quality and customer satisfaction rates. Ford was the first automaker to implement Six Sigma methodology into its business operations on a large scale.

A pressing problem facing Ford when the company implemented Six Sigma was 20,000 plus opportunities for defects that came with the manufacture of automobiles. Despite a system of quality control, defects showed up in cars. The company aimed to reduce its defect rate to a single defect per 14.8 vehicles, and they attained this goal. Furthermore, customer-satisfaction goals were also attained. Six Sigma also helped Ford reduce consumption of vital resources. By committing to a green work culture with Six Sigma, the company reduced waste, thereby also saving money.[46]

Six Sigma can help an organization achieve reliable products and services. However, the program must fit into the company culture. Companies more attuned to Six Sigma are those where the culture emphasizes discipline and measurement, such as Xerox, Bank of America and Honeywell International. A concern about pushing too far with Six Sigma is that it sometimes takes away from the innovation and customer relationships partially because of its heavy emphasis on measurement and paperwork (or electronic work). At the same time, critics of Six Sigma claimed that the system has been overhyped, and has lost popularity in recent years.[47]

Six Sigma
A data-driven method for achieving near-perfect quality with an emphasis on preventing problems.

SUMMARY OF KEY POINTS

1 **Describe the bureaucratic organization structure and discuss its advantages and disadvantages.**

The most widely used form of organization is the bureaucracy, a multi-level organization in which authority flows downward and rules and regulations are carefully specified. Bureaucracies can be highly efficient organizations that are well suited to handling repetitive, recurring tasks. People know who is responsible for what, and vertical integration of the company is possible Also, a bureaucracy fits the human need for order and security, among other needs. However, they may be rigid in terms of handling people and problems, and decision-making delays are frequent in bureaucracies.

2 **Explain the major ways in which organizations are divided into departments.**

The usual way of subdividing effort in organizations, particularly in bureaucracies, is to create departments. Three common types of departmentalization are functional, geographic (or territorial) and product-service. Product-service departmentalization also takes the form of creating groups to better service customer needs.

3 **Describe four modifications of the bureaucratic structure.**

Projects are temporary groups of specialists. The matrix organization consists of a project structure superimposed on a functional structure. Personnel assigned to the projects within the matrix report to a project manager, yet they report to a functional manager also. Flat organizations have fewer layers than traditional hierarchies and are often the result of downsizing. They are created for such purposes as reducing human resource costs and speeding up decision making. Downsizing can also be looked at as a way of simplifying an organization to make it less bureaucratic. Unless downsizing is done carefully, it can backfire in terms of efficiency. By outsourcing, a company can reduce its need for employees, physical assets and associated payroll costs. Outsourcing is part of globalization but is also part of the organization structure by having other companies perform part of your work.

Another approach to organization structure is to organize horizontally, or for a group of people to concern themselves with a process, such as filling an order or development of a new product. Team members focus on their purpose rather than their specialty and take collective responsibility for customers.

In addition to the formal structures, organizations also have informal structures that consist of personal relationships and networks to accomplish work. Information technology facilitates communication in all types of organization structures.

4 **Identify key factors that influence the selection of organization structure.**

The most effective structure depends on four key factors. The organization's strategy and goals are the most influential factor. High technology favors a flexible structure, whereas low technology favors bureaucracy. Large size often moves a company toward bureaucracy. Finances influence structure because flatter structures lower costs. An unstable environment favors a flexible structure.

5 **Specify how delegation, empowerment, and decentralization spread authority in an organization.**

Delegation is assigning formal authority and responsibility for accomplishing a task to another person. Delegation fosters empowerment. The manager remains accountable for the result of subordinates' efforts. Effective delegation includes assigning duties to the right people and obtaining feedback on the delegated task. Decentralization stems from delegation. It is the extent to which authority is passed down to lower levels in an organization. Decentralization sometimes refers to geographic dispersion. Although units may be decentralized and autonomous, in some organizations these units cooperate with each other for the common good.

6 **Identify major aspects of organizational culture.**

The organizational culture is shaped by such forces as the values and personality of the founder, the attitudes of top-level managers, society and the industry. Nine key dimensions of organizational culture are values, relative diversity of behavior, resource allocation and rewards, degree of change, a sense of ownership, organizational ambidexterity, extent of fear, joy and happiness, and the strength of culture. Employees learn the culture primarily through socialization, including story telling.

Culture has important consequences and implications for factors, such as competitive advantage, productivity, quality, morale, ease of recruitment and direction of leadership activity.

7 **Describe key aspects of managing change, including gaining support for change.**

Change can take place at the individual and small group levels as well as at the organizational level. A model of change suggests the process has three stages: unfreezing attitudes, followed by attitude change, then refreezing to point out the success of the change. People resist change for reasons they think are important, the most common being the fear of an unfavorable outcome.

Seven techniques for gaining support for change are as follows: allow for discussion and negotiation; allow for participation; point out compelling reasons for the change including the financial benefits; establish a sense of urgency; avoid change overload; get the best people behind the program; and inspire group members by presenting a compelling vision for the future.

Six Sigma is another organizational change strategy. It is a data-driven method for achieving near-perfect quality and is administered by Six Sigma teams with the cooperation of most managers and executives.

Key Terms and Phrases

Questions

1. If you are not a C-suite executive, what relevance does understanding organization structure have for you?

2. Over the years, large business organizations have steadily reduced the number of layers in the organization structure. What purposes has this profound change in structure served?

3. Small- and medium-sized companies are often eager to hire people with about five years of experience working in a large, successful bureaucratic firm like IBM or General Foods. What might be the reason behind the demand for these workers with experience in a bureaucracy?

4. Some management experts who think departmentalization has become an obsolete organization structure still would rush a family member to a hospital urgent care center following an accident. How are these experts being hypocrites?

5. What can first- and middle-level managers, as well as team leaders, do about shaping a firm's culture?

6. What can you tell about the organizational culture of a large retailer just by visiting a couple of stores?

7. In recent years, many small- and medium-size business firms have encouraged employees to use their own mobile devices at work. Why has this change to "bring your own device" encountered such little resistance?

Skill-Building Exercise 8-A: Comparing Organization Structures

Work individually or in groups to find the organization structure at a local company or any type of organization. It may be possible to accomplish the task by e-mail and telephone. Whatever structure you find, provide some kind of explanation for why the particular structure is useful for the organization. For example, a department store would have a departmental structure such as "girls' clothing" and "office supplies." The reason would be that the departments serve clientele with radically different needs. Compare your organization structures in class and see how many different types of structures were found.

Skill-Building Exercise 8-B: Reactions to Organizational Change

Although the term "organizational change" seems straightforward, what type of difference in a policy, procedure, rule, attitude, or physical object, workers actually perceive to be a change is difficult to specify. Your role in this exercise is to pin down examples of what workers actually perceive to be a change. Ask four people in your network to give you an example of both a positive and a negative change they have experienced on the job. Include yourself in your network if you would like. Ask your respondents to be a specific as possible. You might compare your findings to those of a classmate. Next, answer two questions:

- What type of workplace changes do people like?
- What type of workplace changes do people dislike?

Management Now—Online Skill-Building Exercise: Analyzing an Organizational Culture

Every organization has a culture, even if the organization has not developed a description of its culture. Search the Internet for several articles posted within the last 12 months about one of your favorite companies, as well as the company website. Find at least three statements that describe its culture, such as, "this is a highly disciplined organization where every worker keeps focused on the goal," or, "this place is a bunch of cowboys and cowgirls running wild." Arrive at a tentative conclusion about the company's culture based on your findings.

Aspiring Hotel Executive Annabelle Wants to Know if She Would Fit the Culture

Twenty-eight-year-old Annabelle has worked for four years as an assistant hotel manager at a hotel chain. One of her major career goals was to move up to a senior executive position at a major hotel and resort chain. The hotel she works at currently is franchise operated, and several family members are work at key positions at the hotel. Annabelle therefore feels that she is an outsider who will not be promoted to hotel manager in the near future. As she sees it, working as a hotel manager is the next step toward becoming a hotel and resort executive.

Based on these considerations, Annabelle elected to conduct a job search, including a careful use of the job-search website, Indeed. To her delight, her skills and experience were in strong demand in the healthy service economy at the time.

The second company she interviewed with for a hotel manager position was a Milwaukee location of an international hotel chain, only a twenty-minute commute from where she lives. After a series of telephone interviews, video interviews, and face-to-face interviews, Annabelle received an attractive offer at 20 percent higher pay than she was receiving at her current hotel. As is typical in the hotel industry, the manager position required some work at night and on weekends. Annabelle said she was excited about the offer but wanted one week to reach a final decision.

Annabelle thought highly of the job offer and the hotel but believed that she should learn more about the hotel's culture to see if she would be a good fit. She thought, "I should be diligent before taking a big leap." Annabelle's first step in checking out the organizational culture was to ask one of the hotel's receptionists what he thought of the hotel. He responded, "Amazing. Anything else I can help you with?"

Next, Annabelle had lunch at the hotel restaurant. She explained to her server that she was considering working for the hotel in an administrative position, and she wanted the server's input into what it was like working there. The server responded, "Hotel management believes in a fair work on your shift to earn fair pay. If you do your job right, you will earn good tips. To keep your job, you have to work well with the other servers and the kitchen staff."

Annabelle also asked the dining room hostess about working conditions at the hotel. The hostess responded, "If you are looking for an easy job, go someplace else. They expect a lot out of you here. There are plenty of other hotels in Milwaukee, and there is pressure on you to go out of your way to please customers."

Annabelle then asked 10 people in her network if they knew anybody who worked for this prospective employer. She finally identified three people: an accountant, a banquet manager, and a housekeeping supervisor, along with their contact information. When asked about the type of hotel atmosphere, the accountant replied, "Only hard workers survive here. You have to attain good results to justify your compensation."

The banquet manager said, "If you are serious about running a hotel, you have to be totally committed. You face one emergency after another from a snow storm that results in cancellations to five employees quitting at the same time. You also have to deal with outrageous hotel guests who want a refund for any little inconvenience they have encountered. The housekeeping supervisor said, "Our hotel is a nice place to work, but you earn every dollar you get. My staff and I are expected to keep the rooms spotless, and keep guest complaints to an absolute minimum."

Annabelle thought she was learning a lot about the corporate culture, but she wanted one more vital input. Through a couple of people in her network, Annabelle identified a family that had recently stayed at the hotel. When asked about what she thought of the hotel in question the mother in the family said, "The hotel staff is fine, and the hotel has all the amenities you would expect. My husband, my two children and I had an enjoyable four-night stay at the hotel. We weren't expecting Disneyland at a downtown Milwaukee hotel."

Annabelle concluded, "I have uncovered no skeletons in the closet, and what I hear impresses me. I'm going to phone in my acceptance at 9:00 tomorrow morning."

Case Questions

1 What do you think of Annabelle's approach to sizing up the organizational culture at her prospective employer?

2 What other approach would you recommend that Annabelle could have taken to assess the organizational culture at the hotel?

3 Based on the evidence that Annabelle collected, what is your assessment of the organizational culture at the hotel where she will be working?

Redesigning the Kellogg Company

Kellogg's (also referred to as the Kellogg Company) is a giant multinational food company, headquartered in Battle Creek, Michigan. Kellogg's produces a wide variety of well-known cereal and convenience foods. Among these famous brands are Corn Flakes, Frosted Flakes, Rice Krispies, Kashi, and Cheez-it. The company's products are manufactured in 18 countries and marketed in 180 countries.

Assume CEO and Chairman Steven Cahillane comes to your class and says, "Folks, as you know we produce some of the world's most recognized brands. I bet that every member of your class and the professor has enjoyed a Kellogg cereal or snack at some point in his or her life. Yet, company management is worried. Too many people are eating bagels, toast, or natural goods for breakfast, as well as for other meals. We may have to become a nimbler company. Maybe we should begin with our organization structure. Right now, 20 people report directly to me, as shown in the organization chart. Please suggest a simplified organization chart that might help us uncomplicate Kellogg."

Your job is to simplify the Kellogg's organization structure and chart, perhaps with an eye toward faster decision making in the company. Use the most efficient medium for your drawing, including paper and pencil, flip chart, or computer graphic.

Case Questions

1 What do you think of Steven Cahillane's span of control?
2 Why will your new organizational structure help Kellogg become more effective?

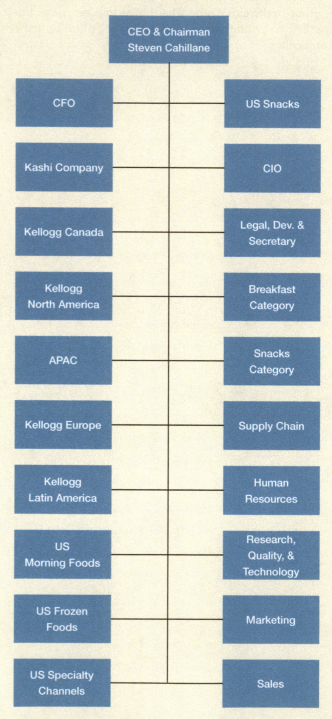

ENDNOTES

1. Original story created from facts and observations in the following sources: Ron Miller, "After 5 Years, Microsoft CEO Satya Nadella has Transformed More than the Stock Price," TC (https://techcrunch.com), February 4, 2019, pp. 1–4; Simone Stolzoff, "How Do You Turn Around the Culture of a 130,000-person Company? Ask Satya Nadella," *Quartz at Work* (https://qz.com), February 1, 2019, pp. 1–7; Harry McCraken, "Transforming Culture at Microsoft: Satya Nadella Sets a New Tone," *Intheblack* (www.intheblack.com), June 1, 2018, pp. 1–19; Alex Konrad, "Microsoft's New Groove," *Forbes*, December 31, 2018, pp. 68–70; Marco della Cava, "Nadella Counts on Culture Shock to Drive Microsoft Growth," *USA Today*, February 20, 2017, p. 4B; Scott Anthony and Evan I. Schwartz, "What the Best Transformational Leaders Do," *Harvard Business Review* (https://hbr.org), May 8, 2017, p. 7.

2. Harold J. Leavitt, "Why Hierarchies Thrive," *Harvard Business Review*, March 2003, p. 99; Leavitt, *Top Down: Why Hierarchies Are Here to Stay and How to Manage Them More Effectively* (Boston: HBS Press, 2004).

3. Russ Buchanan, "Examples of Vertically Integrated Companies," *Chron* (http://smallbusiness.chron.com), p. 1. © Copyright 2016 Hearst Newspapers, LLC.

4. Daisy E. Chung and Beth Bechky, "Latitude or Latent Control? How Occupational Embeddedness and Control Shape Emergent Coordination," *Administrative Science Quarterly*, August 8, 2017 (doi).

5. Rana Foroohar, "We've All Got GM Problems," *Time*, June 23, 2014, p. 24.

6. Shelia Simsarian Webber and Maria T. Torti, "Project Managers Doubling as Client Account Executives," *Academy of Management Executive*, February 2004, p. 70.

7. Jay R. Galbraith, *Designing Matrix Organizations That Actually Work: How IBM, Procter & Gamble, and Others Design for Success* (San Francisco: Jossey-Bass, 2009), p. 247.

8. Michael Bazigos and Jim Harter, "Revisiting the Matrix Organization," *McKinsey Quarterly* (www.mckinsey.com), January 2016, p. 2; Aaron De Smet, Sarah Kleinman, and Kirsten Weerda, "The Helix Organization," *McKinsey Quarterly*, (www.mckinsey.com), October 2019, p. 2.

9. Shelly Frost, "The Disadvantages of Corporate Downsizing," *Chron* (http://smallbusiness.chron.com), p. 1. © 2016 Hearst Newspapers LLC.

10. Suzanne Kapner and Ann Aisha Al-Muslim, "Macy's Plans Managerial Culling," *The Wall Street Journal*, February 27, 2019, p. B5.

11. Thomas Tunstall, "Where the New Jobs Will Come From" *The Wall Street Journal*, November 5, 2015, p. A15; Lauren Weber, "The End of Employees," *The Wall Street Journal* (www.wsj.com), February 2, 2017, pp. 1–2.

12. Carter Dougherty, "Porsche Finds Fortune from Unlikely Outsourcing," *The New York Times* (www.nytimes.com), April 3, 2009.

13. "Outsourcing Logistics Can Pay Off Big Time," *UPS Compass* (http://compass.ups.com), November 2013, p. 2; UPS Staff Writer, "3 Tips When Outsourcing Your Supply Chain," UPS (www.ups.com), February 1, 2017, pp. 1–2.

14. Frank Ostroff, *The Horizontal Organization: What the Organization of the Future Actually Looks Like and How It Delivers Value to Customers* (New York: Oxford University Press, 1999); Ann Majchrzak and Qianwei Wang, "Breaking the Functional Mind-Set in Process Organizations," *Harvard Business Review*, January 1998, p. 21.

15. Rob Cross and Laurence Prusak, "The People Who Make Organizations Go—or Stop," *Harvard Business Review*, June 2002, p. 104.

16. Jena McGregor, "The Office Chart That Really Counts: Mapping Informal Relationships at a Company is Revealing and Useful," *Business Week*, February 27, 2006, pp. 48–49.

17. Valdis Krebs, "Social Network Analysis: A Brief Introduction," 2009.

18. Abhishek Srivastava, Kathryn M. Bartol, and Edwin A. Locke, "Empowering Leadership in Management Teams: Effects on Knowledge Sharing, Efficacy, and Performance," *Academy of Management Journal*, December 2006, pp. 1239–1251.

19. Sharon Gazda, "The Art of Delegating," *HR Magazine*, January 2002, pp. 75–77; "Boost Delegation with this Master List," *Manager's Edge*, June 2002, p. 7; "The Power of Power Sharing," *HR/OD*, July–August 1998, p. 2; Bob Frisch and Cary Greene, "To Hold Someone Accountable, First Define What Accountable Means," *Harvard Business Review* (https://hbs.org) , June 28, 2016, pp. 1–4.

20. "Johnson & Johnson CEO William Weldon: Leadership in a Decentralized Company," *Knowledge@Wharton*, June 25, 2008; "Decentralized Management Approach," *Johnson & Johnson* (www.jnj.com), p. 1. © Copyright Johnson & Johnson Services Inc. 1997–2015.

21. Aileen Williams, "The Power of Positive Culture," *HR Magazine*, May 2015, pp. 24–25.

22. J. Steven Ott, *The Organizational Culture Perspective* (Chicago: Dorsey Press, 1989), pp. 20–48; Personal communication from Lynn H. Suksdorf, Salt Lake City Community College, October 1998.

23. James O'Toole and Warren Bennis, "What's Needed Next: A Culture of Candor," *Harvard Business Review*, June 2009, pp. 54–61.

24. Pankaj C. Patel, Jake G. Messersmith, and David P. Lepak, "Walking the Tightrope: An Assessment of the Relationship between High-Performance Work Systems and Organizational Ambidexterity," *Academy of Management Journal*, October 2013, p. 1421.

25. Dori Meinert, "Scared Stiff: Do You Have a Workplace Culture of Fear?" *HR Magazine*, December 2015/January 2016, p. 12.

26. Sigal Barsade and Olivia A. O'Neil, "Managing Your Emotional Culture," *Harvard Business Review*, January–February 2016, p. 62.

27. Michael Naor, Susan Goldstein, Kevin Linderman, and Roger Schroeder, "The Role of Culture as Driver of Quality Management and Performance: Infrastructure Versus Core Quality Practices," *Decision Sciences*, Vol. 39, 2008, pp. 671–702.

28. Julie Goran, Laura LaBerge, and Ramesh Srinivasan, "Culture for a Digital Age," *McKinsey & Company* (www.mckinsey.com), June 2017, pp. 3–5.

29. William Boston, Hendrik Varnholt, and Sarah Sloat, "VW Says 'Culture' Flaw Led to Crisis," *The Wall Street Journal*, December 11, 2015, p. B1.

30. Edith Onderick-Harvey, "5 Behaviors of Leaders Who Embrace Change," *Harvard Business Review* (https: hbr.org), May 18-2018, p. 2.

31. Rhonda Abrams, "A Great Small Business Culture Shows Values," *USA Today Money*, September 7, 2015, p. 4B.

32. Amy L. Kristof-Brown, Ryan D. Zimmerman, and Erin C. Johnson, "Consequences of Individuals' Fit at Work: A Meta-Analysis of Person–Job, Person–Organization, Person–Group, and Person–Supervisor Fit," *Personnel Psychology*, Summer 2005, p. 310; Sue Shellenbarger, "The Perils of 'Cultural Fit'," *The Wall Street Journal*, September 24, 2019, p. A12.

33. "Will You Be My Friend?" *Bloomberg Businessweek*, January 7–January 13, 2013, pp. 64–65.

34. Robert H. Schaffer, "All Management is Change Management," *Harvard Business Review* (https://hbr.org), October 26, 2017, p. 2.

35. Beth Sears, "Strategic Cultural Change," *Democrat and Chronicle*, July 5, 2015, p, 5E.

36. Quoted in "The Wrong Ways to Strengthen Culture," *Harvard Business Review*, July-August 2019, p. 24.

37. Kurt Lewin, *Field Theory and Social Science* (New York: Harper & Brothers, 1951).

38. Jeffrey D. Ford and Laurie W. Ford, "Decoding Resistance to Change," *Harvard Business Review*, April 2009, p. 100.

39. Anita Baggio, Eleftheria Digentiki, and Rahul Varma, "Organizations Do Not Change, People Change," *McKinsey& Company* (www.mckinsey.com), pp. 1–4.

40. John Kotter, *A Sense of Urgency* (Boston: Harvard Business School Press, 2008).

41. Jon R. Katzenbach, Ilona Steffen, and Caroline Kronley, "Cultural Change that Sticks," *Harvard Business Review*, July–August 2012, pp. 113–114.

42. Nate Boaz and Erica Ariel Fox, "Change Leader, Change Thyself," *McKinsey & Company* (www.mckinsey.com), March 2014, p. 6.

43. Mel Fugate and Guillaume Soenen, "Predictors and Processes Related to Employees' Change-Related Compliance and Championing," *Personnel Psychology*, Number 1, 2018, pp. 111–112

44. Morgan Galbrath, "Don't Just Tell Employees Organization Changes Are Coming—Explain Why," *Harvard Business Review* (https://hbr.org), October 8, 2018, p. 3.

45. Sara Fister Gale, "Building Frameworks for Six Sigma Success," *Workforce*, May 2003, pp. 64–69.

46. "Six Sigma Case Study: Ford Motors," *Six Sigma* (www.6sigma.us), pp. 1–6.

47. Oliver Stanley, "Whatever Happened to Six Sigma?" *Quartz at Work* (https://qz.com), September 3, 2019.

CHAPTER 9

Human Resource and Talent Management

OBJECTIVES

After studying this chapter and doing the exercises, you should be able to:

1 Explain how human resource management is part of business strategy.

2 Describe the components of a human resource management model.

3 Present an overview of recruitment and selection.

4 Present an overview of employee orientation, training, and development.

5 Explain the basics of a performance evaluation system.

6 Summarize the components of employee compensation.

7 Understand the role of labor unions in human resource management.

Hilton Worldwide is the world's largest hospitality company, and it continues to expand. Hilton has 18 brands, nearly 6,000 properties, in 117 countries, and more than 169,000 team members (employees) including both owned and managed properties, and corporate offices. To effectively operate such a vast enterprise, Hilton devotes enormous resources to training and developing managers as well as employees holding many other positions. Many of these programs are offered through Hilton Worldwide University (not a true university) that is sanctioned by the government. Others are offered through a few colleges and universities.

The Management Development Program (MDP) is a six-month program offered through the Florida Atlantic College of Business to prepare graduating seniors for a career in hospitality. The trainee spends the first six to eight weeks of the program participating in a general rotation through all functions of the hotel to better understand the hospitality business. The next 16 to 18 weeks focus on specialization areas, which include event services, finance and accounting, food and beverage, front office, housekeeping, revenue management, sales and marketing, and human resources. During the last four weeks, trainees are given probationary (position not guaranteed) management assignments at high revenue-generating hotels in New York, Washington, D.C., Orlando, Chicago, or New Orleans.

Among the qualifications for being accepted into the MDP are (a) fluency in reading, writing and speaking English, (b) strong problem-solving skills, (c) self-starting ability, (d) critical thinking, (d) creative thinking, (e) positive attitude, (f) visionary with passion about the hospitality industry, and (g) ability to collaborate with team members. To get into the program the candidate must also be a graduating senior with a degree in hospitality, business or related field, and have a cumulative GPA of 3.0 or higher, and a willingness to relocate.

The Leadership College of the Hilton Worldwide University provides executive and leadership development programs and experience for senior leadership in the company. The purpose is to provide a leadership pipeline for general managers. The General Studies College offers a wide variety of training programs and learning experiences for all team members. The broad range of subjects is geared toward enabling ongoing career developed via the School of Management.

Hilton partners with Cornell University's School of Hotel Administration to provide online programs in leadership development for the global hospitality leader. The subjects offered to Hilton Worldwide senior executives and hotel general managers are hospitality management, revenue management, and strategic leadership. Matt Schuyler, Chief Human Resources Officer, Hilton Worldwide says, "eCornell and Cornell University's School of Hotel Administration have already proven to be essential partners in the professional development of our team members." The network of more than 3,800 hotels across 88 countries enables business leaders to access a wide variety of training programs online.[1]

The description of the varied components of the Hilton Worldwide University illustrates the importance some companies place on the human resource activity of training and development. This chapter deals with key aspects of human resource management, including how it fits into business strategy, recruitment and selection, training, development, evaluation and compensation. All managers engage in human resource management (HRM) to some extent because they participate in activities including, recruiting, selecting, training and evaluating employees. The human resource department assists in these activities and also provides direction for such programs as leadership development and diversity training.

Many of the activities that have been included in human resource management are now referred to as **talent management** because employees represent the talent the organization needs to function. An instructive definition of talent management is "a deliberate approach to attract, develop, and retain people with the aptitude and abilities to meet current and future organizational needs."[2]

talent management
A deliberate approach to attract, develop, and retain people with the aptitude and abilities to meet current and future organizational needs.

HUMAN RESOURCE MANAGEMENT AND BUSINESS STRATEGY

Today's human resource professionals partner in helping the organization implement its business strategy. In the words of many HR professionals, "We finally have a seat at the executive table." The implication is that human resource management is an integral part of business strategy. Without effective human resource management, the company cannot accomplish high-level goals such as competing globally, grabbing market share and being innovative. For example, unless talented and imaginative employees are recruited (even through outsourcing recruitment) innovation cannot be sustained. (This helps explain the emergence of the term *talent* management.)

A major purpose of HRM is to maximize human capital so workers can achieve the goals of the organization. It has been recommended that the chief human resource officer (CHRO) work alongside the CEO and CFO to manage human capital with a rigor equivalent to that applied to financial capital.[3]

LEARNING OBJECTIVE 1

Explain how human resource management is part of business strategy.

In contrast, many human resource managers and professionals are still seen as occupying a minor operational role, carrying out activities, such as processing payroll, filing government forms about equal employment opportunity and recruiting and selecting entry-level workers. Also, in small enterprises the HR function might be part of the office manager's or owner's responsibility.

Several developments have contributed to the shrinking number of HR professionals in many firms, even though the human resource functions remain as important as ever. One is the outsourcing of HR tasks, such as training or compensation and benefits to firms specializing in human resource management. Another development is more HR activities are being absorbed by other departments and functions, such as a financed unit doing its own recruiting and selection. Furthermore, the surge in HR software availability has made it easier to automate personnel-related functions, such as benefits administration and payroll.

A specific way in which HRM contributes to business strategy is by helping to build high-performance work practices. Several of these approaches were mentioned in Chapter 7 about designing jobs for high performance and establishing flexible working hours. Aspects of high-performance work practices described in the present chapter include selection, incentive compensation and training. An integration of 92 studies found organizations can increase their performance 20 percent by implementing high-performance work practices. The results demonstrate that human resource methods contribute substantially to an organization's performance goals.[4]

LEARNING OBJECTIVE 2

Describe the components of a human resource management model.

THE HUMAN RESOURCE MANAGEMENT MODEL AND STRATEGIC HUMAN RESOURCE PLANNING

Figure 9-1 shows the human resource management process flows in a logical sequence. Although not every organization follows the same steps in the same sequence, talent management ordinarily proceeds in the way we discuss in this section. Software is available to support every aspect of human resource and talent management. For example, tools are available to facilitate evaluating performance by making it easier to record feedback, and algorithms can aid in selection. Also, an applicant tracking system (ATS) is used to find, collect, organize and screen applications the company receives. Although all this software may be impressive from a technical standpoint, it does not necessarily mean that: (a) human judgment is not required in making judgments about people, and (b) the content in the software was prepared by a human resource professional.

The arrows pointing to "Retention" in the model suggest a major strategy of human resource management is to retain valuable employees. During a strong economy, retention of talented employees becomes more difficult, and that any aspect of such management can contribute to retention. All components of the model can contribute to employee retention. For example, selecting the right person for the job increases the probability he or she will enjoy the job and stay with the firm. Hal Gregerson, a lecturer at the MIT Sloan School of Management, suggests that giving more personal space to employees will aid retention. The trend toward bare-boned work stations and open office space creates job dissatisfaction and unhappiness for many employees.[5]

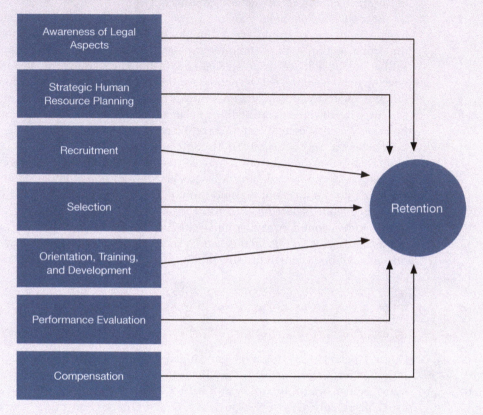

Figure 9-1 The Human Resource Management Model

Under ideal circumstances, organization staffing would proceed through the stages as shown, and improve employee retention. Terminating employees might also be considered part of staffing.

Legal Aspects of Staffing

Federal, state, provincial and local laws influence every aspect of talent management. Managers and human resource specialists must keep the major provisions of these laws in mind whenever they make decisions about any phase of employment. Figure 9-2 summarizes major pieces of U.S. federal legislation that influence various aspects of staffing—not just employee selection. Canada has comparable legislation at both the federal and provincial levels. Managers need to be aware that such legislation exists and be familiar with the general provisions of each law or executive order. When a possible legal issue arises, the manager should review the relevant legislation in depth and confer with a company specialist in employment law.

A key aspect of implementing the spirit and letter of employment discrimination law in the United States has been affirmative action programs. To comply with the Civil Rights Act of 1964, employers with federal contracts or subcontracts are required to develop such programs to end discrimination. **Affirmative action** consists of

affirmative action
An employment practice that complies with antidiscrimination law and correcting past discriminatory practices.

Figure 9-2 Federal Laws Prohibiting Job Discrimination

- Title VII of the Civil Rights Act of 1964 (Title VII) prohibits employment discrimination based on race, color, religion, sex, or national origin.

- The Equal Pay Act of 1963 (EPA) protects men and women who perform substantially equal work in the same establishment from sex-based wage discrimination.

- The Age Discrimination in Employment Act of 1967 (ADEA) protects individuals who are 40 years of age or older.

- Title I and Title V of the Americans with Disabilities Act of 1990 (ADA) prohibits employment discrimination against qualified individuals with disabilities in the private sector, and in state and local governments.

- Sections 501 and 505 of the Rehabilitation Act of 1973 prohibits discrimination against qualified individuals with disabilities who work in the federal government.

- The Civil Rights Act of 1991, which, among other things, provides monetary damages in cases of intentional employment discrimination.

- The federal Family and Medical Leave Act (1993 and updated 2015) entitles eligible employees of covered employers to take unpaid, job-protected leave for specified family and medical reasons with continuation of group health insurance coverage under the same terms and conditions as if the employee had not taken the leave. A key provision is that employees are entitled to take 12 workweeks of leave in a 12-month period for the birth of a child and to care for the newborn child within one year of birth. (The FMLA is classified here as prohibiting discrimination because employees cannot be discriminated against for taking family leave.)

Source: http://www.eeoc.gov/abouteeo/overview_laws.html.

---

complying with antidiscrimination law and correcting past discriminatory practices. Under an affirmative action program, employers actively recruit, employ, train and promote minorities and women who may have been discriminated against by the employer in the past, which resulted in their underrepresentation in certain positions.

Complying with affirmative action requires extensive documentation, such as an analysis of compensation paid to minority group members and recruitment and hiring goals for affected groups. Part of an affirmative action plan may include a career development program for Native American workers to help them qualify for management positions.

A debate continues over whether any person in a competitive situation deserves a preference because of race, ethnicity, or sex. The opposing point of view to affirmative action programs is that race, ethnicity, or sex should not be a factor in making employment or business decisions. For example, a job candidate should not be given an edge over other applicants because she is a Latina. What is your opinion on this issue?

An effective way of understanding how these laws might affect the individual is to specify the discriminatory practices prohibited by these laws. Under Title VII, the ADA, and the ADEA, it is illegal to discriminate in any aspect of employment, including hiring and firing; compensation, assignment, or classification of employees; transfer, promotion, layoff, or recall; job advertisements; recruitment; testing; use of company facilities; training and apprenticeship programs; fringe benefits; pay, retirement plans, and disability leave; or other terms and conditions of employment.

Although all of the above forms of discrimination may appear clear-cut, a good deal of interpretation is required to decide if a given employee is the subject of discrimination. For example, assume a woman files a charge of sex discrimination. Later on, she is bypassed for promotion. She claims she is now the victim of discrimination, yet the company claims she did not have the appropriate interpersonal skills to be promoted to a supervisory position.

Strategic Human Resource Planning

Staffing begins with a prediction about how many and what types of people will be needed to conduct the work of the firm. Such activity is referred to as **strategic human resource planning**. It is the process of anticipating and providing for the movement of people into, within, and out of an organization to support the firm's business strategy. Through planning, management attempts to have the right number and right kinds of people at the right time. Long-range planning is important in HR as well as other business functions, but agile (more nimble and flexible) models are now prevalent.[6] HR is now adapting more swiftly to talent management needs. For example, a long-range plan developed five years ago might not have seen the need to recruit data scientists to develop artificial intelligence capability for the company. The full engagement of business unit leaders and line managers is required for workforce (human resource) planning to be effective.

Human resource planning addresses the question, "What skills are needed for the success of this business?" Planning helps identify the gaps between current employee competencies and behavior and the competencies and behavior needed in the organization's future. Forecasting is needed to develop these plans, such as predicting the future size of the organization. Two types of human resource planning follow:

1   *Planning for future needs.* A human resource planner estimates how many people, and with what abilities the firm will need to operate in the foreseeable future.

2   *Planning for recruitment, selection, and layoffs.* The organization must engage in recruitment, employee selection, or layoffs to attain the required number of employees. A major choice between the commitment strategy in which the firm seeks to develop its own human capital and the secondary strategy of acquiring human capital in the market must be made. Most firms find a balance between training, promoting current employees and hiring needed talent from the outside.

Human resource planning can be a strategic objective in itself. For example, one strategic objective of PepsiCo is the development of talented people. Human resource planning contributes to attaining this objective by suggesting on- and off-the-job experiences to develop talent.

RECRUITMENT

Recruitment is the process of attracting job candidates with the right characteristics and skills to fit job openings. The preferred recruiting method is to begin with a large number of possible job candidates and then give serious consideration to a much smaller number. However, if few candidates are available, the recruiter must be less selective or not fill the position.

Purposes of Recruitment

A major purpose of recruiting and selection is to find qualified employees who fit well into the culture of the organization. Most job failures are attributed to workers being a "poor fit" rather than because of poor technical skills or experience. The poor fit often implies poor relationships with co-workers. A positive person–organization fit

---

strategic human resource planning
The process of anticipating and providing for the movement of people into, within, and out of an organization to support the firm's business strategy.

Present an overview of recruitment and selection.

recruitment
The process of attracting job candidates with the right characteristics and skills to fill job openings.

is usually based on a mesh between the person's values and those of the organization. For example, a person who values technology and diversity among people—and is qualified—would be a good candidate to work for AT&T or Verizon. A synthesis of many studies indicates that person–organization fit is positively related to job satisfaction, commitment to the firm and intention to quit.[7] An important implication is that a good person–organization fit helps increase retention.

Another key purpose of recruiting is to sell the organization to high-quality prospective candidates. Recruiters must select candidates who can function in one job today and be retrained and promoted later, as company needs dictate. Flexible candidates of this type are in demand; therefore, a recruiter may need to sell the advantages of his or her company to entice them to work there. However, an important principle of successful recruiting is to present an honest picture of the firm about such factors as growth opportunities, the amount of travel and the type of culture.

Job Descriptions and Job Specifications

A starting point in recruiting is to understand the nature of the job to be filled and the qualifications sought. Toward this end, the recruiter should be supplied with job descriptions and job specifications. The job description explains in detail what the jobholder is supposed to do. It is therefore a vital document in human resource planning and performance evaluation. An exception is that in some high-level positions, such as CEO, the person creates part of his or her own job description. Job titles are closely related to job descriptions. In an attempt to attract more applicants, several companies attempt to freshen their image to young recruits by using interesting job titles. A product manager position might be retitled as a "product evangelist," and an analyst as "data wrangler." The revamped job titles are also aimed at showing recruits they can make an impact in their roles.[8]

job specification
A statement of the personal characteristics needed to perform the job.

A **job specification** (or person specification) stems directly from the job description. It is a statement of the personal characteristics needed to perform the job. A job specification usually includes the education, experience, knowledge and skills required to perform the job successfully.

Many firms see job descriptions and job specifications decreasing in relevance, as explained in the study of job design in Chapter 7. Organizations often expect workers to occupy flexible roles rather than specific positions, to meet the need for rapid change. An example of flexibility might be a worker whose role is to learn new job-related software, whereas a job description might mention specific software that must be mastered.

Recruiting Sources

The term *recruitment* covers a wide variety of methods for attracting employees to the firm, even such methods as a manager handing out business cards to people she meets while skiing. Recruiting sources are classified into four major categories, as described below.

1 *Present employees.* As a standard recruiting method, companies post job openings so the current employees may apply. Managers also recommend current employees for transfer or promotion. A human resources information system can identify current employees with the right skills and competencies, which minimizes the need to reject unqualified internal applicants. Internal job boards are useful in finding strong candidates already on the payroll,

and promoting from within is less expensive than hiring from outside the organization.[9] Temporary workers are another source of potential full-time workers, providing the company has a temp-to-hire agreement with the employment agency.

2 *Referrals by present and former employees.* For established firms, present employees can be the primary recruiters, as shown by a Society for Human Resource Management survey. It was found that 96 percent of companies with 10,000 or more employees, and 80 percent of companies with fewer than 100 employees, indicate that referrals are their number one recruitment source.[10] Satisfied employees may be willing to nominate relatives, friends, acquaintances and neighbors for job openings. The effectiveness of current employees in the recruiting process comes from their ability to explain the culture of the firm to prospects, such as pointing out that the company expects its employees to work hard and long. Former employees can be effective recruiting sources, providing they left the company on good terms. An angry former employee might be prompted to refer poorly qualified candidates. Present and former employees can sometimes be helpful in identifying recent retirees with vital skills who would like to get back into the labor market.

3 *Online recruiting including company websites.* The Internet is a standard source of recruiting job candidates. It offers hundreds of websites free to job candidates, and sometimes to employers. Online recruiting includes listing open positions on company websites, on job boards, or surfing sites for possible candidates. A key part of online recruiting is the job board for posting openings to which candidates submit their credentials. Job search engines are useful because they consolidate job seekers across a variety of sources, particularly job boards. Many companies focus their online recruiting on the career section of the company website. Also, many job seekers go directly to company websites instead of using job boards.

Another form of online recruiting is for companies to create pages on social networking websites such as Facebook, LinkedIn and Twitter to attract possible candidates. Information posted by employers on websites is usually made mobile friendly because so many job seekers rely almost exclusively on their smartphones for electronic communication. The social website offers the advantage of allowing for continuing dialogue with potential job candidates. Some recruiters scan social networking sites looking for potential talent. LinkedIn's premium tools help recruiters filter searches to find just the right candidates. A potential employer might find an interesting person on a social networking site and proceed to track down any blogs that individual may have posted to learn more about the prospect.[11]

4 *External sources other than online approaches.* Potential employees outside an organization can be reached in many ways. The best known of these methods is a recruiting advertisement, including print, radio and sometimes television. Other external sources include: (a) placement offices, (b) private and public employment agencies, (c) labor union hiring halls, (d) walk-ins (people who show up at the firm without invitation), and (d) write-ins (people who write unsolicited job-seeking letters). Labor union officials believe they simplify the hiring process for employers because only qualified workers are admitted to the union.

Finding employees or finding a job is best done through a variety of methods mentioned here. A major consideration in which recruiting source will be the most effective is whether the company is seeking active job seekers, or passive candidates—those who are not looking for a job but could be enticed. In many cases, people with the appropriate skills and talent to fill a given position are still employed. They may not be fully content with their present position but have not yet begun a job search.[12] Referrals and the scanning of social networking sites are likely to be the most effective in tracking down passive candidates. Websites that advertise jobs as well as other external sources tend to be more effective in recruiting active job seekers.

Many recruiting activities are now integrated through an *applicant tracking system* that enables electronic management of a company's recruiting needs. The tracking system facilitates the organizations ability to collect and store candidate data and track and monitor all stages of the hiring process. One application of the system is to post job openings on a job board or company website.[13]

SELECTION

Selecting qualified candidates is the lifeblood of the firm. An important goal of selection is to fill as many positions as possible with "A" players, or top-level performers.[14] Even in the most basic jobs, some people outperform others, such as some custodial technicians exceeding standards for creating a clean workplace.

Selecting the right candidate for a job is part of a process that includes recruitment, as shown in Figure 9-3. The figure is a general model. It is not followed completely by all employers, such as many omitting psychological testing. Recruiting sources such as websites and print ads typically result in hundreds of unqualified applicants, along with a few valuable candidates. A hiring decision is based on information gathered in two or more of these steps. For instance, a person might receive a job offer if he or she was impressive in the interview, scored well on the tests, and had good references. Another important feature of this selection model allows for an applicant to be rejected at any point. An applicant who is abusive to the employment specialist might not be asked to fill out an application form.

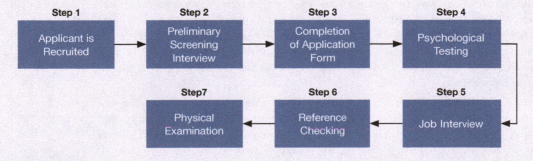

Figure 9-3 A Model for Selection

The selection process generally proceeds in the steps as indicated here, yet many exceptions can occur in terms of which steps are included and in what order. For example, some employers do not use psychological testing, and others have candidates complete the application form first.

Step 1: Applicant is Recruited → Step 2: Preliminary Screening Interview → Step 3: Completion of Application Form → Step 4: Psychological Testing → Step 5: Job Interview → Step 6: Reference Checking → Step 7: Physical Examination

Preliminary Screening Interview and Texting

Selection begins as soon as candidates come to the attention of the recruiter, often by cover letter and job résumé. Some employers require an online application in addition to, or even instead of the cover letter and résumé. If candidates come close to fitting the job specifications, a brief screening interview follows, frequently by telephone, Skype, or Messenger. The purpose of the screening interview is to determine whether the candidate should be given further consideration. One area of disqualification would be for the candidate to demonstrate such poor oral communication skills over the phone that the person is excluded from consideration for a job requiring considerable customer contact. "Knockout" questions are sometimes used to quickly disqualify candidates. Assume a person applying for a supervisory position in a nursing home is asked, "How well do you get along with senior citizens?" A candidate who responds, "Very poorly," is immediately disqualified.

Many employers now use texting to replace preliminary screening interviews by telephone. For many people in the applicant pool, texting is more natural than being interviewed over the phone, or even responding to an e-mail. Some recruiters report than many applicants do not bother to answer phone calls. A texting app might ask a question such as, "What motivates you?" or "Why do you want to work for us?"[15] A text response might be useful as a screening device because it could reveal that the applicant writes, spells, and thinks incoherently.

Psychological Testing

Hundreds of different tests are used in employment testing, and such testing is standard practice in about one-half of firms. All tests are psychological tests in the sense that measuring human ability is an important part of psychology.

Types of Psychological Tests

The four principle types of psychological tests used in employment screening are situational judgment, aptitude, personality, and honesty and integrity.

1 *Situational judgment tests* are a method of measurement typically composed of job-related situations or scenarios that describe a dilemma or problem representative of the job under consideration. As such, they can be considered job samples or performing a task that the applicant would encounter on the job. Dealing with the problem requires the application of relevant knowledge, skills, abilities and perhaps personality characteristics. Situational judgment tasks may be presented in written, oral, video-based, computer-based, or virtual reality formats. The applicant often has to choose among alternatives, such as the best way to deal with an angry customer. Areas of competence typically measured by situational judgment tests include job knowledge and skills, interpersonal skills, teamwork, leadership and personality tendencies such as agreeableness.[16] An advantage of situational judgment tests is they tend to be perceived as fair by job applicants because the simulations appear to be relevant.

2 *Aptitude tests* measure the potential for performing satisfactorily on the job, given sufficient training. Mental ability tests, the best-known variety of aptitude tests, measure the ability to solve problems and learn new material. Mental ability tests measure such specific aptitudes as verbal reasoning, numerical reasoning and spatial relations (the ability to visualize in three dimensions).

Tests of *emotional intelligence* are widely used whereby the candidate is measured on the ability to deal with people's feelings and emotions. However, emotional intelligence can also be classified as an aspect of personality.

3 *Personality tests* measure personal traits and characteristics that could be related to job performance, such as extraversion. The use of personality tests still sparks controversy, but research shows positive connection between certain personality tests and subsequent job performance. Critics express concern that these tests invade privacy and are too imprecise to be useful. Nevertheless, personality factors can profoundly influence job performance. Personality tests are increasingly used to screen applicants for entry-level jobs at call centers, retail stores and other customer-contact positions.

4 *Honesty and integrity tests* are designed to measure a person's honesty or integrity as it relates to job behavior. (Honesty relates most specifically to lying, whereas integrity refers to sticking with your principles.) These tests are frequently used in workplaces such as retail stores, banks and warehouses, where employees have access to cash or merchandise. Other types of work in which employees may potentially damage computers or access secret documents also require a prediction of employee honesty. A major factor measured by integrity tests is social conscientiousness. People who score high on this personality factor show a much greater likelihood of following organizational rules.

Validity and Usefulness of Psychological Tests

The most consistent finding about the effectiveness of psychological tests in predicting job performance stems from a long series of studies concerning general intelligence and conscientiousness. Research has shown consistently that in general, employees who have good problem-solving ability and are conscientious are likely to perform well in most jobs.[17] (These findings assume the employee also has the necessary education and job skills. Yet for basic jobs, the ability to learn and dependability are more important than experience and already existing skills.) General problem-solving ability is measured by a mental ability test, and conscientiousness by a personality test. A straightforward explanation of these findings is that a bright person will learn quickly, and a conscientious person will try hard to get the job done.

A study with middle managers in an energy company suggests personality tests are good predictors of management performance with respect to both the task and interpersonal aspects of their job. Management performance was measured in terms of judgments by both superiors and subordinates, providing more insight into performance than judgments of performance made by superiors only. Subordinate judgments were made using 360-degree feedback ratings (described later in this chapter).[18]

The Job Interview and Its Replacements

The job interview is more comprehensive than the screening interview, covering topics such as education, work experience, special skills and abilities, hobbies and interests. Interviewers frequently use the candidate's résumé as a source of topics. For example, "I notice you have worked for four employers in three years. Why is that?" Testing results may also provide clues for additional questioning. If a candidate scored low on a scale measuring conscientiousness, the interviewer might ask about the candidate's punctuality and error rate.

Employment interviews are more valid when the interviewer is trained and experienced. Evidence also suggests that when the interviewer carefully follows a format, predictions about job performance tend to be more accurate.[19] A surprising finding is that building rapport through small talk before the formal part of the interview lowers the validity of the interview. The problem appears to be that if the interviewer appears to like or dislike a person based on small talk, observations made later in the interview might be biased.[20]

Job interviews serve a dual purpose. The interviewer tries to decide whether the interviewee is appropriate for the organization. At the same time, the interviewee tries to decide whether the job and organization fit him or her. An important approach to helping both the organization and the individual to make the right decision is to offer a **realistic job preview**, a complete disclosure of the potential negative features of a job to a job candidate.[21] For example, an applicant for a tech support center position might be told, "At times customers will scream and swear at you because a computer file has crashed. Around holiday time many frustrated customers go ballistic." Telling job applicants about potential problems leads to fewer negative surprises and less turnover.

realistic job preview
A complete disclosure of the potential negative features of a job to a job candidate.

Figure 9-4 presents guidelines for conducting a job interview. Several of the suggestions reflect a screening approach referred to as **behavioral interviewing** because the answers to many of the questions reveal actual job behaviors relevant to a given position. An airline marketing manager might be instructed, "Give me an example of what you have done in the past to compete with a lower-price competitor." Behavioral interviewing can also take the form of asking the candidate to display a job competency.[22] Here are two examples: "Show me how you can code in Java." "Develop a marketing plan for a fish product made out of vegetables."

behavioral interviewing
A style of interviewing in which the interviewer asks questions whose answers reveal behaviors that would be either strengths or weaknesses in a given position.

If the candidate lacks much job experience, a behavioral question can be asked about a characteristic important to the job, such as resiliency.[23] The candidate might be asked, "Tell me about how you acted the last time you were rejected for something you really wanted?"

Minimizing and Avoiding Biases During Interviews

Increased emphasis has been placed in recent years in avoiding bias in job interviews as well as in other methods of selection and in recruitment. As implied in the discussion of cultural diversity in Chapter 3, it takes effort to recognize personal biases. Quite often biases take the form of unconscious prejudices that could work against or in favor of candidates from a particular demographic or cultural group. On the negative side, if a hiring manager thinks most women are not well suited to the construction business, the manager might look for reasons to disqualify a woman for a construction supervisor position. On the positive side, if the hiring manager thinks Irish Americans are good natured and witty, the manager might be quick to think an Irish American applicant for a machinery sales position is well qualified.

Biases about race, sex (or gender) and age are the most common, but employment interviews can harbor unconscious prejudices about may other factors. Among them are height and weight, physical status (such as using a wheelchair or cane), foreign accents, where a candidate attends school, and leisure activities.[24] A recommended technique for overcoming biases in recruiting and hiring, is to try going against your intuition a couple of times and observe the results. This could mean having the gut feel that a candidate is not right for the position, and the "gut feel" based on a prejudice such as discrediting candidates with facial tattoos.[25]

Figure 9-4 Guidelines for Conducting an Effective Selection Interview

1. **Prepare in advance.** Prior to the interview, carefully review the applicant's résumé. Keep in mind several questions worthy of explanation, such as, "I notice that you have done no previous selling. Why do you want a sales job now?"

2. **Find a quiet place free from interruptions.** Effective interviewing requires careful concentration. Also, the candidate deserves the courtesy of an uninterrupted interview. Do not access e-mail, look at the computer screen or smartphone, or engage in telephone conversations during the interview.

3. **Take notes during the interview.** Take notes on the content of what is said during the interview, preferably by hand rather than hacking away at a keyboard. In addition, record your observations about the person's statements and behavior. For example, "Candidate gets very nervous when we talk about performance evaluations received in the past." Ensure written observations are factual and fair.

4. **Use a brief warm-up period.** A standard way of relaxing a job candidate is to spend about five minutes talking about a neutral topic such as the weather, and sports preferences of the candidate or his or her family members. A caution, however, is not to make strong judgments about the candidate just because you two have good rapport. For example, if you like field hockey and the candidate played field hockey in college do not conclude that the person is an excellent candidate!

5. **Avoid off-limit interview questions.** You would need to be familiar with job discrimination legislation to figure out which questions might be illegal. Questions should therefore not be related to questions such as the applicant's race, color, national origin, religion, sex, age, disability or sexual orientation. A general guideline is to avoid questions irrelevant to a candidate's ability to perform the job. Here are a few off-limit questions: "How old are you?" "How many times have you been divorced?" "Which sex is your significant other?"" "How far in debt are you?" "What disabilities do you have?" "Do you intend to start a family?"[26]

6. **Ask open-ended questions.** To encourage the employee to talk, ask questions that call for more than a one- or two-word answer. Sometimes a request for information—a statement like, "Tell me about your days at business school"—works like an open-ended question.

7. **Follow an interview format.** Effective interviewers carefully follow a predetermined interview format. They ask additional questions that are based on responses to the structured questions.

8. **Encourage the job candidate.** The easiest way to keep an interviewee talking is to give that person encouragement. Standard encouragements include: "That's very good," "How interesting," "I like your answer," and "Excellent."

9. **Dig for additional details.** When the interviewee brings up a topic worthy of exploration, dig for additional facts. Assume the interviewee says, "I used to work as a private chauffeur, but then I lost my driver's license." Noticing a red flag, the interviewer might respond, "Why did you lose your license?"

10. **Spend most of the interview time listening.** An experienced job interviewer spends little time talking. It is the interviewee who should be doing the talking.

11. **Provide the candidate ample information about the organization.** Answer any relevant questions.

To personalize the job interview process, go through the checklist presented in Figure 9-5 just to assure you are on the top of your game for your next interview.

Replacements for Traditional Interviews

Although interviews will most likely remain a permanent part of selection, they are sometimes being replaced or eliminated for several reasons. One is that the validity of the selection interview for many positions has been questioned, meaning that interview observations might not be highly accurate predictors of job performance. Another reason is that interviewers are subject to bias, and often hire people who are quite similar to them in terms of cultural background and personality. A third reason is that in a tight job market, requiring candidates to visit the organization for an interview is too time consuming. The valuable candidate might take another position before the interview can be completed.

One replacement for the interview, is for the candidate to respond over the phone to automated exchanges in which candidates give recorded responses to a series of questions related to the job. Allstate Insurance Co. uses this technique in selecting candidates for some positions. The questions asked by the automated system might

Figure 9-5 The Job Interviewee Checklist

Most readers are already familiar with most of the behaviors and attitudes associated with having a successful job interview. Nevertheless, going through the checklist of behaviors presented below in the form of questions can serve as a quick reminder of how to be at your best during a job interview.

1. Have I visited the organization's website to learn more about the company, and done an Internet search to read a few articles about the company?
2. Have I investigated which style of clothing (such as business formal versus business casual) would be preferred by HR and the interviewing manager?
3. Do I plan to look relaxed and fresh during the interview by resting, exercising, and showering as close to interview time as feasible?
4. Have I rehearsed a discussion of my strengths and areas for needed development?
5. Have I rehearsed a scenario of how I solved a difficult job problem or took care of an emergency?
6. Can I describe my job and educational history without hesitation?
7. Am I prepared to put away my smartphone (and keep it turned off) during the entire interview?
8. Will I be able to resist the temptation of frequently glancing at the interviewer's computer monitor?
9. Do I have a few intelligent questions in mind to ask the interviewer?
10. Am I prepared to listen to the interviewer as well as ask questions?
11. Will I ask questions about the nature of the work and challenges instead of asking about factors such as vacation time and personal leave time?
12. Will I be able to refrain from making negative statements about people I worked with in the past?
13. Will I be able to give examples of how I have been a team player?
14. Will I be able to give examples of having taken on some leadership responsibility (even for a project)?
15. Am I prepared to look relaxed and smile frequently?
16. Am I prepared to make a few comments about current events if the topic is relevant to the interview?
17. Am I prepared to explain how I would like to make a contribution?
18. Will I be able to refrain from talking about how this job will give me the experience I need to achieve my career goals?
19. Will I make only factual and verifiable statements about myself?
20. If the job interests me, will I have enough courage to indicate that I would accept an offer?
21. After the interview is completed will I remember to thank the interviewer for his or her time?

Interpretation: I can hear you saying "Duh" in response to a few of the above checklist items. Yet, you would be surprised how many candidates—even for top-level executive positions—blow job interviews by violating these suggestions. The more yes answers you gave, and assuming you are qualified for the position, the better your chances are for receiving a job offer.

duplicate those asked in a traditional interview, such as, "Describe your best job skill." The automated interview can be taken at any time, and from any place.[27] A problem with this technique is that the person taking the automated interview is unable to ask questions, which is considered a bedrock principle of job interviews.

Another replacement for the traditional interview is to use only a phone interview to make a hiring decision. The more difficult the position is to fill, the more likely to skip the in-personal interview. Managers at all levels, however, are rarely hired without an in-person interview.

REFERENCE CHECKING AND BACKGROUND INVESTIGATIONS

A **reference check** is an inquiry to a second party about a job candidate's suitability for employment. The two main topics explored in reference checks are past job performance and the ability to get along with co-workers. However, asking about any

reference check
An inquiry to a second party about a job candidate's suitability for employment.

evidence of violent behavior has become more frequent. Laws about what former employers are permitted to reveal about employees exist only at the state level. Employers can typically share information about your time at the company, such as your date of employment, job title, and responsibilities. Some states allow past employers to reveal more about the employee, such as salary, ability, job performance, and the reason the person left the organization. In spite of such legislation, many past employers are hesitant to provide complete references because job applicants have legal access to written references unless they specifically waive this right in writing (Privacy Act of 1974). Also, former employers are usually aware of laws regarding defamation, slander and libel.[28]

Background investigations are closely related to reference checks, except they focus on information from sources other than former employers. The growth of databases accessible through the Internet has facilitated reference checking. Areas investigated include driving record, possible criminal charges or convictions, creditworthiness, disputes with the IRS, and co-workers' and neighbors' comments about a candidate's reputation. Many employers believe a good credit record reflects dependability. A concern for both employers and job candidates is that many credit reports are inaccurate.

Standard practice today is for prospective employers to search the Internet, including social networking websites for potentially negative and positive information about a candidate. Candidates with popular names, such as Susan Johnson or Robert Anderson often advise potential employers in advance as to their full identifying information.

One justification for background investigations is that so many job candidates present untrue information in résumés and job interviews. According to a HireRight employment screening background report, 85 percent of employers caught applicants lying on their résumés or applications. Three of the most common lies related to education embellishments, covering up employment gaps, and stretching their true skills.[29] The many financial scandals in the executive suite in recent years have prompted more thorough background investigations of candidates for top-level management positions. Executives also have misrepresented facts on their résumés, such as claiming a college degree never earned.

Physical Examination and Drug Testing

The physical examination remains a key part of preemployment screening. The exam gives some indication as to the person's physical ability to handle the requirements of particular jobs. For example, a person with a history of two heart attacks would be a poor candidate for a high-stress managerial position. The physical exam also provides a basis for later comparisons. This step lessens the potential for an employee to claim the job caused a particular injury or disease. For example, after one year on the job, an employee might claim the job created a fusion of two vertebrae. If the preemployment physical showed evidence of two fused vertebrae before the employee was hired, the employer would have little to fear from the claim.

Many companies test all job applicants for use of illegal drugs. (Executives as well as entry-level workers can be drug abusers.) Abuse of prescription drugs is also a widespread problem. Testing for substance abuse includes blood analysis, urinalysis, analysis of hair samples, observations of eyes and examination of skin for punctures.

Some people raise the concern that inaccurate drug testing may unfairly deny employment to worthy candidates. A strong argument in favor of drug testing, however, is employees who are drug abusers may create such problems as lowered productivity, lost time from work, and misappropriation of funds. Accident and absenteeism rates for drug (as well as alcohol) abusers are substantial, and they also experience more health problems.

An encouraging note about the type of selection methods described in this section is they are valid if combined with assessor judgment. Judgment here refers to the manager or human resources specialist integrating data from the various sources and then making a decision. For example, algorithms alone should not be the basis for choosing job candidates. A decision about a candidate reached by an algorithm may be based on hundreds of variables common to high performers but might not be good predictors of future performance.[30] A synthesis of 29 validation studies of the assessment of job candidates, found that the validity was higher for managerial than non-managerial occupations. Furthermore, the validity was higher when the assessments included a cognitive (mental) ability test.[31]

After being recruited, job candidates pass through all the selection screens, such as the physical exam before being hired. After making the hiring decision and applicant acceptance, human resource specialists and new employees complete all the necessary forms, such as those relating to taxes and benefits. Next is orientation.

ORIENTATION, TRAINING, AND DEVELOPMENT

LEARNING OBJECTIVE **4**

Present an overview of employee orientation, training, and development.

Most firms no longer operate under a "sink or swim" philosophy when it comes to employee learning. Instead, employees are oriented to the firm, and later trained and developed, as illustrated in the chapter opener about Hilton Worldwide.

Employee Orientation (Onboarding)

An **employee orientation program** (also referred to as **onboarding**) formally acquaints new employees with the company and imparts information about the corporate culture. Integration into the culture of a new firm, such as recognizing whether consensus decision making is expected, is essential for managers new to an organization.[32] The onboarding experience is significant because it starts the process of the new employee feeling committed to the firm, and less likely to leave shortly. Part of the orientation may deal with small but important matters, such as telling the employee how to get a parking sticker, and how to connect to the company network. Large firms offer elaborate orientation programs conducted by human resource specialists. The program may include tours of the buildings, talks by department heads, video presentations, printed and online information and visits to the company website.

employee orientation program (onboarding)
A formal activity designed to acquaint new employees with the organization.

Employee orientation also conveys to new employees the specific nature of their jobs and performance expectations. In some firms, a buddy system is part of the orientation. A buddy, a peer from the new employee's department, shows the new employee around and fills in information gaps. A growing orientation practice is to assign a new employee a mentor who will help him or her better understand the organization, and also serve as a resource person for resolving problems. Your mentor is supposed to check in with you regularly to discuss progress, even by text messaging.

Another aspect of orientation is informal socialization. In this process, co-workers introduce new employees to aspects of the organizational culture. Co-workers might convey, for example, how well motivated a new employee should be or the competence level of key people in the organization. The new employee might also be advised of informal practices such as taking turns at bringing donuts and bagels for co-workers. The disadvantage of informal orientation is that it may furnish the new employee with misinformation.

The most successful onboarding programs work with groups of employees on some aspects of the program, such as having a buddy lasting one to two years. In addition to presenting factual information, the program should help newcomers build relationships with peers and managers, which can help with retention.

Training and Development

training
Any procedure intended to foster and enhance learning among employees, particularly directed at acquiring job skills.

Training and development deals with systematic approaches to improving employee skills and performance. **Training** is any procedure intended to foster and enhance learning among employees and particularly directed at acquiring job skills. Rapid changes in technology and the globalization of business have spurred the growth of training programs. Training programs exist to teach hundreds of different skills such as equipment repair, performance evaluation, software utilization and budget preparation. Training can develop both hard skills (technical, scientific, and numerical) and soft skills (interpersonal skills and attitudes). Employee training and development are both based on the belief that developing talent internally is a good investment.

A high-end example of the emphasis business enterprises place on employee training is AT&T Inc. The company is investing more than $1 billion to retrain over 100,000 employees through a variety of classes and programs to retool the company.[33] The need for companywide training arose because AT&T invested heavily in technology and needed workers with the right skills to run the technology.

Training and development are so important to many big companies that the organizational unit responsible for such activity is labeled a *university*, as illustrated by the Hilton Worldwide University. None of these universities is authorized to grant degrees by the state in which it operates. Jeff Levi, executive director of Trust for America's Health, points to the importance of employee training in these words: "You may be able to buy equipment quickly, but you can't buy trained personnel quickly."[34]

e-learning
A form of computer-based training delivered via the Internet or private Intranets in organizations.

E-Learning. A substantial amount of skills training in industry is delivered using computers, tablets and even phones. **E-learning** is a form of computer-based training delivered via the Internet or private Intranets in organizations. An e-learning course is usually carefully structured, with specific lesson plans for the student. E-learning helps deal with the challenge of training workers who are geographically dispersed. Placing learning modules on social networking websites is a form of e-learning, and it is gaining some momentum. Many e-learning programs are designed so they are in small enough chunks to be used specifically on mobile devices.

Another feature of e-learning is it is often interactive. The computer provides a stimulus or prompt, to which the trainee responds. The computer then analyzes the response and provides feedback to the student. A question in a customer service course might ask trainees to evaluate the following response to a customer complaint: "If you don't like my answer, go speak to my boss." A message would then appear suggesting the trainee take more ownership of the problem.

Despite the substantial contribution and growth of e-learning, many students learn better when they can interact with people, such as fellow students and instructors. Nonverbal cues, so important for many types of learning, are minimal at best when interacting with software.

Many companies are now taking a balanced approach to classroom training combined with e-learning. Internet-based learning is effective in helping workers learn conceptual information, mandatory compliance training and hard skills, such as product information, or principles of customer service. Yet developing interpersonal skills is more effective with classroom and face-to-face practice. For example, The Home Depot relies heavily on e-learning for training cashiers how to make change and process credit cards. In contrast, personal mentoring is used more often to coach store associates about product knowledge and dealing with customers.[35] Also, as with remote working, many workers lack enough self-discipline and self-motivation to follow through with e-learning.

Middle Skills Training. A substantial amount of employee training is conducted by community colleges and career schools working in close collaboration with one company, or a group of local companies. This fits into a key trend of employers, schools and government agencies working together to fill in-demand positions requiring middle skills. Such positions are often relatively high-paying, skilled jobs that require more than a high school diploma, but not a bachelor's degree. An example would be a certificate program to become an industrial engineering technician.[36]

Development is a form of personal improvement that usually consists of enhancing knowledge and skills of a complex and unstructured nature. For example, a development program might help managers become better leaders or develop multicultural skills. Management development, as with other purposes of acquiring knowledge, now deals with two broad types of learner expectations. One extreme is a demand for bite-sized, job-related, on-demand learning, such as consulting a smartphone app to learn how to calculate return on investment. At the other extreme is enrollment in a university program to escape a time-pressured, and often unreflective (no time to think about learning) learning environment.[37]

Employee training and development can also take place through MOOCs, or massive open online courses that are another form of e-learning. MOOC designers take online technology and learning content and package them into free products.[38] The link to employee learning and development is when a MOOC is chosen that fits an organizational need, such as creativity enhancement or understanding financial statements.

Managers play an important role in most types of on-the-job training and development. We return to the topic of the manager as a teacher in discussions about mentoring in Chapter 10 and coaching in Chapter 16.

Most of this text and its accompanying course could be considered an experience in management training and development. The next paragraphs describe two vital aspects of training and development for employees and managers: needs assessment and the selection of an appropriate training program.

Needs Assessment and Selecting an Appropriate Training Program. Before embarking on a training program, an organization needs to determine what type of training is needed. Such an assessment generally benefits from including a job analysis and asking the managers themselves, their managers, and group members about the managers' need for training. For example, many managers need training in the application of data analytics and artificial intelligence. Training and development needs can also be identified for the entire organization, or portions of it. For example,

development
A form of personal improvement that usually consists of enhancing knowledge and skills of a complex and unstructured nature.

an entire organization might be trained in how to use social networking to enhance the company's image.

Despite the importance of matching training and development programs to a specific individual and organizational need, universal training needs also require attention. The training would include elements, such as communication, motivation, decision making, coaching and time management.

After needs are assessed, a program must often be tailored to fit company requirements. The person assigning employees to training and development programs must be familiar with their needs for training and development, know the content of various programs, and enroll employees in programs that will meet their needs. Figure 9-6 presents a sample listing of training and development programs.

Informal Learning. In addition to training and development programs, substantial learning takes place outside the classroom or away from the computer. Many employees learn job skills and information by asking each other questions, sharing ideas and observing each other. Such learning is spontaneous, immediate and task specific. Much **informal learning** takes place in meetings, on breaks, and in customer interactions. Digitized information facilitates informal learning because workers can exchange information so readily. Some companies have installed high round tables and white boards around the company so workers can informally exchange ideas in addition to small talk. Open office spaces also facilitate informal learning because it is easy to ask questions of co-workers than if they were in a cubicle or office.

informal learning
Any learning in which the learning process is not determined or designed by the organization.

The accompanying *Management in Action* insert illustrates how a company whose brand is a household name emphasizes training and development to become a productive organization.

Figure 9-6 A Sample Listing of Training Programs versus Development Programs

Training programs listed in the left column are often included in a program of management development. The programs on the right, however, are rarely considered to be specific skill-based programs.

Training Programs	Management Development Programs
Hospitality skills	Strategic leadership
Human resources legislation	Teamwork development
Preventing and controlling sexual harassment	Building a learning culture
IT certification and training	Strategic marketing management
Social media marketing	Strategic human resource planning
Accident prevention	Employee engagement
Dealing with difficult employees	Building an innovative organization
Writing better reports	Formulating growth strategy ideas
Mindfulness to improve productivity	Implementing data analytics and AI

MANAGEMENT IN ACTION

KitchenAid and Whirlpool Invests in their Promising Workers

Jennifer Hanna, is responsible for the work activities of over 1,000 people at the Greenville, Ohio, manufacturing facility of KitchenAid, a subsidiary of appliance-maker Whirlpool Corp. Every KitchenAid stand mixer in the world is built at this facility. Hanna's career success is linked closely to the emphasis KitchenAid and Whirlpool place on employee training and development. She has worked her way up to being a member of KitchenAid's senior leadership team. Hanna began her employment at KitchenAid when she graduated from high school in 1991, and was searching to find a way to pay for college expenses. During her career, with the help of her employer, she has graduated from community college, a four-year college, and an MBA program. KitchenAid paid her way through community college and the University of Findlay in Ohio.

The company's investment in Hanna has been substantial. In a highly competitive market for manufacturing leadership with 10-20 years of experience, KitchenAid has a prized and rare asset in Hanna, who appears to be committed to the company that took a chance on her.

Training and development are emphasized throughout the workforce at the Greenville facility where workers produce millions of stand mixers annually, painting them in 80 different colors. Hanna says it takes six weeks to learn how to build a stand mixer. She emphasizes that the most important skill a new hire brings to Whirlpool is a strong work ethic. "Everything else can be taught." Without people coming to work every day the operation shuts down.

Maggie Hammaker, a 28-tear-old assembly supervisor, has followed a similar career path at KitchenAid, and she now manages 100 people. Hammaker showed up for a job interview with no idea of the type of job she wanted. After she was hired, she began taking courses at Sinclair Community College in nearby Dayton, Ohio. The course she chose included business, communications, and environmental ethics. The courses Hammaker took helped her work her way up form production technician to supervisor to manager.

Kenneth R, Hossler, the plant leader at Whirlpool in Tiffin, Ohio, began his career over 30 years ago on the production line. He said, "The nice thing about Whirlpool, for me, was that they paid for my college. If you're on the assembly line and you want to take a business course or get an engineering technology degree, Whirlpool will pay for it."

Questions

1 **Why does Whirlpool consider employee training to be a "strategic benefit" for the company?**

2 **What restrictions should KitchenAid and Whirlpool place on the type of courses they will pay for taken by employees?**

Source: Original story based on the following sources: John D. Stoll, "Kitchen Aid's Secret Ingredient: Investment in Its Workers," *The Wall Street Journal*, February 23–24, 2019, p. B5; Mark J. Sagor, "Employee Training: A Strategic Benefit for Employees & Employers," *Comp EAP* (www.compeap.com), March 13, 2019, pp. 1–4; "Mixing It Up the KitchenAid Way," *Manufacturing Business Technology* (www.mbtmag.com), July 22, 2014, pp. 1–9; "Whirlpool Lauded for Learning, Development Programs," *Reliable Plant* (www.reliableplant. com). Accessed January 25, 2019.

PERFORMANCE EVALUATION (OR APPRAISAL)

LEARNING OBJECTIVE **5**

Explain the basics of a performance evaluation system.

Up to this point in the staffing model, employees have been recruited, selected, oriented and trained. The next step is to evaluate performance. A **performance evaluation (or appraisal)** is a formal system for measuring, evaluating, and reviewing performance. The term *performance* appears self-explanatory, yet an analysis of dozens of studies indicates performance has three major components[39]:

performance evaluation (or appraisal)
A formal system for measuring, evaluating, and reviewing performance.

- *Task performance* is the accomplishment of duties and responsibilities associated with a given job (like maintaining inventory at a profitable level).

- *Citizenship performance* is behavior that contributes to the goals of the organization by contributing to its social and psychological environment (like voluntarily helping a co-worker with a technical problem).

- *Counterproductive performance* is voluntary behavior that harms the well-being of the organization (like consistently insulting customers).

When managers evaluate performance, they are thinking of these components even if they are not explicitly aware of them. For example, when a manager rates marketing assistant Maria "outstanding," the manager is most likely reacting to the fact that Maria: (a) accomplished her marketing tasks, (b) was a cooperative company citizen, and (c) did not engage in counterproductive behavior, such as disrupting meetings or regularly arriving late to work.

The emphasis on team structures changes performance evaluations in two major ways. One, groups as well as individuals are now subject to regular evaluation. Another change comes in the widespread use of multi-rating systems, whereby several workers evaluate an individual. The most frequently used multi-rater system is **360-degree feedback**, in which a person is evaluated by most of the people with whom he or she interacts. Used in this fashion, 360-degree evaluation is a form of peer evaluation.

360-degree feedback
A performance appraisal in which a person is evaluated by most of the people with whom he or she interacts.

An evaluation form for a manager might incorporate input from the manager's manager, all group members, other managers at his or her level, and even a sampling of customers when feasible. The manager's manager would then synthesize all the information and discuss it with him or her. Dimensions for rating a manager might include: "gives direction," "listens to group members," "coaches effectively," and "helps the group achieve key results."

The rationale for using 360-degree feedback for performance evaluation is based on its ability to present a complete picture of performance. This technique is used as much for management and leadership development as for performance evaluation. As with most human resource programs, 360-degree evaluations for both evaluation and development work best if it begins with top-level managers and then cascades down through the organization.[40] The system is also dependent on the raters not giving good evaluations to their friends and getting even with people they dislike.

Purposes of Performance Evaluation

Performance evaluations serve a number of administrative purposes and can also help the manager carry out the leadership function. A major purpose is to decide whether an employee should receive merit increases and the relative size of the increases. The evaluation process also identifies employees with potential for promotion. High-performing teams can be identified as well. Employee reviews are widely used to provide documentation for discharging, demoting and downsizing employees who are not meeting performance standards.

Performance evaluations help managers carry out the leadership function in several ways. Suggesting areas for needed improvement can increase productivity. Also, the manager can help employees identify their needs for self-improvement and self-development. Appraisal results can be used to motivate employees by providing feedback on performance. Finally, a performance appraisal gives employees a chance to express their ambitions, hopes and concerns, thereby enhancing career development.

performance management
A set of processes and managerial behaviors aimed at defining, measuring, and motivating the development of good performance.

A broad purpose of performance evaluation is to contribute to **performance management**—a set of processes and managerial behaviors aimed at defining, measuring, and motivating the development of good performance.[41] Performance evaluation is necessary for the measuring component of performance management. Several other key components of performance management are goal setting, communicating with workers, providing feedback, coaching, and providing positive or negative consequences for the performance attained. All of these topics are described later in this book.

Design of the Performance Evaluation System

Performance evaluation methods are usually designed to measure traits, behavior, or results. **Traits** are stable aspects of people, which are closely related to personality. Job-related traits include enthusiasm, dependability and honesty. **Behavior**, or activity, is what people do on the job. Job-related behavior includes working hard, keeping the work area clean, maintaining a good appearance, and showing concern for customer service. A worker's level of activity in company social networking sites might provide clues to how frequently his or her opinion is sought by other workers. The content of the worker's blogs might also provide a few hints about how well he or she represents the company to the community. **Results** are what people accomplish, or the objectives they attain. The following is an example of a performance factor on an employee evaluation form that focuses on results:

5	4	3	2	1
☐	☐	☐	☐	☐
Innovative approach to problem solving.	Consistently unsatisfactory	Occasionally unsatisfactory	Consistently satisfactory	Sometimes superior	Consistently superior

Many performance evaluation systems take into account results, as well as traits and behaviors. For example, a worker might have achieved work goals (results), and also be described as having initiative (a behavior linked to a trait). Another important consideration is the performance evaluation system should encourage some risk-taking behavior even if it could mean not reaching agreed-upon goals. Without prudent risk taking, innovation would be stifled.[42]

A major development in performance evaluation is to rely on extensive data to measure performance. In the past, managerial or supervisory judgments were often the major sources of data for evaluation. Amazon, Accenture and Deloitte revamped their performance review process to adopt a more data-driven approach. Sources of data include more frequent ratings by managers and other internal feedback that can be synthesized and analyzed to provide a fuller picture of performance than a managerial rating. At Amazon, staffers are encouraged to report praise or criticism about co-workers to provide management more data for performance evaluation.[43] (Not everybody likes this Amazon tactic!)

Another data-driven approach to performance evaluation is the use of apps designed to provide employees with continuous 360-degree feedback and goal attainment. The app works like a fitness tracker but is job-related. Using the app, staff members are able to send encouraging real time feedback to co-workers and subordinates on positive as well as negative performance incidents.[44] For example, "Bart, that quality report was outstanding," or "Cindy, we need to discuss your impatience with customers."

Employees are the most satisfied with performance evaluation when they participate in the process. Participation can take a number of forms, such as jointly setting goals with the manager, submitting a self-appraisal as part of the evaluation, and having the opportunity to fully discuss the results.[45]

Many workers dislike having their performance evaluated, and many managers dislike evaluating workers, particularly when negative feedback is involved. Some researchers and managers therefore propose eliminating performance appraisals. Such a move would be tantamount to abolishing grades in school. One alternative to performance appraisals is for managers to have face-to-face conversations with

traits
Stable aspects of people, closely related to personality.

behavior
What people actually do on the job.

results
What people accomplish, or the objectives they attain.

workers about their performance on a regular basis, at a minimum of three or four times annually. Frequent reviews are particularly important during rapidly changing business conditions because priorities may change, such as a sudden need to cut costs or increase sales. Managers also have the option of providing performance feedback to workers whenever it is thought necessary. One approach to frequent reviews in a project-based organization is to provide a performance snapshot at the end of each project. When projects are longer term, quarterly reviews can be implemented.[46]

Managers must make written notes of any problems that workers experience, which creates the necessary documentation to support any necessary discipline or termination. Regular conversations that accommodate documentation of poor performance simply translate into an informal system of performance evaluation, not its replacement. Feedback on performance as needed may be useful for employee development but it is difficult to integrate the feedback for deciding on salary increases and bonuses—a key use of performance evaluation results.

LEARNING OBJECTIVE **6**

Summarize the components of employee compensation.

COMPENSATION

Compensation, including pay and benefits, plays a major role in talent management that includes attracting and retaining valued employees in general, and particularly during a labor shortage. Even when a firm is downsizing, key employees will be recruited and retained by juggling benefits. Compensation also attracts considerable management attention because it constitutes about two-thirds of the cost of running most enterprises. Here we look at several types of pay and employee benefits. Chapter 11 will describe how compensation is used as a motivational device.

Types of Pay

Wages and salary are the most common forms of pay. Wages are payments to employees for their services, computed on an hourly basis or on the basis of the amount of work produced. Salary is an annual amount of money paid to a worker and does not depend directly on output or hours worked. Nevertheless, future salary is dependent to some extent on how well the worker produced in the previous year. Many workers are eligible for bonuses or incentives to supplement their salary.

job evaluation
The process of rank-ordering jobs based on job content, to demonstrate the worth of one job in comparison to another.

To determine how much a given job should receive in wages or pay, many companies perform a **job evaluation**, the process of rank-ordering jobs based on job content, to demonstrate the worth of one job in comparison to another. Among the factors contributing to the content of a job are education, skill, mental demands and physical demands. Each factor receives a weight, and the weights are added to determine how many points a job is worth. The greater the total points, the higher the pay.[47]

variable pay
When the amount of money a worker receives is partially dependent on his or her performance.

The major thrust in compensation for workers at all levels is **variable pay**, in which the amount of money a worker receives is partially dependent on his or her performance. A worker might receive a bonus for having surpassed a performance standard, or a salary increase for the same reason. Performance-based compensation is widespread as employers struggle to remain competitive in price yet attract and retain capable workers. The assumption is that a talented worker will accept lower guaranteed pay if higher incentive pay is possible.

Employee Benefits

An **employee benefit** is any noncash payment given to workers as part of compensation for their employment. Benefits are a major contribution to job satisfaction and retention.[48] Employee benefits cost employers about 35 percent of salaries. Therefore, an employee earning $40,000 per year in salary probably receives a combined salary and benefit package of $54,000. Under ideal circumstances, employee benefits should be linked to business strategy, meaning that these benefits should reward employees for achieving key business goals. Some companies offer tuition assistance only for courses that directly improve job performance. Honda of America would thus reimburse an engineer for studying fuel cell technology but would not reimburse an engineer for a course in acupuncture.

Figure 9-7 presents a representative list of employee benefits, organized by type and frequency. Organizations vary considerably in the benefits and services they offer employees. No one firm is likely to have the same portfolio of benefits, particularly for nonstandard benefits, such as back massage services, or on-company-premises dry-cleaning. One of the most humanitarian benefits, is a rainy-day fund to hand out

employee benefit
Any noncash payment given to workers as part of compensation for their employment.

Figure 9-7 A Variety of Employee Benefits

Employers find that the right package of benefits for an individual worker will increase the chances he or she will stay with the firm for a relatively long time.

Common Healthcare Benefits
Health and dental insurance
Life insurance
Drug prescription program
Employee assistance program
Wellness program including weight reduction, stress management, blood pressure control, and smoking cessation
Healthcare benefits for domestic partners

Frequent Financial Benefits
Credit union
Tuition assistance
Defined-contribution retirement plan
Incentive bonus plan
Employee stock ownership
Financial counseling for employees in financial difficulty
Financial wellness to improve money management
Rainy-day fund assistance

Frequent Family-Friendly Benefits
Dependent care flexible spending account
Flexible working hours
Compressed workweeks
Remote work option
Bring child to work in emergency
Childcare referral service
Paid parental leave beyond the Family and Medical Leave Act

Frequent Personal Services
Professional development opportunities (seminars, conferences, courses, etc.)
Professional memberships
Casual dress everyday
Casual dress one day per week
Organization-sponsored sports teams
Food services/subsidized cafeteria
Club memberships

Infrequent Benefits of All Types
On-site healthcare clinics
Free lunches served on premises
Massage therapy at work area
Lactation rooms for mothers of infants
Company-supported childcare center
Company-supported eldercare center
Subsidize cost of elder care
Naptime during the workday
Bringing babies to work permitted
Animal pet allowed on company premises
Take-your-dog to work days
Animal pet health insurance

cash to financially-strapped families when they face emergencies. Offering financial advice and counseling is gaining in frequency, partly in recognition of the reality that financial problems are a major stressor that can affect job performance. Also, financial fitness is a major component of personal well-being.

Many business firms in recent years have either decreased benefits to current employees or required them to pay a larger share, particularly with respect to healthcare. High deductible plans are often combined with a health savings account. The latter plan allows money to go in, grow, and go out to pay medical bills, all tax free.[49]

The Affordable Care Act (ACA) of 2010 has influenced the administration of medical insurance benefits to employees. The bill is complex with 2,700 original pages, and 20,000 additional pages in regulations and adjustments. Many organizations need to hire consultants to help them interpret and comply with the ACA. The employer mandate to the law requires companies with at least 50 full-time employees to offer affordable healthcare benefits to those employees who work an average of 30 hours per week. "Affordable" means the amount each employee pays in annual health premiums for single coverage cannot exceed 9.5 percent of that employee's household income. The 9.5 percent figure will be adjusted annually.

The fine for not complying with the ACA is a maximum $3,000 per employee who is not offered coverage and instead seeks to be covered through a public exchange for purchasing an insurance policy that conforms to the law. Most large employers already offer health insurance to employees, so the ACA has minimal impact on employee health benefits.

The individual mandate went into effect in 2014, requiring almost all Americans to maintain health insurance coverage unless they were eligible for an exemption. Up until the individual mandate was eliminated by the Tax Cuts and Jobs Act of 2017, individuals who did not maintain health coverage were fined by the Internal Revenue Service. After the individual mandate was eliminated, five states and the District of Columbia implemented their own mandates and penalties.[50] Although the removal of penalties for not purchasing health insurance was important to many individuals, it had a negligible impact on employer health insurance plans.

Few companies today offer the traditional benefit plan in which retirees are given a fixed pension for life, adjusted upward annually for inflation. Instead, most employers offer a defined contribution plan, often referred to as a 401(k) plan. The employee contributes to the plan, and the employer often matches the employee contribution in part or full. The money paid into the plan is tax deferred, and earnings accrue on a tax-deferred basis. Employees usually have a broad choice of investments. Should the employee quit he or she takes the 401 (k) with him or her just like a personal investment. For the employer, a 401(k) plan avoids such costs as paying $65,000 a year in pension to a worker who leaves at 55 and lives until 100. If employees are diligent enough to invest seriously during their career, their portable 401(k) nest egg will be sufficient for retirement.

A strategic perspective when considering employee benefits (combined with other human management practices, such as empowerment and recognition) is they should contribute to worker sustainability. Workers stay healthier physically and mentally, and live longer when they are treated well. Stanford University Professor of Organization Behavior Jeffrey Pfeffer notes that humane treatment of employees is therefore socially responsible.[51]

THE ROLE OF LABOR UNIONS IN HUMAN RESOURCE MANAGEMENT

When a public or private organization is unionized, the labor union influences almost all human resource programs and practices. The major purpose of a **labor union** is to attain fair treatment for workers in such areas as compensation, including health and retirement benefits, safe working conditions, working hours, job security, and work-life programs.

According to the United States Bureau of Labor Statistics, about 10.3 percent of wage and salary workers are union members, a level that has remained stable for several years. The union membership rate has declined from a high of 20.1 percent in 1983, partially because of the manufacturing decline in North America. The unionization rate for government workers is 33.6 percent, whereas the rate for private sector workers is 6.2 percent. The most heavily unionized public sector workers is protective service occupations (33.8 percent) and in education, training, and library occupations (33.1 percent). The most heavily unionized occupations include police officers, firefighters, and teachers. Among private industries, utilities, transportation, telecommunication and construction have the highest union membership rate.

Because the manufacturing sector has been the hardest hit by foreign competition, union leaders are often unable to push for improved compensation including wages and health retirement benefits. Company executives can use the threat of sending work offshore when union demands are too high. Another alternative for an American employer is to threaten to relocate operations to a state where union membership is low, such as South Carolina (2.1 percent), or North Carolina (3.0 percent).[52]

Low-wage workers appear to be important to future union organizing because many of these workers are performing jobs that cannot be globally outsourced. The union movement for a higher minimum wage in recent years could result in more workers earning enough money to be able to afford union dues. Also, low-paid service workers represent growth potential for unions, with only 1.3 percent of workers in the food industry being organized.[53]

A concern management has had about unions for many years, particularly in manufacturing, is that union leaders attempt to avoid flexible work rules that allow workers to rotate jobs or shifts in work assignments. For example, a welder would not be allowed to pitch in as a parts assembler. Another concern is that in some industries, union demands for compensation have made it difficult for companies to remain competitive. As a result, foreign car makers have established manufacturing facilities in several Southern states in recent years by utilizing generous tax benefits and laws that make it easier to build a largely non-union workforce.[54] Two union counterarguments are that workers should: (a) receive a fair share of profits, and (b) not be expected to receive low wages to compensate for management bungling.

A reasonably balanced point of view is when employers offer workers what they want and need, employee desire to unionize diminishes. Human resource strategies and policies like these discourage union activities, as they address the type of demands labor unions typically seek.

- Fair and consistent policies and practices
- Open-door management policies (workers are free to discuss problems with management)
- Competitive pay and benefits
- Employee trust and recognition

LEARNING OBJECTIVE **7**

Understand the role of labor unions in human resource management.

labor union
An organization formed to attain fair treatment for workers in such areas as compensation, including health and retirement benefits, safe working conditions, working hours, job security, and work-life programs.

Many instances exist of healthy partnerships between management and labor unions in which both sides gain advantage. One example is Costco Wholesale Corporation and the International Brotherhood of Teamsters. Costco provides wages and benefits higher than industry standards and demonstrates that treating employees well is good for business. The annual membership fees Costco collects from customers helps fund their generous benefits. Perhaps not every business firm is in a position to have such progressive labor relations, yet the message is clear that working well with all stakeholders is associated with business success.

1 **Explain how human resource management is part of business strategy.**

Human resource and talent management is an integral part of business strategy. Without effective human resource management, the company cannot accomplish high-level goals, such as competing globally, grabbing market share and being innovative.

2 **Describe the components of a human resource management model.**

The human resource management model consists of seven phases: awareness of the legal aspects of staffing; strategic human resource planning; recruitment; selection; orientation, training and development; performance appraisal; and compensation. All phases can influence employee retention.

3 **Present an overview of recruitment and selection.**

Recruitment is the process of attracting job candidates with the right characteristics and skills to fit job openings and the organizational culture. Job descriptions and job specifications are necessary for recruiting. External and internal sources are used in recruiting, including extensive use of online recruiting, encompassing job boards, job search engines, company websites, and social networking sites.

Selecting candidates who will perform well is the lifeblood of the firm. Selecting the right candidate from among those recruited may involve a preliminary screening interview or texting, psychological and personnel testing, a job interview, reference checking and a physical examination. Traditional job interviews are sometimes replaced by automated exchanges over the telephone, or hiring a candidate through a phone interview only.

The four types of psychological and personnel tests used most frequently in employee selection are situational judgment, aptitude, personality, and honesty and integrity. Validity studies indicate that tests measuring problem solving ability and conscientiousness are likely to show good job performance.

Interviews are more valid when the interviewer is trained and experienced. Job interviews help both the interviewer and the interviewee acquire important information. Behavioral interviewing helps make the interview job-related, and sometimes take the form of a job tryout. Reference checks and background investigations are useful in making sound selection decisions, as does the physical examination.

4 **Present an overview of employee orientation, training, and development.**

An employee onboarding program helps acquaint the newly hired employee with the firm. Training includes any procedure intended to foster and enhance employee skills. Development is a form of personal improvement that generally enhances knowledge and skills of a complex and unstructured nature. A needs assessment should be conducted prior to selecting training and development programs.

5 **Explain the basics of a performance evaluation system.**

A performance evaluation (or review) is a standard method of measuring, evaluating and reviewing performance of individuals as well as teams. The 360-degree evaluation involves feedback from many people. Performance evaluations serve important administrative purposes, such as helping managers make decisions about pay increases and promotions and carrying out the leadership function. A broad purpose of performance evaluation is to contribute to performance management. Evaluation systems measure traits, behavior and results, with some systems taking into account more than one factor. A substitute for the traditional performance evaluation is for the manager to provide frequent feedback to employees.

6 **Summarize the components of employee compensation.**

Workers are typically paid salaries, bonuses, and sometimes payment for job skills. The purpose of job evaluations is to determine how much a job is worth. Variable pay is used to motivate employees and reduce company expenses. Employee benefits are a major part of compensation. Compensation is a major factor in recruiting and retaining employees, yet expensive benefits, such as health insurance and pensions have been reduced in recent years to help companies face global competition.

7 **Understand the role of labor unions in human resource management.**

The labor union influences almost all human resource programs and practices. A major purpose of a labor union is to attain fair treatment for workers in such areas as compensation including health and retirement benefits, safe working conditions, flexible working hours, job security, and work-life programs. Companies can counterinfluence unions through offering the type of compensation, policies, and work practices that workers would like to have. Many instances exist of healthy partnerships between management and labor unions, including at Costco.

Key Terms and Phrases

Questions

1. How realistic are the entrance qualifications for the Hilton Worldwide Management Development Program?

2. What potential disadvantages do you see when large companies eliminate their human resources departments?

3. Why should a manager who does not work in the human resources department be familiar with the various aspects of talent management?

4. How might a person applying for a management position prepare for a job interview that will most likely include a job sample?

5. If you were a hiring manager, what would be your attitude toward selecting job candidates without an interview either in-person or over the Internet by video?

6. To end all the controversy about merit pay, why not give all workers in the same job grade, or category, the same compensation?

7. How might a labor union official in a unionized company demonstrate to company management that the union is making a contribution to organizational effectiveness?

Skill-Building Exercise 9-A: Presenting Yourself in 30 Seconds

A well-accepted belief about recruiters, hiring managers and employment interviewers is they form a quick impression of a candidate, often within the first 10 seconds. With this fact in mind, develop a 30-second opening presentation about yourself with the goal of creating a favorable impression on people making judgments about your job qualifications. (This 30-second presentation is often referred to as an elevator pitch.) Facts to pack into your 30-second statement might include your name, type of work sought, education, experience and key accomplishments. However, be creative. Many job seekers have found the 30-second self-promotion speech invaluable when meeting with recruiters or attending job fairs. Give your 30-second presentation to a few fellow students to obtain their feedback and return the favor to them.

Skill-Building Exercise 9-B: The Selection Interview

Assume the role of the owner of an athletic club with four locations. You need to fill the position of general manager for the club's most successful location. After thinking through the job demands of an athletic club general manager, conduct a 15-minute interview of a classmate who pretends to apply for the position. Before conducting the interview, review the guidelines in Exhibit 9-5. Other students on your team might observe the interview and then provide constructive feedback.

Management Now—Online Skill-Building Exercise: Recruiting on the Internet

Place yourself in the role of a manager who is recruiting qualified job applicants to fill one or more of the following positions: (a) sales representative of industrial robots, (b) customer service supervisor who speaks English and Spanish, (c) and social networking marketing specialist. Use the Internet to conduct your search for a pool of candidates. A good starting point might be the job boards, job search engines (such as Indeed), and social media sites. Limit your search to candidates who appear to have posted their credentials within the last 90 days. Remember, in this exercise you are looking for job candidates, not a position for yourself. Try to determine whether you can locate any job applicants without paying an employer fee.

Should We Hire Wanda as Our Supervisor of Consumer Loan Collection?

Dion, the VP of Consumer Loans at a financial services company, is interviewing several candidates for the position of supervisor of consumer loan collection. Among the key responsibilities of the consumer loan collector are contacting customers who are delinquent in repayment of their loans and obtaining a repayment plan or agreement. In some cases of default on vehicles, motorcycles, boat loans, the consumer loan collector works with repossession specialists ("repo" workers) to take back the property. The supervisor will be responsible for about 10 consumer loan collectors.

Dion's first interview this morning is with Wanda, whose job résumé and preliminary screening interview make her a plausible candidate for the position. An excerpt from the interview follows:

Dion: Good morning, Wanda. We appreciate your applying for this position, but why should we hire you?

Wanda: I know that I can work with the loan collectors to improve their collection rates. In my present position as a customer-care supervisor, I am considered to be a terrific motivator. And besides, I need the salary increase that this job would pay.

Dion: How is your credit record with respect to paying back loans?

Wanda: Pretty good. I would have an almost perfect credit score except for a dispute I had with my smart-phone carrier. I was hit with an unjustified $750 bill one month. We finally settled for $350 after six months of haggling.

Dion: Tell me about a time you really helped an employee reporting to you to improve his or her performance.

Wanda: I supervise a customer-care technician right now who was falling behind schedule in terms of the number of cases he was handling each week. I listened in on a sampling of his calls. It seemed to me he was wasting too much time making small talk with customers. I coached him on this problem and he was soon making quota.

Dion: We need somebody who can devote full energy to this position. Distractions at home could be a problem. Do you plan to have any children soon?

Wanda: No plans for another child right now. I already have three children.

Dion: I noticed you have an interesting last name. Where were your parents born?

Wanda: I'm proud to say that my mother was born in Mexico, and my father in Cuba.

Dion: Do you think that a customer who has not made a loan payment on a car in three months should have the car repossessed?

Wanda: If the customer is facing some financial hard times, I might give that person a break. After all, even a loan company has to be a little bit human.

Dion: The supervisor of consumer loan collection has to get involved with all sorts of electronic recording keeping and reporting. How good are your technology skills?

Wanda: I get what needs to be done after I have learned the system. When I'm stuck, I ask the youngest worker in the department for help (said with a laugh).

Dion: What questions do you have of me?

Wanda: I have two questions for now. How soon after starting will I get a raise? Is this a dead-end job?

Case Questions

1 Based on the limited evidence from this interview, how qualified does Wanda appear to be for the position of supervisor of consumer loan collection?

2 What questions has Dion asked Wanda that appear to be inappropriate or illegal?

3 Which one of Dion's questions could be classified as behavioral or as a job-sample question?

Abigail Believes in As-Needed Evaluations

Abigail is the manager of a large bank branch located in Brooklyn, New York. She considers herself a modern manager, in these words: "As a native New Yorker, I am outspoken and hard-hitting. I believe in management as a profession, and I keep up to date on management trends. I don't wait for a bank-wide program to guide me on how to manage." Abigail believes strongly that as-needed feedback to subordinates is the most effective type of performance evaluation.

Quinn is a licensed banker responsible for retirement accounts for certificates of deposit. She has an office with a full-length window overlooking a busy street. Abigail sent her a text one day with this message: "Saw you gazing out the window again. Shouldn't you be studying your computer or be talking on the phone?"

Carlos is a licensed banker responsible for broker accounts involving investment in equities. Abigail sent him an e-mail 9 a.m. on a Monday with the central message, "Bad week Carlos? What went wrong? The total investments by your customers for the week were well below average. You need to do better to justify your salary."

Mia is a twenty-one-year old bank teller who has been on the job for three months. As she was walking to the bus after work, she noticed a text from Abigail that read, "The outfit you wore today was a little too racy for a bank. We're not a sports bar."

Nathan is a banker responsible for automotive and personal loans. After three consecutive days of heavy activity at his desk, he received an e-mail from Abigail that contained four positive emoji faces, and these words, "Keep your foot on the pedal of car loans. The pace at which you are closing on loans could put you on track for a fat year-end bonus."

Katrina is a bank security guard who is a contractor because she works for a security company, not the bank. As Abigail walked past Katrina one morning, she said to her, "How about a few more smiles at our customers. We haven't had any bank robberies so your job could be a little bit boring. But we still need a warm, friendly face near the door."

Case Questions

1 How appropriate is the type of performance feedback Abigail is giving to bank employees?

2 Identify what you consider to be the best and the worst feedback Abigail has delivered.

3 What could be a problem if Abigail is using her regular feedback as a substitute for year-end or six-month-end evaluations?

ENDNOTES

1. Original story created from facts and observations in the following sources: "Management Development Program (MDP) – 2020," "Hilton's Management Development Program," *WIZBII.com*. Accessed January 125, 2020, pp. 1–4; *Florida Atlantic University College of Business*, January 1, 2015, pp. 1–2; "Discover a World of Opportunity," *Hilton Worldwide News* (www.hiltonworldwide.com), January 2016, pp. 1–2; "Hilton Worldwide Expands Leadership Development Training Partnership with eCornell," *http://news.hiltonworldwide.com*, January 24, 2012, pp. 1–2.

2. Derek Stockley, "Talent Management Concept—Definition and Explanation," *www.derekstockely.com*, accessed February 25, 2010.

3. "Talent First: It's Up to CHROs to Set a Truly Talent-Driven Tone for their Organizations," *HR Magazine*, April 2018, p. 24.

4. James Combs, Yongmei Liu, Angela Hall, and David Ketchen, "How Much Do High-Performance Work Practices Matter? A Meta-Analysis of Their Effects on Organizational Performance," *Personnel Psychology*, Autumn 2006, pp. 501–528.

5. Hal Gregersen, "The Key to Retaining Your Best Employees," *The Wall Street Journal*, December 13, 2019, p. R4.

6. Peter Cappelli and Anna Tavis, "HR Goes Agile," *Harvard Business Review*, March–April 2018, pp. 46–52.

7. Amy L. Kristof-Brown, Ryan D. Zimmerman, and Eric C. Johnson, "Consequences of Individuals' Fit at Work: A Meta-Analysis of Person–Job, Person–Organization, Person-Group, and Person–Supervisor Fit," *Personnel Psychology*, Summer 2005, p. 310.

8. Te-Ping Chen, "Offbeat Job Titles Become Hiring Tool," *The Wall Street Journal*, November 15, 2008, p. B6.

9. Peter Cappelli, "Your Approach to Hiring is All Wrong," *Harvard Business Review*, May–June 2019, pp. 48–57.

10. Tony Lee, "Follow the Leaders: 12 Tips from Talent Acquisition Pros," *HR Magazine*, July/August 2018, p. 49.

11. Mark Henricks, "Recruiting 2.0," *Entrepreneur*, February 2009, p. 56.

12. Julie Bos, "Rebuilding Recruitment: Top Strategies in a Recovering Economy," *Workforce Management*, January 2010, p. 30.

13. Dave Zielinski, "7 Reasons to Love Your ATS," *HR Magazine*, October 2015, p. 31.

14. Michelle V. Rafter, "Get Your 'A' Players Here!" *Workforce Management*, March 3, 2008, pp. 1, 20–28.

15. Kelsey Gee, "Texting Might Help You Land a Job," *The Wall Street Journal*, June 21, 2017, p. B7.

16. Michael S. Christian, Bryan D. Edwards, and Jill C. Bradley, "Situational Judgment Tests: Constructs Assessed and a Meta-Analysis of their Criterion-Related Validities," *Personnel Psychology*, Spring 2010, p. 84; Sarah Fister Gale, "It's Tourney Time—For Hiring," *Workforce*, March/April 2018, p. 10.

17. Paul R. Sackett, Filip Lievens, Chad H. Van Iddekinge, and Nathan R. Kuncel, "Individual Differences and their Measurement: A Review of 100 Years of Research," *Journal of Applied Psychology*, March 2017, pp. 254, 259.

18. In-Sue Oh and Christopher M. Berry, "The Five-Factor Model of Personality and Managerial Performance: Validity Gains Through the Use of 360 Degree Performance Ratings," *Journal of Applied Psychology*, November 2009, pp. 1498–1513.

19. Richard A. Posthuma, Frederick P. Morgeson, and Michael A. Campion, "Beyond Employment Interview Validity: A Comprehensive Narrative Review of Recent Research and Trends Over Time," *Personnel Psychology*, Spring 2002, p. 42.

20. Julia Levashina, Christopher J. Hartwell, Frederick P. Morgeson, and Michael A. Campion, "The Structured Employment Interview: Narrative and Quantitative Review of the Research Literature," *Personnel Psychology*, November 1, 2014, pp. 249–251.

21. Robert D. Bretz Jr. and Timothy A. Judge, "Realistic Job Previews: A Test of the Adverse Self-Selection Hypothesis," *Journal of Applied Psychology*, April 1998, pp. 330–337.

22. Jennifer Arnold, "Hiring for Skills, Not Pedigree," *HR Magazine*, March 2018, p. 46.

23. Andrea C. Poe, "Graduate Work: Behavioral Interviewing Can Tell You If an Applicant Just Out of College Has Traits Needed for the Job," *HR Magazine*, October 2003, pp. 95–100.

24. Dana Wilkie, "Bringing Bias into the Light," *HR Magazine*, December 2014, p. 24.

25. Jack B. Soll, Katherine L. Milkman, and John W. Payne, "Outsmart Your Own Biases," *Harvard Business Review*, May 2015, pp. 65–66.

26. "The 25 Off-Limits Interview Questions," *Manager's Legal Bulletin*, October 1, 2015, pp. 1,4.

27. Chip Cutter, "A Job Interview, With Nobody," *The Wall Street Journal*, November 29, 2018, p. B6.

28. Eric Titner, "What Are Former Employers Allowed to Say About You?" *thejobnetwork.com*, September 22, 2019.

29. "85 percent of Job Applicants Line on Resumes. Here's How to Spot a Dishonest Candidate," *Inc.*, (www.inc.com), August 15, 2017, pp. 1–2; "The Biggest Resume Lies to Avoid," *Monster.com*, 2020.

30. "Data Science Can't Fix Hiring (Yet)," *Harvard Business Review*, May–June 2019, pp. 56–57.

31. Scott B. Morris et al., "A Meta-Analysis of the Relationship Between Individual Assessments and Job Performance," *Journal of Applied Psychology*, January 2015, pp. 5–20.

32. Mark Byford, Michael D. Watkins, and Lena Triantogiannis, "Onboarding Isn't Enough," *Harvard Business Review*, May–June 2017, pp. 78–86.

33. Aaron Pressman, "AT&T," *Fortune*, March 12, 2017, pp. 124–131.

34. Quoted in John Tozzi and Brendan Greeley, "Making It Up as We Go," *Bloomberg Businessweek*, October 20–October 26, 2014, p. 27.

35. George Anders, "Companies Find Online Training Has Its Limits," *The Wall Street Journal*, March 2007, p. 83; Steven Beggs, "Implementing Mobile Performance Support at Home Depot Canada," *The eLearning Guild* (www.elearningguild.com), February 20, 2014, pp. 1–3.

36. Peter Coy, "Job Training that Works," *Bloomberg Businessweek*, November 24–November 30, 2014, pp. 6–7.

37. Steven J. Armstrong and Eugene Sadler-Smith, "Learning on Demand, at Your Own Pace, in Rapid Bite-Sized Chunks: The Future of Management Development?" *Academy of Management Learning & Education*, December 2008, p. 573.

38. Robert J. Grossman, "Are Massive Open Online Courses In Your Future?" *HR Magazine*, August 2013, p. 34.

39. Maria Rotundo and Paul R. Sackett, "The Relative Importance of Task, Citizenship, and Counterproductive Performance to Global Ratings of Job Performance: A Policy-Capturing Approach," *Journal of Applied Psychology*, February 2002, pp. 66–80.

40. John W. Fleenor, Sylvester Taylor, and Craig Chappelow, *Leveraging the Impact of 360-Degree Feedback* (San Francisco: Pfeiffer, 2008).

41. Angelo Kinicki, Kathryn J. L. Jacobson, Suzanne J. Peterson, and Gregory E. Prussia, "Development and Validation of the Performance Management Behavior Questionnaire," *Personnel Psychology*, November 1, 2013, p. 1.

42. Jena McGregor, "The Midyear Review's Sudden Impact," *Businessweek*, July 6, 2009, pp. 050–052.

43. Mae Anderson, "Amazon's Data-Driven Approach Becoming More Common," *Associated Press*, August 30, 2015.

44. Elizabeth Dunn, "Performance Anxiety," *Entrepreneur*, May 2018, pp. 18-19.

45. Brian D. Cawley, Lisa M. Keeping, and Paul E. Levy, "Participation in the Performance Appraisal Process and Employee Reactions: A Meta-Analytic Review of Field Investigations," *Journal of Applied Psychology*, August 1998, pp. 615–633.

46. Marcus Buckingham and Ashley Goodall, "Reinventing Performance Management," *Harvard Business Review*, April 2015, p. 48.

47. Deborah Keary, Saundra Jackson, and Vicki Neal, "Job Evaluations, Health Coverage, Discipline," *HR Magazine*, January 2004, p. 39.

48. Henry G. Jackson, "Are Benefits the New Wages?" *HR Magazine*, September 2015, p. 4.

49. Patty Kujawa, "Do You Know the Way to HSA?," *Workforce*, February 2015, p. 38.

50. Louise Norris, "Is There Still a Penalty for Being Uninsured in 2020?" *Verywell Health* (www.verywellhealth.com), December 24, 2019, p. 2.

51. Jeffery Pfeffer, "Building Sustainable Organizations: The Human Factor," *Academy of Management Perspectives*, February 2010, p. 43.

52. This section follows closely, "Union Membership (Annual) News Release," *U.S. Bureau of Labor Statistics* (www.bls.gov), January 22, 2020, pp. 1–4.

53. Eric Morath, "Unions Bet on Low Wage Workers," *The Wall Street Journal*, May 24, 2017, p. A2.

54. "Labor-Management Cooperation Essential for American Business," *Cabot Institute for Labor Relations Inc.* (http://laborrelationsexpert.com), October 17, 2012, pp. 1–4.

Part Four

Leading

CHAPTER 10

Leadership in Organizations

OBJECTIVES

After studying this chapter and doing the exercises, you should be able to:

1 Differentiate between leadership and management.

2 Describe how leaders are able to influence and empower team members.

3 Identify important leadership characteristics.

4 Describe participative leadership, authoritarian leadership, entrepreneurial leadership, and servant leadership.

5 Describe transformational and charismatic leadership.

6 Explain the leadership role of mentoring and coaching.

7 Pinpoint leadership approaches to dealing with adversity and crises.

8 Identify several skills that contribute to leadership.

Shake Shack sees itself as a modern "roadside" burger stand featuring 100 percent all-natural Angus beef burgers, chicken sandwiches, and flat-top Vienna beef dogs made without hormones or antibiotics. Other Shake Shack offerings include frozen custard, crinkle cut fries, craft beer, and wine. The company's mission is to Stand for Something Good®. Since opening in New York City in 2004, Shake Shack has expanded to more than 250 locations (stores) in the United States and more than a dozen countries.

In 2019, Tara Comonte was promoted from Chief Financial Officer to the expanded role of President and CFO. Her new role increases her strategic leadership and operational responsibilities as Shake Shack continues to expand with new stores in Mainland China and Mexico. As president, Comonte focuses on expanding the company, broadening support of day-to-day operations, and executing strategy. At the same time, she continues to oversee finance, accounting, technology, internal audit, and the legal department.

Comonte joined Shake Shack in 2017, and played a key role in the company's digital innovation, as well as providing direction to the enterprise-wide technology upgrade. She also has worked on Shake Shack's diversity and inclusion initiatives. Before joining Shake Shack, Comone had more than 20 years of strategy, finance, technology, and operations experience in the public and private sectors. Most of her managerial experience was at global media and advertising companies. Cumonte's marketing and brand experience made her a good fit for Shake Shack.

On her first day on the job, Comonte worked the grill. Every new employee, regardless of job title, has to spend some of his or her training period in a restaurant at different stations learning how to make burgers, fries, and milkshakes. Comonte continues to spend time at the stores to get insight into what processes can be centralized to increase efficiency.

At the time of her expanded role to both CFO and president, Randy Garutti, CEO of Shake Shack said about Comonte, "She's had a tremendously positive impact across the company, over the last few years. Combined with her proven track record, Tara's expanded role will now benefit so many other areas of our business while allowing me to focus even more on where we are headed. In addition to excellence in her field, Tara's commitment to diversity and inclusion, empowerment, and accountability are core to the very special culture we have here at Shake Shack."

Based on her broad experience, Comonte offers advice to the aspiring leader, including these ideas. Be willing to follow a different career path than your fellow students if the traditional path does not bring you happiness. Look to join an organization with a work culture that you find satisfying. Hard work and real engagement in what you are stepping up to do is important for leadership success. If you want to make it to the c-suite listening to more experienced people is imperative.[1]

The story about the fast-casual restaurant executive and her popular casual food chain illustrates that leadership at the top of a company can be a demanding position. It requires a variety of skills, including choosing the right technology for the company and promoting diversity and inclusion.

leadership
The ability to inspire confidence and support among the people who are needed to achieve organizational goals.

Leadership is the ability to inspire confidence and support among the people who are needed to achieve organizational goals.[2] A leader therefore collaborates with other people to accomplish work goals. Leadership is not confined to people of high rank, but is dispersed throughout all levels of the organization.[3] For example, an office manager who is an effective leader helps keep the company running smoothly by motivating and encouraging the office workers to perform at their best. Successful professionals, regardless of their job titles, generally possess leadership capabilities. To cope with frequent change and to solve problems, people exercise initiative and leadership in taking new approaches to their job. Furthermore, in the modern organization, people slip in and out of leadership roles, such as a temporary assignment as a task force leader.

In this chapter we describe the characteristics and behaviors of organizational leaders, as well as useful leadership theories, leadership during times of adversity, and key leadership skills.

Differentiate between leadership and management.

THE LINK BETWEEN LEADERSHIP AND MANAGEMENT

Today's managers must know how to lead as well as manage in order to have an effective organization. (You will recall that leadership—along with planning, organizing, and controlling—is one of the basic functions of management.) Two representative distinctions between leadership and management follow[4]:

- Management is more formal and scientific than leadership. It relies on universal skills, such as planning, budgeting and controlling. Management is a set of explicit tools and techniques based on reasoning and testing that can be used in a variety of situations.

- Managing focuses on continuous improvement of the status quo, whereas leadership is a force for change that compels a group to innovate and depart from routine. Leadership requires having a vision.

The leadership aspects of management also focus heavily on inspiring constituents to attain organizational goals, often by appealing to the emotions of others, and being charismatic (as described later in the chapter). The other functions of management, such as controlling, usually require less inspiration.

Effective leadership and management are both required in the modern workplace because to be an effective leader, one must also be an effective manager. Managers must be leaders, but leaders must also be good managers. Workers need to be inspired and persuaded, but they also need assistance in developing a smoothly functioning workplace.

HOW LEADERS USE POWER AND AUTHORITY

Leaders influence people to do things through the use of power and authority. **Power** is the ability or potential to influence decisions and control resources. Powerful people have the potential to exercise influence, and they exercise it frequently. For example, a powerful executive might influence an executive from another company to do business with his or her company. **Authority** is the formal right to get people to do things or the formal right to control resources. Factors within a person, such as talent or charm, help them achieve power. Only the organization, however, can grant authority. To understand how leaders use power and authority, we examine the various types of power, influence tactics, and how leaders share power with team members. Understanding these different approaches to exerting influence can help a manager become a more effective leader.

Types of Power

Leaders use various types of power to influence others. However, the power exercised by group members, or subordinates acts as a constraint on how much power leaders can exercise. The list that follows describes the types of power exercised by leaders and sometimes by group members.[5]

1   *Legitimate power* is the authentic right of a leader to make certain types of requests. These requests are based on internalized social and cultural values in an organization. It is the easiest type of influence for most subordinates to accept. For example, virtually all employees accept the manager's authority to conduct a performance evaluation.

2   *Reward power* is a leader's control over rewards of value to the group members. Exercising this power includes giving salary increases and recommending employees for promotion. Being wealthy leads to having considerable reward power and being an extremely wealthy leader has become almost synonymous with power.

3   *Coercive power* is a leader's control over punishments. Organizational punishments include assigning undesirable working hours, demotion and firing. Effective leaders generally avoid heavy reliance on coercive power because it creates resentment and sometimes retaliation.

LEARNING OBJECTIVE **2**

Describe how leaders are able to influence and empower team members.

power
The ability or potential to influence decisions and control resources.

authority
The formal right to get people to do things or the formal right to control resources.

4 *Expert power* derives from a leader's job-related knowledge as perceived by group members. This type of power stems from having specialized skills, knowledge, or talent. Expert power can be exercised even when a person does not occupy a formal leadership position. An advertising copywriter with a proven record of writing winning ad slogans has expert power, and so does a marketing manager who knows how to create demand for a product.

5 *Referent power* refers to the ability to control based on loyalty to the leader and the group members' desire to please that person. Having referent power contributes to being perceived as charismatic, but expert power also enhances charisma.[6] Part of the loyalty to the leader is based on identification with the leader's personal characteristics. Referent power and charisma are both based on the subjective perception of the leader's traits and characteristics.

6 *Subordinate power* is any type of power that employees can exert upward in an organization, based on justice and legal considerations. This type of power restricts the extent to which power can be used to control them. For example, certain categories of workers cannot be asked to work overtime without compensation, and a worker does not have to put up with being sexually harassed by the boss.

The preservation of power can be important to executives, even for an exemplary leader. A frequent example is that many executives prefer to hold both the CEO and chair positions simultaneously, rather than having another person serve as chair. The chairperson (or chairman, or chairwoman) oversees the CEO, therefore diluting some of his or her power. A recent trend is for more major companies to divide the chair and CEO roles. For example, a few years ago, Wells Fargo & Co, hired Charles Scharf as CEO to help rebuild the bank's reputation after a fake account scandal. The company also kept the board's independent chairwoman Elizabet Duke in her role.[7]

Influence Tactics

In addition to various types of power, leaders use many other influence tactics to get things done. Influence tactics are especially important, because in the modern organization you often have to influence people over whom you lack formal authority. Various groups team up informally to accomplish work without the benefit of a command-and-control hierarchy. Here are eight frequently used influence tactics:

1 *Leading by example* means the leader influences group members by serving as a positive model of desirable behavior. A manager who leads by example shows consistency between actions and words. The manager's words and actions provide a consistent model. A popular connotation of leading by example is for the manager to demonstrate a strong work ethic by working long and hard, and expecting others to do the same.

2 *Leading by values* means the leader influences people by articulating and demonstrating values that guide the behaviors of others. Using values to influence others is similar to the organizational culture guiding behavior. The ideal values for a leader to pursue would be mutual respect, trust, honesty, fairness, kindness and doing good.[8] According to Bill George, former Medtronic executive and now Harvard Business School professor, an important part of leading by values is to be authentic by staying true to your values. This includes

being more concerned about employee welfare than trying to appease outside financial analysts.[9]

3   *Assertiveness* refers to being forthright in your demands. It involves expressing what you want done and how you feel about it. Assertiveness also refers to making orders clear. A supervisor might say, for example, "This break room is a mess. It nauseates me, and I want it cleaned up by tomorrow morning at 8:30." It is easier to be assertive when you are extraverted.

4   *Rationality* means appealing to reason and logic. Strong leaders use this tactic frequently. Pointing out the facts of a situation to group members to get them to do something is an example of rationality. For example, a middle-level manager might tell a supervisor, "If our department goes over budget this year, we are likely to be cut further next year." Knowing this information, the supervisor will probably become more cost conscious. Appealing to reason and logic works best when the leader is perceived as knowledgeable.

5   *Ingratiation* refers to getting somebody else to like you, often through the use of political skill. A typical ingratiating tactic would be to act in a friendly manner just before making a demand. Ingratiation works well as an influence tactic because it is a basic principle of persuasion: If people like you, perhaps because they sense you like them or have common interests, they are more apt to say yes to your demands.[10]

Effective managers treat people well consistently to get cooperation when it is needed. A representative example is Timothy D. Cook, the CEO at Apple Inc. Part of his ability to influence others is based on his being so well liked. A comment made about Cook earlier in his career was that he has "the courtly demeanor of a Southern Gentleman."[11]

6   *Exchange* is a method of influencing others by offering to reciprocate if they meet your demands. Leaders with limited expert, referent, and legitimate power are likely to use exchange and make bargains with subordinates. A manager might say to a group member, "If you can help me out this time, I'll go out of my way to return the favor." Using exchange is like using reward power. The emphasis in exchange, however, is that the manager goes out of his or her way to strike a bargain that pleases the team members.

7   *Coalition formation* is a way of gaining both power and influence. A **coalition** is a specific arrangement of parties working together to combine their power, thus exerting influence on another individual or group. Coalitions in business are a numbers game—the more people you can get on your side, the better. For example, a manager might band with several other managers to gain support for a major initiative, such as merging with another company.

8   Joking and kidding are widely used to influence others on the job. Good-natured ribbing is especially effective when a straightforward statement might be interpreted as harsh criticism. In an effort to get an employee to stop excessive Internet surfing during the work day, the supervisor said, "I know that you have over 7,000 friends on Facebook, but please just stay in touch with only your business contacts during the day."

coalition
A specific arrangement of parties working together to combine their power, thus exerting influence on another individual or group.

So which influence tactic should a leader choose? Leaders are unlikely to use all the influence tactics in a given situation. Instead, they tend to choose an influence tactic that fits the demands of the circumstances. For example, leading by values works best when a manager is highly placed in the organization and the influencing does not have to be done in a hurry. Rationality might work best in a fast-paced team setting, such as a meeting to discuss a product introduction.

Although influence tactics are presented here from the standpoint of the leader using them, recognize that in today's organization, influence runs in many directions. Leaders influence subordinates, subordinates influence leaders, and people at various organization levels influence other. Many workers are considered to be active agents who influence and are influenced by others.[12] Relevant examples here include a group member influencing the manager to try a new system of minimizing inventory, and one division manager influencing another to give remote work a try in her division.

Employee Empowerment and the Exercise of Power

Chapter 8 emphasized empowerment as a way of distributing authority in the organization. Empowerment is similarly a way for leaders to share power, and empowerment is also referred to as shared leadership. When leaders share power, employees experience a greater sense of personal effectiveness and job ownership. Sharing power with group members enables them to feel better about themselves and become better motivated. The extra motivation stems from a feeling of being in charge. An important use of empowerment is to enhance customer service. As employees acquire more authority to take care of customer problems, these problems can be handled promptly, or sometimes right on the spot.

A cornerstone belief underlying empowerment is that leadership in a team can and should be shared. Shared leadership also means leadership should flow between individuals on teams, depending on the nature of the task and the skills of the team members.[13] Not only does the leader share power with team members, but they share power with each other. According to management professors Craig L. Pearce, Charles C. Manz, and Henry P. Sims, Jr., teams that share leadership consistently outperform those whose leadership is centralized in the hands of a top-down designated leader.[14]

A key component of empowerment is the leader's acceptance of the employee as a partner in decision making. Because the team member's experience and information are regarded as equal to those of the leader, he or she shares control. Both the leader and team member must agree on what is to be accomplished. Trust is the bedrock of shared leadership in groups and teams.[15] Stated simply, it is easier to share leadership when you trust the people who share the leadership responsibility. Mark Pincus, the founder and chief executive of Zynga, a provider of online social games, practices empowerment regularly. He provides this example:

> *"We had this really motivated, smart receptionist. She was young. We kept outgrowing our phone systems, and she kept coming back and saying, "Mark, we've got to buy a whole new phone system." And I said: 'I don't want to hear about it. Just buy it. Go figure it out.' She spent a week or two meeting every vendor and figuring it out. She ended up running our whole office."*[16]

Self-Leadership and Empowerment

self-leadership
The process of influencing oneself.

For empowerment to work well, people have to exercise **self-leadership**, the process of influencing oneself.[17] Self-leadership is possible because most people have the capacity to lead themselves particularly when faced with difficult yet important tasks. At the same time, people are intrinsically (internally) motivated to perform well when they engage in challenging tasks, as in job enrichment. A manager could give the group an opportunity to practice self-leadership with an assignment such as this: "We need to find a way to boost productivity 10 percent in our division starting next month. I am going to Ireland on a business trip for ten days. You can stay in touch with me by e-mail if you like, but the assignment is yours. When I return, I will accept your three best suggestions for boosting productivity."

Managers can help group members practice effective self-leadership through three core steps.[18] First, the leader must set an example of self-leadership through such means as setting his or her own goals, making work enjoyable, and accepting rather than avoiding challenges. Second, the leader should give encouragement and instruction in self-leadership skills. Asking appropriate questions can be helpful, such as, "What goals have you established?" "What aspects of your work give you the biggest kick?" and "What obstacles have you overcome lately?"

Third, the leader should reward accomplishment in self-leadership, such as giving feedback on progress and praising initiative. The manager above upon returning from a trip might say (if true), "These two productivity-boosting suggestions you made look like winners. I really appreciate the way you followed through on this project."

Cross-Cultural Factors and Empowerment

Empowerment as a leadership technique works better in some cultures than in others. To the extent that cultural values support the manager sharing power with group members, the more likely empowerment will lead to higher productivity and morale. In contrast, in a culture where most workers believe the leader should make all the key decisions, empowerment is less likely to be motivational.

A meta-analysis of 105 studies conducted in 30 countries found that empowering leadership practices had a more beneficial impact on the performance of routine tasks in Western rather than in Eastern cultures. The authors of the study suggested that in Eastern societies such as China, India, and the Republic of Korea, those in more powerful positions are expected to assist and support those in lower positions. At the same time, subordinates are expected to be loyal and obey their leader. In contrast, in Western societies, such as the United States, United Kingdom, and Germany, employees may prefer and expect greater independence from their leader. Extensive care and concern shown by an empowering leader could be seen as an intrusion.[19]

CHARACTERISTICS, TRAITS, AND BEHAVIORS OF EFFECTIVE LEADERS

LEARNING OBJECTIVE **3**

Identify important leadership characteristics.

Understanding leadership requires an understanding of leaders as individuals even if leadership is a process among people. This section will highlight findings about the personal characteristics and behaviors of effective managerial leaders. An assessment of the characteristics and behaviors of leaders translates into the idea that these same positive attributes of a leader will facilitate his or her effectiveness in comparable settings, such as customer service departments in different companies.

The term *effective* is essential for understanding the relevance of leadership. An effective leader makes a positive impact on the organization or group, in terms of productivity and morale. Having the right traits and characteristics facilitates effectiveness, but these traits, characteristics and behaviors alone do not constitute leadership effectiveness. And fortunately for students of leadership, an analysis of 20 years of studies show that the right type of leader does improve organizational performance.[20] A key point to recognize in your development as a leader is that leadership encompasses a wide variety of personal qualities and behaviors that could be relevant in a given situation.

Characteristics and Traits of Effective Leaders

Possessing certain characteristics and traits does not in itself guarantee success. Yet effective leaders differ from others in certain respects. Studying leadership traits is also important because a person who is perceived to embody certain traits is more likely to be accepted as a leader. For example, people see managers whom they believe to be good problem solvers as able to help overcome obstacles and create a better workplace. Scholarly writing emphasizes that leadership effectiveness arises from the combined influence of several characteristics.[21] For example, to develop strategy the leader should need high intelligence and self-confidence, yet would also need effective interpersonal skills to implement the strategy. Here we present a sampling of characteristics and traits relevant to many work settings.[22]

power motivation
A strong desire to control others and resources or get them to do things on your behalf.

1 *Drive and passion.* Leaders are noted for the effort they invest in their work and the passion they have for work and work associates. The drive and passion often expresses itself as an obsession for achieving company goals. Many leaders begin their workday at 6:00 a.m. and return to their homes at 7:00 p.m. After dinner they retreat to their home offices to conduct business for about two more hours.

2 *Power motive.* Successful leaders exhibit **power motivation**, a strong desire to control others and resources or get them to do things on your behalf. A leader with a strong power need enjoys exercising power and using influence tactics. A manager who uses power constructively would more likely be promoted rapidly in an ethical corporation. Jeff Bezos of Amazon exemplifies a power-obsessed leader who aggressively pursues a market domination strategy. He and his executive team continually penetrate new markets such as the cloud, space travel, and online supermarket shopping.

3 *Self-confidence combined with humility.* Self-confidence contributes to effective leadership in several ways, in addition to being part of leadership efficacy. Above all, self-confident leaders project an image that encourages subordinates to have faith in them. Self-confidence also helps leaders make some of the tough business decisions they face regularly. When a dose of humility is combined with self-confidence, the leader is likely to be even more influential. A key aspect of humility as a leader is being able to put other people in the limelight, thereby enhancing their self-esteem. A leader with humility is considered to be humble.

A humble leader focuses on the needs of others without being self-centered. The humble leader recognizes that he or she does not have all the answers to problems facing the group. Instead, he or she listens carefully to the opinions and viewpoints of others before making a decision. A humble leader or professional may have creative ideas for moving the group or organization forward, but also welcomes the input of others.[23]

To personalize the importance of humility for leadership effectiveness, take the self-quiz presented in Figure 10-1. The answers in the direction of humility may appear obvious, but that is our intention. The purpose of this self-quiz as well as those presented in the other chapters is for you to engage in self-reflection, rather than to surprise you with the results of the quiz.

Figure 10-1 Self-Evaluation of My Humility

Humble people, of course, find it difficult to perceive themselves as being humble. Nevertheless, taking this self-quiz will help sensitize you to aspects of your own behavior and attitudes that could reflect your level of humility.

Statement Related to Humility and Humbleness	Mostly Agree	Mostly Disagree
1 Almost everybody who knows me well thinks that I have exceptional interpersonal skills.	☐	☐
2 I carefully listen to people without finishing their sentences for them.	☐	☐
3 I enjoy listening to other people describe their accomplishments.	☐	☐
4 When things go wrong, I look first to blame other people.	☐	☐
5 It annoys me when other people give me advice on the job.	☐	☐
6 I rarely applaud other people's accomplishments.	☐	☐
7 I usually laugh louder than other people at my own jokes.	☐	☐
8 It annoys me when others on the job do not say positive things about my accomplishments.	☐	☐
9 I have a strong desire to learn and improve.	☐	☐
10 With few exceptions, I am the smartest person in the room.	☐	☐
11 I get very upset whenever I am in conflict with other people.	☐	☐
12 I am willing to admit my mistakes and limitations.	☐	☐
13 I tend to ignore information that might require me to change my plans.	☐	☐
14 I would lose respect if I admitted my limitations to others,	☐	☐
15 I deserve a lot of respect from other people.	☐	☐
16 I have much more talent than most of my coworkers.	☐	☐
17 I have many more useful skills than most of my coworkers.	☐	☐
18 I welcome feedback on my performance.	☐	☐
19 I welcome feedback on my job-related behavior.	☐	☐
20 I am willing to learn from others.	☐	☐
21 I admit when I do not know how do something.	☐	☐
22 Unless another person is an established expert in his or field, I do not take that person's advice seriously.	☐	☐
23 It is difficult for a person with talent like mine to be humble.	☐	☐
24 I pay careful attention to the strengths of other people.	☐	☐
25 I brag about myself a lot on social media.	☐	☐

Scoring and Interpretation:

Score yourself one point for each of the following questions you answered:

"Mostly Agree": 2, 3, 9, 12, 18, 19, 20, 21, and 24.

"Mostly Disagree": 1, 4, 5, 6, 7, 8, 10, 11, 13, 14, 15, 16, 17, 22, 23, and 25.

If you scored 20 points or higher your self-evaluation suggests that you have an appropriate degree of humility to facilitate your leadership effectiveness. If you scored between 6 and 19 points, you might need to practice more humility to facilitate your leadership effectiveness. If you scored 5 or less points, you might be projecting an image of a person so humble and lacking in self-confidence that it detracts from your leadership and professional effectiveness.

Source: A few of the ideas for the statements in this quiz are based on the following sources: Arménio Rego, Miguel Pina E Cunha, and Ace Volkmann Simpson, "The Perceived Impact of Humility On Team Effectiveness: An Empirical Study," *Journal of Business Ethics*, March 2008, pp. 205–218; Bradley P. Owens, Michael D. Johnson, and Terence B. Mitchell, "Expressed Humility in Organizations," *Organization Science*, September–October 2013, pp. 1317–1338.

4 *Proactivity.* Leadership is almost synonymous with taking the initiative and being proactive includes taking the initiative to work on problems. A person with a proactive personality has a relatively stable tendency to effect environmental change. He or she makes things happen as part of his or her work role.[24] As a result, the leader with a proactive personality is more likely to be able to influence people and bring about constructive change. A study conducted in a large, consumer, packaged-goods company found proactive senior managers establish more challenging goals for their business units. The higher goals were, in turn, associated with higher sales.[25]

5 *Trustworthiness and honesty.* Trust is regarded as one of the major leadership attributes. Effective leaders know they must build strong employee trust to obtain high productivity and commitment. A major strategy for being perceived as trustworthy is to make your behavior consistent with your intentions, because our behavior instills trust in others, not our intentions. Such behavior is also referred to as behavior integrity, because words and actions are consistent. Practice what you preach and set the example. Allowing group members to participate in decisions is another trust builder.[26] Sharing information with group members is another fundamental trust-builder—sharing detailed information about plans for the expansion or construction of the organization or organizational unit.

Dishonesty has been described as having a major negative impact on trustworthy leadership. Trustworthiness means keeping promises, not gossiping, and telling the truth. Being dishonest makes it very difficult to gain the trust of group members.[27]

Closely related to trustworthiness and honesty is being open with employees about the financial operations and other sensitive information about the company. In an **open-book company** every employee is trained, empowered, and motivated to understand and pursue the company's business goals. In this way employees become business partners. The key to open-book management is to teach employees to understand financial statements and what they can do to improve profits and rewarding them for their accomplishments.[28]

open-book company
A firm in which every employee is trained, empowered, and motivated to understand and pursue the company's business goals.

6 *Good intellectual ability, knowledge, and technical competence.* Effective leaders are good problem solvers and knowledgeable about the business or technology for which they are responsible. They are likely to combine analytical intelligence with practical intelligence (the ability to solve everyday problems based on experience). A comprehensive analysis of research about leadership concluded how leaders think, including their intelligence, can be a key factor determining the behavior of leaders.[29] For example, a leader has to be smart to develop a plan for shaping the company's culture.

Recent research confirms a long-held belief that an optimum level of intelligence exists between intelligence and leadership effectiveness, referred to as a *curvilinear relationship*. It is usually better for the leader to have higher cognitive ability than the average group member, but not too much higher. The study sample consisted of mid-level leaders from multinational private sector companies. Intelligence was measured by the Wonderlic Personnel Test, and leadership behavior was measured through ratings by people who worked with the leader. The perceived effectiveness of leaders was found to be highest at a score equivalent to an IQ of 120. Below and beyond that score, leaders were perceived to be less effective for midlevel managerial positions.[30]

Technical competence, or knowledge of the business, often translates into close attention to details about products and services, and operations. A representative example of a leader with technical competence and knowledge of the business is Jeff Williams, an Apple veteran who became chief operating officer. He has overseen the company's supply chain, its service and support functions, and played key roles with the iPhone and the Apple Watch. "Jeff is hands-down the best operations executive I've ever worked with" said Apple CEO Tim Cook.[31]

7 *Sense of humor and mindfulness.* An effective sense of humor is an important part of a leader's job. In the workplace, humor relieves tension and boredom, defuses hostility, and helps build relationships with group members. The manager who makes the occasional witty comment is likely to be perceived as approachable and friendly. Humor also helps build positive relationships with subordinates, which, in turn, results in a higher amount of organizational citizenship behavior.[32] (This type of behavior is about going beyond your job description to help individuals and the organization.)

Serial entrepreneur Rob Emrich explains that humor is a function of being mindful. **Mindfulness** is about being totally aware of the present situation and blocking out the past and future. As a way of being mindful, a leader will often observe the tension that has built up in an interpersonal interaction and look for an absurdity to help relieve the tension.[33] Imagine a general manager is listening to a dispute between manufacturing and marketing over the pricing of a product. The manufacturing head says the product cannot be produced at the low cost demanded by marketing. At the same time, the marketing head says the product cannot be sold if manufacturing does not lower the product cost. To relieve the tension, the general manager says, "Good enough. We have an impasse. Let's shut down the plant and open a frozen yogurt stand."

mindfulness
Being totally aware of the present situation and blocking out the past and future.

8 *Emotional intelligence.* Effective leaders demonstrate good emotional intelligence, the ability to manage themselves and their relationships effectively. Emotional intelligence broadly encompasses many traits and behaviors related to leadership effectiveness, including self-confidence, empathy, passion for the task and visionary leadership. Being sensitive to the needs of others (and not insulting or verbally abusing them) is another part of emotional intelligence.

Travis Bradberry, the president of a firm that provides emotional testing and training has conducted research with more than one million people, finding that 90 percent of top-performing leaders have high emotional intelligence. Although this evidence is impressive, it is helpful to recognize emotional intelligence is regarded by some researchers as a mixture of personality traits and problem-solving ability. Its strong association with leadership could therefore be exaggerated.[34]

Richard Anderson, the former chief executive of Delta Airlines, provides us an everyday example of the relevance of emotional intelligence. He says that the most important leadership lesson he has learned is to be patient and not lose his temper. Anderson notes that when a leader loses his or her temper, it squelches debate and sends the wrong signal about how you want your organization to run.[35]

Another important aspect of emotional intelligence is to create good feelings in those they lead. The good moods and positive emotions help group members perform at their best because they become excited about the task, and might even be more creative. One way in which the leader fosters good moods is to encourage the positive expression of feelings in others, and avoid being cranky, hostile and miserable most of the time himself or herself.[36]

9   *Leadership efficacy.* A good way of concluding how personal characteristics contribute to leadership effectiveness is the comprehensive trait of **leadership efficacy**. It refers to a specific form of efficacy (or feeling effective) associated with the level of confidence in the knowledge, skills, and abilities associated with leading others. It helps to believe you can accomplish the job when you take on a leadership role. The feeling of efficacy can be based on some of the traits already described, including being self-confident and having the intellectual ability suited to the leadership task.

leadership efficacy
A specific form of efficacy (or feeling effective) associated with the level of confidence in the knowledge, skills, and abilities associated with leading others.

Behaviors and Skills of Effective Leaders

Traits alone are not sufficient to lead effectively. A leader must also behave in certain ways and possess key skills. The actions or behaviors described in the following list are linked to leadership effectiveness. Recognize, however, that behaviors are related to skills. For example, in giving emotional support to team members, a leader uses interpersonal skills. The present discussion should not be interpreted to mean leadership is basically a function of a set of skills. Instead, these skills may facilitate attaining the set of human connections that are essential for effective leadership.[37] For example, a leader who gives frequent constructive feedback will connect better with group members.

A valuable part of understanding leadership behaviors for your career is that they are activities that can be learned because they can be translated into doable tasks.[38] In reality, leaders are neither born nor made, but a combination of genetic predisposition and learning. For example, you might have good native cognitive intelligence but you have to cultivate thinking big to become an effective executive. Here are additional traits of effective leaders:

1   *Is adaptable to the situation.* Adaptability reflects the contingency viewpoint: A tactic is chosen based on the unique circumstances at hand. Research with trauma resuscitation teams (as in an emergency room) at a medical center documents this tried and true observation about leadership behavior. Empowering leadership was found to be more effective when severity of the trauma was low (e.g., broken leg) and team experience was high. In contrast, directive leadership was more effective when trauma severity was high (e.g., gunshot wound to head) or when the team was inexperienced.[39] Another important aspect of adaptability is for a leader to be able to function effectively in different situations, such as leading in a manufacturing or office setting or even with a different cultural group. The ability to size up people and situations and adapt tactics accordingly is a vital leadership behavior.

2   *Establishes a direction for and demands high standards of performance from group members.* A major contribution of the leader at any level is to point the group in the right direction, or work with them to figure out what the group should be doing. The direction becomes a clear vision of the future, such as point a consumer products company into the direction of one that focuses on business-to-business products.

After setting a direction, effective leaders consistently hold group members to high standards of performance, which raises productivity. (However, the leader might also set high standards for directions already in place.) Setting high expectations for subordinates becomes a self-fulfilling prophecy. People tend to live up to the expectations set for them by their superiors. Setting high expectations might take the form of encouraging team members to establish difficult objectives.

3   *Is visible and maintains a social presence.* An effective way of making an impact as a leader is to be visible to group members, thereby maintaining the perception of being present. There is a strong temptation for leaders to stay in their own work area performing analytical work or dealing with e-mail. Being visible allows for spontaneous communication with group members, and a relaxed atmosphere in which to hear about problems. Being visible also creates the opportunity for coaching group members.

4   *Provides emotional support to group members.* Supportive behavior toward subordinates usually increases leadership effectiveness. A supportive leader frequently gives encouragement and praise, such as, "Jack, if it were not for your super effort over the weekend we could have never opened the store today." The emotional support generally improves morale and sometimes improves productivity. Being emotionally supportive comes naturally to the leader who has empathy for people and who is a warm person.

5   *Gives frequent feedback and accepts feedback.* Giving group members frequent feedback on their performance is another vital leadership behavior. The manager rarely can influence the behavior of group members without appropriate performance feedback. Feedback helps in two ways. First, it informs employees of how well they are doing, so they can take corrective action if needed. Second, positive feedback encourages subordinates to keep up the good work. (More will be said about feedback in the chapter section about mentoring and coaching.)

6   *Asks powerful questions to invite exploration.* Powerful questions are open-ended and do not have an obvious answer, but instead are designed to stimulate critical thinking and stimulate discussion. Assume a logistics specialist says to her manager, "I don't know how we can ever get all the components from our suppliers here on time to meet our production schedule." A powerful question might be, "What additional support do you need to achieve your goals?"

Another aspect of making questions powerful is to respond to a request for help with a question instead of an answer.[40] Using this technique, when a group member asks about how to solve a problem, you pause, and the comeback with a question that helps the person reframe or rethink the problem. In the above request from the logistics manager, you might respond, "What approach have you tried so far?"

7   *Uses political skill to advantage.* Many of the skills of an effective leader are encompassed in political skill. The term refers to a combination of social astuteness with capacity to adjust and adapt behavior to the demands of different situations. As a result, the leader with political skill inspires trust and support and controls and influences the responses of others. At the same time, he or she appears genuine and sincere.[41] A leader with strong political skill would therefore combine such skills as adaptability to the situation and providing emotional support with the traits of intellectual ability and emotional intelligence.

Describe participative leadership, authoritarian leadership, entrepreneurial leadership, and servant leadership.

leadership style
The typical pattern of behavior that a leader uses to influence his or her employees to achieve organizational goals.

participative leader
A leader who shares decision making with group leaders.

LEADERSHIP STYLES

Another important part of the leadership function is **leadership style**. It is the typical pattern of behavior that a leader uses to influence his or her employees to achieve organizational goals. Several approaches to describing leadership styles have developed over the years. Most of these involve how much authority and control the leader turns over to the group. The historically important Theory X and Theory Y presented in Chapter 1 can be interpreted as two contrasting leadership styles. This section will describe two basic leadership styles, the participative and the autocratic, followed by a section on entrepreneurial and servant leadership styles.

Participative Leadership Style

A **participative leader** is one who shares decision making with group members. The modern organization generally favors the leader sharing decision making with group members. One key reason is that in this complex world, the leader does not have all the answers. Shared leadership mentioned in relation to empowerment might be considered an approach to carrying out the participative style. Team leaders use the participative style so frequently that participative leadership is also referred to as the *team leadership style*. Participative leadership takes many forms. The group decision making techniques described in Chapter 5 are participative because group input is relied on heavily.

Three closely related subtypes of participative leaders include consultative, consensus and democratic. *Consultative leaders* confer with subordinates before making a decision. However, they retain the final authority to make decisions. *Consensus leaders* encourage group discussion about an issue and then makes a decision that reflects the general opinion (consensus) of group members. All workers who will be involved in the consequences of a decision have an opportunity to provide input. A decision is not considered final until all parties involved agree with the decision. *Democratic leaders* confer final authority on the group. They function as collectors of opinion and take a vote before making a decision. Consensus and democratic leadership styles both run the risk of being time consuming because of the time spent in physical and electronic meetings.

Participative leadership works well with people who want to share decision making, and whose cultural values accept group members sharing leadership. Avoiding participative leadership under these conditions can be dysfunctional for the organization.

Autocratic Leadership Style

autocratic leader
A task-oriented leader who retains most of the authority for himself or herself and is not generally concerned with group members' attitudes toward decisions.

Autocratic leaders retain most of the authority for themselves. They make decisions in a confident manner and assume group members will comply. An autocratic leader is not usually concerned with the group members' attitudes toward the decision. Typical autocratic leaders tell people what to do, assert themselves, and serve as models for group members. A recent scholarly review of autocratic leadership supports the idea that directive (autocratic) leadership styles are sometimes warranted and often effective.[42] During a crisis, autocratic leadership is often welcomed because group members want someone to point them in the right direction in a hurry. Also, the situation may be so dire the leader does not have sufficient time to attain consensus on a recovery plan.

Many autocratic leaders practice hands-on-management, meaning they get involved in the details of the operation. When the leader has good expertise, the hands-on approach can be helpful in teaching others and in getting key tasks accomplished. A strong example is Elon Musk of Tesla (and a few other notable companies) who intervenes in such matters as car design and launching a space satellite. Pushed to an extreme, the hands-on style can create morale problems because many workers feel that their role is too limited.

Entrepreneurial Leadership Style

Interest in entrepreneurial leadership is intense because startup companies and other small enterprises are an important source of new employment. Many new small businesses arise to meet the demand of larger firms that outsource work. Managers who initiate one or more innovative business enterprises show several similarities in leadership style. Entrepreneurs often possess the following personal characteristics and behaviors:

1   *A strong achievement need.* Entrepreneurs have stronger achievement needs than most managers. Building a business is an excellent vehicle for accomplishment. The high achiever shows three consistent behaviors and attitudes. He or she: (a) takes personal responsibility to solve problems, (b) attempts to achieve moderate goals at moderate risks, and (c) prefers situations that provide frequent feedback on results (readily found in starting a new enterprise).[43] As part of their achievement need, entrepreneurs are often in a hurry to get projects accomplished and move on to the next project.

2   *High enthusiasm, creativity, and visionary perspective.* Related to the achievement need, entrepreneurs are typically enthusiastic, creative and visionary. Their enthusiasm, in turn, makes them persuasive. As a result, entrepreneurs are often perceived as charismatic by their employees and customers. The enthusiasm of entrepreneurs propels them into a hurrying mode much of the time. Creativity is needed to find new business ideas. Successful entrepreneurs carefully observe the world around them, in constant search for their next big marketable idea, leading to a vision. They see opportunities others fail to observe.

3   *Uncomfortable with hierarchy and bureaucracy.* Entrepreneurs, by temperament, are not ideally suited to working within the mainstream of a bureaucracy. Many successful entrepreneurs are people who were frustrated by the constraints of a bureaucratic system. Once the typical entrepreneur launches a successful business, he or she often hires a professional manager to take over the internal workings of the firm. The entrepreneur is then free to concentrate on making sales, raising capital and pursuing other external contacts. One of the reasons entrepreneurs have difficulty with bureaucracy is that they focus their energies on products, services and customers. Some entrepreneurs are gracious to customers and moneylenders but brusque with company insiders.

4   *Addiction to work.* A potential problem for many entrepreneurs is that they become addicted to work thereby neglecting personal life, rest, and proper physical exercise. The enterprise the entrepreneur founded becomes important enough to become an obsession. Many entrepreneurs work 70 to

80 hours per week to sustain their enterprise. During a period of production problems with the Tesla, Elon Musk was reported to have worked over 100 hours per week, and slept at the factory. Among the findings for the dark side of entrepreneurship is that some entrepreneurs experience extreme feelings of loneliness. Furthermore, they repeatedly put their family and personal relationships at risk because of their pursuit of entrepreneurship.[44] A contributor to entrepreneurial addiction is that the entrepreneur lacks the fund to properly staff the enterprise.

Servant Leadership Style

Some effective leaders believe their primary mission is to serve the needs of their constituents, including employees, customers and communities. They measure their effectiveness in terms of their ability to help others. Servant leaders see themselves as stewards of the organization who seek to grow the organizations physical, financial, and human resources. Among the many business firms implementing servant leadership practices in at least part of the organization are Starbucks, Southwest Airlines, Container Store, Intel, and Marriott.

Servant leaders usually show qualities, such as patience, honesty, good listening skills and appreciation of others. Instead of seeking individual recognition, servant leaders see themselves as working for the group members. Another defining characteristic of servant leaders is their high level of integrity. The servant leader uses his or her talents to help group members. For example, if the leader happens to be a good planner, he engages in planning because it will help the group attain its goals.

An important contribution of the servant leader is to build a sense of kinship in the group, similar to the feeling of belonging to a family or closely-knit sports team. The kinship within the group helps members feel that their well-being and growth are prioritized. As a result, they are more committed to their work, and tend to perform better.[45]

In research studies, the assessment of whether a given person is a servant leader is made by group member responses to questions, such as the following:

- My leader makes my career development a priority.
- My leader puts my best interests ahead of his or her interests.
- My leader emphasizes the importance of giving back to the community.[46]

A study of how servant leaders contribute to individual and organizational unit performance was conducted in 71 restaurants of a large chain. A major finding was that leaders who established a serving culture within the store (restaurant) had a positive impact on employee and restaurant performance, creativity and positive customer service. A key explanation of the findings was that group members model the servant leader behaviors of their formal leaders, creating a service culture at the store level.[47] (In short, the serve staff serves better under a servant leader!)

Many academic administrators see themselves as servant leaders; they take care of administrative work so instructors can devote more time to teaching and scholarship. To be an effective servant leader, a person needs the many leadership traits and behaviors described in this chapter.

The accompanying *Management in Action* insert describes a prominent business executive who shows elements of being a both a participative and servant leader.

MANAGEMENT IN ACTION

Merck CEO Kenneth Frazier Pushes Hard to Grow the Company and Help Humanity

Kenneth C. Frazier is chairman of the board and CEO of Merck & Co, and also a director of a couple of major business corporations, a member of the board of overseers of a medical college, and a trustee of a private high school. (The company is referred to as Merck in the United States and Canada.) He is the first African American to be CEO of a major pharmaceutical firm. Merck & Co. Inc. is a global healthcare leader that develops and manufactures prescription medicines, vaccines, biologic therapies, and consumer care and animal health products. Founded in 1891, the company operates in more than 140 countries to provide medicine and healthcare solutions, and has 69,000 employees worldwide.

Frazier's strategy for the pharmaceutical giant Merck is to expand its pipeline of breakthrough drugs, expand its international business, and save millions of lives throughout the world. He notes, "When one runs a company like Merck that has long lead times in terms of development, you're not necessarily running the company for the immediate reaction of the stock market." Frazier hopes Merck will be first to market with life-saving drugs, but he is also happy when a competitor contributes to combatting disease and saving lives.

Prior to being appointed CEO and Chairman, Frazier was president of Merck with responsibility for three major divisions: global human health, manufacturing and the research laboratories. Frazier's joining Merck stemmed from representing the company as a partner in a large Philadelphia law firm.

Several people who have worked with Frazier credit his analytical yet accessible leadership style with creating an innovative and highly disciplined organization. Mirian Graddick Weir, the executive vice president of human resources at Merck, describes Frazier as being the right combination of, "head, heart, and guts." On the head side he is good at asking the right questions so the executive team can focus on core issues and carrying out the company mission. On the heart side he has exceptional ability to connect with people at all levels in the organization. He helps people be optimistic about the future but also recognize challenges. The guts component refers to his candor and not being afraid to make tough decisions.

As the CEO, Frazier professes a deep commitment to letting the company scientists do their job, recognizing they are the backbone to producing new pharmaceuticals. Frazier says, "I am a person who does not subscribe to the hero-CEO school of thought." Instead of reducing costs to boost profits, Frazier invests heavily in research and development hoping the company will discover the next effective drug for combatting disease and early death.

Frazier is recognized for saving the company as general counsel because he successfully managed thousands of lawsuits related to the alleged harmful effects of the painkiller, Vioxx. This accomplishment led to his becoming chairman and CEO of Merck. Frazier is noted for his humanitarian approach to business. For example, he spearheaded donations to a program to treat millions of people in African and South American countries who suffered from the parasitic disease, "river blindness." In recent years, Frazier has led the company through a period of growth fueled partly by the highly successful cancer drug Keytruda, that surpassed sales of $7 billion in 2018.

Although Frazier has had a long and distinguished career the company, in 2020, the Merck board began preliminary planning for his eventual replacement, with a preference for an internal candidate.

Frazier received a B. A. degree from Pennsylvania State University and a J. D. degree from Harvard Law School.

Questions

1 **What evidence do you find that Frazier should be classified as a servant leader?**

2 **What evidence do you find that Frazier should be classified as a participative leader?**

3 **How ethical do you think it is for the general counsel of a pharmaceutical firm to actively combat lawsuits against the firm in relation to the side effects of a pain-killing drug?**

Source: Original story created from facts and observations in the following sources: "Kenneth Frazier—The 25 Most Influential People In Biopharma Today," *FierceBiotech* (www.fiercebiotech.com) pp. 1–2. © 2016 Fierce Markets; Eric Sagonowsky, "Merck Scouts Replacements for CEO Frazier Less than a Year After Scrapping Retirement Rule: Report," *Fierce Pharma* (www.fiercepharma.com), June 19, 2019, pp. 1–3; Robert Hanfield, "Leadership Personified: Jen Frazier, CEO of Merck," *https://scm.ncsu.edu/scm-articles/article/leadership-personified-ken-frazier-ceo-of-merck*, October 18, 2017, pp. 1–4; "Kenneth Frazier's Prescription for Growth," *Black Enterprise*, July/August 2014, pp. 52–58.

Describe transformational and charismatic leadership.

transformational leader
A leader who helps organizations and people make positive changes in the way they do things.

TRANSFORMATIONAL AND CHARISMATIC LEADERSHIP

The study of leadership often emphasizes the **transformational leader**—one who helps organizations and people make positive changes in the way they do things. According to transformational leadership theory, exceptional performance takes place because of a sense of mission and new ways of thinking and learning.[48] Transformational leadership combines charisma, inspirational leadership and intellectual stimulation. It plays an especially critical role in the revitalization of existing business organizations. The transformational leader develops new visions for the organization and mobilizes employees to accept and work toward attaining these visions. Transformational leadership is usually required for bringing about large-scale organizational change, as described in Chapter 8.

Transformational leadership often takes the form of turnaround management in which the leader spearheads the rescue of a failing firm. The late Jack Byrne is regarded as the best turnaround artist in insurance. Today, most people have heard of Geico because of their incessant television advertising. In 1976, the auto insurance company, the Government Employees Insurance Co. was close to bankruptcy. Geico had lost $124 million the previous year. As newly appointed CEO, Byrne cut costs by closing offices and laying off employees. He increased premiums and jettisoned money-losing operations while negotiating a reinsurance agreement with other insurance companies. He also issued $75 million in stock to raise capital. Berkshire Hathaway (with Warren Buffet as CEO) became the major investor in Geico, and eventually acquired the company. After Geico, Byrne turned around another major insurer, the Fireman's Fund Insurance Co.[49]

This section will describe how transformations take place, the role of charisma, how to become charismatic, and the downside of charismatic leadership.

How Transformations Take Place

The transformational leader attempts to overhaul the organizational culture or subculture, and to make a difference in people's lives. To bring about the overhaul, transformations take place in a few different ways.[50] First, the transformational leader raises people's awareness of the importance and value of certain rewards and how to achieve them. He or she points out the pride workers would experience if the firm became number one in its field. Second, the transformational leader gets people to look beyond their self-interests for the sake of the work group and the firm. Such a leader might say, "I know you would like more healthcare benefits. But, if we don't cut expenses, we'll all be out of a job." Third, the transformational leader helps people go beyond a focus on minor satisfactions to a quest for self-fulfillment. He or she might explain, "I know that a long lunch break is nice. But, just think, if we get this project done on time, we'll be the envy of the company."

One of many studies indicating that transformational leadership makes a difference in performance was conducted by Robert T. Keller with 118 research and development project teams from five firms. Subordinate perceptions of transformational leadership (including charisma) were measured by a standard measure of such leadership. The results demonstrated transformational leadership was positively related to the technical quality of the projects produced and on-schedule performance one year later. Even more impressive, perceptions of transformational leadership were associated with five-year profitability of the products developed by the project teams, as well as product speed to market.[51]

Transformational leaders put so much energy and time into bringing about transformations they sometimes suffer personally. A study conducted with leaders and their direct reports found leaders who engaged in transformational behaviors were subject to emotional exhaustion (or burnout) and thoughts about quitting. When followers were low on conscientiousness and competence, the probability of emotional exhaustion and quitting were higher.[52] No surprise here!

Charismatic Leadership

A leader's personality can be a big part of his or her effectiveness. **Charisma** is the ability to lead or influence others based on personal charm, magnetism, inspiration and emotion. To label a leader as charismatic does not mean everybody shares that opinion. Even the most popular and inspiring leaders are perceived negatively by some members of their organization or their constituents. Quite often these negative perceptions are communicated on blogs and social networking sites. Charismatic leadership is important because it often leads to enhanced motivation and satisfaction among subordinates. A study with firefighters demonstrated that the firefighters under the command of an officer they perceived to be charismatic were happier than their counterparts working for an officer perceived to be non-charismatic.[53] The list that follows presents leaders' qualities that relate specifically to charisma.[54]

charisma
The ability to lead or influence others based on personal charm, magnetism, inspiration, and emotion.

1 *Vision.* Charismatic leaders offer an exciting image of where the organization is headed and how to get there. A vision is more than a forecast, because it describes an ideal version of the future for an organization or organizational unit. Being visionary is almost synonymous with charisma. Jeff Bezos of Amazon.com created a vision for his company becoming the world's most important store that has come true. Along the way he turned e-commerce from a far-fetched idea into a method of delivering goods that has changed the world marketplace.[55]

2 *Masterful communication style.* To inspire people, charismatic and transformational leaders use colorful language and exciting metaphors and analogies. A former CEO of Coca-Cola told people, "We give people around the world a moment of pleasure in their daily lives." Another key aspect of the communication style of transformational leaders is that they tell captivating stories that relate to the goals of the firm. For example, some leaders use the fairy tale, "The Three Little Pigs," to illustrate how business firms must make products and services stronger to withstand competitive force. Telling interesting stories with a message is also part of the masterful communication style. For instance, a division head might tell a true story of how workers at the division once saved the company by working 60 hours a week to win a vital government contract.

3 *Elicits trust.* People believe so strongly in the integrity of charismatic leaders that they will risk their careers to pursue the leader's vision. Also, when a charismatic leader leaves an organization, several subordinates often follow the leader to his or her next firm.

4 *Energy and action orientation.* Similar to entrepreneurs, most charismatic leaders are energetic and serve as a model for getting things done on time.

5 *Inspiring leadership.* Partly as a result of the four preceding characteristics, transformational and charismatic leaders emotionally arouse people to the point that they want to achieve higher goals than they thought of previously. In short, the charismatic leader stands as an inspiration to many others.

6 *A touch of narcissism.* A narcissistic leader is typically thought of as being too self-absorbed to care about the welfare of others and the organization. Yet when narcissism is combined with a touch of humility, the leader will often be perceived as effective, as demonstrated in a study of a large health insurance company.[56] Personality psychologist Scott Barry Kaufman reports narcissism and leadership go hand in hand. The fun-loving narcissist often enjoys widespread networking and being dominant in a group, not solely for the purpose of wanting to exploit others. The narcissist's real motive is to receive positive reinforcement from many people.[57]

Charisma may indeed be related to personality factors, but often a leader is perceived as charismatic because he or she attained outstanding performance. A study of 33 team leaders and 142 team members demonstrated this relationship. Team leaders were perceived as more charismatic when they bring about constructive change, such as improving a work process.[58] Self-sacrificing leaders also tend to be perceived as charismatic. Followers tend to perceive leaders who exhibited more sacrifice and less self-benefit as more charismatic. As a result, group members develop stronger commitment to and support of the leader.[59]

Katrina Lake, the founder and CEO of Stitch Fix, the clothing and accessories subscription service, is an example of a transformational and charismatic leader. The company uses algorithms and expert stylists to select a box of clothing for clients. Lake is a likeable, stylish and energetic person who built the company into an over $1 billion sales powerhouse by combining data analytics with a human touch. She still takes the time to helps clients individually.[60] Her charisma is reflected in the devotion she engenders in employees, and the many people wanting to work for and with her, and her high number of social media followers.

Developing Charisma

Managers can improve their image as charismatic by engaging in favorable interactions with group members through a variety of techniques.[61] A starting point is to *use visioning.* Develop a dream about the future of your unit and discuss it with others. *Make frequent use of metaphors.* Develop metaphors to inspire the people around you. A commonly used one after the group has experienced a substantial setback is to say, "Like the phoenix, we will rise from the ashes of defeat." *It is important to inspire trust and confidence.* Get people to believe in your competence by making your accomplishments known in a polite, tactful way. *Focus on the positive.* Charismatic people are optimists who minimize complaints and emphasize what positive steps can be taken to overcome a problem.

Be highly energetic and goal oriented so your energy and resourcefulness become contagious. To increase your energy supply, exercise frequently, eat well and get ample rest. It is important to express your emotions frequently. Freely express warmth, joy, happiness, and enthusiasm. *Smile frequently*, even if you are not in a happy mood. A warm smile indicates a confident, caring person, which contributes to perceptions of charisma. *Make everybody you meet feel important.* For example, at a company meeting shake the hand of, or give a fist bump to every person you meet. Another way of making people feel important is giving them assignments in which they have a high chance of succeeding, and then giving positive feedback.

A relatively easy characteristic to develop is to *multiply the effectiveness of your handshake.* Shake firmly without creating pain and make enough eye contact to notice the color of the other person's eyes. When you take that much trouble, you project care and concern. Finally, *stand up straight and use nonverbal signs of self-confidence.* Practice good posture and minimize fidgeting and speaking in a monotone. Finally, maintaining eye contact frequently and a relatively long period with other people has been scientifically demonstrated to being perceived as charismatic.[62]

The Downside of Charismatic Leadership

Charismatic business leaders are seen as corporate heroes when they can turn around a failing business or launch a new enterprise. Charismatic leaders whose efforts benefit others are sometimes referred to as socialized charismatics. Nevertheless, this type of leadership has a dark side. Some charismatic leaders manipulate and take advantage of people, such as by getting them to invest retirement savings in risky company stock. Some charismatic leaders are unethical and lead their organizations toward illegal and immoral ends. People are willing to follow the charismatic leader down a quasi-legal path because of his or her charisma. An historically significant example is Bernard Madoff, the former CEO and chairman of his own investment company as well as the ex-president of NASDAQ. Madoff was perceived as charming and persuasive. He encouraged individual consumers as well as stockbrokers to invest money in his firm, and swindled people out of an estimated $50 billion.

Another concern about some charismatic business leaders is that they begin to perceive themselves as superstars who accomplish most of the company leadership by themselves. Some of these charismatic executives become so caught up in receiving publicity and mingling with politicians and investors, they neglect the operations of the business. Because of this, more low-key executive leaders—especially those who focus on internal operations—are more in style than previously. Tara Comonte of Shake Shack (described in chapter opener) is one such executive who digs into her job with little concern about attaining celebrity.

THE LEADER AS A MENTOR AND COACH

Another vital part of leadership is directly assisting less experienced workers to improve their job performance and advance their careers. A **mentor** is a more experienced person who develops a protégé's abilities through tutoring, coaching, guidance and emotional support. The mentor helps the person being mentored grow by challenging him or her to deal with difficult situations (such as joining a task force) or deal with a difficult work problem. The idea of mentoring traces back to ancient Greece when a warrior entrusted his son to a tutor, named Méntōr.

LEARNING OBJECTIVE **6**

Explain the leadership role of mentoring and coaching.

mentor
A more experienced person who develops a protégé's abilities through tutoring, coaching, guidance, and emotional support.

Although never out of style, mentoring is more important than ever as workers face complex and rapidly changing job demands.

As with all forms of communication in organizations, a good deal of mentoring takes place online, such as sending a manager an e-mail asking for help with a specific problem. It is also possible to use an online mentoring program that facilitates asking for help with a specific problem. In this way the person asking for guidance might have access to multiple mentors.

Coaching deals with helping others improve performance, and will be described more fully in Chapter 15. Quite often the mentor is also a coach, but a manager who coaches another person may not be a mentor. Lou Holtz, one of the most successful coaches in college football history, and later an advisor to managers, offers leaders important justification for mentoring and coaching: "Your job is to make people the very best they can be. And that is when you get them out of their comfort zone because most people don't know how good they can be."[63]

A mentor, a trusted counselor and guide, is typically a person's manager or team leader. For mentorship to succeed there has to be a good relationship, or good chemistry, between the mentor and mentee. Research suggests that even the best-designed mentoring programs are not a substitute for a genuine, comfortable relationship between the two parties.[64] Mentors are typically within the field of expertise of the protégé, but can also come from another specialty. For example, a manufacturing manager might mentor an accountant. A leader can be a mentor to several people at the same time, and successful individuals often have several mentors during their career.

Helping the protégé solve problems is an important part of mentoring. Mentors help their protégés solve problems by themselves and make their own discoveries. A comment frequently made to mentors is, "I'm glad you made me think through the problem. You put me on the right track." A mentor can also give specific assistance in technical problem solving. If the mentor knows more about the new technology than the protégé, he or she can shorten the person's learning time.

Mentoring has traditionally been an informal relationship based on compatibility between two personalities. As with other trusted friends, good chemistry should exist between the mentor and the protégé. Many mentoring programs assign a mentor to selected new employees. Formal mentors often supplement the work of managers by assisting a newcomer to acquire job skills and understand the organization culture.

shadowing
Directly observing the work activities of the mentor by following the manager around for a stated period of time, such as one day per month.

A popular approach to mentoring is **shadowing**, or directly observing the work activities of the mentor by following the manager around for a stated period of time, such as one day per month. The protégé might be invited to strategy meetings, visits with key customers, discussions with union leaders, and the like. The protégé makes observations about how the mentor handles situations, and a debriefing session might be held to discuss how and why certain tactics were used.

To capitalize on the potential advantages of mentoring, develop or build on good relationships with superiors and request feedback on performance at least once a year. Find and identify an informal mentor who is willing to be an advocate for your upward mobility within the organization, help you learn the informal rules of the workplace, and help you make valuable contacts. Your mentor will help you identify the informal rules of the company that are helpful in navigating through the organization. (An example would be "Never turn down a request from upper management.")

LEADERSHIP DURING ADVERSITY AND CRISIS

As suggested at many places in this book, an important role of both managers and leaders is to help the group deal with adversity and crisis. Adversity and crises may take such forms as a downturn in business, a sudden surge in workload that workers perceive as overwhelming, hurricanes, fire damage, a massive product recall, and workplace violence. Almost all the principles and techniques of leadership would be helpful during difficult times, but here we pinpoint nine behaviors and actions that are particularly relevant for a leader dealing with adversity and crisis.[65]

1 *Directive leadership.* The best accepted principle of crisis leadership is that the leader should take decisive action to remedy the situation. The graver the crisis, the less time the leader has to consult a wide array of people. Crisis leadership provokes a centralization of authority. A key part of managing a crisis well is for the leader to present a plan for dealing with the crisis, and at the same time to be calm and reassuring. To implement a plan for coping with adversity, the management team must be extra disciplined in terms of paying attention to operational details, listening to customer complaints, and communicating new developments with each other.

2 *Serve as a model by being resilient.* Effective managerial leaders are resilient: Resilience is both an attitude and a skill.[66] They bounce back quickly from setbacks such as budget cuts, demotions and being fired. Leadership resiliency serves as a positive model for employees at all levels when the organization confronts difficult times. During such times effective leaders sprinkle their speech with clichés such as, "Tough times don't last, but tough people do," or, "When times get tough, the tough get going." Delivered with sincerity, such messages are inspirational to many employees and therefore may help stabilize morale.

3 *Appear confident and trustworthy.* Group members must trust that the leader or leaders can deal with the crisis. Trust can often be attained by communicating openly, honestly and often about the crisis. In dealing with a crisis, it is helpful for the leader to project confident body language, such as appearing relaxed while delivering the crisis plan.

4 *Focus on the future.* Part of being visionary is focusing on the future when the present is filled with difficulty. The leader of a software company might tell the group that technology investment has dipped for the present, but companies will soon recognize they cannot compete well in the long run if they do not upgrade their information technology soon. A bold move to focus on the future is to get into the scavenger mode. For example, a CEO might buy out a struggling competitor and hire talented people who have been laid off from competitors. Top management might also purchase real estate at distressed prices to later earn a big increase in market value. Focusing on the future can be considered an act of transformational leadership.

5 *Communicate widely about the problem.* When tough times hit, it pays to increase communication about the problems facing the company or unit, and what might be done to improve the situation. By communicating with workers throughout the organization, managers will have an opportunity to provide leadership. In one company, a technician suggested the company focus more on servicing existing equipment than attempting to sell new equipment during

LEARNING OBJECTIVE 7

Pinpoint leadership approaches to dealing with adversity and crises.

the recession. Communicating with customers as well as their customers can bring forth useful information about how long the tough times will remain. The business can be reconfigured to meet the new reality, such as finding the least painful ways to cut costs.

6 *Change to meet the changing circumstances.* A bold leadership move is to change the thrust of a company's activities to adapt to changing circumstances. In many geographic locations the operators of shopping malls have faced a crisis because so many retail stores have closed their physical stores. The surviving malls changed their tenant mix by marketing with success to replacement renters such as medical offices, gyms, education centers, and government offices.

7 *Stick with constructive core values.* Leaders who keep their company or division focused on core values are likely to endure difficult times. Lowering core values to help overcome adversity can create permanent damage. Take this humble example: A well-known underwear company decided to cope with lower sales volume by cutting costs on the manufacture of men's briefs. The lower-cost briefs looked fine, but they tore apart at the waistband after several washings. Word spread quickly about the defective briefs, and the company lost accounts with several major retail chains. The core value compromised here was offering only high-quality goods to the public.

8 *Divide major problems into smaller chunks.* Give workers bits of the major problem to work on so they feel less overwhelmed by the adversity facing them and the company. For example, if the company is hurting for cash, one group of employees might search for items in the office or factory that could be sold on an auction website. Another group of workers might search for ways to reduce shipping costs by 10 percent. Other groups would be assigned different adversity-fighting tasks. When an obstacle is framed as too large, too complex, or too challenging, workers might feel overwhelmed and therefore freeze in their tracks.

9 *Lead with compassion.* Crises can take a heavy emotional toll on workers. Compassionate leadership encompasses two related sets of actions. The first is to create an environment in which affected workers can freely discuss how they feel, such as a group meeting to talk about the adversity, crisis, or disaster. The second is to create an environment in which the workers who experience or witness pain can find a method to alleviate their own suffering or that of others. The leader might establish a special fund to help the families who were victims of a disaster, such as a hurricane or earthquake, or give workers the opportunity to receive grief counseling.

LEADERSHIP SKILLS

LEARNING OBJECTIVE 8

Identify several skills that contribute to leadership.

Leadership involves personal qualities, behaviors, and skills. A skill refers to a present capability, such as being able to resolve conflict or create a vision statement. Many of these leadership skills have been mentioned or implied throughout the book. A prime example would be the five general skills for managers described in Chapter 1: technical, interpersonal, conceptual, diagnostic, and political. For example, to exercise strategic leadership, a manager would need to have strong conceptual skills. To inspire people, a leader would need interpersonal skills. To negotiate well, he or she would need good political skills. To be an effective face-to-face leader, the manager would need coaching skills, as described in Chapter 16.

The leadership roles presented in Chapter 1 directly associated with leadership skills are as follows: negotiator, coach, team builder, technical problem solver and entrepreneur. The following checklist provides some additional skills that can contribute to leadership effectiveness, depending on the people and the task.

- Sizing up situations in order to apply the best leadership approach.
- Exerting influence through various approaches such as rational persuasion, inspirational appeal, and being assertive.
- Motivating team members through such specific techniques as goal setting and positive reinforcement.
- Motivating people from diverse cultures and nations.
- Resolving conflict with superiors and group members.
- Solving problems creatively in ways that point group members in new directions.
- Developing a vision statement that inspires others to perform well.
- Displaying empathy to communicate better with constituents and gain their commitment.

As implied by this discussion, leadership involves dozens of different skills. The skills are particularly useful when they help build human connections. An effective manager's toolkit combines various skills according to the leader's needs and the situation. Holding a leadership position offers a wonderful opportunity for personal growth through skill development.

1 Differentiate between leadership and management.

Management is a set of explicit tools and techniques based on reasoning and testing that can be used in a variety of situations. Leadership is concerned with vision, change, motivation, persuasion, creativity, inspiration and influence.

2 Describe how leaders are able to influence and empower team members.

Power is the ability to get other people to do things or the ability to control resources. Authority is the formal right to wield power. Six types of power include legitimate, reward, coercive, expert, referent (stemming from charisma) and subordinate. Through subordinate power, team members limit the authority of leaders. To get others to act, leaders also use tactics such as leading by example, leading by values, assertiveness, rationality, ingratiation, exchange, coalition formation, and joking and kidding.

Empowerment is the process of sharing power with team members to enhance their feelings of personal effectiveness. A key belief of empowerment is that leadership in a team can and should be shared. Empowerment increases employee motivation, because the employee is accepted as a partner in decision making. For empowerment to work well, people have to exercise self-leadership, and cross-cultural factors in the acceptance of empowerment must be considered.

3 Identify important leadership characteristics.

Certain personal characteristics are associated with successful managerial leadership in many situations, including the following: drive and passion; power motive; self-confidence combined with humility; proactivity, trustworthiness and honesty; good intellectual ability, knowledge, and technical competence; sense of humor and mindfulness, emotional intelligence; and leadership efficacy.

Effective leaders need to demonstrate adaptability, establish a direction and set high standards of performance, be visible and maintain a social presence, and provide emotional support to group members. They should give and accept feedback, ask powerful questions to invite exploration, and use political skills to best advantage.

4 Describe participative leadership, authoritarian leadership, entrepreneurial leadership, and servant leadership.

Leadership style is the typical pattern of behavior that a leader uses to influence employees to achieve organizational goals. Participative leaders share decision making with the group. One subtype of participative leader is the consultative leader, who involves subordinates in decision making but retains final authority. A consensus leader also involves subordinates in decision making and bases the final decision on group consensus. A democratic leader confers final authority on the group. Autocratic leaders attempt to retain most of the authority.

Entrepreneurial leaders often have a strong achievement need, high enthusiasm and creativity, and a visionary perspective. They are uncomfortable with hierarchy and bureaucracy, often because they focus their energies on products, services and customers. Work addiction is a potential problem for entrepreneurial leaders.

Servant leaders have the primary mission of serving the needs of their constituents. They measure their effectiveness in terms of their ability to help others. Instead of seeking recognition, they see themselves as working for group members, including the use of their talents to be helpful.

5 Describe transformational and charismatic leadership.

The transformational leader helps organizations and people make positive changes. He or she combines charisma, inspirational leadership and intellectual stimulation. Transformations take place by pointing to relevant rewards, getting people to look beyond self-interest, and encouraging them to work toward self-fulfillment. Charismatic leaders provide vision and masterful communication. They can inspire trust and help people feel capable, and they are action-oriented. Performing well may lead to being perceived as charismatic. Some charismatic leaders are unethical and use their power to accomplish illegal and immoral ends. Managers can improve their image as charismatic by engaging in favorable interactions with group members through a variety of techniques including visioning, and having an effective handshake.

6 **Explain the leadership role of mentoring and coaching.**

Mentoring is more important than ever, as workers face complex and rapidly changing job demands. Coaching is part of mentoring. Mentors help protégés solve problems by themselves and make their own discoveries. Mentoring can be an informal or formal relationship. Shadowing is a useful part of mentoring.

7 **Pinpoint leadership approaches to dealing with adversity and crises.**

An important role of leaders and managers is to help the group deal with adversity and crisis. This requires leaders to: be directive; be a model of resilience; plan for adversity or crisis; appear confident and trustworthy; focus on the future; communicate widely about the problem; change to meet changing circumstances; stick with core values; divide problems into chunks; and lead with compassion.

8 **Identify several skills that contribute to leadership.**

To be an effective leader, a manager must possess a wide variety of skills, many of which are described throughout this chapter and this book. Among these diverse skills are exerting influence, motivating others, solving problems creatively, and displaying empathy.

Key Terms and Phrases

leadership 291

power 292

authority 292

coalition 294

self-leadership 295

power motivation 297

open-book company 299

mindfulness 300

leadership efficacy 301

leadership style 303

participative leader 303

autocratic leader 303

transformational leader 307

charisma 308

mentor 310

shadowing 311

Questions

1. Shake Shack, as well as other fast-casual and fast-food restaurants, insist that their managers get some experience working the front lines. Why might such experiences be important for a future executive?

2. In what way does a first-level supervisor play an important leadership role in the organization?

3. Which of the influence tactics described in this chapter do you think will work in dealing with corporate professionals? Explain your reasoning.

4. How would a leader know whether a given subordinate, or group of subordinates, is trustworthy enough to be empowered?

5. The entrepreneurial spirit has become increasingly embraced in corporations of all sizes. What could you do to develop your entrepreneurial spirit?

6. Suppose you believe you would be more effective as a leader or potential leader if you were more charismatic. What would be a realistic action plan for you to begin this month to become more charismatic?

7. What experiences have you already had in life that would prepare you for leading subordinates through adversity?

Skill-Building Exercise 10-A: My Leadership Journal

A potentially important aid in your development as a leader is to maintain a journal or diary of your experiences. Make a journal entry within 24 hours after you have carried out a significant leadership action or failed to do so when the opportunity arose. You will have entries dealing with leadership opportunities both capitalized upon and missed. An example, "A few of my neighbors were complaining about all the vandalism in the neighborhood. Cars were getting dented and scratched, and lamplights were being smashed. A few bricks were thrown into home windows. I volunteered to organize a neighborhood patrol. The patrol actually helped cut back on the vandalism." Or, in contrast: "A few of my neighbors'

windows were broken. I thought to myself someone else should take care of the problem. My time is too valuable."

Also include in your journal such entries as feedback you receive on your leadership ability, leadership traits you appear to be developing, and key leadership ideas you read about. Review your journal monthly and make note of any progress you think you have made in developing your leadership skills. Also consider preparing a graph of your leadership skill development. The vertical axis can represent skill level on a 1-to-100 scale, and the horizontal axis might be divided into time intervals, such as calendar quarters.

Skill-Building Exercise 10-B: My Self-Leadership Tendencies

Directions: Indicate the extent to which each of the following statements describes your behavior or attitude by circling one number. The numbers refer to disagree strongly (DS), disagree (D), neither agree nor disagree (N), agree (A), and agree strongly (AS). Consider enlisting the help of someone who knows your behavior and attitudes well to help you respond accurately to the statements.

Statement Related to Self-Leadership	DS	D	N	A	AS
1 I frequently take the initiative to work on a problem that appears to need fixing, even if not strictly assigned the problem.	1	2	3	4	5
2 I prefer to consult with my manager before taking action when I face a controversy.	5	4	3	2	1
3 Without a clear company vision, it would be difficult for me to figure out what to do most workdays.	5	4	3	2	1
4 I work best when I have a detailed and unambiguous job description.	5	4	3	2	1
5 I establish many of my work goals.	1	2	3	4	5
6 I look for work activities that I find personally rewarding.	1	2	3	4	5
7 I often set my own performance goals.	1	2	3	4	5
8 I often set goals for my personal life.	1	2	3	4	5
9 I keep careful track of how well I am performing an assigned or self-generated project.	1	2	3	4	5
10 I reward myself for a job well done.	1	2	3	4	5
11 I think of myself successfully performing a task before getting started.	1	2	3	4	5
12 I often doubt whether I can reach a goal I have set.	5	4	3	2	1
13 When working on a difficult assignment, I sometimes say to myself "I know I can do it."	1	2	3	4	5
14 I typically ask permission before doing any activity out of the ordinary.	5	4	3	2	1
15 I would enjoy working for a person I only saw two or three times a year.	1	2	3	4	5
16 When I have not performed well on a task, I tend to be self-critical.	1	2	3	4	5
17 It would be very difficult for me to work from home because I need frequent supervision.	5	4	3	2	1
18 It would be very difficult for me to work from home because I am easily distracted.	5	4	3	2	1
19 I have performed at about the same level no matter what kind of boss was supervising me.	1	2	3	4	5
20 I need a lot of feedback along the way to perform well on a project.	5	4	3	2	1

Scoring and interpretation: Calculate your score by adding up the numbers circled.

90–100 Your self-leadership attitudes and behaviors are quite strong. These attributes should be notable assets in your career and studies.

70–89 Your self-leadership attitudes and behaviors are above average. These attributes should be assets in your career and studies.

16–69 Your self-leadership attitudes and behavior are below average. Your job performance would probably improve if you enhanced your self-leadership.

1–15 Your self-leadership attitudes and behavior are quite low. Another possible explanation for your low score is that you happened to take this quiz when you are in a bad mood and not feeling good about yourself. A self-leadership score this low suggests you need considerable supervision and leadership to perform well.

Skill development: The quiz you just completed is also an opportunity for skill development. Review the 20 questions and look for implied suggestions for engaging in self-leadership. For example, question 5 has to do with goal setting. If you rarely set goals for yourself, being more active in setting goals for yourself might enhance your self-leadership.

Skill-Building Exercise 10-C: Learning from a Successful Leader

Find a written story about a business or sports leader who achieved a high degree of success in his or her leadership role. Identify several traits or behaviors that contributed to the leader being successful. Identify also what you learned from the leader that could help you succeed in a present or future leadership role.

Management Now—Online Skill-Building Exercise: Charisma Tips from the 'Net

A section in this chapter offered suggestions for becoming more charismatic. Search the Internet for additional suggestions and compare them to the suggestions in the text. Use a search phrase, such as, "How to become more charismatic." Be alert to contradictions and offer possible explanations for them. You might want to classify the suggestions into two categories: those dealing with the inner person, and those dealing with more superficial aspects of behavior. A suggestion of more depth would be to become a visionary, and a suggestion of less depth would be to wear eye-catching clothing.

Tyler Asks Loads of Questions

Tyler majored in business administration with a concentration in marketing, and he is delighted with his career progress. He joined the pet food division of a large company 10 years ago as a product specialist for biscuits that help remove plaque from the teeth of dogs. Tyler says with a smile, "I was torn between studying dentistry and marketing. My first job was therefore a perfect fit for my interests."

Tyler now holds the position of general manager of pet foods, with a team of six people directly reporting to him, and 450 total employees. Tyler has learned that a leader does not have all the answers, so he or she should ask lots of questions. He also believes the right questions will get people thinking.

During a recent meeting with his sales manager, Ashley, Tyler asked, "What's to prevent consumers from serving mostly table food to their dogs and cats instead of purchasing our expensive products?" Ashley responded, "Let me think about that one. It never occurred to me that our industry was in jeopardy."

The next day Tyler sent a text message to José, a new product development specialist, that asked, "How have you justified your pay this month?" José sent a message back, "I've been working 45 hours a week. Isn't that enough?"

The following day, Tyler dropped by the cubicle of Alicia, the department administrative assistant, and asked her, "How can I improve my communication with you?" Alicia responded, "I thought that our communication was pretty good."

While having lunch with Calvin, the director of human resources, Tyler asked, "Can you please explain to me how your group is increasing our revenue, improving our products or saving us money?" Calvin replied, "With all due respect Tyler, you need more information about what HR does for an organization."

The following week during a staff meeting, Tyler asked his team, "What should I be doing to help make our division the best pet food division in the industry?" Chelsea, the director of supply chain management, replied: "I'm going to need time to think about this one."

Case Questions

1 How effective does Tyler appear to be in his approach of asking tough questions as a leadership technique?

2 What suggestions can you offer Tyler to make his questioning technique more effective?

3 What style of leadership does Tyler appear to be demonstrating when he asks his team, "What should I be doing to help make our division the best pet food division in the industry?"

Servant Leader Nicole

Nicole is the manager in charge of the mortgage department of a financial services firm. While studying for an MBA part time, she heard and read a lot about the importance of servant leadership. Nicole decided that she would strive to be a servant leader on the job whenever feasible. Her first act as a servant leader was to send an e-mail to her ten direct reports stating, "I may hold the title of mortgage department manager, but I am also a colleague who wants you to achieve your goals." Nicole received a few positive replies, including four smiley faces or similar emojis.

A few days later Brooklyn, the customer service manager, said that she would be absent Friday of the current week to attend a neighbor's funeral. Nicole told Brooklyn not to worry because she (Nicole) had experience in customer service, and would take over her responsibilities on Friday. Brooklyn thanked Nicole for her understanding and willingness to help.

The following week, Nicole was conducting a performance evaluation of Frank, a loan officer who wanted to advance his career. Nicole told Frank that she would do what she could to find an opportunity for Frank to work in the commercial mortgage department so he could broaden his experience. Nicole also told Frank that she would investigate what money might be available in the budget so he might attend an advanced seminar in his specialty.

A few days later, Nicole noted that Ruby, the office assistant, was seated in her cubicle with tears in her eyes. Nicole asked Ruby to tell her the cause of her sadness. Ruby explained that she was behind two payments on her car. She said also that the car would be repossessed if she did not make the two payments within ten days. Nicole patted Ruby on the shoulder and said, "This is awful. You need your car to get to work and take care of family responsibilities. I'll see if the company can offer you a crisis advance. If not, I will make the payments for you, and you can pay me back sometime in the future. I don't want you to suffer."

The following week Nicole called a meeting of her direct reports to discuss a new initiative from top-level management. She explained to the group that the company was falling a little short on revenue for the current fiscal year. The mortgage department was assigned a target of increasing revenues by 5 percent for the rest of the fiscal year. Nicole explained to the group, "I'm not the smartest person in the room. I want you to individually and collectively tell me how we can reach this 5 percent goal."

Case Questions

1. What is your evaluation of Nicole's approach to servant leadership?
2. Explain which incident of servant leadership you think is the most effective.
3. Explain which incident of servant leadership you think is the least effective.

ENDNOTES

1. Original story created from facts and observations in the following sources: "Shake Shack Promotes Tara Comonte to Expanded Role of President and Chief Financial Officer," *Shake Shack* (https:investor. shaekshack.com), October 2, 2019pp. 1–3; Frances Bridges, "Shake Shack CFO Tara Comonte's Career Advice For Aspiring Leaders," *Forbes* (www.forbes.com), August 29, 2019, pp. 1–6; Sam Danley, "Shake Shack C.F.O. Promoted to President," *Food Business News* (www.foodbusinessnews.net), October 2, 2019, pp. 1–2; Rheaa Rao, "Burger Chain To Serve Up Changes," *The Wall Street Journal*, July 8, 2017, p. B5.

2. W. Chan Kim and Renee A. Maubourgne, "Parables of Leadership," *Harvard Business Review*, July–August 1992, p. 123.

3. Julian Barling, *The Science of Leadership: Lessons from Research for Organizational Leaders* (New York: Oxford University Press, 2014), p. 24.

4. John P. Kotter, *A Force for Change: How Leadership Differs from Management* (New York: Free Press, 1990); Herminia Ibarra and Otilia Obodaru, "Women and the Vision Thing," *Harvard Business Review*, January 2009, p. 65.

5. John R. P. French Jr. and Bertram Raven, "The Bases of Social Power," in Dorwin Cartwright and Alvin Zander (eds.), *Group Dynamics: Research and Theory* (New York: Harper & Row, 1960), pp. 607–623.

6. Jeffrey D. Kudisch et al., "Expert Power, Referent Power, and Charisma: Toward the Resolution of a Theoretical Debate," *Journal of Business and Psychology*, Winter 1995, p. 189.

7. Thomas Gryta and Theo Francis, "More Big Companies Divide Their Chairman, CEO Roles," *The Wall Street Journal*, November 5, 2019, p. B3.

8. Manuel London, *Principled Leadership and Business Diplomacy: Value-Based Strategies for Management Development* (Westport, CT: Quorum Books, 1999).

9. Bill George, *Authentic Leadership: Rediscovering the Secrets to Creating Lasting Value* (San Francisco: Jossey-Bass, 2003).

10. Robert Cialdini, "The Uses (and Abuses) of Influence," *Harvard Business Review*, July–August 2013, p. 79.

11. Nick Wingfield, "Apple's No. 2 Has Low Profile, High Impact," *The Wall Street Journal*, October 16, 2006, p. B9.

12. Robert G. Lord et al., "Leadership in Applied Psychology: Three Waves of Theory and Research," *Journal of Applied Psychology*, March 2017, pp. 434–451.

13. Analysis by Richard Osburn in book review of May Uhl-Bien and Russ Marion, *Complexity Leadership: Conceptual Foundations* (Charlotte, NC: Information Age Publishing, 2008). The review appears in *Academy of Management Review*, October 2008, p. 1015.

14. Craig L. Pearce, Charles C. Manz, and Henry P. Sims Jr., "Where Do We Go from Here? Is Shared Leadership the Key to Team Success?" *Organizational Dynamics*, July–September 2009, pp. 234–239.

15. Craig L. Pearce, Christina L. Wassenaar, and Charles C. Manz, "Is Shared Leadership the Key to Responsible Leadership?" *Academy of Management Perspectives*, August 2014, p. 284.

16. "Corner Office—Mark Pincus—Every Worker Should be CEO of Something," *The New York Times* (www.nytimes.com), February 3, 2010, p. 2.

17. Charles C. Manz and Christopher P. Neck, *Mastering Self-Leadership: Empowering Yourself for Personal Excellence*, 3rd ed. (Upper Saddle River, NJ: Pearson Prentice Hall, 2004), p. 5; Neck and Manz, *Mastering Self-Leadership*, 4th ed., 2007.

18. Manz and Neck, *Mastering Self-Leadership*, pp. 138–139; Charles Manz and Henry P. Sims Jr., "Self-Management as a Substitute for Leadership: A Social Learning Theory Perspective," *Academy of Management Review*, No. 5, 1980, pp. 361–367.

19. Allan Lee, Sara Willis, and Amy Wee Tian, "Empowering Leadership: A Meta-Analytic Examination of Incremental Contribution, Mediation, and Moderation," *Journal of Organizational Behavior*, Vol. 18, 2017.

20. Robert B. Kaiser, Robert Hogan, and S. Bartholomew Craig, "Leadership and the Fate of Organizations," *American Psychologist*, February–March 2008, pp. 96–110.

21. Stephen J. Zaccaro, "Trait-Based Perspectives on Leadership," *American Psychologist*, January 2007, p. 12.

22. Several of the items in this list are from Sean T. Hannah, Bruce J. Avolio, Fred Luthans, and P.D. Harms, "Leadership Efficacy: Review and Future Directions," *Leadership Quarterly*, December 2008, pp. 669–692; Timothy A. Judge, Ronald F. Piccolo, and Tomek Kosalka, "The Bright and Dark Sides of Leader Traits: A Review and Theoretical Extension of the Leader Trait Paradigm," *The Leadership Quarterly*, December 2009, pp. 855–875; Lord et al., "Leadership in Applied Psychology: Three Waves of Theory and Research," *Journal of Applied Psychology*, March 2017, pp. 435–437.

23. Robert Hogan as cited in Neal Burgis, "Importance of Humility in Your Leadership," *www.successful-solutions.com*, February 29, 2019, p. 1.

24. Thomas S. Bateman and J. Michael Grant, "The Proactive Component of Organizational Behavior: A Measure and Correlates," *Journal of Organizational Behavior*, March 1993, p. 103.

25. Craig D. Crossley, Cecily D. Cooper, and Tara S. Wernsing, "Making Things Happen through Challenging Goals: Leader Proactivity Trust, and Business-Unit Performance," *Journal of Applied Psychology*, May 2013, pp. 540–549.

26. Tony Simons, Michael Palanski, and Linda Treviño, "Toward a Broader—but Still Rigorous—Definition of Leader Integrity: Commentary," *The Leadership Quarterly*, June 2013, p. 39; Kurt T. Dirks and Donald L. Ferrin, "Trust in Leadership: Meta-Analytic Findings and Implications for Research and Practice," *Journal of Applied Psychology*, August 2002, p. 622; Joanna Barish and Johanna Lavoie, "Lead At Your Best," *McKinsey & Company* (www.mckinsey.com), April 2014, p. 3.

27. Randy Conley, "Trust is the Essential Ingredient for Leadership Success," *https://leading with trust.com*, January 20, 2019, p. 3.

28. Dori Meinert, "An Open Book," *HR Magazine*, April 2013, p. 44.

29. Michael D. Mumford, Logan L. Watts, and Paul J. Partlow, "Leader Cognition: Approaches and Findings," *The Leadership Quarterly*, June 2015, p. 301.

30. John Antonakis, Robert J. House, and Dean Keith Simonton, "Can Super Smart Leaders Suffer From Too Much of a Good Thing? The Curvilinear Effects of Intelligence on Perceived Leadership Behavior," *Journal of Applied Psychology*, July 2017, pp. 1003–1021.

31. Jena McGregor, "Apple Names a New Chief Operating Officer In Management Shuffle," *The Washington Post* (www.washingtonpost.com), December 17, 2015, p. 1.

32. Cecily D. Cooper, Dejun Tony Kong, and Craig D. Crossley, "Leader Humor as an Interpersonal Resource Integrating Three Theoretical Perspectives," *Academy of Management Perspectives*, April 2018, pp. 769–796.

33. Rob Emrich, "The One Leadership Tool Entrepreneurs Don't Use Enough," *Chicago Tribune Business*, November 8, 2015, p. 6.

34. Travis Bradberry and John Antonakis, "Is Emotional Intelligence a Good Measure of Leadership Ability?", *HR Magazine*, November 2015, pp. 22–23.

35. Cited in Adam Bryant, "He Wants Subjects, Verbs and Objects," *The New York Times* (www.nytimes.com), April 26, 2009, p. 1.

36. Daniel Goleman, "Leadership That Gets Results," *Harvard Business Review*, March–April 2000, p. 80; Daniel Goleman, Richard Boyatzis, and Annie McKee, *Primal Leadership: Realizing the Power of Emotional Intelligence* (Boston: Harvard Business School Press, 2002).

37. Gianpiero Petriglieri and Jennifer Louise Petriglieri, "Can Business Schools Humanize Leadership?" *Academy of Management Learning & Education*, December 2015, pp. 625–647.

38. Sharon Daloz Parks, *Leadership Can Be Taught: A Bold Approach for a Complex World* (Boston: Harvard Business School Press, 2005).

39. Seokhwa Yun, Samer Faraj, and Henry P. Sims Jr., "Contingent Leadership Effectiveness of Trauma Resuscitation Teams," *Journal of Applied Psychology*, November 2005, pp. 1288–1296.

40. Hal Gregerson, "To Be a Better Leader, Ask Better Questions," *The Wall Street Journal*, May 14, 2019, p. R2.

41. Timothy P. Munyon, James K. Summers, Katina M. Thompson, and Gerald Ferris, "Political Skill and Work Outcomes: A Theoretical Extension, Meta-Analytic Investigation, and Agenda for the Future," *Personnel Psychology*, Spring, 2015, p. 145.

42. P. D.Harms, et al., "Autocratic Leaders and Authoritarian Followers Revisited: A Review and Agenda for the Future," *The Leadership Quarterly*, February 2018, p. 114.

43. David C. McClelland, *The Achieving Society* (New York: Van Nostrand Reinhold, 1961).

44. April J. Spivack and Alexander McKelvie, "Entrepreneurship Addiction: Shedding Light on the Manifestation of the 'Dark Side' in Work-Behavior Patterns," *Academy of Management Perspective*, August 2018, p. 359.

45. Robert K. Greenleaf, *The Power of Servant Leadership* (San Francisco: Berrett-Koehler Publishers Inc., 1998); Robert C. Liden, Sandy J. Wayne, Haoi Zhao, and David Henderson, "Servant Leadership: Development of a Multidimensional Measure and Multi-Level Assessment," *Leadership Quarterly*, April 2008, pp. 161–171; Nathan Eva et al., "Servant Leadership: A Systematic Review and Call for Future Research," *The Leadership Quarterly*, February 2019, pp. 111–132.

46. Robert C. Liden et al., "Servant Leadership: Validation of a Short Form of the SL-28," *The Leadership Quarterly*, April 2015, p. 256.

47. Robert C. Liden, Sandy J. Wayne, Chenwei Liao, and Jeremy D. Meuser, "Servant Leadership and Serving Culture: Influence on Individual and Unit Performance," *Academy of Management Journal*, October 2014, pp. 1434–1452.

48. Lord et al., "Leadership in Applied Psychology," p. 441.

49. Stephen Miller, "Man Who Saved Floundering Geico," *The Wall Street Journal*, March 12, 2013, p. B9.

50. John J. Hater and Bernard M. Bass, "Superiors' Evaluations and Subordinates' Perceptions of Transformational and Transactional Leadership," *Journal of Applied Psychology*, November 1988, p. 69; Nick Turner et al., "Transformational Leadership and Moral Reasoning," *Journal of Applied Psychology*, April 2002, pp. 304–311.

51. Robert T. Keller, "Transformational Leadership, Initiating Structure, and Substitutes for Leadership: A Longitudinal Study of Research and Development Project Team Performance," *Journal of Applied Psychology*, January 2006, pp. 202–210.

52. Szu-Han (Johanna) Lin, Brent A. Scott, and Fadel K. Matta, "The Dark Side of Transformational Leader Behaviors for Leaders Themselves: A Conservation of Resources Perspective," *Academy of Management Journal*, October 2019, pp. 1556–1582.

53. Amir Erez et al., "Stirring the Hearts of Followers: Charismatic Leaders and the Transferal of Affect," *Journal of Applied Psychology*, May 2008, pp. 602–613.

54. Alan J. Dubinsky, Francis J. Yammarino, and Marvin A. Jolson, "An Examination of Linkages Between Personal Characteristics and Dimensions of Transformational Leadership," *Journal of Business and Psychology*, Spring 1995, p. 315; Timothy A. Judge and Joyce E. Bono, "Five-Factor Model of Personality and Transformational Leadership," *Journal of Applied Psychology*, October 2000, pp. 751–765; Stephen Denning, "Stories in the Workplace," *HR Magazine*, September 2008, pp. 129–132.

55. "World's Greatest Leaders: Jeff Bezos," *http://fortune.com*, 2015.

56. Bradley P. Owens, Angela S. Wallace, and David A. Waldman, "Leader Narcissism and Follower Outcomes: The Counterbalancing Effect of Leader Humility," *Journal of Applied Psychology*, July 2015, pp. 1203–1213.

57. Scott Barry Kaufman, "The Paradox Peacock," *Psychology Today*, April 2011, p. 60.

58. Christoph Nohe, "Charisma and Organizational Change: A Multilevel Study of Perceived Charisma, Commitment to Change, and Team Performance," *The Leadership Quarterly*, April 2013, pp. 378–389.

59. Lord et al., "Leadership in Applied Psychology," p. 442.

60. Sara Spellings, "How I Get It Done: Stitch Fix CEO Katrina Lake," *The Cut* (thecut.com), December 30, 2019, pp. 1–2; "The World's Most Innovative Companies: Stitch Fix: For Sizing Up Its Customers," *Fast Company*, March/April 2018, p. 44.

61. Andrew J. DuBrin, *Personal Magnetism: Discover Your Own Charisma and Learn How to Charm, Inspire, and Influence Others* (New York: AMACOM, 1997), pp. 93–111; Robert A. Eckert, "The Two Most Important Words," *Harvard Business Review*, September 2013, p. 144; Elizabeth Holmes, "The Charisma Boot Camp," *The Wall Street Journal*, August 6, 2014, p. D1.

62. Thomas Maran, "In the Eye of a Leader: Eye-Directed Gazing Shapes Perceptions of a Leader's Charisma," *The Leadership Quarterly*, December 2019, pp. 101–337.

63. "A Coach's View of Leadership," *The Wall Street Journal*, November 24, 2015, p. R12.

64. Anthony K. Tjan, "What the Best Mentors Do," *Harvard Business Review* (https:/hbr.org), February 27, 2017, p. 2.

65. Andrew J. DuBrin, "Personal Attributes and Behaviors of Effective Crisis Leaders," in DuBrin (editor), *Handbook of Research on Crisis Leadership in Organizations* (Cheltenham UK: Edward Elgar, 2013), pp. 3–22; James O'Toole and Warren Bennis, "What's Needed Next: A Culture of Candor," *Harvard Business Review*, June 2009, pp. 54–61; Ronald Heifetz, Alexander Grashow, and Marty Linsky, "Leadership in a Permanent Crisis," *Harvard Business Review*, July–August 2009, pp. 62–69.

66. Kim Wilborn, "Resilience Is an Attitude and a Skill," *Democrat and Chronicle*, October 27, 2015, p, 4B.

CHAPTER 11

Motivation

OBJECTIVES

After studying this chapter and doing the exercises, you should be able to:

1 Explain how employee engagement is part of employee motivation.

2 Present an overview of major theories of need satisfaction in explaining motivation.

3 Explain how goal setting is used to motivate people.

4 Describe the application of positive reinforcement including recognition and praise to worker motivation.

5 Explain the conditions under which a person will be motivated according to expectancy theory.

6 Describe the role of financial incentives and profit sharing in worker motivation.

When Pamela Fletcher was the executive chief engineer at General Motors (GM), she oversaw the development of the Chevrolet Bolt, all-electric vehicle. She said that her approach to leading her team was to operate like a small startup within GM. Fletcher dealt with such issues as having a vision of what "better" means in practice. She also helped formulate the team's portfolio of technologies and products, and what would be a winning product for customers. Fletcher believed that her team was inspired by the mind-blowing revolution into electric vehicles going on in the industry. She said, "I just can't imagine a more exciting place to be."

While head of electric vehicles she received the 2017 Henry Ford II Distinguished Award for Excellence in Automotive Engineering from the Society of Automotive Engineers. She also played a key role in developing plans for future GM electric vehicles, with the goal of putting 20 new battery-electric vehicles on the road by 2023. Another of Fletcher's responsibilities that facilitated team members feeling they had a vital purpose was to aid in the development of the GM Super Cruise semi-autonomous driving system.

Fletcher also worked on executing her plan move GM along the pathway to a world of zero emissions, zero crashes and zero congestion. She and her team devoted considerable energy into self-driving cars that could cut down on auto fatalities. Fletcher said, "These things are big. They're game changing. They will really change the world." Her team members perceived these kinds of statements to be purpose-driven and highly motivational.

In October 2018, Fletcher was appointed to the newly-created role of vice president of innovation. She reports directly to Mary Barra, the CEO of GM. Fletcher's key responsibility is to identify, integrate, and accelerate business opportunities that make the life of GM customers easier. At the same time Fletcher is charged with driving long-term value to GM shareholders.

Fletcher leads teams at GM whose mission is to disrupt the traditional automotive industry ways of producing cars. She concentrates on business model innovation and oversees new businesses from startup to growth. In the Research & Development part of her job, Fletcher directs seven laboratories around the world with a focus on developing technologies such as battery chemistry, mixed material science, smart manufacturing systems, and vehicle infrastructure technology.

Fletcher received a bachelor's degree in engineering at Kettering University in Flint, Michigan, and a master's degree in engineering from Wayne State University in Detroit, Michigan. She is also a graduate of executive development programs at Northwestern University and Stanford University.[1]

The story about the automotive engineering executive illustrates how managers can motivate workers by offering them an inspiring purpose. For many managers, the purpose of motivation is to get people to work hard toward achieving company objectives. Understanding motivation is also important because low motivation contributes to low-quality work, superficial effort, indifference toward customers, and high absenteeism and tardiness.

The term motivation refers to two different but related ideas. From the standpoint of the individual, motivation is an internal state that leads to the pursuit of objectives. Personal motivation affects the initiation, direction, intensity and persistence of effort. (A motivated worker gets going, focuses effort in the right direction, works with intensity and sustains the effort.) From the standpoint of the manager, motivation is the process of getting people to pursue objectives. Both concepts have an important meaning in common. **Motivation** is the expenditure of effort to accomplish results. The effort results from a force that stems from within the person. However, the manager or team leader, or the group can be helpful in igniting the force.

Many people believe the statements, "You can accomplish anything you want," and, "Think positively and you will achieve all your goals." In truth, motivation is but one important contributor to productivity and performance. Abilities, skills, and the right equipment are also essential. An office assistant might be strongly motivated to become a brand manager for Cheerios at General Mills, but she must first acquire knowledge about marketing and project management, develop her leadership skills, and make the right connections—among other factors.

If group norms and organizational culture encourage high motivation and performance, the individual worker will feel compelled to work hard. To do otherwise isolates the worker from the group and the culture. Group norms and an organizational culture favoring low motivation will often lower individual output.

This chapter will present several theories or explanations of motivation in the workplace. In addition, it will provide descriptions of specific approaches to motivating employees. All the ideas presented in this chapter can be applied to motivating oneself as well as others. For instance, when you read about the expectancy theory of motivation, ask yourself: "What rewards do I value strongly enough for me to work extra hard?"

motivation
The expenditure of effort to accomplish results.

Explain how employee engagement is part of employee motivation.

work engagement
An extension of motivation, referring to the level of commitment workers make to their employers.

EMPLOYEE ENGAGEMENT AND MOTIVATION

The major thrust in recent years for motivating and satisfying employees is to find ways to engage them in their work and the organization. **Work engagement** is essentially an extension of motivation, referring to the level of commitment workers make to their employers. Engagement is reflected in employee willingness to stay with the firm and go beyond the call of duty.[2] The engaged employee also works joyfully toward achieving organizational objectives. Worker engagement shows some variation from time to time. Research conducted in a variety of industries suggests that work engagement fluctuates day-to-day around an average level of engagement.[3] A study with NASA crew members also found that engagement may not stay at a consistent level. The workday of a crew member consists of the performance of a wide array of tasks and transitions between the tasks. For example, a crew member might be highly engaged in a simulated moon walk but less engaged in the task of asteroid sampling analysis. The study also found that being highly engaged in one task might lead to being less engaged on the next task.[4]

About eight years ago survey results were frequently cited indicating that employee commitment was a major problem. Recent data suggest a more optimistic view of engagement. During a conference of the Society for Industrial Psychology, specialists from five separate firms shared consistent survey results about employee engagement. All studies indicated that between 61 percent and 70 percent of employees are work engaged even though the psychologists used different data collection methods.[5]

Programs and Managerial Actions to Enhance Work Engagement

A wide variety of programs and managerial actions are aimed at enhancing employee engagement, and therefore motivation and satisfaction. Benefits, compensation, work and family programs, employee recognition, and providing career guidance are all major approaches to engagement. The techniques described in this chapter are designed to help employees commit to the organization, and therefore experience work engagement. High-performance work design as described in Chapter 7 also leads to commitment. High motivation for a given task is different from emotional commitment, which translates into intense motivation for a long period of time. The process works as follows:

Day-by-day motivation and good treatment of workers	→	Long-term motivation of workers	→	Emotional commitment to the firm	→	Competitive advantage	→	Elevated profits and stock price

A major driver of employee engagement is the opportunity to perform work they perceive to be meaningful, as was mentioned in Chapter 4 about the vision aspect of strategy. A study involving 23,000 employees in 45 countries across different industries explored what made for positive work experiences and happy workers. The findings about meaningful work were closely related to engagement. When employee's skills and talents are being fully utilized there is a greater alignment to shared core values. When employees agree that their work is consistent with the organization's core values, 80 percent report more positive experiences. Of the employees who agree that their jobs make good use of their skills and experiences, 81 percent report a more positive employee experience.[6]

Daniel M. Cable, a professor of organizational behavior at the London Business School emphasizes that to inspire and engage employees, managers should keep two things in mind. First, purpose is a feeling, so it helps to show workers the impact they can make on their jobs, such as having them visit a customer who uses their product or service. Second, authenticity matters so make frequent mention of the pursuit of purpose rather than a one-off initiative.[7]

Two less publicized approaches to enhancing work engagement are to promote small wins and listen to employees. We mention these approaches to illustrate that many day-by-day managerial practices can enhance worker engagement. A study of 238 knowledge workers in 26 project teams in three different industries collected e-mail diaries about how these workers felt about their work. The feeling of making progress toward attaining important work goals was the key to employee engagement.[8]

Kevin Elkenberry, a leadership consultant, observes that when a manager listens to employees, and shows care and concern about them and their ideas, employees become more engaged. Asking questions contribute to the process, such as, "What is the most challenging part of this project for you?"[9]

As hard as managers strive to engage employees, we should recognize that engagement is also related to personality. This explains why two individuals may have different levels of engagement even though their job situations are almost identical. An individual who brings to the job a strong work ethic and desire to succeed will most likely show a high level of work engagement.[10] The message to the manager is that effective selection methods facilitate high engagement.

LEARNING OBJECTIVE **2**

Present an overview of major theories of need satisfaction in explaining motivation.

need
A deficit within an individual, such as a craving for water or affection.

MOTIVATION THROUGH NEED SATISFACTION

The simplest explanation of motivation is one of the most powerful: People are willing to expend effort toward achieving a goal because it satisfies one of their important needs. A **need** is a deficit within an individual, such as a craving for water or affection. Self-interest is thus a driving force. The principle is referred to as "What's in it for me?" or WIIFM. Reflect on your own experiences. Before working hard to accomplish a task, you probably want to know how you will benefit. If your manager asks you to work extra hours to take care of an emergency, you will most likely oblige. Yet underneath you might be thinking, "If I work these extra hours, my boss will think highly of me. As a result, I will probably receive a good performance evaluation and maybe a better-than-average salary increase."

Our behavior is ruled partly by our need intensity, such as having an intense desire for recognition. This might propel a person to put forward greater effort to win an employee-of-the month award.[11] People are motivated to fulfill needs that are not currently satisfied. The need-satisfaction approach requires two key steps when motivating workers. First, you must know what people want—what needs they are trying to satisfy. To learn what the needs are, you can ask directly or observe the person. You can obtain knowledge indirectly by getting to know employees better. To gain insight into employee needs, find out something about the employee's personal life, education, work history, outside interests and career goals.

Second, you must give each person a chance to satisfy needs on the job. To illustrate, one way to motivate a person with a strong need for autonomy is to allow that person to work independently.

This section examines needs and motivation from three related perspectives. First, we describe the best-known theory of motivation, Maslow's need hierarchy. Then we discuss several specific needs related to job motivation, and move on to an updated version of another cornerstone idea, Herzberg's two-factor theory.

Maslow's Need Hierarchy

Based on his work as a clinical psychologist, Abraham M. Maslow developed a comprehensive view of individual motivation.[12] **Maslow's need hierarchy** arranges human needs into a pyramid-shaped model with basic physiological needs at the bottom and self-actualization needs at the top. (See Figure 11-1.) Before higher-level needs are activated, the lower-order needs must be satisfied. The five levels of needs are described next.

1 *Physiological needs* refer to basic bodily requirements, such as nutrition, water, shelter, moderate temperatures, rest and sleep. Most office jobs allow us to satisfy physiological needs. Naps to reduce stress and boost productivity help workers satisfy an important physiological need. Firefighting is an occupation with potential to frustrate some physiological needs. Smoke inhalation can block the satisfaction of physiological needs.

2 *Safety needs* include the desire to be safe from both physical and emotional injury. Many workers who hold dangerous jobs would be motivated by the prospects of attaining safety. For example, people who keyboard most of the workday and are suffering from cumulative trauma disorder would prefer jobs that require less intense pressure on their wrists. Any highly stressful job can frustrate the need for emotional safety.

3 *Social needs* are the needs for love, belonging and affiliation with people. Managers can contribute to the satisfaction of these needs by promoting teamwork and allowing people to discuss work problems with each other. Many employees see their jobs as a major source for satisfying social needs.

4 *Esteem needs* reflect an individual's desire to be seen by themselves and others as a person of worth. Occupations with high status are a primary source for the satisfaction of esteem needs. Managers can help employees satisfy their esteem needs by praising the quality of their work, or as we learned from Bank of America, from various forms of recognition.

5 *Self-actualization needs* relate to the desire to reach one's potential. They include needs for self-fulfillment and personal development. True self-actualization is an ideal to strive for, rather than something that automatically stems from occupying a challenging position. Self-actualized people are those who are becoming all they are capable of becoming. Managers can help group members move toward self-actualization by giving them challenging assignments and the chance for advancement and new learning.

Maslow's need hierarchy is a convenient way of classifying needs and it has spurred thousands of managers to take the subject of human motivation more seriously. Its primary value lies in recognizing the importance of satisfying needs in order to motivate employees. Furthermore, Maslow shows why people are difficult to satisfy. As one need is satisfied, people want to satisfy other needs or different forms of the same need.

The need hierarchy is relevant in the current era because so many workers have to worry about satisfying lower-level needs. Job security and having limited or no healthcare benefits are still concerns for many workers who do not qualify for the Affordable Care Act, or cannot afford its premiums and deductibles. Even when finding new employment is relatively easy, many workers feel their security is jeopardized when they have to worry about conducting a job search to pay for necessities.

Maslow's need hierarchy
The motivation theory that arranges human needs into a pyramid-shaped model with basic physiological needs at the bottom and self-actualizing needs at the top.

Figure 11-1 Maslow's Need Hierarchy

As you move up the hierarchy, the needs become more difficult to achieve. Some physiological needs could be satisfied with pizza and a soft drink, whereas it might take becoming rich and famous to satisfy the selfactualization need.

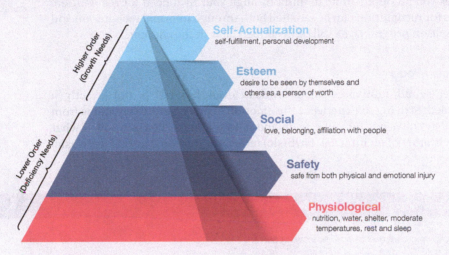

Specific Needs People Attempt to Satisfy

Maslow's need hierarchy refers to classes of needs, and represents but one way of understanding human needs. The work setting offers the opportunity to satisfy dozens of psychological needs. This section will describe six of the most important of these needs.

Achievement, Power, and Affiliation

achievement need
The need that refers to finding joy in accomplishment for its own sake.

affiliation need
A desire to have close relationships with others and to be a loyal employee or friend.

According to David McClelland and his associates, much job behavior can be explained by the strength of people's needs for achievement, power and affiliation.[13] The power need (or motive) has already been described in relation to leadership. The **achievement need** refers to finding joy in accomplishment for its own sake. High achievers find satisfaction in completing challenging tasks, attaining high standards, and developing better ways of doing things. Entrepreneurs and product developers typically have strong achievement needs. The **affiliation need** is a desire to have close relationships with others and to be a loyal employee or friend. Affiliation is a social need, while achievement and power are self-actualizing needs.

A person with a strong need for affiliation finds compatible working relationships more important than high-level accomplishment and the exercise of power. Successful executives, therefore, usually have stronger needs for achievement and power than for affiliation. Workers with strong affiliation needs, however, typically enjoy contributing to a team effort. Befriending others and working cooperatively with them satisfies the need for affiliation.

Recognition

The workplace provides a natural opportunity to satisfy the **recognition need,** the desire to be acknowledged for one's contributions and efforts and to feel important. A manager can thus motivate many employees by making them feel important. Figure 11-2 gives you an opportunity to think through your own need for recognition. Employee needs for recognition can be satisfied both through informal recognition and by formal recognition programs, as will be described later in the chapter.

recognition need
The desire to be acknowledged for one's contributions and efforts and to feel important.

The Need to Feel Proud

Wanting to feel proud motivates many workers even if *pride* is not exactly a psychological need. Striving to experience the emotion of pride most likely stems from the desire to satisfy the needs for self-esteem and self-fulfillment. Being proud of what you accomplish is more of an internal (intrinsic) motivator than an external (extrinsic)

Figure 11-2 How Much Do I Crave Recognition?

Respond to the following statements on the following scale:
DS – disagree strongly; D – disagree; N – neutral, A – agree; AS –agree strongly.

	DS	D	N	A	AS
1 I keep (or would keep) almost every plaque, medal, trophy I have ever received on display in my living quarters.	1	2	3	4	5
2 I feel a nice warm glow each time somebody praises my efforts.	1	2	3	4	5
3 When somebody tells me "nice job," it makes my day.	1	2	3	4	5
4 When I compliment someone, I am really looking for a compliment in return.	1	2	3	4	5
5 I would rather win an "employee-of-the-month" award than receive a $200 bonus for my good work.	1	2	3	4	5
6 If I had the resources to make a large donation to charity, I would never make the donation anonymously.	1	2	3	4	5
7 Thinking back to my childhood, I adored receiving a gold star or similar acknowledgment from my teacher for my good work.	1	2	3	4	5
8 I would rather be designated as *Time* magazine's "Person of the Year" than be one of the world's richest people.	1	2	3	4	5
9 I love to see name on social media or in print.	1	2	3	4	5
10 I do not receive all the respect I deserve.	1	2	3	4	5
Total Score	___	___	___	___	___

Scoring and interpretation: Add the circled numbers to obtain your total score.

45–50   You have an above-average recognition need. Recognition is therefore a strong motivator for you. You will be happiest in a job where you can be recognized for your good deeds.

25–44   You have an average need for recognition and do not require constant reminders that you have done a good job.

10–24   You have a below-average need for recognition and likely to have your good deeds speak for themselves. When you do receive recognition, you would prefer that it be quite specific to what you have done, and not too lavish. You would feel comfortable in a work setting with mostly technical people.

motivator, such as receiving a gift. Giving workers an opportunity to experience pride can therefore be a strong internal motivator.

> *Imagine you are the assistant service manager at a company that customizes corporate jets to meet the requirements of individual clients. Your manager asks you to prepare a PowerPoint presentation of trends in equipment problems. You make your presentation to top management, the group applauds, executives shake your hand, and later you receive several congratulatory e-mail messages. One of the many emotions you experience is likely to be pride in having performed well. You are motivated to keep up the good work.*

Workers can also experience pride in relation to external motivators. For example, a worker might receive a crystal vase for having saved the company thousands of dollars in shipping costs. The vase might be more valuable to the worker as a symbol of accomplishment than as a household decoration. The feeling of pride stems from having accomplished a worthwhile activity (saving the company money) rather than from being awarded a vase.

According to consultant Jon R. Katzenbach, managers can take steps to motivate through pride. A key tactic is for the manager to set his or her compass on pride, not money. It is more important for workers to be proud of what they are doing day by day, than for them to be proud of reaching a major goal. The manager should celebrate "steps" (or attaining small goals) as much as the "landings" (the major goal). The most effective pride builders are masters at identifying and recognizing the small achievements that will instill pride in their people.[14]

Risk Taking and Thrill Seeking

The willingness to take risks and pursue thrills is a need that has grown in importance in the high-technology era. Many people work for employers, start businesses, and purchase stock with uncertain futures. Both the search for giant payoffs and daily thrills motivate these individuals, and they are attracted to high-stress careers, such as computer security specialists or investment banking.[15] A strong craving for thrills may have some positive consequences for the organization, including willingness to perform such dangerous feats as setting explosives, capping an oil well, controlling a radiation leak, and introducing a product in a highly competitive environment. However, extreme risk takers and thrill seekers can create problems, such as being involved in a disproportionate number of vehicular accidents and making imprudent investments. Risk takers in the financial field sometimes get involved in developing and selling high risk investments that can bankrupt a firm and lead to criminal investigations.

A manager can appeal to the need for risk taking and thrill seeking, and therefore enhance the motivation of a person so inclined by rewarding good behavior with adventuresome assignments such as:

- Dealing with an irate, hostile customer.
- Working on a product development team under time constraints.
- Repairing equipment under heavy time pressures and customer demands.
- Attending dangerous team-building activities, such as cliff hanging and race car driving.

If you are a thrill seeker, you will have to be on guard for your own safety and that of others while on the job. Or seek thrills off the job, such as in mountain climbing or betting on changes in foreign currencies!

The Pep Talk and Motivational Speech as Need Satisfiers

The most widely used motivational device of all, the pep talk, is not found in scholarly writings about motivation. Yet, many managers, especially sales managers, attempt to motivate workers by giving them enthusiastic encouragement, much like athletic coaches. A substantial number of companies hire motivational speakers from time to time to boost the motivation of workers. The pep talked is usually directed at one person or a small group, whereas the motivational speech is given to a large group.

Steve Ballmer, now the owner of the basketball team, the Los Angeles Clippers, was CEO of Microsoft from 2000 to 2014, and had also been in charge of sales and support. At a company meeting, he would engage in such antics as screaming as loud as he could, "Windows, Windows, Windows," perhaps ten consecutive times. Many Microsoft workers found his pep talks to be motivational, whereas others thought he was foolish, describing one of his pep talks as, "The Monkey Dance," and posting Ballmer's antics on YouTube.

Katherine Razzi recommends that to develop a pep talk that actually motivates employees is to show them a deeper understanding of the impact of their work (following the idea of task significance in job enrichment). Customer service representatives will often benefit from a pep talk that helps them connect their work to the bigger picture of improving the lives of customers.[16]

Pep talks and motivational speeches can contribute to need satisfaction, and therefore be motivational, with several illustrations to follow. When directed at a small group the pep talk can appeal to the affiliation need because the group or team members might feel they are working toward the same goal as a result of the inspirational message. The pep talk or motivational speech can also appeal to the need for achievement because the talk or speech might inspire the listener to accomplish something worthwhile. Above all the talk or speech can satisfy the need to feel proud because the pep talker or speaker will often emphasize the excellent qualities of the individual or group.

Herzberg's Two-Factor Theory

The study of the need hierarchy led to the **two-factor theory of work motivation**, which focuses on the idea of two different sets of job factors. One set of factors can satisfy and motivate people. The other can only prevent dissatisfaction. The late industrial psychologist Frederick Herzberg and his associates discovered that some factors of a job give people a chance to satisfy higher-level needs. Such elements are satisfiers or motivators.[17] A *satisfier* is a job factor that, if present, leads to job satisfaction. Similarly, a *motivator* is a job factor that, if present, leads to motivation. When a motivator is not present, the effect on motivation is neutral rather than negative.

Satisfiers and motivators generally refer to the content (the heart or guts) of a job. These factors are achievement, recognition, challenging work, responsibility and the opportunity for advancement. All the factors are self-rewarding. The important implication for managers is that most people can be motivated by providing an opportunity to do interesting work or to be promoted. The two-factor theory thus underlies the philosophy of job design through job enrichment and the job characteristics model, as described in Chapter 7.

Herzberg also discovered that some job elements are more relevant to lower-level needs than upper-level needs. Referred to as dissatisfiers, or maintenance factors, these elements are noticed primarily by their absence. A *dissatisfier* is a job element that,

two-factor theory of work motivation
The theory which focuses on the idea of two different sets of job factors. One set can satisfy and motivate people, the other can only prevent dissatisfaction.

when present, prevents dissatisfaction; it does not, however, create satisfaction. People will not be satisfied with their jobs just because maintenance factors are present. For example, not having a handy place to park your car would create dissatisfaction. But having a place to park would not make you happier about your job.

Dissatisfiers relate mostly to the context of a job (the job setting or external elements). These include relationships with co-workers, company policy and administration, job security, and money. All these factors deal with external rewards. Money, however, does work as a satisfier for many people.

The two-factor theory has prompted managers to ask, "What really motivates our employees?" Nevertheless, Herzberg's assumption—that all workers seek more responsibility and challenge on the job—may be incorrect. It is more likely that people in higher-level occupations strive for more responsibility and challenge. A key take-away from Herzberg's theory is that intrinsic motivation is a major form of motivation, and is the basis for job enrichment as well as job crafting. But even in a given occupational group, such as managers or production workers, not everybody has the same motivational pattern. Many workers are motivated by a secure job when they have heavy financial obligations.

The two-factor theory becomes more current when we look at job factors that are considered important today for attracting, motivating, and retaining professional workers of the millennial generation (born in 1981 or later), such as giving workers more responsibility and the opportunity for professional growth. Also, Generation Z, the youngest members of the workforce, tend to be strongly motivated by having a social purpose to their work, such as providing nutritious food to poor people. Where the two-factor theory no longer fits the modern workplace, is that compensation including benefits have become a much stronger motivator to many people today. For example, many workers are willing to exert effort on the job for an employer who provides a generous medical and dental insurance program.

MOTIVATION THROUGH GOAL SETTING

LEARNING OBJECTIVE **3**

Explain how goal setting is used to motivate people.

goal

An overall condition one is trying to achieve, or a conscious intention to act.

Goal setting plays an important role in most formal motivational programs and managerial methods for motivating employees. The premise underlying goal theory is that behavior is regulated by values and goals. A value is a strongly held personal standard or conviction. It is a belief about something important to the individual, such as dignity of work or honesty. Our values create within us a desire to behave consistently with them. If an executive values honesty, the executive will establish a goal of trying to hire only honest employees. He or she would therefore make extensive use of reference checks and honesty testing. A **goal** is an overall condition one is trying to achieve, or a conscious intention to act. Figure 11-3 summarizes some of the more consistent findings and the following list describes them.[18] The suggestions in Chapter 4 (Figure 4-6) for establishing goals and objectives are a useful supplement to goal theory.

1 *Specific goals lead to higher performance than generalized goals.* Telling someone to, "do your best" is a generalized goal. A specific goal would be, "Decrease the turnaround time on customer inquiries to an average of two working days."

2 *Performance generally increases in direct proportion to goal difficulty.* Setting high goals for group members is equivalent to setting high standards. The harder the goal, the more one accomplishes. An important exception occurs, however, when goals are too difficult. Difficulty in reaching the goal leads to frustration, which in turn leads to lower performance. On the other hand, lofty goals can be

inspirational. A vision can be an inspiring goal for many people, such as "Our company will make workplaces safer throughout the world."

At the c-suite level, it is important to set stretch (difficult but still feasible) goals that take into account the impact on other business functions. For example, reducing inventory to meet the goal of having more working capital can lead to lost sales if the production group cannot respond fast enough to a sudden large order.

3   *For goals to improve performance, the employee must accept them.* If you reject a goal, you will not incorporate it into your planning. For this reason, it is often helpful to discuss goals with employees, rather than just imposing the goals on them. Participating in setting goals has no major effect on the level of job performance, except when it improves goal acceptance. Yet participation is valuable because it can lead to higher satisfaction with the goal-setting process.

4   *Goals are more effective when they are used to evaluate performance.* When workers know their performance will be evaluated in terms of how well they have attained their goals, the impact of goals increases. Management by objectives is built around this important idea.

5   *Goals should be linked to feedback and rewards.* Workers should receive feedback on their progress toward goals and be rewarded for reaching them. Rewarding people for reaching goals is perhaps the best-accepted principle of management. Feedback is also important because it is a motivational principle within itself. The process of receiving positive feedback encourages us to repeat the behavior; receiving negative feedback encourages us to discontinue the behavior. A practical way of building more feedback into goal setting is to set achievable short-term goals. In this way, goal accomplishment gets measured more frequently, giving the goal setter regular feedback. Short-term goals also increase motivation because many people do not have the patience and self-discipline to work long and hard without seeing results.

Figure 11-3 The Basics of Goal Theory

Goals that meet the illustrated conditions have a positive impact on motivation, as revealed by a wide variety of research studies.

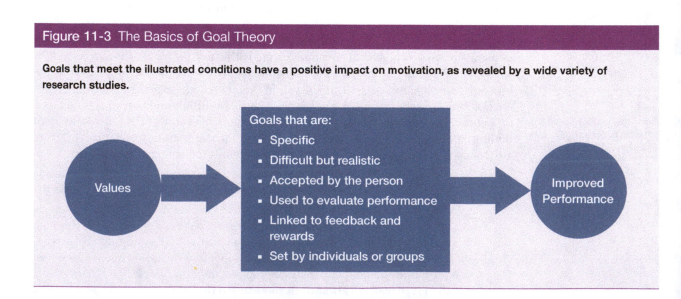

Values → Goals that are:
- Specific
- Difficult but realistic
- Accepted by the person
- Used to evaluate performance
- Linked to feedback and rewards
- Set by individuals or groups

→ Improved Performance

6 *Group goal setting is as important as individual goal setting.* Having employees work as teams with a specific team goal, rather than as individuals with only individual goals, increases productivity. Furthermore, the combination of the compatible group and individual goals is more effective than either individual or group goals.

Pygmalion effect
The idea that people live up to the expectations set for them.

Closely related to goal theory is the **Pygmalion effect**—the idea that people live up to the expectations set for them. If the manager establishes high goals and projects confidence that these goals will be achieved, the workers will rise to the occasion. The confidence might be projected though such means as a firm handshake, a fist bump, or an accepting smile. Holding high expectations for employees can help overcome some of the motivational problems of a low work ethic. Many employees with a low work ethic will change their attitudes and behaviors if management expects these employees to perform well.[19]

A potential problem with relying on goals to motivate workers is they might use unethical means to attain goals. In the words of a team of researchers, "Goal setting is a prescription-strength medication that has both powerful positive effects and formidable negative side effects."[20] Examples of negative effects of clinging to goals include booking sales for a quarter in which the money is yet to be received, and using low-quality components to attain a cost goal for a part.

To meet profit goals, some CEOs will cut back on research and development, fire capable workers, and sell off valuable company assets. Goal setting in the public sector can sometimes encourage unethical behavior. Such behavior may occur when police officers are assigned very high quotas for writing traffic tickets to meet revenue goals set by local officials. The high quota places pressure on police officers to write traffic tickets that may not be entirely justified.[21] Another problem with goals is that the continual pursuit of goals that stretch your capability can be stressful, as workers keep extending their workweek to "make their numbers."

To overcome this potential problem with goals, it is important for the worker pursuing the goal and the goal setter to agree on how to attain the goal. Unethical and dysfunctional methods might be declared out of bounds.

POSITIVE REINFORCEMENT AND RECOGNITION PROGRAMS

positive reinforcement
Increasing the probability that behavior will be repeated by rewarding people for making the desired response.

Motivating workers for doing the right thing is a widely accepted and time-tested principle. **Positive reinforcement** is increasing the probability that behavior will be repeated by rewarding people for making the desired response. A *reward* is something of value received as a consequence of having attained a goal. The phrase, "increases the probability" is noteworthy. No motivation strategy guarantees people will always make the right response in the future. However, it increases the chance they will repeat the desired behavior. The term *reinforcement* means the behavior (or response) is strengthened or entrenched. For example, your response in pressing F7 in Word to reach the spelling and grammar function has been reinforced so many times that the response is now probably automatic. However, for many people pressing F5 to refresh a website is probably done so infrequently that the person has to pause and think before making the response.

Here we describe the successful application of positive reinforcement, and using recognition and praise to motivate workers. Both recognition and praise are part of reinforcement. We will also describe cross-cultural differences in the effectiveness of specific rewards.

Rules for Application of Positive Reinforcement

Motivating through positive reinforcement is most likely to take the form of a rewards and recognition program. Managers use positive reinforcement more frequently, on an informal, daily basis. The following list presents suggestions for making effective use of positive reinforcement, whether as part of a company program or more informally.

1 *State clearly what behavior will lead to a reward, and supply ample feedback.* The nature of good performance, or the goals must be agreed to by both manager and group member. Clarification could take this form: "What I need are inventory reports without missing data. When you achieve this, you'll be credited with good performance." As workers attain the performance goals, they should receive frequent feedback. Telling workers they have done something correctly, or notifying them by e-mail, are both efficient forms of feedback.

2 *Use appropriate rewards.* An appropriate reward proves effective when it is valued by the person being motivated. Examine the list of rewards in Figure 11-4. Note that some appeal more to you than others. The best way to motivate people is to offer them their preferred rewards for good performance. Managers should ask employees what they are interested in attaining.

3 *Make rewards contingent on good performance.* Contingent reinforcement means that getting the reward depends on giving a certain performance. Unless a reward is linked to the desired behavior or performance it will have little effect on whether the behavior or performance is repeated. For example, saying, "You're doing great" in response to anything an employee does will not lead to good performance. Yet if the manager reserves the, "doing great" response for truly outstanding performance, he or she may reinforce the good performance.

4 *Administer rewards intermittently.* Positive reinforcement can be administered under different types of schedules. The most effective and sensible type is an intermittent schedule, in which rewards are administered often, but not always, when the appropriate behavior occurs. A reward loses its effect if given every time the employee makes the right response. Intermittent rewards sustain desired behavior for a longer time by helping to prevent the behavior from fading away when it is not rewarded. In addition to being more effective, intermittent rewards are generally more practical than continuous rewards. Few managers have enough time to dispense rewards every time team members attain performance goals.

5 *Administer rewards promptly.* The proper timing of rewards may be difficult because the manager is not present at the time of good performance. In this case, an e-mail message, text message, or phone call of appreciation within several days of the good performance is appropriate. Some managers are posting tweets these days to post public notes of appreciation.

6 *Change rewards periodically.* Rewards grow stale quickly; they must be changed periodically. A repetitive reward can even become an annoyance. How many times can one be motivated by the phrase "nice job?" Suppose the reward for making a sales quota is a fitness tracker. How many fitness trackers can one person use (assuming the award is not re-gifted)?

Figure 11-4 Rewards Suitable for Use in Positive Reinforcement

A large number of potential rewards can be used to motivate individuals and teams, and many of them are low-cost or no-cost. An important condition for a reward is the perception of its value by the individual being motivated. The viewpoint of the reward giver alone about the value of a reward is not sufficient.

Monetary
Performance raise or bonus
Salary increase
Profit sharing
Stock options
Added vacation days
Gift cards, including restaurant or coffee shop cards
Gift selection from online catalogue
Instant cash award for exceptional performance on a given
    task
Concert, theater, or sporting event tickets
Company-paid weekend vacation at resort

Job and Career Related
Challenging work assignment
Opportunities for advancement
Empower the employee
Change of job status from temporary to permanent
Assignment to high-prestige project
Favorable performance evaluation
Flexible working hours
Authorize remote working part of the time
Job rotation
Seminars and continuous education
Tuition assistance

Recognition and Pride Related
Compliments in private or publicly
Appreciative feedback for high-quality work
Open note of thanks distributed electronically
Hand shake, fist bump. high-five, or pat on back
Object, such as clock, from company recognition program
Employee-of-the-month award
Team uniforms, hats, or T-Shirts
Thank-you note posted on cubicle
"ABCD" card when worker goes, "Above the Call of Duty"
Standing ovation at start of next staff meeting
Recognition parties

Status Symbols
End-cubicle, bigger cubicle, or movement to a private office
Freedom to personalize work area
Private parking space

Time Off
Three-day weekend
Personal leave days for events chosen by employee

Food and Dining
Business luncheon paid by company
Company picnic
Department parties or banquets
Lunch catered into office
After work socials or happy hour

Source: Some of these rewards are from mentions in the following sources: Heather Lonczak, "Positive Reinforcement in the Workplace," *www.positivepsychology.com*, October 7, 2019, pp. 1–23; Kevin Kruse, "25-Low-Cost Ways to Reward Employees," *Forbes* (www.forbes.com), March 1, 2013. pp. 1–3; Julie Davoren, "What Type of Rewards Would Motivate Workers in an Organization?" *Chron* (*www.smallbusiness.chron. com*) pp.1–2; © Copyright 2016 Hearst Newspapers, LLC.

7 *Make the rewards visible.* When other workers notice the reward, its impact multiplies because other people observe what kind of behavior is rewarded. Assume you were informed about a co-worker's exciting assignment, given because of high performance. You might strive to accomplish the same level of performance.

8 *Reward groups and teams as well as individuals.* To improve organizational productivity, groups as well as individuals should receive rewards for good performance. A combination of group and individual rewards encourages teamwork, yet does not discourage outstanding individual performance.

Positive Reinforcement Effectiveness

The power of positive reinforcement to change behavior is being successfully applied to develop a healthier workforce in many companies. Approximately one-half of employers offering wellness incentives tie rewards to completion of lifestyle modification programs, including weight loss, smoking cessation and physical fitness.[22] Incentives from $51 to $100 can increase participation in smoking cessation and weight management programs and encourage workers to get biometric screenings. Incentives of greater than $100 are associated with higher participation in health risk appraisals.[23] The payoff to the company includes lower health-insurance costs as well as higher productivity because healthy workers can concentrate better, have more energy and are absent less frequently.

Employee Recognition and Reward Programs and Informal Recognition

As indicated in Figure 11-4, positive reinforcement for workers often takes the form of tangible rewards as well as recognition and praise. A combination of recognition and rewards along with informal praise is likely to be the most motivational. Here we describe these two related approaches separately.

Recognition and Reward Programs

A large majority of companies of all sizes have formal *recognition* and *reward* programs. The broader purpose of rewards and recognition is to enhance employee engagement. A well-designed reward-and-recognition program can help increase revenue, boost worker productivity, and improve employee retention.[24] Recognition programs are also important because managers want to keep workers productive who worry about losing their jobs or having no private work areas.

These recognition programs usually include the term "reward" because good performers are recognized with rewards. These can include dinner certificates, watches and jewelry, candles, plaques, and on-the-spot cash awards (around $25 to $50) for good performance. Employee recognition programs are so widespread, that several companies including O. C. Tanner Maritz Inc. specialize in developing reward incentive and recognition programs for other companies.

Yum Brands, the world's largest restaurant company whose divisions include Taco Bell, KFC and Pizza Hut, is widely recognized for its programs of rewards and recognition. When Chairman and CEO David C. Novak became president of KFC, he wanted to break through the clutter of recognition so he gave away rubber chickens. He would give an outstanding KFC chef a rubber chicken along with a $100 check, and the event was photographed. Novak now gives away big sets of smiling teeth with legs on them for people walking the talk on behalf of the customer. Part of his reasoning is that many people quit because they do not feel appreciated.[25]

More sophisticated recognition programs recognize behavior that supports organizational values so the awards are a reminder of what is important to the company. A GE program called Ecomagination fits this idea because individuals and teams are recognized for accomplishments related to environmental sustainability.

Teams, as well as individuals, should receive recognition to enhance motivation. Motivation consultant Bob Nelson recommends that to build a high-performing team, the manager should acknowledge the success of all team members. As with individual recognition, a personal touch works best. Examples include a manager thanking group members for their involvement, suggestions and initiatives. Holding a group luncheon for outstanding team performance is also a potential motivator.[26] *Potential* is emphasized because team recognition does not take into account individual differences in preferences for rewards. For example, some employees object to group luncheons because it diverts time they might want to use for personal purposes.

Peer-to-peer recognition is facilitated by technology that enables employees to use their smartphones, or log into their computers or kiosks to praise coworkers. Shared websites are helpful in making recognition public, rather than only an interaction between a manager and the employee.[27]

As with most motivation and retention programs, recognition and rewards have to be carefully planned, otherwise they may backfire and lose money for the company. One example is giving out turkeys or gift baskets of food during the holidays that many employees perceive to be insulting and patronizing. Vegans and vegetarians, as well as people who do not eat poultry based on religious values, may object to such rewards. An advanced procedure is to ask employees what types of recognition they prefer.

The accompanying *Management in Action* insert describes a reward and recognition program at a prominent yogurt maker.

MANAGEMENT IN ACTION

Employee Recognition at Yogurt Maker Chobani

Ten years after Hamdi Ulukaya, raised in Turkey, bought a shuttered yogurt factory in upstate New York, Chobani became the top-selling brand of Greek yogurt in the United States. Chobani also became the second-largest overall yogurt manufacturer in the country. In addition to producing world-class yogurt, the company focuses on keeping its 2000-person workforce motivated and satisfied. A Great Place to Work® survey had indicated five years ago that the employees wanted a more robust employee recognition system.

Up to 2016, HR manager Andrew Schrader had been administering staff recognition through e-mail and delivering gold balloons as rewards, without attaining visible results. Chobani needed a recognition system that was meaningful and more rapidly tied to exceptional behavior for retail teams, factory workers, and corporate employees. The acronym for great feedback at the company is RISE: Regular, Immediate, Specific, and Encouraging.

Schrader and Chobani's People Team launched a recognition program called Bonusly in 2017. The workforce was spread across Chobani headquarters in New Berlin, New York, a yogurt plant in Twin Falls, Idaho, and a corporate office and retail locations in New York City. The Chobani core values are craftsmanship, integrity, leadership, innovation, giving back, and our people. Whenever an employee exhibits one of these values on the job, teammates are authorized to recognize him or her with a small bonus.

The bonuses are of several types: small cash bonuses. written praise, and verbal (spoken) praise. Each employee has a monthly allowance of four cups (a form of currency worth five dollars) to distribute at their discretion. Team leaders receive an additional boost in allowance for cups during major projects so they can adequately recognize everybody who contributes to

the project. Awards can be cashed in for gift cards, Chobani gear, or donated to a charitable cause.

The recognition rewards are generously distributed. Seventy-three percent of Chobani employees receive at least one bonus each month. About one-third of the bonuses are sent via a mobile app. Because production employees are not allowed to use smartphones while working, the bonuses are placed on kiosks in the break room. The annual rate of bonuses is over 63,000. Everyone who put the app on their phone received a Chobani wristband, and everyone who gave their first cup received a Chobani hat. Having the ability to recognize another employee immediately is considered to be the most valuable part of Bonusly. According to Schrader, the recognition program has contributed to a employee loyalty.

Questions

1. **Why might the recognition program at Chobani contribute to engagement as well as motivation?**

2. **What concern might you have that the Bonusly program might be perceived as a "hokey" by many employees?**

Source: Original story based on facts and observations in the following sources: Will Gardner, "Employee Recognition Comes Fast and Frequently at Chobani," *https://willgardner.com*, February 22, 2018, p. 1; Stephanie Strom, "At Chobani, Now It's Not Just the Yogurt That's Rich," *The New York Times* (www.nytimes.com), April 26, 2016, 1–5; Andrew Schrader, "Chobani," *Bonusly* (http://go.bonus.ly/hubfs, accessed February 10, 2020, pp. 1–6; Simon Mainwaring, "Purpose at Work: How Chobani Builds a Purposeful Culture around Social Impact," *Forbes* (www.forbes.com), August 27, 2018, pp. 1–3.

Informal Recognition Including Praise

Praising workers for good performance is a major type of informal recognition. An effective form of praise describes the worker's performance rather than merely making an evaluation. Describing good performance might take this form: "You turned an angry customer into an ally who has referred new business to us." A straightforward evaluation would be, "You did a great job with that angry customer." Even more effective would be to combine the two statements.

Generic praise, such as telling all workers on the team they are doing a great job can be discouraging, because the team members will not feel they are being recognized as individuals. A useful principle of effective praise is that it should be true, sincere, deserved and meaningful. Here is an example of praising good performance:

Karla, you made a terrific presentation this morning. I especially liked the charts you use to illustrate the budget choices we are facing. That really helped me make sense of a complicated issue, and I appreciate the work you put it.[28]

Jana Gallus, assistant professor of strategy and behavioral decision making at the UCLA Anderson School of Management, recommends that managers use *discretionary* rewards to informally recognize good performance. Discretionary rewards refer to honors where a manager, under no obligation, chooses to recognize noteworthy behavior that goes beyond what is expected and isn't already acknowledged by other rewards. For example, a high level of collaboration can be recognized with teamwork honors. The element of surprise increases the potency of the award for the winners.[29]

Although praise costs no money and only requires a few moments of time, many workers feel they do not receive enough praise. Managers therefore have a good opportunity to increase motivation by the simple act of praising good deeds. Other informal approaches to recognizing good performance include taking an employee to lunch, a handshake from the manager or team leader, and putting flowers on an employee's desk. E-mail and text messages are also handy tools for giving praise and recognition. Figure 11-5 provides a list of statements of praise that might be used with team members.

Figure 11-5 Twenty Ways to Say "Well Done"

Sometimes, offering praise is harder than it should be. In a busy office, it's easy to forget to compliment and voice your appreciation. But praise can really make a team member's day. Here are some reminders of how easy it really is to say, "Thanks, well done."

1. I'm proud you're on my team.
2. Congratulations on a terrific job.
3. You're so helpful. Thank you.
4. You really made a difference by …
5. Thanks so much for your considerate effort.
6. I really admire your perseverance.
7. You've made my day because of …
8. You're a champion.
9. Wow, what an incredible accomplishment.
10. Great effort. You make us all look good.
11. I have great confidence in you.
12. You've grasped the concept well.
13. Your customer service skills are sensational.
14. Your sales results are outstanding.
15. You're a valuable part of the team.
16. Your efforts are really making a difference.
17. You are hitting high productivity.
18. Our customers are crazy about you.
19. You have helped us attain our goals.
20. Your work ethic motivates the team.

Cross-Cultural Differences in Needs and Suitable Recognition Awards

A person's culture can influence which needs are strongest for him or her, and therefore which approach to recognizing and motivating that person is the most effective. A manager can study different cultures in general to get some ideas but it is also important to make some observations within the work group. According to popular stereotype, a worker raised in Japan would more likely be motivated by recognition in private than by public recognition. In contrast, an American-raised worker would be more likely to experience need satisfaction when given public recognition, such as during a staff or town hall meeting.

Cross-cultural differences in standards of living also influence the effectiveness of recognition awards. In the United States, an outstanding performer might be rewarded with a luxury item like a Mont Blanc pen or watch worth about $1,000 retail. Yet in India or China, where standards of living are still rising and bicycles remain an important mode of transportation, $1,000 might be better invested by buying a motor bike for a top employee. Incentives consultant Eugene Less says, "You might not give a moped away in the U.S. but giving one in China or India is a huge thing."[30]

Despite cultural and geographic differences, the manager must still investigate. In general, a moped is a better gift than an expensive fountain pen for a high-performing Chinese worker. Nevertheless, beauty products direct seller Mary Kay has found that pink mobile phones, pink Buicks, and pink Cadillacs are cherished gifts for outstanding sales consultants in China.[31]

A concern about recognition programs is the same as for financial incentives (as described later in this chapter). Focusing too much on potential awards or rewards can lower internal motivation for the task. A study was conducted in five industrial plants that were using an attendance reward program. It found that the external reward crowded out the internal motivation of those employees who had previously demonstrated excellent attendance.[32] An example of internal, or intrinsic, motivation would be a laundry worker enjoying the folding and packing of freshly cleaned uniforms.

LEARNING OBJECTIVE 5

Explain the conditions under which a person will be motivated according to expectancy theory.

expectancy theory of motivation
The belief that people will put forth the greatest effort if they expect the effort to lead to performance that, in turn, leads to a reward.

EXPECTANCY THEORY OF MOTIVATION

According to the **expectancy theory of motivation**, people will put forth the greatest effort if they expect the effort to lead to performance that, in turn, leads to a reward. The various versions of expectancy theory suggest that a process similar to rational gambling determines choices among courses of action. Employees are motivated by what they expect will be the consequences of their efforts. Expectancy theory assumes that people are rational and will seek to maximize pleasure and minimize pain with the choices they make. At the same time, they must be confident they can perform the task.[33]

A Basic Model of Expectancy Theory

Expectancy theory integrates important ideas found in other generally accepted motivation theories, including those presented in this chapter. Figure 11-6 presents a basic version of expectancy theory. According to the version of expectancy theory developed by Victor H. Vroom, four conditions must exist for motivated behavior to occur.[34]

> ### Figure 11-6 Basic Version of Expectancy Theory of Motivation
>
> An individual will be motivated when:
>
> A. The individual believes effort (E) will lead to favorable performance (P)—that is, when $E{\rightarrow}P$ (also referred to as expectancy).
>
> B. The individual believes performance will lead to favorable outcome (O)—that is, when $P{\rightarrow}O$ (also referred to as instrumentality).
>
> C. Outcome or reward satisfies an important need (in other words, valence is strong).
>
> D. Need satisfaction is intense enough to make effort seem worthwhile.

Condition A refers to *expectancy*, which means that people will expend effort because they believe it will lead to performance. In this $E{\rightarrow}P$ expectancy, subjective probabilities range between 0.0 and 1.0. Rational people ask themselves, "If I work hard, will I really get the job done?" If they evaluate the probability as being high, they probably will invest the effort to achieve the goal. People have higher $E{\rightarrow}P$ expectancies when they have the appropriate skills, training and self-confidence.

Condition B is based on the fact that people are more willing to expend effort if they think good performance will lead to a reward, referred to as $P{\rightarrow}O$ instrumentality. It too ranges between 0.0 and 1.0. (*Instrumentality* refers to the idea that the behavior is instrumental in achieving an important end.) The rational person says, "I'm much more willing to perform well if I'm assured that I'll receive the reward I deserve." A cautious employee might even ask other employees if they received their promised rewards for exceptional performance. To strengthen a subordinate's $P{\rightarrow}O$ instrumentality, the manager should give reassurance that the reward will be forthcoming.

Condition C refers to *valence*, the value a person attaches to certain outcomes. The greater the valence, the greater the effort. Valences can be either positive or negative. If a student believes receiving an A is important, he or she will work hard. Also, if a student believes that avoiding a C or a lower grade is important, he or she will work hard. Valences range from –1 to + 1 in most versions of expectancy theory. A positive valence indicates a preference for a particular reward. A clearer picture of individual differences in human motivation spreads valences out over a range of –100 to +100.

Most work situations present the possibility of several outcomes, with a different valence attached to each. Assume a project manager is pondering whether becoming a project management professional (PMP) would be worth the effort. The list that follows cites possible outcomes or rewards from achieving certification, along with their valences (on a scale of –100 to +100).

- Status from being a PMP, 75
- Promotion to senior project manager, 95
- Plaque to hang on office wall, 25
- Bigger salary increase next year, 90
- Letters of congratulations from friends and relatives, 50
- Expressions of envy from one or two co-workers, –25

Valences are useful in explaining why some people will put forth the effort to do things with low expectancies. For example, most people know the chance of winning a lottery, inventing something as successful as Facebook, or writing a best-selling novel is only one in a million. Nevertheless, a number of people vigorously pursue these goals. They do so because they attach an extraordinary positive valence to these outcomes (perhaps 100!).

Condition D indicates that the need satisfaction stemming from each outcome must be intense enough to make the effort worthwhile. Would you walk two miles on a hot day for one glass of ice water? The water would undoubtedly satisfy your thirst need, but the magnitude of the satisfaction would probably not be worth the effort. Similarly, a production technician turned down a promotion to the position of inspector because the raise offered was only 50 cents per hour. The worker told his supervisor, "I need more money. But I'm not willing to take on that much added responsibility for $30 a week."

Implications for Management

Expectancy theory has several important implications for the effective management of people. The theory helps pinpoint what a manager must do to motivate group members and diagnose motivational problems.[35]

1. *Individual differences among employees must be taken into account.* Different people attach different valences to different rewards, so a manager should try to match rewards with individual preferences. Positive reinforcement also makes use of this principle.

2. *Help workers feel they are making progress toward their goals.* One of the components of expectancy theory deals with feeling that your effort will lead to good performance, so workers have a desire to believe they are making headway in their jobs. A multiyear study tracking hundreds of knowledge workers found that the top motivator of performance is the feeling of making progress. The study found that when workers feel they are making headway in their jobs, or when they receive support that helps them overcome obstacles, their drive to succeed is at its highest.[36] (The same study was mentioned above in relation to work engagement.)

3. *Rewards should be closely tied to those actions the organization sees as worthwhile.* For example, if the organization values customer service, people should be rewarded for providing good customer service.

4. *Employees should be given the appropriate training and encouragement.* An investment in training will strengthen their subjective decision making which, in turn, will lead to good performance.

5. *Employees should be presented with credible evidence that good performance does lead to anticipated rewards.* Similarly, a manager should reassure employees that good work will be both noticed and rewarded. As part of this implication, managers must listen carefully to understand the perceived link employees have between hard work and rewards. If instrumentality is unjustifiably low, the manager must reassure the employee that hard work will be rewarded.

6. *The meaning and implications of outcomes should be explained.* It can be motivational for employees to know the values of certain outcomes. If an employee knows that a high rating on a performance evaluation increases the chances of receiving favorable assignments and promotions, plus a bigger salary increase, he or she will strive harder to perform well.

MOTIVATION THROUGH FINANCIAL INCENTIVES

LEARNING OBJECTIVE **6**

A natural way to motivate workers at any level is to offer them financial incentives for good performance. The more a person needs money, the stronger the motivational power of financial incentives. Using financial incentives to motivate people fits principles of positive reinforcement. Financial incentives, however, predate positive reinforcement. The paragraphs that follow discuss linking pay to performance, profit sharing, employee stock ownership and stock options, and problems associated with financial incentives. Figure 11-7 outlines this information.

Describe the role of financial incentives and profit sharing in worker motivation.

A useful principle for using financial incentives to motivate workers at all levels is to investigate which incentives are most appealing to groups as well as individuals. Many workers are motivated to work hard for salary increases, yet some others would work harder for the opportunity to obtain a bonus or stock options. Another group of workers might value increased health benefits more than a salary increase. Another key principle is for managers to explain clearly to employees how performance is linked to pay, including the fact that unethical behavior will not be tolerated as a way of attaining a performance goal.

Linking Pay to Performance Including Bonuses

Financial incentives are more effective when they are linked to (or contingent upon) good performance. Production workers and sales workers have long received contingent financial incentives. After meeting a quota, many production workers receive bonuses per unit of production. Most industrial sales representatives receive salary plus commissions.

Managers increasingly use bonuses to retain and motivate employees. Bonuses help control fixed costs, and also tend to keep employees focused on business objectives. Today about 12.5 percent of payroll is allotted to incentive and bonus pay, and about 80 percent of large North American companies award bonuses.[37] Human resources specialists also see equitable salaries and merit pay as a way of keeping employees engaged. Conversely, the lack of merit pay can readily disengage workers. When times are tight, pay for performance can be used to focus on the most valuable contributors so they can be recognized, motivated and retained.[38]

Figure 11-7 Linking Pay to Performance, Including Bonuses

Multiple approaches to motivate workers by using financial incentives are possible.

Linking Pay to Performance

Employee Stock Ownership Plans

Profit Sharing

Stock Options

Figure 11-8 Guidelines for Performance-Based Merit Increases at a Hospital

Merit pay is additional income earned for meeting performance standards.

Performance Level of Staff Members	Merit Increase (Percentage of Pay)
Demonstrate exceptional performance and make outstanding contributions during the year.	4.75–5.50
Give consistently productive performance that meets all standards and exceeds some.	3.75–4.74
Give consistently productive performance that meets expectations.	2.00–3.74
Demonstrate performance that is not wholly satisfactory, even though some expectations may be met or even exceeded.	1.00–1.99
Generally fail to meet key expectations and standards; substantial improvement is necessary and essential.	0.00

Note: To help equalize wages more, some organizations assign an absolute amount of salary increase to each performance category. For example, all workers in the top category would receive a $2,500 increase; those in the second category $1,500; those in the third category, $1,000; and those in the fourth category, zero dollars. Assigning absolute dollar amounts to each category prevents junior workers receiving relatively small increases because their base pay is so much lower. Under the new system a more junior top-performing worker making $30,000 per year would receive a new salary of $32,500 ($30,000 + $2,500). Under the old percentage system, his or her maximum new salary might be $31,650 ($30,000 + 0.055 × $30,000).

merit pay
A method of distributing wage and salary increases based on results.

Figure 11-8 presents a typical approach to linking employee pay to performance, a plan that is often referred to as **merit pay**. Such a plan has become an almost universal method of distributing wage and salary increases in the United States and in many other countries. Note carefully in Figure 11-8 the information about assigning lump sum payments, rather than percentages to each performance category. This approach helps more junior workers receive large merit increases. A cost-of-living adjustment is not considered merit pay because it is not related to performance. Merit pay for both individual contributors and managers is based on actual results.

An increasing effort of managers and compensation specialists to link pay to performance supports many business strategies—workers receive financial incentives for performing in ways consistent with the business strategy. For example, if part of a company's strategy is to build a more culturally diverse workforce, financial incentives would be paid for recruiting culturally diverse workers.

For a pay-for-performance plan to be successful, performance must be measured carefully and regularly. Most pay-for-performance plans are based somewhat on qualitative measures, such as supervisory ratings. Whenever possible, quantitative measures of performance should also be included, such as sales completed, productivity, turnover, patents, return on investment and customer satisfaction results.

As implied above, individual and group differences often influence the type of pay for performance that is most likely to be an effective motivator. For example, a person with high risk-taking tendencies might be willing to accept a higher proportion of pay based on performance.

Profit Sharing

profit-sharing plan
A method of giving workers supplemental income based on the profitability of the entire firm or a selected unit.

The pay plans mentioned so far link rewards to individual effort. Many organizations attempt to increase motivation and productivity through a company-wide plan linking incentive pay to increases in performance. **Profit-sharing plans** give workers supplemental income based on the profitability of the entire firm or a selected unit. The motivational principle is that employees will work harder to contribute to profitability when they will eventually share some of the profits. The larger the company, the more difficult it is for the individual employee to visualize how his or her work efforts translate into corporate profits. Ideally, all employees need to be committed to working for a common good. Employee contributions to profits may take a variety of forms, such as product quantity, product quality, reducing costs, or improving business processes.

A major challenge in administering profit-sharing plans as well as any of the other financial incentives described here is making precise judgments about who should receive how much, and whether the variable pay contributes to organizational performance.

Employee Stock Ownership and Stock Option Plans

Another way of motivating workers with financial incentives is to make them part owners of the business through stock purchases. Two variations of the same idea of giving workers equity in the business are stock ownership and stock option plans. Stock ownership can be motivational because employees participate in the financial success of the firm as measured by its stock price. If employees work hard, the company may become more successful and the value of the stock increases. Executives are supposed to be strongly motivated by stock ownership because if the stock increases in price, the executives earn so many company shares. If the stock increases substantially in value, the executive can sell the stock and earn millions of dollars.

Under an *employee stock ownership plan* (ESOP), employees at all levels in the organization are given stock. The employer either contributes shares of its stock or the money to purchase the stock on the open market. Stock shares are usually deposited in employee retirement accounts. Today there are about 7,000 ESOPs in the United States with over 14 million participants.[39] Upon retirement, employees can choose to receive company stock instead of cash. ESOPs are also significant because they offer tax incentives to the employer. For example, a portion of the earnings paid to the retirement fund are tax deductible. Chobani, the yogurt company described earlier in this chapter, relies heavily on an ESOP to motivate and retain workers. Many Chobani workers have become rich because of the ESOP.

Employee stock ownership plans are popular because they are easy to understand, and contribute to an ownership culture. The only notable downside is that employees might rely too heavily on company stock in their investment portfolio, thereby forgoing the advantages of having a diversified investment portfolio. If the company stock plunges dramatically, the value of the employee's investments shrinks to almost nothing.

Employee stock options are more complicated than straightforward stock ownership. Stock options give employees the right to purchase company stock at a specified price at some future point. If the stock rises in value, you can purchase it at a discount. If the stock sinks below your designated purchase price, your option is worthless. Thousands of workers in the information technology field, particularly in Silicon Valley have become millionaires and multimillionaires with their stock options—particularly those who cashed in their options at the right time. Because of a tax-accounting rule, stock options are rarely granted to employees earning less than $100,000 per year.

For many workers, cash is more attractive than stock ownership as a form of compensation, particularly if they lack a long-range perspective about personal finance. One problem is that if part of compensation is based on stock, the employee has less cash immediately available for personal use. Also, cash has a more stable value than stocks.

Problems Associated with Financial Incentives

Although financial incentives are widely used as motivators, they can create problems. A major problem is that workers may not agree with managers about the value of their contributions. Financial incentives can also pit individuals and groups against each other. The result may be unhealthy competition rather than cooperation and teamwork. Some managers believe that giving equal increases to all members of the team promotes teamwork.

Another concern is that merit pay decisions are based on performance evaluations which may be too subjective. As implied in the criticisms of goals, huge financial incentives can prompt financial managers to make high-risk investments that can result in major losses for investors, such as selling securities based on mortgages held by people with poor credit.

Many critics of financial incentives are concerned that American business executives siphon off too much money from corporations that could go to shareholders, employees, and to customers in the form of lower prices. Top-level managers may deserve large financial rewards for good performance, but how much is too much? For example, does a CEO deserve compensation of $60 million in one year?

People who justify such high executive compensation say the large payments are necessary to attract and retain top talent, and to keep executives motivated. And besides, executive pay is a small percentage of total revenues. You have probably heard the same argument for paying some professional athletes $20 million per year. Another argument in favor of giant compensation for executives is that managerial skills are highly valued in society, and top business managers and leaders are worth at least as much as entertainment stars.

The most researched argument against financial rewards is that it focuses the attention of workers too much on the reward such as money or stocks. In the process, the workers lose out on intrinsic rewards, such as the joy in accomplishment. Instead of being passionate about the work they are doing, people become overly concerned with the size of their rewards. This distinction is important because intrinsic motivation is more intense and longer lasting than the external motivation of pursuing financial incentives.[40]

One argument is that external rewards do not create a lasting commitment. Instead, they create temporary compliance, such as working hard in the short run to earn a bonus. A frequent problem with merit pay systems is that a person who does not receive a merit increase for one pay period then feels that he or she has been punished.

In reality, workers at all levels want a combination of internal (intrinsic) rewards and financial rewards along with other external rewards, such as praise. Workers also want a work environment that enables them to manage their life well off the job, such as ample vacation time and some flexibility in working hours. Workers also search for meaning and satisfaction as well as financial rewards.[41] The ideal combination is to offer exciting (intrinsically motivating) work to people, and simultaneously pay them enough money so they are not preoccupied with matters, such as salary and bonuses.

A useful perspective for managers is that for financial rewards to be effective motivators, they must be combined with meaningful responsibility, respect for the worker, constructive relationships on the job and recognition. All these factors combined make for an effective motivation strategy.[42]

SUMMARY OF KEY POINTS

1 **Explain how employee engagement is part of employee motivation.**

Work engagement is essentially an extension of motivation, referring to employee commitment. Recent studies have found that most Americans are engaged in their work. Employee engagement can have a payoff to the organization. A wide variety of programs and managerial actions are aimed at enhancing employee engagement. Benefits, compensation, work and family programs, recognizing employees, and giving them career guidance are major approaches to engagement. Showing workers the impact of their jobs helps inspire and engage them. Promoting small wins and listening to employees also facilitates engagement.

2 **Present an overview of major theories of need satisfaction in explaining motivation.**

Workers can be motivated through need satisfaction, particularly because most people want to know, "What's in it for me?" First, needs must be identified. Second, the person must be given an opportunity to satisfy those needs.

Maslow's need hierarchy states that people strive to become self-actualized. However, before higher-level needs are activated, certain lower-level needs must be satisfied. When a person's needs are satisfied at one level, he or she looks toward satisfaction at a higher level. Specific needs playing an important role in work motivation include achievement, power, affiliation, recognition, pride, risk taking and thrill seeking. Pep talks and motivational speeches can sometimes satisfy needs, such as affiliation and achievement.

The two-factor theory of work motivation includes two different sets of job motivation factors: Satisfiers and motivators, when present, increase satisfaction and motivation. Satisfiers and motivators generally relate to the content of a job. Dissatisfiers, or maintenance factors, prevent dissatisfaction, but they do not create satisfaction or motivation. Dissatisfiers relate mostly to the context of a job.

3 **Explain how goal setting is used to motivate people.**

Goal setting is an important part of most motivational programs, and it is a managerial method of motivating group members. It is based on these ideas: (a) specific goals are better than generalized goals; (b) difficult goals improve performance, yet excessive difficulty is frustrating except that lofty goals are important; (c) only goals that are accepted improve performance; (d) goals are more effective when used to evaluate performance; (e) goals should be linked to feedback and rewards; and (f) group goal setting is important. The Pygmalion effect contributes to goal setting. Too strong a focus on goals can lead to unethical behavior to attain them.

4 **Describe the application of positive reinforcement including recognition and praise to worker motivation.**

Positive reinforcement focuses on rewarding workers for the right responses. Suggestions for the informal use of positive reinforcement in a work setting include: (a) state clearly what behavior leads to a reward, and supply feedback, (b) use appropriate rewards, (c) make rewards contingent on good performance, (d) administer intermittent rewards, (e) administer rewards promptly, (f) change rewards periodically, (g) make rewards visible, and (h) reward the team as well as the individual. Positive reinforcement is being successfully applied to develop a healthier workforce in many companies.

Motivating employees through recognition takes the form of both reward and recognition programs as well as managers giving recognition and praise informally. Peer recognition can be helpful as a motivator. Cross cultural differences in needs and suitable recognition awards should be taken into account.

Servant leaders have the primary mission of serving the needs of their constituents. They measure their effectiveness in terms of their ability to help others. Instead of seeking recognition, they see themselves as working for group members, including using their talents to be helpful.

5 **Explain the conditions under which a person will be motivated according to expectancy theory.**

Expectancy theory contends that people will expend effort if they expect it will lead to performance and the performance will lead to a reward. According to the expectancy model presented here, a person will be motivated if the person believes effort will lead to performance, the performance will lead to a reward, the reward satisfies an important need, and the need satisfaction is intense enough to make the effort seem worthwhile.

6 **Describe the role of financial incentives and profit sharing in worker motivation.**

A natural way to motivate workers at any level is to offer financial incentives for good performance. Linking pay to performance improves the motivational value of financial incentives. Individual and group differences often influence the type of pay for performance that is most likely to be an effective motivator.

Profit-sharing plans give out money related to company or large-unit performance. Employee stock ownership plans set aside a block of company stock for employee purchase, often redeemable at retirement. Stock option plans give employees the right to purchase company stock at a specified price at some future time. Both plans attempt to motivate workers by making them part owners of the business.

Financial motivators can create problems, such as executives siphoning off too much money from shareholders and employees, and even customers. Financial incentives also encourage workers to focus on the reward instead of the work. For best results, financial incentives should be combined with internal motivators, such as meaningful responsibility and recognition.

Key Terms and Phrases

Questions

1. Assume that a well-known company hires a group of professional workers into high-paying positions. To what extent should the company worry about "engaging" these workers?

2. Suppose you, as a manager, figure out that Jennifer, one of your team members, has strong intrinsic motivation. What would you do with this information to motivate Jennifer to higher levels of performance?

3. A hotel and resort manager finds out that a management trainee on his staff has a strong need for risk taking and thrill seeking. How might the manager make good business use of this trainee?

4. What would you consider to be one or two aspects of a manager's job to be the most meaningful?

5. Visualize a business owner of a chain of hair-styling salons, and she wants to get her salon managers to keep her hair stylists motivated by using positive reinforcement. Identify a few forms of positive reinforcement she might recommend the salon managers use.

6. What information does this chapter have to offer the manager who is already working with a well-motivated team?

7. Some managers object to systematic approaches to motivating employees by expressing the thought, "Why should we have to go out of our way to motivate workers to do what they are paid to do?" What is your reaction to this objection?

Skill-Building Exercise 11-A: Recognizing the Good Work of Others

The evidence about the effectiveness of recognition and other forms of positive reinforcement is impressive. However, we want you to study the results of recognition first hand. Think of someone who performs a service for you whom you might have an opportunity to see more than once or twice. Examples here include cashiers at a supermarket, servers at a restaurant, or bank tellers. When you receive good service from that person, give him or her appropriate recognition (or a super tip if tipping is expected). When you encounter that person again, see if he or she behaves differently, or performs at an even higher level. If no change occurs, analyze the reason for the lack of change. For example, is there a possibility that you did not deliver the recognition effectively.

Skill-Building Exercise 11-B: Identifying the Most Powerful Motivators

The class divides itself into small groups. Working alone, group members first attach a valence to all the rewards in Figure 11-4. Use the expectancy theory scale of −100 to +100. Next, do an analysis of the top ten motivators identified by the group, perhaps by calculating the average valence attached to the rewards that at first glance were assigned high valences by most group members. After each group has identified its top ten motivators, the group leaders can post the results for the other class members to see. After comparing results, answer these questions:

1. What appears to be the top three motivators for the entire class?

2. Do class members tend to favor internal or external rewards?

3. Did career experience or gender influence the results within the groups?

4. Of what value to managers would this exercise be in estimating valences?

Management Now—Online Skill-Building Exercise: Evaluating the Effectiveness of a Motivational Appeal

Search YouTube for a motivational speaker, a business executive, athletic coach, or personal trainer who is delivering a motivational pitch. To what extent do you think this person would be effective at motivating his or her target audience? Explain why. Also, carefully review the video to see what motivational theory might possibly support the presenter's approach to motivation.

The 10-for-10 Program at Mason Appliances

Dennis is the chief sales manager at Mason Appliances, a well-established American firm that manufactures a variety of home appliances including stoves, refrigerators, washing machines, dishwashers, and garbage disposers. Some of the appliances are made in the United States, but with the majority of manufacturing outsourced to companies in China, South Korea, and Malaysia. Mason home appliances have a high-quality reputation, and are priced between high-end appliances and the least expensive. Mason sells most of its appliances through appliance stores, retail stores, and a small percentage through online stores.

Dennis is concerned about declining sales, with sales volume showing an average decrease of 8 percent during the past three years. In a conference with the CEO and chief marketing officer (CMO), the three managers agreed that sales need to improve by 10 percent to keep Mason profitable and to avoid layoffs. The CEO and the CMO agree to give appliance stores and department stores more advertising support. The CMO also said that she might start a program of more brand advertising on television and social media that was not linked to specific stores. Dennis recognized, however, as the sale manager he carried the major responsibility for finding a way to increase sales. Mason has 60 sales representatives across the United States.

Dennis decides on a straightforward plan to motivate the sales reps to increase sales by 10 percent. He will assign a sales goal to each representative to increase sales by 10 percent for the next 12 months. Representatives will have the option of increasing sales by 5 percent for each six-month period. To motivate the reps to attain their goal, Mason will award a 10 percent commission bonus for reaching the goal. Mason decides to label his sales campaign, "10 for 10."

After clearing his program with the CEO and CMO, Dennis communicates the program to the sales reps by phone, e-mail, and text message. Shortly after announcing the 10-for-10 program, Dennis receives back 40 messages from reps who say they will do what they can to increase sales by 10 percent. The idea of a 10 percent bonus is well received. In contrast, Dennis also receives a variety of negative feedback from the other 20 sales reps. The objections center around several points, as illustrated by this feedback:

- "A 10 percent sales increase would be impossible. Five of my customer stores have closed this year. I am doing the best I can to hold on to only a 10 percent decrease."

- "I am trying as hard as I can to sell more appliances. But you have to understand local conditions. Our region is suffering a population decline, and that means fewer people are setting up new household. So fewer people are purchasing new appliances."

- "My customers want bigger and bigger discounts from Mason. If they don't get what they want they will shift to no-name appliances from overseas."

In frustration, Dennis fired back to the negative replies that it was the responsibility of the reps to find a way to reach the new sales goals. Yet at the same time Dennis wondered of his 10-for-10 program would be effective.

Case Questions

1 From the standpoint of goal theory what might Dennis be doing wrong?

2 From the standpoint of goal theory what might Dennis be doing right?

3 Suggest another approach to motivation that might help Mason Appliances boost sales by 10 percent.

Energizing the Vending Machine Team

Pam is the regional manager for Automatic Food Delivery (AFD), a large vending machine management company. She is responsible for the operations of installing and maintaining food and beverage vending machines in four states. AFD customers are typically institutions, such as schools, hotels, offices and factories. Pam's responsibilities include running the office and making sure the company fleet of delivery vans is running smoothly.

The van drivers are the heart of the vending-machine business because they stock and maintain the vending machines, and collect the cash inserted by customers. Wages of the van drivers have been flat for several years because competition makes it difficult to increase prices for services. Also, there has been a slight decline in the sale of food in vending machines because more people are carrying their own food to work, and many consumers have shifted toward healthier snacks. Pam also recognizes that other workers at AFD are experiencing similar problems about flat wages, and a business in slight decline.

Pam notes, "Vending machines may be convenient but they are losing a little of their past popularity. It is much cheaper to store a can of soft drink in the office fridge than pay two bucks for a vended drink." Pam has been in contact with HR director Morgan to discuss the challenges of keeping the van drivers charged up when raises and bonuses will be almost non-existent for the foreseeable future.

Pam says she and the CEO believe that recognition in the form of praise should be an effective way to motivate almost any van driver. Morgan said he would be sending instructions to Pam about praising drivers by both e-mail and the company intranet. Pam

believes she does use praise, but would now do it more systematically, following some of the ideas in the information disseminated by Morgan.

Two days later, Pam dropped by the cubicle of Melissa, the supervisor of customer billing. After a couple of minutes of talk about her work, Pam said, "Melissa, it's just great how you keep the money flowing into the company bank account. Without your efforts AFD would have to shut down." Melissa replied, "Thanks Pam, have a great day."

Later that day, Pam visited a nearby company warehouse where the drivers load their vans before taking off on their route. Pam said to Luis, a van driver, "Top job. Without you making timely stops at your vending machine, we have no business." Luis smiled and said, "Thanks Pam. It feels great to make a contribution."

Pam liked the way her praise was going, so when she ran into Conrad, the sales manager, she said, "You're doing great. It's so much fun to be working with a cool and talented guy." Conrad replied with a quizzical look, "Good enough Pam, whatever you think."

During a visit to the field, Pam commented to Nick, a supervisor of van drivers, "I like how hard and fast your drivers work. You set a high standard for our operations." Nick replied, "Right on, Pam."

Case Questions

1 How well is Pam praising her workers? What advice can you offer her to be more effective in her praise?

2 Which statement of praise do you think was the most effective, and why?

3 Which statement of praise do you think was the least effective, and why?

ENDNOTES

1. Original story based on facts and observations in the following sources: "The 100 Most Creative People In Business: Pamela Fletcher For Electrifying the Auto Industry," *Fast Company*, June 2017, pp. 4041; Aaron Brzozowski, "GM Electric Vehicles Chief Pam Fletcher Made 'Vice President of Innovation'," *GM Authority* (https://gmauthority.com), September 24, 2018, pp. 1–2; "GM VP Pamela Fletcher Earns SAE International's Henry Ford II Distinguished Award for Excellence in Automotive Engineering," *SAE International* (www.sae.org), June 2, 2018, pp. 1–3; Emma Sarran Webster, "Pamela Fletcher on Being a Female Executive in the Auto Industry," *Teen Vogue* (www.teenvogue.com), April 20, 2018, pp. 1–4; "Pamela Fletcher Joins HRL Laboratories Board of Directors," *HRL Laboratories* (www.hrl.com), February 19, 2019, pp. 122.

2. Michael S. Christian, Adela S. Garza, and Jerel E. Slaughter, "Work Engagement: A Quantitative Review of Its Relation with Task and Contextual Performance," *Personnel Psychology*, No. 1, 2011, p. 89.

3. Ibid, p. 94.

4. Daniel W. Newton et al., "Taking Engagement to Task: The Nature and Functioning of Task Across Transitions," *Journal of Applied Psychology*, January 2020, pp. 1–18.

5. Alexander Alonso, "Busting the Engagement Myth," *HR Magazine*, September/October 2018, p. 80.

6. Marcel Schwantes, "Science Found the 5 Things That Drive Employees to Go Above and Beyond," *www.inc.com*, April 19, 2017, p. 5.

7. Daniel M. Cable, "Helping Your Team Find a Purpose in Their Work," *Harvard Business Review* (hrrps://hbr.org), October 22, 2019, pp. 1–6.

8. Teresa Amabile and Steven Kramer, *The Progress Principle: Using Small Wins to Ignite Joy, Engagement, and Creativity at Work* (Boston, MA: Harvard Business School Press, 2011).

9. Kevin Elkenberry, "Questions Are Like Diamonds," *Executive Leadership*, December 2014, p. 7.

10. Thomas Chamorrow-Premuzic, Lewis Garrad, and Didier Elzinger, *Harvard Business Review* (https://hbr.org), November 28, 2018, p. 2.

11. Piers Steel and Cornelius J. König, "Integrating Theories of Motivation," *Academy of Management Review*, October 2006, pp. 895–897.

12. Abraham M. Maslow, "A Theory of Human Motivation," *Psychological Review*, July 1943, pp. 370–396; Abraham M. Maslow, *Motivation and Personality* (New York: Harper & Row, 1954), Chapter 5.

13. Michael J. Stahl, "Achievement, Power, and Managerial Motivation: Selecting Managerial Talent with Job Choice Exercise," *Personnel Psychology*, Winter 1983; David C. McClelland, *Power: The Inner Experience* (New York: Irvington, 1975).

14. Cited in John A. Byrne, "How to Lead Now," *Fast Company*, August 2003, p. 66.

15. Christopher Munsey, "Frisky, but Risky," *Monitor on Psychology*, July/August 2006, p. 40.

16. Katherine Razzi, "The Good Old-Fashioned Pep Talk," *https://employmentinsights.wordpress.com*, January 31, 2013, p. 1.

17. Frederick Herzberg, *Work and the Nature of Man* (Cleveland: World, 1966).

18. Edwin A. Locke and Gary P. Latham (Eds.) *New Developments in Goal Setting and Task Performance* (New York, N.Y.: Routledge, 2013); Gary P. Latham, "Goal Setting: A Five-Step Approach to Behavior Change," *Organizational Dynamics*, Vol. 32, No. 3, 2003, pp. 309–317; Ryan Davies, Hugues Lavandier, and Ken Schwartz, "In Search of a Better Stretch Target," *McKinsey & Company* (www.mckinsey.com), November 2017, pp. 1–7.

19. Dov Eden, *Pygmalion in Management: Productivity as a Self-fulfilling Prophecy* (Lexington, MA: Lexington Books, 1990).

20. Lisa D. Ordóñez, Maurice E. Schweitzer, Adam D. Galinksy, and Max H. Bazerman, "On Good Scholarship, Goal Settings, and Scholars Gone Wild," *Academy of Management Perspectives*, August 2009, pp. 82–87.

21. Eric Schmitt, "'Taxation by Citation Undermines Trust Between Cops and Citizens," *The Wall Street Journal*, August 8, 2015, p. A9.

22. Steven Aldana, "Wellness Program Incentives: The Complete Guide," *www.wellsteps.com*, January 2, 2020, pp. 1–9; Katie Thomas, "Companies Get Strict on Health of Workers," *The New York Times* (www.nytimes.com), March 25, 2013, pp. 1–3

23. Susan J. Wells, "Getting Paid for Staying Well," *HR Magazine*, February 2010, p. 59.

24. Patty Kujwa, "Rewards and Recognition 'Bow' Flex: The Gifts that Rewards Bring You Back," *Workforce*, December 2015, p. 48.

25. Kevin Kruse, "Leadership Secrets from Yum! Brands' CEO David Novak" *www.forbes.com*, June 25, 2014, pp. 1–4; Geoff Colvin, "Great Job! Or How Yum Brands Uses Recognition to Build Teams and Get Results," *Fortune*, August 12, 2013, pp. 62–66.

26. Bob Nelson, "Does One Reward Fit All?" *Workforce*, February 1997, pp. 67–70.

27. Kujawa, Rewards and Recognition 'Bow Flex', p. 50.

28. "Raise Workplace Morale Without Spending a Dime," *Communication Briefings*, April 2010, p. 1.

29. Jana Gallus, "The Best Ways to Give Employees Performance Awards," *The Wall Street Journal*, October 30, 2018, p. R9.

30. Irwin Speizer, "Incentives Catch On Overseas, But Value of Awards Can Too Easily Get Lost in Translation," *Workforce Management*, November 21, 2005, p. 46.

31. Martin Booe, "Sales Force at Mary Kay China Embraces the American Way," *Workforce Management*, April 2005, pp. 24–25; "Mary Kay Cosmetics in China," *The Pink Truth* (www.pinktruth.com), July 26, 2012, pp. 1–8.

32. Timothy Gubler, Ian Larkin, and Lamar Pierce, *Social Science Research Network* (Harvard Business School NOM Unity Working Paper No. 13-069), December 28, 2015, pp. 1–41. © 2016 Social Science Electronic Publishing Inc.

33. Ruth Kanfer, Michael Frese, and Russell E. Johnson, "Motivation Related to Work: A Century of Progress," *Journal of Applied Psychology*, March 2017, pp. 343–344.

34. Victor H. Vroom, *Work and Motivation* (New York: Wiley, 1964).

35. Walter B. Newsom, "Motivate Now!" *Personnel Journal*, February 1999, pp. 51–52.

36. Teresa M. Amabile and Steven J. Kramer, "What Really Motivates Workers," *Harvard Business Review*, January–February 2010, pp. 44–45.

37. Paul Davidson, "Got as Small Raise? Rest May Be In Your Bonus," *USA Today*, June 10, 2017.

38. Fay Hansen, "Merit-Pay Payoff?" *Workforce Management*, November 3, 2008, p. 33.

39. Patty Kujawa, "No Fable: ESOPs Gaining Favor Among Business Owners Looking to Retire," *Workforce*, July/August 2018, p. 17.

40. One such argument is presented in Daniel H. Pink, *Drive: The Surprising Truth About What Motivates Us* (New York: Riverhead, 2010).

41. Gardiner Morse, "Why We Misread Motives," *Harvard Business Review*, January 2003, p. 18.

42.. R. Brayton Bowen, "Today's Workforce Requires New Age Currency," *HR Magazine*, March 2004, p. 101.

CHAPTER 12

Individual and Organizational Communication

OBJECTIVES

After studying this chapter and doing the exercises, you should be able to:

1 Describe the steps in the communication process.

2 Recognize the major types of nonverbal communication in the workplace.

3 Explain and illustrate organizational communications channels and directions.

4 Identify major communication barriers in organizations.

5 Develop tactics for overcoming communication barriers.

6 Describe how to conduct more effective meetings.

7 Describe how organizational (or office) politics affect interpersonal communication.

Workers at LinkedIn often hold business meetings while strolling and talking with each other on the bike path at the company's Mountain View, California, headquarters. It takes approximately 25 minutes to circle the path which fits well in a one-on-one meeting with a colleague or a meeting of up to five people. The walking meetings offer several benefits in addition to getting physical exercise. Walking helps break down formalities, helps people feel less inhibited and fosters camaraderie among the participants. Without eye contact, meetings can feel a little more personal. While walking workers are less likely to access their phones, e-mail, and text messages. Physical exercise can also stimulate creative thinking.

Igor Perisie, the vice president of engineering, recalled a time when he and a colleague were attempting to resolve an issue with the LinkedIn search engine. The two spent hours in a white-board equipped room trying to find a solution, but Perisie still felt something was missing. "So we went on a walk and talked about it," said Perisie. After returning indoors, they had the solution that seemed to be the obvious choice.

Perisie said that sometimes he needs to use a whiteboard to work on a project. Also, when having a difficult conversation that another person's performance is lacking, it is better to converse in a more formal setting.

LinkedIn CEO Jeff Weiner thinks it is energizing to get outside for a one-half hour walk a few times during the working day, saying that the "whole state of things change." At LinkedIn, as well as other companies, walking meetings level the playing field. As people walk side by side, the environment becomes less formal, and the conversation can become more genuine and personal. Some workers believe that fresh air motivates fresh thinking.

Wiener also thinks that conducting a meeting while walking helps you stay focused. "In addition to the obvious fitness benefits," he posted on LinkedIn, "this meeting format essentially eliminates distractions, so I find it to be a much more productive way to spend time."[1]

The above story illustrates how managers look for ways to improve the effectiveness of meetings, a major type of organizational communication. (A walking meeting, however, is limited by the weather and the mobility of its participants.) Communication has been described as the glue that holds the organization together. Looking at the negative side, poor communication is the number one problem in virtually all organizations and the cause of most problems. An interview survey of 1,000 workers conducted by Dynamic Signal, found that 80 percent of workers feel stressed because of ineffective company communication.[2] Considering that negative stress can lower productivity, the communication problems have a strong impact.

Communication is an integral part of all managerial functions. Unless managers communicate with others, they cannot plan, organize, control, or lead. Effective communication is a leader's most potent tool for inspiring workers to take responsibility for creating a better future (implementing the vision).[3] Person-to-person communication is as much a part of managerial, professional, technical, and sales work as running is a part of basketball and soccer. Furthermore, the ability to communicate effectively relates closely to career advancement. Employees who are poor communicators are often bypassed for promotion, particularly if the job includes people contact. Legendary investor and business executive Warren Buffet told a group of business students that good communication skills are the most important skills needed to succeed.[4]

The information in this chapter is designed to improve communication among people in the workplace. Two approaches are used to achieve this end. First, the chapter describes key aspects of the process of organizational communication, including communication channels and barriers, and the use of social networking sites for internal communication. Second, the chapter presents many suggestions about how managers and others can overcome communication barriers and conduct effective meetings. We also study a subtle aspect of communications called organizational politics.

THE COMMUNICATION PROCESS

LEARNING OBJECTIVE **1**

Describe the steps in the communication process.

communication

The process of exchanging information by the use of words, letters, symbols, or nonverbal behavior.

Anytime people send information back and forth to each other they are communicating. **Communication** is the process of exchanging information by the use of words, letters, symbols, or nonverbal behavior. Sending messages to other people, and having the messages interpreted as intended, generally proves to be complex and difficult. The difficulty arises because communication depends on perception. People may perceive words, symbols, actions, and even colors differently, depending on their background and interests.

A typical communication snafu took place at a product-improvement meeting. The supervisor said to a technician, "Product desirability is in the eye of the beholder." The technician responded, "Oh, how interesting." Later the technician told the rest of the team, "It's no use striving for product improvement. The boss thinks product desirability is too subjective to achieve." The supervisor's message—that the consumer is the final judge of product desirability—got lost in the process; communication failed.

Steps in the Communication Process

Figure 12-1 illustrates the complexity of the communication process. This diagram simplifies the baffling process of sending and receiving messages. The model of two-way communication involves four major steps, each subject to interference, or noise. The four steps are encoding, transmission, decoding, and feedback.

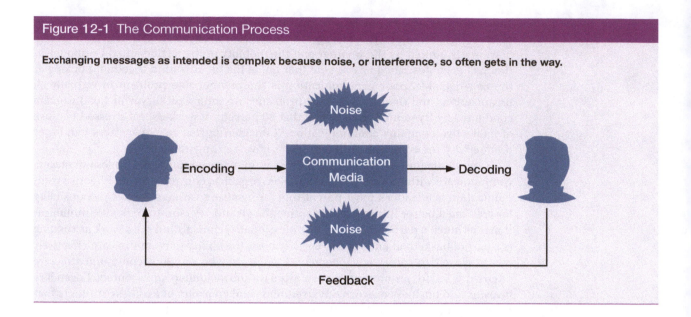

Figure 12-1 The Communication Process

Exchanging messages as intended is complex because noise, or interference, so often gets in the way.

Encoding the Message

Encoding is the process of organizing ideas into a series of symbols, such as words and gestures designed to communicate with the receiver. Word choice strongly influences communication effectiveness. The better a person's grasp of language, the easier it is for him or her to encode. Appropriate choices of words or any other symbol increases the chances that communication will flow smoothly. The supervisor mentioned at the beginning of this section chose to use the somewhat vague phrase: "Product desirability is in the eye of the beholder." A more effective message might be "Product desirability is measured by customer acceptance."

encoding
The process of organizing ideas into a series of symbols designed to communicate with the receiver.

Communication Media

The message is sent via a communication medium, such as voice, e-mail, text message, blog, or phone. Selecting a medium that fits the message contributes to its effectiveness. In general, more emotional, sensitive, and negative topics are better communicated face-to-face, such as offering a worker a promotion or disciplining him or her. It would be appropriate to use the spoken word to inform a co-worker that his shirt was torn. It would be inappropriate to send the same message through e-mail or voice mail because the message might appear too harsh and ridiculing. Many messages in organizations are communicated nonverbally, through the use of gestures and facial expressions. For example, a smile from a superior in a meeting effectively communicates the message, "I agree with your comment."

Decoding the Message

In **decoding**, the receiver interprets the message and translates it into meaningful information. Barriers to communication often surface at the decoding step. People may interpret messages according to their psychological needs and motives. The technician mentioned earlier may have been looking for an out—a reason not to be so

decoding
The communication stage in which the receiver interprets the message and translates it into meaningful information.

concerned about achieving high standards. So he interpreted the message in a way that minimized the need to strive for product desirability.

After understanding comes action—the receiver does something about the message. If the receiver acts in the manner the sender wants, the communication process is successful. From the manager's perspective, the success of a message is measured in terms of the action taken by a group member. Understanding alone is not sufficient. Many people understand messages but take no constructive action.

Feedback

feedback
The communication stage in which the receiver responds to the sender's message.

The receiver's response to the sender's message is referred to as **feedback**. Without feedback, it is difficult to know whether a message has been received and understood. Also, many people are offended when they are forced to listen to a message but not given the opportunity for feedback. The feedback step also includes the reactions of the receiver. If the receiver takes actions as intended by the sender, the message has been received satisfactorily.

Action represents a form of feedback, because it results in a message sent to the original sender from the receiver. Suppose a small business owner receives this message from a supplier: "Please send us $450 within 10 days to cover your overdue account. If we do not receive payment within 10 days, your account will be turned over to a collection agent." The owner understands the message but decides not to comply because the parts for which the $450 is owed were defective. The owner's noncompliance is not due to a lack of understanding.

The feedback from the receiver to the sender is likely to be better accepted when it contains an analysis, rather than merely an opinion.[5] An opinion would be, "Your idea about sending home appliance ads exclusively online is bad." An analysis on the same subject would be, "Although practically all our customers use the Internet, marketing research shows that direct mail is more influential than e-mail and other online ads for the purchase of appliances."

noise
In communication, unwanted interference that can distort or block a message.

Many missteps can occur between encoding and decoding a message. **Noise**, or unwanted interference can distort or block the message. Later in the chapter, the discussion of communication barriers will examine the problem of noise and how it prevents the smooth flow of ideas between sender and receiver.

LEARNING OBJECTIVE **2**

Recognize the major types of nonverbal communication in the workplace.

nonverbal communication
The transmission of messages by means other than words.

NONVERBAL COMMUNICATION IN ORGANIZATIONS

The most obvious modes of communication are speaking, writing, and sign language. A substantial amount of interpersonal communication also occurs through **nonverbal communication**, the transmission of messages by means other than words. Nonverbal communication usually supplements rather than substitutes for writing, speaking, and sign language. The general purpose of nonverbal communication is to express the feeling behind a message, such as nodding one's head vigorously to indicate an emphatic "yes." Here are seven of the most frequently used forms of nonverbal communication:

1 *Hand and body gestures.* Your hand and body movements convey specific information to others. Frequent gesturing shows a positive attitude toward another person. In contrast, dislike or disinterest usually produces few gestures. An important exception here occurs when some people wave their hands while in an argument, sometimes to the point of making threatening gestures. The type of gesture displayed also communicates a specific message. For example,

moving your hand toward your body in a waving motion communicates the message, "Come here, I like you," or, "Tell me more." Palms spread outward indicate perplexity. Putting hands palms down indicates that someone means business. For instance, when negotiating over price, "palms down" indicates a potential buyer intends to walk away.[6]

Related to hand gestures is the handshake that we all know is part of how people judge your self-confidence. A study involving college students enrolled in a career course found that the rated quality of a handshake was directly related to interviewer hiring recommendations. The relationship between a firm handshake and being recommended for hire was stronger for women than men. Interviewers apparently were particularly impressed by a woman with a firm handshake.[7]

Gesturing with the entire body adds emphasis to making a point. In addition to waving the hands, the body and wrists can be involved in movements. Raising the shoulders can also be used for emphasis, particularly when disagreeing about a person's ideas.[8]

2 *Facial expressions and movement.* The particular look on a person's face and movements of the person's head provide reliable cues as to approval, disapproval, or disbelief. A smile from the receiver often indicates support for what you are saying.

3 *Posture.* Another widely used clue to a person's attitude is his or her posture. Leaning toward another person suggests a favorable attitude toward the message a person is trying to communicate. Tilting your head and leaning in indicates your concern and attentiveness. Leaning backward communicates the opposite. Standing up straight generally conveys self-confidence, while slouching can be interpreted as a sign of low self-confidence.

4 *Body placement.* The placement of one's body in relation to someone else is widely used to transmit messages. Facing a person in a casual, relaxed style indicates acceptance. Moving close to another person also generally indicates acceptance. Yet moving too close may be perceived as a violation of personal space, and the message sender will be rejected. Speechwriter and speaking coach Nick Morgan says that to effectively relate to an audience, you need a kinesthetic connection (effective movement of the body). This would include the other forms of nonverbal communication as well as moving around effectively. For example, vary the distance between yourself and your audience, and do not turn away from the audience to cue your next slide.[9]

5 *Voice quality.* Aspects of the voice such as pitch, volume, tone, and speech rate may communicate confidence, nervousness, and enthusiasm. Voice tone is particularly significant in terms of how a message is interpreted.[10] Visualize how the word "good" can be expressed in several different tones to have positive or negative meanings, especially in combination with a facial expression. When "good" is dragged out it is likely to be interpreted as almost an insult. When "good" is expressed quickly, it usually is interpreted as genuine approval.

People often judge intelligence by how a person sounds. The most annoying voice quality is a whining, complaining, or nagging tone.[11] Many professionals hire speech pathologists to serve as coaches for improving their voice, and thereby improve their chances for advancing their career. The emphasis is not on speech therapy but on voice beautification to come across as more intelligent and persuasive.[12]

6 *Clothing, dress, and appearance.* The image a person conveys communicates such messages as, "I feel powerful," and, "I think this meeting is important." For example, wearing one's best business attire to a performance evaluation interview would communicate that the person thinks the meeting is important. Another important meaning of dress is it communicates how willing the employee is to comply with organizational standards. By deviating too radically from a standard, such as wearing a suit on casual dress day, the person communicates indifference.

7 *Mirroring or imitating a conversation partner.* To mirror is to build rapport with another person by imitating his or her voice tone, breathing rate, body movement, and language. Mirroring relies 10 percent on verbal means, 60 percent on voice tone, and 30 percent on body physiology, thus making it largely nonverbal. A specific application of mirroring is to conform to the conversation partner's posture, eye movements, and hand movements. The person feels more relaxed with you as a result of your imitation.

Aside from helping people communicate effectively, nonverbal communication has other applications. One example is to assist in screening airline passengers who might be a security threat. Unusual body language, such as trembling, lack of eye contact with security officials, and a swollen carotid artery (in the neck) could suggest a passenger with evil intent. Wearing a big coat on a summer day would be an example of unusual and suspicious behavior. Odd gestures and split-second expressions could indicate an attempt to conceal emotions. Passengers displaying any of the preceding behaviors would then be interviewed for further screening. Screening for possible security threats by nonverbal communication rather than by cultural stereotypes is much more acceptable to defenders of civil liberties.[13]

Keep in mind that many nonverbal signals are ambiguous. For example, a smile usually indicates agreement and warmth, but at times it can indicate nervousness. Even if nonverbal signals are not highly reliable, they are used to judge your behavior, particularly in meetings. Also, as described later in the chapter, cultural differences in nonverbal communication can be significant. For example, when a Korean smiles it may simply mean he or she is accepting your right to an opinion, not necessarily agreement.

LEARNING OBJECTIVE **3**

Explain and illustrate organizational communications channels and directions.

ORGANIZATIONAL CHANNELS AND DIRECTIONS OF COMMUNICATION

Messages in organizations travel over many different channels, or paths. Communication channels can be formal or informal, and can be categorized as downward, upward, horizontal, or diagonal. The widespread use of communication technology including e-mail, instant messaging, text messaging, intranets, and web conferencing has greatly facilitated sending messages in all directions.

Formal Communication Channels

formal communication channels
The official pathways for sending information inside and outside an organization.

Formal communication channels are the official pathways for sending information inside and outside an organization. The organization chart formally indicates the channels messages are supposed to follow. By carefully following the organization chart, a maintenance technician would know how to transmit a message to the chief operating officer. In many large organizations, the worker may have to go through as many as eight management or organizational levels. Modern organizations, however, make it easier for lower-ranking workers to communicate with high-level managers.

Specific Channels for Exchanging Information Including Social Media

Formal channels include media, such as intranets, e-mail, instant messaging, video-conferences, web conferences and physical meetings. Intranets are widely used for a variety of internal company communications including information about products, services, and company benefits. Instant messages (IM) are usually longer than text messages. A challenge for many companies is to get workers to use company technology rather than employee devices to communicate with each other about business topics. For example, Slack is widely used to send instant messages.[14]

The company *blog* is a widely used formal communication channel. A point of potential confusion here is that the blog, a formal channel, is written in a casual, informal way. Blogs were first used by businesses to communicate with customers in a personal, direct manner. The blog communicates professional information, but with a soft, human touch. For example, a product manager for a laser surgery device might say, "Just the other day we heard from an ophthalmology clinic in Arkansas that our device saved the sight of three patients who had severe glaucoma." Employees as well as customers can interact with the blog by providing comments that can be a source of valuable feedback to management and communicated directly to other visitors to the site.

If an employee publishes a blog with company information, but the blog is not authorized by the company, this does not constitute a formal communication channel. Many employees have been fired for making nasty statements about the company on their blogs. Revealing trade secrets on your blog can also get you fired.

Many companies now use social media websites, particularly Twitter and Facebook to supplement or as a substitute for their own blog. Even when a company does not have its own Facebook page, Facebook contains a link to the company's website. One of thousands of possible examples is that if you look for the general store, Dollar General, you will be directed to their website. You will also find hundreds of mentions of Dollar General, but these are not formal company communications.

Social networking sites are sometimes used as a vehicle for employees to communicate with each other. To supplement e-mail, employees would send each other posts on Twitter or Facebook. (A potential problem, of course, is that workers who send and receive company messages on social networking sites can readily become distracted by outside messages.) A variation of this technique is that some companies establish an internal website that resembles a social networking site used by the public. The Twitter-like system called Yammer is for workers to see what others are doing, share information, collaborate, and brag about their successes without exposure to outside the organization.

Formal channels such as web conferencing are particularly important for companies with a large number of employees who are geographically dispersed. In a web conference, a number of people log in to a designated website at the same time to join an interactive discussion or presentation, often with voice capability. A prime example of web conferencing use is the consulting firm Accenture, with 595,000 employees and offices in 51 countries throughout the world. Professional staff members spend most of their time at client sites, so staying in touch electronically is particularly useful.[15]

The accompanying *Management in Action* insert describes a creative use of an intranet by a non-profit organization.

Management by Walking Around

One important communication channel can be classified as both formal and informal. With *management by walking around*, managers intermingle freely with workers on the shop floor, in the office, with customers, and at company social events. By being accessible and spending time in personal contact with employees, the manager enhances open communication. Because management by walking around is systematic, it could be considered formal. However, a manager who circulates throughout the company without careful consideration to the type of informal communication he or she invites, may violate the chain of command.

MANAGEMENT IN ACTION

The San Diego Humane Society & SPCA Relies on FeTCH, Its Intranet

Elkie Wills, who is now the Director of Community & Partnership at the San Diego Humane Society & SPCA, was responsible for planning and implementing an intranet for the nonprofit organization. She designed the intranet, nicknamed FeTCH, to fit the SDHS brand and to highlight its focus on finding homes for domestic animals. Although SDHS had a limited software budget, management decided to work with the vendor Intranet Connections because the intranet was regarded as a critical collaboration and communication tool for the staff.

The society's intranet is playful and stays consistent with the humane society purpose. Wills assigned names to its features such as "Meow Madness," "Most Pawsitive Purpose," and "In the Mews." FeTCH developed into the major resource for information about SDHS career opportunities, benefits, worker compensation, and calendars, all with links on FeTCH's home page. One of the intranet's most popular features is the opportunity to upload photos to FeTCH for photo-of-the-week contests.

Another FeTCH feature, *Happy Tails*, shares animal adoption success stories which give employees the opportunity to see how well animals are adapting to their new homes. FeTCH also has an employee recognition feature, enabling co-workers to fill out "High Five" forms to nominate peers for good work.

During adoption campaigns, Elkie holds employee contests to encourage creativity. A Valentine's Day contest asked employees to create a card for one of their favorite animals. A contest for "Meow Madness" asked employees to write a fairytale ending for their favorite animal.

Wills thinks that FeTCH has increased employee engagement through its fun elements, and information about SDHS achieving its purpose of finding homes for animals (via *Happy Tails*). She also believes that FeTCH has helped employees form strong connections among different locations and departments. Elkie also offers advice for the successful use of a company intranet. She says it is important to take the time to get to know your intranet software. Talk to support or use the implementation packages for one-on-one guidance.

Questions

1 **To what extent do you think a playful intranet would work in a company in another industry, such as an investment bank?**

2 **How should management at the San Diego Humane Society & SPCA deal with the potential problem of employees spending too much time looking at cute photos of and stories about domestic animals?**

Source: Original story based on facts and observations in the following sources: "8 Highly Effective Intranet Examples," *IC* (https://icthrive.com), January 1, 2020, pp. 1–2; "How to Fetch a Better Intranet," *IC* (https://icthrive.com), June 21, 2018, pp. 1–3; Melissa Del Monte, "3 Intranets Your Organization Should Emulate," *Ragan* (www.ragan.com), November 25, 2014, pp. 1–2; "An Interview with Non-Profit Intranet Manager Elkie Wills," *IC* (https://icthrive.com), December 14, 2012, pp. 1–3.

Informal Communication Channels

Organizations could not function by formal communication channels alone. Another system of communication, called an **informal communication channel** is also needed. The informal organization structure is created from informal communication networks. Informal communication channels form the unofficial network across an organization that supplements the formal channels. Most of these informal channels arise out of necessity. For example, people sometimes depart from the official communication channels to consult with a person with specialized knowledge, such as a marketing manager consulting with a worker from another department who is up to date on adolescent culture or a new piece of technology. Anytime two or more employees consult each other outside formal communication channels, an informal communication channel has been used.

Here we look at four aspects of informal communication channels: networks created by leaders, capitalizing on informal networks, chance encounters, and the grapevine, including rumors.

informal communication channel
An unofficial network that supplements the formal channels in an organization.

Networks Created by Leaders

Leaders make extensive use of informal networks to accomplish goals. Successful leaders have a knack for knowing whom to tap to get things done. For example, Melissa in finance might be highly creative when cost-cutting ideas are needed, and Tim in human resources might be outstanding at negotiating with union leaders. Current practice is for managers and leaders to sometimes ask their counterparts in other organizations for advice via texting.[16] For example, a manager might ask someone else in his advisory group, "Our costs have risen 10 percent because of tariffs. Should we pass these costs along to our customers?"

Based on a study of 30 emerging leaders, Herminia Ibarra and Mark Hunter identified three distinct forms of networking.[17] *Operational networking* is aimed at doing one's assigned task more effectively. It involves cultivating stronger relationships with coworkers whose membership in the network is clear. Some of these relationships may be part of the formal structure, such as getting cost data from a member of the finance department. *Personal networking* engages cooperative people from outside the organization in a person's effort to develop personally and advance. This type of networking might involve being mentored on how to deal with a challenge, such as dealing with the problem of sexual harassment by a senior manager or learning about new marketing tactics used elsewhere in the industry. *Strategic networking* focuses networking on attaining business goals directly. At this level, the manager creates a network that will help identify and capitalize on new opportunities for the company, such as breaking into the Nigerian market.

Capitalizing on Informal Networks

In Chapter 8, social network analysis was described in relation to the informal organization structure. Here we present a few additional ways in which managers can capitalize on the potential contribution of informal networks. A somewhat confusing fact to keep in mind, however, is that in-house networks of experts, or *communities of practice*, are becoming integrated into formal management structures in many companies. Richard McDermott and Douglas Archibald, two consultants and adjunct professors at the Warwick Business School, offer several suggestions for making best use of these informal networks (that are sometimes formal). Two of these suggestions are described next.

1 *Focus on issues important to the organization.* Sustainable communities of practice tackle real problems that have been defined by upper management, rather than working completely on their own. At the pharmaceutical firm Pfizer, communities of practice work on the vital issue of drug safety. They are divided into safety councils and networks, with membership in the networks being voluntary.

2 *Establish community goals and deliverables.* As informal networks have become more formal, they should be assigned goals and deliverables (or end products). At ConocoPhillips a functional group might be responsible for a major goal, whereas the network group contributes to its attainment. For example, when the company planned to improve the performance of its well operations, the functional team formed a well-optimization network. The network then figured out how to reduce unplanned losses in relation to impaired equipment by 10 percent annually.[18]

Chance Encounters

Unscheduled informal contact between managers and employees can be an efficient and effective informal communication channel.[19] Spontaneous communication events may occur in the cafeteria, near the water fountain, in the halls, on the elevator, or walking from the parking lot into the office or factory. For example, during an elevator ride, a manager might spot a purchasing agent and ask, "Whatever happened to the just-in-time inventory purchasing proposal?" In two minutes, the manager might obtain the information that would typically be solicited in a meeting or e-mail exchange. Also, the chance meeting might trigger the manager's thinking of the topic. A chance encounter differs from management by walking around in that the latter is a planned event; the former occurs unintentionally.

The Grapevine and Rumor Control

Two key aspects of informal communication channels are the grapevine and the gossip and rumors it carries; and how to control them.

The Grapevine, Gossip, and Rumors

grapevine
The informal means by which information is transmitted in organizations.

The **grapevine** is the informal means by which information is transmitted in organizations. As such, it is the major informal communication channel. The term grapevine refers to tangled pathways that can distort information. Rumors and gossip are the two major components of the grapevine. Conditions of anxiety and uncertainty breed rumors. Rumors are typically about something people wish to happen (such as double bonuses this year) or something people dread (such as jobs being outsourced).

Gossip is fueled by the need for affiliation, and helps people bond because by sharing information we develop a sense of trust and intimacy.[20] Gossip is usually spread by word of mouth, but electronic transmission is also a vehicle. Positive gossip (Did you hear that our accounts payable supervisor at age 57 is getting married for the first time?) travels over the grapevine. The negative type (Did you hear that our chief ethics officer was convicted of DWI?) travels even faster.

According to workplace psychology professor and rumor expert, Nicholas DiFonzo, gossip can help workers by alerting them to problems. Informing a co-worker, for example, about the boss' negative idiosyncrasies can help her avoid later unpleasantness, such as being reprimanded for having used clipart in a PowerPoint presentation.[21]

The grapevine often creates a bigger impact on employees than messages sent over formal channels. Messages received through formal communication channels often carry the perception of stale news. Information usually travels along the grapevine with considerable speed.

Approximately three-fourths of messages transmitted along the grapevine are true. Because so many grapevine messages are essentially correct, employees believe most of them. Nevertheless, messages frequently become distorted and misunderstood. By the time a rumor reaches the majority of employees, it is likely to contain false elements. An example would be the case of a company CEO who gave a personal donation to a transgender rights group. The funds were to be used to promote local legislation in favor of equal employment opportunities for transgender people. The last version of the story that traveled over the grapevine took this form: "The CEO is getting ready to transition into a man."

Rumor Control

False rumors can be disruptive to morale and productivity and can create employee stress. Some employees take actions that hurt the company and themselves in response to a rumor. Employees might leave a firm in response to rumors about an impending layoff. The valuable workers often leave first because they have skills and contacts in demand at other firms. Severe negative rumors dealing with products or services, especially about product defects or poisonings, must be neutralized to prevent permanent damage to an organization. Many rumors have circulated recently about restaurant food being contaminated by a deadly virus.

Rumors can be combated by enhancing formal communication. Employees naturally seek more information during times of intense rumors. Managers should move quickly on reaching a decision rather than waiting for workers throughout the organization to create their own version of final events. Management should explain to employees when they cannot comment or provide full information on a topic. For example, during the preliminary stages of a merger, management is legally obligated to make no comment.

Confirm the rumor. For example, "Yes, it is true. We are going to outsource the manufacture of all paper clips and staples." Encourage employees to discuss rumors they hear with you. Be readily accessible, including management by walking around. Make it clear that you are willing to clear up rumors, and that you will investigate whatever facts you do not have at hand.[22]

Communication Directions

Messages in organizations travel in four directions: downward, upward, horizontally, and diagonally. Over time, an organization develops communication networks corresponding to these directions. A **communication network** is a pattern or flow of messages that traces the communication from start to finish.

In *downward communication*, messages flow from one level to a lower level. For example, a supervisor gives orders to a team member, or top-level managers send an announcement to employees. A guiding principle of downward communication is for

communication network
A pattern or flow of messages that traces the communication from start to finish.

the company to be transparent (rather than opaque or hidden) in terms of revealing information to company insiders and outsiders. For example, the CEO of a small cloud software firm might explain to employees that it is true that Google has expressed interest in purchasing the company at a premium price.

Upward communication transmits messages from lower to higher levels in an organization. Although it may not be as frequent as downward communication, it is equally important. Upward communication tells management how well messages have been received. The upward communication path also provides an essential network for keeping management informed about problems. Management by walking around and simply speaking to employees facilitate upward communication. Many companies develop their own programs and policies to facilitate bottom-up communication. Four such approaches follow:

1 *Open-door policy.* An open-door policy allows any employee to bring a gripe to top management's attention—without first checking with his or her immediate manager. The open-door policy can be considered a grievance procedure that helps employees resolve problems. However, the policy also enhances upward communication because it informs top management about problems or misperceptions employees are experiencing.

2 *Town hall meetings.* Top-level executives at many companies meet with employees in a town hall format to gather employee concerns and opinions. A town hall meeting in a large company might be held with a sampling of company personnel. In larger companies, the meetings are often held using a combination of onsite audience and videoconference or webcasting for virtual employees. The key for a successful town hall meeting in terms of upward communication is that company management engage in a dialog with employees rather than making presentations. An example of a dialog-provoking question would be, "How do you folks feel about the direction we are headed?"

3 *Complaint programs and hotlines.* Many organizations institute formal complaint programs. Complaints sent up through channels include those about supervisors, working conditions, personality conflicts, sexual harassment, and inefficient work methods.

4 *Blogs.* Blogs are useful vehicles for upward communication, while at the same time being a vehicle for downward communication. The employee has the opportunity to interact with the message sent by management, such as, "We plan to base more of your compensation on variable pay next year." The employee might comment, "Sounds good to me so long as I have the opportunity to earn more money."

Upward communication is also framed as employees having a *voice*, referring to the idea that they can speak up, or that their voice can be heard. A series of studies suggested it is best for employees to speak up about issues that would not require enormous resources to implement.[23] Assume that an employee thinks the current office building has poor air circulation. It would be better for the employee to suggest that the company install ceiling fans, rather than suggest the company relocate to a more modern building.

Through *horizontal communication*, managers as well as other workers send messages to others at the same organizational level. Horizontal communication frequently takes the form of co-workers from the same department talking to or sending e-mail and intranet messages to each other. Co-workers who fail to share information with and respond to each other are likely to fall behind schedules and miss deadlines. Horizontal communication facilitates cooperation. People need to communicate with each other to work effectively in joint efforts. For example, they advise each other of work problems and ask each other for help when needed. Moreover, extensive lateral communication enhances creativity. Exchanging and, "batting around" ideas with peers sharpens imagination and innovation.

Diagonal communication is the transmission of messages to higher or lower organizational levels in different organizational units. A typical diagonal communication event occurs when the head of the marketing department needs some pricing information. She sends an e-mail to a supervisor in the finance department to get his input. The supervisor, in turn, sends an e-mail to a specialist in the data processing department to get the necessary information. The marketing person has thus started a chain of communication that goes down and across the organization.

Organizational Learning and Knowledge Management as Part of Communication

An important output of both formal and informal communication channels is to transmit information to other workers to advance knowledge and learning throughout the organization. An effective organization engages in continuous learning by proactively adapting to the external environment. In the process, the organization profits from its experiences. Instead of repeating the same old mistakes, the organization learns. A **learning organization** is skilled at creating, acquiring, and transferring knowledge. It also modifies its behavior to reflect new knowledge and new insights.[24] All of these activities are facilitated by effective communication.

> **learning organization**
> An organization that is skilled at creating, acquiring, and transferring knowledge.

Learning throughout the organization is more likely when a learning culture has been established. A learning culture consists of a large number of workers who have a growth mindset. Such individuals want to learn, apply what they learned to their jobs, and share knowledge. They attempt to squeeze learning out of as many interactions as possible, such as listening to a worker explain why he is recommending that his sister apply to the company for a job.

Learning organizations find ways to manage knowledge more productively and encourage organizational members to share information by communicating relevant topics to each other. IBM defines **knowledge management** as the ways and means by which a company leverages its knowledge resources to generate business value. More simply, knowledge management involves, "getting the right knowledge to the right people at the right time."[25] Knowledge management has surged in importance with so many boomers retiring, thereby leaving organizations with a "brain drain." The transfer of this "tacit" knowledge between retiring managers and professionals to their younger counterparts therefore becomes an important activity. A representative example is the Bank of America onboarding program, designed to facilitate new executives adapting to the corporate culture by capturing some of the wisdom of senior executives.[26]

> **knowledge management**
> The ways and means by which a company leverages its knowledge resources to generate business value.

Most organizations employ many people with useful knowledge, such as how to solve a particular problem. Because this information may be stored solely in the person's brain, other workers who need the information do not know who possesses it. Systematizing such knowledge develops a sort of corporate yellow pages.

In addition to the specialized work of the *chief learning officer* in a learning organization, managers also manage knowledge. They should actively contribute to knowledge management. Firms that fail to codify and share knowledge lose the knowledge of workers who leave. Shared knowledge, such as knowing who the real decision makers are within a particular customer's business can be retained. In a learning organization, considerable learning takes place in teams, as members share expertise. A major block to knowledge sharing is when workers jealously guard their best ideas, believing their creative ideas are their tickets to success. So the chief information officer and the manager have to work hard to overcome people's natural resistance to sharing their best ideas.

LEARNING OBJECTIVE **4**

Identify major communication barriers in organizations.

BARRIERS TO COMMUNICATION

Barriers to communication influence the receipt of messages, as shown in Figure 12-2. The input is the message sent by the sender. Barriers to communication, or noise, affect throughput, or the processing of input. Noise poses a potential threat to effective communication because it can interfere with the accuracy of a message. The output in this model is the message as received.

Interference occurs most frequently when a message is complex, arouses emotion, or clashes with a receiver's mindset. An emotionally arousing message deals with such topics as money or personal inconvenience, such as a change in working hours. A message that clashes with a receiver's usual way of viewing things requires the person to change his or her typical pattern of receiving messages. To illustrate this problem, try this experiment. The next time you order food at a restaurant, order the dessert first and the entrée second. The server will probably not hear your dessert order.

Low Motivation and Interest

Many messages never get through because the intended receiver is not motivated to hear the message or is not interested. The challenge to the sender is to frame the message in such a way that it appeals to the needs and interests of the receiver. This

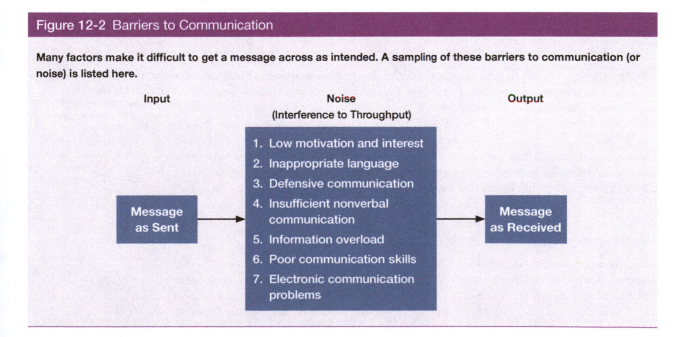

Figure 12-2 Barriers to Communication

Many factors make it difficult to get a message across as intended. A sampling of these barriers to communication (or noise) is listed here.

Input

Noise
(Interference to Throughput)

Output

Message as Sent

1. Low motivation and interest
2. Inappropriate language
3. Defensive communication
4. Insufficient nonverbal communication
5. Information overload
6. Poor communication skills
7. Electronic communication problems

Message as Received

principle can be applied to conducting a job campaign. When sending a message, the job seeker should emphasize the needs of the prospective employer. An example would be: "If I were hired, what problem would you like me to tackle first?" Many job seekers send low-interest messages of this type: "What advancement opportunities would there be for me?" Sending a message at the right time contributes to motivation and interest. Messages should be sent at a time when they are most likely to meet with good reception, such as asking for new equipment when the company is doing quite well.

Inappropriate Language

The language used to frame a message must be suited to the intended receivers. Language can be inappropriate for a host of reasons. Two factors of language that are of particular significance in a work setting—semantics and difficulty level—may affect appropriateness.

Semantics is the study of meaning in language forms. The message sender should give careful thought to what certain terms will mean to receivers. Take, for example, the term *productive*. To prevent communication barriers, you may have to clarify this term. Assume a manager says to the group members, "Our department must become more productive." Most employees will correctly interpret the term to mean "more efficient," but some employees will interpret it as, "work harder and longer at the same rate of pay." Consequently, these latter employees may resist the message.

The difficulty level of language also affects receiver comprehension. Communicators are typically urged to speak and write at a low level of difficulty. At times, however, a low difficulty level is inappropriate. For instance, when a manager communicates with technically sophisticated employees, using a low difficulty level can create barriers. The employees may perceive the manager as patronizing, or worse uninformed, and may tune him or her out. The use of jargon, or insider language, is closely related to difficulty level. When dealing with outsiders, jargon may be inappropriate; with insiders (people who share a common technical language), it may be appropriate.

Defensive Communication

An important general communication barrier is **defensive communication**—the tendency to receive messages in a way that protects self-esteem. Defensive communication also allows people to send messages to make them look good. People communicate defensively through the process of *denial*, the suppression of information one finds uncomfortable. It serves as a major barrier to communication because many messages sent in organizations are potentially uncomfortable. Top management might decide, for example, to require employees to enroll in a physical fitness program so the company might be able to reduce healthcare costs. Many physically unfit employees might dismiss the requirement as simply a joke.

defensive communication
The tendency to receive messages in a way that protects self-esteem.

Insufficient Nonverbal Communication

Effective communicators rely on both verbal and nonverbal communication. If verbal communication is not supplemented by nonverbal communication, messages may not be convincing, as the following situation illustrates. For example, if the manager expresses approval for an idea with a blank expression on his or her face the approval message might not get through. As one worker said, "My manager is a zombie, so I never know what she is really thinking."

Information Overload

Information overload occurs when an individual receives so much information that he or she becomes overwhelmed. As a result, the person does a poor job of processing information and receiving new messages. A contributing factor to errors made on the job, such as not following through on sending a needed document, is that so many workers are suffering from information overload. Many managers suffer from information overload too because of extensive e-mails and text messages, in addition to the phone messages, intranet postings, blogs, and regular receipt of documents and industry information.

Many managers receive over 150 e-mail and text messages daily, and many of them are processed outside of regular office hours. The problem of being overloaded by e-mail is intensified by including too many people on the distribution list. Many workers are learning how to manage e-mail better, such as dealing with e-mail during certain blocks of time, yet information overload is still a widespread problem. Even collaborative software can contribute to overload because each member of the team feels obliged to look through messages that might not really be relevant to him or her. "Notifications" are a substantial contributor to information overload because they can flash on the computer or smartphone screen every few minutes.

Poor Communication Skills

A message may fail to register because the sender lacks effective communication skills. The sender might garble a written or spoken message so severely that the receiver cannot understand it, or the sender may deliver the message so poorly that the receiver does not take it seriously. Documents prepared by human resource departments and lawyers are difficult to understand because the terminology has to be precise to meet legal requirements. Yet, for most purposes the average reader should be able to understand the intent of the written message. Unclear voicemail messages, particularly speaking too rapidly, are a widespread problem. Another form of poor communication skill stems from not focusing on the receiver while sending a message. When speaking on the phone, it is helpful to focus on the other person rather than reading e-mails or doing other work at the same time. Lacking skill in persuasive communication can also create barriers.

The excessive use of jargon is another source of poor communication skill. Business writer Jon Marcus contends that the epidemic of business jargon probably started innocently when complex concepts had to be shared among expert colleagues. Since then the use of jargon has accelerated.[27] A sprinkling of jargon helps a person be perceived as identifying with the group. Too much jargon, however, suggests that the message sender relies on automatic rather than original thinking. A prime example is the current excessive utilization on the word *curate* to refer to any type of gathering of information or objects. A stylist from Stitch Fix might say that she *curates* a selection of clothing for her clients, and a custodial supervisor might say that his staff *curates* refuse while making his rounds. Two other words that suffer from overuse are *space* (referring to an industry sector) and *at the end of the day*. The latter has come to refer to any conclusion, whether taking place just before evening or at any time.

Evidence for the relevance of good communication skills was found in an analysis of real-estate listings at $1 million and up, conducted by Redfin, a national real estate brokerage. It found that "perfect listings"—written in complete sentences without spelling or grammatical errors—sold on average three days faster, and were 10 percent more likely to sell for more than their list price.[28]

Electronic Communication Problems

Information technology plays a major role in workplace communication, yet it creates several problems, including information overload. The problems associated with e-mail are representative of these barriers, particularly impersonality. Many people conduct business with each other exclusively by e-mail and messaging, thus missing out on the nuances of human interaction. According to an analysis conducted by McKinsey & Company, managers and professionals spend about one-third of their workweeks managing e-mail.[29] Some managers and staff professionals discourage face-to-face meetings with workers who ask for help, and instead demand communication by e-mail. (The multi-tasking problems associated with electronic communication are also discussed in Chapter 16 in relation to personal productivity.)

Face-to-face communication offers the advantage of a smile and an expression of sympathy through a nod of the head. When somebody asks or answers a question in person, it is easier to probe for more information than if the interaction took place through e-mail or messaging. Many people supplement their e-mail messages with emoticons to add warmth and humor. Yet many times, an electronic message can seem much harsher than a spoken message. Face-to-face communication is also important for the manager because many activities such as coaching and giving encouragement work better in personal than electronically.

E-mail, in general, is better suited to communicating routine rather than complex or sensitive messages. When dealing with sensitive information it is better to deliver the message face-to-face or at least in a phone conversation. In this way both parties can have questions answered and minimize misunderstandings. Electronic communication is poorly suited for expressing disagreement because you cannot react immediately to the receiver's response. Don G. Lents, the chairman of an international law firm says, "You should never engage in disagreement electronically. If you are going to disagree with somebody, you certainly don't want to do it by e-mail, and if possible you don't even want to do it by phone. You want to do it face-to-face."[30] Laying off workers through e-mail or text messaging is particularly insensitive and creates a poor company reputation.

Videoconferencing is another example of an electronic device that has built-in communication problems despite its many productivity advantages. Exchanging information back and forth through webcams is perceived as too impersonal by some businesspeople. The motivation to save money on travel expenses, as well as reliance on so many remote workers, has given videoconferencing another surge and even spurred technology improvements to make these tools more friendly and effective.

Computer graphic presentations, such as PowerPoint, present problems of their own. In most organizations, PowerPoint presentations are the standard presentation tool. Some major suggestions for communicating effectively with slide presentations are first to maintain eye contact with your audience, and avoid looking too much at your slides which gives the impression that you are reading the slides to your audience. Another suggestion is to present enough slides to keep the audience interested and focused, but do not overwhelm them with slides containing considerable detail.

Develop tactics for
overcoming commu-
nication barriers.

OVERCOMING BARRIERS TO COMMUNICATION

Most barriers to communication are surmountable. First, however, you must be aware that these potential barriers exist. Then as part of a strategy to overcome the barriers, you must develop a tactic to deal with each one. For example, when you have an important message to deliver, make sure you answer the following question from the standpoint of the receiver: "What's in it for me?" This section will describe seven strategies and tactics for overcoming communication barriers. Figure 12-3 lists these strategies.

Understand the Receiver

A common communication error is to think about communication as tool for getting others to agree with you. It is more effective to strive for understanding rather than agreement. Understanding the receiver provides a strategy that can assist in overcoming every communication barrier. For example, part of understanding the receiver comes from an awareness that he or she may be overloaded with information or be poorly motivated.

Achieving understanding takes empathy, the ability to see things as another person does. Empathy leads to improved communication, because people more willingly engage in dialogs when they feel understood. Also, communication improves because empathy builds rapport with the other person. Rapport, in turn, substantially improves communication. You may notice that conversation flows more smoothly when you achieve rapport with a work associate or friend.

Communicate Assertively and Directly

Many people create their own communication barriers by expressing their ideas in a passive or indirect mode. If instead they explain their ideas explicitly and directly—and with feeling—the message is more likely to be received. Being assertive also contributes to effective communication because assertiveness enhances persuasiveness. When both sides are persuasive, they are more likely to find a shared solution.[31] Notice

Figure 12-3 Overcoming Communication Barriers

The chances of getting around the noise in the communication process increase when the sender uses specific strategies and tactics.

1. Understand the receiver
2. Communicate assertively and directly
3. Use two-way communication and ask for clarification
4. Elicit verbal and nonverbal feedback
5. Enhance listening skills
6. Unite with a common vocabulary
7. Be sensitive to cultural differences

Effective
Communication

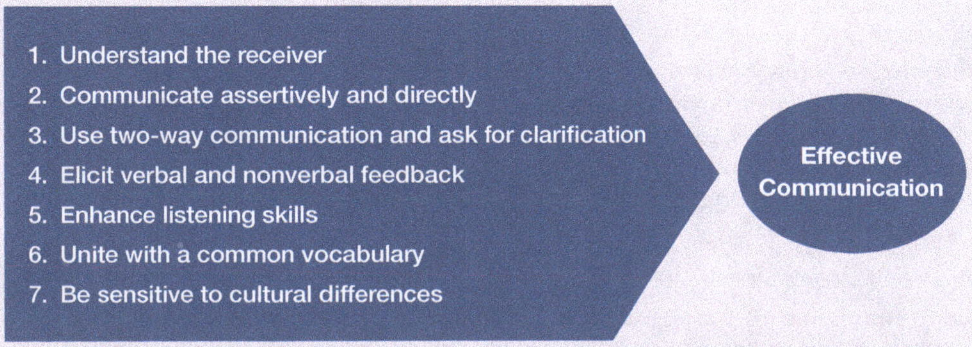

the difference between a passive (indirect) phrasing of a request versus an assertive (direct) approach:

Passive

Team member: By any chance would there be some money left over in the budget? If there would happen to be, I would like to know.

Manager: I'll have to investigate. Try me again soon.

Assertive

Team member: We have an urgent need for a high-speed color copier in our department. Running to the document center to use their copier is draining our productivity. I am therefore submitting a requisition for a high-speed color copier.

Manager: Your request makes sense. I'll see what's left in the budget right now.

Informative Confrontation

Another use of assertiveness in overcoming communication barriers in the workplace is **informative confrontation**, a technique of inquiring about discrepancies, conflicts, and mixed messages.[32] Confronting people about the discrepancies in their message provides more accurate information. As a manager, here is how you might handle a discrepancy between verbal and nonverbal messages: You're talking with a team member you suspect is experiencing problems. The person says, "Everything is going great" (verbal message). At the same time the team member is fidgeting and clenching his fist (nonverbal message). Your informative confrontation might be: "You say things are great, yet you're fidgeting and clenching your fist."

informative confrontation
A technique of inquiring about discrepancies, conflicts, and mixed messages.

Repeating Messages and Using Multiple Channels

As another way of being assertive, you repeat your message and use multiple channels. By being persistent, your message is more likely to be received. An important message should be repeated when it is first delivered and repeated again one or two days later. Repetition of the message becomes even more effective when more than one communication channel is used. Effective communicators follow up spoken agreements with written documentation. The use of multiple channels helps accommodate the fact that some people respond better to one communication mode than another. For example, a supervisor asked an employee why she did not follow through with the supervisor's request that she wear safety shoes. The employee replied, "I didn't think you were serious. You didn't send me an e-mail."

Being Direct

Being assertive also includes being direct, rather than indirect and evasive, when delivering bad news. A manager might say, "Today is a good day for a change," when he has to deliver some bad news about demoting a few staff members, or the loss of a major customer. Indirect communication of this type is often referred to as *spin*, which is intended to look at the bright side of a bad situation.

Powerful Words and Expressions

Closely related to communicating assertively is to sprinkle speaking and writing with words and expressions that connote power. Frank Luntz, a business communications specialist, has discovered five words that really resonate in today's world of business. These five power-packed words are: (1) consequences, (2) impact, (3) reliability, (4) mission, and (5) commitment.[33] So to impress a subordinate, you might say, "The consequences of your work will have an impact on the reliability of our service, thereby fulfilling our mission, and enhancing your commitment." Other powerful words these days include sustainability, recession-resistant, transparent, user-friendly, and seamless.

An approach to using powerful expressions is to present big-picture perspectives rather than details, as many CEOs and politicians do. Research suggests that communicating in abstractions conveys more power than filling an argument with details (at least some of the time).[34] A big-picture statement would be, "Our vision is to become the most sustainable company in the meat-packing industry." A little-picture statement would be, "Let's develop a plan for reducing pollution from our processing plants by four percent this year."

Use Two-Way Communication and Ask for Clarification

A dialog helps reduce misunderstanding by communicating feelings as well as facts. At times a brief amount of small talk, such as commenting on a popular movie or sporting event can set the stage for comfortable two-way communications. Both receiver and sender can ask questions of each other in two-way communications. Here is an example:

Manager: I want you here early tomorrow. We have a big meeting planned with our regional manager.

Employee: I'll certainly be here early. But are you implying that I'm usually late?

Manager: Not at all. I know you come to work on time. It's just that we need you here tomorrow about 30 minutes earlier than usual.

Employee: I'm glad I asked. I'm proud of my punctuality.

A manager who takes the initiative to communicate face-to-face with employees encourages two-way communications. Two-way interaction also overcomes communication barriers because it helps build connections among people. Interaction is also useful in obtaining clarification on what the other person means by a phrase, such as "you need to provide better customer service." Some small enterprises have even moved to a "no e-mail Friday" to encourage more personal and two-way communications among their employees.

Elicit Verbal and Nonverbal Feedback

To be sure the message has been understood, ask for verbal feedback. A recommended managerial practice is to conclude a meeting with a question such as, "to recap, what have we agreed to this morning?" The receiver of a message should also offer feedback to the sender. The expression, "This is what I heard you say," is an effective feedback device. Feedback can also be used to facilitate communication in a group meeting. After the meeting, provide everyone in attendance with written follow-up to make sure they all left with the same understanding.

It is also important to observe and send nonverbal feedback. Nonverbal indicators of comprehension or acceptance can be more important than verbal indicators. For example, the manner in which somebody says, "Sure, sure" can indicate if that person is truly in agreement. If the, "Sure, sure" is a brush-off, the message may need more selling. The expression on the receiver's face can also be due to acceptance or rejection. Avoiding eye contact with you by looking down could also suggest that your message is not being accepted. When the receiver's nonverbal behavior suggests non-acceptance you might ask tactfully, "What problems do you see with my suggestion?"

Enhance Listening Skills

Many communication problems stem from the intended receiver not listening carefully. Managers need to be good listeners because so much of their work involves eliciting information from others to solve problems. Based on his 65 years of consulting and writing, Peter Drucker said a rule for managers is to listen first, speak last.[35] Furthermore, a recent synthesis of studies indicates that managers in the workplace rank listening as a more important oral communication skill than spoken presentations and conversing.[36] Reducing communication barriers takes active listening. **Active listening** means listening for full meaning, without making premature judgments or interpretations. Here are six suggestions that should be followed[37]:

active listening
A technique of inquiring about discrepancies, conflicts, and mixed messages.

1 *The receiver listens for total meaning of the sender's message.* By carefully analyzing what is said, what is not said, and nonverbal signals, you will uncover a fuller meaning in the message. Taking notes during a meeting helps the receiver focus carefully on the meaning of a message.

2 *The receiver reflects the message back to the sender.* Show the sender that you understand by providing summary reflections such as, "You tell me you are behind schedule because our customers keep modifying their orders." Reflecting the message back to the sender shows empathy, because you indicate you understand the sender.

3 *The sender and receiver both understand the message and engage in a concluding discussion.* In the preceding situation, the manager and the employee would converse about the challenges of making on-time deliveries despite changes in customer requirements.

4 *The sender asks open-ended questions instead of making statements.* For example, do not say, "Maurice, don't forget that the Zytex report needs to be completed on Friday morning." Rather, ask, "Maurice, how is the Zytex report coming along? Any problems with making the deadline?" By asking questions you will start the type of dialog that facilitates active listening. (A closed question in contrast to an open-ended one, asks for yes-or-no answers, such as "Maurice, have you finished the Zytex report?)

5 *The receiver does not blurt out questions as soon as the employee is finished speaking.* Being too quick to ask questions gives the impression that you were formulating your reply rather than listening. Before you ask a question, paraphrase the speaker's words. An example is "So what you're saying is...." Then, ask your question. Paraphrasing followed by asking a question will often decrease miscommunication.

6 *The receiver allows the sender to finish his or her sentence.* Do not interrupt by talking about you, jumping in with advice, or offering solutions unless requested. Almost all people prefer to complete their own thoughts.

Note that active listening also incorporates the two previous suggestions about two-way communication and eliciting verbal and nonverbal feedback.

Unite with a Common Vocabulary

People from the various units within an organization may speak in terms so different that communication barriers are erected. For example, the information technology group and the marketing group may use some words and phrases not used by the other. Steve Patterson recommends that managers first identify the core work of a business, and then describe it in a shared business vocabulary.[38] All key terms should be clearly defined, and people should agree on the meaning. Assume a company aims to provide, "high-quality Wi-Fi service." Workers should agree on the meaning of high quality in reference to Wi-Fi. The various departments might retain some jargon and their unique perspectives, but a common language would unite them.

Be Sensitive to Cultural Differences

Effective communication in a global environment requires sensitivity to cultural differences. Awareness of these potential barriers alerts you to the importance of modifying your communication approach. The list that follows presents several specific ideas to help overcome cross-cultural communication barriers.

- *Show respect for all workers.* An effective strategy for overcoming cross-cultural communication barriers is to simply respect all others in the workplace. A key component of respect is to perceive other cultures as different from but not inferior to your own. Respecting other people's customs can translate into specific attitudes, such as respecting a co-worker for wearing a yarmulke on Friday, or another for wearing native African dress to celebrate Kwanzaa.

- *Use straightforward language and speak clearly.* When working with people who do not speak your language fluently, speak in an easy-to-understand manner. Look for signs of poor comprehension, such as not asking any questions or nodding in agreement with everything you say. Minimize the use of idioms and analogies specific to your language. Particularly difficult for foreigners to interpret are sports analogies, such as "This should be a slam dunk." or "We pulled the hat trick."

- *Be alert to cultural differences in customs and behavior.* To minimize cross-cultural communication barriers, recognize that many subtle job-related differences in customs and behavior may exist. You need to search for these differences if you have regular contact with workers from another culture. For example, Asians may feel uncomfortable when asked to brag about themselves in the presence of others, even during a job interview. From their perspective, calling attention to themselves at the expense of another person is rude and unprofessional.

- *Be sensitive to differences in nonverbal communication.* Be alert to the possibility that a person from another culture may misinterpret your nonverbal signal. To use positive reinforcement or give encouragement, some managers will give a sideways hug to an employee or touch his or her arm. People from some cultures resent touching from work associates and will be offended. Koreans in particular dislike being touched or touching others in a work setting.

- *Do not be diverted by style, accent, grammar, or personal appearance.* Although these superficial factors all relate to business success, they are difficult to interpret when judging a person from another culture. It is therefore better to judge the merits of the statement or behavior.[39] A brilliant individual from another culture may still be learning your language and may make basic mistakes in speaking your language.

- *Pronounce correctly the names of people you interact with from other countries.* Communication is much smoother when you correctly pronounce the name of another person. For many Americans, this is a challenging task because they are accustomed to names with one or two syllables that are easy to pronounce, such as Bob or Ann. A trouble spot for many people whose only language is English is that "H" and "J" might be silent in another language. Suppose one of your work or personal associates has the first name "Hyuntak." After listening to his name for the first time, develop a phonetic spelling that will help you pronounce the name in the future. (How about "High-oon-tack"?)

- *Use an occasional emoji in your digital messages.* Many emojis make sense across different languages, and can therefore be used to emphasize a point you are making in a digital message. As an example, to supplement a written message about wanting to cooperate with someone from someone whose native language is different from yours, you might post clapping hands, arms waving, fireworks, or even the traditional smiley face. In this way you might be able to lessen potential misunderstanding.

HOW TO CONDUCT AN EFFECTIVE MEETING

LEARNING OBJECTIVE **6**

Considerable workplace communication, including group decision making, takes place in meetings. When conducted poorly, meetings represent a substantial productivity drain, including wasted money. Most of the information presented in this chapter and in Chapter 5, which discussed decision making, applies to meetings. The following suggestions apply to those who conduct physical and virtual meetings, and some are also relevant for participants. By following these suggestions, you increase the meeting's effectiveness as a vehicle for collaborative effort and communication.

Describe how to conduct more effective meetings.

1   *Meet only for valid reasons.* Many meetings lead to no decisions because they lack a valid purpose in the first place. Meetings are necessary only in situations that require coordinated effort and group decision making. The purpose of the meeting is usually included in the agenda. E-mail messages and collaborative software can be substituted for meetings when factual information needs to be disseminated and discussion is unimportant. Having clear objectives contributes to the validity of a meeting. Recurring meetings often lack a clear objective other than for the participants to coordinate their efforts. When the purpose of a meeting is clear, it is easier to decide who should attend. Research suggests that the most productive meetings contain only five to eight participants.[40]

2   *The meeting leader should set the tone for the meeting.* To help keep the meeting professional, the team leader should be tactful, gentle, and calm. All participants should be treated with respect in terms of receiving their fair share of being listened to. The meeting leader should not take criticism personally or become defensive.[41] When open communication is encouraged, criticism will probably surface during the meeting.

3   *Start and stop on time, and offer refreshments.* Meetings appear more professional and action-oriented when the leader starts and stops on time. If the leader waits for the last member to show up, much time is lost and late behavior is rewarded. Stopping the meeting on time shows respect for the members' time. Offering refreshments is another tactic for emphasizing the importance of the meeting, and also enhances satisfaction with the meeting.

4 *Keep comments brief and to the point.* A major challenge facing the meeting leader is to keep conversation on track. Verbal rambling by participants creates communication barriers because other people lose interest. An effective way for the leader to keep comments on target is to ask the contributor of a non sequitur, "In what way does your comment relate to the agenda?"

5 *Avoid electronic distractions.* Many people attending meetings pretend to be focused on the meeting but instead are doing other work on their laptops, tablets, or smartphones. Getting the group to agree not to perform other work has become the policy at many companies. As a reward, offer briefer meetings with more accomplished. The unauthorized use of smartphones in meetings has been referred to as Electronic Display of Insensitivity.[42]

6 *Capitalize on technology when appropriate.* Although electronic devices can be distracting at meetings, they can also make a major contribution, as in group decision making software. Websites are now used by boards of governors at several large companies. Often board members need to consult masses of information that previously required hauling oversized briefing binders to the meetings.

7 *Encourage critical feedback and commentary.* Meetings are more likely to be fully productive when participants are encouraged to be candid with criticism and negative feedback. Openness helps prevent groupthink and also brings important problems to the attention of management.

8 *Strive for wide participation.* One justification for conducting a meeting is to obtain a variety of input. Although not everybody is equally qualified to voice a sound opinion, everyone should be heard. A key role for the meeting leader is to facilitate the meeting so that participation is widespread. Asking participants for their point of view is a good facilitation technique. During a virtual meeting, people from various sites can be asked a question, such as, "What do you think about this issue?"

   A skillful leader may have to limit the contribution of domineering members and coax reticent members to voice their ideas. Beginning the meeting with a question will often set the tone for an interactive meeting. Asking participants to bring several questions to the meeting will usually spur participation. If the meeting leader spends the entire time making a PowerPoint presentation, participation will be discouraged. The slides should supplement the meeting and be the starting points for discussion.

9 *Solve small issues ahead of time with e-mail.* Meetings can be briefer and less mundane when small issues are resolved ahead of time. E-mail is particularly effective for resolving minor administrative issues and for collecting agenda items in advance.

10 *Consider "huddling" when quick action is needed.* A huddle is a fast-paced, action-oriented way of bringing workers together into brief meetings to discuss critical performance issues. A department store manager might bring together five floor managers 10 minutes before opening to say, "We have a line-up of about 500 customers waiting to get in because of our specials today. Is everybody ready for the rush of excitement? What problems do you anticipate?" The huddle is particularly important when it would be difficult for the workers to attend a long meeting.

The walking meetings described in the chapter opener are another alternative to a sit-down meeting. Meeting while walking may be effective in some situations but there are limits in terms of weather, the physical mobility of the participants and the difficulty of serving refreshments while participants are walking.

11 *During a virtual meeting, discourage the use of the mute function.* A problem noted in virtual meetings is that some participants use the mute function so they can better concentrate on other work. Their behavior reflects the attitude, "I've got you on mute and I'm doing several other tasks."[43]

12 *Ensure all follow-up action is assigned and recorded.* All too often, even after a decision has been reached, a meeting lacks tangible output. Distribute a memo summarizing "next steps" and who is responsible for taking what action by what date.

ORGANIZATIONAL POLITICS AND INTERPERSONAL COMMUNICATION

LEARNING OBJECTIVE **7**

Describe how organizational (or office) politics affect interpersonal communication.

At various places in our study of management, we mention political factors. For example, Chapter 1 describes political skill as essential to managerial success, and Chapter 5 describes the role of political factors in decision making. Politics also affects communication because so much interpersonal communication in organizations is politically motivated. Our communication is often shaped by a desire to gain personal advantage. As used here, **organizational politics** refers to informal approaches to gaining power or some other advantage through means that don't involve merit or luck.

As managers rely more on personal influence and less on hierarchy, people tend to recognize the more positive aspects of organizational politics. The positive nature of organizational politics is implied by the term, **leader political support**. It refers to political acts and influence techniques by the leader to provide followers with the resources they need to accomplish individual, group, and organizational objectives.[44] A series of studies showed that if political skills are wielded effectively, it can enhance one's reputation. (This is true because working smoothly with others is a valuable skill.) And having a positive reputation was shown to improve job performance ratings.[45]

In this section, we describe a sampling of political tactics, classified as relatively ethical versus relatively unethical. We also mention what managers can do to control politics. Figure 12-4 gives you an opportunity to think through your own political tendencies.

organizational politics
Informal approaches to gaining power or some other advantage through means that don't involve merit or luck.

leader political support
Political acts and influence techniques by the leader to provide followers with the resources they need to accomplish individual, group, and organizational objectives.

Relatively Ethical Political Tactics

A political tactic might be considered relatively ethical if used to gain advantage or power that serves a constructive organizational purpose. An example would be getting an influential executive on your side so you can implement a company wellness program. We list useful and relatively ethical tactics below.

1 *Develop power contacts.* After you have identified which powerful people are in your network, establish alliances with them. To use this tactic, you may need to bring influential people into your network. Cultivating friendly, cooperative relationships with organizational members and outsiders can advance the cause of the manager or professional. These people can support your ideas

Figure 12-4 The Positive Organizational Politics Questionnaire

Answer each question "mostly agree" or "mostly disagree," even if it is difficult for you to decide which alternative best describes your opinion.

	Mostly Agree	Mostly Disagree
1 Pleasing my boss is a major goal of mine.	_____	_____
2 I go out of my way to flatter important people.	_____	_____
3 I am most likely to do favors for people who can help me in return.	_____	_____
4 Given the opportunity, I would cultivate friendships with powerful people.	_____	_____
5 I will compliment a co-worker even if I have to think hard about what might be praiseworthy.	_____	_____
6 If I thought my boss needed the help, and I had the expertise, I would show him or her how to operate an electronic gadget for personal use.	_____	_____
7 I laugh heartily at my boss's humor, so long as I think he or she is at least a little funny.	_____	_____
8 I would not be too concerned about following a company dress code, so long as I looked neat.	_____	_____
9 If a customer sent me a compliment through e-mail, I would forward a copy to my boss and another influential person.	_____	_____
10 I smile only at people in the workplace whom I genuinely like.	_____	_____
11 An effective way to impress people is to tell them what they want to hear.	_____	_____
12 I would never publicly correct mistakes made by the boss.	_____	_____
13 I would be willing to use my personal contacts to gain a promotion or desirable transfer.	_____	_____
14 It is always a good idea to send a congratulatory note to someone in the company who receives a promotion to an executive position.	_____	_____
15 Office politics is only for losers.	_____	_____

Scoring and interpretation: Give yourself a +1 for each answer that agrees with the keyed answer. Each question that receives a score of +1 shows a tendency toward playing positive organizational politics. The scoring key is as follows:

1. Mostly agree	6. Mostly agree	11. Mostly agree	1–6	Below-average tendency to play office politics
2. Mostly agree	7. Mostly agree	12. Mostly agree	7–11	Average tendency to play office politics
3. Mostly agree	8. Mostly disagree	13. Mostly agree	12 and above	Above-average tendency to play office politics; strong need for power
4. Mostly agree	9. Mostly agree	14. Mostly agree		
5. Mostly agree	10. Mostly disagree	15. Mostly disagree		

Skill development: Thinking about your political tendencies in the workplace is important for your career because most successful leaders are moderately political. The ability to use politics effectively and ethically increases with importance in the executive suite. Most top players are effective office politicians. Yet being overly and blatantly political can lead to distrust, thereby damaging your career.

or directly assist you with problem solving. Power contacts are also essential because they can recommend you for promotion or high-visibility assignments. Social media websites, such as LinkedIn and Facebook are only a starting point in developing useful contacts. In-person meetings are still the medium of choice for building truly useful contacts. For example, Sheryl Sandberg, the chief operating officer of Facebook holds networking events with other powerful women in her living room.[46]

2   *Be courteous, pleasant, and positive.* Having good interpersonal relations skills create many more friends than enemies and can help you be chosen for good team assignments and staying off the downsizing list. It is widely acknowledged by human resource specialists that courteous, pleasant, and positive people are the first to be hired and the last to be fired (assuming they are also technically qualified).

3   *Create a positive image.* A positive image can be cultivated by keeping your voice calm and well-modulated, dressing fashionably, and matching your humor to those around you. Speaking well is critical, and being courteous, pleasant, and positive also contributes to a positive image.

4   *Ask satisfied customers to contact your boss.* A favorable comment by a customer receives considerable weight because customer satisfaction is a top corporate priority. If a customer says something nice, the comment will carry more weight than one from a co-worker or subordinate, because they might praise a person for political reasons. Customers' motivation, on the other hand, is assumed to be pure because they have little concern about pleasing suppliers.

5   *Be politically correct.* Political correctness involves being careful not to offend or slight anyone, and being extra civil and respectful.[47] An effective use of political correctness would be to say that, "We need a ladder in our department because we have workers of different heights who need access to the top shelves." It would be politically incorrect to say, "We need ladders because we have some short workers who cannot reach the top shelves." Carried too far, political correctness can push a person to become too bland and imprecise in language. The ultra-politically correct person, for example, will almost never mention a person's race, sex, ethnicity, or health status when referring to another worker. Ultra-political correctness also involves using supposedly correct terms to describe people even if a given individual rejects the label. For example, many black people are incorrectly referred to as "African American" when in fact they are citizens of Africa, Haiti, England, or another country. These people are Africans, Haitians, or English, not African Americans, and might take pride in being referred to as "black."

6   *Minimize political blunders.* To avoid damaging your career, it is important to avoid, or minimize being blatantly tactless toward others, especially influential people. An example would be telling the CEO that he or she is technically challenged. A frequent political blunder is to insult your own company on social media, which might result in being fired. When you feel you are on the verge of being critical, delay your response, and perhaps reword it for later delivery. Similarly, pause before you hit the send button on a very critical or insulting e-mail, text message, or media post. Use your emotional intelligence. If you are needlessly tactless, compensate the best you can by offering a full apology later.[48]

7   *Send thank-you notes to large numbers of people.* One of the most basic political tactics, sending thank-you notes profusely, is simply an application of sound human relations. Many successful people take the time to send hand-written notes to employees and customers. Handwritten notes are warmer than e-mail messages, and can help create bonds with their recipients.

Relatively Unethical Political Tactics

In the ideal organization, each employee works harmoniously with work associates, all focused on achieving organizational goals rather than pursuing self-interest. Furthermore, everyone trusts each other. In reality not all organizations are ideal, and many people use negative political tactics to fight for political advantage. Here we describe four unethical political tactics.

1   *Backstabbing.* The despised yet widely practiced backstab requires that you pretend to be nice, but all the while plan someone's demise. A frequent form of backstabbing is to initiate a conversation with a rival, or someone you just dislike, about the weaknesses of a common boss. You encourage negative commentary and make careful mental notes of what the person says. When these comments are passed along to the manager, the other person appears disloyal and foolish.

E-mail provides a medium for backstabbing. The sender of the message documents a mistake made by another individual and includes key people on the distribution list. A sample message sent by one manager to a rival began as follows: "Hi Ruth. Thanks for being so candid about why you think our corporate strategy is defective. I was wondering if you had any additional suggestions that you think would help the company compete successfully...."

A useful counterattack to the backstab is to ask an open-ended question to justify his or her actions, such as "I'm not sure I understand why you sent that e-mail about my not supporting the corporate strategy. Can you explain why you did that, and what made you think I do not support corporate strategy?" You might also add, "Do you think this situation is serious enough to discuss with the boss?"

2   *Setting up another person to fail.* A highly devious and deceptive practice is to give another person an assignment with the hopes he or she will fail and therefore be discredited. The person is usually told he or she is being chosen to tackle this important assignment because of a proven capability to manage difficult tasks. (If the person does perform well, the "set-up" will backfire on the manager.) A typical example of setting a person up to fail is to assign a supervisor to a low-performing unit, staffed mostly with problem employees who distrust management.

3   *Stealing credit.* For many workers, the most detestable form of office politics is for their boss, or another worker, to take credit for their ideas without acknowledging the source of the idea. The credit stealing breeds distrust, damages motivation, and is sometimes misinterpreted as a perk of power. A good starting point in stopping idea thieves is to hold a one-on-one session with the thief, and confront the issue. If the issue is not resolved, tell the appropriate manager about the idea theft.[49]

4   *Being unpredictable.* Some particularly devious executives behave unpredictably by design to keep people off guard. People are easier to control when they do not know whether you will be nice or nasty. In the words of business commentator Stanley Bing, "This quality of rampaging unpredictability is a well-known tool used by terrorists, authoritarian brainwashers, and those who wish to command and dominate others. It's used because it works better than straight-out intimidation, which can be anticipated and psychologically prepared for."[50]

Any political tactic can be considered unethical if it is used to advance oneself at the expense of others.

Exercising Control of Negative Organizational Politics

Carried to excess, organizational politics can damage productivity and morale and hurt the careers of innocent people. The productivity loss stems from managers and others devoting too much time to politics and not enough time to useful work. Another problem is that when workers perceive too much office politics to be present, their performance may suffer.[51] The perception that extensive politics exist in the organization has also been traced in a number of studies to psychological strain, the intention to leave the employer, and to a weaker commitment (or engagement) while on the job.[52]

Just *being aware of the presence of organizational politics* can help a manager stay alert for its negative manifestations, such as backstabbing. The politically aware manager carefully evaluates negative statements made by one group member about another.

Open communication can also constrain the impact of political behavior. For instance, open communication lets everyone know the basis for allocating resources, thus reducing the amount of politicking. If people know in advance how resources will be allocated, the effectiveness of kissing up to the boss will be reduced. *Avoiding favoritism* (giving the best rewards to the group member you like the most) is a powerful way of minimizing politics within a work group. If trying to be the boss's pet is not effective, people are more likely to focus on good job performance to get ahead.

SUMMARY OF KEY POINTS

1 Describe the steps in the communication process.

The communication process involves four basic elements, all of which are subject to interference, or noise. The process begins with a sender encoding a message and then transmitting it over a channel to a receiver, who decodes it. Feedback from receiver to sender is also essential. In successful communication, the receiver decodes the message, understands it, and then acts on it.

2 Recognize the major types of nonverbal communication in the workplace.

Seven major modes of transmitting nonverbal messages are hand and body gestures; facial expressions and movements; posture; body placement; voice quality; clothing, dress, and appearance; and mirroring. Nonverbal communication has been applied to help screen airline passengers as security risks.

3 Explain and illustrate organizational communications channels and directions.

Formal channels follow the organization chart, and include media, such as intranets, e-mail, videoconferences, web conferences, physical meetings, and the company blog. Social media websites such as Facebook can be used as a formal channel. Web conferences are particularly useful when employees are geographically dispersed. Management by walking around can also be considered both a formal and an informal communication channel.

Informal channels are the unofficial network of communications that supplement the formal pathways. Leaders often use informal networks to accomplish goals. Informal networks, or communities of practice, can help attain important organizational goals. Chance encounters with employees are also useful for communication. The grapevine is the major informal communication pathway, and it transmits gossip and rumors. Management can take steps to neutralize negative rumors by enhancing formal channels. Messages are transmitted in four directions: upward, downward, sideways, and diagonally. Upward communication program and policies include the open-door policy, and town hall meetings.

An important output of both formal and informal communication channels is to transmit information to other workers to advance knowledge and learning throughout the organization. The learning organization creates and transfers knowledge, and knowledge management leverages knowledge to generate business value.

4 Identify major communication barriers in organizations.

Barriers exist at every step in the communication process. Among them are: (1) low motivation and interest, (2) inappropriate language, (3) defensive communication, (4) insufficient nonverbal communication, (5) information overload, (6) poor communication skills, and (7) electronic communication problems.

5 Develop tactics for overcoming communication barriers.

Strategies and tactics for overcoming communication barriers include: (1) understanding the receiver, (2) communicating assertively and directly, (3) using two-way communications and asking for clarification, (4) eliciting verbal and nonverbal feedback, (5) enhancing listening skills, (6) uniting with a common vocabulary, and (7) being sensitive to cultural differences.

6 Describe how to conduct more effective meetings.

To improve communication effectiveness and the decision-making quality of meetings, follow these suggestions: (1) meet only for valid reasons, (2) the meeting leader should set the tone for the meeting, (3) start and stop on time, and offer refreshments, (4) keep comments brief and to the point, (5) avoid electronic distractions, (6) capitalize on technology when appropriate, (7) encourage critical feedback and commentary, (8) strive for wide participation, (9) solve small issues ahead of time with e-mail, (10) consider "huddling" when quick action is needed, (11) during a virtual meeting discourage the use of the mute function, and (12) ensure follow-up action is assigned and recorded.

7 **Describe how organizational (or office) politics affect interpersonal communication.**

Politics is related to communication because so much interpersonal communication in organizations is politically motivated. Relatively ethical political tactics include: (a) developing power contacts, (b) being courteous, pleasant, and positive, (c) creating a positive image, (d) asking satisfied customers to contact your boss, (e) being politically correct, (f) minimizing political blunders, and (g) sending thank-you notes to large numbers of people. Four relatively unethical political tactics are: (a) back-stabbing, (b) setting up another person to fail, (c) stealing credit, and (d) being unpredictable. Used for a negative purpose, any political tactic can be unethical. Managers must take steps to control excessive negative politics. Open communication and avoiding favoritism can help.

Key Terms and Phrases

communication 355

encoding 356

decoding 356

feedback 357

noise 357

nonverbal communication 357

formal communication channel 359

informal communication channel 362

grapevine 363

communication network 364

learning organization 366

knowledge management 366

defensive communication 368

information overload 369

informative confrontation 372

active listening 374

organizational politics 378

leader political support 378

Questions

1. What do you recommend as the maximum and minimum temperatures for holding walking meetings outside?

2. Employers continue to emphasize good communication skills as one of the most important qualifications for screening career-school and business graduates. What are some of the reasons for this requirement?

3. What kind of facial expression do you think might make a person appear intelligent?

4. What do you see as the potential advantages and disadvantages of firing an employee via a text message?

5. If you believe that listening skills contribute to the effectiveness of a manager or corporate professional, what could you do this week to enhance your listening skills?

6. To what extent do you think communication technologies like GoToMeeting.com (an online meeting tool) or join.me will ever virtually eliminate face-to-face meetings in the workplace?

7. Many workers who have been laid off contend that if they had possessed better political skills they could have avoided losing their jobs. What are they talking about?

Skill-Building Exercise 12-A: Practicing Your Active Listening Skills

Before conducting the following role plays, review the suggestions for active listening in this chapter. The suggestion about reflecting the message back to the sender is particularly relevant because the role plays involve emotional topics.

The Elated Co-worker. One student plays the role of a co-worker who has just been offered a promotion to supervisor of another department. She will be receiving 10 percent higher pay and be able to travel overseas twice a year for the company. She is eager to describe full details of her good fortune to a colleague. Another student plays the role of the co-worker to whom the first co-worker wants to describe her good fortune. The second worker decides to listen intently to the first worker. Other class members will rate the second student on his or her listening ability.

The Discouraged Co-worker. One student plays the role of a co-worker who has just been placed on probation for poor performance. His boss thinks his performance is below standard and his attendance and punctuality are poor. He is afraid that if he tells his girlfriend, she will leave him. He is eager to tell his tale of woe to a colleague. Another student plays the role of a co-worker he corners to discuss his problems. The second worker decided to listen intently to his problems but is pressed for time. Other class members will rate the second student on his or her listening ability.

When evaluating the active listening skills of the role players, consider using the following evaluating factors, on a scale of 1 (low) to 5 (high):

	Rating				
Evaluation Factor	**1**	**2**	**3**	**4**	**5**
1. Maintained eye contact					
2. Showed empathy					
3. Reflected back what the other person said					
4. Focused on other person instead of being distracted					
5. Asked questions					
6. Let other person speak until he or she was finished					
Total Points: _____					

Skill-Building Exercise 12-B: Your Personal List of Powerful Words

As explained in the chapter, using powerful words contributes to assertive communication. Develop a list of 10 powerful words you might actually use to communicate at work. Include in your list a few words that are not widely used by many people. Try out a few of these words with people in your network, and observe how they react to this approach to assertive communication.

Management Now—Online Skill-Building Exercise: The Communication Component of Jobs

Search the Internet for a description of any three jobs that might possibly interest you now or in the future. In addition, the job must mention some type of communication component, such as, "good presentation skills." Based on this brief sample of three jobs, reach a conclusion about the communication requirements of the type of work that interests you. An easy starting point might be to enter your preferred job into a job search engine. Restrict your analysis to jobs that appear to have been posted within the last 60 days. If you are currently working, you might use a job description for that position.

Lone Wolf Pamela Gets Passed Over

Pamela was enjoying her career as a real estate agent at Magnum Properties, a real estate development company. The business model of Magnum is to purchase then rehabilitate distressed office buildings. Many of the older buildings that the company has rehabilitated have been converted into mixed-use properties, such as office space, retail space, and lofty condominium properties.

As Magnum Properties continued to expand, seven agents were working full time, all of them reporting to Austin, the company founder. Pamela's major responsibility was to find tenants as well as condominium buyers for the rehabilitated buildings. Her passion for the business, combined with knowledge of the business and sales skills, enabled her to become the leading agent in terms of sales volume.

Austin specialized in supervising the rehabilitation of older buildings. His role required him to spend considerable time with architects, construction firms, and local zoning boards. Jasmine, the other cofounder, concentrated more on finding properties and working with financial institutions to fund properties. Austin and Jasmine agreed that Magnum had expanded enough to warrant hiring a manager to direct the sales group. Austin enjoyed working with the real estate agents but was too occupied to provide much assistance or direction to the agents.

Austin and Jasmine agreed that it would be a plus for the firm to offer the promotion to sales director to one of the seven agents. The new sales director would continue to contribute as a real estate agent, but would also function as the manager of the group. After considerable discussion, the director of sales position was offered to Blake who readily accepted. For the previous year, he had been the third-highest sales producer.

After learning of Blake's appointment, Pamela demanded an explanation from Austin and Jasmine. She said angrily, "I am the number one agent here, and you didn't even discuss the promotion with me. What's going on?"

Austin responded, "Jasmine and I are well aware that you are a star performer. But we needed more of a team player for the sales director position. We see you as an individual star who doesn't get too involved with the rest of the sales group. The buzz we picked up from your colleagues is that you are great with clients, but that you are a lone wolf. You never share your expertise with the guys and gals in the group."

Pamela replied, "I thought the name of the game is to bring in the big bucks. Spending time with colleagues seems less important." Jasmine replied, "Sales volume is obviously very important, but we needed more of an internal person for this position."

Case Questions

1 In what way might Pamela have been more politically astute to have avoided being passed over?

2 What do you think of the logic behind the decision of Austin and Jasmine to pass over Pamela?

3 What political tactics should Pamela use if she wants to reverse her image as a lone wolf?

4 How ethical was it for the cofounders to listen to "buzz" about Pamela to help them reach their promotion decision?

B.S. Bingo at Vitamin Extra

Carlos is the brand manager for Vitamin Extra, a successful vitamin water drink manufactured and distributed by a medium-sized food and beverage company. Vitamin Extra is a small player in the beverage market but has been successfully marketed into supermarkets, convenience stores, service stations, and a scattering of restaurants. As the brand manager, Carlos looks out for the welfare of Vitamin Extra. He strives to make sure the beverage gets enough resources from the company, such as advertising dollars and incentives for supermarkets to distribute the brand.

Carlos holds weekly strategy meetings with four team members to make plans for building the Vitamin Extra brand, to receive feedback on progress, and to investigate any problems in manufacturing, marketing, or distribution. An outsider, such as a representative from manufacturing or the dietitian staff, is invited to most meetings.

Carlos' boss, Larry, the vice president of non-carbonated beverages, was holding a progress meeting with him about the success of Vitamin Extra. Carlos said he was pleased with the progress and the market share he was taking from Coca-Cola, Pepsi, and Dr. Pepper continued to increase. Carlos did comment, however, that he wished his meetings were more effective. When Larry asked for clarification, Carlos lamented:

"We have a creative staff, so they have to be granted leeway in how they behave. I can't rightfully expect them to be self-disciplined all the time. Yet I wonder if they are going too far."

"How about a few specifics?" asked Larry.

"Two meetings ago, the team was playing B.S. Bingo (short for Business Speak Bingo). Jenny, one of the team members, passed out bingo cards filled with business jargon. The idea for the game was that the first person to check off a row of terms used during the meeting was to jump up and say 'B.S. Bingo.' Pete won with a row of the five terms or words, *at the end of the day*, *strategize*, *rocket science*, *innovative*, and *scale*. We didn't conduct much serious work while the team laughed for three minutes.

"Another problem is that I wonder exactly what the team members are doing with their tablets and laptops during the meetings. They look like they are typing away to take notes, but I have the distinct impression there is some web surfing and processing of personal messages going on.

"We more or less agreed that smartphones should not be used during the meeting, but I get the impression several of our team members check their phones for messages periodically during the meeting. They are kind of sneaky about it. Richard, for example, puts his phone on his lap and glances down.

"You would think that Georgia (another team member) has an attention-deficit disorder. During a one-hour meeting she'll leave at least twice. Or maybe she has a bladder problem. I'm not sure. We drink a lot of Vitamin Extra around here.

"You could say that our meetings are not as productive as I would like. Yet if I come down too heavy on the team, the members might not like the work environment."

Larry responded, "I agree that your meetings could be more disciplined, but I also agree that we don't want to hurt morale. Let's both think through this problem a little bit more."

Case Questions

1 What do you recommend Carlos do to have more disciplined meetings? (Or, should he do anything?)

2 Should Carlos conduct his business meeting with language that would make it difficult to win at B.S. Bingo?

3 What stance should Carlos take about multitasking during meetings?

ENDNOTES

1. Original story created from facts and observations in the following sources: Ruth Umoh, "The Meeting Hack Loved By CEOs at Google, Facebook, and LinkedIn," *www.cnbc.com*, August 23, 2018, pp. 1–3; Leena Patel, "How Walking Meetings Boost Workplace Performance and Productivity," *www.linkedin.com*, August 21, 2017, pp. 1–2; Emily Peck, "Why Walking Meetings Can Be Better Than Sitting Meetings," *HuffPost* (www.huffpost.com), December 6, 2017pp. 1–4; Anna Trester, "Walking Meetings Inspired by LinkedIn," *https:blogs.commons.georgetown.edu*, December 18, 2013, p. 1.

2. Survey reported in Ben Tobin. "Poor Office Communication Stresses 4 In 5," *USA Today*, March 24, 2019.

3. John Hamm, "The Five Messages Leaders Must Manage," *Harvard Business Review*, May 2006, p. 114.

4. Josh Funk, "Buffet Devotes Time to College Students," Associated Press, April 14, 2006.

5. Seth Godin, "How to Give Feedback," *Fast Company*, March 2004, p. 103.

6. Anita Raghavan, "Watch Your Body Language," *Forbes*, March 16, 2009, p. 93.

7. Greg L. Stewart et al., "Exploring the Handshake in Employment Interviews," *Journal of Applied Psychology*, September 2008, pp. 1139–1146.

8. Anett Grant, "3 Ways to Use Gestures When Speaking Without Feeling Uncomfortable," *www.fastcompany.com*, March 19, 2015, p. 4.

9. Nick Morgan, "The Kinesthetic Speaker: Putting Action Into Words," *Harvard Business Review*, April 2001, p. 115.

10. Joyce E. A. Russell, "Career Coach: Sometimes It's Now What You Say, but How You Say It that Hurts," *The Washington Post* (www.washingtonpost.com), February 5, 2015, p. 1.

11. Jeffrey Jacobi, *The Vocal Advantage* (Upper Saddle River, NJ: Prentice-Hall, 1996).

12. Jennifer Saranow, "A Personal Trainer for Your Voice," *The Wall Street Journal*, February 3, 2004, pp. D1, D4.

13. Daniel Michaels, "Queues Caused by Airport Searches Spur Calls for Passenger Profiling," *The Wall Street Journal*, August 17, 2006, p. A5.

14. Sue Shellenbarger, "The Instant Message Generation Gap," *The Wall Street Journal*, April 18, 2018, p. A9.

15. "Accenture to Host Conference Call Thursday Dec 17 to Discuss First-Quarter Fiscal Year 2016 Results," *https://newsroom.accenture.com*, December 16, 2015, pp. 1; "Accenture Fact Sheet," *www.newsroom.accenture.com*, 2020, p. 2.

16. Chip Cutter, "Executives Turn to Texting for Advice," *The Wall Street Journal*, October 12, 2019, p. R9.

17. Herminia Ibarr and Mark Hunter, "How Leaders Create and Use Networks," *Harvard Business Review*, January 2007, pp. 40–47.

18. Richard McDermott and Douglas Archibald, "Harnessing Your Staff's Informal Networks," *Harvard Business Review*, March 2010, pp. 82–89.

19. John P. Kotter, *The General Manager* (New York: The Free Press, 1991).

20. Zak Stambor, "Bonding Over Others' Business," *Monitor on Psychology*, April 2006, pp. 58–59.

21. Nicholas DiFonzo, "When Gossip Is Good," *The Wall Street Journal*, December 12–13, 2009, p. W3.

22. "Make the Rumor Mill Work for You," *Executive Leadership*, May 2003, p. 7.

23. Ethan R. Burris, Kevin W. Rockman, and Yurianna S. Kimmons, "The Value of Voice to Managers: Employee identification and the Content of the Voice," *Academy of Management Journal*, December 20127, pp. 2099–2125.

24. David A. Garvin, "Building a Learning Organization," *Harvard Business Review*, July–August 1993, p. 80.

25. Robert J. Grossman, "A Culture of Learning," *HR Magazine*, May 2015, p. 40.

26. Jeff Green, "Chowing Down on Boomers' Brains," *Bloomberg Businessweek*, January 28, 2016, pp. 19–20.

27. Jon Marcus, "The War Against Jargon," *Entrepreneur*, July/August 2017, p. 56.

28. "Grammar Rules in Real Estate," *The Wall Street Journal*, May 9, 2014, p. M12.

29. Leena Rao, "Email: Unloved. Unbreakable," *Fortune*, May 1, 2015, p. 54.

30. Quoted in Joe Sharkey, "E-Mails Saves Time, but Being There Says More," *The New York Times* (www.nytimes.com), January 26, 2010.

31. Jay A. Conger, "The Necessary Art of Persuasion," *Harvard Business Review*, May–June 1998, p. 86.

32. William Cormier and Sherilyn Cormier, *Interviewing Strategies for Helpers* (Monterey, CA: Brooks/Cole, 1990).

33. Frank Luntz, "Words that Pack Power," *BusinessWeek*, November 3, 2008, p. 106.

34. Cheryl Wakslak, Pamela K. Smith, and Albert Han, "Using Abstract Language Signals Power," *Academy of Management Proceedings*, January 2013.

35. Peter F. Drucker, "What Makes an Effective Executive," *Harvard Business Review*, June 2004, p. 63.

36. Kyle E. Brink and Robert D. Costigan, "Oral Communication Skills: Are the Priorities of the Workplace and AACSB-Accredited Business Programs Aligned?", *Academy of Management Learning & Education*, June 2015, pp. 205–221.

37. Niels Van Quaquebeke and Will Felps, "Respectful Inquiry: A Motivational Account of Leading Through Asking Questions and Listening," *Academy of Management Review*, January 2018, p. 7; "Train Yourself in the Art of Listening," *Positive Leadership*, p. 10, sample issue, 2001; "Five Keys to Effective Listening," *Black Enterprise*, March 2005, p. 113.

38. Steve Patterson, "Returning to Babel," *Management Review*, June 1994, pp. 44–48.

39. David P. Tulin, "Enhance Your Multi-Cultural Communication Skills," *Managing Diversity*, Vol. 1 (1992), p. 5.

40. Paul Axtell, "The Most Productive Meetings Have Fewer Than 8 People," *Harvard Business Review* (https://hbr.org), June 22, 2018, p. 2.

41. K. H. Queen, "Let's Vote and Go Home: How to Run an Efficient Meeting," *The Washington Post*, February 26, 2017, p. G8.

42. Kim Lachance Sandor, "4 Ways to Stop People from Using their Phone During Meetings," *www.entrepreneur.com*, April 2, 2014, p. 1.

43. "Meetings: The Good, the Bad and the Ugly," *Knowledge@Wharton* (http://knowledge.wharton.upenn.edu), September 16, 2015, p. 2.

44. B. Parker Ellen III, Gerald R. Ferris, and M. Ronald Buckley, "Leader Political Support: Reconsidering Leader Political Behavior," *The Leadership Quarterly*, December 2013, pp. 842–857.

45. Yongmei Liu et al., "Dispositional Antecedents and Outcomes of Political Skill in Organizations: A Four-Study Investigation with Convergence," *Journal of Vocational Behavior*, 2007, pp. 146–165.

46. Patricia Sellers, "The New Valley Girls," *Fortune*, October 13, 2008, p. 154.

47. Robin J. Ely, Debra Meyerson, and Martin N. Davidson, "Rethinking Political Correctness," *Harvard Business Review*, September 2006, p. 80.

48. Andrew J. DuBrin, "Political Blunders within Organizations," in Eran Vigoda-Gadot and Amos Drory, *Handbook of Organizational Politics*, Second Edition (Cheltenham, UK: Edward Elgar Publishing, 2016), pp. 172–192.

49. "Stopping Idea Thieves: Strike Back When Rivals Steal Credit," *Executive Leadership*, April 2003, p. 3.

50. Stanley Bing, "What Would Machiavelli Do?" *Fortune*, December 5, 1999, pp. 222–223.

51. Darren C. Treadway et al., "The Role of Age in Perceptions of Politics—Job Performance Relationships: A Three-Study Constructive Replication," *Journal of Applied Psychology*, September 2005, pp. 872–881.

52. Chu-Hsiang Chang, Christopher C. Rosen, and Paul E. Levy, "The Relationships between Perceptions of Organizational Politics and Employee Attitudes, Strain, and Behavior: A Meta-Analytic Examination," *Academy of Management Journal*, August 2009, pp. 770–801.

CHAPTER 13

Teams, Groups, and Teamwork

OBJECTIVES

After studying this chapter and doing the exercises, you should be able to:

1 Identify various types of teams and groups, including self-managed work teams and project groups.

2 Describe the characteristics of effective groups and teams.

3 Summarize managerial actions for building teamwork.

4 Pinpoint the actions and attitudes of an effective team player.

5 Point to the potential contributions and problems of teams and groups.

6 Describe the positive and negative aspects of conflict and how team leaders and managers can resolve conflict.

D ogfish Head Craft Brewery Inc. is a successful company that brews and sells beer, and also operates a restaurant. The 20 styles of beers are offered in 25 states through a network of distributors and wholesalers to grocery stores, bars, and restaurants. Dogfish Head was founded in 1995, and is located in Milton, Delaware. Aside from its tasty craft beers, Dogfish Head is known in the industry and by management observers for the cooperative approach to doing business spearheaded by founder and former CEO Sam Calagione.

Part of Calagione's growth strategy has been to view competitors not as enemies but partners in publicizing the merits of craft beer. He reasoned that if other craft brewers prospered, they would help expand the market in which Dogfish Head had a strong niche. Calagione has embraced the marketing strategy of reasonable cooperation with competitors to attain mutual gain. Calagione has written several books about brewing craft beers, in which he includes admiring anecdotes about competitors. In media appearances to promote his books, he has praised competitors, such as New Belgium Brewing. Calagione says, "I really believe there's a lot of good karma in my celebrating other small breweries I believe in; not just Dogfish Head."

The strategy of collaboration and cooperation also includes having united local government officials, educators, historians, farmers and others in the creation of an all-Delaware beer. Dogfish Head has collaborated with other craft breweries to create unique beers, including a brewery in New Zealand. The company has also collaborated with the environmentally conscious company Patagonia to produce high-tech outerwear. Dogfish Head has even teamed with the Grateful Dead band to create a strong pale ale, labeled American Beauty. In 2020, Dogfish joined forces with the Rodenbach brewery in Belgium to carefully combine two beers, and labeled the new beer Vibrant P'Ocean. Calagione claims that the collaboration was 200 years in the making because Rodenbach was founded in 1821.

Calagione believes that his extensive collaboration has been a major factor in making Dogfish Head one of the top dozen craft breweries in the United States.[1]

The story about the brewery founder illustrates the potential benefits of collaboration and teamwork across organizations. Collaboration in the form of teamwork is also important within organizations. As mentioned in relation to creativity in Chapter 5, office space is frequently designed with open spaces to enhance the exchange of ideas and collaboration. The widespread use of collaborative software that enables workers to share ideas with colleagues rapidly is also part of the movement toward making more effective use of groups and teams.

The heavy emphasis on teams and group decision making in the workplace increases the importance of understanding teams and other types of groups. (You will recall the discussion of group decision making in Chapter 5 and the mention of teams throughout the book.) We approach an additional understanding of teams, groups, and teamwork here by presenting a handful of key topics: types of groups and teams, characteristics of effective work groups, building teamwork, and becoming a team player. We also describe the manager's role in resolving conflict that takes place within groups and between groups.

LEARNING OBJECTIVE **1**

Identify various types of teams and groups, including self-managed work teams and project groups.

group

A collection of people who interact with one another, are working toward some common purpose, and perceive themselves to be a group.

team

A special type of group in which members have complementary skills and are committed to a common purpose, a set of performance goals, and an approach to the task.

teamwork

A situation characterized by understanding and commitment to group goals on the part of all team members.

formal group

A group deliberately formed by the organization to accomplish specific tasks and achieve goals.

informal group

A group that emerges over time through the interaction of workers.

TYPES OF TEAMS AND GROUPS

A **group** is a collection of people who interact with each other, are working toward some common purpose, and perceive themselves to be a group. The head of a customer service team and her staff would be a group. In contrast, 12 people in an office elevator would not be a group because they are not engaged in collective effort. A **team** is a special type of group. Team members have complementary skills and are committed to a common purpose, a set of performance goals, and an approach to the task. **Teamwork** is characterized by understanding and commitment to group goals on the part of all team members.[2]

Some groups are formally sanctioned by management and the organization itself, while others are not. A **formal group** is deliberately formed by the organization to accomplish specific tasks and achieve goals. Examples of formal groups include departments, project groups, task forces, committees, and virtual teams. In contrast, **informal groups** emerge over time through the interaction of workers. Although the goals of these groups are not explicitly stated, informal groups typically satisfy a social or recreational purpose. Members of a department who dine together occasionally would constitute an informal group. Yet the same group might also meet an important work purpose of discussing technical problems of mutual interest. A collection of workers who decide to interact on a company social networking site might also be considered an informal group.

All workplace teams share the common element of people who possess a mix of skills, working together cooperatively. No matter what label the team carries, its broad purpose is to contribute to a collaborative workplace in which people help each other achieve constructive goals. Here we describe five types of work groups even though they have many similarities. The groups are self-managing work teams, project teams and task forces, cross-functional teams, top management teams, and virtual teams.

Because of the widespread use of teams, it is helpful for you to be aware of the skills and knowledge needed to function effectively on a team, particularly a self-managing work team. Figure 13-1 presents a representative listing of behaviors and attitudes related to team member effectiveness.

Figure 13-1 My Effectiveness as a Team Member

The following list of behaviors and attitudes are related to team member effectiveness in a wide variety of work and school settings. To personalize the information, note whether each statement appears to be characteristic of you in your activities as a team member. Answer Yes or No.

	Yes	No
1 Performs high quality work, often surpassing expectations	☐	☐
2 Communicates readily with teammates	☐	☐
3 Cares more about team results than individual recognition	☐	☐
4 Displays integrity in dealing with teammates and managers outside the team	☐	☐
5 Maintains focus on achieving results	☐	☐
6 Gets individual work done on time	☐	☐
7 Accepts feedback from teammates in order to improve	☐	☐
8 Helps another teammate resolve a difficult problem	☐	☐
9 Shares useful knowledge with teammates	☐	☐
10 Listens carefully when ideas are challenged by another team member	☐	☐
11 Makes effective use of professional and technical skills when solving problems	☐	☐
12 Believes strongly that the team will achieve its goals	☐	☐
13 Willing to switch assignments with teammates if needed	☐	☐
14 Cheers the team on toward attaining its goals	☐	☐
15 Expresses sincere interest in the ideas and contributions of teammates	☐	☐

Interpretation: The more of these 15 statements to which you responded "Yes," the higher the probability you are an effective team member now, were in the past, and will be in the future.

Source: Several of the items in the list are derived from Matthew W. Ohalalnd et a., "The Comprehensive Assessment of Team Member Effectiveness: Development of a Behaviorally Anchored Rating Scale for Self- and Peer Evaluations," *Academy of Management Learning & Education*, December 2012, pp. 625–626; "Are You a Team Player?," *Communication Briefings*, November 2011, p. 4.

Self-Managed Work Teams

Almost all organizations use some form of team structure in their organizations, often a type of self-managed team. A **self-managed work team** is a formally recognized group of employees who are responsible for an entire work process or segment that delivers a product or service to an internal or external customer.[3] Self-managed work groups originated as an outgrowth of job enrichment. Working in teams broadens the responsibility of team members.

Self-managed work teams usually have an internal leader who is designated as team leader. At the same time, the team is likely to also have an external leader to whom the team reports.[4] This individual is often a middle manager. So even the self-managing work team is not totally independent.

self-managed work team
A formally recognized group of employees who are responsible for an entire work process or segment that delivers a product or service to an internal or external customer.

The key purposes for establishing self-managed teams are to increase productivity, enhance quality, reduce cycle time (the amount of time required to complete a transaction), and respond more rapidly to a changing workplace. Self-managed work teams also present an opportunity to empower employees.

Members of the self-managed work team typically work together on an ongoing, day-by-day basis, thus differentiating it from a task force or committee. The work team often assumes total responsibility or "ownership" of a product or service. A financial services work team might be assigned the responsibility for servicing customers from one industry. At other times, the team takes on responsibility for a major chunk of a job, such as building a truck engine (but not the entire truck). The self-managed work team is taught to think in terms of customer requirements. The team member might ask, "How easy would it be for a left-handed person to use this tire jack?"

To promote the sense of ownership, management encourages workers to be generalists rather than specialists. Each team member learns a broad range of skills and switches job assignments periodically. Members of the self-directed work team frequently receive training in team skills. Cross training in different organizational functions helps members develop an overall perspective of how the firm operates.

The level of responsibility for a product or service contributes to team members' pride in their work and group. At best, the team members feel as if they operate a small business, with the profits (or losses) directly attributable to their efforts. An entry-level worker, such as a data-entry clerk in a government agency, is less likely to experience such feelings.

high-performance work team

A group of employees who have the responsibility and the authority as a team to determine the process by which core tasks are accomplished.

An updated version of the self-managed team is the **high-performance work team**, a group of employees who have the responsibility and the authority to determine the process by which core tasks are accomplished. The high-performance work team (HPWT) has clearly specified values, goals, and shared responsibility among team members. The team also has open communication and information sharing, participative decision making, and responds rapidly to change.

A four-year study was conducted about the effectiveness of HPWTs in 20 manufacturing plants producing automation and control equipment in a Fortune 500 company. Data were collected regarding plant-level productivity and inventory turnover before and after implementing the work teams. A surprising finding was that the growth rate of labor productivity declines immediately after conversion to HPWTs and recovers to the original productivity level, but not higher. The growth rate of inventory turnover does not decline significantly but shows a long-term improvement. The researchers concluded from the study is that management needs to be patient to obtain a return on their investment in a high-performance work team.[5] Another conclusion is that HPWTs do not always improve productivity.

Project Teams and Task Forces

project team

A small group of employees working on a temporary basis in order to accomplish a particular goal.

Project teams comprise the basic component of the matrix structure described in Chapter 8. A **project team** is a small group of employees working on a temporary basis in order to accomplish a particular goal. Being able to manage a project is a core competence for most managers.[6] In many organizations, being certified as a Project Management Professional (PMP) gives an individual additional status and advancement potential. One reason project managers are important is that projects are so frequently used to manage change, such as launching a new product, introducing a new method of delivering service or manufacturing a large product, including a new vehicle launch. Here we present additional details about project teams to help you understand this important type of work group.

1   Project managers operate independently of the normal chain of command. They usually report to a member of top-level management, often an executive in charge of projects. This reporting relationship gives project members a feeling of being part of an elite group.

2   Project managers negotiate directly for resources with the heads of the line and staff departments whose members are assigned to a given project. For example, a project manager might borrow an architectural technician from the building design department. For the team member who likes job rotation, project teams offer the opportunity for different exciting projects from time to time.

3   Project managers act as coordinators of the people and material needed to complete the project's mission, making them accountable for the performance of those assigned to the project. Project members therefore feel a sense of responsibility to their project leader and their team.

4   Members of the project team might be from the same functional area or from different areas, depending on the needs of the project. The members of a new-product development team, for example, are usually from different areas. A cross-functional team might therefore be regarded as a special type of project team. An example of a project team with members from the same functional area would be a group of financial specialists on assignment to revise the company pension program.

5   The life of the project ends when its objectives are accomplished, such as adding a wing to a hospital or building a prototype for a new sports car. In contrast, most departments are considered relatively stable.

Project teams are found in almost every large company. Being part of a project encourages identification with the project, which often leads to high morale and productivity. A frequently observed attitude is, "we can get this important job done." From the standpoint of the organization, a project team offers flexibility. If the project proves not to be worthwhile it can be disbanded quickly, without having committed enormous resources like renting a separate building or hiring a large staff. If the new project is a big success, it can become the nucleus of a new division of the company or a major new product line.

One problem with project teams, as well as other temporary teams, is that people assigned to the project may be underutilized after the project is completed. Unless another project requires staffing, some of those working on the team may be laid off.

A **task force** is a problem-solving group of a temporary nature, usually working against a deadline. It functions much like a project except it is usually a smaller size and more focused on studying a particular problem or opportunity. The task force is often used to study a problem and then make recommendations to higher management. Representative task force assignments include the following: investigating whether stock options are being used illegally and unethically in the company; finding a potential buyer for the company; making recommendations about improved promotional opportunities for minorities and women; and investigating whether the number of suppliers can be reduced. Being a member of a task force is good for your career because you are likely to make good contacts and be noticed if the task force produces useful results.

task force
A problem-solving group of a temporary nature, usually working against a deadline.

Cross-Functional Teams

cross-functional team
A group composed of workers from different specialties at the same organizational level who come together to accomplish a task.

A **cross-functional team** is a group composed of workers from different specialties, at the same organizational level who come together to accomplish a task. (A cross-functional team might be considered a type of project team or even a task force.) A cross-functional team blends the talents of team members from different specialties as they work on a task that requires such a mix. To perform well on a cross-functional team, a person must think in terms of the good of the larger organization, rather than about his or her own specialty. A typical application of a cross-functional team would be to develop a new product like wearable technology for sports clothing. Among the specialties needed on such a team would be computer science, engineering, manufacturing, industrial design, marketing, and finance. (The finance person would help guide the team toward producing wearable technology that could be sold at a profit.)

When members from different specialties work together, they take into account each other's perspectives when making their contributions. For example, if the manufacturing representative knows that wearable technology for sports clothing must sell for about one-fourth the price of a HDTV, then he or she will have to build the device inexpensively.

In addition to product development, cross-functional teams might be used to improve customer service, reduce costs, and improve the workings of a system, such as online sales. Cross-functional teams are used widely in conglomerates, such as Siemens and Tyco, and often include representatives from different companies within the larger organization.

A key success factor for cross-functional teams is that the team leader has both technical and team leadership skills. The leader needs the technical background to understand the group task and to recognize the potential contribution of members from diverse specialties. At the same time, the leader must have the interpersonal skills to facilitate a diverse group of people with limited experience in working collaboratively. The success of a cross-functional team requires collaboration among its members.

A major advantage of cross-functional teams is that they enhance communication across groups, thereby saving time. The cross-functional team also offers the advantage of a strong customer focus, because the team orients itself towards satisfying a specific internal or external customer or group of customers. A challenge with these teams, however, is that they often breed conflict because of the different points of view.

Top-Management Teams

The group of managers at the top of most organizations is referred to as a team, the management team, or the top-management team. Yet as consultant Jon R. Katzenbach observes, few groups of top-level managers function as a team in the sense of the definition presented earlier in this chapter.[7] The CEO gets most of the publicity, along with credit and blame for what goes wrong. Nevertheless, groups of top-level managers are teams in the sense that they make most major decisions collaboratively with all members of the top-management group. Michael Dell (from the company named "Dell") exemplifies a highly visible chairman and CEO who regularly consults with trusted advisors before making major decisions.

Virtual Teams

Workplace teams are no longer tied to a physical location. A **virtual team** is a small group of people who conduct almost all of their collaborative work by electronic communication rather than in face-to-face meetings. E-mail, text messaging and videoconferencing are the usual medium for sharing information and conducting meetings, yet phone conversations are still useful. Collaborative software is another widely used approach to conducting business virtually. Using collaborative software, like Google Docs, several people can edit a document at the same time, or in sequence, and also have access to a shared database. (The *Management in Action* insert later in the chapter mentions more of these technology tools.) Many virtual teams are composed of people who work from remote locations, with the small company they work for having no physical central office.

A more advanced approach is to have an intranet dedicated to the shared project. Members can update each other, and the status of the project is posted daily. A "virtual workspace" of this type can be more effective than sending hundreds of e-mail messages back and forth to each other.

The trend toward forming cross-cultural teams from geographically dispersed units of a firm increases the application of virtual teams. Strategic alliances in which geographically dispersed companies work with each other depend on virtual teams in many regards. The field technician in Iceland who holds a virtual meeting with her counterparts in South Africa, Mexico, and California realizes a significant cost savings over bringing them all together in one physical location. IBM makes some use of virtual teams in selling information technology systems, partially because so many IBM field personnel work from their homes, vehicles, and hotel rooms. Meeting electronically does not cure all the problems of geographically dispersed teams from different cultures. For example, the manager or team leader must often confront the problem of different attitudes toward hierarchy and authority, such as workers from many cultures not feeling comfortable with the flat structure of a team.[8]

Virtual teams are sometimes the answer to the challenge of hiring workers with essential skills who do not want to relocate. The company can accommodate these workers by creating virtual teams, with perhaps one or two members working in company headquarters. A similar application of virtual teams is to integrate employees after a merger. Instead of relocating several employees from the acquired company, a virtual team is formed. In one merger, the company's legal division became a virtual team.

Trust is a crucial component of virtual teams. Managers must trust people to perform well without direct supervision. Team members develop trust in their co-workers without the benefit of face-to-face meetings. Managers face the same challenge as assembling self-managed or high-performance work teams: self-reliant and talented employees must be selected for the team. Getting team members to feel they are part of a team is another challenge that can sometimes be met by the occasional face-to-face meeting.

A challenge for members of the virtual or remote team is how to collaborate effectively with other team members. Workplace behavior specialists Erica Dhwan and Thomas Chamorrow-Premuzic offer several practical suggestions. First, is relying heavily on regular video calls to help reduce the misinterpretation that might take place when reading e-mail and text messages. Second, invest extra effort to make sure that written communications are clear. Brief messages save time, but they often suffer from a lack of clarity. Third, establish communication rules or norms

virtual team
A small group of people who conduct almost all of their collaborative work by electronic communication rather than in face-to-face meetings.

that promote clarity in communications. Merck, or example, has acronyms that guide digital communication, such as "Four Hour Response" (4HR) and "No Need to Respond" (NNTR).[9]

Importance of Good Leader-Member Relationships

As with teams that work together in physical proximity, good relationships between the leaders of virtual teams and the team members enhances team member satisfaction. The quality of the relationship between leaders and team members is often referred to as LMX (leader-member exchange). A study was conducted with 375 workers who volunteered to engage in virtual work. Virtual workers who have a high-quality relationship with their supervisors (as measured by the LMX questionnaire) are likely to be more committed to the organization. In contrast, virtual workers with a low-quality relationship with the leader had a significant reduction in commitment. High-quality relationships with the leader were strongly related to job satisfaction of team members. The presence of a high-quality leader-member exchange was related to job performance mostly for those workers who spent a lot of time working virtually.[10]

Importance of Ample Communication

High-performing virtual teams typically have ample communication among members, as described in relation to collaboration within the team. One study showed that members of successful virtual design teams send significantly more and longer messages to each other than low-performing teams. A key part of these messages was updating each other on the transition of their projects from one phase to another. Another aspect of ample communication was that the leaders of the high-performing teams took responsibility for making summaries of the team's work and sending messages throughout the project.[11]

The consulting firm Aon Hewitt found that virtual teams are 10 to 43 percent more productive than traditional teams, depending on the industry and organization.[12] Virtual teams are inadvisable in industries, such as manufacturing, healthcare, and hospitality. Any type of work that is sequential or integrated would create problems for a virtual team, including project work that emphasizes face-to-face interaction.[13]

LEARNING OBJECTIVE **2**

Describe the characteristics of effective groups and teams.

CHARACTERISTICS OF EFFECTIVE WORK GROUPS AND TEAMS

Groups and teams, like individuals, possess characteristics that contribute to their uniqueness and effectiveness. As shown in Figure 13-2, these characteristics can be grouped into ten categories. Our description of group and team effectiveness follows this framework.

1 *Enriched job design.* Effective work groups and teams follow the principles of job design embodied in job enrichment and the job characteristics model described in Chapter 7. For example, task significance and task identity are both strong. Group members therefore perceive their work as having high intrinsic motivation. In short, exciting, challenging work contributes to group and team effectiveness.

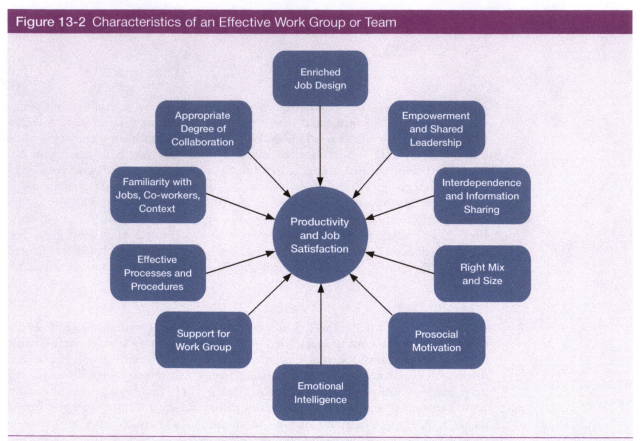

Figure 13-2 Characteristics of an Effective Work Group or Team

Enriched Job Design

Appropriate Degree of Collaboration

Empowerment and Shared Leadership

Familiarity with Jobs, Co-workers, Context

Interdependence and Information Sharing

Productivity and Job Satisfaction

Effective Processes and Procedures

Right Mix and Size

Support for Work Group

Prosocial Motivation

Emotional Intelligence

Sources: Scott Keller and Mary Meaney, "High-Performing Teams: A Timeless Leadership Topic," *McKinsey & Company*, (www.mckinsey.com), June 2017, pp. 1–7; Jia Hu and Robert C. Liden, "Making a Difference in the Teamwork: Linking Prosocial Motivation to Team Processes and Effectiveness," *Academy of Management Journal*, August 2015, pp. 1102–1127; Crystal I. C. Chien Farth et al., "Emotional Intelligence, Teamwork Effectiveness, and Job Performance: The Moderating Role of Job Context," *Journal of Applied Psychology*, July 2012, pp. 890–900; Claus W. Langred, "Too Much of a Good Thing? Negative Effects of High Trust and Individual Autonomy in Self-Managing Work Teams," *Academy of Management Journal*, June 2004, pp. 385–399; Aparna Joshi and Huntak Roh, "The Role of Context in Work Team Diversity Research: A Meta-analytic Review," *Academy of Management Journal*, June 2009, pp. 599–627; Jeffrey A. LePine et al., "A Meta-Analysis of Teamwork Processes: Tests of a Multidimensional Model and Relationships with Team Effectiveness Criteria," *Personnel Psychology*, Summer 2008, pp. 273–307; Rob Cross, Scott Taylor, and Deb Zehner, "Collaboration Without Burnout," *Harvard Business Review*, July-August 2018, pp. 134–137.

2 *Empowerment and shared leadership.* An effective group or team believes in its authority to solve a variety of problems without first obtaining approval from management. An important modern perspective about leadership is that effective leaders require leadership from all team members, as well as the team leader. As described in Chapter 7, group members take turns exerting leadership when the task at hand fits their expertise. Taking turns exerting leadership energizes group members.

3 *Interdependent tasks, information sharing, and rewards.* Effective work groups are characterized by several types of group or team member dependencies on one another. Such groups show task interdependence in the sense that members interact and depend on one another to accomplish work. Goal interdependence refers to the linking of individual goals to the group's goals.

Unless the task requires interdependence, such as building a motorcycle, a team is not needed. For interdependence to work well, group members must share information. An integration of 72 studies involving over 4,500 groups and 17,000 group members demonstrated that information sharing is associated with team performance. The clearer the task, the more likely that information will be shared. Information sharing was also associated with group cohesiveness and job satisfaction.[14]

4 *Right mix and size.* A variety of factors relating to the mix of group members are associated with effective work groups. The diversity of group members' experience, knowledge and education generally improves problem solving. Teams with members who have diverse educational backgrounds are more likely to benefit from the different information that stems from the diversity. For example, a person who majored in fine arts could make a design suggestion that engineers and business specialists might overlook. In general, functional (work specialty) diversity tends to enhance performance. Complementary skills and attitudes also contribute to an effective mix. For example, it is helpful to have as group members both big-picture thinkers as well as those who focus on important details.

Cultural diversity includes attributes, such as gender, race, ethnicity, and age. These factors tend to have a small negative effect on group performance, but the relationship is complex. Cultural diversity tends to enhance creativity by bringing various viewpoints into play. However, only when each team member enjoys high quality interactions can the full benefits of diversity be realized. The interactions relate to both the task itself (such as talking about improving a motorcycle starter) and social interactions (such as chatting about children during a break).[15]

Groups should be large enough to accomplish the work, but when groups become too large, confusion and poor coordination may result. Also, larger groups tend to be less cohesive. Cross-functional teams, work teams, committees, and task forces tend to be most productive with seven to 10 members. Uber chief executive Dara Khosrowshahi points out the disadvantage of excessively large group in these words: "Bigger often means slower: slower decision making, blurry lines of authority, and a tendency to say yes to everything, rather than doing the hard work or prioritization."[16]

Another important composition factor is the quality of the group or team members. Bright people with constructive personality characteristics contribute the most to team effectiveness. A study involving 652 employees composing 51 work teams found that teams with members higher in mental ability, conscientiousness, extraversion, and emotional stability received higher supervisor ratings for team performance.[17] Furthermore, observations made in a variety of industries concluded that putting the best thinkers on a team together can trigger extraordinary creativity.[18] (Put winners on your team and you are more likely to have a winning team.)

5 *Prosocial motivation of group members.* Strong work motivation of group members is a major contributing factor to group performance. Research suggests **prosocial motivation,** or the desire to exert effort to benefit others, is especially important. Studies conducted with 191 teams in work settings and in the laboratory found prosocial motivation enhances cooperation within the group. In turn, the higher level of cooperation facilitates higher

prosocial motivation
The desire to exert effort to benefit others.

performance and organizational citizenship behavior. Prosocial motivation has a strong effect when the work is more interdependent.[19] A logical explanation is that when people depend on each other to accomplish a task, the willingness to help each other is more important.

6 *Emotional intelligence.* The group or team itself should have high emotional intelligence in the sense of being able to build relationships both inside and outside the team and make constructive use of its emotions. Norms that establish mutual trust among group members contribute to an emotionally intelligent group.[20] A potential problem, however, is when group members trust each other too much, they neglect to monitor each other's work and may not catch errors and unethical behavior.[21]

7 *Support for the work group.* One of the most important characteristics of an effective work group is the support it receives from the organization. Key support factors include giving the group the information it needs, coaching group members, providing the right technology, and receiving recognition and other rewards. Training quite often facilitates work group effectiveness. The training content typically includes group decision making, interpersonal skills, technical knowledge, and the team philosophy. Managerial support in the form of investing resources and believing in group effort fosters effectiveness.

8 *Effective processes within the group.* Many processes (activities) take place within the group that influence effectiveness, which is often enhanced when workers provide social support by helping each other have positive interactions. (Prosocial motivation helps here.) Workload sharing is another process characteristic related to effectiveness. Communication and cooperation within the work group also contributes to effectiveness. Collectively, the right amount of these process characteristics contributes to cohesiveness, or a group that pulls together. Without cohesiveness, a group will fail to achieve synergy.

Teams that can be trusted to follow work processes and procedures tend to perform better. Adhering to such processes and procedures is also associated with high-quality output. Although following processes and procedures might appear to be a routine expectation, many problems are created by workers who fail to do so. For example, a group might show a productivity dip if workers fail to follow safety regulations and a group member has a serious accident.

9 *Familiarity with jobs, co-workers, and the environment.* Another important set of factors related to work group effectiveness is familiarity. It refers to the specific knowledge group members have of their jobs, co-workers, and the environment. Familiarity essentially refers to experience, and for many types of job experience—at least to the point of proficiency—familiarity is an asset. The contribution of familiarity is also evident when new members join an athletic team. Quite often the team loses momentum during the adjustment period.

10 *Appropriate degree of collaboration.* Because groups and teams are formed to make collective effort possible, collaboration among everyone involved is essential. Collaboration is also the basis for interdependence within the group. As will be described later in relation to building teamwork, too much collaboration can lead to wasted time and emotional exhaustion because so much time is spent interacting with others. Group and team members still need

time to independently perform analytical work such as preparing a budget, coding, or working out a supply-chain problem. An appropriate degree of collaboration therefore contributes to group and team effectiveness.

collective efficacy
A group's shared belief in its combined capabilities to organize and execute the courses of action required for certain outcomes.

Teams and groups with all or most of these characteristics develop a feeling of **collective efficacy**, a group's shared belief in its combined capabilities to organize and execute the courses of action required for certain outcomes. Collective efficacy is a factor of substantial impact. Results based on over 6,000 groups and 31,000 individuals showed that collective efficacy was significantly related to group performance.[22] A manager is therefore well advised to help the group or team develop some of the above characteristics. Successful organizations are characterized by the presence of many effective work groups and teams.

Effective leadership should supplement the characteristics of an effective work group. Team leaders must emphasize coaching more than controlling. The group as an entity should be coached, not just individual members. An example would be talking with the group about communicating more freely with each other. Frederick P. Morgeson, in a study conducted in three organizations, found that supportive coaching was associated with being perceived as effective by team members. However, coaching in the form of the manager jumping in with suggestions was associated with effectiveness when the team was facing an urgent problem.[23]

LEARNING OBJECTIVE 3

Summarize managerial actions for building teamwork.

MANAGERIAL ACTIONS FOR BUILDING TEAMWORK

Given the importance of teams, managers may need to invest time in building teamwork. The all-time great professional basketball player Michael Jordan made a statement that reinforces considerable scholarly opinion and research about the importance of building an effective team. Jordan said, "Talent wins games, but teamwork and intelligence win championships."[24]

Here we highlight managerial actions and organizational practices that facilitate teamwork.[25] Good teamwork enhances but does not guarantee a successful team. For example, a group with excellent teamwork might be working on improving a service no longer valued by the company or customers. No matter what the output of the team, it will probably be ignored.

1 *Begin with a mission and an agreement on the meaning of success.* A natural starting point in developing teamwork is to have a mission that is accepted by the team, such as one that relates to providing an outstanding experience for customers. A clearly articulated mission translates into the team having an urgent, constructive purpose. Knowing and accepting the mission includes agreeing on what constitutes success. The team leader for snow blowers at Caterpillar, for example, might say, "Do we all agree that our mission is to design and build the safest snow blower in the industry?"

2 *Help the group focus on its strengths.* Teams that experience group efficacy are more likely to be cohesive, therefore working together smoothly. A useful subject for at least a portion of a team meeting is to respond to the question, "What are our team's strengths?" and "What do we do well?" Articulating these positive points might help the team feel stronger.[26] An example of both a team strength and doing something well might be on-time delivery of high-priority projects.

3 *Compete against a common enemy.* Competing against a common enemy is often used to build team spirit. It is preferable that the adversary is external, such as an independent diner competing against franchised family restaurants.

4 *Make teamwork the norm.* A primary strategy for teamwork promotes the attitude that working together effectively is an expected norm. The team leader can communicate the norm of teamwork by making frequent use of words and phrases that support teamwork. Emphasizing the words "team members" or "teammates," and deemphasizing the words "subordinates" and "employees" helps communicate the teamwork norm. A norm of teamwork might also be regarded as a culture favoring teamwork. Ray Dalio, the founder of the world's largest hedge fund, Bridgewater Associates, supports a culture of teamwork. To encourage working well with each other, the staff regularly rate co-workers on 77 qualities, and workers also assess their bosses.[27]

5 *Use consensus decision making and provide information.* Using the consensus decision making style provides another way to reinforce teamwork. A sophisticated approach to enhancing teamwork, feeds team members valid facts and information that motivate them to work together. New information prompts the team to redefine and enrich its understanding of the challenge it is facing, thereby focusing on a common purpose.

6 *Minimize micromanagement.* To foster teamwork, the manager should minimize **micromanagement**, or supervising group members too closely and second-guessing their decisions. Micromanagement can hamper a spirit of teamwork because team members do not feel in control of their own work. Also, morale suffers when the manager is more concerned about the format of a document than its purpose.[28]

micromanagement
Supervising group members too closely and second-guessing their decisions.

7 *Reward the team and individuals.* A high-impact strategy for encouraging teamwork rewards the team as well as individuals. The most convincing team incentive is to calculate compensation partially on the basis of team results. Managers might also apply positive reinforcement whenever the group or individuals engage in behavior that supports teamwork. For example, team members who took the initiative to have an information-sharing session can be singled out and praised for this activity. Research supports the practical idea that individual team members should be rewarded for their individual contributions as well as their contributions to the team effort, referred to as hybrid rewards.[29]

8 *Encourage some face-to-face communication.* A robust approach to enhancing teamwork is to encourage team members to supplement e-mail communication and text messaging with phone calls and face-to-face meetings. The old fashioned method of humans interacting with one another in person has proven to be of value in the era of communication technology.

9 *Show respect for team members.* Showing respect for team members is a general technique for building teamwork. Respect can be demonstrated in such ways as asking rather than demanding something be done. For example, "Jeremy, could you investigate developing a Facebook page for the team?" Giving team members your undivided attention when they come to you with a problem is another demonstration of respect. Making positive comments about other team members, and not talking behind their backs is another way of showing respect. An indirect way of respecting all members is to lead them in approximately the same manner. According to leader-member exchange theory, the successful leader has different relationships with each group member. More recent research suggests, however, that the leader should avoid a high level of differentiation in working with team members. Members should be treated essentially alike to help build teamwork.[30] Yet there will still be a need for differentiated leadership, such as providing more coaching to a less-skilled team member.

10 *Participate in teamwork training.* Another option available to organizations for enhancing teamwork comes through experiential learning, such as sending members to offsite (or outdoor) training. NASA invests two weeks every several years in wilderness training to develop collaboration among astronauts because accomplishing their mission and surviving depends on high-level teamwork.[31] In outdoor training, participants acquire leadership and teamwork skills by confronting physical challenges and exceeding their self-imposed limitations. In rope activities, which are typical of outdoor training, participants attached to a secure pulley with ropes climb ladders and jump off to another spot. Another form of outdoor training for elite teams, is a day at an auto-racing track. This experience provides team members with an opportunity to drive race cars at speeds in some kind of cooperative venture. All of these challenges require teamwork rather than individual effort, hence their contribution to team development.

The benefits of teamwork training can sometimes be accomplished through workers eating together regularly, such as at lunch. A study of 395 firefighters found that eating together is a key component of keeping the teams operating effectively. The collaborative effort of the firefighters preparing the meals also enhanced teamwork.[32]

A problem frequently noted with off-site team building is that the activities can backfire leading to both embarrassment and injury. In one paintballing activity, a participant threw a paintball that accidentally hit his boss. The boss fell to the floor, the game was stopped, and an ambulance was called. Other participants said that the manager suffered potential liver damage or kidney damage. The manager was not seriously hurt, but a pre-existing medical condition had flared up.[33]

Outdoor training generally offers the most favorable outcomes when the trainer helps the team members comprehend the link between such training and on-the-job behavior. Reviewing what has been learned is a key step in this direction. Still, the manager should not impose outdoor training on the growing number of workers who dislike the idea or fear bodily damage. Also, dissent is growing about outdoor activities that require athletic ability because less physically capable team members feel excluded.

11 *Rise to the challenge of teamwork for virtual teams.* Building teamwork within a virtual team creates additional challenges because members rarely meet face-to-face, thereby having less opportunity to build the chemistry often found within traditional teams. Without careful attention to building teamwork, virtual teams can evolve into a frustrating and inefficient way of working.[34] A study involving 15 European and U.S. multinational companies observed that certain factors helped build teamwork in virtual teams. Several of the success factors are as follows:

- First, invest in an online resource where team members can readily learn about each other.

- Second, to capitalize on familiarity, choose a few team members who have worked together previously.

- Third, create an online site where team members can exchange ideas, collaborate, and encourage and inspire each other.

- Fourth, when establishing the team, rely on volunteers as much as possible. Volunteers are more likely to enjoy being virtual team members and will therefore be willing to cooperate with each other.[35]

Effective managers pick and choose from strategies as appropriate to build teamwork. Relying too heavily on one tactic, such as establishing a mission statement or outdoor training, limits the development of sustained teamwork.

An important caution about building teamwork is that it can have diminishing returns. Over the past two decades, the time spent by managers and employees in collaborative activities has surged by at least 50 percent. Most managerial workers spend at least 85 percent of work time on e-mail, meetings, and on the phone. The need for collaboration has been attributed to the increased complexity of products and services, globalization, digital messaging, and the widespread use of collaborative tools and social media. An analysis prepared by the Wharton School of the University of Pennsylvania suggests that the sharp rise in cross-functional collaboration has triggered a difficulty in keeping up with e-mails, text messages, and conference calls.

When demands for collaboration and teamwork are excessive, work flow bottlenecks and employee burnout may occur.[36] For example, too much time spent in meetings, or conversing with co-workers may make it difficult for some workers to complete analytical and creative work.

The accompanying *Management in Action* insert describes how a well-known technology company makes use of virtual (or remote) teams to foster teamwork.

BEING AN EFFECTIVE TEAM PLAYER

LEARNING OBJECTIVE **4**

Pinpoint the actions and attitudes of an effective team player.

Being an effective team player makes collaborative efforts possible. Being an effective team player also affects managerial perceptions because they value such behavior among employees and job applicants. Here we describe a number of skills, actions, and attitudes contributing to effective team play. For convenience, six are classified as task-related, and six as people-related. In reviewing these attributes, remember that all team situations do not have identical requirements.

Task-Related Actions and Attitudes

Task-related actions and attitudes focus on group or teamwork goals and actual work rather than on interpersonal relationships. An effective team player is likely to behave and think in the following ways:

1 *Possesses and shares technical expertise.* Most people are chosen to join a particular work team based on their technical or functional expertise. Using technical expertise to advantage requires a willingness and ability to share that expertise. The technical expert must be able to communicate with team members in other disciplines who lack the same technical background.

2 *Assumes responsibility for problems.* The outstanding team player assumes responsibility for problems. If he or she notices a free-floating problem (not yet assigned to a specific person), the team member says, "I'll do it." The task

MANAGEMENT IN ACTION

Dell Inc. Implements Virtual Teams

Dell Inc. the technology company with over 100,000 employees worldwide, has a culture that emphasizes a connected workplace. Virtual teams are a key part of keeping people connected and offering employees flexibility with respect to where and when to work. Twelve years ago, Dell developed a work flexibility program labeled Connected Workplace. The program offered flexible options to employees that enable teams as well as individuals to work remotely. Company management believes that the program has contributed to a more engaged and productive workforce with a global participation rate of above 50 percent in the program. Dell's program has also created a more collaborative environment that has been as productive as in-office teams.

Jennifer Newbill, Director of Global Employment Branding at Dell, explains that technology tools are crucial for effective team communication, and they make it possible for the "everywhere office" to work smoothly. Being able to send an IM from your phone, PC, or tablet means that you are just a moment away from connecting with your team. Beyond the instant contact, it is still important to set up weekly conversations with key team members, and to connect with network members over Skype, Facebook, video chat Messenger, or in person to keep the relationships current. Videos are an important part of virtual teamwork at Dell. Seeing another person's face makes it possible to form a deep connection with him or her.

Dell relies on technology to help build teamwork with remote workers. The company has a Slack-type tool that lets team members from around the world chat, follow each other, create groups, and share content. Video plays a major role in completing their engaging remote team experience. Dell also uses Adobe Connect or Skype for follow-up sessions, and Dell champion updates. Staff members are encouraged to use the chat feature while using video. Team members can say hello to each other, comment on the content, and ask the presenter a question. All the interaction fosters a team spirit that fits in with the company culture.

Dell uses Salesforce Chatter as an internal social network. There are hundreds of group workers can join depending on their team, business, or outside events. An assist to working remotely is to be able to get help when needed. One morning a Dell staff member was having trouble connecting to his network. He posted his problem on the IT Help Desk Chatter Group. Within minutes another group member e-mailed him with a suggested fix for the problem.

GlobeSmart is another tool Dell uses to help team members connect by understanding better different cultures and work preferences. For example, you can compare with other people how much respect you give to people based on their job titles.

Employee affinity groups are another method used to help remote employees feel more included. As project manager Meredith Burnhill Harrison explains, "Finding your 'tribe' and knowing you have people who share your passions and interests can make a large global corporation feel that much smaller." The employee affinity group Conexus brings together remote team members and hosts virtual career development seminars. The same affinity group has an internal social networking site that swaps tips that enhance remote productivity, and also helps resolve technical problems.

Using social media, team members are encouraged to share their personal experiences working remotely. Employees post about their daily work activities using the tag @Life@Dell.

Questions

1   **In what way does it appear that the tools Dell uses for virtual teams can also be used by individuals working remotely?**

2   **To what extent might so many different tools and approaches to accomplish teamwork confuse employees?**

Source: Original story based on facts and observations in the following sources: "3 Companies with High-Performing Virtual Teams," *Onpoint Consulting* (onpointconsultingllc.com), July 17, 2019, pp. 1–4; Andrea Loubier, "How Microsoft And Dell Use Technology To Manage Their Remote Teams," *Forbes* (www.forbes.com), August 1, 2017, pp. 1–5; "Dell's Tools for a Successful Virtual Team," *Remote.Co* (https://remote.com), December 26, 2015, pp. 1–2; "Virtual Teams," *Intercultural Management Wiki* (https://intercultural management.fandom.com), 2020; 2019, pp. 1–4.

should be suited for independent rather than coordinated activity, such as conducting research.

3   *Is willing to commit to team goals.* The exceptional team player will commit to team goals even if his or her personal goals cannot be achieved for now. For instance, the team member seeking visibility will be enthusiastic about pursuing team goals even if not much visibility will be gained.

4   *Is able to see the big picture.* As described in Chapter 1, a basic management skill is to think conceptually. Exceptionally good team players exhibit this same skill. In team efforts, discussion can get bogged down in small details. As a result, the team might temporarily lose sight of what it is trying to accomplish. The team player (or team leader) who can help the group focus on its broader purpose plays a vital role.

5   *Is willing to ask tough questions.* A **tough question** helps the group achieve insight into the nature of the problem it faces, what it might be doing wrong, and whether progress is sufficient. Tough questions can also be asked to help the group see the big picture. Asking tough questions helps the group avoid groupthink. Here is a representative tough question asked by a team member: "I've been to all our meetings so far. What specifically have we accomplished?"

6   *Is willing to try something new.* An effective team player experiments with new ideas even if the old method works relatively well. Trying something new leads to a spirit of inventiveness that helps keep the group vibrant. In a Harley-Davidson manufacturing team, several of the workers designed a device to guide the brush in painting Harley's trademark striping. Although the more experienced manufacturing technicians had been successful with the hand-painting method, in the spirit of teamwork they were willing to try the new technique.

tough question
A question that helps the group achieve insight into the nature of the problem it faces, what it might be doing wrong, and whether progress is sufficient.

People-Related Actions and Attitudes

Outstanding team players cultivate a conscious awareness of their interpersonal relations within the group. They recognize that effective interpersonal relationships are important for accomplishing tasks. An outstanding team player is likely to do or think the following:

1   *Trust team members.* The cornerstone attitude of the outstanding team player is to trust team members. If you do not believe the other team members have your best interests at heart, it will be difficult to share opinions and ideas. Trusting team members includes believing their ideas are technically sound and rational until proven otherwise. Another manifestation of trust is taking a risk by trying out a team member's unproven ideas. (As cautioned above, however, do not trust teammates to the point that you never monitor their work.)

2   *Share credit.* Sharing credit is authentic because other members of the team usually have contributed to the success of a project. The late Stephen Covey, best-selling author and consultant, said that teamwork is fostered when you don't worry about who gets the credit.[37] To the strong team player, getting the group task accomplished is more important than receiving individual recognition.

3   *Recognize the interests and achievements of others.* A fundamental tactic for establishing yourself as a solid team player is to recognize the interests and achievements of others. Let others know you care about their interests by such means as asking, "How do my ideas fit into what you have planned?" Recognizing the achievements of others can be done by complimenting their tangible accomplishments.

4   *Listen actively and share information.* The skilled team player listens actively both inside and outside of meetings. An active listener strives to grasp both

the facts and feelings behind what is being said. Information sharing helps other team members do their job well and also communicates concern for their welfare. Information sharing can take many forms, such as sending teammates links to useful websites, news clips, and magazine articles, and recommending relevant books.

5   *Give and receive criticism.* The strong team player offers constructive criticism when needed, but does so diplomatically. A high-performance team demands sincere and tactful criticism among members. In addition to criticizing others in a helpful manner, the strong team player benefits from criticism directed toward him or her. A high-performing team involves give and take, including criticism of each other's ideas. The willingness to accept constructive criticism is often referred to as self-awareness. The self-aware team player insightfully processes personal feedback to improve effectiveness.

6   *Don't rain on another team member's parade.* Pointing out the flaws in another person's accomplishments, or drawing attention to your own achievements when somebody else is receiving credit, creates disharmony within the group. When a teammate is in the spotlight, allow him or her to enjoy the moment without displaying petty jealousy.

LEARNING OBJECTIVE 5

Point to the potential contributions and problems of teams and groups.

POTENTIAL CONTRIBUTIONS AND PROBLEMS OF TEAMS AND GROUPS

Given that groups and teams are such an integral part of how organizations function, it is easy not to look critically at their contribution. However, researchers, writers, and managerial workers themselves assess the contributions of groups, both the upside and downside, especially with teams.

Potential Contributions of Teams and Groups

lift outs (in relation to teams)
The practice of recruiting an entire high-functioning team from another organization.

Teams and groups make a contribution to the extent they produce results beyond what could be achieved without a high degree of collaboration among workers. Considerable case history supports the contribution of teams over independent effort. A revealing perspective on the importance of teams is **lift outs**—the practice of recruiting an entire high-functioning team from another organization. The company doing the recruiting believes that the team is more important for attaining its goals than an individual star. It is also believed the recruited team can get up to speed rapidly in the new setting. By hiring a team, the path to productivity is shorter because the group members have a track record of working well together.[38]

Lift outs have been used frequently in such industries as financial services, law, and information technology. Now professional services firms, such as management consulting and accounting firms are hiring more teams. Despite the increase in lift outs, the concept can raise legal issues and might be considered unethical. Is it fair to decimate a competitor by hiring one of its key teams? Or, is it just part of competitive business?

Teams tend to be the most useful as a form of organization under the following conditions[39]:

- When work processes cut across functional lines (as in new-product development).

- When speed is important (assuming not too many meetings are required).
- When the organization faces a complex and rapidly changing environment (as in developing toys and video games for the next holiday season).
- When innovation and learning have high priority (entering a new market or field).
- When the tasks to be accomplished require integration of highly interdependent performers (gathering inputs for a strategic plan).

When these conditions do not exist, the organization is better off assigning the task to more traditional groups, or to individuals working alone. Remember, a team is essentially a super group.

Potential Problems of Teams and Groups

Although the collaborative workplace enjoys popularity, many concerns accompany the use of teams and groups. In Chapter 5, discussing problem solving and decision making, we described two problems with groups: time wasting and groupthink. Here we look at other problems: group polarization, social loafing, limited accountability, ostracism of an occasional member, and career retardation.

Group Polarization

During group problem solving, or group discussion in general, members often shift their attitudes. Sometimes the group moves toward taking greater risks, called the risky shift. At other times the group moves toward a more conservative position. The general term for moving in either direction is **group polarization**, a situation in which post-discussion attitudes tend to be more extreme than pre-discussion attitudes.[40] For example, as a result of group discussion, members of an executive team become more cautious about entering a new market.

Group discussion facilitates polarization for several reasons. Discovering that others share our opinions may reinforce and strengthen our position. Listening to persuasive arguments may also strengthen our convictions. The, "devil-made-me-do-it" attitude is another contributor to polarization. If responsibility is diffused, a person will feel less responsible—and guilty—about taking an extreme position.

Group polarization has a practical implication for managers who rely on group decision making. Workers who enter into group decision making with a stand on an issue may develop more extreme post-decision positions. For example, a team of employees who were seeking more generous benefits may decide as a group that the company should become an industry leader in employee benefits.

group polarization
A situation in which post-discussion attitudes tend to be more extreme than pre-discussion attitudes.

Social Loafing

An unfortunate by-product of group and team effort happens when an under-motivated person squeezes by without contributing his or her fair share. **Social loafing** is freeloading, or shirking individual responsibility, when a person is placed in a group setting and removed from individual accountability. The concept is said to have originated from a sociologist who was studying group behavior among people playing tug-of-war with a rope. Readers who have worked on group projects for courses may have encountered this widely observed dysfunction of collective effort.

social loafing
Freeloading, or shirking individual responsibility, when a person is placed in a group setting and removed from individual accountability.

Two motivational explanations of social loafing have been offered. First, some people believe that because they are part of a team, they can, "hide in the crowd." Second, group members typically believe others are likely to withhold effort when working in a group. As a consequence, they withhold effort to avoid being played for a sucker.

As one approach to minimizing the effects of social loafing, a manager may ask group members to contribute to the evaluation of each other. Concerns about being evaluated as a freeloader by peers would prompt some people to work harder.

Limited Accountability

A curious problem about workplace teams is that they are often given credit for accomplishments, but they are rarely blamed for failures. Instead, individual team members are blamed for team failures, and the group escapes blame. Teams often develop a positive halo, and they are perceived as being able to attain high performance.[41] So when the team does fail, observers (including the manager) look for individuals to blame.

Ostracism of an Unwanted Group Member

ostracism

The extent to which an individual group member perceives that he or she is being ignored by the other group members.

Despite all the team spirit found in many groups, group members can be cruel in ostracizing an unwanted or unpopular member. **Ostracism** is the extent to which an individual group member perceives that he or she is being ignored by other group members. Several surveys have suggested that many employees feel they have been given the silent treatment by other members of the workgroup. A danger is when ostracism is in the form of discrimination based on gender, age, race, ethnicity, or sexual orientation.[42]

At other times ostracism is based on an individual's personality or low work performance. Being ostracized has a strong negative impact on a group member's well-being. Even when ostracism is warranted, it is dysfunctional. It would be better for the other group members to work with the individual to help him or her to be welcomed into the group. Or, the group might ask the manager to get help for the unwanted worker if he or she has a personality or performance problem.

Career Retardation

A final concern about teams arises from focusing too much on group or team effort, rather than individual effort, which can retard a person's career. Some managers tend to classify workers as team players versus leaders. (The perception is somewhat misleading because most effective leaders and managers are also good team players.) Yet it is true that a person who tries too hard to be a good team player might become a conformist and not seek individual recognition. People who do break away from the team and become higher-level managers are typically those known for independent thought and outstanding accomplishment.

For those who want to advance beyond being a team member, or team leader, it is important to be recognized for outstanding performance. As a team member, for example, volunteer to take on leadership roles, such as chairing a team meeting or coordinating a special project. Bring a dossier of your individual accomplishments to your performance review. Every team has a most valuable player (MVP) who is still a good team player.

RESOLVING CONFLICT WITHIN TEAMS AND GROUPS

Although harmony and collaboration are an important goal of groups and teams, some disagreement and dispute are inevitable. **Conflict** is the simultaneous arousal of two or more incompatible motives. It is often accompanied by tension and frustration. Whenever two or more people in the group compete for the same resource, conflict occurs. Two team members, for example, may both want to take the team's one allocated seat on the corporate jet on business trips they are taking on the same day. Conflict can also be considered a hostile or antagonistic relationship between two people.

Another reason conflict often occurs in groups is the existence of different factions within a group, often because group members are from different units within the company. Also, after a merger of acquisition various groups may be composed of people from the acquired company and the company that made the acquisition.[43] A purpose of these types of groups might be to help smooth the integration of two large firms such, as T-Mobile and Sprint.

Here we look at three aspects of conflict particularly relevant to managers and team leaders of small groups: task versus relationship conflict, consequences of conflict, and methods of conflict resolution.

Task Versus Relationship Conflict

Some conflicts within the group deal mostly with disagreements over how work should be done. They are referred to as task or *cognitive* conflicts because they deal mostly with the work itself rather than emotions and relationships. Two group members, for example, might argue over whether it is better to use their limited advertising budget to buy space on the outside of a bus versus on the Internet. **Task conflict** focuses on substantive, issue-related differences related to the work itself. These issues are tangible and concrete and can be dealt with more intellectually than emotionally.

Other conflicts within the group are more people oriented. They occur because people have personality clashes, are rude to each other, or simply view many problems and situations from a different frame of reference. **Relationship conflict** focuses on personalized, individually oriented issues. In these cases, conflict relates to subjective issues that are dealt with more emotionally than intellectually.[44] One symptom that often indicates a relationship conflict exists within the group is when, during a meeting, two people say to each other frequently, "Please let me finish. I'm still speaking." Relationship conflict might also take place based on generational differences, such as young people disliking the fact that older workers prefer e-mail over text messages for most communication.

Task conflict in moderate doses can be functional because it requires teams to engage in activities that foster team effectiveness. Team members engaged in moderate task conflict would critically examine alternative solutions and incorporate different points of view into their goals or mission statement. Because frank communication and different points of view are encouraged, task conflict can encourage innovative thinking. In contrast, relationship (or affective) conflict undermines group effectiveness by blocking constructive activities and processes. By directing anger toward individuals and blaming each other for mistakes, relationship conflict leads to cynicism and distrust.

An analysis of many studies cautions that both task conflict and relationship conflict can be equally disruptive. A little conflict may be beneficial, but this advantage

LEARNING OBJECTIVE 6

Describe the positive and negative aspects of conflict and how team leaders and managers can resolve conflict.

conflict
The simultaneous arousal of two or more incompatible motives.

task conflict
Conflict that focuses on substantive, issue-related differences related to the work itself.

relationship conflict
Conflict that focuses on personalized, individually oriented issues.

quickly breaks down as conflict intensifies.[45] The underlying explanation is that most people take differences of opinion personally, whether the issue is strictly the task, or their personal characteristics.

Consequences of Conflict

Conflict results in both positive and negative consequences. The right amount of conflict may enhance job performance, but too much or too little conflict lowers performance. If the manager observes that job performance is suffering because of too much conflict, he or she should reduce it. If performance is low because employees are too placid, the manager might profitably increase conflict. For example, the manager might establish a prize for top performance in the group.

Positive Consequences of Conflict

Many managers and scholars believe job conflict can have positive consequences. The right amount of conflict is usually quite low—somewhat like fat in your diet. Because a touch of conflict is beneficial, teams need not fear conflict.[46] With the right amount of conflict in the workplace, one or more of the following outcomes can be anticipated.

1 *Increased creativity.* Talents and abilities surface in response to conflict. People become inventive when they are placed in intense competition with others.

2 *Increased effort.* Constructive amounts of conflict spur people to new heights of performance. People become so motivated to win the conflict they may surprise themselves and their superiors with their work output.

3 *Increased diagnostic information.* Conflict can provide valuable information about problem areas in the department or organization. When leaders learn of conflict, they may conduct investigations that will lead to the prevention of similar problems.

4 *Increased group cohesion.* When one group in a firm is in conflict with another, group members may become more cohesive. They perceive themselves to be facing a common enemy.

5 *Opportunity for learning and growth.* Most conflicts hold some opportunity for learning and growth. Managers and team leaders might ask themselves, "What lessons can be learned from this conflict? and "How can we use these lessons to prevent future conflicts?" By asking the right questions, managers can facilitate internal innovation and improve the workplace.[47] If several customers sue the company for having sold dangerous child furniture, managers might investigate defects in the manufacturing process.

Negative Consequences of Conflict

When the wrong amount or type of conflict exists, job performance may suffer. Some types of conflict have worse consequences than others. A particularly bad form of conflict is one that forces a person to choose between two undesirable alternatives. Negative consequences of conflict include the following:

1 *Poor physical and mental health.* Intense conflict is a source of stress. A person under prolonged and intense conflict may suffer stress-related disorders. Many acts of workplace violence stem from highly stressed employees or ex-employees who experienced conflict with supervisors or co-workers.

Many who return to the workplace to shoot former co-workers, and or the manager, were dismissed for poor performance.

2 *Wasted resources.* Employees and groups in conflict frequently waste time, money, and other resources while fighting their battles. One executive took a personal dislike to one of his managers and ignored his cost-saving recommendations.

3 *Sidetracked goals.* In extreme forms of conflict, those involved may neglect the pursuit of important goals. Instead, they focus on winning their conflicts. A goal displacement of this type took place within an information technology group. The rival factions spent so much time squabbling over which new hardware and software to purchase they neglected some of their tasks.

4 *Heightened self-interest.* Conflict within the group can result in extreme demonstrations of self-interest at the expense of the group and the larger organization. Here, individuals or groups place their personal interests over those of the rest of the firm or customers. One common result of this type of self-interest is hogging resources. A team member might attempt to convince the team leader to place him on an important customer troubleshooting assignment even though he knows his rival on the team is better qualified.

Methods of Conflict Resolution

Managers spend as much as 20 percent of their work time dealing with conflict. A leader who learns to manage conflict effectively can increase his or her productivity. In addition, being able to resolve conflict enhances one's stature as a leader. Employees expect their boss to be able to resolve conflicts. Here, we describe the five basic styles or methods of resolving conflict: forcing, accommodation, sharing, collaboration, and avoiding. An effective manager will choose the best approach for the situation.

Forcing

The forcing, or competitive style, is based on the desire to win one's own concerns at the expense of the other party, or to dominate. A person with a forcing style is likely to engage in win-lose ("I win, you lose") power struggles, resulting in poor teamwork. Steve Jobs, the late legendary leader of Apple Inc., relied on forcing to resolve conflict, such as questions about design direction. Because of his stature and power, subordinates were usually willing to accept the forcing style of Jobs.

Accommodation

The accommodative style favors appeasement, or satisfying the other's concerns without taking care of one's own. People with this orientation tend to be generous or self-sacrificing just to maintain a relationship. An irate customer might be accommodated with a full refund, "just to shut him (or her) up." The intent of such accommodation might also be to retain the customer's loyalty.

Sharing

The sharing style is midway between domination and appeasement. Sharers prefer moderate but incomplete satisfaction for both parties. The result is compromise.

The term *splitting the difference* reflects this orientation. The sharing style of conflict resolution is commonly used in such activities as purchasing a house or car. Within the work group, sharing might take the form of each team member receiving the same percentage salary increase rather than haggling over dividing the available pool of money for increases.

Collaboration

In contrast to the sharing style, collaboration reflects an interest in fully satisfying the desire of both parties. It is based on an underlying win-win philosophy, the belief that after conflict has been resolved both sides should gain something of value. For example, a small company president might offer the management team more stock options if they are willing to take a pay cut to help the firm through rough times. If the firm succeeds, both parties have scored a victory. All parties benefit from collaboration, or a win-win approach to resolving conflict. In addition, compliance with the solution occurs readily, and the relationship between those in conflict improves.

A conflict-resolution technique built into the collaboration style is *confrontation and problem solving*. Its purpose is to identify the real problem and then arrive at a solution that genuinely solves it. First the parties are brought together and the real problem is confronted.

Another collaborative approach involves asking what action can break an impasse. When a conflict reaches a point where progress has reached a standstill, one of the parties asks, "What would you like me to do?" The other side often reacts with astonishment and then the first party asks, "If I could do anything to make this situation okay in your eyes, what would that be?" Frequently, the desired action—such as, "Treat me with more respect"—can be implemented.

A frequent example of win-win conflict resolution is when a restaurant chain wants to move into a neighborhood. The local government does not want a structure that disrupts the ambience of the neighborhood, but would like to have the tax revenue and employment the restaurant provides. The win-win solution is to build a restaurant storefront that blends into the neighborhood, an approach favored by chains, such as Starbucks or McDonald's.

Avoiding

The avoider combines uncooperativeness and unassertiveness. He or she is indifferent to the concerns of either party. The person may actually be withdrawing from conflict or relying upon fate. Managers sometimes use the avoiding style to stay out of a conflict between team members. The members are left to resolve their own differences.

Experience and research suggest the more cooperative approaches to resolving conflict (sharing and collaboration) work more effectively than the competitive approaches (forcing and accommodation). A study conducted with 61 self-managing teams involved 489 employees from the production department of a leading electronics manufacturer, found that a cooperative (focus on mutual benefits or win-win) approach to conflict resolution led to confidence in skills for dealing with conflict. The heightened confidence in dealing with conflict, in turn, led to more effective performance as evaluated by managers.[48]

Resolving Conflicts Between Two Group Members

A high-level managerial skill is mediation; helping two or more group members resolve conflict between or among them. Much of the time a manager invests in conflict resolution is geared toward helping others resolve their conflicts. The most useful approach is to get the parties in conflict to engage in confrontation and problem solving. The manager sits down with the two sides and encourages them to talk to each other about the problem— not talk directly to him or her. This approach is preferable to inviting each side to speak with the manager alone, as this scenario encourages each side to attempt to convince the manager that he or she is right. An abbreviated example follows:

Manager: I've brought you two together to see if you can overcome the problems you have about sharing the workload during a period in which one of you is overloaded.

Melissa: I'm glad you did. Luke never wants to help me, even when I'm drowning in customer requests.

Luke: I would be glad to help Melissa, if she ever agreed to help me. If she has any downtime, she runs to the break room so she can chat on her smartphone.

Melissa: Look who's talking. I have seen you napping in your SUV when you have a little down time.

Manager: I'm beginning to see what's going on here. Both of you are antagonistic toward each other, and look for little faults to pick at. With a little more respect on both sides, I think you would be more willing to help each other out.

Luke: Actually, Melissa's not too bad. And I know she can perform well when she wants to. Next time I see her needing help, I'll pitch in.

Melissa: I know that the name "Luke" can sound like a tough guy, but our Luke really has a warm heart. I'm open to starting with a fresh slate. Maybe Luke can ask me politely the next time he needs help.

Conflict specialist Patrick S. Nugent believes that being able to intervene in the conflicts of group members is a management skill that grows in importance. Such competencies are useful in an emerging form of management based less on traditional hierarchy and more on developing self-managing subordinates and teams.[49]

SUMMARY OF KEY POINTS

1 **Identify various types of teams and groups, including self-managed work teams and project groups.**

Formal groups are deliberately formed by the organization, whereas informal groups emerge over time through worker interaction. Representative types of work teams include self-managed work teams and high-performance work teams, project teams, task forces, cross-functional teams, top-management teams, and virtual teams.

2 **Describe the characteristics of effective groups and teams.**

Effective work group characteristics are well documented. Member jobs are enriched, and workers feel empowered to solve problems including sharing leadership. Group members operate interdependently in terms of tasks and rewards. Culturally diverse members enjoy task and social interaction. The right size of the group, as well as the intelligence and personality of group members, pro-social motivation, and emotional intelligence of the group as a whole contribute to effectiveness. The work group requires support from management. Effective group processes include team spirit, workload sharing, and communication and cooperation. Following work processes and procedures also aids effectiveness, as does familiarity with jobs and co-workers, and an appropriate degree of collaboration.

3 **Summarize managerial actions for building teamwork.**

Managers and leaders can enhance teamwork through many behaviors, attitudes, and organizational actions, including the following: begin with a mission statement and an agreement on the meaning of success; help the group focus on its strengths; compete against a common adversary; make teamwork the norm; use a consensus decision-making style, and provide information; minimize micromanagement; reward the team and individuals; encourage some face-to-face communication; show respect for team members; participate in offsite teamwork training; and rise to the challenge of building teamwork for virtual teams. Too much teamwork can lead to the problem of not having sufficient time for individual work.

4 **Pinpoint the actions and attitudes of an effective team player.**

Task-related actions and attitudes of effective team players include: sharing technical expertise; assuming responsibility for problems; committing to team goals; seeing the big picture; asking tough questions; and trying something new. People-related actions and attitudes include trusting team members; sharing credit; recognizing others; listening and information sharing; giving and receiving criticism; and not downplaying the success of others.

5 **Point to the potential contributions and problems of teams and groups.**

Teams and groups make a contribution when they lead to results that could not be achieved without collaboration. Evidence indicates that collective effort leads to enhanced productivity. Lift outs of competitive teams suggest that teams are productive. Groups and teams also have potential problems. Group polarization (taking extreme positions) may occur, and members may engage in social loafing (freeloading). Groups too often escape blame for their mistakes, with individuals being blamed instead. Unwanted group members are frequently ostracized. Also, focusing too much on group or team efforts instead of attaining individual recognition can retard a person's career.

6 **Describe the positive and negative aspects of conflict and how team leaders and managers can resolve conflict.**

Although harmony and collaboration are important goals of groups and teams, some conflict is inevitable. Task or cognitive conflict focuses on substantive, issue-related differences. Relationship or affective conflict focuses on personalized, individually oriented issues that are dealt with more emotionally than intellectually. Task conflict in small doses leads to such positive outcomes as creative problem solving. Positive consequences of conflict also include increased effort, obtaining diagnostic information, increased group cohesion, and opportunity for learning and growth. Negative consequences of conflict include wasting resources and heightened self-interest.

Five major modes of conflict management have been identified: forcing, accommodation, sharing, collaboration, and avoiding. Each style is based on a combination of satisfying individual concerns (assertiveness) and the concerns of others (cooperativeness). Confrontation and problem solving is a widely applicable collaborative technique of resolving conflict. Managers often need to resolve conflict between and among group members, with confrontation and problem solving being useful.

Key Terms and Phrases

Questions

1. In what way is participating on a sports team, musical band, or orchestra good preparation for being a member of a work group on the job?

2. Why is experience working on a cross-functional team particularly valuable for a person who aspires to a career in management?

3. Identify two actions you would be willing to take to impress upon your manager that you are a good team player.

4. Why do you think a project manager has to be effective at working under pressure?

5. Give an example of a manager leading by example for a team.

6. Provide two examples of interdependent (or collaborative) tasks in the workplace where teams are well suited.

7. Describe an example of conflict you have witnessed as a team member, at work, for a class project, or a sports team. How might this conflict have been resolved?

Skill-Building Exercise 13-A: Housing for the Homeless

Organize the class into teams of about six people. Each team takes on the assignment of formulating plans for building shelters for the homeless. The task will take about one hour and can be done inside or outside of class. The dwellings you plan to build, for example, might be two-room cottages with electricity and indoor plumbing. During the time allotted to the task, formulate plans for going ahead with Housing for the Homeless. Consider dividing up work by assigning certain tasks to each team member. Sketch out tentative answers to the following questions:

1. How will you obtain funding for your venture?

2. Which homeless people will you help?

3. Where will your shelters be located?

4. Who will do the actual construction?

After your plan is completed, evaluate the quality of the teamwork that took place within the group. Specify which teamwork skills were evident and which ones did not surface. Search the chapter for techniques you might use to improve teamwork. The skills used to accomplish the house-for-the-homeless task could relate to the team skills presented in Self-Assessment Quiz 13–1 or some team skill not mentioned in this chapter. Here is a sampling of the many different skills that might be relevant in this exercise:

☐ Speaks effectively

☐ Listens to others

☐ Innovates solutions to problems

☐ Thinks outside the box

☐ Displays a high level of cooperation and collaboration

☐ Provides knowledge of the task

☐ Sees the big picture

☐ Focuses on deadlines

Skill-Building Exercise 13-B: The Good Samaritans

The Good Samaritans ("people helper") exercise will have to be performed outside of a classroom setting, and could require transportation expenses of a few dollars, as well a few hours. Select a team of about four to look for one or more people needing help in a public setting, such as a mall parking lot, a park or a neighborhood. Examples of situations needing help could be removing snow from a driveway, loading packages into an automobile, controlling a child's temper tantrum, or getting a parallel-parked car out of a tight space. Introduce yourself to the person or persons you want to help. Explain that you are a team of problem solvers who work for free for the good of society (and, perhaps as a class assignment).

After you have worked on the problem, hold a debriefing session on how well you worked as a team. Answer such questions as the following: Did you assign tasks based on relevant skills within the group? How cooperatively did you work with each other? Did working as a team save any time, or make the task easier?

Management Now—Online Skill-Building Exercise: Productivity of Teams and Groups

The U.S. Department of Labor regularly publishes information about the productivity of workers. Yet there is much less information published about the productivity of teams and work groups. Conduct an Internet search to find two sources of information on team or workgroup productivity that have been published within the last 12 months. See if you can find information other than that provided by consulting and training firms that specialize in team building. Compare your findings with those of a few classmates. If you cannot find any evidence about group productivity in general, at least find a case history of any successful work group posted within the last year.

Kevin Cultivates His Co-workers

Kevin was happy to find a position as a scanning technician at a business-process-outsourcing company, Employee Resource, Inc. A major part of the Employee Resource's business was converting paperwork related to human resource management into digital form. Clients would mail their forms, such as medical claims, to Employees Resiources. Scanning technicians would then insert the claim forms into large scanning machines to make the conversion to digital. Clients would then have digital instead of paper documents for health claims and other human resource records.

The scanning technicians had to interact with other employees in several ways. Many of the claims received contained illegible identifying information, so they had to be sent to a security department that attempted to obtain the proper identification for the forms. The scanning technicians were expected to help level the workload among the technicians. For example, if one of the technicians was overwhelmed, and another was caught up, the latter was supposed to help out the former. Also, the company frequently held small celebrations in the office. A typical celebration would be to hold a brunch in honor of a new employee joining the company.

Kevin believed that if he performed well in the scanning technician, he would be eligible for promotion to the information technology department. Eventually being promoted to a supervisory position was also within the realm of possibility. Kevin also recognized that having good skills and speed in scanning documents were not sufficient to be promoted to a supervisory position. His size-up of the situation was that being a good team player would be required to be considered for promotion. Kevin then set out to develop the reputation of being a good team player.

The next Monday morning, Kevin arrived at the office with a box of donuts that he placed in the break room, with a note attached that said, "Enjoy your coffee or tea this morning with a treat from your co-worker Kevin." Several of the other scanning technicians thanked Kevin; however, one technician said to him, "Why did you bring us donuts? You're not our supervisor."

A week later, Kevin implemented another tactic designed to boost his reputation as a team player. He sent an e-mail to the other technicians informing them that they were free to send him an e-mail or text message anytime they were overloaded with documents to scan. Kevin said that he would help the overloaded co-worker so long as he was caught up on her own work.

A week later Kevin reflected, "I think I am developing a reputation as a good team player, but I can't give up yet. I think I know a way to really cement being regarded as a strong team player." Kevin then wrote an e-mail to the other scanning technicians, as well as his supervisor. The e-mail read in part:

"We all know that it takes a village to raise a child. But did you also know that it takes a group of friendly and cooperative co-workers to get a scanning technician up to speed? I want to thank you all for your cooperation and friendliness. You have been very helpful to me."

Case Questions

1 How effective do you think Kevin's initiatives are in helping him develop a reputation as a strong team player?

2 If you were Kevin's supervisor, how would you react to the e-mails he sent to the group?

3 What advice might you offer Kevin to help him advance his reputation as a team player?

The Big Battle Over Conference Room Space

Brenna is the vice president of administrative services and human resources at Mercury Voyages, a national travel agency serving corporations and large government agencies. Although the Internet has replaced most travel agencies, Mercury has found a niche in organizing travel for business meetings and controlling travel costs. Brenna is facing a bothersome problem related to internal conferences.

"Like so many of our clients," said Brenna, "we have a small amount of office space for our number of employees, particularly with respect to the availability of conference rooms. Our people love to meet in person and thrash out problems and plan our next moves. We conduct some virtual meetings, but there is still a high demand for in-person meetings."

Asked what specific problems the shortage of conference room space created, Brenna answered, "You wouldn't believe it. You should see those angry faces. One group is in the conference room running a little late, and the next group is knocking on the door or trying to barge into the meeting and take over the space. Some of our people conduct their meetings at a Starbucks, McDonald's or Dunkin' Donuts. We have found small groups of people conducting brief meetings in the building lobby, or even under a stairwell."

"When one group can't find a place to meet, we get all sorts of angry e-mails and intranet posts directed at me and other department heads. We spend far too much time fighting about conference room space. We are wasting a lot of time that should be spent serving customers."

Asked what Mercury Voyages has done so far to deal with the meeting room shortage, Brenna said, "We are using online calendars to allocate space, but the results can be ugly. Some groups get scheduled for a Monday 7:30 meeting which doesn't go over very well. Neither does a meeting set for 4:45 on a Friday. Then you've got the problem of deception and trickery. A few groups book space, just in case they might have a meeting. It's like booking a second airplane flight just in case there will not be space available with one carrier.

"I asked the CEO if he would consider keeping a trailer in the parking lot for meetings, but he said it would look too crude for a travel agency. Whatever we decide to do, my job is to reduce some of this time-wasting and stressful conflict."

Case Questions

1 How can conflict about conference rooms exist in this age of high technology?

2 Which method of conflict resolution should Brenna recommend to resolve the conflicts mentioned in this case?

3 So, what's wrong with company employees meeting at a nearby coffee shop or restaurant?

ENDNOTES

1. Original story created from facts and observations in the following sources: "Company Profile: Dogfish Head Craft Brewed Ale," *www.dogfish.com*, © 1995–2020 Dogfish Head Craft Brewery Inc.; "Company Overview of Dogfish Head Craft Brewery Inc., *www.bloomerg.com*, March 1, 2016, p. 1; "Try 'Co-Petition' with Rival Firms," *Executive Leadership*, September 2014, pp. 1, 2; Sam Calagione, as told to Nitasha Tiku, "The Way I Work: Dogfish Head's Sam Calagione," *Inc* (www.inc.com), July 1, 2009, pp. 1–10; "Our Cross-Atlantic Collaboration with Rodenbach is Finally Here," *dogfish.com/blog*, January 10, 2020, pp. 1–2.

2. Jon R. Katzenbach and Douglas K. Smith, "The Discipline of Teams," *Harvard Business Review*, March–April 1993, p. 113.

3. Richard S. Wellings, William C. Byham, and Jeanne M. Wilson, *Empowered Teams: Creating Self-Directed Work Groups That Improve Quality, Productivity, and Participation* (San Francisco: Jossey-Bass, 1991), p. 3.

4. Frederick P. Morgeson, "The External Leadership of Self-Managing Teams: Intervening in the Context of Novel and Disruptive Events," *Journal of Applied Psychology*, May 2005, p. 497.

5. The definition and the study are from Sarv Devaraj and Kaifeng Jiang, "It's About Time – A Longitudinal Adaption Model of High-Performance Work Teams," *Journal of Applied Psychology*, March 2019, pp. 443–447.

6. Robert Buttrick, "Project Management," in Perseus Publishing's *Business: The Ultimate Resource* (Cambridge, MA: Perseus, 2002), p. 165.

7. Jon R. Katzenbach, "The Myth of the Top Management Team," *Harvard Business Review*, November–December 1997, pp. 82–99.

8. Jeanne Brett, Kristin Behfar, and Mary C. Kern, "Managing Multi-cultural Teams," *Harvard Business Review*, November 2006, pp. 87–88.

9. Erica Dhawan and Tomas Chamorro-Premuzic, "How to Collaborate Effectively If Your Team Is Remote," *Harvard Business Review* (https://hbr.org), February 27, 2018, pp. 1–7.

10. Timothy D. Golden and John F. Veiga, "The Impact of Superior-Subordinate Relationships on the Commitment, Job Satisfaction, and Performance of Virtual Workers," *Leadership Quarterly*, February 2008, pp. 77–88.

11. "Ramp Up for Virtual Teams," *Manager's Edge*, August 2009; Jerry Fjermestad, Chief Learning Officer, *www.clomedia.com*.

12. Cited in, "Leaders Notes for Virtual Teams," *IEDP*, (www.iedp.com), September 11, 2011, p. 1.

13. Carla Johnson, "Managing Virtual Teams," *HR Magazine*, June 2002, p. 70; Cristina B. Gibson, and Susan G. Cohen (eds.), *Virtual Teams That Work: Creating Conditions for Virtual Team Effectiveness* (San Francisco: Jossey-Bass, 2003).

14. Jessica R. Messner-Magnus and Leslie A. DeChurch, "Information Sharing and Team Performance: A Meta-Analysis," *Journal of Applied Psychology*, March 2009, pp. 535–546.

15. Priscilla M. Ellsass and Laura M. Graves, "Demographic Diversity in Decision-Making Groups: The Experience of Women and People of Color," *Academy of Management Review*, October 1997, p. 968.

16. Quoted in Heather Sommerville and Mark Mauer, "Uber Slashes Hundreds of Technical Jobs," *The Wall Street Journal*, September 11, 2019, p. B3.

17. Murray R. Barrick et al., "Relating Member Ability and Personality to Work-Team Processes and Team Effectiveness," *Journal of Applied Psychology*, June 1998, pp. 377–391; Leslie DeChurch and Jessica R. Mesmer-Magnus, "The Cognitive Underpinnings of Effective Teamwork: A Meta-Analysis," *Journal of Applied Psychology*, January 2010, pp. 32–53.

18. Michael Mankins, Alan Bird, and James Root, "Making Star Teams Out of Star Players," *Harvard Business Review*, January–February 2013, pp. 74–78.

19. Jia Hu and Robert C. Liden, "Making a Difference in the Teamwork: Linking Team Prosocial Motivation to Team Processes and Effectiveness," *Academy of Management Journal*, August 2015, pp. 1102–1127.

20. Vanessa Urch Druskat and Steven B. Wolff, "Building the Emotional Intelligence of Groups," *Harvard Business Review*, March 2001, pp. 80–90.

21. Claus W. Langred, "Too Much of a Good Thing? Negative Effects of High Trust and Individual Autonomy in Self-Managing Work Teams," *Academy of Management Journal*, June 2004, pp. 385–399.

22. Alexander D. Stajkovic, Dongseop Lee, and Anthony J. Nyberg, "Collective Efficacy, Group Potency, and Group Performance: Meta-Analyses of Their Relationships, and Test of a Mediation Model," *Journal of Applied Psychology*, May 2009, pp. 814–828. The definition of collective efficacy is based on Albert Bandura, *Self-Efficacy: The Exercise of Control* (Englewood Cliffs, N.J.: Prentice Hall, 1997).

23. Frederick P. Morgeson, "The External Leadership of Self-Managing Teams: Intervening in the Context of Novel and Disruptive Events," *Journal of Applied Psychology*, May 2005, pp. 497–508.

24. Quoted in Scott Keller and Mary Meaney, "High-Performing Teams: A Timeless Leadership Topic," *McKinsey & Company*, (www.mckinsey.com), June 2017, p. 1.

25. Some of the key research support for this section stems from Katzenbach and Smith, "The Discipline of Teams," p. 112; "Build Teamwork by Showing Employees You Respect Them," *Manager's Edge*, April 2002, p. 1; DeChurch and Mesmer-Magnus, "The Cognitive Underpinnings of Effective Teamwork: A Meta-Analysis," pp. 32–53.

26. "Ask Positive Questions," *Manager's Edge*, March 2010, p. 1.

27. Brian Patrick Eha, "Build a Culture of Teamwork," *Entrepreneur*, March 2016, p. 52.

28. Jared Sandberg, "Bosses Who Fiddle With Employees' Work Risk Ire, Low Morale," *The Wall Street Journal*, April 25, 2006, p. B1.

29. Matthew J. Pearsall, Michael S. Christian, and Aleksander P. J. Ellis, "Motivating Independent Teams: Individual Rewards, Shared Rewards, or Something in Between?" *Journal of Applied Psychology*, January 2010, pp. 184–185.

30. Joshua R. Wu, Anne S. Tsui, and Angelo J. Kinicki, "Consequences of Differentiated Leadership in Groups," *Academy of Management Journal*, February 2010, pp. 90–106.

31. Robert Levine, "The New Right Stuff," *Fortune*, June 12, 2006, pp. 116–118.

32. "Team Building in the Cafeteria," *Harvard Business Review*, December 2015, p. 24.

33. Katie Morell, "What's Your Most Awkward Team-Building Experience?" *Bloomberg Businessweek*, April 10–April 23, 2017, p. 78.

34. Comment made in review of Silvester Ivanaj and Claire Bozon, *Managing Virtual Teams* (Cheltenham, England: Edward Elgar Publishing, 2016). Review appears in *Personnel Psychology*, Number 3, 2018, pp. 486–488.

35. Lynda Gratton, "Working Together...When Apart," *The Wall Street Journal*, June 16–17, 2007, p. R4.

36. Rob Cross, Reb Rebele, and Adam Grant, "Collaborative Overload," *Harvard Business Review*, January–February 2016, pp. 74–79; Rob Cross, Scott Taylor, and Deb Zehner, "Collaboration without Burnout," *Harvard Business Review*, July–August 2018, pp. 134–137; "Too Much Togetherness? The Downside of Workplace Collaboration," *Knowledge@Wharton*, (www.knowlege.wharton.upenn.edu) November 9, 2019, pp. 1–7.

37. Steven Covey, "Team Up for a Superstar Office," *USA Weekend*, September 4–6, 1998, p. 10.

38. Boris Groysberg and Robin Abrahams, "Lift Outs: How to Acquire a High-Functioning Team," *Harvard Business Review*, December 2006, pp. 133–140; Bridget Miller, "Why You Should Consider Hiring Teams," *HR Daily Advisor* (www.hrdailyadvisor.blr.com), January 5, 2018, pp. 1–4.

39. Russ Forrester and Allan B. Drexler, "A Model for Team-Based Performance," *Academy of Management Executive*, August 1999, p. 47.

40. Gregory Moorhead and Ricky W. Griffin, *Organizational Behavior: Managing People and Organizations*, 4th ed. (Boston: Houghton Mifflin, 1995), pp. 52–62.

41. Charles E. Naquin and Renee O. Tynan, "The Team Halo Effect: Why Teams Are Not Blamed for Their Failures," *Journal of Applied Psychology*, April 2003, pp. 332–340.

42. D. Lance Ferris et al., "The Development and Validation of the Workplace Ostracism Scale," *Journal of Applied Psychology*, November 2008, pp. 1348–1366.

43. Jiato Li and Donald C. Hambrick, "Factional Groups: A New Vantage on Demographic Faultlines, Conflict, and Disintegration in Work Teams," *Academy of Management Journal*, October 2005, p. 794.

44. Carsten K. W. De Dreu and Laurie R. Weingart, "Task Versus Relationship Conflict, Team Performance, and Team Member Satisfaction: A Meta-Analysis," *Journal of Applied Psychology*, August 2003, pp. 741–749.

45. De Dreu and Weingart, "Task Versus Relationship Conflict," *Journal of Applied Psychology*, Aug 2003, p. 746.

46. Patrick M. Lencioni, *The Five Dysfunctions of a Team* (San Francisco: Jossey-Bass, 2002).

47. Zak Mustpha, "Managing Conflict in the Workplace," *Business.com*, February 22, 2017, p. 2.

48. Steve Alper, Dean Tjosvold, and Kenneth S. Law, "Conflict Management, Efficacy, and Performance in Organizational Teams," *Personnel Psychology*, Autumn 2000, pp. 625–642.

49. Patrick S. Nugent, "Managing Conflict: Third-Party Interventions for Managers," *Academy of Management Executive*, February 2002, p. 152.

Part Five

Controlling

CHAPTER 14

Essentials of Controlling

OBJECTIVES

After studying this chapter and doing the exercises, you should be able to:

1 Explain how controlling relates to the other management functions.

2 Understand the different types and strategies of control.

3 Describe the steps in the control process.

4 Explain the use of nonbudgetary control techniques.

5 Have an awareness of the various types of budgets, and the use of budgets and financial ratios for control.

6 Explain how managers and business owners manage cash flow and control costs, and use nontraditional measures of financial performance.

7 Describe a computer-based monitoring system.

8 Specify several characteristics of effective controls.

A few years ago, the giant food maker Kraft Heinz was struggling to generate sales growth in its well-known collection of brands, such as Oscar Mayer and Kraft Mac & Cheese. Several of the company's brands were seen as out of step with trends toward more natural and healthful food items. According to former employees, a major cost-cutting drive after the merger of Kraft and Heinz had diminished the company's ability to promote new or improved products. In 2019, Kraft Heinz had marked down the value of its brands by close to $17 billion after reporting slowing sales and a federal investigation into inaccuracies in stating the cost of goods sold. Among the major brands with declining sales were Miracle Whip, Oscar Mayer, Jell-O, and Velveeta.

To help deal with declining revenues, and find productive ways of trimming costs, in 2019 Kraft Heinz promoted Nina Barton to the newly appointed position of chief growth officer. Just before the promotion, she was the President of both Kraft Heinz Canada and Digital Online Growth. As the chief growth officer, Barton is responsible for accelerating organic growth that includes leading all aspects of the company's global e-commerce and digital businesses. She also oversees innovation, channel growth, marketing services, and research and development (R&D).

At the same time Kraft Heinz appointed Barton as the chief growth officer, the new CEO Miguel Patricio announced that he planned to halve the number of new product introductions. "My role is to simplify this business. Fewer, bigger bets." Patricio said that some low-selling or unprofitable products would be discontinued whereas other more profitable products would receive more funding for development and marketing. Barton and Patricio said they are willing to sacrifice some profit to improve the sales of promising brands. For example, Barton praised new snack packs that combine Philadelphia cream cheese with bagel chips. "It's a very different mindset," she said.

Barton holds a bachelor's degree in commerce from McGill University and an MBA from the Wharton School at the University of Pennsylvania.[1]

The story about a major food company looking to grow in certain areas and reduce other costs at the same time illustrates how carefully organizations monitor performance. The control function of management involves measuring performance and then taking corrective action if goals are not being achieved.

Controls make many positive contributions to the organization. Controlling aligns the actions of workers with the interests of the firm. Without the controlling functions, managers cannot know whether people are carrying out their jobs properly. Controls enable managers to gauge whether the firm is attaining its goals. Controls often make an important contribution to employee motivation. Achieving the performance standards set in a control system leads to recognition and other deserved rewards. Accurate control measurements give the well-motivated, competent worker an opportunity to be noticed for good work.

In this chapter we emphasize the types and strategies of controls, the control process, budgets and controls, how managers manage cash flow and cut costs, and the use of computer-aided monitoring in control. Finally, we describe characteristics of effective controls.

LEARNING OBJECTIVE 1

Explain how controlling relates to the other management functions.

CONTROLLING AND THE OTHER MANAGEMENT FUNCTIONS

Controlling, takes place after the other functions have been completed. Controlling is most closely associated with planning, because planning establishes goals and the methods for achieving them. By using controls, managers know whether planning was successful.

The links between controlling and other major management functions are illustrated in Figure 14-1. Controlling helps measure how well planning, organizing, and leading have been performed. The controlling function also measures the effectiveness of the control system. On occasion, the control measures are inappropriate. For example, suppose one measure of sales performance is the sales volume. Such a

Figure 14-1 The Links Between Controlling and Other Major Management Functions

The control function is extremely important because it helps managers evaluate whether all four major management functions have been implemented.

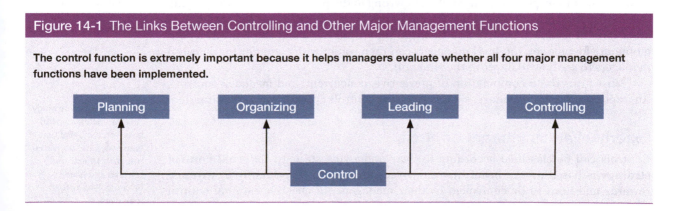

measure might encourage a sales representative to push easier to sell products instead of helping the company establish a few new products. Spending more time developing a market for the new products would probably boost the sales representative's effectiveness. More will be said about effective control measures later.

The planning and decision-making tools and techniques described in Chapter 6 can be used as tools and techniques of control as well. For example, a Gantt chart keeps track of how well target dates for a project are being met. Keeping track is a control activity. If an event falls behind schedule, a project manager usually takes corrective action.

TYPES AND STRATEGIES OF CONTROL

LEARNING OBJECTIVE **2**

Understand the different types and strategies of control.

Controls can be classified according to the time at which the control is applied to the activity—before, during, or after. Another way of describing controls relates to the source of the control—external versus internal.

The Time Element in Controls

A **preventive control** takes place prior to the performance of an activity and prevents problems that result from deviation from performance standards. Preventive controls are generally the most cost-effective. A manufacturer that specifies quality standards for purchased parts establishes a preventive control. By purchasing high-quality parts, the manufacturer prevents many instances of machine failure. Preventive controls are also used in human resource management. Standards for hiring employees are preventive controls. For example, a company may require that all job candidates are nonsmokers. This preventive control helps decrease lost productivity due to smoking breaks outside the building and smoking-related illnesses. The company might also save some money on health insurance premiums because smokers are likely to have a high number of health claims, leading to high premiums based on claims experience.

preventive control
A control that takes place prior to the performance of an activity.

Concurrent controls monitor activities while they are carried out. A typical concurrent control takes place when a supervisor observes performance, spots a deviation from standard, and immediately makes a constructive suggestion. For example, suppose a telemarketing manager overhears a telemarketing specialist fail to ask a customer for an order. On the spot, the manager would coach the telemarketer about how to close an order.

concurrent control
A type of control that monitors activities while they are carried out.

Feedback controls evaluate an activity after it is performed. Feedback controls measure history by pointing out what went wrong in the past. The process of applying the control may provide guidelines for future corrective action. Financial statements are a form of feedback control. If a financial report indicates one company in a conglomerate lost money, top-level managers can then confer with company (or division) managers to see how to improve the situation.

feedback control
A control that evaluates an activity after it is performed.

Most firms use a combination of preventive, concurrent, and feedback controls. An important part of a manager's job is choosing controls appropriate to the situation.

External Versus Internal Controls

Controls can be classified according to their underlying strategy. **External control strategy** is based on the belief that employees are motivated primarily by external rewards and need to be controlled by their managers. An effective external control

external control strategy
An approach to control based on the belief that employees are motivated primarily by external rewards and need to be controlled by their managers.

system involves three steps. First, the objectives and performance standards need to be relatively difficult in order to gain optimum effort of team members and leave little leeway in performance. Second, the objectives and measures must be set in such a way that they cannot be manipulated or distorted. For instance, top-level management should conduct its own investigation of customer satisfaction rather than take the word of field personnel. Third, rewards must be directly and openly tied to performance.

An external control strategy produces several different effects. On the positive side, employees may channel considerable energy into achieving objectives. Employees do so because they know that good performance leads to a reward. A tightly structured control system translates into a high degree of control over employee behavior.

External control can create problems, however. Employees may work toward achieving performance standards, but they may not develop a commitment to the firm. They may reach standards but not be truly productive. Reaching standards without being productive is sometimes referred to as "looking good on paper," or "looking good digitally." Suppose the marketing and sales director of a telecommunications company establishes a performance standard for a high number of customers processed. To achieve this standard, the customer service manager might instruct the customer service representatives, "Take care of as many calls as you can. And minimize the time customers are kept on hold." As a result, the customer service reps spend brief amounts of time on the phone attempting to resolve problems with most customers. Instead of customers being happy with customer service, many of them are dissatisfied with the abrupt treatment. The standard of taking care of more customers is met, yet at the same time customer service deteriorates.

internal control strategy
An approach to control based on the belief that employees can be motivated by building their commitment to organizational goals.

Internal control strategy is based on the belief that employees can be motivated by building their commitment to organizational goals. Empowerment of individuals and teams depends on an internal control strategy. Management may impose the controls, but the employees are committed to them. Hyundai Corp. provides an instructive example of employees being committed to controls, especially in the form of high quality and cleanliness. Adhering to high quality is part of the Hyundai culture, so the majority of Hyundai manufacturing workers enjoy meeting the quality standards imposed by management.

Building an effective internal control system requires three steps. First, group members must participate in setting goals. These goals are later used as performance standards for control purposes. Second, the performance standards (control measures) must be used for problem solving rather than for punishment or blame. When deviations from performance are noted, superiors and subordinates work together to solve the underlying problem. Third, although rewards should be tied to performance, they should not be tied to only one or two measures. An internal control strategy calls for evaluation of an employee's total contribution, not one or two quantitative aspects of performance.

An internal control system is not necessarily good, and an external control system is not necessarily bad. Internal controls work satisfactorily for a high-caliber, well-motivated workforce. External controls compensate for the fact that not everybody is capable of controlling their own performance (or self-leadership), or is committed to organizational goals. If applied with good judgment and sensitivity, external control systems work quite well. The effective use of controls thus follows a contingency, or "if..., then..," approach to management.

STEPS IN THE CONTROL PROCESS

LEARNING OBJECTIVE **3**

Describe the steps in
the control process.

The steps in the control process follow the logic of planning: (1) performance standards are set, (2) performance is measured, (3) performance is compared to standards, and (4) corrective action is taken if needed. The following discussion describes these steps and highlights the potential problems associated with each one. Figure 14-2 presents an overview of controlling.

Setting Appropriate Performance Standards

A control system begins with a set of performance standards that are realistic and acceptable to the people involved. A **standard** is a unit of measurement that is used to evaluate results. Standards can be quantitative, such as cost of sales, profits, or time to complete an activity. Standards can also be qualitative, such as the visual appeal of an advertisement. Laws are often the basis for standards because performance must comply with laws and regulations such as those relating to disposal of toxins, fair employment practices, and safety. An effective standard shares the same characteristics as an effective objective (see Chapter 4). Figure 14-3 presents two of the performance standards established for a customer service representative unit within a telecommunications company.

standard
A unit of measurement
that is used to evaluate
results.

Historical information about comparable situations often provides the basis for setting initial standards. Assume a manufacturer wants to establish a standard for the percentage of machines returned to the dealer for repair. If the return rate for other machines with similar components is three percent, the new standard might be a return rate of no more than three percent.

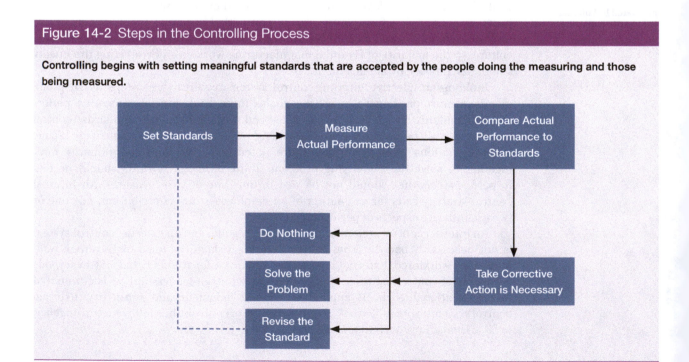

Figure 14-2 Steps in the Controlling Process

Controlling begins with setting meaningful standards that are accepted by the people doing the measuring and those being measured.

Figure 14-3 Two Performance Standards Established for a Customer Service Operation

The performance standards shown here give customer-service representatives precise targets for meeting organizational objectives. Performance evaluation is based on how well customer-service representatives, individually and as a group, meet these standards.

CSR Objectives	Distinguished Performance (4 points)	Above-Standard Performance (3 points)	Standard Performance (2 points)	Below-Standard Performance (1 point)
Customer Satisfaction	89% or higher overall customer satisfaction	86%–88% overall customer satisaction	83%–85% overall customer satisfaction	<83% overall customer satisfaction
Calls Answered in 30 Seconds	Group consistently answers 80% or more of calls within 30 seconds	Group consistently answers 75%–79% of calls within 30 seconds	Group consistently answers 70%–74% of calls within 30 seconds	Group consistently answers <70% of calls within 30 seconds

At times, profit-and-loss considerations dictate performance standards. A case in point is the occupancy-rate standard for a hotel. Assume break-even analysis reveals the average occupancy rate must be 75 percent for the hotel to cover costs. Hotel management must then set an occupancy rate of at least 75 percent as a standard.

Measuring Actual Performance

To implement the control system, performance must be measured. Evaluations are one of the major ways of measuring performance. Supervisors often make direct observations of performance to implement a control system. A simple example would be observing to make sure a sales associate always asks a customer, "What else could I show you now?" A more elaborate performance measure would be a 10-page report on the status of a major project submitted to top-level management. The aspects of performance that accountants measure include manufacturing costs, profits, and cash flow (available cash on hand). Measurement of performance is much more complex than it would seem on the surface. The list that follows presents three important conditions for effective performance measurement[2]:

1 *Agree on the specific aspects of performance to be measured.* Top-level managers in a hotel chain might think occupancy rate is the best measure of performance. Middle-level managers might disagree by saying, "Don't place so much emphasis on occupancy rate. If we try to give good customer service, the occupancy rate will take care of itself. Therefore, let's try to measure customer service."

2 *Agree on the accuracy of measurement needed.* In some instances, precise measurement of performance is possible. Sales volume, for example, can be measured in terms of customer billing and accounts paid. The absolute number or percentage of customer returns is another precise measurement. In other instances, precise measurement of performance may not be possible. Assume top-level managers of the hotel chain buy the idea of measuring customer service. Quantitative measures of customer satisfaction—including the ratings

guests submit on questionnaires and the number of formal complaints—are available. However, many measurements would have to be subjective, such as observing the behavior of guests, including their spontaneous comments about service. These qualitative measures of performance might be more relevant than the quantitative measures.

3   *Agree on who will use the measurements.* In most firms, managers at higher levels have the authority to review performance measures of people below them in the hierarchy. Few people at lower levels object to this practice. In a team-based organization, peers might be allowed to see each other's performance measurements. Another issue centers on the level of staff access to control reports. Line managers sometimes believe too many staff members make judgments about their performance.

Comparing Actual Performance to Standards

After establishing standards and taking performance measurements, the next step is to actually compare performance to standards. Key aspects of comparing performance to standards include measuring the deviation and communicating information about it.

Deviation in a control system indicates the size of the discrepancy between performance standards and actual results. It is important to agree beforehand how much deviation from the standard is a basis for corrective action. When using quantitative measures, statistical analysis can determine how much of a deviation is significant. Recall the 75 percent occupancy rate standard in the hotel example. A deviation of plus or minus three percent may not be considered meaningful but rather caused by random events. Deviations of four percent or more, however, would be considered significant. Taking corrective action only in the case of significant deviations applies the exception principle.

Sometimes a deviation as small as one percent from the standard can have a big influence on company prosperity. If a business unit fails by one percent to reach $100 million in sales, the firm has $1 million less money than anticipated. At other times, deviations as high as 10 percent might not be significant. A claims department might be 10 percent behind schedule in processing insurance claims because of an unanticipated event, such as a hurricane. However, the claims manager might not be upset, knowing that all the claims will eventually be processed.

When statistical limits are not available, it takes wisdom and experience to diagnose a random deviation. Sometimes factors beyond a person's influence lead to a one-time deviation from performance. In such a case, the manager might ignore the deviation. For example, a person might turn in poor performance one month because he or she faced a family crisis.

For the control system to work, the results of the comparison between actual performance and standards must be communicated to the right people, including the employees themselves and their immediate managers. At times, the results should also be communicated to top-level managers and selected staff specialists. They need to know about events, such as exceptional deviations from safety and health standards. For example, nuclear power plants are equipped with elaborate devices to measure radiation levels. When a specified radiation level is reached or exceeded, several key people are notified automatically.

deviation
In a control system, indicates the size of the discrepancy between performance standards and actual results.

Taking Corrective Action

An evaluation of the discrepancy between actual performance and a standard presents a manager with three courses of action: do nothing, solve the problem, or revise the standard. Each of these alternatives may be appropriate, depending on the results of the evaluation.

Do Nothing

The purpose of the control system is to determine whether the plans are working. No corrective action is required if the evaluation reveals events are proceeding according to plan. Doing nothing, however, does not mean abdicating, or giving up responsibility. A manager might take the opportunity to compliment employees for having achieved their objectives (thus increasing employee motivation), but do nothing about their approach to reaching objectives because performance measurements show it to be effective.

Solve the Problem

The big payoff from the controlling process concerns the correction of deviations from substandard performance. If a manager decides a deviation is significant (non-random), he or she starts problem solving. Typically, the manager meets with the team member to discuss the nature of the problem. Other knowledgeable parties might participate in the problem-solving process. At times, a significant deviation from a performance standard demands a drastic solution. A severe shortfall in cash, for example, might force a retailer to sell existing inventory at a loss.

Sometimes a manager can correct the deviation from a performance standard without overhauling current operations. An office manager in a group dental practice used a control model to measure the percentage of professional time allotted to patient care. The analysis revealed that non-billed time exceeded 10 percent—an unacceptable deviation. The corrective action involved two steps. First, workers scanned dental records to find patients overdue for cleaning and checkups. Second, the office manager sent emails or phoned these people and asked whether they would like to schedule an appointment for cleaning and a checkup. The successful e-mail and telemarketing campaign filled virtually all the slack time within 10 days.

Revise the Standard

Deviations from standard are sometimes attributable to errors in planning rather than to performance problems. Corrective action is thus not warranted because the true problem is an unrealistic performance standard. Consider an analogy to the classroom: If 90 percent of the students fail a test, the real problem could be an unrealistically difficult test.

Standards often must be revised because of changes in the external environment. As more and more companies shifted to e-commerce, standards of hotel occupancy rates had to be lowered. The reason is that business travel decreased as more business was conducted over the Internet rather than in person. The use of videoconferences to substitute for in-person meetings also bit into hotel occupancy. Planning for a new task can also create a need for revised standards. Performance quotas may be based on "guesstimates" that prove to be unrealistically difficult or overly easy to reach. A performance standard is too difficult if no employee can meet it. A performance standard may be too easy if all employees can exceed it. As we saw in Figure 14-2, revising standards means repeating the control cycle.

NONBUDGETARY CONTROL TECHNIQUES

LEARNING OBJECTIVE **4**

Explain the use of nonbudgetary control techniques.

One way of classifying control techniques is to divide them into those based on budgets versus those not based on budgets. In this section we describe nonbudgetary techniques, and classify them into two types. **Qualitative control techniques** are methods based on human judgments about performance that result in a verbal rather than a numerical evaluation. For example, customer service might be rated as "outstanding." Even using a 1-to-5 rating scale could be interpreted as a qualitative technique because the rating is based on an overall human judgment. **Quantitative control techniques** are methods based on numerical measures of performance, such as number orders processed per hour.

Figures 14-4 and 14-5 summarize qualitative and quantitative control techniques, respectively. The purpose in listing them is primarily to alert you to their existence. Chapter 6 provided details about four of the quantitative control techniques described in Figure 14-5. When interpreting the results of an audit, it is necessary to evaluate carefully the processes used to provide the information. A key factor to investigate is the political motivation of the people conducting the audit. Are the auditors going out of their way to please management? Are they out to make management look bad? Or are they motivated only to be objective and professional?

The auditing process has come under considerable scrutiny because of many reported cases of unethical and illegal reporting of financial information by business firms. The auditors are dependent on the client for their fees, and also the same firm that audits a company's books might be selling consulting services to them. Auditors, being human, suffer from an unconscious bias to see what they want to see and not

qualitative control technique
A method of controlling based on human judgments about performance that result in a verbal rather than a numerical evaluation.

quantitative control technique
A method of controlling based on numerical measures of performance.

Figure 14-4 Qualitative Control Techniques

The competence and ethics of people collecting information for qualitative controls influence the effectiveness of these controls.

Technique	Definition	Key Features
External audit	Verification of financial records by an external agency or individual	Conducted by an outside agency, such as a CPA firm
Internal audit	Verification of financial records by an internal group of personnel	Wide in scope, including evaluation of control system
Management audit	Use of auditing techniques to evaluate the overall effectiveness of management	Examines a wide range of management practices, policies, and procedures
Personal observation	Manager's firsthand observations of how well the plans are carried out	Natural part of a manager's job
Performance evaluation	Formal method or system of measuring, evaluating, and reviewing employee performance	Points out areas of deficiency and areas for corrective action; manager and group member jointly solve the problem

Figure 14-5 Quantitative Control Techniques Used in Production and Operations

Quantitative control techniques are widely accepted because they appear precise and objective.

Technique	Definition	Key Features
Gantt chart	Chart depicting planned and actual progress of work on a project	Describes progress on a project
PERT	Method of scheduling activities and events using time estimates	Measures how well the project is meeting the schedule
Break-even analysis	Ratio of fixed costs to price minus variable costs	Measures an organization's performance and gives basis for corrective action
Economic-order quantity (EOQ)	Inventory level that minimizes ordering and carrying costs	Avoids having too much or too little inventory
Variance analysis	Major control device in manufacturing	Establishes standard costs for materials, labor, and overhead, and then measures deviations from these costs

displease the clients they serve.[3] It is sometimes difficult to be objective because of our unconscious tendencies to survive by not biting the hand that feeds us. As they say, "Whose bread I eat, whose song I sing." The Sarbanes-Oxley Act of 2002 includes provisions for making auditors more independent, and puts the accounting industry under tightened federal oversight.

Have an awareness of the various types of budgets, and the use of budgets and financial ratios for control.

budget
A spending plan expressed in numerical terms for allocating resources.

BUDGETS AND BUDGETARY CONTROL TECHNIQUES

When people hear the word *budget*, they typically think of tight restrictions placed on the use of money. The car rental agency name Budget was chosen because of popular thinking that the adjective budget means conservative spending. In management, a budget does place restrictions on the use of money, but the allotted amounts can be quite generous. A **budget** is a plan, expressed in numerical terms for allocating resources. The numerical terms typically refer to money, but they could also refer to such things as the amount of energy or the number of laser cartridges used. A budget typically involves cash outflow and inflow.

Virtually every manager assumes some budget responsibility, because a budget outlines a plan for allocating resources. Without budgets, keeping track of how much money is spent in comparison to how much money is available would be nearly impossible. A company's performance against budget, or anticipated results, is also important because this is one way outside analysts and business reporters judge a CEO's performance. As described in the chapter introduction, the CEO of Kraft Heinz was taking initiatives to increase the probability that sales of major brands would meet expectations.

Here we look at different types of budgets and how to use budgets for control. Readers familiar with accounting and finance will find much of this information a review.

Types of Budgets

Budgets can be classified in many ways. For example, budgets are sometimes described as either fixed or flexible. A *fixed budget* expenditure is based on a one-time allocation of resources. The organizational unit receives a fixed sum of money that must last for the budget period. A *flexible budget* allows for variation in the use of resources on the basis of activity. Under a flexible budget, an e-commerce department would receive an increased information technology budget if the department increased the scope of its program. Any type of budget can be classified as fixed or flexible.

Many different types of budgets help control costs in profit and nonprofit firms. Figure 14-6 presents a tabular summary of eight commonly used budgets. Most other budgets are variations of these basic types. Figure 14-7 provides an example of one of the revenue-and-expense budgets.

Suggestions for Preparing a Budget

Although budgets give the appearance of being factual, objective documents, judgment and political tactics all enter into budget preparation. When preparing a budget, a manager can impress higher-ups if he or she tracks variables with care and makes sound assumptions. In contrast, if the manager allocates resources poorly or permits too much flab, he or she will lose credibility. Here are several recommendations for preparing a sensible budget[4]:

- *Leave wiggle room.* Optimistic projections with little basis in reality will come back to haunt you. Budget conservatively for income and liberally for expenses. Using this approach, you will be impressive if you constrain costs and generate more revenue than you anticipated.

Figure 14-6 Budgets Commonly Used in Organizations

Type of Budget and Definition	Notable Characteristics
Master budget — consolidates budgets of various units.	Purpose is to forecast financial statements for entire company.
Cash budget — forecast of cash receipts and payments.	Important control measure because it reflects a firm's ability to meet cash obligations and to invest in new opportunities.
Cash flow budget — prediction of a business firm's cash inflow and outflow over a specified time.	Primary purpose is to predict the firm's capacity to take in more cash than it dispenses.
Revenue-and-expense budget — describes in currency amounts plan for revenues and operating expenses.	Most widely used budget, such as a sales budget to forecast sales and estimate expenses.
Production budget — a detailed plan that identifies the products and services needed to match sales forecast and inventory requirements.	Follows the sales forecast and can be considered a production schedule.
Materials purchase/usage budget — identifies the raw materials and parts that must be purchased to meet production demands.	When accurate, leads to smooth production. Can be used in retailing to purchase merchandise.
Human resource budget — provides a schedule to identify human resource needs for future and the compensation requirements.	Needed to satisfy sales and production demands, and predicts whether hiring or layoffs will be required.
Capital expenditure budget — a plan for spending money on assets used to produce goods or services.	Are usually regarded as major expenditures and are tied to long-range plans.

Figure 14-7 March Revenue-and-Expense Budget for Nightclub and Restaurant

Item	Budget	Actual	Over	Under
Revenues	$40,000	$42,000	$2,500	
Beginning inventory	3,500	3,500		
Purchases	19,250	19,000		$250
End inventory	3,000	3,000		
Cost of goods sold	19,750	19,500		
Gross profit	20,250	23,000	2,750	
Salaries expense	10,500	10,500		
Rent and utilities expense	1,500	1,500		
Miscellaneous expense	100	250	150	
Maintenance expense	650	650		
Total operating expenses	12,750	12,900	150	
Net income before tax	7,500	10,100	2,600	
Taxes (40%)	3,000	4,040		1,040
Net income	$4,500	$6,060		

- *Research the competition.* Do some fact-finding to determine how your competitors at other firms arrive at their budget estimates. For example, find out how others adjust for inflation or an industry slump. Managers who submit the best budgets show comparisons to the competition and explain how they can outperform and why.

- *Embrace reality.* Study the facts carefully, and take a historical perspective in arriving at the correct estimates for any given financial period. For example, if your industry traditionally experiences high turnover, factor these costs into your budget forecast.

- *Do not neglect intuition.* Future sales are contingent on many factors including the competition, the local economic climates, and your own internal operations and capacity. Past experience is important but so is intuition. Estimates must be based on reality and yet contain a little creativity, and optimism if warranted.

- *Identify all the costs that are necessary and reasonable to complete the work described in your plan or proposal.* This step is particularly important when applying for a grant from a government agency, but is also meaningful in the private sector.[5]

Budgets and Financial Ratios as Control Devices

The control process relies on the use of budgets and financial ratios as measures of performance. To the extent that managers stay within budget or meet their financial ratios, they perform according to standard.

Budgets and the Control Process

Budgets are a natural part of controlling. Planned expenditures are compared to actual expenditures, and corrective action is taken if the deviation is significant. Figure 14-7 shows a budget used as a control device. The nightclub and restaurant owner operates with a monthly budget. The owner planned for revenues of $40,000 in March. Actual revenues were $42,500, a positive deviation. The discrepancy is not large enough, however, for the owner to change the anticipated revenues for April. Expenses were $150 over budget, a negative deviation the owner regards as insignificant. In short, the performance against budget looks good. The owner will take no corrective action on the basis of March's performance.

Financial Ratios and the Control Process

A more advanced method of using budgets for control is to use financial ratio guidelines for performance. Four such ratios are presented here.

Gross profit margin. One commonly used ratio is **gross profit margin**, expressed as the difference between sales and the cost of goods sold, divided by sales:

$$\text{Gross profit margin} = \frac{\text{Sales} - \text{Cost of goods sold}}{\text{Sales}}$$

gross profit margin
A financial ratio expressed as the difference between sales and the cost of goods sold, divided by sales.

This ratio measures the total money available to cover operating expenses and to make a profit. If performance deviates significantly from a predetermined performance standard, corrective action must be taken. Gross profit margins are highly regarded by many managers because sales volume can present a misleading figure of company health. A company can sell loads of merchandise and still lose money. Assume the nightclub owner needs to earn a 30 percent gross profit margin. For March, the figures are as follows:

$$\text{Gross profit margin} = \frac{\$42,500 - \$19,500}{\$42,500} = \frac{\$23,000}{\$42,500} = 0.54 \text{ or } 54\%$$

The night club owner is quite pleased with the gross profit margin of 54 percent, and will take no corrective action. However, for the next budgeting cycle, the owner might raise expectations.

Profit margin. One could argue that the gross profit margin presents an overly optimistic picture of how well the business is performing. Another widely used financial ratio is the **profit margin**, or return on sales. Profit margin measures profits earned per dollar of sales as well as the efficiency of the operation. In the business press, the profit margin is usually referred to as simply the margin and calculated as profits divided by sales. Companies with impressive sales sometimes have negative profits. For example, in the first quarter of 2019, Uber had sales of $3 billion, yet the company had spent $4 billion to attain those sales.[6]

profit margin
A financial ratio measuring return on sales, or net income divided by sales.

$$\text{Profit margin} = \frac{\text{Net income}}{\text{Sales}} = \frac{\$6,060}{\$42,500} = 0.14 \text{ or } 14\%$$

A profit margin of 14 percent would be healthy for most businesses. It also appears to present a more realistic assessment of how well the nightclub in question performs as a business.

return on equity
A financial ratio measuring how much a firm is earning on its investment, expressed as net income divided by owner's equity.

Return on equity. The **return on equity** is an indicator of how much a firm is earning on its investment. It is the ratio between net income and the owner's equity, or

$$\text{Return on equity} = \frac{\text{Net income}}{\text{Owner's equity}}$$

Assume the owner of the nightclub and restaurant invested $400,000 in the restaurant, and that the net income for the year is $72,500. The return on equity is $72,500/$400,000 = 50.181 or 18.1 percent. The owner should be satisfied, because few investments offer such a high return on equity.

Revenue per employee. A simple financial ratio that is widely used by business managers is **revenue per employee**, expressed as

revenue per employee
Total revenues divided by number of employees.

$$\text{Revenue per employee} = \frac{\text{Total revenues}}{\text{Number of employees}}$$

A company with 100 employees that generated $40 million in sales would have revenue per employee of $400,000, a reasonably representative figure. Here are two company examples: In 2019, Apple Inc. reported annual revenue of $260.2 billion for 137,000 employees. The revenue per employee was therefore $1,899,270—an impressive figure even for a high-technology company. For the year 2019, the Burger King restaurant chain had revenues of $1.3 billion dollars for 30,500 employees, resulting in a revenue per employee of $42,623. The general reason for the difference in revenue per employee between Apple and Burger King is that an information technology worker usually generates much more revenue than a food worker. Also, an iPhone or Apple computer has a much higher price than a Burger King Whopper and French fries!

Revenue per employee is often used to measure the productivity of the firm. Top management at Cisco Systems, for example, uses revenue per employee as their primary productivity measure. A more recent trend is to use the measure of profit per employee, rather than revenue per employee, because profit is usually a more meaningful metric than revenue.

The ratios presented above offer a traditional view of the financial health of an organization because they emphasize earning a profit. Many startups in the telecommunications, information technology, and biotechnology fields with revenues far below their expenses pay salaries and other expenses out of investor capital. Dozens of other companies do not pay their bills at all because they lack the necessary cash. Without cash to pay bills and profits to pay investors, most companies eventually fail. Ratios such as profit margin and return on equity are therefore still relevant in today's economy.

Other Measures of Financial Health

Several other measures of financial success in addition to financial ratios are widely used by managers. The purpose of most of these measures is to portray the company in a favorable light and impress investors. Economic value added, however, is a conservative measure of a company's financial performance.

economic value added (EVA)
Measures how much more (or less) a company earns in profits than the minimum amount its investors expect it to earn.

Economic value added (EVA). A measure of financial health that works much like a financial ratio is **economic value added (EVA)**. EVA refers to how much more (or less) the company earns in profits than the minimum amount its investors expect it to earn. The index can also be regarded as a measure of the company's efficiency in using resources, or its true economic profit. The minimum amount, also known as the cost of capital, represents what the company must pay the investors to use their capital. Cost of capital is also calculated as the overall percentage cost of the funds used to finance a firm's assets. If the sole source of financing were junk (high risk) bonds that paid investors seven percent, the cost of capital would be seven percent. All earnings beyond the minimum are regarded as excess earnings.

For example, assume investors give their company $2 million to invest and the investor's minimum desired return is seven percent, or $140,000 per year. The company earns $300,000 per year. The EVA is $160,000 as follows:

Earnings: $300,000
– Cost of capital: $140,000 (7% × $2 million capital)

Excess earnings: $160,000

To put the matter quite simply, if you could earn two percent on your investment just by purchasing CDs in a bank, why invest that money in a business that does not return much more than two percent? Investors expect higher excess earnings when they invest in a risky venture, such as a company with unproven technology entering a new industry. An example might be manufacturing electronic communication systems for space stations. Investors willing to settle for lower excess earnings usually invest in a company with proven technology in a stable industry, such as construction supplies. EVA is a frequently used control measure because it focuses on creating shareholder value.

Earnings before interest, taxes, depreciation, and amortization (EBITDA). A rough measure of the success of a company is how much it earns after deducting all expenses but interest, taxes, depreciation, and amortization. **EBITDA** is earnings before interest, taxes, depreciation, and amortization. The figure is sometimes used to evaluate the financial health of a company that might be for sale. In 2018, when weight-loss brand Jenny Craig was seeking a buyer, it hired an investment bank to explore strategic alternatives including selling the company. An analysis showed that Jenny Craig was projected to generate approximately $400 million in revenue and $35 million in earnings before interest, taxes, depreciation, and amortization. One year later, Jenny Craig was sold to the private equity firm H.I.G. Capital, suggesting that the weight-loss company had a favorable EBITDA.[7]

EBITDA
Earnings before interest, taxes, depreciation, and amortization.

Another use of EBITDA is to provide financial justification for bold management actions. In 2020, the fashion retailer Express said it would close about 100 stores by 2022. At the time, Express operated 411 regular stores and 215 factory outlet stores. Company management said that the store closures would reduce sales by 2022, but the cost reductions could boost its earnings before interest, taxes, depreciation, and amortization by $15 million.[8]

EBITDA paints an optimistic picture of a company's financial health because it excludes important costs. Imagine how profitable many businesses would be if they did not have to pay taxes or interest on their debts.

Pro forma earnings. Another way of "putting lipstick on a pig" is to report earnings that exclude nonrecurring items, such as restructuring and merger costs. **Pro forma** is a financial statement that excludes write-downs or goodwill and other one-time charges not relevant to future earnings. (*Goodwill* refers to the premium a company pays when it purchases another company for more than the value of its net assets.) Pro forma earnings remove the negative impact from a one-time event. A large depreciation cost might also be excluded, such as a computer company downgrading the value of a warehouse full of desktops that are not powerful enough to run Microsoft's latest operating system.

pro forma
A financial statement that excludes write-downs or goodwill and other one-time charges not relevant to future earnings.

Pro forma is also referred to as "earnings excluding bad stuff." The use of pro forma earnings has been criticized because it does not follow generally accepted accounting principles (GAAP). In its early days when Amazon.com was struggling to produce a profit, company management published pro forma earnings. Eventually, Amazon.com became a highly profitable company, and management no longer emphasized pro forma earnings—so in this case the pro forma statement made sense.

Net debt. Yet another measure of the financial health of an organization is how much money it owes after taking into account how much money is on hand to eliminate the debt if necessary. **Net debt** refers to a company's debt minus the cash and cash equivalents it has on hand. The net debt calculation might be considered a cosmetic device to make corporate debt appear slimmer. Yet, informing the public that debt could be lowered immediately, if necessary, seems like a reasonable assertion.

net debt
A company's debt minus the cash and cash equivalents it has on hand.

Explain how managers and business owners manage cash flow and control costs, and use nontraditional measures of financial performance.

cash flow
Amount of net cash generated by a business during a specific period.

MANAGING CASH FLOW AND COST CUTTING

In addition to developing and monitoring the cash budget, many managers pay special attention to keeping cash on hand to prevent over-reliance on borrowing and being perceived by investors as a firm in financial trouble. Both cash flow and controlling, or cutting, costs help meet these objectives. We look at these two major business processes separately.

Managing Cash Flow

Cash is so vital to keep almost any type of organization running that cash has been analyzed in many ways. **Cash flow** is the amount of net cash generated by a business during a specific period. Paychex founder and philanthropist B. Thomas Golisano advises entrepreneurs to focus on finding customers. "If you're an entrepreneur who doesn't realize that, sooner or later you're going to end up with what they call a cash flow problem,"[9] Although the definition just presented appears straightforward, many other definitions of cash flow add to its complexity. For example, cash flow can also be described as the excess of cash revenues over cash outlays. Another complexity is that cash flow is calculated in many ways. A useful and readily understandable approach is to divide a corporation's cash flow statement into three sections, each specifying a different source of cash, with a fourth section that combines the first three.[10]

1 *Cash provided by (or used in) operating activities.* This section indicates how much cash a business uses (a loss), thereby containing clues to the health of earnings. Cash from operating activities is the heart of cash flow and includes subsections: net income, provision for uncollectible money owed to the company, tax benefit from stock options, receivables, inventories, and accounts payable. When most people think of cash flow, they are referring to cash generated by earnings.

2 *Cash provided by (or used in) financing activities.* This section records cash from or paid to outsiders, such as banks or stockholders.

3 *Cash provided by (or used in) investing activities.* Recorded here is the cash used to buy or received from selling stock, assets, and businesses, plus capital expenditures.

4 *Summary.* This revealing section lists cash at the beginning and end of the specific period, plus the change in cash position.

A subtle problem with the four types of cash flow listed above is that accounting firms do not always agree with managers as to the definition of *cash*. Of course, money deposited in a bank or in the cash registers or safes is cash, but what about money invested in short-term money market funds, certificates of deposit, or bonds? Are these investments really the equivalent of cash? The Big Four accounting firms are strict about what they count as cash equivalents. Short-term or highly liquid investments are generally classified as cash.[11]

Firms with large cash flows make attractive takeover targets because acquiring firms are likely to use the cash to pay off the cost of the acquisition. A company that does not want to be taken over might deliberately lower its cash flow by taking on a lot of debt. A large cash flow for a business owner contributes to peace of mind because the owner can keep operating without borrowing during a business downturn. In turbulent times, having cash in the bank gives managers a feeling of tranquility. With stocks and other investments being so volatile in recent years, "cash is royalty" is truer than ever. Cash on hand is a key measure of financial well-being. For large companies, having abundant cash available makes purchasing another company at a bargain much more feasible, and the acquiring company can act quickly.

Cash flow analysis is well accepted because it provides a more accurate picture of financial health than sales volume. A company frequently makes a sale but then does not receive payment for a minimum of 30 days. Cash flow analysis provides an important tool because it is less subject to distortion than is a statement of revenues. Many managers use the questionable accounting practice of classifying as "revenue" goods in the hands of distributors, which have not yet been sold, and contracts for which no money has yet been exchanged.

Cash flow analysis helps keep managers focused on the importance of managing cash. Paying suppliers too quickly wastes money, as does paying too slowly. The latter may lead to penalties or higher prices because the supplier needs to compensate for late payments. Taking steps to receive prompt payment from customers is an essential part of cash management.

A refinement of cash flow is **free cash flow**, or the cash from operations minus capital expenditures. The capital expenditures in this context are the investments necessary to maintain or expand the company's fixed assets. Free cash flow therefore takes into account the idea that managers should be thinking of needed expenditures, such as purchasing a modern call center before they brag about how much cash is on hand. A few years ago, GE halved its quarterly dividend, partly to be able to cover its obligations from the free cash flow it generates.[12] Following the logic of free cash flow, if you were a home owner, before calculating how much cash you have available, set aside a reserve for the inevitable replacement of your roof or furnace.

free cash flow
A refinement of cash flow that measures the cash from operations minus capital expenditures.

A heavy concern with cash flow, or preserving cash, can lead to business practices that some people might consider unsavory, such as the delay of paying bills in order to keep cash on hands as long as possible.

The accompanying *Management in Action* insert illustrates the cash flow problems of a well-known company.

Cost Cutting to Improve Financial Health

The ideal way to improve cash flow is to generate more revenue than expenses. However, generating more revenue can be an enormous challenge. For example, additional advertising might not pay off, a new product might flop, and offering huge discounts may evaporate profits. Many companies therefore trim costs to improve

MANAGEMENT IN ACTION

Netflix Tackles Cash Flow Issue

Netflix Inc., the best-known video streaming service, used to be equally well-known for offering CD rentals via the mail. Less well-know about Netflix is how much more money it spends than it earns. The company's operations and investments have regularly burned through cash since 2011, resulting in a large and growing amount of debt. In 2019, Netflix expected its operations and investments to consume $3.5 billion beyond its cash generation. Revenues for that year were $20.1 billion. Its content budget alone for 2019 was $15 billion. Netflix spends heavily to produce original movies, TV series, and other exclusive content. It takes approximately two years to get a new show from production to viewing on screen, meaning that revenue with no returns is tied up for that period.

Netflix has relied on debt to fund its negative free cash flow amid its spending spree. CEO Reed Hastings said in 2019, "Our plan is to continue to use the debt market in the interim to finance our investment needs." At the time Netflix was already over $12 billion in debt. Yet management was optimistic that it would be able to slowly narrow its free cash flow gap starting in 2020, based on is growing revenue base and expanding operating margins. Outside business analysts estimated that Netflix could manage to close its cash gap between 2021 and 2024. Another prediction was that Netflix would hit break-even on free cash flow by 2024.

Analyst John Blackledge predicted that Netflix will turn free cash flow positive by about $305 million by 2021 as the company moves from licensing to more original content (such as filmmaking). Predictions were also made that more popular originals will enable Netflix to further boost is subscription price despite less-expensive competitors, such as Amazon. com. Another analyst, Michael Pachter was more pessimistic

about Netflix overcoming its cash burn problems. He said, "We expect the company to continue to increase its marketing and content spending over the next several years in order to maintain the pace of its subscriber growth."

Top management at Netflix hopes that its efforts to convert original content into more subscriptions and profits will resolve its cash-flow problems.

Questions

1 **Why should a popular company like Netflix with over $20 billion in annual revenue worry about cash flow and debt?**

2 **How might a drive to crack down on password sharing by customers improve Netflix's cash flow problems?**

Source: Original story based on facts and observations in the following sources: Georg Szalai, "When Will Netflix Finally End Its Cash Burn?" *Hollywood Reporter* (www.holllywoodreporter.com), October 30, 2019, pp. 1–5; Todd Spangler, "Netflix to Raise Another $2 Billion Through Debt to Fund Massive Content Spending," *Variety* (www.variety.com), October 21, 2019, pp. 1–5; Troy Wolverton, "Netflix Now Expects to Burn through $3.5 Billion in Cash this Year. That's about $500 Million More than It Previously Forecast," *www.businessinsider.com*, April 16, 2019, p. 1; Patrick Seitz, "Netflix Stock Downgraded On Negative Cash Flow Problem," *www.investorbusinessdaily.com*, November 25, 2019, pp. 1–2; Tatyana Shumsky, "New Netflix CFO to Tackle Cash-Flow Issues," *The Wall Street Journal*, January 4, 2019, p. B4.

cash flow. Even when revenues are increasing, some firms reduce costs to remain more competitive. As you may have noticed, the less cash you spend, the more you have on hand. How do managers know when it is time to cut costs? Obviously, when a firm has low cash flow or is losing money, costs need to be cut pronto. In addition, managers can use ratios as rules of thumbs. For example, a company might want to keep sales expenses at or below 10 percent of sales.

Here we look at positive approaches for making the right type of investment that can reduce costs, and the potential hazards of cost reduction. Figure 14-8 presents a broad sampling of cost-cutting measures.

Investing in Positive Approaches to Cost Reduction

Investing money in the right process or equipment can often lead to useful cost reductions. A small example is that if a company invests in a new printer that consumes less inkjet or laser cartridges, the company might start saving money within a few months. A bigger example is that over 50 airlines have hired the Pratt & Whitney unit

Figure 14-8 A Variety of Ways to Cut Costs

Saving money can greatly affect profit levels, so managers look for many ways to trim costs without damaging productivity or morale. Annual savings range from a few hundred dollars to millions, depending on the measures used. As noted below, cost-cutting carried to the extreme can backfire in terms of product quality and morale.

Techniques Focused Mostly on People

- Offer more opportunities for remote work which on a large scale will reduce the need for office space because fewer workers will be at the office at a given time. Use virtual teams when workers are geographically dispersed.

- Minimize business travel by using e-mail, phone, company Websites, or videoconferencing when possible. Have business travelers fly coach instead of first class, and stay at budget hotels and motels. Establish per diem rates for meal allowances instead of an open-ended travel account substantiated by receipts.

- Keep offices, factories, and laboratories at the coolest or warmest temperature that does not lower morale or productivity, or damage equipment. Encourage employees to wear warm clothing in cold months, and light clothing in warm months.

- Place frequent business travelers on hoteling status, so they do not have a permanent office or cubicle when in the office.

- Ask employees to conduct bimonthly brainstorming sessions to find ways to reduce costs. Offer rewards for the best savings.

- Drop customers who cost you money because of their constant demands for service despite modest purchases.

- Automate wherever possible to reduce payroll costs so long as the automation does not drive away business, such as in many call centers that rely heavily on menus driven by voice-recognition.

Techniques Focused Mostly on Material and Equipment

- Use remanufactured parts wherever feasible. As a general rule, 70 percent of the cost to build something new is in the materials, and 30 percent in the labor. Salvaging and rebuilding typically gets the material costs down to 40 percent.[13]

- Eliminate battery-operated office clocks, as well as other battery-operated electronic devices whenever feasible.

- To save on telephone bills, use Internet phones or recommend that employees use their own mobile devices. Eliminate voice mail for many employees.

- Instead of owning advanced hardware and software, use information technology on demand (cloud computing) to provide for information technology requirements.

- Lease equipment when it is less expensive than owning.

- Sell surplus and obsolete equipment on an online auction site.

- Subcontract manufacturing and services that can be done less expensively by other firms.

- Sell the corporate jet and limousines, and ask executives to fly on commercial airlines and drive their own vehicles for business (or take the bus or train). When it is more economical, have company representatives use their own vehicles at IRS mileage rates instead of renting vehicles.

- For retailers, close unprofitable stores, and relocate from shopping malls to lower rent areas (if the relocation does not drive away customers).

- Introduce only those new products or services that appear to have a high probability of success.

Techniques Focused Mostly on Money Management

- Merge with or acquire another company, and eliminate or greatly reduce duplicate functions, such as having two IT or human resource groups.

- Relocate to another geographic area where the costs are lower or where taxes are lower.

- Downsize the office and shift some workers to shared working facilities such as WeWork.

- Centralize purchasing to obtain better prices on bulk purchases, as done by Home Depot and many other large, geographically dispersed firms. At the same time, reduce the number of suppliers to obtain volume discounts because each surviving vendor will get more business.

- Try eBay and other auction sites when making purchases, or use a reverse auction in which suppliers bid on providing you the equipment or supplies you need.

- Ask suppliers for discounts on early payments.

- Drop products or services that lose money for the company, or if possible, sell these business lines to another company to raise cash.

of United Technologies Corp. to wash their engines with a machine that can deep clean while simultaneously collect and purify the hazardous runoff. Clean engines burn less fuel, and fuel is the largest component of operating costs.[14]

Investing money in videoconferencing equipment is a widespread practice for reducing travel expenses. Accenture, the worldwide consulting firm makes extensive use of videoconferencing to both enhance communication and reduce costs. The company saves several thousand business trips annually through the use of videoconferencing.

Many human resource managers believe an investment in the physical and mental health of employees saves money in the long run, even when short-term savings are not evident. Researchers studied the effects of a wellness program at BJ's Wholesale Club, a retail chain of discount warehouses. After 18 months employees who participated in the wellness program, 8.3 percent said they were more likely to report that they were engaging in physical exercise, and 13.6 percent were more likely to report that they were trying to maintain their weight. Yet the wellness program participants were not significantly different from other employees with respect to measures such as cholesterol, blood pressure, and healthcare spending. A note for optimism with respect to cost cutting is that in the long run, employees who engage in physical exercise and weight control will be healthier and spend less on healthcare.[15]

Automation is generally a positive investment that often reduces costs, such as the reduction in the number of store associates required with automated, self-service checkout counters. The lean manufacturing movement exemplifies how investing in automation can reduce costs. For example, many manufacturing plants operated by Parker Hannifin Corp require only a handful or only a single highly trained worker. As a result, revenue per employee has moved up from $125,000 to $200,000 during a nine-year period. The early successes with lean manufacturing have prompted Parker Hannifin to continue with the program, thereby generating more cash and freeing up working capital.[16]

Potential Hazards of Cost Reduction

A caution about cost cutting is that it can lead to low morale, lower-quality goods and services, and foster the image of being a cheap company. For example, using old newspapers as packing material is environmentally friendly and saves money but does not fit with a high-quality image.

Before Kraft Heinz appointed a chief growth officer (described in the chapter introduction), the company experienced negative consequences from an intense cost-cutting campaign. The company had reduced investment in marketing to support its brands which contributed to a 1 percent decline in revenues during a one-year period. Kraft-Heinz also lowered its non-production related costs from 10 percent to 8 percent of sales. Gross margins dropped by 3.5 percent, as private-label brands squeezed its profits on such key brands as Oscar Mayer hotdogs.

3G Capital, the private equity firm that had bought both Heinz and Kraft slashed the workforce. Another cost-cutting scheme was to use zero-based budgeting, a procedure that requires managers to frequently justify cost regardless of previous spending levels to eliminate $1.7 billion in expenses. To pinch pennies further, the company stopped employee perks such as free cheese sticks and Jell-O. An analyst at Edward Jones said this about the strategy 3G used with Heinz and Kraft: "You can't just cut and buy, cut and buy—it's a packaged food company, all you have is the value of your brands."[17]

We caution about managers resorting to cost-cutting measures that make the company appear cheap. The situation is worsened when everybody but top-level managers and selected professionals are expected to trim costs. Cynicism can mount, as illustrated by the following fictitious lodging standard for business travel[18]:

> *All employees are encouraged to stay with relatives and friends while on business travel. If weather permits, public areas, such as parks should be used as temporary lodging sites. Bus terminals, train stations, and office lobbies may provide shelter in periods of inclement weather.*

TWO NONTRADITIONAL MEASURES OF FINANCIAL PERFORMANCE

As managers continue to look for ways to measure the financial performance of the companies or units they manage, several nontraditional measures of financial performance have emerged. Two such indicators are the balanced scorecard, and relative standing against the competition.

The Balanced Scorecard

Many researchers and managers have abandoned their exclusive reliance on financial ratios and related indices to measure the health of a firm. Managers continue to look for ways to overcome the limited view of performance sometimes created by budgets. An accounting professor and a technology consultant worked with hundreds of companies to devise a **balanced scorecard**—a management system that enables organizations to clarify their vision and strategy and translate them into action.[19] Managers using the balanced scorecard do not rely on short-term financial measures as the only indicators of a company's performance. The balanced scorecard is a strategic approach and performance management system that helps an organization set goals and measure performance from four perspectives that are vital to all businesses, as outlined in Figure 14-9.

balanced scorecard
A set of measures to provide a quick but comprehensive view of the business.

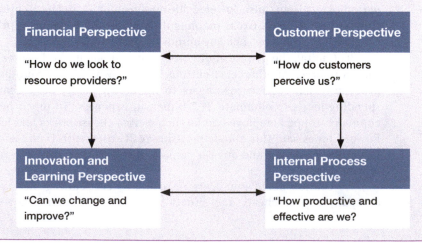

Figure 14-9 A Basic Version of the Balanced Scorecard

The balanced scorecard suggests we view the organization from four perspectives We also develop measures of each perspective, and analyze data to see if these perspectives are being attained.

Financial Perspective

"How do we look to resource providers?"

Customer Perspective

"How do customers perceive us?"

Innovation and Learning Perspective

"Can we change and improve?"

Internal Process Perspective

"How productive and effective are we?"

The balanced scorecard continues to broaden its use in helping companies widen their horizon about what constitutes success. A high-level application of the scorecard is to help alliances work more effectively. The problem solved is that only about 50 percent of alliances are successful. Furthermore, most alliances are defined by service level agreements that identify what each side agrees to deliver rather than what each hopes to gain from the partnership. The balanced scorecard helps partners in the alliance wither their focus from contributions and operations to strategy and commitment. For example, building a strategy map can help a company see how attaining objectives at department levels helps the firm achieve business-process, customer, and ultimately financial objectives.[20]

The balanced scorecard supports a strategy to the extent that it directs the company effort toward achieving the four goals of financial health, customer satisfaction, business processes, and learning and growth. Internal business processes are the mechanisms through which performance expectations are achieved. An example of an internal business process would be whether products and services are built to meet customer requirements. Compensation is based on achieving all the factors included in the balanced scorecard. Many managers attend seminars given by the Balanced Scorecard Institute to guide them in using the balanced scorecard approach.

Relative Standing Against the Competition

Performance measures often measure success by comparing this year's results with those attained in previous years, such as a sales increase or decrease in operating costs. Andrew Likierman, the former dean of the London Business School, suggests that comparing one's performance against the competition is more meaningful. For example, if your sales decreased five percent this year, you might be doing quite well because your two biggest competitors experienced decreases of nine percent and eight percent.

Likierman suggests that measuring performance in terms of anticipated market share is a valuable performance metric. One way to obtain such information is to ask customers. Enterprise, the car rental company relies on the Enterprise Service Quality Index, which measures the intention of customers to return. An employee at each Enterprise branch phones a random sample of customers and asks whether they plan to use Enterprise again. When the index rises, the company is gaining market share; when it falls, other rental companies will be getting a piece of Enterprises' business. Branch managers place the results next to profitability numbers on monthly financial statements, and factor them into criteria for promotion.[21] (We caution here that customer surveys should not be taken too frequently because they can be annoying.)

LEARNING OBJECTIVE **7**

Describe a computer-based monitoring system.

computer-based monitoring system
A computer-based system to monitor the work habits and productivity of employees.

COMPUTER-BASED MONITORING SYSTEM

A **computer-based monitoring system** gathers data about the work habits and productivity of employees. Managers using employing monitoring through software can measure productivity, track attendance, ensure security, and obtain proof of hours worked. The content of electronic messages is also monitored frequently. Employee monitoring systems capitalize on the networking of computer terminals to monitor the work of employees who use computer terminals in their jobs or who operate complex machine tools. Remote workers can also be tracked with a computer-based monitoring system. Once the monitoring software is installed, the central computer processes information from each terminal and records the employee's efficiency and effectiveness. At its best, data gathered by a computer-monitoring system improves decision making, in areas such as assigning performance bonuses, and deciding on the optima team size.[22]

Employee Internet use is frequently monitored, with more than three quarters of U.S. companies monitoring such use. A major problem is that time spent on websites unrelated to the task at hand can drain productivity. (Yet, at times a quick glance at a website unrelated to the job can be a refreshing pause that enhances productivity.) Another problem is that visiting objectionable sites, such as pornography or gambling sites, on company time can place the company at legal risk. A specific risk is harassment suits from employees who may be exposed to the risk.[23]

A contributing factor to electronic monitoring of work is that an increased number of employees conduct their work far from their manager's gaze, including at home and in hotel rooms. Also, in the face of global competition and tight budgets, managers are forced to boost worker productivity. Another boost to the use of electronic monitoring is that electronic evidence plays an important role in lawsuits and regulator investigations, including insider trading.

Workers Most Likely to Be Monitored

Office workers, including those in frequent telephone contact with the public, are the most likely to be monitored. An everyday example of electronic work monitoring is when you telephone customer service and hear the words, "This message may be monitored for quality assurance." Word processing specialists are measured by such factors as words keyed per minute, the number of breaks taken, and the duration of each break.

The reservation center for JetBlue Airways consists of reservation agents who work from home, using computers and phone systems provided by the company. These employees are referred to as Customer Support crew members. JetBlue management is able to attain exceptional productivity with the assistance of software that enables it to track each agent's telephone activity. When an agent receives a call, the telephone system logs data, such as the duration of the call, who hangs up first, and whether the agent is immediately available to answer another call. Also, to monitor quality, every month a supervisor listens to about 10 calls, recorded at random, for each worker supervised.[24]

Computer-aided monitoring is also used for purposes of data-loss prevention—the unauthorized transmission of sensitive data to company outsiders. Leaks are a major concern in healthcare and law, but also in product development and marketing. Software keeps track of all computer activities, including the use of detachable devices like USB flash drives. The software can also be set to automatically enforce security policies, including the blocking of certain phrases.[25] An example of a phrase that might be blocked would be, "Great new product coming down the pike."

A general guideline is that high-technology monitoring tools can be applied best with workers who perform discrete, measurable tasks during prescribed hours, such as employees in call centers, finance departments, and insurance claims. Monitoring workers whose jobs primarily involve thinking is much more difficult. For example, a chemist might be looking out the window with his feet on the desk—yet at the same time developing an idea for a drug that will prevent high blood pressure. When monitoring is used for purposes of data-loss prevention, whether or not work is measurable is irrelevant.

Concerns about Electronic Monitoring Systems

The major advantage of an electronic monitoring system is the close supervision it allows managers. Some employees welcome computerized monitoring because it supplements arbitrary judgments by supervisors about their productivity. Computerized work-monitoring systems have substantial disadvantages, however. Many argue these systems invade employee privacy and violate their dignity. As a result, many lawsuits are being filed against companies. Moreover, electronic monitoring often contributes to low levels of job satisfaction, absenteeism, high turnover, and job stress.

As the technology of computer-aided monitoring of work has become more technologically advanced, it has raised more concerns about privacy issues. What bothers many employees is they typically do not expect the company will monitor them on password-protected sites using non-work computers, including those on their smartphones.[26] For example, a worker might think he has the right to express his frustration with his job and supervisor by posting a Tweet via his Samsung Galaxy during a rest break. The company might think otherwise.

Another concern about electronic monitoring is that executives are usually not monitored even though they are in a better position than other workers to commit fraud, such as stealing company money and selling trade secrets. Finally, some people are concerned that members of the IT group involved in security have too much power to monitor the electronic communications of other workers. For example, a worker shopping for lingerie on the Internet during the workday could be accused of accessing pornography by a vindictive information technology specialist. The results of computer-aided monitoring of work are often used to take action that seems unduly harsh against employees who violate company rules, such as firing workers for misusing the Internet.

Despite these concerns, computer-based monitoring usually does not involve privacy infringement in the legal sense. An IT law opinion is that workplace activities that are monitored by software are inherently public activities, many of which were monitored by supervisors before the advent of computers. Yet privacy and access questions could arise related to the ability of employees to see or challenge work-related records.[27]

Gaining Acceptance for Computer-Aided Monitoring

An important recommendation to managers about electronic monitoring of workers is to establish an Acceptable Usage Policy and an employee monitoring policy. The usage policy defines appropriate and inappropriate uses of corporate resources, including telecommunication devices. For example, setting up an eBay business with your employer's desktop is out of bounds. The monitoring policy explains exactly where and when inappropriate Internet access is blocked, and when the company monitors telephone, computer, and Internet usage. In some workplaces, employees accept computer monitoring as a tool that helps them gain control of their work and be judged fairly by their supervisors.[28]

CHARACTERISTICS OF EFFECTIVE CONTROLS

LEARNING OBJECTIVE **8**

Specify several characteristics of effective controls.

An effective control system improves job performance and productivity by helping workers correct problems. A system that achieves these outcomes possesses distinct characteristics. The greater the number of the following characteristics a given control system contains, the better the system will be at providing management with useful information and improved performance:

1 *The controls must be accepted.* For control systems to increase productivity, employees must cooperate with the system. If employees are more intent on beating the system than on improving performance, controls will not achieve their ultimate purpose. For example, the true purpose of a time-recording system is to ensure employees work a full day. If workers are intent on circumventing the system through such means as having friends punch in and out for them, the time-recording system will not increase productivity.

2 *The control measures must be appropriate and meaningful.* People tend to resist control measures that they believe do not relate to performance in a meaningful way. The number of visitors to a website is sometimes used as a performance measure for the developers of the site. A glitzy website might attract a lot of business because it is recommended by network members to each other, yet the visitors may not necessarily purchase from the merchants advertising on the site. For the website to continue to generate ad revenue, a more meaningful performance measure is the number of visitors who click on the advertisers' links and make a purchase. A less glitzy site that attracted fewer but more serious buyers would indicate the website developer is doing a better job.

3 *An effective control measure provides diagnostic information.* If controls are to improve performance, they must help people correct deviations from performance. A sales manager might be told that he or she was performing well in all categories except selling to small business owners. This information might prompt the manager to determine what services the company sells that would have more appeal to small businesses.

4 *Effective controls allow for self-feedback and self-control.* A self-administering control system saves considerable time. Employees can do much of their own controlling if the system permits them access to their own feedback. An example is a system whereby clients complain directly to the employee instead of going to management.

5 *Effective control systems provide timely information.* Controls lead to positive changes in behavior if the control information is available quickly. It is more helpful to give workers daily, rather than monthly estimates of their performance against quota. Given day-by-day feedback, an employee can make quick adjustments. If feedback is withheld until the end of a month or a quarter, the employee may be too discouraged to make improvements.

6 *Control measures are more effective when employees have control over the results measured.* People rebel when held responsible for performance deviations beyond their control. For example, a resort hotel manager's profits might fall below expectations because of a factor beyond his or her control, such as a sudden shift in weather that results in cancellations.

7 *Effective control measures do not contradict each other.* Employees are sometimes asked to achieve two contradictory sets of standards. As a result, they resist the control system. Employees told to increase both quantity and quality, for example, may experience confusion and chaos. A compromised approach would be to improve quality with the aim of increasing net quantity in the long run. Care taken in doing something right the first time results in less rework. With less time spent on error correction, eventually the quantity of goods produced increases.

8 *Effective controls allow for random variations from the standard.* If a control allows for random variations that do not differ significantly from the standard, then it is more effective. An ineffective way of using a control system is to quickly take action at the first deviation from acceptable performance. A one-time deviation may not indicate a genuine problem. It could simply be a random or insignificant variation that may not be repeated for years. For example, would you take action if a team member exceeded a $3,000 travel expense allowance by $2.78?

9 *Effective controls are cost-effective.* Control systems should result in satisfactory returns on investment. In many instances they don't because the costs of control are too high. Having recognized this fact, some fast service restaurants allow employees to eat all the food they want during working hours. The cost of trying to control illicit eating is simply too high. (This policy provides the added benefit of building worker morale.)

10 *The controls do not limit innovation.* Controls aimed at the executive level can sometimes restrict innovation because they emphasize short-term profits at the expense of investing money in ways that might pay off in the future. The emphasis on short-term earnings per share helps boost the stock price but may restrict investments in long-term growth opportunities.[29] A CEO whose success is measured by this quarter's profits might think, "Why spend $4 million on research and development that might never pay off when I can look good by reporting the $4 million as profit for this quarter?"

In short, the intelligent and sensible use of controls enhance organizational and individual effectiveness without creating morale problems and resentment. Managers must control and lead at the same time.

SUMMARY OF KEY POINTS

1 **Explain how controlling relates to the other management functions.**

Controlling is used to evaluate whether the manager is effective in good job planning, organizing, and leading. Controls can also be used to evaluate control systems.

2 **Understand the different types and strategies of control.**

Controls can be classified according to the time when they are applied. Preventive controls are applied prior to the performance of an activity. Concurrent controls monitor activities while they are being carried out. Feedback controls evaluate and prompt corrective action after activity performance.

Controls can also be classified according to their underlying strategy. An external control strategy is based on the assumption that employees are motivated primarily by external rewards and need to be controlled by their managers. An internal control strategy assumes managers can motivate employees by building commitment to organizational goals.

3 **Describe the steps in the control process.**

The steps in the controlling process include setting standards, measuring actual performance, comparing actual performance to standards, and taking corrective action if necessary. To measure performance, agreement must be reached on the aspects of performance to be measured, the degree of accuracy needed, and who will use the measurements.

The three courses of action open to a manager are do nothing, solve the problem, or revise the standard. Taking corrective action on significant deviations only is called the exception principle.

4 **Explain the use of nonbudgetary control techniques.**

Nonbudgetary control techniques can be qualitative or quantitative. Qualitative techniques include audits, personal observations, and performance evaluations. The auditing process has come under considerable scrutiny in recent years because of many cases of unethical and illegal reporting of financial information by business firms. Quantitative techniques include Gantt charts, PERT, and economic-order quantity.

5 **Have an awareness of the various types of budgets, and the use of budgets and financial ratios for control.**

A budget is a spending plan for a future period of time, expressed in numerical terms. A fixed budget allocates expenditures based on a one-time allocation of resources. A flexible budget allows variation in the use of resources based on the level of activity. Eight types of budgets are summarized in Figure 14-6 for reference purposes. Budgets function as a natural part of controlling. Managers use budgets to compare planned expenditures to actual expenditures, and they take corrective action if the deviation is significant.

Three key financial ratios are gross profit margin, profit margin, return on equity, and revenue per employee. Other ways of measuring financial performance are economic value added (EVA); EBITDA (earnings before interest, taxes, depreciation, and amortization) pro forma earnings; and net debt.

6 **Explain how managers and business owners manage cash flow and control costs, and use nontraditional measures of financial performance.**

Closely tied in with the cash budget, is the special attention managers pay to cash flow. Cash flow measures how much actual cash is available for conducting business. The three sections of a cash flow statement are cash provided by (or used in) operating activities, financing activities, and investing activities. A firm that writes off many income deductions will have a bigger cash flow. Many companies trim costs to improve cash flow. Too much cost cutting can lead to low morale, low quality, and a company image of cheapness.

Many researchers and managers no longer rely exclusively on financial ratios and related indices to measure the health of a firm. Instead, they use a balanced scorecard that measures the various aspects of an organization's performance, and is also a management system for implementing vision and strategy. Another approach to determining a firm's wealth measures relative standing against the competition.

7 Describe a computer-based monitoring system.

Although a computer-based monitoring system helps managers monitor employee performance, and protect secrecy, it has been met with considerable criticism. Computer-based monitoring usually does not involve privacy infringement in a legal sense. An effective monitoring policy explains exactly where and when inappropriate Internet access is blocked, and when the company monitors telephone, computer, and Internet usage.

8 Specify several characteristics of effective controls.

An effective control system results in improved job performance and productivity because it helps people correct problems. An effective control measure is accepted by workers, appropriate, provides diagnostic information, allows for self-feedback and self-control, and provides timely information. It also allows employees some control over the behavior measured, does not embody contradictory measures, allows for random variation, is cost-effective, and does not limit innovation.

Key Terms and Phrases

preventive control 426

concurrent control 426

feedback control 426

external control strategy 426

internal control strategy 427

standard 428

deviation 430

qualitative control technique 432

quantitative control technique 432

budget 433

gross profit margin 436

profit margin 436

return on equity 437

revenue per employee 437

economic value added (EVA) 437

EBITDA 438

pro forma 438

net debt 439

cash flow 439

free cash flow 440

balanced scorecard 444

computer-based monitoring system 445

Questions

1. Provide an example of how feedback from customers can be used as part of a control system.

2. Tony works full time as a computer-repair technician and makes onsite repairs for individuals and small businesses. He says his gross profit margin is 94 percent because last year his total revenues were $150,000 and his expenses were $9,000. "I'm actually doing better than Microsoft. They talk about gross profit margins of 80 percent," said Tony. What is wrong with Tony's estimate of his gross profit margin?

3. Which one or two of the financial ratios mentioned in this chapter could be a good motivational tool if revealed to employees?

4. Prominent CEOs and management scholars have often said, "You can't achieve greatness by cutting costs." What are these people talking about?

5. Managers of some businesses save costs by suggesting employees bring their own electronic device (BYOD) to work, including smartphones and tablet computers. What do you see as the advantages and disadvantages of this approach to cost cutting?

6. How might the use of "revenue per employee" provide useful information to the owner of a professional sports team, such as hockey, football, or baseball?

7. Provide an example of how cash flow might be incorporated into a performance standard.

Skill-Building Exercise 14-A: Constructive and Destructive Cost Cutting

Using in-person interviews, phone conversations, or emails, text messages, or social networking sites, do some live research on cost cutting with several individuals. Ask your respondents for examples of useful, or constructive, cost cutting they have observed on the job. You might include yourself as an interviewee for this exercise. Do the same for useless, or destructive, cost cutting. Look for patterns. What types of cost-cutting measures are likely to be well accepted by workers? What types of cost-cutting measures are likely to be resisted by workers?

Skill-Building Exercise 14-B: Financial Ratios

Cadence invested a $50,000 inheritance as equity in a franchise print and copy shop. Similar to well-established national franchises, the shop also offers desktop publishing, digital printing, and computer graphics services. Cadence's revenue-and-expense statement for her first year of operation follows.

Working individually or in small groups, compute the following ratios: gross profit margin, profit margin (return on sales), and return on equity. Groups may compare answers. Discuss whether you think Cadence is operating a worthwhile business.

Item	Financial Result
Revenues	$255,675
Beginning inventory	15,500
Purchases	88,000
End inventory	14,200
Cost of goods sold	89,300
Gross profit	166,375
Salaries expense	47,000
Rents and utilities expense	6,500
Miscellaneous expense	1,100
Maintenance expense	750
Total operating expenses	55,350
Net income before taxes	111,025
Taxes (40%)	44,410
Net income	66,615

Management Now—Online Skill-Building Exercise: Checking Out the Profit of Your Favorite Companies

Here is an opportunity to check out the profit margins, or return on sales, of two of your favorite companies. We recommend two approaches to finding a statement of the profit margin of the companies. One is to search for their annual report of the companies. Another approach is to use the search phrase, "Profit margin of (your target companies)." Based on your analyses, what is your opinion of the financial health of the companies you researched? What recommendations can you make to management? Also, what explanation can you offer if you find that the profit margins between the two companies vary and are quite different?

"Let's Boost Our Revenue Per Employee"

Cecilia is the CEO of Practical Design, a company that manufactures and sells low-priced furniture for the office and home. The company employees 98 employees, and has annual revenues of $16 million. Last week, Cecilia sent a message on a shared website expressing her concern about the relatively modest revenue per employee of $163,265. She wanted her top-management team to prepare for a Tuesday morning meeting to discuss how to enhance the revenue per employee at Practical Design.

Cecilia began the meeting by stating, "I am pleased with our company's financials in general, but it seems our revenue per employee is on the low side. I understand we are in a labor-intensive industry, so we can't have revenue per employees similar to an investment bank or a software company. Any ideas, folks?"

Dion, the manufacturing head offered this comment: "I see room for automating a few of our manufacturing processes, but that would take quite a big investment in new machines."

Stacey, the head of sales and marketing said, "I think we could improve our commission structure for our best sales representatives. If the sales representatives generate more revenue, our revenue per employee would increase automatically."

Mason, the head of office administration and human resources suggested, "We might be able to reduce our headcount a little. We could consolidate a few jobs, and dismiss a few of our worst performers. Also, we might be able to get by without replacing a few of the employees who will quit or retire in the next year or so. Having fewer employees translates into more revenue per employee."

Lia, the head of information systems, said, "I wonder if we are focusing too much on revenue per employee. It is somewhat of an arbitrary metric that detracts from the success of Practical Design in a highly competitive industry."

Roman, the head of finance, offered this idea: "Before we make a decision, I am going to review the company records for 10 years, and determine the pattern of our revenue per employee. I am also going to try to dig up information on the revenue per employee of our competitors."

Cecilia concluded, "All your ideas have merit. I am going to carefully review your suggestion, and get back to you within 10 days."

Case Questions

1 Explain which suggestion you think Cecilia should implement.

2 What other suggestions might you offer Practical Design for boosting its revenue per employee?

3 What do you think of Lia's suggestion to not worry about revenue per employee?

Business Owner Jeremy Needs More Cash

Jeremy owns and operates a small regional trucking company, Magenta Trucking. His company has a fleet of six trucks, two full-time employees, and a bank of 15 contract drivers who he hires as needed. Jeremy earns enough money to make what he considers an acceptable living. Revenue for the company is sporadic because demand for his trucking service is unpredictable. At times he does not have enough trucks and drivers to meet demand. At other times he might have four or five trucks not in use for a week.

As with other business firms, Jeremy is required to pay estimated taxes each quarter. His federal and state tax payments are due in April, June, September, and January. When revenues have been high, Jeremy has enough money to pay the estimated taxes. When he does not pay the estimated taxes on time, he has to pay late penalties to the U.S. Treasury. Jeremy keeps enough cash on hand to last about two weeks.

In late March of a recent year, Jeremy met with his tax attorney Rebecca to review the documentation necessary to file his federal and state income taxes for the year. She noted that for two of the quarters, Jeremy sent the United States Treasury and the New Jersey Income tax bureau about $50 each. Rebecca said that she would have to run Jeremy's tax return through the appropriate software, yet she could see that Jeremy had a big tax liability. "It wouldn't surprise me," she said, "that you will owe about $9,000 on federal taxes, and $2,000 in state taxes." Looking grim, Jeremy responded, "It's horrible, but I was expecting bad news."

Rebecca then asked Jeremy why doesn't he make reasonable estimated tax payments when they are due. Jeremy said, "When revenue comes in, I usually need it for an urgent purpose, like paying for rent, paying the truckers, paying salaries, maintaining my trucks, and paying the utility bills. I also need to take enough of our sales revenues to pay my living expenses. I guess I pay taxes with whatever is left over."

Rebecca responded, "I hear you Jeremy, but you have got to fix your cash flow problem."

Case Questions

1 What is your opinion about whether or not Jeremy has a cash flow problem?

2 What would you recommend that Jeremy do from a management standpoint to have enough money to pay his taxes?

3 What budgeting mistakes might Jeremy be making?

ENDNOTES

1. Original story created from facts and observations in the following sources: Ben Miller, "Beleaguered Kraft Heinz Makes a Change at Its CFO Position," *Chicago Business Journal* (www.bizjournals,com), 2020, pp. 1–3; Annie Gasparro, "Kraft Plans to Slash Bets on New Brands," *The Wall Street Journal*, January 27, 2020, pp. B1, B2; Heather Haddon and Micah Maidenberg, "Kraft Heinz Replaces Finance Chief," *The Wall Street Journal* (www.wsj.com), August 26, 2019, pp. 1–4; "Nina Barton: Chief Growth Officer," *The Kraft Heinz Company* (www.ir.kraftheinzcompany.com), 2020, p. 2.

2. Richard O. Mason and E. Burton Swanson, "Measurement for Management Decision: A Perspective," *California Management Review*, Spring 1979, pp. 70–81.

3. Jonathan Weil, "Behind the Wave of Corporate Fraud, A Change in How Auditors Work," *The Wall Street Journal*, March 25, 2004, p. A1.

4. The first three suggestions are from, "Master the Art of Budget Projection," *WorkingSMART*, March 1999, p. 6; the fourth one is from Edward Lowe Foundation, "How to Prepare a Cash Budget," *eSmallOffice*, copyright © 2020.

5. "Developing Your Budget," U.S. Department of Health & Human Services, National Institutes of Health (*http://grants.nih.gov*), 2016.

6. Clifton Leaf, "Follow the Money," *Fortune*, July 2019, p. 8.

7. Elise Reuter, "Private Equity Firm Acquires Jenny Craig Inc." *San Diego Journal* (www.sdbj.com), April 4, 2019, p. 1; Jaewon Kang and Lillian Rizzo, "Jenny Craig Weighs Sale as Performance Improves," *The Wall Street Journal*, September 13, 2018, p. B3.

8. Robert Barba and Colin Kellaher, "Express to Close 100 Stores By 2022," *The Wall Street Journal*, January 28, 2020, p. B3.

9. Quoted in Georgie Silvarole, "Billionaire Tom Golisano Opens Up about New Book, Greenlight Investment and 'no regrets'," *Democrat and Chronicle*, February 23, 2020, p. 12A.

10. Anne Tergesen, "The Ins and Outs of Cash Flow," *BusinessWeek*, January 22, 2001.

11. Steven D. Jones, "Firms Ponder What Constitutes Cash," *The Wall Street Journal*, July 27, 2006, p. C3.

12. Charley Grant, "GE's Light Bulb Finally Goes On," *The Wall Street Journal*, November 14, 2017, p. B11.

13. Brian Hindo, "Everything Old is New Again," *BusinessWeek*, September 25, 2006, p. 65.

14. J. Lynn Lunsford, "Engine Washing Cuts Airline Fuel Costs," *The Wall Street Journal*, June 11, 2008, p. B1.

15. Zirui Song and Katherine Baicker, "Effects of a Workplace Wellness Program on Employee Health and Economic Outcomes," *Journal of the American Medical Association*, April 16, 2019, pp. 1491–1501.

16. Timothy Aeppl and Justin Lahart, "Lean Factories Find It Hard to Cut Jobs Even in a Slump," *The Wall Street Journal*, March 9, 2009, p. A1; "Parker-Hannifin (PH): 59 Straight Dividend Increases and Plenty of Runaway Growth," *Simply Safe Dividends*, Copyright © 2016 Simply Safe Dividends, p. 4.

17. Shawn Tully, "Kraft-Heinz: A Cautionary Tale," *Fortune*, April 1, 2019, p. 10; Craig Giammonna and Katherine Chiglinsky, "3G Capital Gets Indigestion," *Bloomberg Businessweek*, March 4, 2019, pp. 28–29.

18. "Work Place Notices: New Corporate Cost-Cutting Policy," *http://www.home.att.net/~angryoldman*. Accessed January 14, 2007.

19. Robert S. Kaplan and David P. Norton, "Using the Balanced Scorecard as a Strategic Management System," *Harvard Business Review*, January–February 1996, pp. 75–77; "Balanced Scorecard Example," *Intrafocus* (www.intraficus.com), June 9, 2016, pp. 1-4.

20. Kaplan, Norton, and Bjarne Rugelsjoen, "Managing Alliances with the Balanced Scoreboard," *Harvard Business Review*, January–February 2010, pp. 114–120.

21. Andrew Likierman, "The Five Traps of Performance Measurement," *Harvard Business Review*, October 2009, p. 98.

22. "What Is Employee Monitoring?" *Hubstaff* (www.hubstaff.cim), copyright © 2020, p. 1.

23. Robert Strohmeyer, "How to Monitor Your Employees' PCs Without Going Too Far," *PC World*, pp. 1–4. Accessed March 10, 2016.

24. The information about JetBlue and the few preceding statements are from Riva Richmond, "It's 10 a.m. Do You Know Where Your Workers Are?", *The Wall Street Journal*, January 12, 2004, pp. R1, R4; "A Day in the Life of Customer Support," (*http://blog.jetblue.com*), 2016, pp. 1–7.

25. Amanda C. Cooser, "On Watch," *Entrepreneur*, September 8, 2008, p. 31.

26. Dionne Searcey, "Employers Watching Workers Online Spurs Privacy Debate," *The Wall Street Journal*, April 27, 2009, p. A13.

27. "Computer-Based Monitoring System," *The IT Law Wiki* (www.itlaw.wikia.org), copyright © 2020, Fandom Inc., p. 1.

28. Gary S. Millefsky, "Employee Monitoring Facts Every CIO Should Know," *www.SearchCIO.com*, July 2006, p. 3; "Computer-Based Monitoring System," p. 2.

29. Clayton M. Christensen, Stephen P. Kaufman, and Wily C. Shih, "Innovation Killers: How Financial Tools Destroy Your Capacity to Do New Things," *Harvard Business Review*, January 2008, pp. 98–105.

CHAPTER 15

Managing Substandard Performers

OBJECTIVES

After studying this chapter and doing the exercises, you should be able to:

1 Identify factors contributing to poor performance.

2 Describe the control model for managing ineffective performers.

3 Know what is required to coach and constructively criticize employees.

4 Understand how to discipline employees.

5 Develop an approach for dealing with difficult people, including cynics.

6 Explain the recommended approach to terminating employees.

Plante Moran, based in Southfield, Michigan, is among the largest public accounting and management consulting firms in the United States, with over 6,300 employees domestically and internationally. For 22 consecutive years the firm has been recognized as one of the country's "100 Best companies to Work For" by FORTUNE magazine. The company believes that it provides an exceptional opportunity and organizational culture for talented and motivated individuals who have a passion to serve and a hunger to thrive. Company leadership emphasizes that Plante Moran lives each day by the Golden Rule, where its, "relatively jerk-free policy" provides the firm with a unique opportunity for teamwork, caring, and an exceptional culture. (A "jerk" defined as a person who makes life difficult for others, often by being obstinate, inflexible, and insensitive to their needs.) The "jerk-free" work environment is part of a commitment to excellence.

The career website, Vault.com, ranked Plante Moran the top firm in six quality-of-life categories; business outlook, culture, company leadership, informal training, internal mobility, and promotion policies. Gordon Krater, the managing partner, said the key to Plante Moran's culture is hiring the right kind of people. "We are relatively jerk-free," he said, "If you act like a jerk, there is no room for you here."

Another large accounting firm, the Bonadio Group, has adopted the Plante Moran idea of keeping the workplace free of annoying workers. Founder and CEO Thomas F. Bonadio said that when his company has a jerk, it gets rid of that person, even if he or she is productive. "I don't care who they are—partner or receptionist."[1]

The initiative taken by these two accounting firms to keep difficult people out of the firm points to another important part of a manager's job—minimizing the potential negative influence of some workers. In addition to dealing with "office jerks," managers have to deal with a variety of workers who perform below expectations.

Managerial control requires dealing constructively with **ineffective job performance,** defined as performance that does not meet standards for the position. Ineffective performers are also referred to as problem employees because they create problems for management. Management consultant, Ron Ashkenas reinforces the importance of improving ineffective job performance in these words: "As a manager your primary responsibility is to the organization and the achievement of its performance targets." He also notes that a manager's success depends on the success of team members.[2]

Ineffective performers lower organizational performance directly by not accomplishing their fair share of work. They also lower organizational productivity indirectly. Poor performers decrease the productivity of their superiors by consuming excessive managerial time. Additionally, the productivity of co-workers is often decreased because co-workers must take over some of the ineffective performer's tasks. In this chapter we address ineffective performance as a control problem for which the manager can take corrective actions.

ineffective job performance
Job performance that lowers productivity below an acceptable standard.

LEARNING OBJECTIVE **1**

Identify factors contributing to poor performance.

FACTORS CONTRIBUTING TO INEFFECTIVE PERFORMANCE

Employees are, or become ineffective performers for many different reasons. The cause of poor performance can be rooted in the person, the job, the manager, or the organization. At times, the employee's personal traits and behaviors create so much disturbance that he or she is perceived as ineffective. Performance is sometimes classified as ineffective, or substandard, because of an arbitrary standard set by management, such as being in the bottom 10 percent of workers.

Figure 15-1 lists a variety of factors that can contribute to ineffective performance, divided into four categories: related to the employee, the job, the manager, or the organization. Usually, the true cause of ineffective performance is not a single issue, but a combination of several factors. Assume an employee is late for work so frequently that his or her performance becomes substandard. The contributing factors in this situation could be the worker's disrespect for work rules, an unchallenging job, or an unduly harsh supervisor. One factor may be more important than others, but they are all contributors.

The following list expands on how the factors listed in Figure 15-1 are related to ineffective performance:

The Employee

- *Insufficient problem-solving ability and education.* The employee lacks the problem-solving ability necessary to do the job, such as not being able to understand the software used to run a machine. Poor communication skills are included here, such as the inability to listen carefully to instructions or speak clearly to customers and co-workers. Insufficient mental ability and education of the available U.S. workforce for basic jobs has become a major challenge for managers.

- *Insufficient job knowledge.* The employee is a substandard performer because he or she comes to the job with insufficient training or experience. The employee

Figure 15-1 Factors Contributing to Ineffective Performance

Dozens of factors can lower job performance. The factors listed contribute to the majority of ineffective performance.

Factors Related to the Employee
- Insufficient problem-solving ability and education
- Insufficient job knowledge
- Poor fit between vocational interests and the demands of the position.
- Job stress and burnout
- Low motivation and loafing
- Excessive absenteeism and tardiness
- Emotional problem or personality disorder
- Alcoholism and drug addiction
- Tobacco addiction or withdrawal symptoms
- Conducting outside business on the job
- Family, personal, and financial problems
- Physical limitations
- Preoccupying office romance
- Fear of traveling
- Poor organizational citizenship behavior

Factors Related to the Job
- Ergonomics problems and repetitive motion disorder
- Repetitive, physically demanding job, including heavy travel
- Built-in conflict
- Night-shift work assignments
- Substandard industrial hygiene

Factors Related to the Manager
- Inadequate communication about job responsibilities
- Inadequate feedback about job performance
- Inappropriate leadership style
- Negative and untrusting attitude
- Abusive supervision

Factors Related to the Organization
- Organizational culture that tolerates poor performance
- Poor ethical climate
- Counterproductive work environment
- Negative work group influences
- Violence or threats of violence
- Sexual harassment
- Workplace harassment in general
- A compensation/reward structure that encourages deviant
- behavior
- Unrealistically performance standards for positions throughout the organization

might be smart enough to learn but lacks the skills to perform the job today. Insufficient job knowledge includes technological obsolescence in which the employee does not keep up with the state of the art in his or her field. He or she avoids using new ideas and techniques and becomes ineffective.

- *Poor fit between vocational interests and the demands of the position.* Research has reinforced the traditional idea that when a worker's vocational interests fit the position the worker performs better. When there is a poor fit, the worker is more likely to perform poorly.[3] For example, a worker with strong interests in working with people, but spends almost the entire day staring at a computer screen might perform poorly.

- *Job stress and burnout.* Severe, short-term stress leads to errors in concentration and judgment. As a result of prolonged job stress, an employee may become apathetic, negative, and impatient. He or she can no longer generate the energy to perform effectively.

- *Low motivation and loafing.* An employee who is poorly motivated will often not make the effort to accomplish the amount of work required to meet standards. Closely related to low motivation is goofing off and loafing. Many employees spend too much time surfing the Internet or engaging in some other diversionary activity, such as making personal phone calls and running personal errands during working hours.

- *Excessive absenteeism and tardiness.* The employee is often not at work for a variety of personal or health reasons. Productivity, deadlines, and morale may suffer by increasing workloads, hiring replacements, and causing overtime.[4]

- *Emotional problem or personality disorder.* The employee may have emotional outbursts, periods of depression, or other abnormal behaviors that interfere with human relationships and work concentration. A Gallup study indicated that about 12 percent of full-time American workers have been diagnosed with depression at some point in their careers.[5] Even without a certifiable emotional problem, workers experiencing strongly negative emotions, such as anger, may become counterproductive.[6] Cynical behavior may lower the performance of an entire work group if the negative attitude spreads to others.

- *Alcoholism and drug addiction.* The employee cannot think clearly because his or her mental or physical condition has been temporarily or permanently impaired by alcohol or other drugs. Attendance is also likely to suffer. A national U.S. survey indicated that approximately 6.5 percent of the working population are heavy drinkers. The survey also found that 3.1 percent of employed adults use illicit drugs on the job and 9.2 percent of workforce members are illicit drug users off the job.[7] Opioid addiction is another threat to adequate job performance because it can negatively affect productivity and absenteeism.[8] Managers must be aware that not every drug user is impaired as many workers develop tolerance to drugs, including prescription drugs.

- *Tobacco addiction or withdrawal symptoms.* The employee who smokes is often fatigued and takes so many cigarette breaks that his or her work is disrupted. Sick leave may also increase. Even workers who stop smoking may suffer performance problems for a while. However, as smokers drop the habit, they may become more productive.

- *Conducting outside business on the job.* The employee may be an "office entrepreneur" who sells merchandise to co-workers or spends time on the phone, e-mail, and social media working on investments or other outside interests. Operating an eBay business or other online auction site during working hours is a notable distraction. Time spent on these activities lowers productivity.

- *Family, personal, and financial problems.* The employee is unable to work at full capacity because of preoccupation with an off-the-job problem, such as a marital dispute, conflict with children, a broken romance, or indebtedness.

- *Physical limitations.* Job performance decreases as a result of injury or illness. For example, according to the American Council on Exercise, low-back pain is a leading cause of job-related disability and absenteeism in the United States.[9] Many problems of physical limitations are self-imposed such as obesity or high blood pressure due to limited physical exercise and poor eating habits.

- *Preoccupying office romance.* For many people, a new romance is an energizing force that creates positive stress, resulting in a surge in energy directed toward work. For others, an office romance becomes a preoccupation that detracts from concentration. Time spent together in conversation and long lunch breaks can lower productivity.

- *Fear of traveling, especially flying.* In an era of worldwide terrorism, some employees refuse to travel for business, particularly by airplane, because of their perception of the potential danger. Others are hesitant to visit tall office towers. During a disease epidemic some workers refuse to travel out of fear of catching germs. Yet to meet the full requirements of the job, many employees are required to visit remote locations.

- *Poor organizational citizenship behavior.* A subtle cause of low performance is that some employees will not inconvenience themselves to provide assistance not strictly related to their job descriptions. As such, they are poor organizational citizens. **Organizational citizenship behavior** is employee behavior that is discretionary and typically not recognized or rewarded but helps the organization. A small example would be taking it on your own to repair a broken chair that might create an accident. An analysis of 49 different groups found that workers low on organizational citizenship behavior were more likely to engage in counterproductive workplace behaviors.[10] The latter include any activities that harm the organization, such as wasting resources and stealing money.

organizational citizenship behavior
Employee behavior that is discretionary and typically not recognized or rewarded but nevertheless helps the organization.

The Job

- *Ergonomics problems and repetitive motion disorder.* If equipment or furniture used on the job contributes to fatigue, discomfort, or injury, performance problems result. For example, if an employee develops neck pain and eyestrain from working at a poorly designed computer configuration, performance will suffer. As described in Chapter 7 about job design, repetitive motion disorder, including carpal tunnel syndrome is a major problem stemming from poorly designed or poorly utilized computer equipment.

- *Repetitive, physically demanding job.* A repetitive, physically demanding job can cause the employee to become bored and fatigued, leading to lower performance. Many workers report feeling burned out from working for package-delivery services because of the constant heavy physical demands and pressure to stay on schedule; leading to mental stress. The problem has become more acute as online shopping increases, particularly during the holiday season.

- *Built-in conflict.* The nature of the job involves so much conflict that job stress lowers performance. The position of collection agent for a consumer-loan company might fit this category. So would a telemarketer who receives a high percentage of rejections, including rudeness and slammed-down telephone receivers.

- *Night shift work assignments.* Employees assigned to all night shifts suffer many more mental lapses and productivity losses than those assigned to daytime or evening shifts. A major problem is that night shift work interrupts the natural rhythms of the body.

- *Substandard industrial hygiene.* Excessive noise, fumes, uncomfortable temperatures, inadequate lighting, high humidity, and fear of injury or contamination engender poor performance.

The Manager

- *Inadequate communication about job responsibilities.* The employee performs poorly because he or she lacks a clear picture of what the manager expects. For example, a worker might spend the entire day defragging the hard drive on her desktop computer because the manager did not explain that he really wanted her to consolidate the accounts of a few suppliers. As a result, the worker is accused of wasting time.

- *Inadequate feedback about job performance.* The employee makes a large number of errors because he or she does not receive the feedback—early enough or at all—to prevent them.

- *Inappropriate leadership style.* The employee performs poorly because the manager's leadership style is inappropriate to the employee's needs. For example, an immature employee's manager gives him or her too much freedom and little direction; the result is poor performance. This employee needs closer supervision.

- *Negative and untrusting attitude.* Some managers believe employees cannot be trusted to behave ethically or in the best interest of the company. As a result, these managers will often exert too much control, leading some employees to retaliate by such means as personally slowing down production. Also, when managers expect the worse from employees, they can often live down to the manager's expectations.[11]

- *Abusive supervision.* As perceived by subordinates, abusive supervisors engage in hostile verbal and nonverbal behaviors excluding physical contact. Such hostile behaviors include temper tantrums, public criticisms, and unwarranted blame.[12] Furthermore, many employees perceive that they are intimidated and bullied by their managers to the point that they cannot work effectively. Bullying and intimidation go far beyond being firm and setting high standards. They include such behaviors as publicly insulting group members, frequent yelling, and showing insensitivity toward personal requests, such as time off to handle a severe personal problem.

The Organization

- *Organizational culture that tolerates poor performance.* An organization culture that has low expectations from workers creates an atmosphere conducive to substandard performance. A closely related problem is when an organization has a history of not imposing sanctions on employees who perform poorly. When managers clearly articulate better performance, many employees may not respond to the new challenge.

- *Poor ethical climate.* An unethical climate sets the tone for employees to engage in deviant behavior that can produce poor performance, as suggested by a study of working business graduates. Among these behaviors are attending to personal matters during work time, and intentionally slowing down the work pace.[13]

- *Counterproductive work environment.* The employee lacks the proper tools, support, budget, or authority to accomplish the job. An example would be a telecommuter whose company-provided computer is plagued with viruses, and the company hesitates to take care of the problem.

- *Negative work group influences.* Group pressures restrain good performance or the work group penalizes a high-performance worker. Similarly, peer-group social pressure may cause an employee to take overly long lunch breaks, neglecting job responsibilities. A study conducted in 20 organizations showed that antisocial behaviors, such as lying, spreading rumors, loafing, and absenteeism were more frequent when co-workers exhibited the same behavior.[14]

- *Violence or the threat of violence.* Employees witness violent behavior in the workplace, such as physical assaults, knifings, shootings, or threats of violence. Even employees not directly affected are nevertheless distracted and fearful, leading to lowered productivity.

- *Sexual harassment.* The employee who is sexually harassed usually experiences enough stress to decrease concentration and performance in general. Both men and women are sexually harassed. Textual harassment is a new form of sexual harassment that consists of inappropriate, and sexually toned, text messages on the job.[15] In situations where the manager is the harasser, resentment toward the manager may lead to lowered performance. The person who commits sexual harassment and is under investigation for or charged with the act is likely to experience stress and preoccupation about the charges.

- *Workplace harassment in general.* A continuing problem in the workplace is that people are harassed, or verbally and physically attacked because of their membership in a group, such as being black, female, Latino, gay, trans-sexual, young, or old. Workplace harassment is distinct from sexual harassment because the bothersome behavior is not sexually toned. All types of harassment can lower job performance because the harassed worker might become overly stressed and distracted. Two studies showed that when workers are subject to more than one form of harassment, such as gender and age, the negative effects on well-being are even stronger.[16]

- *A compensation/reward structure that encourages deviant behavior.* A compensation/reward structure, similar to an ineffective control standard, might encourage workers to perform in counterproductive ways. Too much of compensation based on commissions might encourage some sales workers to engage in counterproductive practices. Studies of sales representatives in a variety of industries whose income was over 80 percent based on commissions found evidence of workplace deviance, including undercharging for services, lying about meeting quotas, and padding expense accounts. For example, automobile service technicians who work on commission might be encouraged to recommend unnecessary repairs ultimately leading to a poor reputation for the service center.[17]

You are invited to take the self-quiz in Figure 15-2 to ponder tendencies of your own that could ultimately contribute to substandard performance. Many sports figures, elected officials, and business executives experience the problems pinpointed in this questionnaire.

THE CONTROL MODEL FOR MANAGING INEFFECTIVE PERFORMERS

LEARNING OBJECTIVE 2

Describe the control model for managing ineffective performers.

The approach to improving ineffective performance presented here follows the logic of the control process shown in Figure 14-2. Problem identification and problem solving lie at the core of this approach. The control process for managing ineffective performers is divided into the eight steps illustrated in Figure 15-3, and should usually be followed in sequence. This section will describe each of these steps in detail. Another key method of improving ineffective performance—employee discipline—receives separate attention later in the chapter.

Figure 15-2 The Self-Sabotage Questionnaire

Directions: Indicate how accurately each of the following statements describes or characterizes you, using a five-point scale: (0) very inaccurately, (1) inaccurately, (2) midway between inaccurately and accurately, (3) accurately, (4) very accurately. Consider discussing some of the questions with a family member, close friend, or work associate. Another person's feedback may prove helpful in providing accurate answers to some of the questions.

1 Other people have said that I am my own worst enemy. _____
2 If I don't do a perfect job, I feel worthless. _____
3 I am my own harshest critic. _____
4 When engaged in a sport or other competitive activity, I find a way to blow a substantial lead right near the end. _____
5 When I make a mistake, I can usually identify another person to blame. _____
6 I have a strong tendency to procrastinate. _____
7 I have trouble focusing on what is really important to me. _____
8 I have trouble taking criticism, even from friends. _____
9 My fear of seeming stupid often prevents me from asking questions or offering my opinion. _____
10 I tend to expect the worst in most situations. _____
11 Many times I have rejected people who treat me well. _____
12 When I have an important project to complete, I usually get sidetracked and then miss the deadline. _____
13 I choose work assignments that lead to disappointments even when better options are clearly available. _____
14 I frequently misplace things such as my keys and then get very angry at myself. _____
15 I am concerned that if I take on much more responsibility, people will expect too much from me. _____
16 I avoid situations, such as competitive sports, where people can find out how good or bad I really am. _____
17 People describe me as the "office (or class) clown." _____
18 I have an insatiable demand for money and power. _____
19 When negotiating with others, I hate to grant any concessions. _____
20 I seek revenge for even the smallest hurts. _____
21 I have a giant-size ego. _____
22 When I receive a compliment or other form of recognition, I usually feel I don't deserve it. _____
23 To be honest, I choose to suffer. _____
24 I regularly enter into conflict with people who try to help me. _____
25 I'm a loser. _____

Total Score _____

Scoring and Interpretation: Add your answers to all the questions to obtain your total score. Your total score provides an approximate index of your tendencies toward being self-sabotaging or self-defeating.

0–25   You appear to have few tendencies toward self-sabotage. If this interpretation is supported by your own positive feelings toward your life and yourself, you are in good shape with respect to self-defeating behavior tendencies. However, stay alert to potential self-sabotaging tendencies that could develop at later stages in your career.

26–50   You may have some mild tendencies toward self-sabotage. It could be that you do things occasionally that defeat your own purposes. A person in this category, for example, might write an angry e-mail memo to an executive, expressing disagreement with a decision that adversely affects his or her operation. Review actions you have taken during the past six months to decide if any of them have been self-sabotaging.

51–75   You show signs of engaging in self-sabotage. You probably have thoughts, and carry out actions, that could be blocking you from achieving important work and personal goals. People whose scores place them in this category characteristically engage in negative self-talk that lowers their self-confidence and makes them appear weak and indecisive to others. For example, "I'm usually not good at learning new things." People in this range frequently experience another problem. They sometimes sabotage their chances of succeeding on a project just to prove that their negative self-assessment is correct.

76–100 You most likely have a strong tendency toward self-sabotage. (Sometimes it is possible to obtain a high score on a test like this because you are going through an unusually stressful period in your life.) You might discuss your tendencies toward undermining your own achievements with a mental health professional.

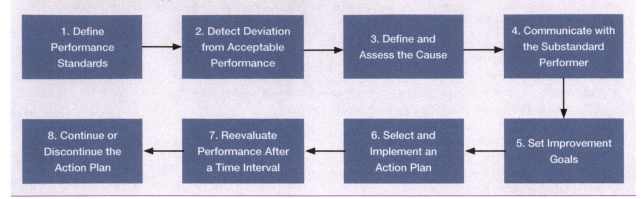

Figure 15-3 The Control Model for Managing Ineffective Performers

The most systematic and effective method for bringing ineffective performance up to standard is to follow the control process, referred to in this application as the control model.

1. Define Performance Standards → 2. Detect Deviation from Acceptable Performance → 3. Define and Assess the Cause → 4. Communicate with the Substandard Performer

8. Continue or Discontinue the Action Plan ← 7. Reevaluate Performance After a Time Interval ← 6. Select and Implement an Action Plan ← 5. Set Improvement Goals

Two cautions are in order when using the control model for improving ineffective performance. First, the model may need slight modification to follow company procedures. Company policy, for example, might establish certain procedures about documenting poor performance and reporting it immediately to higher levels of management. Second, the control process is not designed to deal with mental illness. An employee who suddenly begins to neglect the job because of a sudden change in personality should be referred immediately to a human resource specialist. The specialist, in turn, will make an appropriate referral to a mental health professional.

Define Performance Standards

Penalizing employees for not achieving performance standards without first carefully communicating those standards is unfair. Therefore, the first step in the control model for managing ineffective performers is to clearly define what is expected of employees. Performance standards are commonly established through job descriptions, work goals, production quotas, and formal discussions of what is to be accomplished in a position.

Detect Deviation from Acceptable Performance

Detection is the process of noting when an employee's performance deviates from an acceptable standard. Managers use the various control measures described in Chapter 14 to detect deviations from acceptable performance. For performance to be considered ineffective or poor, it must deviate significantly from the norm.

At times, quantitative measures can be used to define ineffective performance. For some jobs, ineffective performance might begin at 30 percent below standard. For other jobs, the cutoff point could be 20 or 50 percent, or any other percentage of deviation that fits the situation. What percentage of deviation from standard do you think would be acceptable for a commercial airline pilot? For a bank teller?

Personal observation plays a key role in detecting ineffective performance. One reason that observation is so important is that it is a concurrent control. By the time quantitative indicators of poor performance have been collected, substantial damage may have been done. Assume a bank manager observes that one of the mortgage loan officers is taking unduly long lunch hours on Fridays. Upon return, the officer appears to be under the influence of alcohol. Eventually, this unacceptable behavior will show up in quantitative indicators of performance. However, it might take a year to collect these data.

An important caution about observing substandard performance or counterproductive behavior is that it can often go undetected by the supervisor or co-workers. It is therefore important for the supervisor to make frequent observations to accurately detect problems. A study found that many counterproductive work behaviors go undetected by supervisors and co-workers. The least likely to be observed were "spends too much time fantasizing or daydreaming instead of working" and "discussed confidential company information with an unauthorized person. More observable behaviors were "cursed someone at work" and "acted rudely toward someone at work."[18]

Define and Assess the Cause

At this stage, the manager attempts to diagnose the real cause of the problem. Following the logic of Figure 15-1, the primary contributor to the problem could be a personal factor or a factor related to the job, the manager, or the organization. A discussion with the employee (the next step in the control model) may be necessary to reveal the major cause of the problem. For example, an office assistant was absent so frequently that her performance suffered. She claimed that photocopying made her sick. The supervisor investigated further and called in the company health and safety expert. A medical examination confirmed that the office assistant was allergic to the trace fumes from the toner in the large-volume photocopier. After the office assistant was reassigned, her attendance became satisfactory.

Communicate with the Substandard Performer

After detecting unacceptable performance or behavior, the manager must communicate concern to the worker. At times, a simple discussion will suffice. At other times, a more sensitive form of feedback may be necessary. **Confrontation** means dealing with a controversial or emotional topic directly. Confrontation is necessary whenever the employee does not readily admit to experiencing a problem.

confrontation
Dealing with a controversial or emotional topic directly.

Managers often avoid confrontation for several reasons. They may have limited skill in criticizing employees. Or, they may prefer not to deal with the anger and resentment that confrontation is likely to trigger. A third reason is the manager not wanting to make the employee feel uncomfortable. Another concern about confrontation is that the rights of the employee might be violated if he or she is suffering from a problem covered by the Americans with Disabilities Act, such as alcoholism. Some employees have claimed their poor performance could be attributed to Internet addiction disorder.[19] In reality, the law allows employers to confront employees with disabilities, and to hold those, in the case with an alcohol problem, to the same performance standards of other employees.[20]

A recommended confrontation technique is to communicate an attitude of concern about the confronted person's welfare. To use this technique, confront the person in a sincere and thoughtful manner. Using the words *care* and *concern* can be helpful. For instance, a manager might begin by saying: "The reason I'm bringing up this problem is that I care about your work. You have a good record with the company, and I'm concerned that your performance has slipped way below its former level."

Set Improvement Goals

The fifth step in the control model is to set improvement goals. An **improvement goal** is one that, if attained, will correct an unacceptable deviation from a performance standard. The goals should be documented on paper or electronically. Improvement goals should have the same characteristics as other objectives (see Chapter 4). Above all, improvement goals should specify the behavior or result that is required. Vague improvement goals are not likely to cause changes in performance.

An example of a specific improvement goal is, "During this month, nine of your 10 customer service reports must be in on time." This specific goal is likely to be more effective than a general improvement goal, such as, "become more prompt in submitting customer service reports."

If the ineffective performer expresses an interest in improvement, joint goal-setting is advisable. By providing input into goal-setting, the substandard performer stands a good chance of becoming committed to improvement. At times, managers need to impose improvement goals on substandard performers, especially in cases involving a motivation problem. If substandard employees were interested in setting improvement goals, they would not have a motivation problem.

improvement goal
A goal that, if attained, will correct an unacceptable deviation from a performance standard.

Select and Implement an Action Plan

The setting of improvement goals leads logically to the selection and implementation of action plans to attain those goals. Much of the art of remedying ineffective performance is contained in this step. Unless appropriate action plans are developed, no real improvement is likely to take place. Many attempts at improving substandard performance fail because the problem is discussed and then dropped. Thus, the employee has no concrete method of making the necessary improvements.

Types of Action Plans

An action plan for improvement can include almost any sensible approach tailored to the specific problem. An action plan could be formulated to deal with every cause of ineffective performance listed in Figure 15-1.

Action plans for improving ineffective performance can be divided into two types. One type is within the power of the manager to develop and implement the action plan. Plans of this type include coaching, encouraging, and offering small incentives for improvement. The second type of action plan is offered by the organization or outsourced. These include training programs, stress-management programs, or stays at alcoholism-treatment centers. Figure 15-4 lists a selection of feasible corrective actions.

When attempting to improve ineffective performance resulting from a variety of personal problems, the preferred action plan for many managers is to refer the troubled worker to an **employee assistance program (EAP)**. The EAP is an organization-sponsored service to help employees deal with personal and job-related problems that interfere with job performance. Professionals who specialize in dealing with particular problems staff an employee assistance program. Many companies that do not have an EAP of their own refer employees to such a program that serves firms in the area. Employee assistance programs offer extensive services to employees.

employee assistance program (EAP)
An organization-sponsored service to help employees deal with personal and job-related problems that hinder performance.

Figure 15-4 Corrective Actions for Ineffective Performers

When attempting to bring ineffective performers up to standard or beyond, managers can either take action by themselves or refer employees to a company program designed to help them with performance problems.

Managerial Actions and Techniques

- **Coaching.** The manager points out specifically what the performer could be doing better or should stop doing. In daily interaction with the team members, the manager makes suggestions for improvement. Coaching is the most widely used technique for performance improvement.

- **Closer supervision.** The manager works more closely with the subordinate, offering frequent guidance and feedback.

- **Reassignment or transfer.** The manager reassigns the ineffective performer to a position that he or she can handle better. Another approach is to assign a low-performing worker to a group of high-performing workers. Quite often the low performer will rise to the expectations of the high-performing environment. Also, the former low performer will recognize that the group needs him or her to perform well.[21]

- **Motivational techniques.** The manager attempts to improve employee motivation by using positive reinforcement or some other motivational technique.

- **Corrective discipline.** The manager informs the employee that his or her behavior is unacceptable and that corrections must be made if the worker is to remain employed by the firm. The employee is counseled as part of corrective discipline.

- **Lower performance standards.** If performance standards have been too high, the manager lowers expectations of the team member. Consultation with higher management would probably be necessary before implementing this step.

- **Job rotation.** If ineffective performance results from staleness or burnout, changing to a different job of comparable responsibility may prove helpful.

Organizational Programs

- **Wellness programs.** The organization encourages employees to participate in specialized programs that help them stay physically and mentally healthy. Physical exercise and nutrition instruction are typically included. By focusing on wellness, employees may prevent or cope with health problems—such as heart disease or an eating disorder—that interfere with job performance or lead to absenteeism. The wellness program usually includes stress management.

- **Career counseling and outplacement.** The employee receives professional assistance in solving a career problem, including being counseled on finding a job outside the firm.

- **Job redesign.** Specialists in human resource management and industrial engineering redesign job elements that could be causing poor performance. For example, the job is changed so that the employee has less direct contact with others, leading to reduced conflict.

- **Training and development programs.** The employee is assigned to a training or development program linked directly to his or her performance deficiency. For example, a reserved sales representative might receive assertiveness training.

- **Executive or personal coaching.** The company hires a personal coach who helps the professional or managerial worker with such problems as poor interpersonal relationships, resolving conflict, and ineffective approach to problem solving.

- **Anger-management programs.** The company sends a worker whose anger results in poor performance to an anger-management workshop, where the worker learn how to control anger and express it in constructive ways. The problem is that anger creates a less cohesive workplace and damages morale. Anger also interferes with focused attention, therefore impairing judgment and decreasing reaction time.[22]

For example, three of the services offered by the EAP that are associated with Federal Occupational Health are as follows:

- Seven-day, 24-hour telephone access for employees and family members to professional counselors for assessment, consultation, referral, and crisis management.

- Professional assessment of issues related to mental health, substance abuse, and other workplace or challenges in living.

- Face-to-face, short-term focused counseling for individuals, couples, and families.[23]

Employees and their families use assistance programs to cope with a variety of personal and family problems and illnesses. Among them are alcoholism and other substance abuse, financial and legal difficulties, emotional problems, chronic illness, such as AIDS or cancer, compulsive gambling, and weight control. Employees also use EAPs to deal with job-related concerns, such as work stress, chronic job dissatisfaction, and sexual harassment.

When supervisors refer employees to the EAP, workplace problems should be the focus. The manager should be aware that some employees may feel embarrassed about visiting an EAP. It is therefore important for the manager to destigmatize the EAP and mention that anyone can benefit from this type of service.[24] The supervisor should not say, "I am encouraging you to go to the EAP. The EAP can help you with any personal problems you may have." Say instead, "I encourage you to go to the EAP. The EAP may be able to help you solve your workplace problems."[25] The second approach usually creates less defensiveness than the first.

Implementation of the Action Plan

After the action plan is chosen, it must be implemented. As shown in Figure 15-3, implementation begins in Step 6 and continues through Step 8. The manager utilizes the approaches listed under "Managerial Actions and Techniques" in Figure 15-4. Human resources specialists outside the manager's department usually implement organizational programs.

An important part of effective implementation is continuation of the remedial program. Given the many pressures facing a manager, it is easy to forget the substandard performer who needs close supervision or a motivational boost. Often, a brief conversation is all that is needed.

Reevaluate Performance After a Time Interval

Step seven in the controlling process helps ensure the process is working. In this step the manager measures the employee's current performance. If the remedial process is working, the team member's performance will move up toward standard. The greater the performance problem, the more frequent the reevaluations of performance should be. In instances of behavior problems, such as alcoholism, weekly performance checks are advisable.

Formal and Informal Reviews

A reevaluation of performance can be formal or informal. A formal progress review takes the form of a performance-evaluation session. It might include written documentation of the employee's progress and samples of his or her work. Formal reviews are particularly important when the employee has been advised that a dismissal review is pending unless improvements are made. Reviews are critical to avoid lawsuits over a dismissal.

The first level of informal review consists of checking on whether the employee has started the action plan. For example, suppose a reserved sales representative agreed to attend an assertiveness-training program. One week later, the manager could ask the rep, "Have you signed up for or started the training program yet?" The next level of informal review is a discussion of the employee's progress. The manager can ask casual questions such as, "How much progress have you made in accounting for the missing inventory?"

Positive Reinforcement and Punishment

If the employee makes progress toward reaching the improvement goal, positive reinforcement is appropriate. Rewarding an employee for progress is the most effective way of sustaining that progress. The reward might be praise, encouragement, or longer intervals between review sessions. The longer time between reviews may be rewarding because the employee will feel that he or she is, "back to normal."

Giving rewards for improving generally proves more effective than punishing an employee for not making improvement. Yet if the problem employee does not respond to positive motivators, some form of organizational punishment is necessary. More will be said about punishment in the discussion about employee discipline.

Continue or Discontinue the Action Plan

Step eight in the control model for managing ineffective performers is deciding whether to continue or discontinue the action plan. This step can be considered the feedback component of the control process. If the performance review indicates the employee is not meeting improvement goals, the action plan is continued. If the review indicates goal achievement, the action plan is discontinued and documented.

An important part of using the control model to manage ineffective performers is realizing that positive changes may not be permanent. Performance is most likely to revert to an unacceptable level when the employee is faced with heavy job pressures. For instance, suppose an employee and a manager formulated an action plan to improve the employee's work habits. The employee's performance improved as a result. When the employee is under pressure, however, his or her work may once again become badly disorganized. The manager should then repeat the last five steps of the process, beginning with confrontation.

LEARNING OBJECTIVE **3**

Know what is required to coach and constructively criticize employees.

coaching
A method for helping employees perform better, which usually occurs on the spot and involves informal discussion and suggestions.

constructive criticism
A form of criticism designed to help improve performance or behavior.

COACHING AND CONSTRUCTIVE CRITICISM

Most performance improvement takes place as a result of a manager dealing directly with the worker not meeting standards. The usual vehicle for bringing about this improvement is **coaching**. It is a method for helping employees perform better, which usually occurs on the spot and involves informal discussion and suggestions. Workplace coaching is much like coaching on the athletic field or in the performing arts. Coaching involves considerable **constructive criticism**, a form of criticism designed to help improve performance. To be a good coach, and to criticize constructively, requires considerable skill.

Business psychologists James Waldroop and Timothy Butler point out that good coaching is simply good management. Coaching requires the same skills that contribute to effective management, such as keen observation skills, sound judgment, and an ability to take appropriate action. Coaching and effective management share the goal of making the most of human resources.[26] A key reason is that coaching unlocks a person's potential to elevate his or her performance. The following suggestions will help you improve your coaching skill if practiced carefully:

1 *Focus feedback on what is wrong with the work and behavior rather than the employee's attitude and personality.* When the feedback attacks a person's self-image, he or she is likely to become hostile. A defensive person is more likely to focus on getting even rather than getting better. Another way to upset the

person being coached is to exaggerate the nature of the poor performance, such as saying, "You've committed the same mistake 100 times," when you have only observed the mistake four times.

2 *Give on-the-spot positive feedback as warranted.* A recent synthesis of information about effective feedback suggests that performance is most likely to improve when team members are told what is working.[27] Assume that a marketing analyst is being coached by her manager about providing more depth to her reports about the appeal of certain products. When the manager receives a report that contains the depth he is seeking, the manager sends a text message to the analyst saying, "Nice work on the coco butter report. Just the depth I need."

3 *Be timely with negative feedback.* Negative feedback should be given close in time to the incident of poor performance. If you observe a worker being rude to a customer, do not wait until the annual performance evaluation to share your observation. Schedule a coaching session as soon as feasible. The worker might be rude to many more customers until he or she receives your criticism.

4 *Listen actively and empathize.* An essential component of coaching employees requires careful listening to both their presentation of facts and feelings. Your listening will encourage the employee to talk. As the employee talks about his or her problem, you may develop a better understanding of how to improve performance. As you listen actively, the opportunity to show empathy will arise naturally. Suppose the employee blames being behind schedule on the servers being down so frequently. You might show empathy by saying, "Yes, I know it is frustrating to have a computer crash when faced with a deadline. Yet we all have to deal with this problem."

5 *Ask good questions.* An effective workplace coach asks questions that help people understand their needs for improvement. Start the coaching session by asking a question, thereby encouraging the person being coached to be an active participant immediately. Consultant Marilyn J. Darling says that effective coaching is based on asking good questions. She notes that the simpler the question, the better (notice that the questions are open-ended, therefore encouraging conversation).

- What are you trying to accomplish?
- How will you know if you have succeeded?
- What obstacles do you believe are stopping you?
- How can I help you succeed?[28]

6 *Engage in joint problem solving.* Work together to resolve the performance problem. One reason joint problem solving is effective is that it conveys a helpful and constructive attitude on the part of the manager. Another is that the employee often needs the superior's assistance in overcoming work problems. The manager is in a better position to address certain problems than is the employee.

7 *Offer constructive advice.* Constructive advice can be useful to the employee with performance problems. A recommended way of giving advice is first to ask an insightful question. You might ask the employee, "Could the real cause of your problem be poor work habits?" If the employee agrees, you can then offer some specific advice about improving work habits. As part of giving advice,

it is more effective to suggest a person do something rather than try to do something. For example, it is more persuasive to say, "Be at our staff meetings on time," than to say, "Try to be at our staff meetings on time." "Trying" something gives a person an excuse not to succeed.

An especially effective aspect of constructive advice is to help the person who is performing poorly understand the link between the negative act and attaining key goals, such as increased revenue and productivity.[29] Suppose a store manager typically neglects to respond to questions asked by customers using the "Contact Us" function. His or her manager/coach might point out, "Customers who are ignored will soon ignore us, leading to the loss of some important customers, along with some important sales. We need every customer we can get or keep."

8. *Give the poor performer an opportunity to observe and model someone who exhibits acceptable performance.* A simple example of modeling would be for the manager to show the employee how to operate a piece of equipment properly. A more complex example of modeling would be to have the poor performer observe an effective employee making a sale or conducting a job interview. In each case, the ineffective performer should be given opportunities to repeat the activity.

9. *Obtain a commitment to change.* Ineffective performers frequently agree to make improvements but are not really committed to change. At the end of a session, discuss the employee's true interest in changing. One clue that commitment may be lacking is when the employee too readily accepts everything you say about the need for change. Another clue is agreement about the need for change but with no display of emotion. In either case, further discussion is warranted.

10. *When feasible, conduct some coaching sessions outside of the performance evaluation.* The coaching experience should focus on development and improvement, whereas the performance review is likely to be perceived by the ineffective performer as a time for judging his or her performance. Despite this perception, performance evaluations should include an aspect of development.

11. *Applaud good results.* Effective coaches on the playing field and in the workplace are cheerleaders. They give encouragement and positive reinforcement by applauding good results. Some effective coaches shout in joy when a poor performer achieves standard performance; others clap their hands in applause.

EMPLOYEE DISCIPLINE

LEARNING OBJECTIVE **4**

Understand how to discipline employees.

discipline
Punishment used to correct or train.

summary discipline
The immediate discharge of an employee because of a serious offense.

Up to this point, this chapter has emphasized positive approaches to improving substandard performance. At times, however, using the control model requires a manager to discipline employees in an attempt to keep performance at an acceptable level. It is also part of an effective manager's role to be willing to take harsh and unpopular action when the situation requires such behavior. **Discipline**, in a general sense, is punishment used to correct or train. In organizations, discipline can be divided into two types.

Summary discipline is the immediate discharge of an employee because of a serious offense. The employee is fired on the spot for rule violations, such as stealing, fighting, selling illegal drugs on company premises, or hacking into computer files.

In unionized firms, the company and the union have a written agreement specifying which offenses are subject to summary discipline.

Corrective discipline allows employees to rectify their behavior before punishment is applied. Employees are told their behavior is unacceptable and they must make corrections if they want to remain with the firm. The manager and the employee share the responsibility for solving the performance problem. The controlling process for managing ineffective performers includes corrective discipline. Steps 4 through 7 in Figure 15-3 are based on corrective discipline. Corrective discipline sometimes includes a written letter to an employee summarizing what has taken place so far. The letter is similar to the written warning aspect of progressive discipline (described in the following section) but the letter is less explicit about the consequences of no improvement by the employee.

Taking disciplinary action is often thought of in relation to lower-ranking employees. Managers, professionals, and other salaried employees, however, may also need to be disciplined, such as in backdating stock options for themselves and harassing employees.

The paragraphs that follow will describe three other aspects of discipline. First, we describe the most widely used type of corrective discipline—progressive discipline. Second, we explain the rules for applying discipline. Third, we examine the positive consequences of punishment to the organization.

corrective discipline
A type of discipline that allows employees to correct their behavior before punishment is applied.

Progressive Discipline

Progressive discipline is the step-by-step application of corrective discipline, as shown in Figure 15-5. Progressive discipline alerts the employee that a performance problem exists, such as not properly documenting claims on an expense report. The manager confronts and then coaches the poor performer about the performance problem. If the employee's performance does not improve, the employee is informed in writing that improvements must be made. The written warning contains more specific information than the oral warning. Some of this specific information might be documentation of the problem. The written notice often includes a clear statement of what will happen if performance does not improve. The "or else" could be a disciplinary layoff or suspension. If the notice is ignored and the disciplinary action does not lead to improvement, the employee may be discharged.

Progressive discipline, an old concept, continues to be widely used for two key reasons. First, it provides the documentation necessary to avoid legal liability for firing poorly performing employees. Second, many labor-management agreements require progressive discipline because of the inherent fairness of the step-by-step procedure. Employees are not harshly punished for first offenses that fall outside the realm of summary discipline.

progressive discipline
The step-by-step application of corrective discipline.

Rules for Applying Discipline

This chapter discussed discipline as it relates to the correcting ineffective performance. However, discipline is more frequently used to deal with policy and rules infractions. The employee in these situations may not necessarily be a poor performer. The administration of discipline, whether for poor performance or infractions, should adhere to certain time-tested rules. Before applying these rules, a manager in a unionized firm must make sure they are compatible with the employee discipline clauses in the written union agreement.

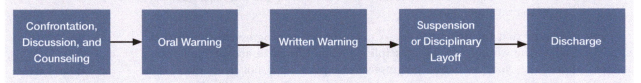

Figure 15-5 Steps in Progressive Discipline

Progressive discipline is a standard practice that remains important because it gives the worker a chance to improve, and it documents poor performance. Should discharge be necessary, it would be more difficult for the employee to claim unfair treatment and wrongful discharge.

Confrontation, Discussion, and Counseling → Oral Warning → Written Warning → Suspension or Disciplinary Layoff → Discharge

The red-hot-stove rule offers an old-fashioned but still valid principle in administering discipline. According to the *red-hot-stove rule*, employee discipline should be the immediate result of inappropriate behavior, just as a burn is the result of touching a very hot stove. The employee should receive a warning (the red metal), and the punishment should be immediate, consistent, and impersonal. A manager should keep this rule and those that follow in mind when disciplining employees. Several of these suggestions incorporate the red-hot-stove rule.

1. *All employees should be notified of what punishments will be applied for what infractions.* For example, paralegals might be told that discussing the details of client cases with outsiders, a violation of company policy, will result in discharge.

2. *Discipline should be applied immediately or shortly after the infraction is committed.* As soon as is practical after learning of a rule violation, the manager should confront the employee and apply discipline.

3. *The punishment should fit the undesirable behavior.* If the punishment is too light, the offender will not take it seriously. If, on the other hand, it is too severe, it may create anxiety and actually diminish performance. Research conducted in China indicates that when punishment is contingent, it tends to enhance job performance. *Contingent* in this sense means the punishment is commensurate with the deficit in performance. However, this positive effect of punishment is more likely to occur if the employee feels committed to the organization.[30]

4. *Managers should be consistent in applying discipline for each infraction.* Every employee who violates a certain rule should receive the same punishment. Furthermore, managers throughout the organization should impose the same punishment for the same rule violation. An employment law newsletter advises that the key to a sound discipline policy is equal treatment for all who commit equal offenses.[31]

5. *Disciplinary remedies should be applied impersonally to offenders.* "Impersonal" in this context implies that everybody who is a known rule violator should be punished. Managers should not play favorites.

6. *Documentation of the performance or behavior that led to punishment is required.* Justification for the discipline must be documented in substantial detail. Documentation is essential for defending the company's action in the event of an appeal by the employee or the union or in the case of a lawsuit.

7 *When the discipline is over, return to usual work relations.* The manager should not hold a grudge or treat the rule violator as an outcast. How the person who violated the rule is treated could become a self-fulfilling prophecy. Treating the person who was disciplined as an outcast may make that person feel alienated, causing his or her performance to deteriorate. If the person is treated as someone who is expected not to commit mistakes, he or she will most likely try to live up to that expectation.

You will know that the effort you invest in corrective or progressive discipline is successful when the worker you have disciplined has returned to acceptable performance. In contrast, your efforts in progressive discipline have not been successful when the worker does not improve or his or her performance deteriorates. If progressive discipline proceeds in the spirit of coaching, it is more likely to be successful. In contrast, if progressive discipline results in a legalistic battle with each side fighting for its rights, changes in performance are unlikely.

Positive Consequences of Punishment

Conventional wisdom is that punishment should be avoided in the workplace or used only as a last resort because of its negative side effects. Workers who are punished may become anxious, fearful, revengeful, and even violent. Evidence, however, suggests that punishment perceived in certain ways can actually benefit the organization.[32]

A key factor in whether punishment is beneficial is the employee's belief in a just world, or that people get the rewards and punishments they deserve. Employees who believe in a just world are likely to accept punishment when they violate rules or perform poorly because they believe they deserve to be punished. As a consequence, they do not complain about punishment, and might even spread the word that the organization is fair.

When employees observe that another employee has been punished justly (fairly), they will often rally on the side of management. The employees may think the offending employee deserved the punishment. In some instances, other employees may desire that a rule violator be punished because it fits their sense of justice.

Just punishment also informs employees that certain types of misconduct will not be tolerated, as documented in an interview study conducted with 77 managers from different organizations. Many managers therefore regard punishment as an opportunity to promote vicarious learning (in this sense, learning through others).[33] For example, if one employee receives a 10-day suspension for racial harassment, other employees learn the organization takes racial harassment seriously.

The accompanying *Management in Action* insert describes one of the ways in which the world's largest retailer manages substandard performance.

DEALING WITH DIFFICULT PEOPLE, INCLUDING CYNICS

So far this chapter has focused on dealing with substandard performers. Another group of employees, however, may perform adequately yet be annoying and waste managers' time as well as that of co-workers. At times their performance slips below standard because they divert their energy from accomplishing work. A person in this category is often referred to as a **difficult person**, an individual whose personal

MANAGEMENT IN ACTION

Amazon.com Systematically Approaches Substandard Performance

Several years ago, Amazon launched the "Pivot" program with the purpose of retaining underperforming employees with additional coaching and training. Before Pivot, if an employee was placed into Amazon's performance-improvement program it meant that termination was likely to happen. Pivot is considered by management to be a strengthening of the performance improvement program, and has been interpreted as an employee appeals process.

Management at Amazon wrote that "Pivot is a uniquely Amazonian program that was thoughtfully designed to provide a fair and transparent process for employees who need support. When employees are placed in Pivot, they have the option of working with their manager and HR professional to improve with a clear plan forward, or leaving Amazon with severance, or of appealing if the feel they shouldn't be in the program."

With Pivot, employees can take advantage of coaching with a "career ambassador" who might be able to bring their performance up to standard. The career ambassador is a subject-matter expert who gives guidance and support for a fixed period of time A rigorous work-improvement plan is assigned to the substandard employee. The employee might also be helped by a team of career ambassadors rather than one coach. Career ambassador positions require over seven years of experience in HR, mediation, and social services.

An employee enrolled in Pivot is given two months to show the ability to meet expectations of his or her manager. Two other alternatives employees have to working with an ambassador are to quit and receive severance pay, or to appeal the manager's decision to place him or her in Pivot. Employees who accept severance pay must sign an agreement not to sue Amazon.

The appeal is presented to a three-person panel of Amazon workers who are often unknown to the worker making the appeal, with the appeal being made through a videoconference. The manager and worker make separate presentations to the panel, going point-by-point through the boss's disappointments about the worker's performance. The panel watches the presentation and then decides who made the better case. In 2019, the upfront option appeal being placed in the program was eliminated, leaving the worker with two options: severance or the performance improvement program. Yet workers can still appeal if they are not satisfied with the improvement program. An employee who is successful with the appeal and the performance-improvement plan is then assigned to another manager.

A favorable perspective on Pivot is that Amazon is setting a positive example for other companies that have fast-paced, competitive work environments. Because not all employees can adapt to such an environment, coaching might help them improve their performance. Pivot also helps retain more talent as fewer workers are available to fill positions.

A negative perspective is provided by a Seattle employment lawyer who represented an Amazon employee. He raised this objection to Pivot: "It's a kangaroo court. My impression is that the process is that it's totally unfair." About 70 percent of employees lose their appeal. Another negative opinion of Pivot is that is used as a method of edging out employees for many reasons unrelated to low performance.

Questions

1 **In what way might the Pivot program strengthen the quality of the workforce at Amazon?**

2 **Why do you think many outside observers, including employment lawyers, have a negative view of Pivot?**

Source: Original story based on facts and observations in the following sources: Tess Taylor, "Amazon Launches 'Pivot' Program to Help Underperforming Employees," *HR Dive* (www.hrdive.com), January 24, 2017, p. 1; Bill Murphy Jr. "You Don't Just Get Fired at Amazon: What Happens is Brilliant (Or Maybe Insane: Your Choice)," *Inc.* (www.inc.com), June 26, 2018, pp. 1–5; Casey Coombs, "How Amazon Stacks the Deck Against Workers Fighting to Keep Their Jobs," *Daily Beast* (www.thedailybeast.com), August 9, 2019, pp. 1–8; Spencer Soper, "Inside Amazon's People's Court," *Bloomberg Businessweek*, July 2, 2019, pp. 22–23; "Amazon Just Launched a New Training Program to help Employees In Danger of Being Fired," *Business Insider* (www.businessinsider.com), January 19, 2017, pp. 1–4.

characteristics disturb other people. Difficult people are such a drain on productivity and personal well-being that they are studied frequently in both the business press and in research journals. Approximately 10 percent of all employees can be classified as difficult, a statistic that highlights the importance of this topic.[34] The "jerks" referred to in the chapter opener are difficult people.

Six Types of Difficult People

Difficult people have been placed into many different categories or types. Among them are whiners and complainers, naysayers, know-it-alls, office bullies, pessimists, poor team players, back stabbers, and saboteurs. A common feature of difficult people is that they focus on their own needs and agenda, such as wanting to control and manipulate others. For example, the office bully who insults and intimidates others is attempting to control them. Here we focus on six of the most frequently found types of difficult employees, and later we highlight cynics because of their unusual nature.

Workplace bullies are people who try to control their victims through fear and intimidation. They frequently interrupt others, rant in a loud voice, excessively tease, make threats, and use hostile glances. A bullying boss will often mandate that things be done his or her way or find another job. ("My way or the highway.") Bullying is often triggered by a person facing considerable pressure such as a sales manager attempting to attain a difficult sales goal during a business downturn.

Disgruntled workers are angry and often see themselves as victims. They justify their feelings by blaming work associates, including supervisors, co-workers, and customers. Typically, they isolate themselves from those around them.[35] Extremely disgruntled employees with low emotional stability may engage in workplace violence.

The *passive-aggressive worker* on the other hand, expresses anger and hostility by neglecting to take care of an emergency or sitting silently in a meeting without making a contribution.

Uncivil workers have grown rapidly as standards for civility in society continue to diminsh. Representative examples of uncivil behavior include dealing with your request while talking on the phone with another person, processing e-mail while talking to you, insulting you in public, and barging past you from the other direction as you exit a door. According to a Civility in America survey, 86 percent of respondents described their workplaces as civil and respectful. Despite this positive statistic, one-quarter of the 1,100 respondents said they quit a job because of an uncivil work environment.[36] Uncivil behavior can sometimes be triggered by mistreatment from customers. One study found that customer service employees tend to react negatively to customer incivility by being uncivil in return. Customer-service quality can therefore suffer.[37]

Change resisters tend to live in the past and have difficulty learning new procedures and adjusting to new initiatives.[38] They will often cling to old technologies or processes when the rest of the unit or organization has immersed in newer versions. Years ago, change resisters might have been the last to accept direct deposit of their paychecks. In the present, they might resist communicating with work associates through social media. Instead, they cling to e-mail and the telephone.

Destructive heroes or heroines are high-performing people whose contributions to the organization make it difficult to fire them, despite being egotists, prima donnas, and/or poor team players. A destructive hero or heroine can also be characterized as a brilliant jerk. Destructive heroes and heroines intimidate co-workers and lower morale.[39]

Tactics for Dealing with Difficult People

Much of the advice about dealing with difficult people centers on certain tactics, as described next. It will often be necessary to use a combination of these tactics to help a difficult person become more cooperative. The more the difficult behavior is an ingrained personality pattern, the more difficult it will be to change. In contrast, it is easier to change difficult behavior that stems from the pressures of a given situation. For example, a worker might be sulking because he was not appointed as team leader, rather than being a long-term passive-aggressive personality.

Pick and choose from the following tactics as needed to fit the situation. Despite the many categories of difficult people, the approach to dealing with them is about the same for each type. The medical analogy is that the same antibiotic works successfully for a wide variety of infections.

- *Give feedback about the difficult behavior and stay focused on the issues at hand.* Providing timely feedback about the problems the difficult person is creating is essential to bring about change. Do not react specifically to the problem maker's antics, but instead stay focused on work issues. Describe the behavior you want changed, and explain why the behavior is disruptive. Be extra clear in your communication, and pinpoint the difficult behavior.[40] Pause for a moment, next wait for a response. Acknowledge what the person says, next state what needs to be changed, such as, "Please stop giving customers an exasperated look and a loud exhale when they make a special request." Ask how the difficult person will make the change, and then get a commitment to change. (Notice the good coaching technique.)

- *Use tact and diplomacy.* Team members who irritate you rarely do annoying things on purpose. Tactful actions on your part can sometimes take care of these problems without having to go through the controlling process. For example, if a co-worker is engaging in a tirade about how terrible the company is, you might say, "I am really interested in your observations, but I will not attain my goals today if I don't get these e-mails out by 5 this afternoon." (Notice here how you are using "I" statements instead of "you" statements. In this way you are focusing on the problem being created rather than on the individual's character.[41]) When subtlety does not work, you may have to confront the person. Incorporate tact and diplomacy into the confrontation. For example, as you confront a team member, point out one of his or her strengths.

- *Use non-hostile humor.* Non-hostile humor can often be used to help a difficult person understand how his or her behavior annoys or blocks others. The humor should point to the person's unacceptable behavior but not belittle him or her. You might say to a subordinate who is overdue on a report: "I know we are striving for error-free in our company. But if you wait until your report is perfect before submitting it, we may not need it anymore." Your humor may help the team member realize that timeliness is an important factor in the quality of a report.

- *Give recognition and attention.* Difficult people, like misbehaving children, are sometimes crying out for attention. Give them recognition and attention, and their difficult behavior will sometimes cease. For example, in a staff meeting, mention the person's recent contributions to the department. If the negative behavior is a product of a deeper-rooted problem, recognition and attention alone will not work. The employee may have to be referred for professional counseling.

- *Listen and then confront or respond.* When discussing the problem with the difficult person, allow the individual a full expression of feelings. Allow the person to finish talking because interrupting may escalate the problem.[42] Next, acknowledge your awareness of the situation, and confront the person about how you size up the situation. Finally, specify what you would like changed, such as: "Please stop complaining so much about factors beyond our control." Avoid judging the person ("You shouldn't be like that") or generalizing ("You always act this way"). Part of managing confrontation includes standing up to a difficult person, especially a bully. Include a statement such as, "I've listened to you, now I have something to say."[43]

- *Stand fast and do not make unwarranted concessions.* A variety of difficult people, but particularly bullies, expect you to sacrifice your position or standards, such as breaking the rules just for them. If a person insults you, don't laugh it off or sidestep the remarks. Instead, say, "That's not called for. I cannot let your lack of professionalism pass unnoticed." If you are not intimidated, and do not appear insecure, the difficult person is less likely to keep pushing for the advantage.[44]

- *Boost the difficult worker's self-confidence.* Many workers who complain and make excuses frequently or exhibit other forms of difficult behavior are suffering from low self-confidence. They may not stay focused on work because of fear of failure. Assign these employees an easy task so they can succeed and begin to build self-confidence. Then move up the scale with a more difficult task. Administer praise and recognition after each success.[45]

- *If the difficult person is your boss, defend yourself without a defensive tone.* A difficult person with formal authority over you will sometimes attack you in a mean-spirited way. Assume your boss finds a mistake in your work, and then says to you, "You're totally screwing up." You can defend yourself without a defensive tone by saying, "It is true that I made a mistake, and I appreciate constructive feedback to minimize errors in the future." Defend yourself by acknowledging the error, but refuse to be incorrectly labeled as a screw-up.[46]

- *Do not feel shamed or inadequate by a bully's intimidating behavior toward you.* Bullies attack the self-worth of others to compensate for their own inadequacies. Recognize that your own mental and physical well-being remain essential. Simply pausing and taking a deep breath can help you get through challenging interactions with a bully.[47]

Dealing with Cynical Behavior

Many employees carry extremely negative attitudes toward their employers, and these negative attitudes often take the form of cynicism. Much of the cynicism appears to be a reaction to top-level management actions, such as boosting their own compensation substantially while laying off lower-ranking workers to save money. Hiring so many contract and temporary workers at the expense of offering full-time employment also leads to cynicism. Global outsourcing creates cynicism because executive positions are rarely sent overseas. Cynics are classified as difficult people because they express their cynicism more negatively and persistently than others.

Cynicism is usually expressed by finding something negative about even the best intentions of others. An investigation into the topic concludes that workplace cynicism is shown on any of three dimensions:

- *A belief that the organization lacks integrity* (The cynic might say, "Our advertising is a pack of lies.")

- *A negative affect toward the organization* (Cynics frequently make such comments as "This company is the pits." or "Who in his right mind would join this company today?")
- Tendencies toward *disparaging and critical behaviors* directed at the organization that are consistent with these beliefs (The cynic might use a competitor's consumer product and brag about it.)[48]

Managers may not want to suppress dissent, but too much cynicism in the workplace can lower the morale of others and interfere with recruiting positive people. Cynicism can also be distracting enough to harm productivity. One promising approach to dealing with cynics is to ignore cynical comments, and move on to another subject. If the cynic is seeking attention by being cynical, the lack of response will defeat the purpose of the sarcastic comments.

Cynical commentary can sometimes be reduced by demanding evidence to support harsh comments. Ask for the facts behind the opinion. A cynic might say, "I doubt there will be any money in the bonus pool this year. As usual, top management is taking care of itself first and leaving little money for the rest of us." You might respond, "I seriously doubt top management is going to deny us raises. Where did you get your information?" As in dealing with most difficult people, changing the individual substantially is unlikely. However, you can work toward enough improvement to bring about a more positive working relationship.

TERMINATION

LEARNING OBJECTIVE **6**

Explain the recommended approach to terminating employees.

termination
The process of firing an employee because of poor job performance, unacceptable behavior, or interpersonal problems.

good cause
A legally justifiable or good business reason for firing an employee.

wrongful discharge
The firing of an employee for arbitrary or unfair reasons.

Termination is the process of firing an employee because of poor job performance, unacceptable behavior, or interpersonal problems. Employees, however, can be laid off as part of downsizing, and they are not classified as being fired. Dismissing an employee is considered part of the control process because it is a corrective action, and is the last alternative when corrective action fails. It represents a failure in staffing and managing ineffective performers. Nevertheless, to maintain discipline and control costs, a firm is often forced to terminate nonproductive employees. Spending too much time to help an ineffective performer up to acceptable performance might take too much of a manager's time away from other responsibilities.[49] When substandard performers are discharged, it communicates the message that adequate performance must be maintained.

Termination usually takes place only after the substandard performer has been offered the types of help described throughout this chapter. In general, every feasible alternative—such as retraining and counseling—should be attempted before termination. A manager must also accumulate substantial written documentation of substandard performance. Appropriate documentation includes performance evaluations, special memos to the file about performance problems, e-mail messages written to the employee about his or her performance, and statements describing the help offered the employee.

Employees must be fired for **good cause**, a legally justifiable or good business reason. For example, it is easy to fire an employee who is caught taking bribes from a vendor or because management decides to close a unit of the company. Without documentation of substandard performance, the employer can be accused of **wrongful discharge**, the firing of an employee for arbitrary or unfair reasons, such as age. Many employers face wrongful discharge suits. When a termination is mismanaged, the employer may be subject to a lawsuit even though the reasons for termination were well-founded.[50] To minimize major errors in firing an employee, it is prudent to follow these guidelines:

- *Document carefully the substandard performance that led to the termination.* To repeat, this is the most fundamental rule for avoiding retaliation, including a lawsuit by the fired employee. Adequate documentation would include well below-average performance evaluations over a period of time, as well as such objective data as a branch manager not hitting financial targets for a couple of years despite written action plans for performance improvement.

- *Never fire an employee when you are angry.* Words said in anger may be too harsh, and could also reveal a prejudice, such as, "I'm getting rid of you, Harry, because we need some fresh young thinkers in this department."

- *Never fire anyone based on second-party information.* For your own legal protection, you should have first-hand knowledge and evidence of the employee's unsatisfactory, immoral, or illegal behavior. For example, a frequent reason for firing a worker today is based on accusations of sexual harassment by one person. Managers need to collect solid evidence before firing an employee stemming from only accusations.

- *Be direct and clear in your language.* Inform the employee explicitly that he or she is being fired and why. Yet ease the blow with a few reassuring phrases such as, "I am sorry this job did not work out for you. Good luck in your next job."

- *Avoid surprises.* Employees should never be totally surprised by being terminated for poor performance. They should receive regular feedback on their performance, as well as suggestions for improvement. Poor performance reviews help take the surprise element out of being terminated.[51] (Good management counts even when terminating workers.)

- *Do not shift the blame.* Joel Peterson, the Chairman of JetBlue and professor of management at the Stanford University Graduate School of Business, advises against shifting the blame for firing the individual. He observes that when firing someone, the manager will sometimes imply that he or she is only the messenger. Even though firing someone is usually a collaborative decision, the manager communicating the decision should feel and express personal responsibility for the firing.[52]

SUMMARY OF KEY POINTS

1 **Identify factors contributing to poor performance.**

Job performance is ineffective when productivity falls below a standard considered acceptable at a given time. Ineffective performers consume considerable managerial time. The causes of poor job performance can be rooted in the employee, the job, the manager, or the organization. Usually, ineffective performance is caused by a combination of several factors.

2 **Describe the control model for managing ineffective performers.**

The approach to improving ineffective performance presented in this chapter is a control process. It consists of eight steps that should be followed in sequence: (1) define performance standards, (2) detect deviation from acceptable performance, (3) define and assess the cause, (4) confront the substandard performer, (5) set improvement goals, (6) select and implement an action plan for improvement, (7) reevaluate performance after a time interval, and (8) continue or discontinue the action plan.

Corrective actions for ineffective performers are divided into managerial actions and techniques, and organizational programs. Managerial actions include coaching, close supervision and corrective discipline. Organizational programs include employee assistance programs (EAPs), counseling, outplacement, job redesign, and anger-management programs.

3 **Know what is required to coach and constructively criticize employees.**

Coaching and constructive criticism are useful approaches to managing poor performers. Coaching consists of giving advice and encouragement. Most coaching includes constructive criticism. Skill is required to coach ineffective performers and criticize them constructively. Among the components of good coaching are offering advice and applauding good results.

4 **Understand how to discipline employees.**

The controlling process may also call for discipline. Summary discipline is the immediate discharge of an employee who commits a serious offense. Corrective discipline gives employees a chance to correct their behavior before punishment is applied. Both the manager and the employee share the responsibility for solving the performance problem. Corrective discipline involves counseling.

The major type of corrective discipline is called progressive discipline. It represents a step-by-step application of corrective discipline. The manager confronts the ineffective performer about the problem and then coaches him or her to correct the issue. If the employee's performance does not improve, the employee is given a written warning. If this fails, the employee is suspended or given a disciplinary layoff. The next step is discharge.

The *red-hot-stove rule* refers to administering discipline right away. The situation should include a warning and consistent, impersonal punishment administered immediately after the infraction is committed.

Punishment can help an organization because many employees believe a rule violator should be punished. Also, punishment emphasizes certain types of misconduct will not be tolerated.

5 **Develop an approach for dealing with difficult people, including cynics.**

Difficult people exist in many different types, including the workplace bully, disgruntled, passive-aggressive workers, uncivil people, change resisters, destructive heroes and heroines, and cynics. When dealing with difficult people, give feedback about the behavior and stay focused on the issue at hand. Use tact, diplomacy, and humor, while giving recognition and attention. Listen to the difficult person and confront the person about your evaluation of the situation. Do not make unwarranted concessions. Boost the difficult person's self-confidence by starting with an easy task to perform. If your boss is a difficult person, defend yourself without using a defensive tone. Do not feel shamed or inadequate because of a bully. One approach to dealing with cynics is to ignore cynical comments. However, the cynic might also be challenged to support the basis for his or her cynicism.

Explain the recommended approach to terminating employees.

Termination should take place only after the substandard performer has been offered the type of help built into the control model. Documentation of poor performance is required. Co-workers should be offered a performance-based explanation of why the substandard performer was terminated. Never fire anyone based on second-hand information. Employees should never be totally surprised by being terminated for poor performance. Do not shift the blame for having fired a worker.

Key Terms and Phrases

ineffective job performance 457

organizational citizenship behavior 460

confrontation 465

improvement goal 466

employee assistance program (EAP) 466

coaching 469

constructive criticism 469

discipline 471

summary discipline 471

corrective discipline 472

progressive discipline 472

difficult person 474

termination 479

good cause 479

wrongful discharge 479

Questions

1. What is a potential fallacy behind the idea that workers in the bottom 10 percent or five percent of the workforce are substandard performers?

2. What is the link between managing ineffective performers and organizational productivity?

3. Think of any ineffective performer you have observed on the job. What appeared to be the reason for his or her ineffective performance?

4. When executives meet with outside financial analysts to evaluate the company's prospects, should the executives provide an estimate of the percentage of ineffective performers on the payroll? Why or why not?

5. During a period when there is a shortage of employees to fill a wide variety of positions, to what extent should managers lower their standards for what they consider to be acceptable job performance?

6. Who should decide whether a specific employee is an "office jerk"?

7. What is your opinion of the merits of using an outside consultant to terminate substandard performers?

Skill-Building Exercise 15-A: Managing Ineffective Performance Role Play

Imagine you are the team leader, and one of the team members frequently fails to show up when a critical task has to be performed. He or she usually has an excuse, such as having to perform a task for higher-level management that demands his or her attention, having to attend a funeral, or having a medical appointment. You and the other team members are concerned that this team member is a social loafer. One person plays the role of the teammate with

excuses; one person plays the role of the team leader; and three or four other students play the role of the rest of the team members. At your meeting today, you intend to confront the errant team member, and develop a plan for improvement. Being a true team, all team members will contribute to dealing with the problem member. Run the session for about 10 to 15 minutes.

Skill-Building Exercise 15-B: How Does A Person Qualify as a Workplace Jerk?

Categorizing a worker as a *jerk* is somewhat subjective because the term lacks a scientific definition. Your task is to ask five people with work experience, what a person has to do to qualify as a workplace jerk. Ask your respondents to provide an example of someone

they consider to be a workplace jerk. After synthesizing the information you collect, see how your criteria for a workplace jerk matches the definition provided in the chapter introduction.

Management Now—Online Skill-Building Exercise: Finding a C-Level Manager Worthy of Being Terminated

It is easy to talk in the abstract about what type of behavior by a high-level manager warrants the manager being fired. Your assignment is to search the Internet for a story published within the last 12 months of a specific C-level executive who you think

should be fired from his or her position. Document in about 50 words why you think the executive should be terminated. Also, estimate what you think adequate severance pay should be for the executive in question.

Melissa, the Destructive Heroine

Melissa works as a sales consultant in the wealth management group of a large branch of an investment bank. She does financial planning and portfolio management for about three dozen clients. Melissa manages about $250 million in client assets, and is therefore the leading producer in the wealth management group. She has frequently hinted to management that if she is not treated nicely by the firm, she might join a competitor and that her clients would follow her.

Melissa's boss, Jenkins, admits that Melissa is an outstanding producer, and a savvy financial professional. Yet at the same time, Melissa is a disruptive influence within the wealth-management group. "The office administrators call her a financial diva," said Jenkins. "But I call her a destructive heroine because she is truly a heroine in terms of job performance. Yet she is destructive to morale."

When asked for a couple of examples of how Melissa is destructive, Jenkins said, "Any time we have a gathering, such as a meeting or business dinner, she talks incessantly about how great she is. She drones on about how she has created exceptional wealth for her clients, and how we might all learn from her. Yet, Melissa almost never shares her investment knowledge with the rest of the professional staff."

Chelsea, the office manager, offered this description of how Melissa is over the top: "She acts like she is the CEO of the bank who gives all the orders. She even told me a couple of times that my outfits aren't professional enough for the office. Melissa often demands the office assistants order her lunch, and run personal errands for her."

Jenkins said that Melissa is a big problem, and that he has asked her to be a little more courteous with the staff, but she won't change. "I need to do something with Melissa, but I don't know what action to take. Her clients love her, and she's our outstanding producer."

Case Questions

1 How about Jenkins sending Melissa to an employee assistance program, so the counselors could work on her personality problem?

2 Would you advise Jenkins to tell Melissa to "shape up or ship out"? Why or why not?

3 What would you advise Jenkins to better manage the job behavior of his destructive heroine?

Blunt Manager Elijah

Elijah is the manager of the mortgage department at the downtown headquarters of a bank. He has seven direct reports, including three mortgage consultants. Although these consultants work full-time hours at the bank, they are classified as contractors who work only on commissions, without any salary or benefits. A consequence of this compensation arrangement is that the mortgage consultants are under considerable pressure to sell home mortgages to bank customers. Until a mortgage is approved, the consultant receives no financial compensation.

Christina, a 30-year-old mortgage consultant, asked for an appointment to speak to Elijah about her recent problems in finalizing mortgages. Elijah was eager to meet with Christina because he was also under pressure for the mortgage department to secure more mortgages. A partial transcript of their meeting follows:

Christina: I've come to you for help. For several months, I haven't been closing enough mortgages to make a living. My husband and I have three children, and we can't pay all our expenses on his salary alone. Is there any way the bank can put me on salary? Or maybe give me a few months' worth of advance commissions? I've been a great producer in the past.

Elijah: Grow up, Christina. When you took this job, you knew it did not include a salary and that the bank does not allow advances. We need you to produce, but we can't change the bank rules. We are not a small community bank.

Christina: Do you know how brutal it is out there? Home sales are down 10 percent in our area. I don't have enough warm leads coming into the bank to pursue for a mortgage. More potential bank customers are taking out mortgages online. Besides that, our mortgage approval committee has been shooting down too many deals on me lately.

Elijah: Wake up, Christina—the mortgage business has changed in recent years. We can't add any more high-risk loans to our portfolio. It is very difficult to sell those mortgages to other institutions.

Christina: Okay, then what do you suggest I do to generate more mortgage applications that the committee will approve?

Elijah: Do what you do best. You're a professional. Just bear down harder on good mortgage prospects who visit your desk. Be persuasive. Turn up the heat. Do something good, or be gone.

Christina: I'm trying. I want my commissions just as much as the bank wants its mortgages.

Elijah: Just keep trying, and get back to me with results, not excuses.

Case Questions

1 What is your evaluation of the usefulness of Elijah's criticism of Christina?

2 How should Christina respond to the criticism she is receiving from Elijah?

3 To what extent do you think that Elijah is effective in helping Christina bring her performance up to standard?

ENDNOTES

1. Original story created from facts and observations in the following sources: Beecher Tuttle, "'No Jerks' and Work-Free Fridays: Meet the Happiest Accounting Firms," *efinancial-careers*, April 15, 2014, pp. 1–4; Plante Moran, *www.glassdoor.com*. p.1. Accessed March 15, 2016; Adrienne Gonzalez, "The Secret to Plante Moran's Success is a Jerk-Free Environment," *Going Concern*, http:goingconcern.com, April 22, 2014. Accessed March 17, 2016; Scott Talley, "Culture of Caring Give Plante Moran Workers their Mission" *Detroit Free Press* (www.freep.com), November 9, 2018, pp. 1–4; Mathew Daneman, "CEOs Share Do's and Don'ts," *Democrat and Chronicle*, March 28, 2014, p. 71.

2. Ron Ashkenas, "How to Handle Underperformers on a Team You Inherit," *Harvard Business Review* (https://hbr.org), June 15, 2017, p. 1.

3. Dragos Iliescu, Dan Ispas, Coralia Sulea, and Alexandra Ilie, "Vocational Fit and Counterproductive Work Behaviors: A Self-Regulation Perspective," *Journal of Applied Psychology*, January 2014, pp. 21–39.

4. Drew Robb, "Absence Makes HR's Job Harder," *HR Magazine*, March 2015, p. 67.

5. Dan Witters, Diana Liu, and Sangeeta Agrawal, "Depression Costs U.S. Workplaces $23 Billion In Absences," *Gallup* (www.gallup.com/poll), July 24, 2013, p. 2.

6. Jixia Yang and James Diefendorf, "The Relations of Daily Counterproductive Workplace Behavior with Emotions, Situational Antecedents, and Personality Moderators: A Diary Study in Hong Kong," *Personnel Psychology*, Summer 2009, p. 286.

7. "Results from the 2012 National Survey on Drug Use and Health: Summary of National Findings," *U.S. Department of Health and Human Services*, pp. 1–3.

8. Rita Pyrillis, "Office Detox," *Workforce*, Winter 2020, pp. 30–34.

9. "Protecting Your Back at Work," *Fit Facts* (American Council on Exercise), www.acefitness.org. Accessed April 6, 2010.

10. Reeshad S. Dalal, "A Meta-Analysis of the Relationship Between Organizational Citizenship Behavior and Counterproductive Work Behavior," *Journal of Applied Psychology*, November 2005, pp. 1241–1255.

11. Jean-François Manzoni and Jean-Louis Barsoux, "The Set-Up-to-Fail Syndrome," *Harvard Business Review*, March–April 1998, pp. 101–113.

12. Angela J. Xu, Raymond Loi, and Long W. Lam, "The Bad Boss Takes It All: How Abusive Supervision and Leader-Member Exchange Interact to Influence Employee Silence," *The Leadership Quarterly*, October 2015, pp. 763–774.

13. Dane K. Peterson, "Deviant Workplace Behavior and the Organization's Ethical Climate," *Journal of Business and Psychology*, Fall 2002, pp. 47–61.

14. Sandra L. Robinson and Anne M. O'Leary-Kelly, "Monkey See, Monkey Do: The Influence of Work Groups on the Antisocial Behavior of Employees," *Academy of Management Journal*, December 1998, pp. 658–672.

15. Hemanshu Nigam, "Textual Harassment—Another Form of Bullying," *The Huffington Post*, (www.huffingtonpost.com), June 10, 2013, pp. 1–3.

16. Jana L. Raver and Lisa H. Nishii, "Once, Twice, or Three Times as Harmful? Ethnic Harassment, Gender Harassment, and Generalized Workplace Harassment," *Journal of Applied Psychology*, March 2010, pp. 236–254.

17. Barrie E. Litzky, Kimberly A. Eddleston, and Deborah L. Kidder, "The Good, the Bad, and the Misguided: How Managers Inadvertently Encourage Deviant Behaviors," *Academy of Management Perspectives*, February 2006, pp. 93–94.

18. Nichelle C. Carpenter, Bertha Rangell, Gahyun Jeon, and Jonathan Cottrell, "Are Supervisors and Coworkers Likely to Witness Employee Counterproductive Work Behavior? An Investigation of Observability and Self-Observer Convergence," *Personnel Psychology*, Number 4, 2017, pp. 843–889.

19. "Internet Addiction: An ADA-Protected Disability?" *The HR Weekly*, March 17, 2014, p. 1.

20. Saundra Jackson, Ruhal Dooley, and Diance Lacy, "Substance Abuse, Ethics, Intermittent Leave," *HR Magazine*, July 2003, p. 41.

21. Bernhard Weber and Guido Hertel, "Motivation Gains of Inferior Group Members: A Meta-Analytical Review," *Journal of Personality and Social Psychology*, June 2007, pp. 973–993.

22. Linda Wasmer Andrews, "When It's Time for Anger Management," *HR Magazine*, June 2005, p. 132.

23. "Documenting the Value of Employee Assistance Programs," Federal Occupational Health Program Support Center, *http://www.foh.dhhs.gov*, April 2010.

24. Sarah Fister Gale, "Anxiety and the Employee Assistance Program," *Workforce*, May/June 2018, p. 48.

25. Jonathan A. Segal, "I'm Depressed—Accommodate Me!" *HR Magazine*, February 2001, p. 148.

26. James Waldroop and Timothy Butler, "The Executive as Coach," *Harvard Business Review*, November–December 1996, p. 111.

27. Marcus Buckingham and Ashley Goodall, "The Feedback Fallacy," *Harvard Business Review*, March–April 2019, pp. 92–101.

28. Marilyn J. Darling, "Coaching Helps People Through Difficult Times," *HR Magazine*, November 1994, p. 72.

29. Gary P. Latham, Joan Almost, Sara Mann, and Celia Moore, "New Developments in Performance Management," *Organizational Dynamics*, Vol. 34, No. 1, 2005, p. 85.

30. Hong Deng and Kwok Leung, "Contingent Punishment as a Doubled-Edged Sword: A Dual-Pathway Model from a Sense-making Perspective," *Personnel Psychology*, No. 4, 2014, pp. 951–980.

31. "Track All Discipline to Show Unbiased Process," *HR Specialist: New York Employment Law*, March 2010 Special Issue, p. 1.

32. Gail A. Ball, Linda Klebe Treviño, and Harry P. Sims Jr., "Just and Unjust Punishment: Influence on Subordinate Performance and Citizenship," *Academy of Management Journal*, April 1994, pp. 300–301.

33. Kenneth B. Butterfield, Linda Klebe Treviño, and Gail A. Ball, "Punishment from the Manager's Perspective: A Grounded Investigation and Inductive Model," *Academy of Management Journal*, December 1996, p. 149.

34. Tim McClintock, "Dealing with Difficult People," *Projects@Work* (www.projectsatwork.com), November 17, 2008, p. 1.

35. Paul Falcone, "Welcome Back Disgruntled Workers," *HR Magazine*, February 2001, p. 133.

36. Leslie Gaines-Ross, "Offices Can Be Bastions of Civility in an Uncivil Time," *Harvard Business Review* (https://hbr.org), July 14, 2017, p. 2; "Why We Need to Kick Incivility Out of the Office," (Interview with Christine Porath, *Knowledge@Wharton* (https://knowledgewharton.upenn.edu), June 20, 2017, pp. 1–3.

37. David D. Walker, Danielle D. van Jaarsveld, and Daniel P. Skarlicki, "Sticks and Stones Can Break My Bones but Words Can Also Hurt Me: The Relationship Between Customer Verbal Aggression and Employee Incivility," *Journal of Applied Psychology*, February 2017, pp. 163–179.

38. "Tame Team Tigers: How to Handle Difficult Personalities," *Manager's Edge*, Special Issue 2008, p. 8.

39. John Grossman, "The Long Odds of Reforming an Employee Who is a 'Destructive Hero,'" *The New York Times* (www.nytimes.com), October 29, 2014, pp. 1–4.

40. "Difficult Employee? Time for 'the Chat'," *Managing People at Work*, February 1, 2016, p. 1.

41. "Keep Conflicts from Festering," *Manager's Edge*, August 2009, p. 5.

42. Michelle Juergen, "Battle of the Button-Pushers," *Entrepreneur*, April 2014, p. 26.

43. "Fighting Off Bullies," WorkingSMART, September 1997, p. 1; *http://www.kickbully.com.*

44. "How to Deal with 'Problem' Workers," *Positive Leadership*, Sample Issue 2004, p. 6.

45. McClintock, "Dealing with Difficult People," p. 3.

46. Nando Pelusi, "Dealing with Difficult People," *Psychology Today*, September/October 2006, p. 69.

47. John Young, "Pulling the Curtain Back on the Workplace Bully," *Insead Knowledge* (https://knowledge.insead.edu/blog), March 3, 2020, pp. 2–3.

48. James W. Dean Jr., Pamela Brandes, and Ravi Dharwadkar, "Organizational Cynicism," *Academy of Management Review*, April 1998, pp. 341–352.

49. Joann S. Lublin, "Being Fix-It Boss to Staff Doesn't Work," *The Wall Street Journal*, November 2, 2017, p. B6.

50. Margaret Fiester, "Terminating Employees, Fostering Culture, Paying for Training Time," *HR Magazine*, August 2009, p. 25.

51. "How to Avoid the 5 Classic Firing Mistakes," *The HR Specialist*, March 2008, p. 6.

52. Joel Peterson, "Firing with Compassion: Do's and Don'ts," *Harvard Business Review*, March–April 2020. P. 139.

Part Six

Managing for Personal Effectiveness

CHAPTER 16
Enhancing Personal Productivity
and Managing Stress

Enhancing Personal Productivity and Managing Stress

OBJECTIVES

After studying this chapter and doing the exercises, you should be able to:

1 Identify techniques for improving work habits and time management.

2 Explain why people procrastinate and identify techniques for reducing procrastination.

3 Understand the nature of stress and burnout, including their consequences.

4 Explain how stress can be managed effectively.

Sleek privacy pods that resemble phone booths of yesteryear are popping up in many workplaces that have open-floor plans. These pods that enable you to talk on the phone without being overheard have been installed in company offices ranging from tech startups to media companies. Office pods are self-contained nearly soundproof and ventilated booths available in a variety of sizes. The privacy pod is usually constructed of glass and contains a seat and a small table along with Internet capability. Most privacy pods are entirely see-through. Spending time in a pod gives workers some quiet time away from the noise and interruptions of many offices. There is also the opportunity to concentrate intently on a demanding task. Many employers have learned during the last decade that eliminating partitions in the office to both cut costs and enhance collaboration left workers with no outlet for peace and quiet.

A lawyer, Talia Cohen, who works in-house for the flexible office-space startup Knotel Inc., was running late for a confidential call at her office. She spotted a colleague in a pod who was not making a call. Cohen tapped on the door. "I said I'd put her contracts first in the queue if she would give me her phone booth (pod). You have to be a quick negotiator to get inside one."

Kyle DeMilo is an information technology specialist at a textbook publisher in New York who sometimes occupies a pod for several hours at a time. "You move in with your laptop, cellphone, and maybe a snack. You can't crank out something with good grammar when the person behind you is slurping soup," he said.

Privacy pods are in demand even at trade show displays. SnapCab Inc. sometimes found that attendees were squatters in the company's display booths. Glenn Bostock, SnapCab's CEO says, "We're trying to sell the booths, but they don't care." One time a woman who was making a video call in a demonstration booth shoved Bostock away with an arm gesture after he knocked on the glass door, seeking to get inside. Bostock wanted to give a demonstration to a prospective customer who was thinking about placing a $10 million order. The woman still refused to leave until she completed her video call.

The privacy pods range in price from about $3,000 to $13,000, yet are still considered less expensive than renovating an office to create more space. The pods can also be moved from one part of the office to another as needed. Zen Booth, a manufacturer of privacy pods, explains that when in an office privacy pod, teleconferencing, videoconferencing, and Skype meetings are of much higher quality. Workers can more easily focus entirely on the conversation, with no disturbances.[1]

The story about the privacy pods illustrates that managers need to find ways to keep all workers productive, even if it means finding an unusual way to accommodate their workstyle preferences. At the same time, the story illustrates how working alone in privacy is sometimes required for a person to attain high personal productivity. In this chapter, we describe methods for both improving productivity and managing stress, because the two are as interlocked as nutrition and health. If you are well organized, you will avoid much of the negative stress that stems from feeling your work and life are out of control. If your level of stress is about right, you will be able to concentrate better on your work and be more productive.

The emphasis in this final chapter of the book is about managing yourself; rather than managing other people or managing a business. Unless you have your work under control, and effectively manage stress, it is unlikely you can be an effective manager or leader.

LEARNING OBJECTIVE **1**

Identify techniques for improving work habits and time management.

productivity
How effectively you use your resources to achieve your goals.

IMPROVING YOUR WORK HABITS AND TIME MANAGEMENT

High personal productivity leads to positive outcomes, such as higher income, more responsibility, and recognition. **Productivity** in this sense is how effectively you use your resources to achieve your goals.[2] Furthermore, in an era of work streamlining, downsizing and company consolidations, the demand for high productivity among managerial workers has never been greater. Productivity enhancers, such as daily planners are still widely used. Individual productivity is also important because an economy's long-term growth is determined by the number of workers in the economy and how much they produce.[3] (From the standpoint of a labor economist, productivity is the output per hour of the non-farm business sector.)

Good work habits and time management can also facilitate helping co-workers. A study with business-to-business sales representatives in the hospitality industry found time-management skills helped representatives avoid the potential negative consequences of organizational citizenship behavior. A specific finding was that helping others was less likely to decrease task performance, if the sales rep managed time well.[4] High job productivity also allows you to devote more worry-free time to your personal life and hobbies, resulting in the ability to lead a more balanced life.

Here we describe how developing more effective work habits can improve time management. In the next section, productivity improvement is approached from the perspective of reducing procrastination. Improving your work habits and time management is much like applying scientific management to boost personal productivity.

Develop a Mission, Goals, and a Strong Work Ethic

A major starting point in becoming a better organized and more productive person is to have a purpose and values that propel you toward being productive. In the words of the late Stephen Covey, without a personal mission statement, you have nothing to plan and act for.[5] Assume that a person says, "My mission in life is to become an outstanding office supervisor and a caring, constructive spouse and parent." The mission serves as a compass to direct that person's activities (such as getting done on time) to developing a reputation that will lead to promotion to supervisor. Goals are more specific than mission statements, and support the mission statement, but the effect is the same. For example, the person in question might set a goal one day to respond to 75 different customer inquiries that have accumulated on the company website by the end of the day. Accomplishing that amount of work today would be one more step toward being promoted to supervisor.

In establishing goals to enhance your productivity, it is helpful to choose the most important performance metrics to use as goals. You then track these metrics to see how well you are performing. Technology researcher Alexandra Samuel recommends that weekly tracking works best for most people. Examples of metrics include the number of PowerPoint decks created, sales that are closed, employee evaluations completed, and lines of code written.[6]

Closely related to establishing goals is to have a strong **work ethic**—a firm belief in the dignity and value of work. Developing a strong work ethic may lead to even higher productivity than goal setting alone. For example, one might set the goal of earning a high income. It would lead to some good work habits, but not necessarily to a high commitment to quality. A person with a strong work ethic believes in producing work or high quality service, is highly motivated, and minimizes time-wasting activities. Having a strong work ethic also implies you are an engaged worker, or are committed to your employer and willing to put in extra effort on the job.[7]

work ethic
A firm belief in the dignity and value of work.

Practice Self-Discipline

Part of having a strong work ethic is to practice **self-discipline**, the ability to work systematically and progressively toward a goal until it is achieved. Without a reasonable degree of self-discipline, most time-management techniques will have a negligible impact on personal productivity. If you are self-disciplined, you work toward achieving your goals without being derailed by daily distractions. Assume that Caleb downloads a productivity app to his Apple watch. The app sends notifications to the user about progress toward work goals. If Caleb does not have the self-discipline to pay attention to the notifications, and act on goal attainment, the slick productivity tool will have no positive impact.

self-discipline
The ability to work systematically and progressively toward a goal until it is achieved.

Clean Up Your Work Area and Sort Out Your Tasks

People sometimes become inefficient because their work area is messy. They waste time looking for things and neglect important papers. Desk accessories that allocate spaces for pencils pens, paperclips, and small notes are helpful in controlling clutter.[8] Electronic documents can also be lost, even if not as readily. The chance of losing or misplacing electronic documents increases mostly because many people create so many different files and documents that cause disorganization. It is best to store never used or rarely used files in a place other than your hard drive. So, to get started on improving personal productivity, clean up your work area and sort out what tasks you need to accomplish.

Most documents are stored on computers, on external drives, or on the servers of cloud computing services. Yet most companies still have many paper documents that need to be carefully filed so they can be retrieved on demand. Paper copies are legally required for some financial and medical records. Having well organized physical files remains an important part of cleaning up your work area.

"Getting Things Done" is a popular system for improving productivity that hits on many of the principles described in this chapter. The starting point for uncluttering your life is to collect everything you must do that is unfinished or undecided. After that, you begin sorting out the tasks and assigning priorities in terms of their accomplishment[9] (as described below).

Get rid of as much clutter as possible, including personal souvenirs. Cleaning up your work area includes your briefcase, your file of phone numbers, your hard drive, and your e-mail files. Having loads of e-mail messages stacked in your inbox, sent, and deleted files can easily lead to overlooking important new messages. Weeding out your mail list is also important. Ask to be removed from the distribution of paper and e-mail that is of no value. Rebel against being burdened with junk mail. Many people begin their workday by immediately deleting unwanted e-mail messages. Deleting these messages is a bigger task for people who work at home or at smaller firms that lack elaborate protections against unwanted e-mail messages.

Recognize that the issue of avoiding clutter is controversial. Many workers believe that working in the midst of a mess is effective so long as you are organized—being able to find what you need within the mess. Research suggests the amount of clutter might simply reflect differences in cognitive or mental style, so a clutter-free environment may mean fighting against a natural tendency.[10] Another problem with avoiding clutter by filing away papers is that many people work by the principle, "out of sight, out of mind." If something is put into a drawer or other file, it will be neglected.

Prepare a To-Do List and Assign Priorities

A to-do list lies at the heart of every time-management system and is a building block for planning because it records what needs to be accomplished. In addition to writing down tasks you need to do, assign priorities to them. A simple categorization, such as top priority versus low priority, works well for most people. In general, take care of top-priority tasks before low-priority ones. There are so many things to do on any job that some very low-priority items may never get done. Keep your to-do list on a desk calendar, in your computer, or in a mobile device. Setting deadlines for accomplishment is also helpful in directing your efforts, so long as the deadlines are real rather than arbitrary. A real deadline would be one imposed by your boss or legal requirements, or one that is necessary to attain so you can start on another project by a particular date.

Although many managers and professionals keep to-do lists on their computers or smartphones, there are still many executives who appreciate the value of to-do lists placed on index cards. A case in point is Ken Washington, the chief technology officer at Ford Motor Company. He has a Ph.D. in nuclear engineering and was previously a rocket scientist at Lockheed Martin. Washington says that there is no substitute for paper. "You don't need a Wi-Fi hot spot to get it to work. It never runs out of batteries. I start each week with a list of the things I want to accomplish and a list of key actions."[11]

Taking care of a small, easy-to-do task first—such as sharpening pencils—has a hidden value. It tends to be relaxing because it gives you the emotional lift of having accomplished at least one item on your list. Also, accomplishing small tasks helps reduce stress. It is also less stressful to take care of easy items on the to-do list when you are at less than peak energy. An example would be deleting unimportant messages at the end of your workday.

Because the to-do list has such a big impact on productivity, many time-management specialists continue to develop refinements including incorporating more technology. For example, hundreds of list-making apps are available for smartphones. A modification of the to-do list that appears to be effective for many people is the **time box**—a period of time to work on a task when you declare it completed.[12] You may be familiar with speed dating or speed networking in which you allocate a brief period of time to spend into exchanging introductions with another person. Both of these activities are timeboxing but preceded the term. One item on a manager's time box list might be "Locate and hire contractor to replace heating-and-air conditioning unit." The amount of time allocated to the task might be 50 minutes. In this way the manager will not spend two days on a task that could probably be accomplished in 50 minutes.

time box
A period of time to work on a task when you declare it completed.

A variation on the to-do list with enormous consequences for productivity and safety is the checklist. The checklist prescribes steps that must be taken while executing a procedure when a deviation for this procedure could have strong negative consequences. According to productivity consultants Dan Heath and Chip Heath, checklists are effective because they inform workers about the best course of action, showing them the ironclad way to do something.[13] In a hospital, a valid checklist would help avoid infections in surgical patients, and cutting off the wrong limb during surgery. In a retail store, a checklist would help avoid accepting a bogus check. In a factory, a checklist would help avoid shipping a defective product.

Streamline Your Work

An essential work habit and time-management principle is **work streamlining**—eliminating as much low-value work as possible and concentrating on activities that add value for customers or clients. To streamline work, justify whether every work procedure, e-mail message, report, meeting, or ceremonial activity contributes value to the firm. The number of group luncheon meetings away from the office might be cut in half, giving staff members more time during the day to conduct urgent work. A basic example of work streamlining would be to take advantage of the United States Postal Service package pick-up service instead of visiting the post office to ship packages.

work streamlining
Eliminating as much low-value work as possible and concentrating on activities that add value for customers or clients.

A method of streamlining meetings so more important work gets accomplished is to minimize talking about topics not on the agenda. Yet if this policy is followed too rigidly, the company might lose out on a few spontaneous ideas that could benefit the group or the firm. For example, during a meeting about cost cutting, somebody might think of an idea that would bring in more revenue.

Work at a Steady, Rapid Pace

Although a dramatic show of energy (as in "pulling an all-nighter") is impressive, the steady worker tends to be more productive in the long run. The spurt employee creates many problems for management; the student who works in spurts is in turmoil at examination time or when papers are due. Managers who expend the same amount of effort day-by-day tend to stay in control of their jobs. When a sudden problem or a good opportunity comes to their attention, they can fit it into their schedule. Working at a steady pace often means always working rapidly. To be competitive, most organizations require that work be accomplished rapidly.

An important exception about working rapidly all the time is that some decisions require careful deliberation and should not be rushed. A team of researchers studied for 19 months the decision making of an Internet startup. Making decisions too rapidly resulted in many errors in purchasing software and hiring people.[14]

The recommendations about working rapidly yet making major decisions deliberately are compatible. After you take enough time to make a major decision, work rapidly to accomplish the tasks necessary to implement the decision. A manager might carefully weigh the evidence about the value of outsourcing some call center operations to the Philippines. After the decision is made, the manager and his or her staff work rapidly to make the outsourcing a reality.

Minimize Time Wasters and Interruptions

An important strategy for improving personal productivity is to minimize time wasters. Each minute invested in productive work can save you from working extra hours. A major time waster is interruptions from others. One of the benefits of remote working is that interruptions from other workers are minimized. When doing intellectually demanding work, getting the appropriate flow of thought is difficult. When interrupted, people lose momentum and must launch themselves again. The definition of what constitutes an *interruption* is tricky. A co-worker asking you to participate in a basketball pool is certainly an interruption but socializing with him or her might strengthen your network. Some executives feel that a demand from a customer should never be classified as an interruption. A sudden demand from a boss may also not be classified as an interruption. The privacy pods described in the chapter opener are one approach to help deal with the interruptions of co-workers when difficult work needs to be accomplished.

A contingency perspective on interruptions is that most of them are harmful to work, but some are helpful. For example, if somebody walks into your cubicle while you are attempting to calculate a gross profit margin that your boss wants in 10 minutes, the interruption is dysfunctional. Yet at another time, chatting with an intruder could result in some useful information sharing that is functional.

A considerable time waster is searching the Internet for information not strictly related to work, or otherwise known as Internet surfing. Lost productivity is a major problem as workers who surf the Internet for non-work reasons. A CareerBuilder survey of a representative sample of 3,022 fulltime employees found that 39 percent perceived the Internet to disrupt concentration.[15]

Minimize Distractions Including Nonproductive Multitasking

A frequent distraction is using several electronic devices at once because it often interferes with a person's ability to concentrate carefully on the major problem at hand. Computerized information encourages multitasking to the point that many managers feel they are wasting time unless they are attempting two tasks at once, such as talking on a smartphone and accessing e-mail at the same time. The problem is that diminished concentration often leads to poorer-quality work. "Multitasking doesn't look to be one of the great strengths of human cognition," according to James C. Johnston, a research psychologist at NASA. "It's almost inevitable that each individual task will be slower and of lower quality."[16] Another problem with multitasking is its inherent rudeness, such as when a manager peeks at his or her smartphone while talking to a subordinate about a problem. Accidents, such as car crashes while talking on a cell phone or sending a text message are another serious problem.

According to Basex, an IT research and consulting firm, the average worker dealing with information loses 2.1 hours of productivity each workday to electronic interruptions and distractions (that includes Internet surfing). Multitasking costs the U.S. economy an estimated $650 billion annually, as workers frequently switch back and forth between different tasks. Lost also is about $28 billion in work time. The primary productivity drainers are e-mail alerts, instant messages, buzzing smart-phones, and mobile phones. (Yet, used properly these productivity drainers can be productivity enhancers, as explained later in the chapter.) A contributing problem is that the more you multitask by checking your messages, the more you feel the need to check them.[17]

Another way to understand the potential hazards of multitasking is to personalize the problem. If you were a passenger in an airplane going through a storm would you want the pilot to be chatting on the cell phone or reading e-mail while commandeering the plane?

Productivity trainer Maura Thomas has developed a method to help workers overcome the distraction habit, such as checking your e-mail every five minutes *when your job does not require it*. Pay attention to how frequently you are distracted. Note when you switch away from a task before your intended stopping point. Also jot down the cause of your distraction. After you become aware of these cues, you will probably develop ways of overcoming distractions. For example, you might decide that a good way to avoid grabbing for your phone every five minutes is to keep it out of sight and reach. Or, you might decide to exert the self-discipline to check your phone only every 30 minutes. When you find an effective anti-distraction technique, deploy it frequently enough to make it a habit.[18]

Figure 16-1 presents a list of significant ways to reduce wasted time, including distractions. Many of the other suggestions in this chapter can also help you save time directly or indirectly.

The accompanying *Management in Action* insert presents a novel approach taken by a small technology firm to increase productivity by decreasing wasted time on the job.

Concentrate on One Task at a Time

Productive managers develop their capacity to concentrate on the problem facing them at the moment, however engulfed they are with other obligations. Intense concentration leads to sharpened judgment and analysis and also decreases the chances of making major errors. Another useful by-product of concentration is reduced absent-mindedness. The person who concentrates on the task at hand is more likely to remember what he or she intended.

Multitasking has become a typical mode of operation for many workers. However, multitasking is best reserved for routine tasks such as discarding unwanted e-mail messages and cleaning your desk at the same time. A major problem with multitasking is that it can lead to accidents and death both on and off the job. If you are driving

Figure 16-1 Ways to Prevent and Overcome Time Wasting

Wasted time is a major productivity drain, so it pays to search for time wasters in your work activities. The following list suggests remedies for some of the major time wasters in the workplace.

1 Use a time log for two weeks to track time wasters.

2 Minimize daydreaming on the job by forcing yourself to concentrate.

3 Avoid the computer as a diversion from work, such as sending jokes back and forth to network members, including your friends and followers; playing video games; and checking out recreational and shopping websites during working hours.

4 Batch tasks together such as responding to e-mail messages or returning phone calls. For example, in most jobs it is possible to be productive by reserving two or three 15-minute periods per day for taking care of e-mail correspondence. Checking e-mail too frequently, such as every five minutes, is a major time waster unless necessary for your job.

5 E-mail filters can be helpful, providing you do not simply go to "junk mail" or its equivalent to review which messages have been blocked.

6 Socialize on the job just enough to build your network. Chatting with co-workers is a major productivity drain and one of the reasons so many managers work at home part of the time when they have analytical work to get done.

7 Be prepared for meetings by having a clear agenda and sorting through the documents you will be referring to. Make sure electronic equipment is in working order before attempting to use it during the meeting.

8 Keep track of important names, places, and things to avoid wasting time searching for them. For example, have a permanent place for your keys and flash (or thumb) drive, both at home and at work. Also, visualize where you placed items, such as, "I am putting my sunglasses over the visor on the driver's side of my car."

9 Set a time limit for tasks after you have done them once or twice.

10 Prepare a computer template for letters and computer documents that you send frequently. (The template is essentially a form letter, especially with respect to the salutation and return address.)

11 Avoid perfectionism, which leads you to keep redoing a project. Let go and move on to another project.

12 Make use of free time, such as five minutes between appointments. Invest those five minutes in sending a business e-mail, or revising your to-do list. (Note the exception to the batch principle.)

13 Decrease grabbing for your smartphone at every conceivable moment, such as when you exit the building. Some of the time devoted to chatting on the phone could be invested in planning your work or searching for creative ideas.

14 Minimize procrastination, the number one time waster for most people.

15 Avoid asking the same question even after you have received a satisfactory answer. Redundant questioning wastes both your time, and the other person's time.

16 Turn off push notifications unless they are absolutely necessary to accomplish your work. Notifications or alerts that include a "ping" are particularly distracting and often waste time.

Source: Suggestion 5 is based on Alexandra Samuel, "Fight Fire with Fire," *Harvard Business Review*, June 2015, p.113. Suggestion 8 is based partly on, "How to Boost Your Brainpower," *TopHealth*, October, 2009, p. 2. Suggestion 16 is from Steve Glaveski, "Quick Productivity Hack: Turn Off Your Push Notifications," *Harvard Business Review* (https://hbr.org), March 18, 2019, pp. 1–5.

your car for company business and talking on your cell phone or texting at the same time, your employer is liable if you get into an accident.

Notice the important difference between multitasking, which refers to doing two or more tasks at the same time, versus working on multiple tasks in sequence. For example, it is the usual case for a manager or corporate professional to be assigned to two different projects, such as one for product development, and another for environmental protection. Multitasking would be doing a spreadsheet on product development while talking on the phone to a co-worker about office relocation. Working

MANAGEMENT IN ACTION

German Tech Consulting Firm Decreases Wasted Time to Enable Five-Hour Workday

Lasse Rheingans, a German entrepreneur, recognized that taking time to check Facebook or responding to reply-all e-mails distracted from his main work. These activities also caused him to spend extra time at the office rather than with his daughters. In 2017, he acquired a small tech consulting firm, Rheingans Digital Enabler, and therefore reduced the regular workday in the office to five hours. (The company develops websites, apps, and e-commerce platforms.) Rheingans modified the workday for his 16 employees from 8 a.m. to 1 p.m. without slashing any staff member's salary or benefits including vacation time. He said that at first employees thought he was kidding. "Some of them thought I was testing them. But yeah, I was being serious."

To make the 5-hour workday feasible, Rheingans thinks the workplace must be as distraction-free as possible. Small talk is discouraged, and the use of social media and smartphones are forbidden with the latter being kept in backpacks. Staff members are permitted to check company e-mails no more than twice a day, and most meetings are scheduled to last a maximum of 15 minutes. Each workday a monitor at the office counts down the remaining hours and minutes. At 1 p.m. the display changes to the "#high5, #feierabend," the German term for closing time.

Digital Enabler employees say it takes an adjustment to get accustomed to not texting family members during the workday, producing the same amount of work in three fewer hours, and not taking short breaks. The workers contend that they experience pressure to produce the same amount of work in fewer hours. Yet the staff members seem happier, and are using the extra hours of nonwork time for such activities as spending time with children, tackling chores, and engaging in physical exercise. The 25-hour workweek also makes it easier to recruit in Germany's tight labor market.

Rheingans observes that with the shortened working hours, employees feel less overworked even though they are still attaining their productivity goals. He has also seen productivity increases, and output has held consistent with the 40-hour workweek. He also says that profits have increased since shifting to the 25-hour workweek. Rheingans has said the experiment has changed the way people work in the office: "We sit in the office, out of energy, reading newspapers online or Facebook, just in need of the little pauses to recharge, but you don't really recharge. My idea is focusing on the first five hours and then just leave and have a proper break."

Questions

1 **How much do you agree with Lasse Rheingans' opinion about how people work?**

2 **How effective do you think the 5-hour workday would be in a large American firm such as Ford Motor Company?**

3 **How would a 5/25 workweek fit your style of work and personal life?**

Source: Original story based on facts and observations in the following sources: Erik Morath, "Five-Hour Workday Gets Put to the Test," *The Wall Street Journal*, October 24, 2019, p. B6; Michael Tedder, "5-Hour Workday Could Transform the Office and Make Life Better," *Money* (www.msn.com), October 24, 2019, pp. 1–4; HR Exchange Network Editorial Team, "HR News: 5 Hour Workday Experiment a Success?" *HR Exchange* (www.hrexchangenetwork. com), October 25, 2019, pp. 1–3; "A German Company is Testing a 5-Hour Workday Where Employees Only Check Email Twice and Small Talk is Banned," *Business Insider* (www.businessinsider.com), October 25, 2019, pp. 1–3.

on multiple projects would include spending the morning on product development, and the afternoon on office relocation.

In contrast to the problems just stated, multitasking for routine tasks can lead to productivity gains. A growing form of multitasking is to work with two computer monitors. You use one monitor to go about your regular work, and the other monitor for e-mail. In this way you do not have to constantly minimize and maximize your document to access e-mail. However, if you are working on a document that requires full attention, it is hazardous to continually glance at the e-mail monitor. For example, if you are analyzing tax data for the company, do not keep looking at your second monitor.

Concentrate on High-Output Tasks

Many people interpret time-management techniques as a way of becoming a tidy perfectionist who never lets a detail slip by. In contrast, a major time-management principle is to become more productive on the job or in school, concentrate on tasks in which superior performance could have a large payoff. For a manager, a high-output task would be to develop a strategic plan for the department or finding ways to obtain a high return on investment for surplus cash. For a student, a high-output task would be to think of a creative idea for an independent study project. Expending your work effort on high-output items is analogous to looking for a good return on investment for your money. The high-output strategy also follows the Pareto principle, described in Chapter 6.

Do Creative and Routine Tasks at Different Times

Similar to concentrating on high-output tasks, to improve productivity, organize your work so you do not shift between creative and routine tasks. For many people it is best to work first on creative tasks because they require more mental energy than routine tasks. A minority of people prefer to get minor paperwork and e-mail chores out of the way so they can get to the pleasure of doing creative tasks. Whichever order you choose, it is important not to interrupt creative (or high-output) tasks with routine activities, such as deleting spam or rearranging the desk.

It is also helpful to tackle creative tasks when you are typically at your best. For many people, their mentally best time is the morning; for others the afternoon is best. The reason for selecting your high-energy time for creative work is that creativity requires considerable mental energy. Routine work can then be performed when you are not at your best mentally.

Stay in Control of Paperwork, E-mail, and Voice Mail

No organization today can accomplish its mission unless paperwork, including the electronic variety, receives appropriate attention. If you handle paperwork improperly, your job may get out of control. Once your job is out of control, the stress level will increase greatly. Invest a small amount of time in paperwork and electronic mail every day. Avoid becoming a paper shuffler or frequently rereading e-mail messages. The ideal is to handle a piece of paper or an e-mail message only once. When you read an electronic memo or a piece of postal mail, take some action: delete it or throw it away, route it to someone else, write a short response to the sender, or flag it for action later. Loose ends of time can be used to take care of the flagged memos.

Although many managers and corporate professionals have shifted some e-mail to collaboration tools, e-mail has not been eliminated as a natural way of conducting business. You therefore need to manage e-mail well rather than fight the system.

Staying in control of voice mail messages is also important to stay productive. Stacked up voice mail messages will often detract from your ability to concentrate on other work. Not returning voice mail messages promptly also creates the problem of perceived rudeness and poor customer service. Disciplining yourself to answer voice mail messages in batches, as mentioned in Figure 16-1 will help you manage these messages productively.

Make Effective Use of Digital Technology Including Productivity Tools

Used properly, most information technology devices in the office improve productivity. According to a Pew Research Center report, 46 percent of workers who use online and digital tools say they feel more productive. The five electronic tools and digital technology tools used were e-mail, the Internet, a landline phone, a cell phone or smartphone, and social media sites. Thirty percent of respondents said they were working longer hours because of these tools.[19]

How you use these ubiquitous devices is the key to increased productivity. A relevant example is real estate agents. They facilitate sales by consulting their mobile devices when working with potential clients in the field. Their specific productivity booster is to have real time access to information about other listings that might interest the client if they choose not to purchase the home being show at the moment.

Making good use of digital technology also implies avoiding those tools most likely to drain productivity. At the top of the list are those beeps and alerts that pop up onto your screen to announce e-mails, collaborative software inputs from other workers, or that someone from your Skype network is now online. A key exception is that if your job requires paying immediate attention to such messages. An example would be when an engineering support technician receives an alert that her help is needed in closing a heavy-equipment sale.

Productivity tools refer more specifically to information technology devices, including apps aimed directly at enhancing productivity. Among the most popular is Slack, an office-messaging service that enables co-workers to communicate through via private or group messages. As a result, the individual worker is often flooded with messages from around the organization. Used selectively and with self-discipline, many of these tools can enhance productivity. In contrast, when these productivity tools are used as an end in themselves and occupy too much of a worker's time, they become a productivity drain. A related suggestion is to use just one collaboration tool. Research suggests that workers often resist using multiple collaboration services because they do not want to open one more window on their computer or load another app on their mobile device.[20]

Another problem is that these tools often consume more time than they are worth. Little by little, the information technology enthusiast begins to think that using productivity tools is his or her job. Such an individual will often boast about organizing 100 files into one device, communicating with 10 people simultaneously, and always being connected. All this activity might not translate into useful work outcomes, such as satisfying customers or improving a business process. A major reason many workers do not achieve productivity gains with information technology is that they do not invest the time saved into other productive activity.

Digital technology devices are attractive and intriguing. It is also important to know when simple mechanical or handwritten procedures are faster than office technology. For example, the simple 3×5 index card remains a powerful low-technology way of preparing and executing a to-do list. Managers and professionals who move from one location to another may find it a time waster to access a computer just to check their daily lists. Even checking a mobile device can be more disruptive than simply glancing at an index card attached to a pocket calendar.

Practice the Mental State of Peak Performance

peak performance
A mental state in which
maximum results are
achieved with minimum
effort.

To achieve maximum potential productivity, one must transcend ordinary levels of concentration and devotion to duty. That occurs in **peak performance**, a mental state in which maximum results are achieved with minimum effort. People who achieve peak performance typically have an important mission in life—such as building a top-quality company.[21]

Peak performers remain mentally calm and physically at ease when challenged by difficult problems. They focus intensely and stay involved, much like they would be in playing the best tennis game of their lives. Peak performance also involves careful planning for the task to be accomplished, including obtaining input from others. For example, if you had an upcoming meeting with a major customer, you might research the type of information that would be important to that customer. You may have experienced the state of peak performance when totally involved with a problem or task. At that moment, nothing else seems to exist.

To achieve peak performance, you must continually work toward being mentally calm and physically at ease. Concentrate intensely, but not so much that you choke. In addition to frequent practice, peak performance can be achieved through visualization. In visualization you develop a mental image of how you would act and feel at the point of peak performance. For example, imagine yourself making a flawless presentation to top-level management about the contributions of your department.

Take Naps or Meditate

A productivity booster is to take a nap of about 15 to 30 minutes designed to recharge the individual. Naps of 30 minutes or more may create grogginess and lower productivity for many people. Well-placed naps actually enhance rather than diminish productivity, and they are also an excellent stress reducer. An experiment conducted at the University of Michigan found that napping can be a cost-effective and easy technique to increase workplace productivity, especially safety. Nap pods and extended break times are especially useful for workplace naps. An advantage cited of napping is that it helped workers cope better with frustration, and they were therefore more likely to stay with a difficult problem until it was solved.[22]

The organizational nap taker must use discretion in napping so as not to be perceived as sleeping on the job. Toward this end, some workers nap in their cars or in a storeroom during lunch breaks. In companies where the organization accepts such behavior, some employees nap with their heads resting on their desks or worktables during breaks. Many workers continue to nap under their desks. Some companies offer nap rooms or other nap-friendly devices, such as the nap pods mentioned above. The nap pod blocks out light and sound.

Closely related to the productivity-boosting value of napping is *meditation*. The process physically changes neurological connections between parts of the brain and allows for a deep state of relaxation. Workers who meditate before and after work often find they can think more clearly about job challenges. A frequently used form of meditation is to get in a physically relaxed state and keep repeating a word or mantra. Yoga is essentially another form of meditation. Meditation, like striving for peak performance and napping, helps you concentrate and focus, thereby boosting your productivity, assuming that you have the right talent and skills to perform well.

Increase Your Supply of Mental Energy

Closely related to taking naps is the broader tactic of increasing your energy supply to boost you toward higher levels of productivity. An aspect of a manager's job that requires high energy is attending face-to-face meetings, or videoconferences, 25 hours per week. Many workers are not as productive as they or the company would like them to be largely because they lack enough energy for the demands of their work. Among the 540 business leaders who participated in a Leadership Pulse study, 61 percent reported working below what they perceived to be their optimal energy levels. Twenty-one percent said they were working above their optimal levels, and only 18 percent reported working at their most productive energy levels.[23] Working above the optimal energy level can be counterproductive because it is not sustainable and can lead to frustration.

Among the recommended techniques for increasing energy are getting sufficient sleep at night, napping during the day, physical exercise, meditation, proper diet, and mindfulness. (The last four will be mentioned in the discussion of work stress, later in this chapter.) A specific technique to enhance energy through physical exercise during working hours is to stand up and walk around for one to two minutes every 25 to 30 minutes. Many workers at New Balance, the athletic shoe and apparel company, participated in a program of walking around approximately one minute each half hour. Approximately one-third of the participants in the program reported higher levels of energy in the middle of the day.[24]

Work Smarter, Not Harder

A comprehensive time-management principle is to plan your activities carefully and discharge them in an imaginative way rather than simply working furiously. Several of the time-management suggestions already presented facilitate working smarter, not harder, such as streamlining your work and concentrating on high-output tasks. A working-smart approach requires that you spend a few minutes carefully planning how to implement your task. An example of working smarter would be the placement of an online or newspaper ad to fill a job vacancy. If you list the qualifications precisely, you can decrease the flood of completely unqualified candidates even though most candidates will still be unqualified.

Another example of working smarter, not harder is to use communication technology that fosters collaboration. A company intranet that allows you to find out what colleagues in other parts of the company are working on will enable you to spend less time in duplicated effort. For example, if you are developing a list of cost-saving suggestions for customer service, and you learn that Kim in Portland, Maine, is also developing such a list, you can share suggestions.

Build Flexibility into Your System

A time-management system must allow some room for flexibility. How else could you handle unanticipated problems? If you work 50 hours per week, build in a few hours for taking care of emergencies. If your plan is too tight, delegate some tasks to others or work more hours. Perhaps you can find a quicker way to accomplish several of your tasks. As with other forms of planning, do not let your to-do list become a straitjacket that prevents you from capitalizing on new opportunities. Suppose an item on today's to-do list is to download the latest antivirus program. A customer calls unexpectedly wanting to place a $150,000 order. Do not reply, "Let me call you back after I have finished checking for new antivirus programs."

Finally, to avoid staleness and stress, your schedule must allow sufficient time for rest and relaxation. The optimum amount of rest and relaxation will often boost productivity because it will enhance your mental energy.

LEARNING OBJECTIVE 2

Explain why people procrastinate and identify techniques for reducing procrastination.

procrastination
The delaying of action for no good reason.

UNDERSTANDING AND REDUCING PROCRASTINATION

The number one time waster for most people is **procrastination**, the delaying of action for no good reason. According to clinical psychologist Christain ljoscha Lukas, the procrastinator usually recognizes there will be future negative consequences because of the delayed action.[25] When we procrastinate, there is a gap between intention and action. Reducing procrastination pays substantial dividends in increased productivity, especially because speed can give a company a competitive advantage. Procrastination also needs to be taken seriously because such tendencies can doom a person to low performance. Figure 16-2 gives you an opportunity to think about your own tendencies toward procrastination, so get to it without delay. Here we consider why people procrastinate, and what can be done about the problem.

Why People Procrastinate

People procrastinate for many different reasons, with some of them being deep-rooted emotional problems, and others more superficial and related directly to the work. Here we look at eight major reasons for procrastination.

1   A major reason for, or explanation of procrastination, is that the person wants immediate gratification instead of longer-range gain. Procrastination researcher Timothy Psychl says the essence of procrastination is, "giving in to feel good."[26] Visualize Tanya who needs to get her department budget prepared by tomorrow night—a difficult and demanding chore. But instead, she wants the immediate gratification of checking out how well her investment portfolio has performed this week. Tanya therefore drops the work on the budget, and logs into her investment portfolio.

2   Some people fear failure or other negative consequences. As long as a person delays doing something of significance, he or she cannot be regarded as having performed poorly on the project. Other negative consequences include looking foolish in the eyes of others or developing a bad reputation. For instance, if a manager delays making an oral presentation, nobody will know whether he or she is an ineffective speaker. Fear of failure can be—but is not always—a deep-rooted personality problem that will make it difficult to overcome procrastination. See the suggestions presented in the following section.

3   Procrastination may stem from a desire to avoid uncomfortable, overwhelming, or tedious tasks. Many people delay preparing their income tax forms for this reason. Wharton School professor and organizational psychologist Adam Grant observes that people procrastinate to avoid negative emotions stirred up by work including anxiety, frustration, confusion, and boredom.[27]

Figure 16-2 Procrastination Tendencies

Circle **Yes** or **No** for each item:

1	I usually do my best work under the pressure of deadlines.	Yes	No
2	Before starting a project, I go through such rituals as sharpening every pencil, straightening up my desk more than once, and discarding bent paper clips.	Yes	No
3	I crave the excitement of the "last-minute rush."	Yes	No
4	I often think that if I delay something, it will go away, or the person who asked for it will forget about it.		
5	I extensively research something before taking action, such as obtaining five different estimates before getting the brakes repaired on my car.	Yes	No
6	I have a great deal of difficulty getting started on most projects, even those I enjoy.	Yes	No
7	I keep waiting for the right time to do something, such as getting started on an important report.	Yes	No
8	I often underestimate the time needed to do a project, and say to myself, "I can do this quickly, so I'll wait until next week."	Yes	No
9	It is difficult for me to finish most projects or activities.	Yes	No
10	I have several favorite diversions or distractions that I use to keep me from doing something unpleasant.	Yes	No

Total yes responses _____

The more **yes** responses, the more likely it is that you have a serious procrastination problem. A score of 8, 9, or 10 strongly suggests that procrastination lowers your productivity.

4 People frequently put off tasks that do not appear to offer meaningful rewards. Suppose you decide that your smartphone apps need a thorough updating. Even though you know it should be done, having a fresh set of apps might not be a particularly meaningful reward to you. A related reason for procrastination is that impulsivity drives the problem. We can receive an immediate reward right now by delaying a task, such as taking the time to get a refreshment or read a tweet. The reward from completing a project is much further into the future.[28]

5 Some people dislike being controlled. When a procrastinator does not do things on time, he or she has successfully rebelled against being controlled by another person's time schedule.

6 People sometimes are assigned tasks they perceive to be useless or needless, such as checking someone else's work. Rather than proceed with the trivial task, the individual procrastinates.

7 A neurological and emotional reason for procrastination is to achieve the stimulation and excitement that stems from rushing to meet a deadline. For example, some people enjoy fighting their way through traffic or running through an airline terminal so they can make an appointment or airplane flight barely on time. They appear to enjoy the rush of adrenaline, endorphins, and other hormones associated with hurrying.

8 Procrastination is sometimes a symptom of a negative emotional state such as self-defeating behavior (see Figure 15-2 about self-sabotage) or depression. The procrastinator may want to fail as a form of self-punishment, or may be so depressed that he or she just cannot get started on an important task. In

such cases, mental-health counseling may be required. Procrastination can also result from a negative form of perfectionism in which a person believes the project at hand has not been polished enough to deliver to another person. A deadline might be missed, as the person thinks, "With just a little more work, my report will be perfect." Another emotional factor driving procrastination is impulsiveness. Instead of remaining focused on an important goal, the person impulsively shifts attention to another activity (as with Tanya and her investment portfolio).

Approaches to Reducing and Controlling Procrastination

Procrastination often becomes a strong habit that is difficult to change. Nevertheless, the following strategies and tactics can be helpful in overcoming procrastination:

1. *Break the task down into smaller units.* By splitting a large task into smaller units, you can make a job appear less overwhelming. This approach is useful, of course, only if the task can be done in small pieces, such as a small business owner preparing tax returns by working on one category of expenses at a time: "Friday I document telephone and Internet expenses; Saturday I'll work on travel and entertainment."

2. *Make a commitment to others.* Your tendency to procrastinate on an important assignment may be reduced if you publicly state that you will get the job done by a certain time. You might feel embarrassed if you fail to meet your deadline.

3. *Reward yourself for achieving milestones.* A potent technique for overcoming any counterproductive behavior pattern is to give yourself a reward for progress toward overcoming the problem. Make your reward commensurate with the magnitude of the accomplishment.

4. *Calculate the cost of procrastination.* You can sometimes reduce procrastination by calculating its cost. Remind yourself, for example, that you might lose out on obtaining a high-paying job you really want if your résumé and cover letter are not ready on time. The cost of procrastination would include the difference in the salary between the job you do find and the one you really wanted. Another cost would be the loss of potential job satisfaction. An indirect approach to calculating the cost of procrastination is to think through how procrastination blocks attaining core values. If a person strongly values becoming wealthy, procrastinating about starting a new investment plan would be less likely.

5. *Post encouraging notes in your work and living area.* Encourage yourself to get something done by a particular time, via small notes, perhaps even using a digital camera to create computer wallpaper. For example, "The plan for recycling laser print cartridges is due September 15, and YOU CAN DO IT!!!!!"

6. *Counterattack.* Another way of combating procrastination is to force yourself to do something uncomfortable or frightening. After you begin, you are likely to find the task is not as onerous as you thought. Assume you have been delaying learning a foreign language even though you know it will help your career. You remember how burdensome it was studying another language in school. You grit your teeth and download the app for the target language. After listening for five minutes, you discover that beginning to study a foreign language again is not nearly as bad as you imagined.

7 *Post a progress chart in your work area.* The time and activity charts presented in Chapter 6 can be applied to combating procrastination. As you chart your progress in achieving each step in a large project, each on-time accomplishment will serve as a reward, and each missed deadline will be self-punishing. The constant reminder of what needs to be accomplished by what date will sometimes prod you to minimize delays. Figure 16-3 presents a basic version of a chart for combating procrastination. The time and activity chart is helpful because it fits into the more general solution to procrastination—get organized.

8 *Get perfectionism under control.* Not letting go of a document or project until it seems perfect will usually result in delays or no action. Visualize a homebuilder who does not want to place an expensive home on the market until "everything is perfect." Because perfection in an object with countless thousands of parts is extraordinarily difficult to attain, the builder will suffer substantial losses because the house cannot be sold if it is not on the market. One way to get perfectionism under control is to recognize that what constitutes perfection is most likely an arbitrary standard. Another approach is to use an evidence-based viewpoint of perfectionism. A recent meta-analysis of 2,300 studies found that in total, high levels of perfectionism are not constructive in the workplace.[29]

THE NATURE OF STRESS AND BURNOUT

Job stress and its related condition, job burnout, contribute to poor physical and mental health. Employee stress is a source of discomfort and a major concern to managers and stockholders. The Centers for Disease Control and Prevention report that stress is the leading workplace health problem, According to a consistent estimate, worker stress costs $300 billion annually due to lost productivity, turnover, psychological depression, and medical insurance costs.[30] A study indicated that work-related problems, such as hypertension, a cardiovascular disease that is often intensified by job stress can lead to about 120,000 deaths in the United States each year.[31]

LEARNING OBJECTIVE 3

Understand the nature of stress and burnout, including their consequences.

Figure 16-3 A Time and Activity Chart to Combat Procrastination

Charting key tasks and their deadlines, along with your performance in meeting the deadlines, can sometimes help overcome procrastination.

Tasks to be Accomplished	Deadlines for Task Accomplishment					
	Jan 1	Jan 31	Feb 15	Feb 28	Mar 15	Mar 31
Expense reports	Did it					
Real-estate estimates		Blew it				
Website installed			One day late			
Replace broken furniture				Made it		
Plan office picnic					On time	
Collect delinquent account						Blew it

stress

The mental and physical condition that results from a perceived threat that cannot be dealt with readily.

To effectively prevent and control stress, you first need to understand the nature and cause of these conditions. A good starting point in understanding stress symptoms is to take the self-quiz presented in Figure 16-4. As used here, **stress** is the mental and physical condition that results from a perceived threat that cannot be dealt with readily. The demands of the situation exceed your personal resources for coping with them. Stress is an internal response to a state of activation. The stressed person is physically and mentally aroused. Stress ordinarily occurs in a threatening

---

Figure 16-4 The Stress Questionnaire

Here is a brief questionnaire to give a rough estimate of whether you are facing too much stress. Apply each question to the last six months of your life. Check the appropriate column.

Mostly Yes	Mostly No	
☐	☐	1 Have you been feeling uncomfortably tense lately?
☐	☐	2 Do you frequently argue with people close to you?
☐	☐	3 Is your romantic life very unsatisfactory?
☐	☐	4 Do you have trouble sleeping?
☐	☐	5 Do you feel lethargic about life?
☐	☐	6 Do many people annoy or irritate you?
☐	☐	7 Do you have constant cravings for candy and other sweets?
☐	☐	8 Is your consumption of cigarettes or alcohol way up?
☐	☐	9 Are you becoming addicted to soft drinks, coffee, or tea?
☐	☐	10 Do you find it difficult to concentrate on your work?
☐	☐	11 Do you frequently grind your teeth?
☐	☐	12 Are you increasingly forgetful about little things, such as answering e-mail or mailing a letter?
☐	☐	13 Are you increasingly forgetful about big things, such as appointments and major errands?
☐	☐	14 Are you making far too many trips to the lavatory?
☐	☐	15 Have people commented lately that you do not look well?
☐	☐	16 Do you get into verbal fights with others too frequently?
☐	☐	17 Have you been involved in more than one breakup with a friend lately?
☐	☐	18 Do you have more than your share of tension headaches?
☐	☐	19 Do you feel nauseated much too often?
☐	☐	20 Do you feel light-headed or dizzy almost every day?
☐	☐	21 Do you have churning sensations in your stomach far too often?
☐	☐	22 Are you in a big hurry all the time?
☐	☐	23 Are far too many things bothering you these days?
☐	☐	24 Do you hurry through activities even when you are not rushed for time?
☐	☐	25 Do you often feel that you are in the panic mode?

Scoring: 0–6 Mostly Yes answers: You seem to be experiencing a normal amount of stress.

7–16 Mostly Yes answers: Your stress level seems high. Become involved in some kind of stress-management activity, such as the activities described in this chapter.

17–25 Mostly Yes answers: Your stress level appears to be much too high. Seek the help of a mental-health professional or visit your family physician (or do both).

or negative situation, such as being fired. However, stress can also be caused by a positive situation, such as receiving a major promotion or bonus.

Symptoms of Stress

A person experiencing stress displays certain symptoms indicating that he or she is trying to cope with a stressor (any force creating the stress reaction). These symptoms can include a host of physiological, emotional, and behavioral reactions.

Physiological symptoms of stress include increased heart rate, blood pressure, breathing rate, pupil size, and perspiration. These symptoms surface because chemical changes in the body that ultimately produce the hormones cortisol and adrenaline activate the body's fight-or-flight response. If these physiological symptoms are severe or persist over a prolonged period, the result can be a stress-related disorder, such as a heart attack, hypertension, migraine headache, ulcer, colitis, or allergy. The underlying problem is that under chronic stress, cortisol weakens muscle, suppresses the immune system and elevates the risk of high blood pressure.[32] Because of the weakened immune system, people may experience difficulty shaking a common cold or recovering from a sexually transmitted disease. In general, any disorder classified as psychosomatic is precipitated by emotional stress.

Emotional symptoms of stress include anxiety, tension, depression, discouragement, boredom, prolonged fatigue, feelings of hopelessness, and various kinds of defensive thinking. Note that anxiety is a general sense of dread, fear, or worry for no immediate reason, and is a symptom of stress. Behavioral symptoms include nervous habits, such as facial twitching, and sudden decreases in job performance due to forgetfulness and errors in concentration or judgment. Increased use of alcohol and other drugs may also occur. Procrastination is another potential symptom of negative stress.

Job Performance Consequences of Stress

Stress has both negative and positive job consequences, and these consequences are closely related to symptoms. For example, if a worker concentrates poorly, or consumes too much alcohol as a result of stress, his or her job performance will suffer. **Hindrance stressors** are those stressful events and thoughts that have a negative effect on motivation and performance. In contrast, **challenge stressors** have a positive direct effect on motivation and performance.[33] A study showed that hindrance stressors will often decrease organizational citizenship behavior and increase counterproductive (poor performance) behaviors.[34] Challenge stressors have been reframed as finding your stress sweet spot, the amount of stress or arousal that enable you to function at your highest level.[35]

People require the right amount of stress to keep them mentally and physically alert. Managers create challenge stressors by challenging workers and being passionate about work.[36] If the stress is particularly uncomfortable or distasteful, however, it will lower job performance—particularly on complex, demanding jobs. An example of a stressor that will lower job performance for most people is a bullying, abrasive manager who wants to see the employee fail.

A person's perception of something (or somebody) usually determines whether it acts as a challenge or hindrance stressor. For example, one person might perceive an inspection by top-level managers to be so frightening that he is irritable toward team members. Another manager might welcome the visit as a chance to proudly display her department's high-quality performance.

hindrance stressors
Stressful events and thoughts that have a negative effect on motivation and performance.

challenge stressors
Sources of stress that have a positive direct effect on motivation and performance.

job burnout

A pattern of emotional, physical, and mental exhaustion in response to chronic job stressors.

After prolonged exposure to job stress, a person runs the risk of feeling burned out—a drained, used-up feeling. **Job burnout** is a pattern of emotional, physical, and mental exhaustion in response to chronic job stressors. Cynicism, apathy, and indifference are the major behavioral symptoms of the burned-out worker. Hopelessness is another key symptom of burnout, with the worker often feeling that nothing he or she does makes a difference, and is not accomplishing much of value. Correspondingly, burnout involves losing a sense of the basic purpose and fulfillment of your work.[37] Supervisors are more at risk for burnout than other workers because they deal primarily with the demands of other people.

Two studies conducted in a variety of organizations showed that burnout in the form of emotional exhaustion leads to lower job performance, less organizational citizenship behavior, and an intention to quit.[38] Have you ever experienced the phenomenon of being so exhausted that your motivation suffered?

Absence of ample positive feedback and other rewards is strongly associated with job burnout. As a consequence of not knowing how well they are doing and not receiving recognition, employees often become discouraged and emotionally exhausted. The result is often—but certainly not always—job burnout. The right type of leader/manager can help prevent the problems of burnout. A study with two different samples of workers suggested that workers who perceive their leaders to be charismatic are less likely to suffer from burnout. Workers who do not feel in control of their own fate are more likely to avoid burnout by having a charismatic leader.[39]

Factors Contributing to Stress and Burnout

Factors within a person, as well as adverse organizational conditions, can cause or contribute to stress and burnout. Personal-life stress and work stress also influence each other. Work stress can create problems—and therefore stress—at home. And stress stemming from personal problems can lead to problems—and therefore stress—at work. Because stress is additive, if you have considerable personal stress you will be more susceptible to job stress, and vice versa.

Figure 16-5 reports the results of a work stress survey of 1,512 adults conducted by the American Psychological Association.

Figure 16-5 Top Sources of Work Stress Among U.S. Workers

Percentage of people reporting consider these are somewhat or very significant sources of stress.

Rank	Potential Stressor	Percentage
1	Low salary	49
2	Lack of opportunity for advancement	46
3	Heavy worklod	42
4 (tie)	Unrealistic job expectations	39
4 (tie)	Hours	39
6	Job insecurity	37
7	Inflexible hours	36
8	Work interfering during person or family life	34

Source: Adapted from "Top Sources of Work Stress," *2018 Work and Family Well-Being Survey*, (www.apaexcellence.org), p. 13.

Factors Within the Individual

Hostile, aggressive, and impatient people find ways of turning almost any job into a stressful experience. Such individuals are labeled Type A, in contrast to their more easygoing Type B counterparts. In addition to being angry, the outstanding trait of Type A people is their strong sense of time urgency, known as "hurry sickness." This sense of urgency compels them to achieve more and more in less and less time. Angry, aggressive (usually male) Type A people are more likely than Type Bs to experience cardiovascular disorders.

Although Type A behavior is associated with coronary heart disease, only some features of the Type A personality pattern may be related to cardiac disorders. The adverse health effects generally stem from hostility, anger, cynicism, and suspiciousness in contrast to impatience, ambition, and drive. Recognize also that not every hard-driving, impatient person is correctly classified as Type A. Managers who love their work and enjoy other people are not particularly prone to heart disease.

Another notable personality characteristic related to job stress is **locus of control**, the way in which people look at causation in their lives. People who believe they have more control over their actions than do external events are less stress prone. For example, a 50-year-old man with an internal locus of control might lose his job and say, "I don't care if a lot of age discrimination in business exists. I have many needed skills and many employers will want me. Age will not be an issue for me in finding suitable employment." This man's internal locus of control will help him ward off stress related to job loss. A 50-year-old with an external locus of control will experience high stress because the person believes that he or she is helpless in the face of job discrimination.

People who have high expectations are likely to experience job burnout at some point in their careers, because they may not receive as many rewards as they are seeking. People who need constant excitement also face a high risk of job burnout, because they bore easily and quickly.

Related to factors within the individual that contribute to stress are personal problems and worries. For example, workers who worry considerably about housing costs bring considerable stress with them into the workplace. A personal worry that creates stress for many people both inside and outside the workplace is **nomophobia**, a form of anxiety stemming from having no access to a smartphone or phone battery being dangerously low. (*Nomophobia* is short for non-mobile phobia and is also referred to as battery anxiety.) The same condition is characterized by the fear people can experience when they are out of mobile contact entirely.[40]

locus of control
The way in which people look at causation in their lives.

nomophobia
A form of anxiety stemming from having no access to a smartphone or phone battery being dangerously low (short for non-mobile phobia; also referred to as battery anxiety).

Adverse Organizational Conditions

Under ideal conditions, workers experience just enough stress to prompt them to respond creatively and energetically to their jobs. Unfortunately, high stress levels created by adverse organizational conditions lead to many negative symptoms.

Work and Information Overload A major contributor to job stress is work overload. Demands on white-collar workers appear to be at an all-time high, as companies attempt to increase work output and decrease staffing at the same time. According to stress specialist, David Posen, the modern trend toward heavy workloads began in the 1990s with the first wave of downsizing due to the global recession and new technologies. Companies trimmed down, and the trend remains.[41] Work overload also comes from working longer hours, which often leads to stroke, as revealed by a review of 17 studies involving 528,908 men and women followed for an average of 7.2 years. Working 55 hours or more per week was linked to a one-third greater risk of stroke compared to a 35–40-hour workweek. The exact cause of experiencing a stroke was difficult to determine, but it appeared that physical inactivity, high alcohol consumption, and repetitive stress all enhance the risk.[42]

A specific overload demand relates to information overload, as many managers and professionals are so bombarded with simultaneous and competing messages that they suffer from *attention deficit trait*. The sheer volume of information combined with the many different ways of accessing information, makes many workers deficient in their ability to pay attention.[43] The brain becomes overloaded leading to symptoms of distractibility, inner frenzy, and impatience. In short, their brains are so loaded they become spastic. (If you are suffering from attention deficit trait, follow the suggestions about personal productivity and stress management presented in this chapter.)

Extreme Interpersonal Conflict Extreme conflict with co-workers, including office politics or with managers is also a stressor. Another annoyance is short lead times—too little notice to get complex assignments accomplished. A powerful stressor today is job insecurity due to the many mergers and downsizings. Worrying about having one's job outsourced to another region, country, or a subcontractor is also a stressor.

Role Ambiguity Not knowing what is expected of you has been long observed as a major job stressor. **Role ambiguity** is a condition in which the job holder receives confusing or poorly defined expectations. The person facing extreme role ambiguity proclaims, "I don't know what I'm supposed to be doing or what will happen to me if I do it." A synthesis of many studies involving over 35,000 employees found that role ambiguity is one of the two job stressors most strongly related to negative job performance. The other is situational constraints, which refer to factors that limit the worker's ability to accomplish the job, such as improper machinery or inadequate supplies.[44]

role ambiguity
A condition in which the job holder receives confusing or poorly defined expectations.

job demand–job control model
A model demonstrating the relationship between high or low job demands and high or low job control. It shows that workers experience the most stress when the demands of the job are high yet they have little control over the activity.

Limited Control Over Work According to the **job demand–job control model**, workers experience the most stress when the demands of the job are high, yet they have little control over the activity.[45] (See Figure 16-6) A customer service representative with limited authority who has to deal with a major error by the firm would fit this category. In contrast, when job demands are high and the worker has a great degree of control, the worker will be energized, motivated, and creative. A branch manager in a successful business might fit this scenario.

Figure 16-6 The Job Demand–Job Control Model

A worker is likely to experience the most job stress when he or she exercises low control over a job with high demands.

	Low Job Demands	High Job Demands
Low Control	Passive Job	High-Strain Job
High Control	Low-Strain Job	Active Job

Adverse Customer Interactions Interactions with customers can be a major stressor. Stressful events include customers losing control, using profanity, badgering employees, harassing employees, and lying. Part of the problem is that the sales associate often feels helpless when placed in conflict with a customer. The sales associate is told, "the customer is always right." Furthermore, the store manager usually sides with the customer in a dispute with the sales associate.

Emotional Labor Another aspect of adverse customer interaction is the stressor of having to control the expression of emotion to please or avoid displeasing a customer. Imagine having to smile at a customer who belittles you or makes unwanted sexual advances. **Emotional labor** is the process of regulating both feelings and expressions to meet organizational goals.[46] Regulation involves both surface acting and deep acting. Surface acting means faking expressions such as smiling, whereas deep acting involves controlling feelings, such as suppressing anger toward a customer you perceive to be annoying or hostile.

emotional labor
The process of regulating both feelings and expressions to meet organizational goals.

Sales workers and customer service representatives experience considerable emotional labor among all workers because so often they have to fake facial expressions and feelings to please customers. The supervisor often dictates the type of emotional display (or display rules). Call center workers are expected to calm down angry callers—a behavior that often requires the suppression of negative feelings. In addition, they are supposed to end calls on a positive note, perhaps with a sale.[47]

When workers experience emotional labor, co-workers might feel the negative impact. A study was conducted about the spillover effects of emotional labor with frontline service employees and their immediate supervisors in a four-star hotel in China. The study showed that surface acting with customers led to ego depletion for the service workers, which in turn prompted harmful behavior toward co-workers. In contrast, deep acting did not lead to ego depletion or the harming of co-workers. A sample questionnaire item for supervisor in relation to employee harming was "This employee is nasty to his/her co-workers."[48]

Work–Family Conflict **Work–family conflict** is a major stressor that represents a combination of individual and organizational factors contributing to stress. It occurs when the individual has to perform multiple roles: worker, spouse, and often parent. The stress comes about because of the difficulty of attempting to fill two roles at the same time, such as having to manage a restaurant on New Year's Eve, while your spouse insists you celebrate the event together. Dual-earner couples are particularly susceptible to work–family conflict because of the demands on their time.

work–family conflict
A major stressor that represents a combination of individual and organizational factors contributing to stress.

Another major contributor to work–family conflict is that because of communication technology, the boundaries between work and family life are often blurred. It is common practice for managers and corporate professionals to initiate or receive work-related communications outside of regular business hours. Another communication technology–based source of work–family conflict is that people bring home into the workplace, such as doing online shopping during working hours, managing personal deadlines (such as an online application for Little League) and sending e-mails back and forth to family and friends.

The more time invested in the job, the greater the exposure to work–family conflict, and the greater the stress. A confusing aspect of work–family conflict is that it works in both directions. Work responsibilities can create conflict with home responsibilities, and family responsibilities can create conflict with work. The conflict in both directions creates stress.[49] Imagine yourself as a marathon runner, who runs a weekend marathon. You are too exhausted to go on a business trip on Monday, so you become stressed about dealing with this conflict.

STRESS-MANAGEMENT TECHNIQUES

LEARNING OBJECTIVE **4**

Explain how stress can be managed effectively.

Everybody experiences stress, so how you manage stress can be the key to your well-being. Constructive techniques for managing job stress on your own can be divided into three categories: control, symptom management, and escape. Companies often provide services, such as wellness programs that give you the opportunity to implement some of these techniques. A telling example is the wellness program run by the Cleveland Clinic. Executive Director Joe Sweet says the clinic's number one request is, "stress support for our clients."[50] Employee assistance programs, as mentioned in Chapter 15, are another resource to help employees manage stress.

A major role for managers in dealing with the stress of workers is to encourage them to pursue stress-management techniques on their own and/or rely on company programs. When choosing methods of stress reduction, it is useful to select methods you truly enjoy so they won't feel like chores.

Methods for Control and Reduction of Stress

The seven control techniques described next consist of both actions and mental evaluations that help people take charge in stressful situations.

1 *Embrace the stress.* A growing body of research suggests that the best way to manage stress is to embrace rather than trying to minimize or get rid of it. Welcoming your stress as a positive force, can boost confidence and improve performance—as described with challenge stressors.[51]

2 *Get social support.* Few people can go it alone when experiencing prolonged stress. Receiving social support—encouragement, understanding, and friendship—from other people is an important strategy for coping successfully with job stress.

3 *Improve your work habits.* You can use the techniques described for improving your personal productivity to reduce stress. People typically experience stress when they feel themselves losing control of their work assignments. Conscientious employees are especially prone to negative stress when they cannot get their work under control.

4 *Develop positive self-talk.* Stress-resistant people are basically optimistic and cheerful. This kind of positivism can be learned by switching to positive self-talk instead of thinking many negative thoughts.

5 *Hug the right people.* Hugging is seriously regarded as vital for physical and mental well-being. People who do not receive enough quality touching may suffer from low self-esteem, ill health, depression, and loneliness. Conversely, quality touching may help people cope better with job stress. The hugging, however, has to be genuine.

6 *Demand less than perfection from yourself.* By demanding less than 100 percent performance from yourself, you will fail less frequently in your own perceptions. Not measuring up to one's own unrealistically high standards creates a considerable amount of stress.

7 *Strive to not neglect aspects of life outside of work.* There is a big difference between a negative type of workaholic and a person who simply works hard and long to attain constructive goals. A negative workaholic usually becomes anxious when not working.[52] When a person neglects other aspects of life outside of work, such as spending time with family, friends, and physical exercise, the person is more likely to suffer from stress symptoms, such as irritability and lack of focus. The ability to set healthy boundaries between work and personal life is often referred to as unplugging from work because so much business is conducted electronically.

Symptom Management

This category of stress management refers to tactics that address the symptoms related to job stress. Dozens of symptom-management techniques have been developed, including the following:

1 *Make frequent use of relaxation techniques, a form of meditation.* Learning to relax reduces the adverse effects of stress. The **relaxation response** is a general-purpose method of learning to relax by yourself and is a form of meditation. The key ingredient of this technique is to make yourself quiet and comfortable. At the same time, think of the word *one* (or any simple chant or prayer) with every breath for about 10 minutes. The technique slows you down both physiologically and emotionally and at the same time reduces the adverse effects of stress. A major contributor of the relaxation response is that it is a physical state of deep rest that counteracts the harmful effects of fighting stressors.[53]

relaxation response
A general-purpose method of learning to relax by yourself.

2 *Practice mindfulness.* Another technique for preventing and reducing stress, as well as enhancing productivity is **mindfulness**. The term refers to concentrating on the present moment without making judgments about what is happening. The use of mindfulness to reduce stress and attain other positive mental states has moved from a Buddhist concept founded approximately 2,000 years ago to a mainstream method. Mindful-Based Stress Reduction (MSRB) is used in thousands of training programs as well as mental health and community settings. Participants are taught a formal daily practice of introspection and self-observation without judgment. A typical approach is to mentally focus on the process of breathing or your foot movements while walking slowly without looking down.[54]

mindfulness
Concentrating on the present moment without making judgments about what is happening.

3 *Get appropriate physical exercise.* Physical exercise helps dissipate some of the tension created by job stress, and it also helps the body ward off future stress-related disorders. A physically fit, well-rested person can usually tolerate more frustration than a physically run-down, tired person. One way in which exercise helps combat stress is that it releases endorphins. These morphine-like chemicals are produced in the brain and act as painkillers and anti-depressants. Workers who travel frequently particularly need physical exercise because travel can damage the body, producing such symptoms as muscle cramps and even blood clots from long airplane trips. More information about the benefits of physical exercise is presented in Figure 16-7.

4 *Try to cure hurry sickness.* People with hurry sickness should learn how to relax and enjoy the present for its own sake. Specific tactics include having at least one idle period every day; eating nutritious, not overly seasoned foods to help decrease nervousness; and finding enrichment in an area of life not related to work.

Figure 16-7 The Benefits of Physical Exercise

- Increases energy and reduces feelings of frequent fatigue.
- Reduces feelings of tension, anxiety, and depression.
- Improves sleep.
- Improves concentration.
- Enhances self-esteem and self-confidence.
- Helps you lose weight or maintain a healthy weight providing you do not consume more food because you have exercised.
- Reduces the risk of heart disease, or improves cardiac function if you have had a heart attack or bypass; reduces harmful cholesterol and raises levels of HDL (good) cholesterol in as little as eight weeks; the good results are most likely to occur when combined with moderate alcohol consumption (two glasses per day for adult males, one for adult females).

- Strengthens your bones and muscles.
- Reduces the risk of colon cancer.
- Lowers pulse rate thereby decreasing high blood pressure and the risk of stroke.
- Controls blood sugar levels if you have, or are at risk for diabetes.
- Improves bone density and lowers the risk of osteoporosis and fractures as you get older.
- Improves muscle tone so you feel better and look better.
- Improves your mental health and mood.
- Slows the effects of aging, such as physical and mental decline, and increases longevity.

Source: "Physical Activity and Health," *Centers for Disease Control and Prevention* (http://www.cdc.gov/chronicdisease/) June 4, 2015, pp.1–4; Tara Parker-Pope, "Doctors' Orders: Ways to Work Exercise Into a Busy Day," *The Wall Street Journal*, January 9, 2007, p. D1; John Cloud, "Why Exercise Won't Make You Thin," *Time*, August 11, 2009, p. 45; Sanjay Gupta, "Work Out and Drink Up," *Time*, February 4, 2008, p. 54.

Removal of the Stressor

Methods of removing the stressor are actions and reappraisals of situations that provide the stressed individual some escape from the stressor. Eliminating the stressor is the most effective escape technique. For example, if a manager is experiencing stress because of serious understaffing in his or her department, that manager should negotiate to receive authorization to hire additional help. Mentally blocking out a stressful thought is another escape technique, but it may not work in the long run.

A strategic method of escaping stress is to identify your work skills, and then find work to match those skills. Assessing your skills and preferences can help you understand why you find some tasks or roles more stressful than others.[55] For example, many people enter the computer science or information technology field without having appropriate skills and interest for that type of work. When they are asked to perform such tasks as coding for nine hours in one day, they become stressed out, because they lack the right aptitude and interest for such work.

Given that you could probably locate 500 million Internet posts on the subject of job stress, we have not mentioned every possible approach to managing stress. Try a few of the techniques mentioned in this chapter that you think would best fit your situation and personality.

1 **Identify techniques for improving work habits and time management.**

One way of increasing your personal productivity is to improve your work habits and time-management skills: develop a mission, goals, and a strong work ethic, and practice self-discipline. Clean up your work area and sort out your tasks. Prepare a to-do list and assign priorities. Also, streamline your work; work at a steady, rapid pace; minimize times wasters and interruptions; minimize distractions including nonproductive multitasking; and concentrate on one task at a time. Concentrate on high-output tasks; do creative and routine work at different times; and stay in control of paperwork, e-mail, and voice mail. Making effective use of office technology is essential. Practice the mental state of peak performance; take naps or meditate; increase your supply of mental energy; work smarter, not harder; and build flexibility into your system.

2 **Explain why people procrastinate and identify techniques for reducing procrastination.**

Avoid procrastinating by understanding why you procrastinate. Take remedial action, including the following: break the task down into smaller units, make a commitment to others, reward yourself for achieving milestones, calculate the cost of procrastination, post encouraging notes in your work and living area, counterattack against an uncomfortable task, and post a progress chart, and get perfectionism under control.

3 **Understand the nature of stress and burnout, including their consequences.**

Stress is the mental and physical condition that results from a perceived threat that cannot be dealt with readily. Symptoms of stress can be physiological, emotional, and behavioral. Stress has job performance consequences. Hindrance stressors are negative, whereas challenge stressors are positive. Job burnout is a pattern of emotional, physical, and mental exhaustion in response to chronic job stressors. Hopelessness is another key symptom of burnout.

Job stress is caused by factors within the individual, such as Type A behavior and an external locus of control, and nomophobia. A variety of adverse organizational conditions, including work overload, role ambiguity, low control over a demanding job, and work–family conflict contribute to stress. People with high expectations are candidates for burnout. Limited rewards and lack of feedback from the organization contribute to burnout.

4 **Explain how stress can be managed effectively.**

Methods of preventing and controlling stress and burnout can be divided into three categories: attempts to control stressful situations, symptom management, and removal of the stressor. Specific tactics include getting social support, improving your work habits, using relaxation techniques, getting appropriate physical exercise, practicing mindfulness, and trying to cure the hurry sickness.

Key Terms and Phrases

productivity 491

work ethic 491

self-discipline 492

time box 494

work streamlining 494

peak performance 501

procrastination 503

stress 507

hindrance stressors 508

challenge stressors 508

job burnout 509

locus of control 510

nomophobia 510

role ambiguity 511

job demand–job control model 511

emotional labor 512

work–family conflict 512

relaxation response 514

mindfulness 514

Questions

1. To what extent are privacy pods an effective solution to the problem that many workers have with working in an open-office plan?

2. What is your mission in life? If you do not have a mission, how might you develop one?

3. Have you noticed the frequency of errors in dealing with business firms, such as billing errors, names spelled incorrectly, and customer problems that were supposed to be fixed, but proved to be unfixed? What work habit explanation can you offer for all these errors?

4. With so many tasks and work processes being automated today, why bother studying about improving personal productivity?

5. Assume it really is possible to be highly productive even if your work area is cluttered and littered. Why might having an uncluttered, tidy work area still help you in your career?

6. Why might mindfulness be useful in both reducing stress and enhancing personal productivity?

7. Why are good work habits and time management so effective in reducing job stress?

Skill-Building Exercise 16-A: Getting Uncluttered

Many time-management experts believe a major contributor to low productivity is that people's lives are too cluttered with material possessions. If you have less clutter around you, your concentration and focus will improve. A specific recommendation is to throw out one object every day, including old newspapers, magazines, and e-mail messages. (Selling some of your clutter in a garage sale or on eBay might be an extra incentive.) Beginning today, throw out something every day from your living quarters or work area. Anything you discard counts, from a few pencil stubs to an obsolete laptop. By the end of two weeks, see how much progress you made in reducing clutter. Of more significance, analyze whether your efforts at becoming uncluttered are enhancing your ability to accomplish work. Also, has this exercise made you feel better and less stressed?

Skill-Building Exercise 16-B: Good and Bad Ways to Reduce Stress

The purpose of this exercise is to help participants understand the difference between constructive and less constructive ways of reducing stress. The materials needed for the exercise are a whiteboard, a blackboard, or a computerized method of projecting information on a screen. One at a time, class members present in front of the class a technique they use for managing or reducing stress that they are willing to share. (Others in the class might have ways of reducing stress they would prefer to keep private.) Participants speak one at a time. As each new technique is suggested, the audience shouts either "Good" or "Bad." Based on majority opinion, the moderator places the technique in the Good or Bad column.

A good technique is defined roughly as one that produces almost all benefits. A bad technique is one that produces short-lived benefits, such as a "high," followed by negative side effects. (An example would be getting drunk to escape a major problem.) For some or all of the techniques, people should justify their classification as Good or Bad.

After the techniques are listed for all to see, the class discusses any conclusions about the difference between good and bad techniques. The group also discusses why knowing the difference is important.

Management Now—Online Skill-Building Exercise: Effectiveness of a Personal Productivity Tool

Dozens of digital personal productivity tools have been developed in recent years, and new tools continue to emerge. Search the Internet to identify one or two personality productivity tools that appear to really pay off in boosting personal productivity. Search for any evidence that the tool does boost productivity rather than just giving the user one more desktop or mobile task to deal with. If possible, try the tool yourself. Or,

look for blogs or comments on the effectiveness of the productivity tool. See if you can find evidence for the value of the productivity tool other than what is presented in statements by its developer. Based on this exercise, reach a conclusion about whether the productivity tool or tools you identify would be worth using.

Lance Wants to Boost His Energy

Lance, 32 years old, has what he regards as a dream job at this stage of his career; the product manager for forklift trucks at a construction equipment manufacturer. Although many people do not regard forklifts as glamorous, these trucks are expensive, and must often be adapted to the demand of a particular purchaser. As product manager, Lance conducts market research, and coordinates with engineering and manufacturing to meet customer requirements. He also works hard to ensure the forklift trucks get their share of company resources.

Lance is married, coaches his daughter's youth soccer team, is a member of three trade associations, and is actively involved with social media to help promote the company's forklift trucks. A major problem Lance faces is having enough energy to get his professional work done successfully and also meet this family and personal life obligations.

Lance says he works about 55 hours per week, and gets an average of 6.5 hours of sleep per night. He travels away from home at least one night per week. He spends about 30 minutes per night processing e-mail messages and searching the Internet for trade information about the forklift industry. Lance said that

for the last six months, he has struggled to find enough energy to perform at his best on the job.

"I'm feeling depleted," says Lance. "I don't have much time for working out, but I do fit in a little running here and there. I also do push-ups before taking a shower. I rely heavily on soft drinks, coffee, and energy drinks to get me through the day. All this caffeine does get me feeling a little sick from time to time, but I need to be pumped up to be on top of my job as a product manager. I'm afraid to ask my manager if I could work a few less hours per week because there would be somebody else to take my place.

"My last physical exam indicates I am in good physical shape. But I'm still looking for an answer to my energy problem."

Case Questions

1 What is your evaluation of Lance's approach to boosting his energy?

2 What do you recommend Lance do about boosting his energy?

3 To what extent do you think Lance should find a new job or career?

Harper, The Busy Office Manager

Harper looked at the kitchen clock and said to Mike, her husband, "Oh no, it's 7:25, and it's my turn to drop off Jason and Gloria at the childcare center. Once again, I'll start my day late for childcare and just barely making it to work on time."

After getting Jason and Gloria settled at the childcare center, Harper dashed off to the public accounting firm where she worked as the office manager. Harper found an e-mail from Gabriella, a partner in the firm: "See you today at 11:30 for the review of overhead expenses. Two other partners will be attending."

According to Harper's calendar, the meeting was one week from today. Harper called Gabriella immediately and said, "My apologies. My schedule says that the meeting is one week from today, at 11:30. I'm just not ready with the figures for today's meeting."

"My calendar says the meeting is today," responded Gabriella harshly. "I am ready for the meeting, and so are Craig and Gunther (the other partners). This isn't the first time you've gotten your weeks moved up. The meeting will go on, however poorly you have to perform."

"I'll be there," said Harper. "It's just a question of reviewing some figures that I've already collected." Harper calculated that she had less than three hours to prepare a report on overhead. She then glanced at her calendar to see what else she had scheduled for the morning. All was clear except for the entry: "PA/LC." Harper quickly recalled that the initials stood for "performance appraisal with Lucy Cruthers," the head bookkeeper at the firm. She then sent Lucy an e-mail suggesting that they meet the following week at the same time.

Harper had a difficult time locating the file she needed. Harper asked Lois, her administrative assistant, to help her locate the file. She scanned about 100 documents and said, "Here's a possibility, a document labeled PTR. The initials could refer to

"preparing for partners." Lois proved to be correct, and Harper dug into preparing the report, now only two hours away.

At the meeting, the partners accepted her analysis of overhead expenses and said they would study her findings further. As the meeting ended, a senior partner said to Harper, "If you had gotten your weeks straight, I think you would have presented your analysis in more depth."

Harper returned from lunch at 2 p.m. and decided to finish the report on overhead expenses that she had prepared for the partners. By 4 p.m., Harper was ready to tackle other tasks listed on her daily planner. However, Lois told her that an employment agency representative was in the building and had decided to drop in and talk about their temporary employment services.

"Might as well let her in," said Harper. "We will soon be hiring some temporary bookkeepers. It's getting too late to do much anyway."

On the way home from the childcare center, the oldest child, Gloria, asked if the family could eat at a fast-food restaurant this evening. Harper said, "OK, but I'll have to stop at an ATM first. We'll ask dad if he wants to eat out tonight before his class." Mike agreed and said to Harper "By the way, how did your day go?"

Harper replied, "I just fell one day further behind schedule. I'll have to do some paperwork after the children are asleep. Maybe we can watch the late news together. We should both be free by then."

Case Questions

1 **What time-management mistakes does Harper appear to be making?**

2 **What does Harper appear to be doing right from the standpoint of managing time?**

3 **What suggestions can you offer Harper to help her get her schedule more under control?**

ENDNOTES

1. Original story created from facts and observations in the following sources: Sarah Holder, "Can 'Pods' Bring Quiet to the Noisy Open Office?" *City Lab* (www.citylab.com), July 2, 2019, pp. 1–13; Catey Hill, "Overworked and Seeking Privacy, American Workers Turn to the Pod," *Market Watch* (www.marketwatch.com), December 13, 2018, pp. 1–4; Sarah E. Needleman, "Sick of Noise, Office Workers Clamor to Think Inside the Box." *The Wall Street Journal*, November 28, 2018, pp. A1, A10; "Office Privacy Pods: Inside Their Truly Unique Design," *Zen Booth* (https://zenbooth.net), January 31, 2019, pp. 1–7.

2. Adaptation of a definition presented in Robert D. Pritchard et al., "The Productivity Measurement and Enhancement System: A Meta-Analysis," *Journal of Applied Psychology*, May 2008, p. 540.

3. Harriet Tory and Sarah Chaney. "Worker-Productivity Gains Lag Behind," *The Wall Street Journal*, November 2, 2018, p. A2.

4. Adam A. Rapp, Daniel G. Bachrach, and Tammy L. Rapp, "The Influence of Time Management Skill on the Curvilinear Relationship Between Organizational Citizenship Behavior and Task Performance," *Journal of Applied Psychology*, July 2013, pp. 668–677.

5. Cited in Ed Brown, "The 'Natural Laws' of Saving Time," *Fortune*, February 1, 1999, p. 138.

6. Alexandra Samuel, "The Power of Personal Metrics," *The Wall Street Journal*, March 2, 2020, p. R11.

7. Ed Frauenheim, "Commitment Issues," *Workforce Management*, November 16, 2009, p. 20.

8. Monica Khemsurov, "Everything in Its Place," *Bloomberg Businessweek*, January 19–January 25, 2015, pp. 74–75.

9. Paul Keegan, "The Master of Getting Things Done," *Business 2.0*, July 2007, p. 77.

10. Research cited in Jay Dixit, "Office Spaces," *Psychology Today*, March/April 2010, p. 49.

11. J.J. McCorvey, "Secrets of the Most Productive People: Ken Washington, VP of Research and Advanced Engineering, Ford," November 2015, p. 84.

12. Kat Boogaard, "What is Timeboxing? Questions (and Answers) About this productivity Strategy," *Toggl Track* (www.toggle.com/blog), February 28, 2019, pp. 1–6.

13. Dan Heath and Chip Heath, "The Heroic Checklist," *Fast Company*, March 2008, pp. 66, 68.

14. Leslie A. Perlow, Gerardo A. Okhuysen, and Nelson P. Repenning, "The Speed Trap: Exploring the Relationship Between Decision Making and Temporal Context," *Academy of Management Journal*, October 2002, pp. 931–955.

15. Luke Siuty, "For Workers, There Are a Lot of Distractions," *Workforce*, April 2014, p. 12.

16. Quoted in Jared Sandberg, "Cubicle Culture: Yes, Sell All My Stocks. No, the 3:15 from JFK. And Get Me Mr. Sister," *The Wall Street Journal*, September 12, 2006, p. B1.

17. Data reported in Patty Ann Tublin, "Multitasking Lowers Your Emotional Intelligence?", *Huffpost Business* (www.huffingtonpost.com), July 14, 2014, p. 1; Susan G. Hauser, "Mindfulness over Matter of Multitasking," *Workforce Management*, December 2012, p. 10.

18. Maura Thomas, "How to Overcome Your (Checks Email) Distraction Habit," *Harvard Business Review* (https://hbr.org), December 4, 2019, pp. 1–8.

19. Study reported in Mike Snider, "Employees' 'Electronic Leash' Getting Tighter," *USA Today*, January 1, 2015, p. 4B.

20. Research reported in Jay Greene, "Collaboration is Great, But One Tool Is Enough," *The Wall Street Journal*, March 13, 2017, p. R6.

21. Ingrid Lorch-Bacci, "Achieving Peak Performance: The Hidden Dimension," *Executive Management Forum*, January 1991, pp. 1–4; Don Straits, "Peak Performers: In Search of the Best," pp. 1–2, *http://www.careerbuilder.com*, accessed March 10, 2006.

22. Jennifer Goldschmied et al., "Napping to Modulate Frustration and Impulsivity," *Personality and Individual Differences*, November 2015, pp.164–167.

23. Dori Meinert, "Work at Ideal Energy Level To Maximize Productivity," *HR Magazine*, September 2014, p. 18.

24. Rebecca Vesely, "Get on Your Feet: Taking a Stand on Moving Around," *Workforce Management*, February 2013, p. 4.

25. Cited in Andrea Petersen, "New Ways to Battle Procrastination," *The Wall Street Journal*, December 12, 2019, p. A13.

26. Steven Berglas, "Chronic Time Abuse," *Harvard Business Review*, June 2004, pp. 96–97.

27. Adam Grant, "Granted: The Real Reason Your Procrastinate," *newsletter@adamgrant.net*, March 10, 2020, p. 1.

28. See note 26.

29. Dana Hararo, "Is Perfect Good? A Meta-Analysis of Perfectionism in the Workplace," *Journal of Applied Psychology*, October 2018, pp. 1121–1144.

30. Gillian Mohney, "Stress Costs U.S. $300 Billion Every Year," *Healthline* (www.healthline.com), January 8, 2018, p. 1.

31. Rita Pyrillis, "Many Workplaces Failing Stress Test," *Workforce*, May 2015, p. 15.

32. Laboratory findings reported in Shirley S. Wang, "Stress Hormone's Surprise Powers," *The Wall Street Journal*, February 2, 2010, p. D2.

33. Jeffery A. Lepine, Nathan P. Podsakoff, and Marcie A. Lepine, "A Meta-Analytic Test of the Challenge-Stressor-Hindrance Stressor Framework: An Explanation for Inconsistent Relationships Among Stressors and Performance," *Academy of Management Journal*, October 2005, pp. 764–775.

34. Jessica B. Rodell and Timothy A. Judge, "Can 'Good' Stressors Spark 'Bad' Behaviors? The Mediating Role of Emotions in Links of Challenge and Hindrance Stressors With Citizenship and Counterproductive Behaviors," *Journal of Applied Psychology*, November 2009, pp. 1438–1451.

35. Vanessa Van Edwards, "Find Your 'Stress Sweet Spot'," *Entrepreneur*, September 2017, p. 18.

36. Peg Gamse, "Stress for Success," *HR Magazine*, July 2003, p. 102.

37. Lin Grensing-Pophal, "HR, Heal Thyself," *HR Magazine*, March 1999, p. 84.

38. Russell Cropanzano, Deborah E. Rupp, and Zinta S. Byrne, "The Relationship of Emotional Exhaustion to Work Attitudes, Job Performance, and Organizational Citizenship Behaviors," *Journal of Applied Psychology*, February 2003, pp.160–169.

39. Annebel H. B. De Hoogh and Deanne N. Den Hartog, "Neuroticism and Locus of Control as Moderators of the Relationships of Charismatic and Autocratic Leadership with Burnout," *Journal of Applied Psychology*, July 2009, pp. 1058–1067.

40. Tripp Mickle, "Your Phone's Nearly Out of Power, Remain Calm, Call a Doctor," *The Wall Street Journal*, May 5–8, 2018, pp. A1, A10.

41. Cited in Donna M. Owens, "Stressed Out," *HR Magazine*, March 2014, p. 44.

42. Mika Kivmaki et al., "Long Working Hours and Risk of Coronary Heart Disease and Stroke: A Systematic Review and Meta-Analysis of Published and Unpublished Data for 603, 838 Individuals," *The Lancet*, October 2013, pp. 1739–1746.

43. Maggie Jackson, "Quelling Distraction," *HR Magazine*, August 2008, p. 44.

44. Simona Gilboa, Arie Shirom, Yitzhak Fried, and Cary Cooper, "A Meta-Analysis of Work Demand Stress and Job Performance: Examining Main and Moderating Effects," *Personnel Psychology*, Summer 2008, pp. 227–271.

45. Marilyn L. Fox, Deborah J. Dwyer, and Daniel C. Ganster, "Effects of Stressful Job Demands and Control on Physiological and Attitudinal Outcomes in a Hospital Setting," *Academy of Management Journal*, April 1993, pp. 290–292.

46. Alicia A. Grandey, "Emotion Regulation in the Workplace: A New Way to Conceptualize Emotional Labor," *Journal of Occupational Health Psychology*, Vol. 5, No.1 (2000), pp. 95–110.

47. Steffanie L. Wilk and Lisa M. Moynihan, "Display Rule 'Regulators': The Relationship Between Supervisors and Worker Emotional Exhaustion," *Journal of Applied Psychology*, September 2005, pp. 917–927.

48. Hong Deng et al., "Spillover Effects of Emotional Labor in Customer Service Encounters Toward Coworker Harming: A Resource Depletion Perspective," *Personnel Psychology*, Number 2, 2017, pp. 469–502.

49. Leslie B. Hammer, Talya N. Bauer, and Alicia A. Grandey, "Work–Family Conflict and Work-Related Withdrawal Behaviors," *Journal of Business and Psychology*, Spring 2003, pp. 419–434.

50. Quoted in Geoff Colvin, "The New Trend? Reducing Stress in the Workplace—by Order of Management," *Fortune*, August 11, 2014, p. 42.

51. Kelly McGonigal, "Stressed Out? Embrace It," *The Wall Street Journal*, May 16–17, 2015, p. C3.

52. Dana Mattioli, "When Devotion to Work Becomes Job Obsession," *The Wall Street Journal*, January 23, 2007, p. B8.

53. Reported in "A Conversation with Mind/Body Researcher Herbert Benson," *Harvard Business Review*, November 2005, p. 54.

54. Ute R. Hülsheger, "Benefits of Mindfulness at Work: The Role of Mindfulness in Emotion Regulation, Emotional Exhaustion, and Job Satisfaction," *Journal of Applied Psychology*, March 2013, p. 310; Lauren Dixon, "Calm Employees' Mind with Mindfulness," *Talent Management*, January 29, 2016, pp. 1–8; "Mindfulness-Based Stress Reduction (MBSR)," *NREPP* (SAMHSA's National Registry of Evidence-Based Programs and Practices), March 2012, p. 1.

55. William Atkinson, "When Stress Won't Go Away," *HR Magazine*, December 2000, pp. 108, 109.

360-degree feedback A performance appraisal in which a person is evaluated by a sampling of all the people with whom he or she interacts.

A

achievement need The need that refers to finding joy in accomplishment for its own sake.

action plan The specific steps necessary to achieve a goal or an objective.

active listening Listening for full meaning, without making premature judgments or interpretations.

activity In the PERT method, the physical and mental effort required to complete an event.

administrative management The use of management principles in the structuring and managing of an organization.

affiliation need A desire to have close relationships with others and to be a loyal employee or friend.

affirmative action An employment practice that complies with antidiscrimination law and correcting past discriminatory practices.

anchoring In the decision making process, placing too much value on the first information received and ignoring later information.

artificial intelligence (AI) The ability of a computer program or machine to think and learn in a manner that emulates human intelligence.

authority The formal right to get people to do things or the formal right to control resources.

autocratic leader A task-oriented leader who retains most of the authority for himself or herself and is not generally concerned with group members' attitudes toward decisions.

B

balanced scorecard A management system that enables organizations to clarify their vision and strategy and translate them into action.

behavior In performance evaluation, what people actually do on the job.

behavioral approach to management An approach to management that emphasizes improving management through an understanding of the psychological makeup of people.

behavioral interviewing A style of interviewing in which the interviewer asks questions whose answers reveal behaviors that would be either strengths or weaknesses in a given position.

Big Data The collection of enormous amounts of data in order to find patterns and insights that are useful in marketing products and dealing customers and employees.

brainstorming A group method of solving problems, gathering information, and stimulating creative thinking. The basic technique is to generate numerous ideas through unrestrained and spontaneous participation by group members.

break-even analysis A method of determining the relationship between total costs and total revenues at various levels of production or sales activity.

budget A spending plan expressed in numerical terms for a future period of time.

bureaucracy A rational, systematic, and precise form of organization in which rules, regulations, and techniques of control are specifically defined.

C

carpal tunnel syndrome The most frequent cumulative trauma disorder that occurs when frequent wrist bending results in swelling, leading to a pinched nerve.

cash flow Amount of net cash generated by a business during a specific period.

centralization The extent to which authority is retained at the top of the organization.

challenge stressors Sources of stress that have a positive direct effect on motivation and performance.

charisma The ability to lead or influence others based on personal charm, magnetism, inspiration, and emotion.

c-level manager A current term to describe top-level managers because they usually have *chief* in their title.

coaching A method for helping employees perform better, which usually occurs on the spot and involves informal discussion and suggestions.

coalition A specific arrangement of parties working together to combine their power, thus exerting influence on another individual or group.

collective efficacy A group's shared belief in its combined capabilities to organize and execute the courses of action required for certain outcomes.

communication The process of exchanging information by the use of words, letters, symbols, or nonverbal behavior.

communication network A pattern or flow of messages that traces the communication from start to finish.

compressed workweek A full-time work schedule that allows 40 hours of work in less than five days.

computer-based monitoring system A computer-based system to gather data about the work habits and productivity of employees.

concurrent control A type of control that monitors activities while they are carried out.

conflict The simultaneous arousal of two or more incompatible motives.

conflict of interest A situation that occurs when one's judgment or objective is compromised.

confrontation Dealing with a controversial or emotional topic directly.

constructive criticism A form of criticism designed to help people improve.

contingency approach to management A perspective on management that emphasizes no single way to manage people or work is best in every situation. It encourages managers to study individual and situational differences before deciding on a course of action.

contingency plan An alternative plan to be used if the original plan cannot be implemented or a crisis develops.

contingent workers Part-time or temporary employees who are not members of the employer's permanent workforce.

corporate social performance The extent to which a firm responds to the demands of its stakeholders for behaving in a socially responsible manner.

corporate social responsibility The idea that firms have obligations to society beyond their economic obligations to owners or stockholders and also beyond those prescribed by law or contract.

corrective discipline A type of discipline that allows employees to correct their behavior before punishment is applied.

creativity The process of developing novel ideas that can be put into action.

critical path The path through the PERT network that includes the most time-consuming sequence of events and activities.

cross-functional team A group composed of workers from different specialties at the same organizational level who come together to accomplish a task.

crowdsourcing The use of collective intelligence gathered from the public, often by the use of social media.

cultural sensitivity Awareness of local and national customs and their importance in effective interpersonal relationships.

culture shock A group of physical and psychological symptoms that may develop when a person is abruptly placed in a foreign culture.

cumulative trauma disorders Injuries caused by repetitive motions over prolonged periods of time.

D

data-driven decision making The idea that decisions are based on facts rather than impressions or guesses.

decentralization The extent to which authority is passed down to lower levels in an organization.

decision A choice among alternatives.

decision making style A manager's typical pattern of making decisions.

decision tree A graphic illustration of the alternative solutions available to solve a problem.

decisiveness The extent to which a person makes up his or her mind promptly and prudently.

decoding The communication stage in which the receiver interprets the message and translates it into meaningful information.

defensive communication The tendency to receive messages in a way that protects self-esteem.

delegation Assigning formal authority and responsibility for accomplishing a specific task to another person.

Delphi Technique A form of group decision making designed to provide group members with one another's ideas and feedback while avoiding some of the problems associated with interacting groups.

departmentalization The process of subdividing work into departments.

development A form of personal improvement that usually consists of enhancing knowledge and skills of a complex and unstructured nature.

deviation In a control system, the size of the discrepancy between performance standards and actual results.

difficult person An individual whose personal characteristics disturb other people.

discipline Punishment used to correct or train.

disruptive innovation The way a new product or service transforms an existing market by bringing new simplicity, convenience, and affordability.

diversity A mixture of people with different group identities within the same work environment.

diversity training Training that attempts to bring about workplace harmony by teaching people how to get along better with diverse work associates.

downsizing The slimming down of operations to focus resources and boost profits or decrease expenses.

E

EBITDA Earnings before interest, taxes, depreciation, and amortization.

economic order quantity (EOQ) The inventory level that minimizes both administrative costs and carrying costs.

economic value added (EVA) Measures how much more (or less) a company earns in profits than the minimum amount its investors expect it to earn.

e-learning A form of computer-based training delivered via the Internet or private intranets in the organization.

emotional intelligence Qualities such as understanding one's feelings, empathy of others, and the regulation of emotion to enhance living. Also, the ability to connect with people and understand their emotions.

emotional labor The process of regulating both feelings and expressions to meet organizational goals.

empathy The ability to understand another person's point of view.

employee assistance program (EAP) An organization-sponsored service to help employees deal with personal and job-related problems that hinder performance.

employee benefit Any noncash payment given to workers as part of compensation for their employment.

employee network group A group composed of employees throughout the company who affiliate on the basis of group characteristics such as race, ethnicity, gender, sexual orientation, or physical ability status.

employee orientation program (or **onboarding**) A formal activity designed to acquaint new employees with the organization and imparts information about the corporate culture.).

empowerment The process by which managers share power with group members, thereby enhancing employees' feelings of personal effectiveness.

encoding The process of organizing ideas into a series of symbols designed to communicate with the receiver.

entrepreneur A person who founds and operates an innovative business.

entropy A concept of the systems approach to management that states an organization will run down and die without continuous input from the outside environment.

ergonomics The science of fitting the worker to the job.

ethically-centered management Management that emphasizes that the high quality of an end product takes precedence over its scheduled completion.

ethics The study of moral obligation, or separating right from wrong.

event In the PERT method, a point of decision or the accomplishment of a task.

evidence-based management The systematic use of the best available evidence to improve management practice.

expectancy theory of motivation The belief that people will expend effort if they expect the effort to lead to performance and the performance to lead to a reward.

expected time The time that will be used on the PERT diagram as the needed period for the completion of an activity.

expected value The average return on a particular decision being made a large number of times.

external control strategy An approach to control based on the belief that employees are motivated primarily by external rewards and need to be controlled by their managers.

F

feedback The communication stage in which the receiver responds to the sender's message.

feedback control A control that evaluates an activity after it is performed.

first-level managers Managers who supervise operatives (also known as first-line managers or supervisors).

flat organization structure A form of organization with relatively few layers of management, making it less bureaucratic.

flow experience The ultimate involvement in work or a condition of heightened focus, productivity, and happiness.

formal communication channels The official pathways for sending information inside and outside an organization.

formal group A group deliberately formed by the organization to accomplish specific tasks and achieve goals.

Fourth Industrial Revolution An economy fueled by the mobile Internet, automation, and artificial intelligence.

free cash flow A refinement of cash flow that measures the cash from operations minus capital expenditures.

functional departmentalization An arrangement that defines departments by the function each one performs, such as accounting or purchasing.

G

Gantt chart A chart that graphically depicts the planned and actual progress of work during the life of the project.

geographic (or territorial) departmentalization An arrangement of departments according to the geographic area or territory served.

gig economy Workers who are involved in some form of freelancing, contracting, or temporary work, often based on outsourcing.

global leadership skills The ability to effectively lead people of other cultures.

global startup A small firm that comes into existence by serving an international market.

goal An overall condition one is trying to achieve, or a conscious intention to act.

good cause A legally justifiable or good business reason for firing an employee.

grapevine The informal means by which information is transmitted in organizations.

gross profit margin A financial ratio expressed as the difference between sales and the cost of goods sold, divided by sales.

group A collection of people who interact with one another, are working toward some common purpose, and perceive themselves to be a group.

group decisions The process of several people contributing to a final decision.

group polarization A situation in which post-discussion attitudes tend to be more extreme than pre-discussion attitudes.

groupthink A psychological drive for consensus at any cost.

H

Hawthorne effect The tendency of people to behave differently when they receive attention because they respond to the demands of the situation.

heuristics A rule of thumb used in decision making.

high-performance work system A way of organizing work so that front-line workers participate in decisions that have an impact on their jobs and the wider organization.

hindrance stressors Stressful events and thoughts that have a negative effect on motivation and performance.

horizontal structure The arrangement of work by teams that are responsible for accomplishing a process.

I

improvement goal A goal that, if attained, will correct unacceptable deviation from a performance standard.

ineffective job performance Job performance that does not meet the standards for the position.

informal communication channel An unofficial network that supplements the formal channels in an organization.

informal group A group that emerges over time through the interaction of workers.

informal learning Any learning in which the learning process is not determined or designed by the organization.

informal organization structure A set of unofficial relationships that emerge to take care of events and transactions not covered by the formal structure.

information overload A condition in which an individual receives so much information that he or she becomes overwhelmed.

informative confrontation A technique of inquiring about discrepancies, conflicts, and mixed messages.

internal control strategy An approach to control based on the belief that employees can be motivated by building their commitment to organizational goals.

intuition An experience-based way of knowing or reasoning in which weighing and balancing evidence are done unconsciously and automatically.

J

job burnout A pattern of emotional, physical, and mental exhaustion in response to chronic job stressors.

job characteristics model A method of job enrichment that focuses on the task and interpersonal dimensions of a job.

job crafting The physical and mental changes individuals make in the task or relationship aspects of their job.

job demand–job control model A model demonstrating the relationship between high or low job demands and high or low job control. It shows that workers experience the most stress when the demands of the job are high yet they have little control over the activity.

job description A written statement of the key features of a job along with the activities required to perform it effectively.

job embeddedness The array of forces attaching people to their jobs.

job enlargement Increasing the number and variety of tasks within a job.

job enrichment An approach to including more challenge and responsibility in jobs to make them more appealing to employees.

job evaluation The process of rank-ordering jobs based on job content, to demonstrate the worth of one job in comparison to another.

job involvement The degree to which individuals identify psychologically with their work.

job rotation A temporary switching of job assignments.

job sharing A work arrangement in which two people who work part-time share one job.

job specialization The degree to which a job holder performs only a limited number of tasks.

job specification A statement of the personal characteristics needed to perform the job.

judgmental forecast A qualitative forecasting method based on a collection of subjective opinions.

just-in-time (JIT) system A system to minimize inventory and move it into the plant exactly when needed.

K

knowledge management The ways and means by which a company leverages its knowledge resources to generate business value.

L

labor union An organization formed to attain fair treatment for workers in such areas as compensation, including health and retirement benefits, safe working conditions, working hours, job security and work-life programs.

lateral thinking A thinking process that spreads out to find many alternative solutions to a problem.

leader political support Political acts and influence techniques by the leader to provide followers with the resources they need to accomplish individual, group, and organizational objectives.

leadership The ability to inspire confidence and support among the people who are needed to achieve organizational goals.

leadership efficacy A specific form of efficacy (or feeling effective) associated with the level of confidence in the knowledge, skills, and abilities associated with leading others.

leadership style The typical pattern of behavior that a leader uses to influence his or her employees to achieve organizational goals.

learning organization An organization that is skilled at creating, acquiring, and transferring knowledge.

lift-outs (in relation to teams) The practice of recruiting an entire high-functioning team from another organization.

locus of control The way in which people look at causation in their lives.

M

management by objectives (MBO) A systematic application of goal-setting and planning to help individuals and firms be more productive.

management The process of using organizational resources to achieve organizational objectives through planning, organizing and staffing, leading, and controlling.

manager A person responsible for the work performance of group members.

Maslow's need hierarchy The motivation theory that arranges human needs into a pyramid-shaped model with basic physiological needs at the bottom and self-actualizing needs at the top.

matrix organization A project structure superimposed on a functional structure.

mentor A more experienced person who develops a protégé's abilities through tutoring, coaching, guidance, and emotional support.

merit pay A method of distributing wage and salary increases based on results.

micromanagement Supervising group members too closely and second-guessing their decisions.

middle-level managers Managers who are neither executives nor first-level supervisors, but who serve as a link between the two groups.

milestone chart An extension of the Gantt chart that provides a listing of the sub-activities that must be completed to accomplish the major activities listed on the vertical axis.

mindfulness Concentrating on the present moment without making judgments about what is happening.

mission The firm's purpose and where it fits into the world.

modified work schedule Any formal departure from the traditional hours of work, excluding shift work and staggered work hours.

moral intensity The magnitude of an unethical act.

moral laxity A slippage in moral behavior because other issues seem more important at the time.

motivation The expenditure of effort to accomplish results.

multicultural worker An individual who is aware of and values other cultures.

multinational corporation (MNC) A firm with operating units in two or more countries in addition to its own.

N

need A deficit within an individual, such as a craving for water or affection.

net debt A company's debt minus the cash and cash equivalents it has on hand.

noise In communication, unwanted interference that can distort or block a message.

nominal group technique (NGT) A group decision making technique that follows a highly structured format.

nomophobia A form of anxiety stemming from having no access to a smartphone or phone battery being dangerously low.

nonverbal communication The transmission of messages by means other than words.

O

offshoring Global outsourcing.

open-book company A firm in which every employee is trained, empowered, and motivated to understand and pursue the company's business goals.

operating plans The means through which strategic plans alter the destiny of the firm.

operational planning Planning that requires specific procedures and actions at lower levels in an organization.

organization structure The arrangement of people and tasks to accomplish organizational goals.

organizational citizenship behavior Employee behavior that is discretionary and typically not recognized or rewarded but nevertheless helps the organization.

organizational culture (or corporate culture) The system of shared values and beliefs that actively influence the behavior of organization members.

organizational politics Informal approaches to gaining power or other advantage through means other than merit or luck.

ostracism The extent to which an individual group member perceives that he or she is being ignored by other group members.

outsourcing The practice of hiring an individual or another company outside the organization to perform work.

P

Pareto diagram A bar graph that ranks types of output variations by frequency of occurrence.

participative leader A leader who shares decision making with group members.

peak performance A mental state in which maximum results are achieved with minimum effort.

performance evaluation (or appraisal) A formal system for measuring, evaluating, and reviewing performance.

performance management A set of processes and managerial behaviors aimed at defining, measuring, and motivating the development of good performance.

policies General guidelines to follow in making decisions and taking action.

positive reinforcement Increasing the probability that behavior will be repeated by rewarding people for making the desired response.

power The ability or potential to influence decisions and control resources.

power motivation A strong desire to control others and resources or get them to do things on your behalf.

preventive control A control that takes place prior to the performance of an activity.

problem A discrepancy between ideal and actual conditions.

procedures A customary method for handling an activity that guides action rather than thinking.

procrastinate To delay taking action without a valid reason.

procrastination The delaying of action for no good reason.

productivity How effectively you use your resources to achieve your goals.

product–service departmentalization The arrangement of departments according to the products or services they provide.

profit margin A financial ratio measuring return on sales, or net income divided by sales.

profit-sharing plan A method of giving workers supplemental income based on the profitability of the entire firm or a selected unit.

pro forma A financial statement that excludes write-downs or goodwill and other one-time charges not relevant to future earnings.

program evaluation and review technique (PERT) A network model used to track the planning activities required to complete a large-scale, nonrepetitive project. It depicts all of the interrelated events that must take place.

progressive discipline The step-by-step application of corrective discipline.

project organization A temporary group of specialists working under one manager to accomplish a fixed objective.

project team A small group of employees working on a temporary basis in order to accomplish a particular goal.

prosocial motivation The desire to exert effort to benefit others.

Pygmalion effect The idea that people live up to the expectations set for them.

Q

qualitative control technique A method of controlling based on human judgments about performance that result in a verbal rather than numerical evaluation.

quantitative approach to management A perspective on management that emphasizes use of a group of methods in managerial decision making, based on the scientific method.

quantitative control technique A method of controlling based on numerical measures of performance.

R

realistic job preview A complete disclosure of the potential negative features of a job to a job candidate.

recognition need The desire to be acknowledged for one's contributions and efforts and to feel important.

recruitment The process of attracting job candidates with the right characteristics and skills to fill job openings.

reference check An inquiry to a second party about a job candidate's suitability for employment.

relationship conflict Conflict that focuses on personalized, individually oriented issues.

relaxation response A general-purpose method of learning to relax by yourself.

results In performance evaluation, what people accomplish, or the objectives they attain.

return on equity A financial ratio measuring how much a firm is earning on its investment, expressed as net income divided by owner's equity.

revenue per employee Total revenues divided by number of employees.

role An expected set of activities or behaviors stemming from a job.

role ambiguity A condition in which the job holder receives confusing or poorly defined expectations.

rule A specific course of action or conduct that must be followed. It is the simplest type of plan.

S

scenario planning The process of preparing responses to predicted changes in conditions.

scientific management The application of scientific methods to increase individual workers' productivity.

self-discipline The ability to work systematically and progressively toward a goal until it is achieved.

self-leadership The process of influencing oneself.

self-managed work team A formally recognized group of employees who are responsible for an entire work process or segment that delivers a product or service to an internal or external customer.

shadowing Directly observing the work activities of the mentor by following the manager around for a stated period of time, such as one day per month.

Six Sigma A data-driven method for achieving near-perfect quality with an emphasis on preventing problems.

small-business owner An individual who owns and operates a small business.

social loafing Freeloading, or shirking individual responsibility, when a person is placed in a group setting and removed from individual accountability.

socialization The process of coming to understand the values, norms, and customs essential for adapting to the organization.

social network analysis The mapping and measuring of relationships and links between and among people, groups, and organizations.

span of control The number of workers reporting directly to a manager.

stakeholder viewpoint The viewpoint on social responsibility contending that firms must hold themselves responsible for the quality of life of the many groups affected by the firm's actions.

standard A unit of measurement used to evaluate results.

stockholder viewpoint The traditional perspective on social responsibility that a business organization is responsible only to its owners and stockholders.

strategic human resource planning The process of anticipating and providing for the movement of people into, within, and out of an organization to support the firm's business strategy.

strategic planning A firm's overall master plan that shapes its destiny.

strategy The organization's plan for achieving its vision, mission, and goals.

stress The mental and physical condition that results from a perceived threat that cannot be dealt with readily.

subculture A pocket in which the organizational culture differs from the dominant culture, as well as other pockets of the subculture.

summary discipline The immediate discharge of an employee because of a serious offense.

superordinate goal An overarching goal that captures the imagination.

SWOT analysis A method of considering the strengths, weaknesses, opportunities, and threats in a given situation.

synergy The whole is greater than the sum of its parts. When the various parts of the organization work together, they can produce will produce much than they could by working independently.

systems perspective A way of viewing aspects of an organization as an interrelated system. It is based on the concept that an organization is a system, or an entity of interrelated parts.

T

tactical planning Planning that translates a firm's strategic plans into specific goals by organizational unit.

talent management A deliberate approach to attract, develop, and retain people with the aptitude and abilities to meet current and future organizational needs.

task conflict Conflict that focuses on substantive, issue-related differences, related to the work itself.

task force A problem solving group of a temporary nature, usually working against a deadline.

team A special type of group in which members have complementary skills and are committed to a common purpose, a set of performance goals, and an approach to the task.

team leader A manager who coordinates the work of a small group of people, while acting as a facilitator and catalyst.

teamwork A situation characterized by understanding and commitment to group goals on the part of all team members.

Telecommuting (or remote work) An arrangement with one's employer to use a computer to perform work at home or in a satellite office.

termination The process of firing an employee because of poor job performance, unacceptable behavior, or interpersonal problems.

time box A period of time to work on a task when you declare it completed.

time-series analysis An analysis of a sequence of observations that have taken place at regular intervals over a period of time (hourly, weekly, monthly, and so forth)

top-level managers Managers at the top one or two levels in an organization.

tough question A question that helps the group achieve insight into the nature of the problem, what it might be doing wrong, and whether progress is sufficient.

training Any procedure intended to foster and enhance learning among employees, particularly directed at acquiring job skills.

traits Stable aspects of people, closely related to personality.

transformational leader A leader who helps organizations and people make positive changes in the way they do things.

triple bottom line The idea that companies should prepare three different and separate bottom lines: the corporate bottom line; people in terms of their well-being; and the planet, referring to environmental responsibility.

two-factor theory of work motivation The theory contending there are two different sets of job factors. One set can satisfy and motivate people, and the other set can only prevent dissatisfaction.

U

unity of command The classic management principle stating that each subordinate receives assigned duties from one superior only and is accountable to that superior.

V

variable pay When the amount of money a worker receives is partially dependent on his or her performance.

vertical thinking An analytical, logical process that results in few answers.

virtual team A small group of people who conduct almost all of their collaborative work by electronic communication rather than in face-to-face meetings.

virtue The human inclination to feel, think, and [behave in] ways that express moral excellence and contribute to the common good.

vision An idealized picture of the future of an organization.

W

whistleblower An employee who discloses organizational wrongdoing to parties who can take action.

work engagement An extension of motivation, referring to the level of commitment workers make to their employer.

work ethic A firm belief in the dignity and value of work.

work–family conflict A major stressor that represents a combination of individual and organizational factors contributing to stress.

work streamlining Eliminating as much low-value work as possible and concentrating on activities that add value for customers or clients.

wrongful discharge The firing of an employee for arbitrary or unfair reasons.

Name Index

Company / Brand Index

Subject Index

Page numbers with an *f* refer to a figure.

CPSIA information can be obtained
at www.ICGtesting.com
Printed in the USA
JSHW060308201122
33283JS00002B/4